SAMUEL BARBER

The Composer and His Music

BARBARA B. HEYMAN

OXFORD UNIVERSITY PRESS

New York ▫ Oxford

Oxford University Press

Oxford New York Toronto
Delhi Bombay Calcutta Madras Karachi
Kuala Lumpur Singapore Hong Kong Tokyo
Nairobi Dar es Salaam Cape Town
Melbourne Auckland Madrid

and associated companies in
Berlin Ibadan

First published in 1992 by Oxford University Press, Inc.,
198 Madison Avenue, New York, New York 10016-4314

First issued as an Oxford University Press paperback, 1994

Oxford is a registered trademark of Oxford University Press

Library of Congress Cataloging-in-Publication Data
Heyman, Barbara B.
Samuel Barber : the composer and his music / Barbara B. Heyman.
p. cm. Includes bibliographical references and index.
ISBN 0-19-506650-2
ISBN 0-19-509058-6 (PBK.)
1. Barber, Samuel, 1910–1981
Criticism and interpretation.
I. Title. ML410.B23H5
1992 780'.92—dc20
91-2454

2 4 6 8 10 9 7 5 3

Printed in the United States of America

To my mother

SUSAN LACHOLTER BRODY

and to the memory of my father

SAMUEL H. BRODY

Preface

Samuel Barber (1910–1981) was one of the most honored and most frequently performed American composers in Europe and the Americas during the mid-century decades. Through most of his career he made his living almost entirely by composing, perhaps one of the few composers who could make this choice. His works—comprising forty-eight opus numbers and more than one hundred unpublished pieces—are representative of nearly every musical genre, and many entered the repertoire soon after he wrote them.

In spite of his position as a major American composer of the twentieth century, there has been a relative paucity of scholarly writings about Barber's music and no exhaustive, documented study of his career and oeuvre. The short biography by Nathan Broder is the most substantial and frequently cited work about Barber. While it covers only up to 1954 and is not dependable in every detail, it is to this time the only biography of the composer based on information provided by Barber, his family, and newsletters from the Curtis Institute of Music. Richard Jackson's general article on Barber in the *New Grove Dictionary of American Music* builds on Broder's work and adds material through 1981. A number of dissertations have focused on selected aspects or genres. Don A. Hennessee's study is largely a bibliography of review excerpts and includes limited (though sometimes inaccurate) material on first performances, a discography, and sketchy biographical information. Over the last five decades, numerous articles, reviews, or record liner notes mostly concern individual works. Several sympathetic profiles of Barber by Hans W. Heinsheimer, of his publisher, G. Schirmer, Inc., offer interesting anecdotes focusing on the composer's personal and creative struggles.

This historical study traces Barber's career in relation to all his published and all but a few of his unpublished works. The considerable biographical material presented is designed to illuminate the course of that career and Barber's compositional process. Information about the circumstances surrounding a work's composition, premiere, critical reception, and revisions is included when available.

It is not my intention to present an analytical study of the music, or to arrive at a critical judgment, but it is part of my documentary purpose to weave in the judgments of Barber's contemporaries as historical context. I have tried to document the genesis of each work and explore the formative stages of composition. Discussion of the music itself is limited to a brief description of the work with some references to existing analytic studies and the relevant holographs. Occasionally more detailed discussion is included to trace the particular influence of performing artists, or when it bears on the nature of revisions after a performance, or when it helps to clarify patterns of stylistic tendencies in Barber's music.

Primary source material for the study consists almost entirely of letters, diaries, journals, sketchbooks, holographs, autograph manuscripts, and other related documents from the Barber estate. Barber was an ardent and eloquent letter writer, and fortunately his family, colleagues, and friends valued his letters enough to preserve most of them. These sources include the extraordinary, rich correspondence (1912–1953) between Barber and his uncle Sidney Homer and numerous letters to his parents, Serge Koussevitzky, William Strickland, Jeanne Behrend, Orlando Cole, Eugene Ormandy, William Schuman, Charles Turner, Henry-Louis de La Grange, and Manfred Ibel, among others.

Other sources include manuscripts from private collections or libraries: the Library of Congress (the largest repository of Barber holographs), the Curtis Institute of Music, the Sibley Library at the Eastman School of Music (housing the G. Schirmer collection), and the Chester County Historical Society, where lie the early sketches of many of Barber's juvenile works, including *The Rose Tree,* his first opera, written when he was ten. Individual manuscripts, or copies of them, were given by Barber as gifts to performers, close friends, or family. The largest number of privately owned manuscripts belonged to Louise Homer and are preserved by her daughter Katharine Homer Fryer.

From 1939 on, Barber was unusually fortunate in that only first-rate performers—proven virtuosos—premiered his works, and therefore most of his instrumental compositions were written with a particular performer or performing group in mind. In this study, interviews were conducted whenever possible with those artists who gave first performances. Thus an oral history emerges that focuses on several themes—discussions between Barber and performers as a piece progressed, its special challenges or innovations, and specific suggestions about its performance.

For the most part, each work is taken up chronologically, following the course of Barber's career. The narrative digresses if there were significant revisions or performances of a work well after its completion. Thus the reader will usually find most of the information about a work in one location in the text. If equal attention is not given to all pieces, it is sometimes because primary source material was sparse or unavailable; this is the case, for example, with some of Barber's songs, which were usually composed with such facility that he rarely wrote about them in his letters.

Future analytic study of Barber's music will be facilitated by the holograph sketches and drafts deposited at the Library of Congress in 1984, which will support work in greater depth than was possible for studies completed before that date. New sources continue to emerge. These and the many inquiries I receive from scholars, performers, and conductors confirm a pressing need for a descriptive catalogue—which I hope to complete at an early date—that can serve as a guide for future Barber research and performances of his music. It will be a thematic *catalogue raisonné* that will provide an entry for each of Barber's published and unpublished compositions, including dates of beginning and completion, instrumentation, first performances, tempi markings, duration, and discography as well as locations, descriptions, and comparisons of manuscripts—holographs, sketches, and revisions. I hope that the present documentary study will prove useful in itself and, in combination with the completed catalogue, will pave the way for future analytical and critical studies of Barber's music.

B. B. H.

New York
September 1991

Acknowledgments

This study owes much to the support of Gian Carlo Menotti, executor of the Estate of Samuel Barber, whose early endorsement of the overall project has made possible much of the documentary investigation on which it is based. I am especially indebted also to Katharine Homer Fryer for her lively recollections and for lending me the extraordinary collection of correspondence between Barber and her father, Sidney Homer, and the treasured manuscripts of her mother, Louise Homer.

The many, many excerpts from Samuel Barber's published works, as well as unpublished manuscript materials, appear by kind permission of G. Schirmer, Inc. I thank Steven Culbertson, Susan Feder, Peter Herb, and Paul Wittke for their help in solving mysteries and unravelling knots.

One of the most gratifying aspects of piecing together Barber's life has been the savoring of his own written words, but the mosaic could not have been fully set without the words of others. Mrs. Eugene Ormandy graciously granted permission to use correspondence from her late husband's papers. The letters of Serge Koussevitzky are quoted with the permission of the Serge Koussevitzky Foundation. The letters of John Nicholas Brown are quoted with the kind permission of Anne S. K. Brown. The letters of William Schuman are quoted with his permission.

The project in its particular form would not have been possible without the enthusiastic participation of the many colleagues, friends, and schoolmates of Barber's who shared with me their recollections in interviews or by letter and in many instances made available their personal copies of his manuscripts, letters, notebooks, and journals: Martina Arroyo, Rose Bampton, Samuel Baron, Herbert Baumel, the late Jeanne Behrend, Ralph Berkowitz, Brunetta Bernard, John Bitter, the late Nellie Lee Bok, Todd Bolender, John G. Briggs, Iso Briselli, John Browning, Leonard Burkat, Paul Callaway, Orlando Cole, Rohini Coomara, Patrick Creagh, Suso Cecchi d'Amico, David Freed, Raya Garbousova, Herbert Harris, Hans Heinsheimer, Valentin Herranz, Lee Hoiby, Stanley Hollingsworth, Joel Honig, Colonel George Howard, Frank M. Hudson, Manfred Ibel, the late Werner Janssen, Stuart Kessler, Henry-Louis de La Grange, Roland Leich, the late Jane Hill Meyer, Dr. Jack Nelson, Phillip Ramey, Muriel Robertson, Richard Roeckelein, Ned Rorem, Daniel Saidenberg, Rudolf Schirmer, Oscar Schumsky, Stephen Spender, the late Eleanor Steber, William Strickland, Ruth Thomas, the late Virgil Thomson, Charles Turner, Katherine Von Hagendorp, Jonathan Williams, and Perry Wolfe. Letters and photographs belonging to the Estate of Rosario Scalero were provided literally as this book went to press through the generosity of Monique Arnoldi, in fulfillment of the intentions of her late stepmother, Maria Teresa Scalero de Ruette.

My appreciation is boundless to the many librarians, archivists, and representatives of other organizations, whose knowledge and spirit of cooperation have enabled my research to move forward with remarkably few delays. At the Curtis Institute of Music Library, Elizabeth Walker provided invaluable assistance in the launching of the research nine years ago and continued to alert me to new materials. Working in the Music Division of the Library of Congress is like going to heaven without dying; Gillian Anderson and Ray White have an uncanny talent for locating elusive manuscripts, Margaret Kieckhefer was diligent in overseeing the photoreproduction of holographs; and my gratitude is enormous to Wayne Shirley for his enthusiastic reading of the manuscript and for providing valuable textual advice on matters beyond music.

Also for their help I thank Floyd K. Harvey, formerly of Bell Telephone Laboratories; Milfred Myhre, carillonneur at the Bok Tower Gardens; former and present research associates of the Institute for Studies in American Music at Brooklyn College, Allen Lott, Emily Good, Carol Oja, and K. Robert Schwarz; Rosemary Philips and Pamela Powell of the Chester County Historical Society; Holly Haswell of the Columbia University Archives; Nicholas Scheetz of the Georgetown University Library; Dan Stehman of Los Angeles Valley College; Robert Tuggle and John Pennino of the Metropolitan Opera Archives; J. Rigbie Turner of the Pierpont Morgan Library; Jean Bowen, Richard Jackson, Channan Willner, and their colleagues at the Music Division of the New York Public Library, Astor, Lenox and Tilden Foundations, as well as Don McCormick of the Rodgers and Hammerstein Archives of Recorded Sound; Ron Jeffers of Oregon State University; Louise Goldberg of the Sibley Music Library; Robert Green at West Chester State University; the Reverend Robert D. Young of the Westminster Presbyterian Church in West Chester; Martin Bookspan and Robert Sherman of WQXR; Vivian Perlis, director of the American Music Oral History Project at Yale University; Harold E. Samuel and Kendall L. Crilly of the Yale University Music Library; and archivists and librarians of the American Academy and Institute of Arts and Letters, the American Academy in Rome New York Office, the Atlanta Public Library, the Carnegie Library in Pittsburgh, the Cleveland Public Library, the Van Cliburn Foundation, the Detroit Free Library, the Martha Graham Center of Contemporary Dance, the Walter Clinton Jackson Library, the Los Angeles Public Library, the University of North Carolina Library, the University of Pennsylvania Library, the Philadelphia Free Library, Rollins College Theater Department, the Boston Symphony Orchestra, the New York Philharmonic, the Philadelphia Orchestra, and the Westminster Choir School.

It is a special pleasure to thank colleagues at the City University of New York: Barry S. Brook, as my earliest mentor and teacher, introduced me to the joys of the scholarly treasure hunt; and beyond the immediacy of giving expert bibliographic and editorial suggestions, his way of thinking about music and musicians in society in general has in large measure influenced the particular focus of this book. I am sincerely grateful to H. Wiley Hitchcock for much valuable advice and for the continuous flow of Barberiana sent in my direction; and to Stephen Blum, Leo Kraft, and Edward O. D. Downes for their helpful criticisms of the manuscript in its early stage.

I am especially indebted and offer my warmest thanks to Teresa Edge, Fred Nichols, and Carl Schachter, who unstintingly gave professional expertise on matters of literature, syntax, translation, and propriety of language—musical and otherwise—and whose wonderful suggestions I mostly took and where I did not I will surely be sorry.

There are others—good friends, some of whom are relatives too—who buoyed me with encouragement and sweet humor during nearly ten years of my obsession with Samuel Barber, and to them I offer an affectionate salute: Natalie and Larry Appel, Adrienne Block, Paul and Linda Brody, Sam Brody, Gretchen Clumpner, Ellen Glass, Albert Glinsky, Charles Gouse, Tim Gura, Daniel Heyman, David and Nadine Heyman, Cary Kaminsky, Linda Kobler, Catherine Morrison, Hannah Rose, Elizabeth Snyder, and my patient children—Jon, Lisa, Ben, and Ruth, Karen and Larry.

To everyone at Oxford University Press who shepherded this book with care through its various stages of production—especially to Sheldon Meyer and Karen Wolny—I offer my sincere gratitude. I thank Michael Steinberg for his early reading of the manuscript. Proofreading by David Bloom and indexing by Marilyn Bliss were funded in part by the Sonneck Society for American Music. The many musical examples were designed by John Davis of Music-Book Associates, whose inventive and artistic solutions are indeed appreciated. India Cooper has greatly enhanced this book with her graceful, unobstrusive editing and sharp eye for details.

And finally, it is with my deepest appreciation that I thank Sherman Van Solkema of the City University of New York, a generous teacher and friend, whose wise counsel helped bring my ideas to fruition. For his forthright, insightful criticisms and provocative questions, I am forever grateful.

B. B. H.

Contents

Musical Examples

G. Schirmer, Inc. is Barber's sole publisher. Unless otherwise indicated, all manuscripts are at the Library of Congress, Music Division, Washington, D.C.

SAMUEL BARBER

INTRODUCTION

> There is a degree of innovation beyond which one does not pass without danger—Lamartine had the gift of seizing the exact point of permissible innovation.[1]
>
> *Franz Liszt*

Nothing could more clearly illuminate the musical aesthetic that guided Samuel Barber throughout his career than this quotation—in effect an undeclared credo—written by the composer on the final page of an early sketchbook.* When, near the end of his life, he said, "I myself wrote always as I wished, and without a tremendous desire to find the latest thing possible. . . . I wrote as I wanted to for myself,"[2] he was acknowledging his insulation from the stylistic trends of his generation.

Barber entered his professional career in the mid-1930s upon the wave of Depression-era conservatism that characterized the music of many American composers who were at least a decade older than he. But unlike many of his contemporaries whose careers came to maturity between the two world wars, he rarely responded to experimental trends that infused music in the 1920s and again after World War II, instead pursuing a path marked by a vocally inspired lyricism and a commitment to the tonal language and many of the forms of late nineteenth-century music. Although he shared the concern of his generation for writing music accessible to a broadly based audience, unlike Copland, Harris, Blitzstein, and Thomson, who searched for a music with national identity and who from the thirties on began incorporating popular, jazz, and folk idioms in their compositions, Barber attempted to communicate to established concert audiences whose taste was based on eighteenth- and nineteenth-century European models. Even an anomaly among his works—"Adventure," scored partially for non-Western instruments—maintains a firm connection to European rather than Asian musics. When he did incorporate Americana into

*The sketchbook, kept by Barber from about 1932 to the early 1940s, is at the Library of Congress, Washington, D.C. Barber donated this book to the library in 1962 and at that time identified many of the works in it.

his music, it was transitory, yielding *Excursions* (1941–42)—stylized pieces based on American idioms—and the Piano Sonata (1949) and the Piano Concerto (1962), both of which lightly display motoric jazz rhythms. His song texts—only occasionally by American poets, overwhelmingly by Irish or English—were usually selected for their inherent musical interest or because they held personal significance. *Knoxville: Summer of 1915*, for example, based on James Agee's memoir and sometimes considered the most "American" of Barber's works, was selected because it evoked an identification with, and nostalgia for, the composer's own childhood. In this regard, he bears a closer resemblance to nineteenth-century Romantics than to his peers, whose choice of subjects was often motivated by social consciousness or a sense of nationalism. His international literary orientation is reflected in the 1945 commencement address he delivered to young musicians at the Curtis Institute of Music: "One might think there were no poets except Sara Teasdale and Walt Whitman. . . . Do you know the poems of Spender, T. S. Eliot . . . W. H. Auden?"[3] Barber not only read their works but became a friend to many poets and writers.

Of the many influences on Barber's music, three seem most prominent in preserving his consistent connection to the nineteenth century. The first is the character of his formal musical education, which was traditional, Europe-oriented, and institutionalized—nine rigorous years of training in composition at the Curtis Institute of Music under the tutelage of Rosario Scalero, a student of Eusebius Mandyczewski, friend and colleague of Brahms.

The second is the impact on his intellectual development of travels to Europe. Beginning in his student years, Barber's affinity for European culture intensified with travel and extended residence abroad and found fulfillment in his close personal relationship and professional collaborations with Gian Carlo Menotti. Although such experiences freed him from the social provincialism and intellectual conservatism of Philadelphia, instead of being attracted to Paris—the "Boulangerie" and the arena of avant-gardism—Barber turned to Italy and mingled with young artists whose temperament and interests were in sympathy with his own Romantic orientation. His conviction that the narrow intellectual interests of American artists, resulting from an "intense vogue for specialization," so limited the vision of a musician that he virtually became "ossified within the very limits of his techniques" led him to form few alliances with composers and, in general, to prefer the company of nonmusician intellectuals (among the few exceptions were Menotti, Francis Poulenc, Alexei Haieff, Rudolf Serkin, and Dimitri Mitropoulos).*

*The quotations are from the Curtis Institute of Music commencement address, 12 May 1945. His delight in long conversations with poets in particular is made clear in a letter of 13 February 1946 to Katherine Garrison Chapin: "I am always interested in talking to poets," he wrote. "It's such a pleasure after musicians!" (Francis and Katherine Biddle Papers, Special Collections Division, Georgetown University Library).

A third force that molded Barber's artistic principles was the personal guidance he received from his uncle, the composer Sidney Homer, whose advice and mentoring can scarcely be overestimated. Homer's importance to his nephew is strongly disclosed by selected letters Barber thought significant enough to transcribe. They demonstrate that, from the time he was twelve until Homer's death in 1953, the younger composer was barraged with specific advice about his training. Early on, Homer held up to him as role models the giants of the nineteenth century, while at the same time directing his nephew to trust the validity of his "inner voice." He counseled him to ignore superficial intellectualism and transient opinions, to shun the mediocre in art. Yet within this context, paradoxically, he preached to his nephew an antielitist, populist point of view.

As much as Barber's nonrevolutionary posture was a product of his experience, however, it derived also from his personal motivation for writing music—to express feelings. From his earliest piano piece, "Sadness," to the song cycle written near the end of his career, *Despite and Still,* self-expression was inseparable from the compositional process:

> I suppose if I'm writing music for words, then I immerse myself in those words, and I let the music flow out of them. When I write an abstract piano sonata or a concerto, I write what I feel. I'm not a self-conscious composer.[4]

This self-projected image of the composer for whom writing music was always spontaneous and easy is contradicted over and over again, however, by Barber's letters and individual testimonies describing the birth-pangs that accompanied many of his large-scale works. Menotti, who knew Barber better than anyone, draws a profile of his friend as "gifted" but "tormented" by his need for perfection.[5]

Exceptions were his songs, which were often composed spontaneously during periods when he was having difficulty beginning a new piece or revising an old one. His facility with this genre is supported statistically: excluding large-scale vocal works—operas, choruses, and orchestral settings—Barber wrote 103 solo songs (of which only 37 are published). These represent more than half of his more than two hundred compositions.

No matter how unfashionable his tenacious loyalty to melody may have been judged from time to time in his career, Barber's impeccably crafted compositions continue to move listeners. Perhaps this is precisely because he had the "gift" of knowing how to merge "permissible innovation" with tradition.

I

BEGINNINGS

I was meant to be a composer

When he was nine years old Samuel Barber left a letter on his desk announcing his intention to become a composer:

> NOTICE to *Mother* and *nobody else*
> Dear Mother: I have written this to tell you my worrying secret. Now don't cry when you read it because it is neither yours nor my fault. I suppose I will have to tell it now without any nonsense. To begin with I was not meant to be an athlet [*sic*]. I was meant to be a composer, and will be I'm sure. I'll ask you one more thing.—Don't ask me to try to forget this unpleasant thing and go play football.—*Please*—Sometimes I've been worrying about this so much that it makes me mad (not very),
>
> *Love,*
> *Sam Barber II**

Although there are many legendary stories about composers, especially if they were child prodigies, this Barber legend is supported by material evidence, for the note itself has been preserved. In his adult years, Barber enjoyed retelling the story whenever interviewed about his career.

Samuel Osborne Barber II—named after his paternal grandfather—was born 9 March 1910 in the quiet town of West Chester, Pennsylvania, thirty miles from Philadelphia. In the mid-nineteenth century West Chester had been an affluent industrial town, but by the turn of the century what remained as a reminder of former wealth were gracious large homes, en-

*This letter is quoted in several different sources: Nathan Broder, in *Samuel Barber* (New York: G. Schirmer, 1956), reports that Barber was eight when he wrote it; the composer on two other occasions said he wrote the note when he was nine (quoted by James Felton in the *Philadelphia Bulletin*, 9 March 1980, and by Phillip Ramey in liner notes for the recording "Songs of Samuel Barber and Ned Rorem," New World Records, NW 229, 1978).

hanced with ornate cupolas, pillared doorways, and grand lawns.[1] The Barbers' three-story red brick house at 107 South Church Street was of generous proportions, fronted by an expansive porch with a decoratively striped awning and bordered along the sidewalk by neatly trimmed low hedges.*

A prevailing moral and cultural conservatism marked community and family life, perhaps an influence of a once dominant Quaker population that still existed in the town. Although a literary figure might be venerated—for example, the novelist Joseph Hergesheimer, West Chester's "most celebrated inhabitant"[2]—musicians and theater people were regarded with suspicion.† Music was considered to be mainly a diversion, "and a rather odd one at that," wrote Barber's cousin Anne Homer about West Chester: "There was a certain attitude toward music, a belittlement, as though it had no valid place in the scheme of things."[3] Nor, according to novelist Owen Wister, was Philadelphia any more open-minded about creative innovation; he is said to have remarked, "proper Philadelphians seem to distrust our own power to do anything out of the common; and when a young man tries to, our minds close against him with a civic instinct of disparagement."‡

This provincialism partially explains the resistance exerted by Barber's maternal relatives, the Beattys, when their daughter Louise, who had married the composer Sidney Homer, went off to Paris to study voice and dramatic acting. She became a celebrated opera singer,§ and during her career with the Metropolitan Opera, which began in 1900 and spanned two decades, she was one of the leading contraltos of her time.

Barber's mother, Marguerite McLeod Beatty Barber, called Daisy, was of English, Scottish-Irish descent, and her family had lived in the United States since Revolutionary times. Her great-great-grandfather, Captain Oliver Brown, had, according to his letters, "stood in front of the first cannon fired by the British on the Americans at Lexington" and was entrusted with "many small adventures" by General Washington. Her grandfather's cousin was Robert Fulton, the inventor of the steamboat.‖ The youngest

*A photograph of the Barber house is in Broder, *Samuel Barber,* between pages 32 and 33. The Barber family moved to this house in January 1919 (*West Chester Daily Local News,* 17 January 1919).

†Anne Homer refers to her grandmother's concern about her daughter Louise's choice of composer Sidney Homer for her husband: "The most stringent of her stipulations was that he should be earning enough to support a wife, for his unconventional, seasonal and somewhat uncertain occupation was looked upon with great suspicion in West Chester" (*Louise Homer and the Golden Age of Opera* [New York: William Morrow, 1974], p. 100).

‡William K. Stevens, "Bashful Philadelphians Changing with Newcomers Who Want to Stand Out," *New York Times,* 6 October 1985, p. 52. Wister and his sister Marina opened their home to Barber during the early 1930s.

§When, during the beginning of her operatic career, she played several *travesti* roles, Louise pacified her family's shock by having costumes specially designed to minimize the masculine character of her dress (see Anne Homer, *Louise Homer,* pp. 172–76).

‖Brown's letters are quoted in detail in Barber's unpublished memoir of his own childhood, "Fadographs of a Yestern Scene," ca. 1974, p. 1.

(Left) Samuel Osmond Barber II, fifteen months old. *(Right)* The Barber family ca. 1916.

of eight children and the daughter of a pastor, Daisy Beatty moved from Minneapolis to West Chester with her widowed mother in 1885, and when on 17 October 1905 she married the young doctor Roy Barber, she lived at 35 High Street, only a few blocks away from her family's home.* Their only son, Sam Barber, as he was called, was reported by a cousin to be "an unusually handsome child, strong, lively, and intelligent."[4] He had one sister, Sara, who was three years younger than he and the close companion of his youth. "I think she really understood my 'makeup' as an artist, about which my parents remained somewhat withdrawn," Barber wrote in his 1974 memoir. Sara was high-spirited, romantic, and by her own account greatly influenced intellectually by her older brother. Barber wrote some of his earliest songs for Sara. A family photograph shows Daisy Barber at the piano, flanked by Sam and Sara with song books in hand.†

* *West Chester Daily Local News,* 18 October 1905. Roy Barber's father, Samuel O. Barber, had come from Philadelphia to West Chester in 1888 to take charge of the Denny Tag Factory. In 1909 the family was considered among the "best known people in West Chester, and highly respected on account of their worth and genial disposition" (*West Chester Daily Local News,* 4 March 1908).

† Among the Beattys, Barber's mother's family, music making was a tradition. Although their father, Will Beatty, a minister and educator (he founded the Pennsylvania Female College, now Chatham College), was dedicated fully to his spiritual mission in the Presbyterian church, he often played the flute for his family (reportedly undergoing an "astonishing transformation") and saw to it that all four of his girls learned to play the piano. Duets were sometimes accompanied by Louise on the tambourine (see Anne Homer, *Louise Homer,* pp. 8–10).

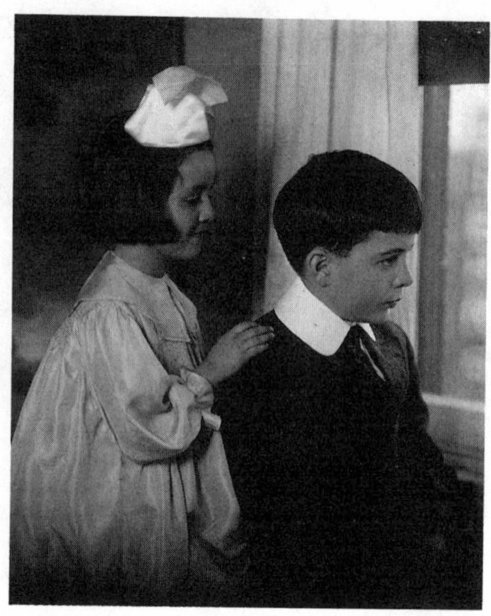

Sara and Sam Barber.

The Barbers handled their warm feelings for one another by gentle, though sometimes unmerciful, teasing: for example, Sara's musical training included singing lessons and years of piano lessons, and when she finally managed to learn the A-major intermezzo by Brahms, her father caused laughter with his remark, "That is the piece I have paid eight hundred dollars for."* But in fact Barber encouraged, sometimes even guided, Sara's musical development, and, although one cannot surmise how deep her commitment actually was, she must have been at least a competent musician.† "I'm so proud of Sara," he wrote from Italy in 1930, "perhaps she will be the first woman orchestra conductor, not a bad idea really."[5]

By the time he was six, Sam Barber was inventing melodies at the piano and his talent was recognized by his family.‡ Daisy Barber wrote proudly

*Barber, "Fadographs," p. 12. Katharine Homer Fryer reports that Sara spent several summers at Lake George studying singing with Louise Homer.

†A letter from Barber to his parents on 27 June 1930, for example, advises, "Tell Sara to learn the Brahms Intermezzo, Op. 116, No. 2. It should be among my music in Vol. II of his works; if not, she can get the single edition from Pressers. It is very easy, and a beauty—in A minor. Tell her not to play the part marked *Ossia* unless she can't possibly get the other."

All letters from Barber to his parents written between 1928 and 1931 cited in this book were made available to the author by the Estate of Samuel Barber through Valentin Herranz, companion to Barber from 1967 to 1981.

‡Broder, *Samuel Barber*, p. 6; Anne Homer (in *Louise Homer*, p. 369) reports, however, that when the young Sam was barely two, Daisy Barber wrote to her family that he was making up tunes on the piano; a news article in the *West Chester Daily Local News*, 13 July 1921, boasts that Barber had been a pianist "since his infancy."

to her relatives of her son's musical accomplishments and helped him write down his first compositions. Because of her aversion to "amateur male pianists," however, for a short time he was given cello lessons.[6]

Barber's father, president and treasurer of the board of trustees of the First Presbyterian Church of West Chester and president of the West Chester School Board for twenty-five years, was a "reserved type of person" who appeared distant until one got to know him.* In his memoir from the mid-1970s, Barber described his father as "a man of exquisite manners, much loved in town, affable, outgoing. . . . He was witty and gentle, with the fine hands of a surgeon, very conventional in his tastes, and devoted to and over-protective of my mother, who was somewhat childlike." Apparently he had other goals for his son than to be a composer. At the very least—as Sam's letter suggests—he wished his young son's preoccupation with music to be tempered by an interest in sports and other more conventional childhood activities.† At the crest of his career, Barber would say: "I was supposed to be a doctor. I was supposed to go to Princeton. And everything I was supposed to do I didn't."‡

From the time he was seven, Sam Barber, as he signed his pieces, had been writing down his own compositions.§ Exemplary of his youthful style are three works written between July and December 1917: two for piano—"Sadness," Op. I, No. 1,|| in C minor, acknowledged by the composer to be his first composition; and "Melody in F," with the melody daringly placed in the left hand—and a song dedicated to Barber's mother, "Sometime," on an affectionate text by Eugene Field. These and other early efforts of the young composer can be found in a leatherbound volume titled "Earliest Compositions" at the Library of Congress.# Of ten youthful pieces written between 1917 and 1919 in the collection, half are for voice (a proportion that would hold for his complete oeuvre) and are based on poems by poets popular with young people—Field being one of Barber's

*This account by John Sepella, a childhood friend of Barber, is recorded in "Samuel Barber: Portrait of a Musical Master," p. 29, an unpublished American history seminar project by students at Henderson High School, West Chester Area School District, 1982–83.

†Dorothy Bates, who was two grades behind Barber in school, recalled hearing Dr. Barber say about his son that he would ask nothing more out of life than to starve in a garret and become a musician ("Samuel Barber: Portrait of a Musical Master," p. 26). Sepella, when interviewed, said about the young Sam Barber: "He didn't quite understand people who didn't love music as he did. You couldn't talk to him about sports. . . . It was that his whole life was dedicated to one purpose and that was composition" (ibid., p. 29).

‡Interview by Robert Sherman, WQXR, 30 September 1978. John Sepella, music director and music supervisor of the West Chester Area School District for thirty-eight years, asked Barber (presumably early in his career) what kind of a mark he wanted to leave on the world; he is reported to have said: "I'm not out to make any mark for anyone or anything but to please myself and what I feel is right about music" ("Samuel Barber: Portrait of a Musical Master," p. 29).

§A complete listing of Barber's earliest compositions is included in my catalogue, in progress.

||Barber numbered his youthful works with Roman numerals.

#The portfolio was given to the library in the 1984 bequest of the Estate of Samuel Barber.

favorites. A waltz set to J. G. Whittier's poem "Isabel" (1919), on the other hand, represents a more sophisticated choice for a nine-year-old and demonstrates an early gift for grateful parlor tunes as well as a budding instinct for building tension through harmonic means.

Barber's interest in the piano was too strong to be denied—he was beginning to teach himself—thus in 1919 his parents obtained lessons for him with the best piano teacher they could find in West Chester, William Hatton Green, a former pupil of Leschetizky in Vienna. Green played an important role in the musical life of West Chester; he frequently gave recitals himself and accompanied Louise Homer and other singers when they performed in the community. Barber studied with Green until he entered Curtis in 1924 and kept in contact with him long after. With the devotion typically accorded by a teacher to a successful student, Green followed Barber's career avidly and kept a clipping file of programs, news articles, and reviews about him.* Barber participated in recitals of Green's students from the time he was nine years old, and on these occasions he sometimes played his own works. At one such recital, on 7 April 1920 at the First Presbyterian Church in West Chester, he played duets and solo piano pieces by Clementi, Bach, Tchaikovsky, Beethoven, and Stephen Heller, and three works of his own: two for piano—"At Twilight" and "Lullaby" (both 1919), a "virtuosic" effort requiring complicated hand crossings and including his first use of dynamic and tempo markings—and a song, "Child and Mother" (on words from the ubiquitous *Book of Knowledge,* vol. 12), in which he was joined by the versatile young soprano Miss Charlsie Eddins. The pair further impressed their audience with a selection of "Auto Harp Duetts." "Sam was at his best," the local paper puffed; "the manner in which he executed different selections. . . . brought round after round of applause."†

Barber's early piano compositions are, as might be expected, modeled on the kind of music Barber himself studied. His "Allegretto on C" (the third movement of "Themes," 1920, see below), for example, coincided with the study of Clementi's Sonatina, Op. 36, No. 1,‡ and bears characteristic bass figurations, decorative turns, and the doubling in thirds of the melodic line. Even these earliest pieces, however, give some hint of Barber's coming individuality. His focus was so strongly on song that many of his instrumental compositions were in fact "songs without words." Most,

*After his death, the collection of clippings was deposited in Philadelphia at the Curtis Institute of Music. The sources of these news articles are not always named or precisely dated but with some detective work could be identified.

†*West Chester Daily Local News,* 10 April 1920. A year later at the Art Alliance in Philadelphia on 25 May 1921 Barber performed three works for piano from Leo Ornstein's *Nine Miniatures.* The program and all other programs of piano recitals by Green's students cited here are in the William Hatton Green clipping file at the Curtis Institute of Music Library.

‡Barber and Charlsie Eddins played a two-piano arrangement of the sonatina in two recitals on 23 June 1919 and 7 April 1920.

up to 1919, are in simple forms—there was a fondness for codas in compound meter—and contain a clearly defined, undecorated diatonic melody, usually placed in the right hand, with an accompaniment of triads in simple cadential harmonies. Dominant and diminished-seventh chords and arpeggios began to appear sparingly, but even his more daring harmonizations suggest that although Barber enjoyed an occasional dissonance as an expressive device, it generally resulted from cross relations or voice leading—based on a linear, rather than vertical, logic.

Barber's precociousness at eight is evident in "War Song," Op. I, No. V (Example 1.1), whose title, year of composition (1918), and character—somber and militaristic—all suggest it was stimulated by his awareness of World War I.

The young composer seemed to enjoy the reiteration of the dissonance C♮ in the left hand against the C♯ in the right (mm. 2–3), for he repeated it several measures later with D and D♭. A suggestion in this piece of the vocabulary that later was intrinsic to Barber's mature style is the shifting between minor and major modes: the first section begins in G minor and ends in F major; the second begins in F minor.

The titles of Barber's piano works during this period reflect their character—"Sadness," "War Song," "At Twilight," "Lullaby," and "Largo"—and suggest that, from the start, even abstract music was for Barber synonymous with expression of feeling. "In the Firelight" (Eugene Field) demonstrates his penchant for melancholy themes, even at a tender age (Example 1.2).

By the time he was eleven Sam Barber was studying the pipe organ and showed some proficiency on the instrument at the First Presbyterian Church, to which his family belonged.[7] The following year he obtained a job as organist for the Westminster Church in West Chester, where he earned $100 a month. One of his compositions, a "Sacred Solo" dedicated "to Auntie,"* was sung by a parishioner, Mrs. Fred Dutt, on words from a little volume of newspaper poetry from the *New York Herald* published under the inspiring title "The Uplands of God." His employment was short-lived, however, for in less than a year he was fired for refusing to hold fermatas in hymns and responses. An elaborate work for organ written in 1923, "To Longwood Gardens," was dedicated to Mr. and Mrs. Pierre DuPont, whose great organ Barber had played on numerous occasions.†

* Mrs. William C. Husted was organist at the First Presbyterian Church for several years. The manuscript is at the Chester County Historical Society.

† The manuscript is at the Library of Congress. The *West Chester Daily Local News* (6 November 1922) reported the young composer's attendance at a concert by John Philip Sousa at the DuPonts' Longwood Conservatories:

> Mr. du Pont, seeing the lad, whom he knows and for whom he has great admiration, realizing that Sam is a musician of no mean note, came forward and took the boy up and introduced him to the March King.

Example 1.1 "War Song," holograph, 1918. *(Library of Congress)*

Sousa was pleased to talk to the chap and learning some facts as to Barber's musical ability, sat down and dashed off three lines . . . of "The Stars and Stripes Forever." He signed the same and presented it to Sam, who is about the proudest boy in town, and would not part with his treasure for a good deal.

Example 1.2 "In the Firelight," holograph, 1918. *(Library of Congress)*

Perhaps the most important personal relationship determining the early course of Barber's career was that with his uncle Sidney Homer. The older composer acted as his mentor from 1922, when Barber showed him his first compositions, up to the time of Homer's death in 1953. From wherever he traveled, Barber wrote in detail to Homer about his music and its compositional progress, and he wrote in greater depth to him than to any other person.* His appreciation for his uncle and his high regard for Homer's own compositions found tangible expression in 1942 when Barber initiated an "all-Homer" radio broadcast,[8] and in 1943 when he arranged for G. Schirmer to publish some of Homer's more popular songs in a volume, *Seventeen Songs by Sidney Homer*.†

Given his family's initial ambivalence toward music as a profession for their son, one might well imagine how important was the time the young Barber spent during the summers with his uncle and aunt at Homeland, on Lake George, in Bolton, New York. Barber recalled that from his childhood on—in Lake George and New York City—he heard his aunt sing her husband's songs integrated into programs of works by more recognized European composers. "She did not give them a place only at the end of her programs, which is the common destiny of most American songs, brought up at the rear, like after dinner mints, for an audience whose best attention has already been given elsewhere."[9] "She was one of the most radiant creatures one could imagine," Barber recalled in the 1970s. "My aunt's voice sounded like no other . . . the rich low voice combined with brilliant high notes that Verdi would have liked and is so rare today."[10]

Compared to the somewhat staid, dry attitude of West Chester, the Homers represented a lively cultural oasis for the young Sam Barber, who was consumed with the idea of being a composer and for whom writing songs "just seemed a natural thing to do." Louise Homer often visited her sister's home in West Chester. Many years later, after he had written his first opera, Barber spoke about her arrivals:

> For a little boy, the sight of the train stopping at Paoli (where the Western express never stopped and where the stationmaster told us it would never stop) was an impressive experience. I knew this was because the Met had arranged it, and I found it exciting. On the other hand, once she got there, she would never sing for us but, with the most endearing smile in the world, would tell us children that she was "out of voice." We thought she was really "out of voice."[11]

* The correspondence between Homer and Barber has been preserved by Sidney Homer's daughter Katharine Homer Fryer and is one of the richest sources of information about Barber's career between 1941 and 1953; all letters from Barber to Homer that are quoted in this book are in Fryer's collection. Barber transcribed selected letters of his uncle's, written from 1912 to 1953; excerpts from these letters are quoted with the permission of Katharine Homer Fryer.

†Homer, born in Boston in 1864, studied there with Chadwick and received further training with Rheinberger in Munich. He wrote at least 103 songs between 1899 and 1915, all of which were published by G. Schirmer. "Throughout his life," his nephew wrote in the introduction to the volume of Homer's songs published in 1943, "a sturdy New England reliance balanced his respect for European tradition."

Barber recalled watching her make a recording for RCA Victor in Camden, New Jersey, in "those pre-electric, pre-patchwork days, when a miss was really a miss, and no splicing could correct it. . . . I saw the exhaustion," he wrote in his memoir in the seventies, "Caruso exhausted, Galli-Curci exhausted. But I was more interested in getting a close-up view of the orchestral instruments." Barber attended his first opera with his uncle Sidney at the Metropolitan Opera House. His memory of the experience was vivid:

> I was six and entranced. It was in New York. The opera: *Aida*. Caruso sang Radames and my aunt, Louise Homer, was Amneris. Even the details are clear in my memory. We missed "Celeste Aida," due to parents' and uncle's irritating habit of lingering over coffee. Once arrived, there was the usual tussle as to who could keep the opera glasses longer (it seemed to me I always had to give them back at just the best moment). And then the kindly old Bishop, in whose box we sat, asked me, at the beginning of the Nile scene, whether I could hear the mosquitoes. This was a signal for me to retrieve my glasses—the best ones. I looked and listened long and hard. I could hear no mosquitoes, only high violins. Ever since that day I have thought that people who listen for too much description in music are rather silly.[12]

At Homeland, Barber and his uncle often reviewed the younger composer's work and sometimes studied music together—a Bach invention or some other classical work. The Homers encouraged Barber "to become acquainted with only the finest music."[13] His aunt did not want him to become a dilettante, and it was only after he entered the Curtis Institute in Philadelphia that she and her husband gave Barber's intention to compose their full support. It was entirely due to Sidney Homer's encouragement that the Barbers allowed their son to be excused from school at noon to travel to Philadelphia to study at the Curtis Institute of Music in its charter year, 1924. Several years earlier, Barber solicited advice from his uncle about a group of songs and part of an opera that he had written. Apparently his uncle's evaluation was crucial to the Barbers' decision to provide professional training for their son.

Barber asked his uncle two questions that were uppermost in his mind: "Do you think from these works of mine that I can become a composer? And if so, what should I do to further my musical career?"[14] Homer weighed his answer carefully, for he did not want to conflict with the interest of Barber's parents. But recognizing the urgency of obtaining early training for a musical profession, even though he couched his persuasive letter in moderate terms, he was explicit in his reply:

> I am returning the Gypsy Dance and the Mother Goose which you sent me. There is no doubt you have the making of a composer in you. There

are touches all through this work which prove it. Therefore, I think it would be fully worth your while to take an intensive course of study with the best man in Philadelphia.

There are three things you must aim for definitely. The first is the development of a taste that should, in time, amount to a passion, for the best in music in all forms. . . . Your whole life will be influenced by the forming of your taste in the next few years.

Taste is formed by coming into close and intimate contact with the great works of the masters. . . . The way to do this is to look ahead and see what programs are to be given in Philadelphia. You can't attend all the concerts, therefore you pick the best. Suppose, for instance, the Flonzaly Quartet is going to play a Beethoven Quartet. You get your ticket and you buy a copy of the quartet beforehand. You then learn more in an hour at the performance than you could possibly learn in any other way in a year.

The second . . . is to have a good teacher in composition. One fairly long lesson a week would be sufficient. Anyone you study with should be a practical composer himself, and as good a man as you can find. If you will write to Mr. Stokowski himself and . . . say that I have asked you to inquire for the best teacher in composition, I am sure [he] will recommend someone to you.

The third thing is that you should master a practical instrument . . . I should say either the piano or the violin, or, better still, both. That is what Mozart and Beethoven did.

If you can't do all three of these things, I should take up the first and third. You must not think that you can fool with music and get anywhere. Sooner or later you will have to do hard work, and you will make more rapid progress now than when you are older.

You can get good books on Harmony and Musical Notation, and they will interest you. For instance, in your last Mother Goose song, I Love Little Pussy, you divide the right hand into groups of three eighth notes, which give the appearance of 6/8 time, but the piece is in 3/4 time. At the beginning of the third measure, you write B natural, whereas it is really C flat. Little mistakes like these sometimes spoil the looks of really good music.

Affectionately yours,
Sidney Homer[15]

Perhaps what Homer appreciated in these pieces was Barber's command of form and the originality of his melodic lines. This is especially apparent in the nursery song, where the vocal part displays a strong sense of direction and interplays graciously with the contrasting arpeggios in a piano accompaniment that often rises above the voice. A manuscript of "I Love Little Pussy" (Example 1.3) shows that Barber made the corrections suggested by Homer. The layout of the piano part suggests he taught himself notation, probably writing the vocal lines first and then adding the accompaniment.

The song is one of a collection titled "Mother Goose Rhymes Set to Music," which Barber eventually bound and illustrated with pictures from nursery books that he hand-colored. (A second manuscript, titled Nursery Songs, Opus VII, is dedicated to Sara.) His models were probably Sidney Homer's "Songs from Mother Goose," written in 1919 as a response to Louise Homer's request for a group of songs that the whole family could sing together and which Barber had undoubtedly heard.* The typewritten preface of Barber's "Mother Goose Rhymes" explains their history:

> From old manuscripts and music books I have collected and copied my Mother Goose Songs. "The Old Man From Jamaica," "The Rockabye Lady," and "I love Little Pussy" have been composed comparatively recently (1922), but the others are much earlier compositions.
>
> The mistakes in notation, the harmonical errors, the poor constructions—they have not been omitted. They are as I first wrote them, before I knew the tiresome rules of harmony.
>
> The ranges are indeed unique. They suit my own Low voice, with an occasional high note beyond my range for effect.
>
> And now I leave you, to sing or play these little child-songs.
>
> *Samuel O. Barber II*
> *April 8, 1923*[16]

The songs were sung by Sara Barber, accompanied by her brother, on 24 March 1923 at a benefit performance for the piano fund of the Sunday school of the First Presbyterian Church in West Chester. A glowing "review" in a local newspaper found "Sam's original compositions particularly interesting, showing a musical conception and feeling which marks him as a budding artist of musical ability. . . . Little Sara Barber sang in a voice marked by its sweetness and clearness. . . . Her manner was unaffected and altogether charming."†

This recital is of special interest because it featured the "Barber Orchestra"—a pair of violins, a cornet, saxophone, drums, and piano—with Sam Barber as "pianist-director" conducting two works by R. H. Bowers and T. H. Morse and, more importantly, selections from *The Rose Tree*, his own opera, written when he was ten.‡ Although the opera never progressed beyond act 1, from its music Barber made many arrangements,

* They were recorded with orchestra in 1922. An earlier recording with piano was never released, but—according to Katharine Fryer—was probably known to the Barber family.

† *West Chester Daily Local News*, 26 March 1923. The box office took in $60.

‡ A manuscript of act 1 of *The Rose Tree* is at the Library of Congress, and the complete libretto and various vocal parts are at the Chester County Historical Society in West Chester. Many of the manuscripts of the score, parts, or arrangements are sewn into cardboard covers decorated with colorful florid designs; the "Gypsy Dance" has a characteristic picture of a Spanish dancer on its cover, a design credited to William Palmer Lear. Lear (who eventually

Example 1.3 "I Love Little Pussy," from "Mother Goose Rhymes set to music," holograph, 1922. *(Library of Congress)*

most for piano, some of which he played in Green's student recitals. One, for violin and piano, was the "Gypsy Dance" he had sent to Sidney Homer in 1922, a habanera with a tricky descending chromatic theme for the violin, imitated at the third by the piano (Example 1.4).

became director of the Chester County Art Association) was reported to be—with Edward Dicks—one of Barber's closest childhood friends. All three young men were born on the same day (*West Chester Daily Local News*, 9 March 1937).

The libretto of *The Rose Tree* was written by Annie Sullivan Brosius Noble, the Barbers' cook, who had been imported from Ireland by the composer's grandmother. She had an unlimited repertoire of Irish songs, which Barber often heard her sing. Her darkly humorous imagination and romantic language were things he never forgot.* From her opera text, one

*Samuel Barber, "On Waiting for a Libretto," *Opera News* (27 January 1958): 6. In this article Barber recounts an example of Annie Noble's parlance: once, when Daisy Barber

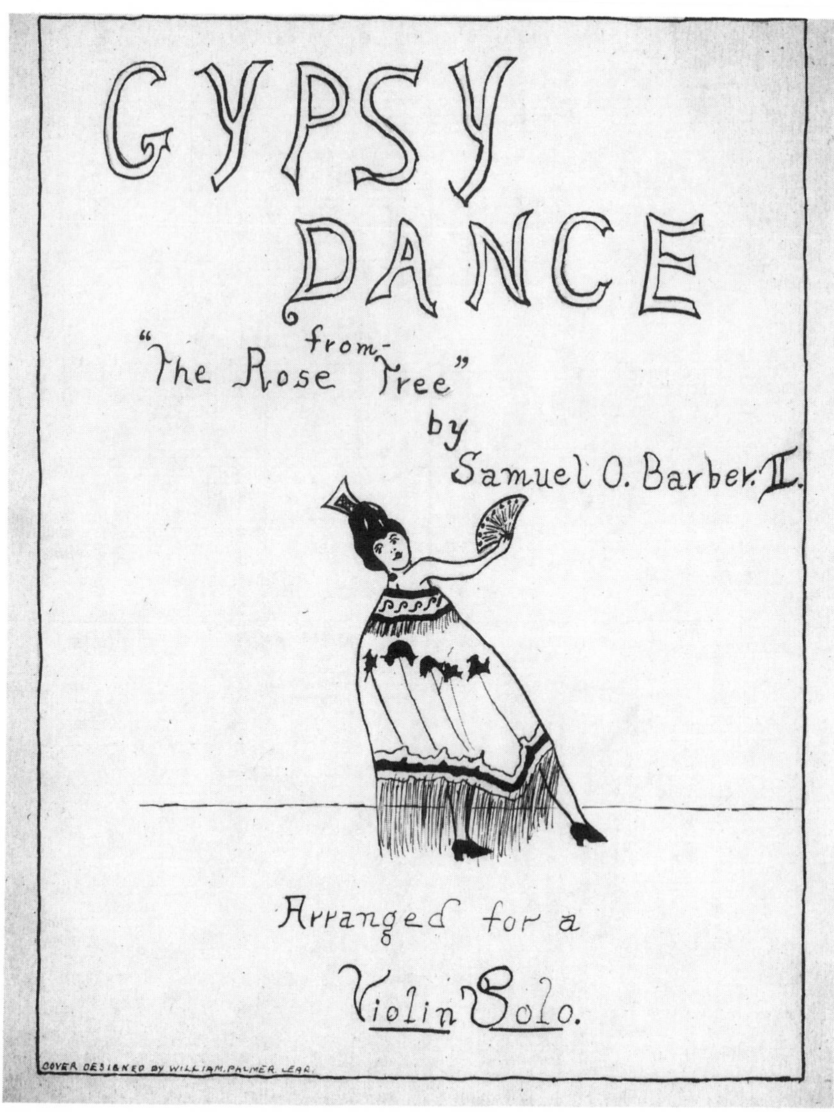

Example 1.4 Cover and title page of "Gypsy Dance," arranged for violin and piano from *The Rose Tree*, holograph, 1922. *(Library of Congress)*

is able to surmise that Annie Noble was quite literate and had read much poetry.* The keen interest in Celtic poetry that emerged in Barber during

inquired what the family was having for dessert, the cook responded, "Madame, a little something of my own. It is called a Bird's Eye View of Death."

*The title itself is significant in that the rose is a favorite symbol with Irish poets in both love poems and addresses to Ireland, and it has given a name to more than one poem in

his teen years may have been as much due to the influence of Annie Noble as that of Sidney Homer, who used Irish texts for his songs.

Interviewed in 1960, Barber recounted the story of his first opera:

Gaelic and Irish. Although Yeats's poem "The Rose Tree" was not published until 1921 (*Michael Robartes and the Dancer* [Ireland: Coala Press, 1921]), he wrote an earlier collec-

It deals with a tenor of the Metropolitan Opera who comes to a small American town on his vacation and falls in love with a local beauty. I wrote the heroine's part for my younger sister, who can still sing every note of it. The hero's part was for me. I was a contralto then! Somehow, after the words and music were written for the first act, Annie ran out of ideas and the opera went no further.[17]

The principal characters are Juanita Alvarado and the Stranger, with a supporting cast of Landlord, Old Man, and a Band of Gypsies (for which Barber wrote a dance and chorus). A description of the opening scene is in the piano score:

The scene is laid in the courtyard of an old Spanish Inn in Florida.* Modern civilization of the nineteenth century has not yet reached Connera and the fashions are very quaint and picturesque. To the left is the inn door. The landlord, servants and a few Spaniards are lounging about the yard. As the curtain rises, a group of wandering gypsies enter upon the scene. They dance, clashing their tambourines, and sing.[18]

Barber never forgot the words of the opening "Gypsy Chorus," and in later years he would occasionally amuse his friends at parties by singing bits of the song:

A wandering gypsy we!
The whole wide world is ours;
We dance and sing with gladsome glee
Through the sunny hours.
We care not for the toilsome way
The world so madly follows,
Our hearts are light, our lives are gay
And free from care as . . . swallows![19]

The vocal score of *The Rose Tree,* musically intriguing with its occasional instructions for "enharmonic change" and a tenor aria for the Old Man, sung to the accompaniment of a lone bass viol, reveals as well an entrepreneurial spirit with the announcement on the inside back cover: "Other Songs by same composer sold at $.60 1.p." The climax of act 1 is the heroine's "Serenade" (in which she is joined by a second voice), which recounts the tale of a "foreigner" who sought romance with Juanita's forebears at the Rose Tree. Annie Noble's language is that of late eighteenth-

---

tion titled *The Rose* (*Poems,* 1895), which Annie Noble may have read. It is more probable, however, that she was merely well versed in Irish and Gaelic folk culture and mythology.

*In later years, Barber, perhaps in jest, incorrectly described the action as taking place in Chester County (Emily Coleman, "Samuel Barber and *Vanessa,*" *Theatre Arts* [January 1958]: 69).

century lyric poets; her poetic meter and sentiment are akin to Robert Burns's "O my luve is like a red, red rose." The foreigner, Alvarado, sings:

> My love is like a rose that blooms, but never dies,
> Like the flaming sun, shalt not perish from the skies
> 'Tis like the fairest flow'r!
> 'Tis like the fairest bird that flew!
> And so I come tonight, to sing my love to you.[20]

Although rooted in parlor song tradition, the aria demonstrates considerable flair for construction of effective vocal lines for the labors of a boy of ten years (Example 1.5). The flowing melody surges through an octave within four measures and arches to a high G (Sara must have had an agile voice). A twice-recurring refrain is borrowed from Longfellow's "Serenade" in *The Spanish Student:* "Stars of the summer Night! / Far in yon azure deeps, / Hide, hide your golden light! / She sleeps! / My lady sleeps! / Sleeps!" The young composer shows admirable sensitivity to the text in using a persistently chanted G for the last lines of the refrain and the momentary color of minor mode on Noble's phrase *the moon steals through the bars.*

The Composer in His Early Teens

By early adolescence, Barber was composing in a variety of genres, and in the few years before he entered the Curtis Institute of Music at fourteen, he had written many pieces for piano, several for organ, a work for two pianos, a cantata, a suite for violin, his first opera, and a plethora of songs.* During this period, too, it was not uncommon for him to rework themes from earlier works into new ones. An example of his inventiveness in exhausting the possibilities of a theme is a minuet of which there are four versions, all written in 1923. Two, in G major, are for piano: the earliest is the second movement of "Themes," Op. X, No. 2;[21] a later, expanded version dedicated to Sara and including a trio (from Beethoven's Minuet No. 2, WoO 10), was published in 1924 as the last of *Three Sketches* (Example 1.6).† A Suite for Violin, Op. XI, No. 2, is unlocated but adver-

* Most of the works from this period are at the Library of Congress; some, including the cantata, "Christmas Eve, Op. XIII, a trio with solos," are at the Chester County Historical Society in West Chester. A complete listing of locations and manuscripts for works written during Barber's youth will be included in my descriptive catalogue now in progress.

† At the Chester County Historical Society, there is a letter from Barber to the U.S. Copyright Office inquiring about how to secure copyright registration of works. Two other sketches in the collection are "Love Song" (April 1924) and "To My Steinway" (June 1923). "Love Song" is an affectionate waltz, dedicated "to Mother," that was later published in a collection of pieces of intermediate-grade difficulty, *American Composers of the Twentieth Century* (Schaum Publications, 1969). Bennett Lerner's description of the piece with performance practice suggestions is published in *Keyboard Classics* (July-August 1986): 4–5. The second of the Sketches—"To My Steinway," dedicated to Number 220601, Barber's piano—is also a waltz, an expansive exploration of the full range of the keyboard.

tised on the manuscript of a "transcription" for piano solo ("easy") under the imprint "Barber and Co" (20 December 1923). Finally, a trio for contralto, soprano, and piano, for which was added a nostalgic text that may have been written by Barber himself, was undoubtedly—as its dog-eared pages suggest—sung many times by Louise Homer and her daughter Louise Stires.*

Several compositions written between 1922 and 1924 mark a leap forward in the young composer's maturation, demonstrating greater variety of color in harmonic language and an interest in more extended forms. *Petite Berceuse,* for example, displays harmonic similarities to Debussy's *En Bateau*—a motion from tonic to submediant in the opening measures (although Barber alternately uses a flat VI chord)—and includes chords with intervals of tenths and thirteenths in parallel motion.†

Barber's first attempt at handling an extended form is a "Fantasie for Two Pianos Written in the Style of Joseph Haydn" (1924).‡ The sectional design, the shape of the themes—triadic or repeated notes decorated abundantly with ornamental turns—suggest that he may have had in mind a model like the C-major sonata of Haydn.§ At fourteen, Barber was so serious about, and so intensely aware of, his own creative process that he detailed the work's complicated four-year evolution in a typewritten introduction dated 23 September 1924 and entitled "The Life of the Fantasie":

> The Fantasie was composed, rather completed on Feb. 15, 1924, because of a request by Mrs. Kerlin for a two-piano piece. Completed, I say, because its history went back to an earlier date than that. As far as I can tell, the "Andante con moto" theme was composed in 1920 for one piano. I looked at it later in 1922 with the idea of arranging it for violin, cello, and piano. Hence why we still call it the "Trio." But it never worked out. I had then the old theme and the introduction to the B-flat part—the little counterpoint, written sometime before, but I was at loss to find a B-flat section and so let the whole thing drop. In January '24, I found it again and finally, about February first, wrote the first section and the B-flat major, from which the introduction is constructed.

*The text reads "Come dance with me the minuet / Slowly as we loved to do / Sing songs I'll ne'er forget / Oh, dance and I'll dance with you." The holograph is in Katharine Homer Fryer's collection of her mother's music.

†The holograph is at the Chester County Historical Society, West Chester, Pennsylvania. A program of a piano recital on 23 March 1923 (about the same time Barber's *Berceuse* was composed), at the Chapel of First Presbyterian Church in West Chester, indicates that, at the time he composed this piece, Barber was playing *Berceuse* by Leo Ornstein (one of his *Nine Miniatures*).

‡The Fantasie is at the Library of Congress, Music Division. The manuscript's cover is decorated in elaborate script reading "from the original of Bach's Well Tempered Clavichord." The material for this work is derived from the earlier "Allegretto on C" (in "Themes," 1920). A manuscript of the second piano part of an earlier version, titled Sonata in Modern Form, Op. XVI, is at the Chester County Historical Society.

§The work is included in the *Sonatina Album* published by C. F. Peters, which also includes the Clementi sonatina that Barber played when he was ten.

Example 1.5 Vocal score of "Serenade," from *The Rose Tree*, holograph, ca. 1920. *(Library of Congress)*

Example 1.6 Minuet (1923) from *Three Sketches for Pianoforte* (private edition, 1924).

legato
molto ritard
Tempo I
dim. e rall.

The Barbers on the boardwalk at Atlantic City, New Jersey, in the late 1920s.

> I wrote the second piano part out one Sunday morning, and Mrs. Kerlin and I played it that afternoon on Mr. Green's [Barber's piano teacher] Two Pianos. Everyone was much impressed and Mother cried a little for lack of something better to do. I was then thirteen years old.
>
> It was first publicly performed at the New Century Club, April 29, with Mother and I playing it on two specially tuned pianos, a Steinway Grand and an Upright. We had to repeat it.
>
> I like it for its simplicity—it was written in the style of Haydn—and Uncle Sid Homer says it is the best thing I have done!*

Undoubtedly, what Barber's uncle recognized about his nephew's longest abstract work to that time was that he had a good grasp of the use of tonal and thematic structure as an effective unifying principle of design. Unlike Barber's earlier instrumental works, "Fantasie" is based on themes of a motivic, rather than lyrical, character and employs developmental procedures. Yet that even so abstract a form should be imbued with drama is evident from his instructions to play a restless transition passage "mysteriously, with foreboding."

What continues to be striking about Barber's songs during this early

*Library of Congress, Music Division. Sonata in Modern Form, Op. XVI is a much shorter version, but it does contain the B♭ section and so is presumably the result of Barber's February 1924 effort. It is possible that the sonata was completed as late as April 1924, since its opus number is later than Barber's Op. XIV ("My Fairyland") dated 29 March 1924.

period is their intuitive lyricism; melody as a means of expression for him was irrepressible. At this time, his songs also demonstrate an increasingly sophisticated skill in fusing music and poetry. Turning toward through-composed songs, he began to write more intricate accompaniments, which often support the voice in a felicitous counterpoint that sometimes rises above the vocal line. Harmonic or modal shifts color or emphasize specific words of the text. Compared to his instrumental works of this period, the songs seem more spontaneous, more personal and related to his own experience. Occasionally he even wrote his own verses, for example, "October-Weather" (ca. 1923), an ingratiating, rip-roaring waltz in E♭ major that celebrates the onset of autumn. An "encore song" in French-Canadian dialect, "Dere Two Fella Joe," was composed while Barber was at Camp Wyanoke in New Hampshire, on "words related to the composer by a White Mountain Guide, spoken by a French-Canadian father, very much excited and mystified by the arrival of twins in his family."*

Sometimes he set to music texts by local poets, for example, Robert T. Kerlin, the controversial head of the English Department at West Chester State Teachers College who was a great supporter of Barber's aspirations during his teen years.† When Barber was barely fourteen he set Kerlin's "My Fairyland," a poem of moralistic bent promising fulfillment through spiritual fortitude, which was sung by the soprano Gertrud Schmidt on an "all-Barber program" on 25 April 1926, two years after its composition.‡ The song's bristling, pulsating piano accompaniment, which suggests the young composer had heard Schumann's *Ich grolle nicht,* and its harmonic

* Manuscripts of both of these songs are at the Library of Congress, Music Division, and also in Louise Homer's private collection (now owned by her daughter Katharine Homer Fryer).

† Barber played two-piano music with Kerlin's wife. Educated at University of Chicago, Johns Hopkins, Harvard, and Yale, Kerlin had served as a minister for three years with the Methodist Episcopal Church South before coming to West Chester in 1922. A promoter of poetry by black writers and the author of several books on labor and racial subjects, he lost his job at West Chester State Teachers College in 1927 because of a heated debate over the military involvement of the United States in Central America. Kerlin was probably largely responsible for introducing Barber to the poetry of Langston Hughes, whose poem "Fantasy in Purple" the young composer set in 1925.

‡ The first "all-Barber" program, with the singers Schmidt and Lilian McD. Brinton, mezzo-soprano, took place in West Chester in the composer's home on 107 South Church Street. Barber wrote: "About a hundred friends heard this program, given at my home. Auntie and Aunt Bess were here, and the Boyles [George Boyle taught Barber piano his first year at the Curtis Institute of Music] drove out from Philadelphia." The program—a facsimile of which can be found in the liner notes of "Songs of Samuel Barber and Ned Rorem" (New World Records, NW 229)—included seventeen songs composed between 1917 and 1926: "Mother Goose Songs" (dedicated to Sara Barber), "Longing" and "Little Children of the Wind" (Macleod), "Sometime (Dedicated to Mother, 1917)," "Lady, When I Behold the Roses" (Wyatt), "*Au Claire de la Lune* (A Modern Setting)," "Dere Two Fella Joe," "October-Weather," "My Fairyland" (Kerlin), "Music, When Soft Voices Die" (Shelley), "Watchers," "Fantasy in Purple" (Hughes), "Youth" (probably "I Never Thought That Youth Would Go," Rittenhouse), "*La nuit*" (Meurath), "Man," "Slumber Song of the Madonna" (Noyes), "Thy Love" (Browning), "Invocation to Youth" (Binyon). Manuscripts of these songs are in the Library of Congress, Music Division.

motion—restless, chromatic, and vacillating between major and minor modes—beautifully underscore the dramatic fervor of the text.*

Among the friends of his youth, Sam Barber was perceived as "an unusual child" whose whole world was music, about which he seemed to know more than anyone else his age. An anecdote told by a former classmate suggests the acuity of Barber's ear when he was in the sixth grade, probably about twelve years old:

> We used to have assemblies and Sam always played the music. At one particular assembly he was so upset because the music was in the wrong key. All the rest of us didn't even know what a key was. The music sounded all right to us.[22]

Even with the rigors of his musical training, he was an outstanding student in high school and a leader in extracurricular activities as well: he was president of the Music Club, literary editor of the quarterly yearbook, president of the Drama Club, and a member of the Latin and French clubs. In addition, he won numerous awards: first prizes in the Junior and Senior Essay Contests and the Webster Meredith Prize Speaking Contest, and honorable mention in the Lincoln Essay Contest. He wrote the class poem and composed his class alma mater, which still stands as the song for West Chester's high school.[23]

Once Barber's parents realized there was no redirecting the goal of their impassioned son, they did everything they could to encourage him and help him obtain a high-quality musical education. When he was about fourteen, soon after he entered high school, Barber played for Harold Randolph, director of the Peabody Conservatory of Music in Baltimore. Randolph recommended he leave school and direct himself toward full-time study of composition and music.[24] Plans were then made for Barber to commute to Philadelphia every Friday for study at the newly founded Curtis Institute of Music while continuing his high school studies in West Chester.

* A copy, bound in yellow construction paper and decorated with a seascape illustration, is among Katharine Homer Fryer's collection of her mother's music.

2

A SERIOUS STUDENT

Against a background of quiet culture

When the doors of the Curtis Institute of Music were opened for the first time on 1 October 1924, Sam Barber was the second person to enter.* Photographs of the fourteen-year-old Barber show him to be lanky and serious, his handsome features hidden behind large spectacles. His hair, parted in the middle, and square chin give him a marked resemblance to his uncle Sidney Homer.

The Curtis Institute was founded by Mary Curtis Bok, born in 1876, the daughter of Louisa Knapp and the prominent publisher Cyrus H. K. Curtis. By the time the institute held its first classes, Mary Bok's wide circle of friends and her knowledge of the musical world enabled her to select an advisory board of great artistic eminence. Included were Felix Adler, Carl Flesch, Walter Fischer, Ossip Gabrilowitsch, Josef Hofmann, Willem Mengelberg, Marcella Sembrich, Leopold Stokowski, Ernest Urchs (of the Steinway Company), and Edward A. Zeigler (then assistant general manager of the Metropolitan Opera).†

Mary Bok's educational philosophy, stated in the institute's catalogue of 1925–26, reflects the educational standard to which Barber was exposed during his nine years at the Curtis Institute:

> It is my aim that earnest students shall acquire a thorough musical education, not learning only to sing or play, but also the history of music, the laws of its making, languages, ear-training and music appreciation.

*Nellie Lee Bok (Mary Bok's daughter-in-law, who was present the opening day of the school), interview with the author, 12 May 1982, Philadelphia. Bok reported that Max Aronoff, a violinist who later played in the Curtis String Quartet and taught on the faculty of the institute, was the first to enter the doors of the institute.

†The Curtis Institute of Music, *Overtones* 11, no. 1, Fiftieth Anniversary Issue (1 October 1974), pp. 9–12. *Overtones* is a newsletter that was started in 1929 and issued on an irregular basis until April 1940. It was written by members of the Curtis faculty, edited by Elsie Hutt, and conceived by Mary Louise Curtis Bok, who presided over the preparation of each issue. It is a valuable source of information about performances of Barber's music and the progress of his career during the 1930s and early 1940s.

> They shall learn to think and to express their thoughts against a background of quiet culture, with the stimulus of personal contact with artist-teachers who represent the highest and finest in their art.
>
> The aim is for quality of the work rather than quick, showy results.[1]

Mary Bok was more than a philanthropist in the traditional sense. Beneath her gentle, calm, wise, and gracious exterior was a forceful spirit that pervaded the institute and was imbibed by its students. She actively dedicated herself to bringing their talents to fruition by giving them personal encouragement as well as financial support.* Her intense loyalty and generosity and the influential network of social connections with other musical patrons in her milieu led to numerous opportunities for her students to perform in the widest public arena, not only in Philadelphia but in Washington, D.C., London, Italy, Florida, and New York.†

When Sam Barber entered the Curtis Institute of Music, he took up three areas of study, in all of which he distinguished himself. Piano studies with George Boyle led to further study, from 1926 to 1931, with Isabelle Vengerova. He studied voice with Emilio de Gogorza from 1926 to 1930 and composition and music theory with Rosario Scalero from 1925 until 1934.‡ Scalero had studied in Vienna with the eminent Austrian musicologist Eusebius Mandyczewski. A composer himself, he had the dubious distinction of having Toscanini comment that his music was "grey."§

* Her personal stereotypes are hinted at by some of her candid remarks; she is reported to have said, for example, "One thing I have learned, is that the talented youngster is no slacker" (*Overtones*, 1 October 1974, p. 12).

† Bok began to take a special interest in Samuel Barber in 1934, shortly before he graduated from the institute, and, beyond financial patronage, actively provided opportunities that promoted his career. Through her came, for example, the introduction to Carl Engel at G. Schirmer, Inc., the firm that became Barber's exclusive publisher. She invited Barber to spend summers at the beautiful harbor village of Rockport, Maine, where she and her husband Edward provided cottages for selected graduates and faculty members who taught their more gifted students over the summer. In 1943 Mrs. Bok married the violinist Efrem Zimbalist, director of the institute. That same year, she enabled Barber and Gian Carlo Menotti to buy Capricorn, the house in Mount Kisco, New York, which until 1973 was both the hermitage of Barber's most productive years and the center of the two composers' social and intellectual life, a gathering place for the numerous gifted artists, poets, musicians, and theater people who were their friends. Upon his patron's death, Barber reflected, "Rather than recall Mary Zimbalist as a philanthropist and social benefactor, I prefer to think of her as a life-long friend who never failed me" (*Overtones*, 1 October 1974, p. 25). Although Bok had encouraged Barber (and Menotti, too) to write letters to her so that his career might be documented, after her death the extensive collection was said to have been destroyed by her son Carey Bok (author's interview with Nellie Lee Bok, 12 May 1982).

‡ Apparently he studied composition with Deems Taylor for a brief period in 1926. Although Taylor's name is absent from Barber's student records at the Curtis Institute, there is a holograph—"A modern setting of the folk tune *Au clair de la lune*"—with the inscription "for Deems Taylor's class" among his "Early Compositions, 1917–1927" at the Library of Congress, Music Division. The composition, for piano, is a dissonant satire of the French folk song, with instructions to be played "mournfully, *con moto*."

§ Jeanne Behrend, interview with the author, 21 September 1982, Philadelphia. All quotations and information attibuted to Behrend in this book are from this interview or one in July 1983.

The rigorous, traditional education Scalero dispensed in counterpoint, the experience in writing for all genres, and training in all musical forms—large and small—unquestionably left an indelible mark on his student Samuel Barber. One consistent observation made about Barber's music throughout his career is of its remarkable sense of form and well-crafted design. With Scalero, too, Barber studied orchestration; his handwritten notes and excerpts from French and Italian orchestration texts are at the Library of Congress. Barber's orchestration—imbued with a striking propensity for haunting melodic lines in solo oboe, English horn, or clarinet parts—reflects a strong vocal orientation.

One is able to gain knowledge of Barber's theoretical and technical studies with Scalero through several sources: the catalogue description of the institute's course of study for composition students, the accounts of other students who studied with Scalero—among them Jeanne Behrend,* Ned Rorem, and Gian Carlo Menotti; and a composition notebook kept by Barber from 1925–33, after which Scalero was "dismissed" from the institute in the wake of the "general reduction of students and faculty because of the financial condition of the institute."[2]

Beginning with music of the sixteenth century, Scalero's students worked on counterpoint, fugue, and motets before graduating to the study of eighteenth- and nineteenth-century works. His students analyzed—in Menotti's words, "it was murder to dissect"—works of Palestrina, Lasso, and Monteverdi. He did not teach harmony as such, because he believed harmony is the result of good counterpoint. Scalero was not, according to Menotti, interested in easy solutions:†

> Contrary to what people thought, Scalero was a very intelligent teacher and he taught in a very original way. He never taught us rules; he wanted us to find out for ourselves what the rules were through the study of great music.
>
> With fugues, for example, when I told him, "But Maestro, I have never written a fugue," he answered, "Don't be ridiculous, do you think that

*Behrend (1911–1987) was a piano student of Josef Hofmann. Talented also as a composer, she reconciled her conflicting career interests by dedicating herself to the dissemination of music by other American composers, giving many concerts of American music, and writing numerous scholarly articles and books on the subject. As an authority on Gottschalk, she was the editor of the reprinted editions of *Louis Moreau Gottschalk: Notes of a Pianist* (Philadelphia, 1881; New York, 1964; 1979, incl. letters). When she toured South America on a grant from the State Department in 1945–46, Behrend was cited by Heitor Villa Lobos as the "heroine of the Americas." The Brazilian government awarded Behrend its Order of the Southern Cross in 1965 in recognition of her services to Brazilian music during her Philadelphia Festival of Western Hemisphere Music, 1959–60, a series of 104 concerts of music in all genres.

†John Gruen, in *Menotti: A Biography* (New York: Macmillan, 1978, p. 22), quotes Scalero as saying to Menotti, "I must cut your wings *now,* so that when they grow back, you can fly farther."

> Bach had someone to teach him how to write a fugue? Just look at his fugues; you have eyes, you have ears." He was very sharp about that. . . . And if your fugue had a dull theme, he wouldn't even look at it. He would say, "How can you write a fugue on such a dull theme? Go home and write another one."*

Menotti reports also that Scalero gave a great deal of importance to the theory that music must "breathe"—the arsis and thesis—"lift your foot and put it down; that is the way music will flow. . . . Don't just breathe in, breathe out."[3]

On Friday afternoons, after his lessons at the institute, Barber was able to hear the Philadelphia Orchestra, for Roy Barber exercised his power as chairman of the local school board in West Chester to pass a rule that any student who was a composer could take Fridays off from school to attend their concerts.[4]

Barber was probably one of the few males and one of the youngest who attended these concerts. Some of the colleges—Bryn Mawr, for example—had reserved seats for their young ladies, who would have been at least three years older than the student composer. By the time he was seventeen or eighteen, however, and had student lodging in Philadelphia, he probably attended the Saturday evening concerts at the Academy of Music, for this, according to Kupferberg, was the place to be for any young Philadelphian with intellectual ambitions. At these concerts there was, in general, a more youthful, heterogeneous audience of professionals and their families and students. The seating was stratified, the less expensive seats in the balcony being occupied by students who had usually studied the scores ahead of time.† In preparation for their attendance at these concerts, Barber and his cousin Katharine Homer would often play four-hand versions of the music they were going to hear and bring orchestral scores to the performances.‡

The Philadelphia Orchestra at this time was still under the direction of

*Menotti, telephone conversation with the author, 11 March 1990. Behrend recalled that Scalero kept Menotti on motets for a solid year, causing him to compose his own music "on the side." Menotti explains that when he began studies at Curtis he was very weak in counterpoint because his Milanese training had focused only on harmony.

†Herbert Kupferberg, *Those Fabulous Philadelphians: The Life and Times of a Great Orchestra* (New York: C. Scribner's Sons, 1969, pp. 51–54), describes the Friday matinee audiences of the Philadelphia Orchestra as almost exclusively composed of middle-aged matrons and elderly women—"Old Philadelphians"—who had lunched at elite clubs before arriving at the concert and often sat and knitted while the music was being played, rustling papers and talking during performances. They were so conservative and undemonstrative in their appreciation of the music that Orville Bullitt, president of the board of directors in 1938, once publicly scolded the ladies for their tepid responsiveness by encouraging them to "let loose at the end of a performance or shout 'bravo' " if they felt like it. Leopold Stokowski, who had been conductor of the orchestra since 1912, was determined to "shape up" the audience and from the podium quite frequently delivered "spontaneous" public admonishments to the "old ladies rushing out at side doors with packages in their hands."

‡A score of Mozart's Symphony No. 41 at the Chester County Historical Society bears the stamp "Prop of S.O.B., 2nd" and a handwritten inscription, "from Uncle Sid Homer."

the young Leopold Stokowski, whose fervent demeanor provided Philadelphians with spirited performances and repertoire that they had not experienced from the Germanic conductors who preceded him. Although when he arrived in Philadelphia in 1913 Stokowski was not yet the innovative conductor he became in his mature years and his taste, as reflected in choice of programs, was still catholic and largely German-oriented, by the time Barber attended his concerts he had introduced Philadelphians to more Russian and French music than had previously been programmed at the Academy of Music. Moreover, he literally put Philadelphia on the musical map with such important United States premieres as Mahler's Eighth Symphony, Schoenberg's *Kammersymphonie,* Scriabin's *Divine Poem,* and Richard Strauss's *Alpine Symphony,* all presented during the 1916 season.

From a program among his memorabilia at the Chester County Historical Society, we know that Barber attended a conservatively oriented Friday afternoon concert on 29 February 1924 that included Respighi's *Sinfonia drammatica,* Tchaikovsky's Piano Concerto in G major, and Borodin's *Polevetski Dances.** But on 30 January 1925, when Stravinsky first conducted the Philadelphia Orchestra in a program entirely of his own works, Barber was among the audience that heard *Fireworks,* the *Scherzo fantastique,* the *Petrouchka Suite,* the *Firebird Suite,* and the *Song of the Nightingale.*† Thus, with the onset of his formal musical education at the Curtis Institute of Music, the student musician had the opportunity for expansion of his musical horizons through exposure to contemporary, as well as standard, orchestral repertoire performed by one of the leading orchestras in the country.

Sidney Homer continued to guide his nephew during this period. A letter he sent to Barber during his first year at the Curtis Institute implies the extent to which Homer's songs, especially, were admired by the student. It reveals Homer as a selfless mentor and illuminates the artistic principles he set forth to the younger composer—principles that shaped Barber's music throughout his career:

> Of course I want you to know all my songs, but as for using them as models that is a different matter. If you write naturally and spontaneously, you will develop a style of your own, without being conscious of it. It is the unconscious charm that is so elusive and valuable, in art, as in Life. . . .
>
> Everything depends, now, on the development of your taste and the

*Program in the Barber collection, Chester County Historical Society. An inscription in a notebook kept by Barber before he began studies at the Curtis Institute reads: "At the Philadelphia Orchestra—Stokowski, April 21, 1924. Played the calliope that morning" (Chester County Historical Society).

†Barber, "Fadographs," p.2. After the concert, Barber rode in a taxi with Stravinsky to a reception at the Bellevue Hotel. The program is cited in Kupferberg, *Those Fabulous Philadelphians,* p. 61. Barber was a student at the Curtis Institute when Stravinsky conducted a fully staged performance of *Le Sacre du printemps* in Philadelphia on 11 April 1930, the first time it was danced in this country.

> refinement of your sensibilities. If you think of music from the point of view of sensationalism and publicity, your work will show it. If you learn to love the poetic under-current and the subtleties of beauty and spirituality which have been expressed in music, your work will show it just as much. The wonderful thing about art is that a man can conceal nothing; it reveals him as naked and unadorned. . . . Sincerity and beauty seem to stand the test, but love for mankind and willingness to serve humbly seem to fill the world with joy.*

Spontaneity and *sincerity,* then, are the key words in Homer's message to his nephew. Two years later, in another letter to Barber, Homer stresses time as the test of quality, and sincerity of feeling as a primary artistic value:

> Your letter warmed up all the little inside cockles of my heart. I am not going to tell you that you are all wrong and that you ought not to love my songs. Here's hoping that you are right in every way and that you will still continue to love them when you are as old as I am. If they are as good as you say they are, this will surely happen. The beautiful thing about art is that quality never fades out. If it is there, it is there to stay, and that is what makes the effort, the patience, persistence, infinite care and scrupulous conscientiousness worth while. . . . The intense desire to tell the truth . . . and to create something which would be an inspiration and an incentive to others, is what has led to the heart-breaking, almost appalling labor on the part of those who honestly felt that they had something to say. . . . Everyone who joins the society in this place pledges himself to just one thing, sincerity. He tries to put into form his real feelings, not feelings he wishes he had. Pretense has no place here.[5]

During his first two years at Curtis Institute, even before beginning studies in composition with Scalero, Barber's creative output was considerable. The imaginative titles of his instrumental pieces (all for piano) and humorous performance instructions scattered through the scores promise more cheekiness than they fulfill, however. Examples are two pieces under the title "Fresh from West Chester (some jazzings)" written the summer after his first year at the institute: the first, "Poison Ivy, a country dance

* 12 November 1924. To the end of his uncle's life, Barber professed that Homer's songs were paradigms of the genre. Even after he composed *Mélodies passagères* and as he began *Hermit Songs*—both closer in style to twentieth-century French art songs than to turn-of-the-century American songs—Barber wrote to Homer with affection: "The edition of your songs, bound in leather, which was given to me years ago . . . was coming apart and . . . looking rather shabby, so I had them bound anew, and included the later songs, which are not in the original volumes. They are in bright red, right next to the Bach Gesellschaft on my shelves, and can be quickly spotted. To prepare them for the binder gave me an added excuse to play them through again, and discover new beauties and play them for new addicts. I played *The Sick Rose* for a very fine musician friend of mine, and asked him to guess who it was by. After a long time, he said that it must be ME. No compliment has given me more pleasure; alas, I wish that were true" (letter, 3 February 1952, from Mount Kisco).

(Left) Sam Barber and Sidney Homer, Lake George, 1924. *(Right)* Barber at age fifteen. Inscription reads "To Mr. Green—always my teacher and friend." *(William Hatton Green Collection, Curtis Institute of Music Library)*

that isn't /Accredited to, and blamed on T. T. Garborinsky," has provocative tempo markings—"As a dog wags his tail," "sock it," "with itching," and "bad memories." The second, "Let's Sit it out, I'd rather watch, a walls," contains such Ivesian instructions as "flirtatiously—molto koketto," "slower, vulgarly, commonly," "shockingly," and "with gushing." A postscript to this set reads "Soon to be released—'Curtis Institute Blues'—the piece that makes people Pray." *

After his second year at the institute, during Barber's sixteenth summer he wrote three "Essays" for piano, their titles foreshadowing the unique orchestral form of his mature years.† Each exploits a single theme ad infinitum—indeed, Essay III introduces its theme with instructions to be played "con moto . . . with monotonous emphasis throughout"—and reflects Barber's continuing interest in colorful, expressive instructions (m. 61 of the second Essay, for example, should be executed "like a very hot summer night"). These are no mere etudes, for the dolorous tone sustained

* To the best of my knowledge, Barber had not seen any of Ives's scores at the time he wrote these pieces.

† These pieces are located in the Library of Congress, Music Division, in the 1984 bequest of the Estate of Samuel Barber, Box 3, in Manuscripts of Sam Barber, 1917–1927 [pp. 153–69].

Sidney and Louise Homer, Gian Carlo Menotti, and Sam Barber at Homeland, Bolton, New York, 1934. *(Curtis Institute of Music Library)*

throughout presages the style of Barber's works written in the early thirties (Two Interludes, for piano; the Cello Sonata; and *Dover Beach*, for example).

At the Curtis Institute Barber was revered by his fellow students, who were dazzled by the versatility of his talents. That he had not one major, but three, and was outstanding in each, astonished them. Some thought him to be, as did Rose Bampton, "extraordinary," others reported him to be a genius.* Of the many talented students at the institute, he was, in Menotti's words, "the star."† His intellectual gifts extended to academic subjects as well: he was well read and accomplished in foreign languages, and, as his letters from this period demonstrate, he wrote with superior

*Unless otherwise indicated, all quotations from, and information attributed to, Rose Bampton in this book are from the author's interview with Bampton on 17 August 1983 in New York. Menotti recalled that when he arrived at the Curtis Institute he learned that Barber was "the absolute idol of the Curtis Institute of Music . . . considered a genius in all three courses" (quoted in Gruen, *Menotti,* p. 20). It was not uncommon in my interviews with his classmates to hear superlatives used in describing the young composer: "extraordinary," "genius," "gifted." Orlando Cole, for example, reported that during his student days at Curtis Institute Barber's name was substituted for that of Brahms as one of the legendary three "B's." (Author's interviews with Orlando Cole, 21 April 1982; Iso Briselli, 11 May 1982; Behrend; and Bampton.)

†Interview with Peter Dickinson, BBC, 23 January 1982. For this "Barber Retrospective," broadcast on the first anniversary of his death, Dickinson also interviewed John Browning, Aaron Copland, H. Wiley Hitchcock, Leontyne Price, William Schuman, Virgil Thomson, and Charles Turner.

ability (receiving an A+ in advanced English composition and A's in English literature).

Though considered aristocratic by his peers, Barber nevertheless was graced with qualities of affability and wit that gained him enormous social acceptance. In spite of Broder's portrayal of the young Barber as shy, withdrawn, and moody, he was, according to his friends from that period, witty and "fun to be with."*

Barber's friends say he possessed a kind of charisma that made each person in his circle feel central to his attention.† This appealing quality was recognized by administrators of Curtis Institute as well, as evidenced by a writer in *Overtones* who in 1936 referred to his "vivid appreciation of beauty, quick perception and keen reactions, the depth of his feeling, and the happy spirit permeating all this, the very qualities that endeared him to his teachers and fellow students."[6] These attractive qualities made it possible for Barber to obtain, throughout his life, intense loyalty from artists who performed his music, many of whom basked in the aura of his friendship as well.

Yet he was selective. He chose as his friends intelligent and gifted artists, respecting their talent and their opinions and suggestions about his work. He would not tolerate less than excellence in himself or others, nor would he tolerate—as he later wrote to one of his classmates—"businessmen and politicians in music, sensationalism, banality, and shoddiness";[7] throughout his life he avoided those musicians he believed displayed these qualities. His wry sense of humor and lemony wit were sometimes mistaken for arrogance, snobbery, and elitism; but those who knew him best perceived this as covering up a deep-rooted shyness in a person who was, after all, really quite humble.‡

One of Barber's most significant attributes during his student years—a talent that was to ensure his early successes—was his ability to draw toward himself gifted musicians who recognized the quality of his music and thus coveted the opportunity to perform his works. Those students at the Curtis Institute who carried his art to the public, in New York, Florida, and

* Bampton, Behrend, and Cole, interviews with the author; Menotti, interview with Peter Dickinson, BBC broadcast, 23 January 1982. Bampton echoed the opinion of her peers when she remarked that Barber was "of a wonderful nature"; in Gruen (*Menotti*, p. 21), Menotti depicts him as "very funny and charming, with a wonderful sense of humor that could set people laughing for hours." Katharine Fryer said about her cousin that he had a unique "Beatty sense of humor" and a love of the ridiculous that made it impossible not to have a good time with him (interview with the author, 9 February 1990).

† Bampton and Behrend, interviews with the author. This personal trait apparently was sustained by Barber throughout his life, as Martina Arroyo, Eleanor Steber, John Browning, and other performers suggested in interviews with the author.

‡ During the latter part of his career, when he withdrew into depression and bitterness, the loyalty of his friends was a source of sustenance. The breadth of his circle is documented by a guest book recording visitors to his New York apartment, 1976–81 (shown to the author by Valentin Herranz).

London as well as in Philadelphia, included notably Rose Bampton, Benjamin de Loache, Jeanne Behrend, and the members of the Swastika Quartet—Gama Gilbert, Benjamin Sharlip, Max Aronoff, and Orlando Cole.* These were the fellow students who saw Barber win his first prizes, confirming what they knew to be his destiny as an internationally renowned composer.

At Curtis Institute, too, began the profound friendship between Gian Carlo Menotti and Barber, a friendship that led to one of the most remarkably productive personal and professional collaborations in contemporary musical life. Menotti told how, when he arrived at the Curtis Institute in fall of 1928, they met:

> I arrived and I spoke very little English. The very first person I met in the school was Sam Barber. He was the only pupil there who spoke fluent French and some Italian.† And so of course we became friends immediately and became friends for life. He was extremely well read and had traveled, and he was very spoiled because not only was he good-looking, but he had many talents. He had a beautiful baritone voice . . . also he was an extraordinary pianist, and of course a star composer. So he was one of the favored pupils of the conservatory.[8]

Menotti recalled further:

> I remember on the night we became friends he made fun of me because I came from Milano and my musical education consisted mainly of opera and the usual classics—Bach, Mozart, Beethoven, Clementi, Mendelssohn. But we didn't know anything about Brahms. Brahms, Debussy, and Ravel were never played at my home or at concerts in Milano. . . . Brahms in Italy was considered a very academic and boring composer. And my friendship with Sam developed under the wings of Brahms's music.[9]

It was through Barber's lovely baritone voice, too, that Menotti heard for the first time many of Schubert's songs—"a revelation," he said, "which influenced my music for ever after."[10]

*The student quartet took its name from the residence of Mary and Edward Bok in Merion, Pennsylvania, where their first concerts were given. The house had been called "Swastika" in the early years of the century by the Boks' friend Rudyard Kipling, in recollection of a drawing of that ancient American Indian symbol made by Kipling's father (*Overtones,* 1 October 1974, p. 84). In the early thirties, when the symbol was adopted by the Nazis, the Boks changed the name of their house and destroyed all household items marked with the swastika. The quartet changed its name to the Curtis Quartet in 1932, when Gilbert resigned to pursue a career in journalism and Jascha Brodsky replaced him as first violinist. Cole, called "Landy" by Barber, was the son of a violinist who played with the Philadelphia Orchestra. Like Barber, Cole entered the Curtis Institute of Music its charter year. A student of Felix Salmond, the distinguished English cellist who had premiered Edward Elgar's Cello Concerto under Elgar's direction in 1919, Cole premiered two works of Barber's in the thirties—*Dover Beach* and the Sonata for Violoncello and Piano, whose evolution he witnessed at almost every step to its completion.

†In fact, Barber's Italian was minimal at that time. He became fluent through his friendship with Menotti and subsequently through their travels together in Europe.

* * *

Between 1924 and 1936—the date of publication of his first group of songs, Op. 2: "The Daisies," "With rue my heart is laden," and "Bessie Bobtail"—Barber wrote more than fifty songs that have been preserved, of which only seven have been published. Although prior to his study at the Curtis Institute Barber had primarily relied on texts by nineteenth-century American poets for his songs, between his fourteenth and sixteenth years his maturing literary tastes broadened to include European writers, in particular the poetry of eighteenth- and nineteenth-century British poets who, as it happens, were poets chosen for Sidney Homer's songs as well: Elizabeth Barrett Browning, Robert Herrick, Sir Thomas Wyatt, Walter Savage Landor, Robert Louis Stevenson, Alfred Tennyson, Percy Bysshe Shelley, Lord Byron, Robert Burns, Charles Kingsley. But his interest turned increasingly to modern poets too, some of whom were American and contemporary to his generation—Alfred Noyes (1880–1958), Louis Untermeyer (1885–1977), Laurence Binyon (1869–1943), George Dillon (1906–1968), Robert Frost (1875–1963)—and others who were post-Victorian British poets: William H. Davies (1871–1940), Fiona Macleod (1855–1905), and A. E. Housman (1859–1936). He chose from a variety of poetic themes—nature and character studies, fantasy, and romance—sensual themes as well as courtly.

Some of Barber's early songs were sung by Louise Homer, as evidenced by well-worn copies in her estate. Barber in 1978 reminisced that he "often had to persuade" his Aunt Louise to try out his songs. She would say her usual, "Sammy, I'm out of voice"; then he would plead with her to sing them until she gave in. He usually had many songs ready for her when she came to visit. Sometimes she would criticize him rather sharply for vagueness in notation: "Write what you mean," she would say, and "though her voice was sharp, it was of such richness that recalcitrant angels might have melted."[11]

In a "never-published group of songs" that Louise Homer sang for her nephew privately there was one called "Watchers," written when he was sixteen, which she did perform in twelve cities on one of her last tours "with most satisfactory results."[12] Barber heard her sing it accompanied by her daughter at Carnegie Hall on 29 January 1927, when it was her only encore. In spite of the good reviews,* he did not believe "Watchers" to be a very good song, even though it was "highly dramatic and had a big range—from low A below C to high A" (Example 2.1).†

*About the songs she sang in English, the *New York Times* review (30 January 1927) carried the accolade: "Mme. Homer proved how vocal and musical the language really is, how expressive it is, and what a fund of pathos and humor it possesses. Samuel Barber's 'The Watchers' (in manuscript) had to be repeated."

†Barber, quoted by Phillip Ramey, liner notes, "Songs of Samuel Barber," NW 229,

Example 2.1 "Watchers," last page of holograph, 1926. *(Library of Congress)*

Recital programs verify that Louise Homer did, in fact, perform more than one of Barber's songs. On 4 June 1927, at the George Morris Philips Memorial Chapel, in West Chester, she sang three—"Only of Thee and Me" (Louis Untermeyer), "Longing" (Fiona Macleod), and, with her daughters Louise Homer Stires and Katharine Homer, "Summer Is Coming" (arranged from Tennyson). Katharine Homer played the piano for all songs except the trio, which Barber accompanied. He also played organ accompaniments for songs by Handel and Bach.[13]

On another occasion, in 1927, Barber accompanied his aunt at the organ for his song "A Slumber Song of the Madonna," text by Alfred Noyes. When Homer took it on nationwide tour, the song was usually received with such success that it had to be repeated.[14] From then on, evidently, her enthusiasm for singing her nephew's songs increased. On his first tour of Europe, summer 1928, Barber met up with the Homers in Paris (Sidney Homer was absent, recovering from a bout of double pneumonia in the American Hospital at Neuilly). That Barber was conflicted about the direction of his career at this time is suggested by an entry in Katharine Homer's diary written on the evening of that meeting:

> Sam gloomy over his future. He doesn't want to be a pianist. Says he can't. Singing still very indefinite, and he's not sure whether he can be better than a second-rate composer.[15]

One day, after a morning of music at a Russian church noted for its *a cappella* choir, Barber, his cousins Anne and Kay, and their mother had dinner together at their pension. "In the midst of all the turmoil," Barber wrote (in a letter to his family, 28 June 1928, from Morgat, Brittany), "Aunt Louise sang my three new songs." It is likely that the three songs he mentioned were "The Daisies" and "There's nae lark," both written in 1927, and "With rue my heart is laden," completed in January 1928.

By the time he was seventeen, Barber's penchant for Celtic poetry was established as a source of texts for his songs—in particular the poems of James Stephens, James Joyce, and William Butler Yeats. Perhaps his earliest venture in this direction had begun in October 1924, shortly after his entrance to the Curtis Institute, with the setting of Fiona Macleod's *Two Poems of the Wind*—"Little Children of the Wind" and "Longing."* These songs are an early expression of the melancholic theme that haunts Bar-

---

1978. The holograph of "Watchers," on a text by Dean Cornwell, is at the Library of Congress, Music Division. The songs by Barber in Louise Homer's collection included the following: "Minuet," for soprano and contralto; "Dere Two Fella Joe," described above; a trio, "Summer Is Coming"; "Longing," from *Two Poems of the Wind* by Fiona Macleod; "My Fairyland"; "The Daisies," published by G. Schirmer in 1936 as Op. 2; and "A Slumber Song of the Madonna."

*Macleod, the pseudonym of the Scottish poet and biographer William Sharp (1855–1905), wrote mystical prose and verse. He was one of a group of Celtic poets who believed in the impending return of the Celtic gods and who—with William Butler Yeats and others—founded a religious cult called Celtic Paganism.

ber's mature music. "Little Children of the Wind" is an especially effective portrayal of Macleod's poignant words within an economical twelve measures of music: "I hear the little children of the wind, crying solitary in lovely places: I have not seen their faces, but I have seen the leaves lying behind—The little tremulous leaves of the wind!" It is to be sung "sorrowfully" to an accompaniment of pulsating seventh chords over an undecorated, chromatic bass line in whole notes. Arpeggios of fourths and fifths conclude "tenderly" with slow chords shifting between major and minor.

"Dance" and Three Songs, Opus 2: "The Daisies," "With rue my heart is laden," and "Bessie Bobtail"

Barber's weekly commute to Philadelphia gave him access to a wide variety of bookstores, and his voracious reading led him to the modern poets who were in vogue with his friends at one time or another. The songs he wrote during the late 1920s suggest he was familiar with the latest published collections of poetry, but lyricism, rhythm, and imagery more often than novelty would continue to draw him to texts.*

Undoubtedly Sidney Homer's choice of poets—in particular Yeats and James Stephens†—influenced the young composer's own selections. Homer had set Stephens's poetry as early as 1917, and he may well have introduced Barber to individual volumes of the Irish poet's works. "The Daisies," for example, first appeared in *Songs from the Clay,*[16] the same collection from which Sidney Homer chose "The King of the Fairy Men."[17] Barber composed "The Daisies" in July 1927 at the windmill where he lived while doing "concert work" at Roger's Rock, a club on Lake George not far from the Homers' residence.‡

Since the settings of "The Daisies" and "Dance" followed by only nine months the arrival of the first American publication of James Stephens's *Collected Poems* in October 1926, that volume was probably Barber's text source for these songs and another he was to compose in 1934, "Bessie Bobtail." Although there is no evidence that Barber heard Stephens speak,

*This could explain why, for example, Barber's keen appreciation of the Georgian pastoral poetry of W. H. Davies peaked in the mid-1930s—leading him to set "Night Wanderers" and "Beggar's Song"—in spite of the fact that by that time Davies's popularity was on the wane.

†James Stephens, who claims to have been born on the same day as James Joyce—2 February 1882—and did eventually establish a friendship with Joyce in 1927, is perhaps best known for *A Crock of Gold* (London: Macmillan, 1912), a fantasy novel, in which he invented an idyllic country of the gods.

‡The holograph, owned by Katharine Homer Fryer, is signed at the end. The *West Chester Daily Local News* (29 June 1927) reported that Barber was one of four students from the Curtis Institute employed by the club, where they would "play two concerts a day, with no dance music, and the compensation [would be] interesting enough to make a special attraction in addition to the pleasure of the work."

he certainly would have heard about him; Stephens's poetry became enormously popular in the United States as the result of the nine tours he made to this country between 1925 and 1935, during which he gave lectures and read his poems. His diminutive stature, puckish vitality, and irreverence for the traditional Irish heroes gained him great popularity with college audiences. A decade later Barber would compose choral settings for five more poems by Stephens, from *Reincarnations* (1917).

"The Daisies" and the never-published "Dance" were sung often by Rose Bampton, who had entered the Curtis Institute the same year the songs were composed. Bampton was as closely associated with Barber's vocal music during the 1930s as Eleanor Steber and Leontyne Price were to become in the middle decades of the century. Barber, of course, had been "spoiled," in that he was used to having his songs sung by a proven artist and moreover an exceptional one—Louise Homer—and so he would naturally continue to seek out the finest voices to perform his songs. Fortunately for Barber, when Bampton auditioned for entrance into the Curtis Institute, a jury dismissed her voice as "nice, but not for opera" and thus "suitable for oratorio or church work," assigning her to courses in Lieder and choral singing.* Her training would benefit Barber, for her familiarity with the Lieder style and the versatility of her vocal range enabled her to present his songs to their advantage.†

Bampton loved singing Barber's songs: "I loved the music, it was well suited to the voice," she said; "but I especially loved the poems. He always chose beautiful poems."‡ It was always with enthusiasm that he announced a new song for her to sing, she recalled, as if indeed something very exciting was happening.

"Dance," although never published and as yet unlocated, was sung nu-

*Bampton, interview with the author. Bampton was a model of Mrs. Bok's "earnest student" in that she was intensely serious about her career. She believed, ultimately, it was a blessing that during her student years she had the time to study art-song literature, to practice her technique and develop her voice without the burden of learning the difficult operatic roles she was destined to play in her eighteen years with the Metropolitan Opera. She recounted with good humor how her friendship with Barber and Menotti was consolidated through two classes they took together—a theory course, in which she considered herself a misplaced, hopeless student, and a course in stage deportment, where her creaking ankles and her awkwardness were a constant source of embarrassment to her and hilarity to the composers.

†Bampton, who began her studies at Curtis as a contralto, was designated in her third year a mezzo-soprano by her teacher Queena Mario and was told she was a soprano at her Metropolitan Opera audition. At the beginning of her career with the Met she distinguished herself by singing the roles of both Aïda *and* Amneris, and Laura in *La Gioconda*. Toward the end of her career she sang a few Wagnerian roles.

‡Bampton, interview with the author. Over the course of Barber's career, Bampton's observation was echoed by other singers: Leontyne Price remarked, "The poetry is so beautiful, he chose his poems so intelligently" (23 January 1982, BBC broadcast); Eleanor Steber said, "He always chose excellent texts" (interview with the author, 2 September 1983); and Martina Arroyo reported that in her preparation for singing *Andromache's Farewell*, Barber and she had long discussions about the text, suggesting his profound regard for psychological aspects of the poetry (interview with the author, 28 November 1987).

Example 2.2a Original version of "The Daisies," mm. 1–12, holograph, 1927. *(Personal collection of Katharine Homer Fryer)*

To Daisy

The Daisies

James Stephens*

Samuel Barber, Op. 2, No. 1

*From *Collected Poems of James Stephens.* Printed by permission of The Macmillan Company, publishers.

Example 2.2b "The Daisies," mm. 1–11 (G. Schirmer, 1936).

merous times by Bampton in the 1930s.* How much of Stephens's four verses Barber set to music is not known. The form of the song was probably strophic, governed by the text. The Stephens poem—with such sentiments as "Happy minions, dancing mad! / Joy is guide enough for you; / Cure the world of good and bad; / And teach us innocence anew!" or "How to banish good and ill / With the laughter of the heart!"—imparts a joyful naïveté not found in the texts of the songs Barber wrote afterwards.

"The Daisies," "Bessie Bobtail," and A. E. Housman's "With rue my heart is laden," published as Op. 2, were among the first works of Barber's brought out by G. Schirmer in 1936. "The Daisies" is dedicated to Barber's mother. Its charm lies in the simplicity of the lyrical setting and its fidelity to the slightly asymmetrical rhythm of the words. A holograph (in the collection of Katharine Homer Fryer) shows an interesting variant at measures 5–8 from the published score at measures 6–9. In the original version, outer voices descend by whole-tones (in parallel tenths), resulting in a slightly pungent, bittersweet harmony against the vocal line (Example 2.2a, beginning at arrows). Why Barber did not include these dissonances in the 1936 edition (Example 2.2b), preferring instead a more conventional harmonization, is not known; he may have been convinced that a diatonic accompaniment would more easily facilitate singing of the vocal line. On the other hand, in the 1936 edition the introduction is improved by the addition of a motive that foreshadows the vocal entrance. The pitch changes at measures 6–8 may have been suggested by Scalero, to whom Barber sent the song for a final review before giving it to Schirmer for publication. The manuscript he submitted for engraving, which is at the Sibley Library at the Eastman School of Music, shows deletions of the accidentals at those measures, suggesting they were made at the last minute.

"Bessie Bobtail," Op. 2, No. 3, written seven years later, was dedicated to Edith and John Braun as a tribute to the winter of 1934 that Barber spent with the couple in Vienna. Edith Evans Braun was a fine pianist and a composer;† her husband was a singer with whom Barber studied Lieder singing. The piano accompaniment of this "narrative song," as Barber called it, evokes a strong pictorial representation of the limping Bessie Bobtail as convincingly as the accompaniment of Schubert's *Der Leiermann* portrays the organ grinder. Musical imagery is vividly realized through rhythmic and harmonic means. Contrary-motion figures in irregular rhythmic groupings alternate between piano and voice in expanding units of three to four to five notes, underlining the character's faltering gait. Well-placed harmonic dissonances—predominantly major and minor seconds—poignantly emphasize the pathos of Bessie's condition and her anguished ap-

* At the time of our interview, Bampton had no recollection of this song.

† Edith Evans Braun was so close a friend of Mary Curtis Bok that in 1940, when Mrs. Bok moved her residence to 1816 Delancey Street, adjacent to the Brauns', a door was built in the common wall of the two houses so that the women might visit each other more easily.

Example 2.3 "There's nae lark," mm. 1–15, holograph, 1927. *(Library of Congress)*

peal for compassion at the climax of the song: the D♮ against E♭ in the caesura on the word *desperate* at measure 25; or the C♯s in the voice part pitted against D♮s in the piano part at measures 44–50; and in the last six measures, the D against E and B♭ against A.

Barber's setting of "With rue my heart is laden," Op. 2, No. 2, one of the best-known poems from A. E. Housman's *A Shropshire Lad,* was dedicated to Gama Gilbert, who was one of Barber's closest friends while at the institute and long after.* The irony of Barber's dedicating this poignant song to Gilbert is that it foreshadowed by a dozen years the painfully premature death of his friend.

Another song set in 1927, "There's nae lark," exists only in manuscript. Sung by Barber in concerts, it is a strophic setting of a poem by Swinburne.[18] A repetitive figure on C and B♭ in the arpeggiated accompaniment is probably meant to suggest a bird call (Example 2.3).

Barber sang three of these early songs himself—"The Daisies," "Bessie Bobtail," and "There's nae lark"—in a performance at the New Century Club, 23 October 1934 in West Chester, upon his return from Vienna where he had studied with Braun (see chapter 4). For this concert he was accompanied by Yvonne Biser.[19] More significantly, however, the three Op. 2 songs were sung by Rose Bampton, accompanied by Elizabeth Westmoreland, on 25 June 1935 at the home of Viscount and Viscountess Astor in London.† Bampton first sang them in the United States with pianist Edith Evans Braun on 7 March 1937 at the Curtis Institute. The occasion was a surprise birthday celebration for Barber, when an entire program was devoted to his music, "an event without precedent" both for the composer and for the institute.

* Gilbert was a talented violinist who was equally talented as a writer. Interested in music criticism, he obtained a job with a Philadelphia newspaper and later became music critic at the *New York Times,* where he worked until his death in 1940. Gilbert admired the music of both Barber and Menotti and was convinced of their talent and future success long before they were known to the general public. Moreover, he had an active commitment to the promotion of contemporary American music, one that derived from a belief in the "great new musical public springing up in this country," where, he perceived, "an unprecedented era in the nation's musical history was at hand" (*New York Times,* 29 September 1940).

†*Overtones,* May 1936, p. 24. See also chapter 5, below, for an account of the performances in London.

3

DISCOVERIES

As far from West Chester as it is in my power to be

During the summer of 1928 Barber made his first trip to Europe, where he planned to travel, study with Scalero, and work on a violin sonata he had begun before he left Philadelphia. The trip awakened a romance with European society and culture that continued for the rest of his life. His letters, rich with the details of his travel, convey exhilaration over his release from the constrictions of West Chester. As a "tourist-third" passenger, he and David Freed* sailed out of the New York harbor early June on the liner SS *de Grasse* destined for Le Havre. The two students "hit it off admirably" and planned to travel together through France, Switzerland, Austria, and Italy, where they would part and Barber would go on to Gressoney to study with Scalero.[1] The Atlantic crossing launched experiences that would forever alter Barber's attitude about American life:

> I sit on the forward bow of the boat looking toward Europe—as far as possible from West Chester as it is in my power to be! There is a quiet swell on the sea and we shoot gaily into the sky and then far down into the waves, with a delicacy of nuance that is never monotonous, and only slightly disastrous to David's intonation when we play Brahms Sonatas for bored first-class passengers. . . . Our whole life is so unreal and so drenched by fantasy that I move around unthinking—unconsciously absorbing, but never collecting or arranging any reactions.[2]

There was a mélange of travelers from all over the world in tourist-class accommodations. The two befriended a Hindu philosopher: "I have rarely met a more crafty, knife-keen knowledge, and withal poetic," Barber wrote to his family, "and we are both fascinated when he talks to us

* David Freed was a cellist and composer who was also a student at the Curtis Institute of Music.

about philosophy or art."[3] At a safe distance from his family for the first time, it is not surprising that he would tease, "there is a liberal atmosphere about the tourist-thirds which would shock West Chester," or that he would appraise the first-class audience who listened to his and David Freed's performances as "blessed by cosmopolitanism, if not by intelligence."[4]

Although Barber's knowledge of French was better than average, he hoped to become still more fluent by reading Flaubert's novels in French and by speaking it as much as possible. Thus in Paris he sought out-of-the-way experiences: "There are little things that thrilled me more," he wrote; "one is always bored by the big things with reputations; it is one's own discoveries—an etching in a book stall, a crooked street in the Latin Quarter—a quaint church in some forgotten corner, these are the things one remembers."[5]

Upon meeting the young Marchese de' Medici, and about his European contemporaries in general, he wrote:

> In fact, I am amazed at the intelligence of the jeunesse abroad; they laugh with as much gaiety as we do, and yet when they stop laughing and begin to talk, one sees that they have an appreciation beyond ours, sad though it may be to say it. A shoemaker must always talk of shoes; when I talk music, they talk, not listen. These young boys and girls—not musicians (ordinary students who go to the movies and adore the Revellers)*—they know all the Wagner operas, Stravinsky, Debussy. Fancy talking like that to an ordinary American college student.[6]

In Paris Barber attended as much theater and as many concerts as he could. He witnessed the great French tragédienne Cécile Sorrel's performance of Daudet's *Sappho*—"terribly sad, and dripping with sentimentality. You would have loved it," he told his mother, "even though you would have understood nothing but the 'Adieu' in the last act, which she said eight times at different pitches, interspersed by sobs."[7] He saw a "fine performance" of Bizet's *Carmen* at the Opéra Comique; from a seat in the top balcony of the Théâtre Sarah Bernhardt, for the price of 6 francs (then equivalent to 24 cents),[8] he watched the ballet *L'Oiseau de feu* performed by the Diaghilev Ballets Russes—"it is fascinating to see it danced by the Russians"—and witnessed Stravinsky himself conduct his new ballet, *Apollon musagète*.† "Only by seeing it danced does his complexity of rhythm and color seem natural," Barber wrote home.[9]

* A male vocal quartet, whose radio broadcasts, recordings, and concerts were popular from the mid-20s to the mid-30s (Roger D. Kinkle, *The Complete Encyclopedia of Popular Music and Jazz 1900–50*, vol. 3 [New Rochelle, NY: Arlington House, 1974], p. 1628).

† Letter to his family, 22 June 1928. Although in his letter he does not name which "new ballet" of Stravinsky he saw the composer conduct, an article by Robert Sabin ("Meet the Composer," *Musical America*, March 1944, p. 7) confirms it was *Apollo*, which was first performed in Europe by the Russian Ballet at Théâtre Sarah-Bernhardt in Paris on 12 June 1928 with choreography by George Balanchine (Eric Walter White, *Stravinsky and His Works*, [Berkeley and Los Angeles: University of California Press, 1966], p. 345).

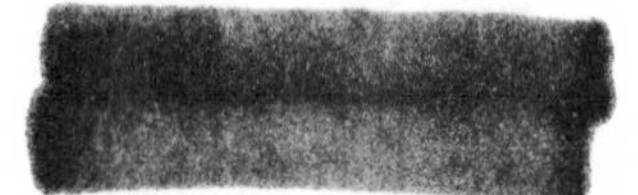

After several weeks in Paris, however, pulled between responsibility and the lust for adventure, the young travelers thought of "some little country place where we may live quietly and work and bicycle." "We must find one. I am not fond of cities by summer," Barber wrote to his family, a theme recurring throughout his life.[10] But their plans were in constant flux: one day an artists' colony in Barbizon appealed to them—it would be a bicycle ride from the music school at Fontainebleau, where they could obtain pianos and live frugally. A day later they changed their plans and thought instead of Beg-Meil, a picturesque village near Quimper, unknown to Americans, where they might be near the sea and have pianos for "almost nothing."[11]

Their indecision resolved, by the end of June the two students settled themselves at the Hôtel de la Montagne in Morgat, Brittany, a coastal village recommended by Louis Bailly, their chamber music coach at Curtis. Although Barber intended to spend several weeks there, the logistics of working in close, nonsoundproof quarters with his cellist schoolmate turned out to be distracting and impractical. Scalero's letters soon lured him to Gressoney, "one of the most beautiful places imaginable," even if it, too, would lack the solitude required for work.[12]

In Gressoney Barber visited the Scaleros daily, where much fuss was made over him as the only American and English-speaking person in the place and the only student as well—"and I *am* fond of attention," he teased his parents.[13] He was enchanted with Scalero's three daughters: "Sandra, an authority on Greek theater, with whom I have daily lessons in German; Liliana, a singer, big in voice and stature, much more intelligent than most of her species, and who is writing a book on the history of singing; and Maria Teresa, physically the most attractive, is an architect."[14] About his teacher he wrote with affection:

> Mr. Scalero is the most striking figure of all. Clad in a brown corduroy mountain suit, and carrying a cane, he leads the way on our daily walks, which often take us far into the mountains; and the wealth of his tales and anecdotes seems to embrace all fields of human knowledge. . . . The first night I arrived, he rushed me into his study to hear the Revellers sing "Chick, chick, chicken,"* which he proceeded to praise with those comments of his which I had heretofore thought most sacred, only for rare occasions, and which I myself have succeeded in inspiring perhaps four times in as many years of study.[15]

Scalero had the new portable Orthophonic record player, which he had brought from the United States with an abundant supply of records. Every evening after dinner the family listened to music. After hearing the Brahms

*The song "Chick, Chick, Chicken" was written in 1925 by Thomas McGhee, Fred Holt, and Irving King (Roger Lax and Frederick Smith, *The Great Song Thesaurus* [New York: Oxford University Press, 1984], p. 188).

C-minor Symphony played by the Philadelphia Orchestra, Barber urged his parents: "I am convinced we must have one; for you especially mother, it should be a source of great pleasure, not to be compared to the bad music on the radio."[16]

At midsummer there were signs that Barber had trouble keeping his mind on composing:

> It is difficult to realize that I was ever a musician. I have no desire to compose and no desire to hear music. Only an occasional letter from a friend or a conversation with Mr. Scalero recalls to me that fantastic world of amusingly bitter illusions which it is my pleasure, as a struggling musician, to inhabit. Mr. Scalero thinks I need a complete rest, but the next minute he talks about the unending industry of anyone from Haydn to Brahms; and I sigh and agree, and forget, and read Anatole France. As I write, a pile of blank manuscript paper eyes me quizzically from the corner; but at once I smother it under a pile of soiled socks.[17]

In one afternoon he turned out a "trivial and jolly scherzo" for his violin sonata,[18] but his letters make no further mention of it. He spent only two weeks in Gressoney and then was off to Venice. Enamored with this magical city that had captured the imaginations of countless artists, Barber filled his letter with lyrical description:

> Here a Spanish woman was singing to a guitar the "Paescatori" Tango:

> and from the other side, the deep baritone of some unknown troubador answered:

> and then voices from every side met in the dark beauty of the night and sent to the stars the ever beautiful measures of the Spanish tango. . . . The Rialto bridge was a blaze of rainbow colors which made reflections of dancing iridescence in the black water below; and it was thronged with singing crowds, watching the procession pass underneath. It was a night of sensuous beauty, heavy with old-world romance.[19]

From Venice he made his way to Vienna, where he plunged into a whirlwind of appointments all relating to his musical life. There he met Dr. Hugo Botstiber, a music critic and a friend of Scalero, who helped him purchase an autograph manuscript of Brahms. He also arranged for Barber to visit the Imperial Library, ordinarily closed for the summer, so that he could examine collections of old volumes of music and autograph manuscripts. More good fortune came to Barber in Vienna when he browsed through an antiquarian book shop and bought the complete works of Brahms in bound volumes for only eleven dollars.[20]

One afternoon, at Scalero's suggestion, Barber visited Eusebius Mandyczewski at his home in Mönichkirchen, a little village in the pine-covered hills outside Vienna. By chance, his visit on 18 August coincided with the seventy-second birthday of the white-bearded "Doktor," who reminded Barber of Brahms himself. Mandyczewski received such "great joy" from the visit of the young composer—"with his spirited, unaffected manner"—that he insisted they send a card to Scalero with both their signatures on it to prove they had been together.[21]

A brief visit to Budapest in August provided Barber the opportunity to hear for the first time a real Gypsy orchestra:

> They began playing some violins, and viola and bass, with a zither. It swept me off my feet; for it was not music; it was an expression of a directness too naïve, too naked and living to be music. It is something I shall never forget, and I left Budapest early for I did not wish to hear it again.[22]

Through Mrs. Bok and Arthur Hice (another of Scalero's pupils) Barber gained an introduction to the composer George Antheil in Vienna. The younger composer received a hearty reception from Antheil and found him to be very "straightforward and sincere."

> Our thoughts about music are surprisingly similar; in fact, even our suits were the same shade of brown. And I thoroughly admire his Symphony, which he played for me, as I previously admired his quartett,* which I heard several times in America. He is ten years older than I, and he says that he is glad to see that my decade of composers is aware of the faults and extravagancies of his own, and that we are profiting by their mistakes. We talked for several hours, and he insisted that I come back the next afternoon with my compositions. This I did, and he went through the Sonata, Prelude and Fugue, and songs with surprising enthusiasm, showing more interest in my work than anyone I have talked with for a long time.† He says he knows all the young American composers thoroughly, but that he could say something to me that he would never say to any of them. He found the musicality, the essence of my music, beyond question; the form, however, is yet archaic. He said that my music was intense, but hampered by my rhetoric. This seems to be a question of technique, but yet he said I had a big technique, in the accepted sense.
>
> Enough of that! He has a growing reputation now in Europe, and says

* Barber frequently used this German spelling through the 1930s. Although Antheil's first quartet was written in 1924 and revised in 1925, Barber was probably referring to the second quartet, which was finished in 1927 and, unlike the first, had been performed in Philadelphia.

† Barber was referring here to his Violin Sonata and his Prelude and Fugue in B minor for organ. The latter was written in the fall of 1927 but not performed until December 1928 (see description below).

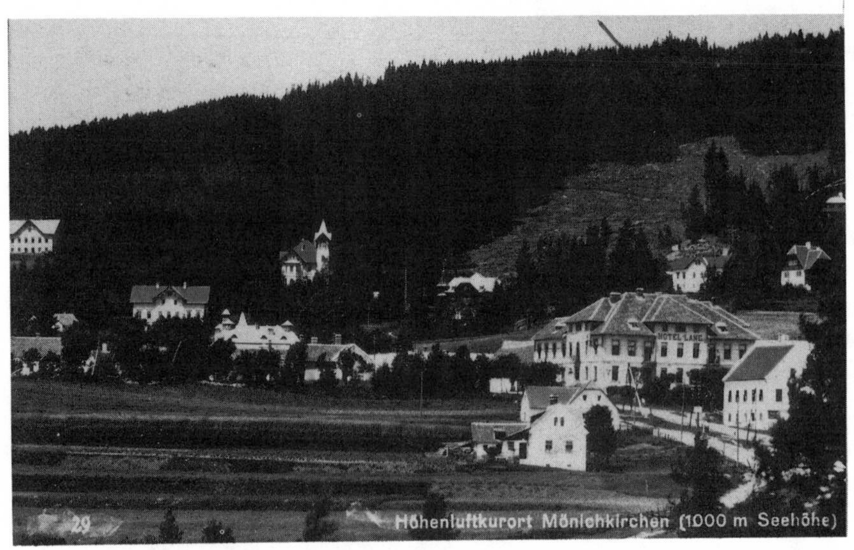

Mönichkirchen 18. 8. 28. Lieber teurer Freund, Ihr lieber junger Barber ist eben bei mir und ich habe große Freude über seinen Besuch wie über sein frisches natürliches Wesen. Ohne es zu wissen überraschte er mich gerade an meinem Geburtstag! Das ist wie ein besonders lieber und herzlicher Gruß von Ihnen. Mit Freuden höre ich von ihm über Sie Gutes und dass es Ihrer Damen auch gut geht. Viele viele herzliche Grüße an Sie alle von Ihrem alten Mandyczewski.

Best greetings to all the Scaleros! Sam Barber

Prof. Rosario Scalero
Villa Gisella
Gressoney St. Jean
(Aosta)
Italien.

Postcard written by Barber and Eusebius Mandyczewski to Rosario Scalero on 18 August 1928 from Mönichkirchen reads:

> *My dear friend* Your dear young Barber is with me now, and I receive great joy from his visit as well as his spirited, unaffected manner. Without knowing it, he surprised me exactly on my birthday. I especially value this warm greeting from you. With pleasure I hear good things about you from him and that your wife is well also. Many, many warm greetings to you all from your old Mandyczewski. *(Author's translation)*

The line on the picture side of the card points to Mandyczewski's house, nestled in the woods, farthest to the right. *(Courtesy of Monique Arnoldi)*

he will do anything in his power to have my works produced or published here.[23]

Afterward Barber met with the piano teacher Marianne Frey and Arnold Schoenberg's pupil Olga Novakovic, for whom he played his sonata. They arranged an appointment for him with Dr. Oskar Adler, a violinist and critic to whom all the younger composers came for criticism. "I wasn't awfully interested in all this," Barber wrote, "for I have my own ideas about my Sonata." Nevertheless, he and Adler played through the sonata together, and the violinist found it to be "a promising student-work, not yet ready for publication, but good in form, and well-written for both instruments." One can only guess from Barber's report to his parents how Adler perceived the style of this lost work:

> He said I must compose very much, and gradually broaden my horizon. At the end he said I must be a good Brahms player, which pleased me, and that he wished to play a Sonata with me. Which we did, and I not too well. All this was translated into English by Frau Frey, for my German is in a pitiful state when it comes to talking of aesthetics.[24]

A stay in Salzburg provided an opportunity to hear productions of *The Magic Flute* and *Fidelio*—"the former I have always found delightful," Barber wrote, "but it was the first time I had heard 'Fidelio,' and I cannot comprehend why it is not more widely produced, especially did I marvel at Beethoven's dramatic sense and so-called 'feeling for the theatre,' which people greatly underestimate."[25] He heard *Così fan tutte* with recitatives played to the accompaniment of "clavichord," "sparkling in its gaiety."

In the square before the cathedral Barber attended the Max Reinhardt production of *Everyman*. At designated times bells tolled all over town, and antiphonal choruses sang from the towers of the cathedral and answered from the turrets of the castle. A symphony orchestra and organ played incidental music. Barber found the supposedly "memorable performance" utterly distasteful, because Reinhardt's "always evident theatricalism" seemed so inappropriate to a drama of "naïveté and sincerity." "And so," he wrote, "I watched the slanting rays of light play on the front of the cathedral; for it was at sunset; and when people asked me how I liked it, I said, 'Yes, very.' "[26]

At the opera in Salzburg Barber met Alexander Steinert, who had won the Prix de Rome and was living at the American Academy. The two had played their compositions for each other at Mrs. Coolidge's several years earlier. "Alas, his music is as French as ever," Barber wrote perceptively.*

That the young composer had no patience for Wagner at this time is

*Letter to his family, 25 August 1928, Salzburg. The mature music of Steinert, who studied with Loeffler, Koechlin, and d'Indy, still bears the imprint of the French modern school.

evident from his description of what seemed an "endless" performance of *Parsifal* in Munich:

> It is true and fine staging of a modern spirit, quite inconsistent with Wagner's pathetic strivings toward realism; but neither Kundry nor the mise-en-scène could re-write the music; and I choked in a maddening mêlée of sickly chromaticism, masquerading under an ironic masque of religion. I advise you never to hear *Parsifal* again, for you will lose your illusions; and I wonder how I will like "Meistersinger" on Friday, for that was always a favorite; but now that my musical ideals have turned so directly from the path of Sir Richard - - - - -.*

As it turned out, he found that *Meistersinger*, "though well produced, was barely supportable."

> Any love for the monarch of Bayreuth, whom I once may have cherished, is now quite definitely vanished and his only effect on me is a wiggling boredom, which crescendos and decrescendos, much as his music, for five long hours. . . . The intermissions between acts are the most enjoyable moments; one strolls through crowds of Germans and visitors trying to be Germans, eating dainty little sandwiches, which taste far from dainty. . . . As the performances start at four in the afternoon, pale tuxedos, which smile wanly by daylight, go through the most singular metamorphosis as the opera progresses, and become brilliantly éclatant at the end of the performance at ten o'clock; at which hour people who have been inveigled into believing "Parsifal" religious, or "Meistersinger" medieval, suddenly wake up, and become themselves, and dance, which is decidedly more intelligent.[27]

In Munich Barber was motivated to work again. With a friend he had met on the boat, he took a room that belonged to a piano student who was on vacation. He practiced every morning: "I am doing the Schumann G-minor Sonata and the Beethoven 32 Variations, and trying to find a technique I never had, which I lost for the summer," he wrote to his family.[28] Afternoons were spent visiting the Alte Pinakothek. Dürer seemed to him the most interesting of the collection, yet he much preferred Italian art: "I recall the sensuous beauty of the Italians . . . of the Bellini altarpiece at the church of the Frari in Venice, which I found most beautiful; there is such a difference of spirit. . . . The Italians were the true artists, I am sure."[29]

* * *

*Letter to his family, 29 August 1928, Munich. Eight years later he was to respond quite differently to Wagner's music: "I am in a very Wagnerian state," he wrote to Scalero. "I went up to Bayreuth with its superb orchestra under Fürtwangler and unforgettable acoustics" (letter, 5 August 1936, St. Wolfgang).

The summer over, Barber returned to Philadelphia and threw himself into his studies with even more intensity. The violin sonata that he had worked on during the summer was finished by the fall and won him his first honor in 1929—the Joseph H. Bearns prize, $1,200 awarded by Columbia University for musical composition in the larger forms.[30] The following letter from Sidney Homer suggests that Barber apparently had doubts about the merit of the sonata and had asked Homer to give an opinion: "I want to hear the sonata and your new work. If I can't stop in Philadelphia, then you and your friend . . . must come to New York."* He gently admonished:

> You speak of having "all sorts of opinions on your work" and wanting ours. I can't imagine why. It sounds like "inferiority complex." You don't need opinions. A little praise is pleasant if you don't have to go too far out of your way to get it, but you will have to learn to get along without opinions. Opinions don't change a note or add to your stature. If you can give pleasure, well and good. Your work is your own affair and yours only. Depending on opinion means less independence in your work. It also means laying yourself open to pinpricks which may be boresome. It can result in uncertainty. Even too much praise can do things—introduce a smirk and too much gush in your style.
>
> The only thing to do is to get down to brass tacks and fight the thing out on your own line, doing, as nearly as you can, that thing that you know you want to do. You are the only one that can see your target, so you are the only one that can sight your gun and, ergo, you will be the only one that will ever know how near you came to the bull's eye.[31]

Barber and Gilbert played the sonata for Homer on 4 May 1929, but apparently the older composer "couldn't make much out of it."[32] Louis Bailly, Barber's chamber music coach at the Curtis Institute, on the other hand, is reported to have said Barber's violin sonata reminded him of Brahms.[33] Despite his respect for Brahms, the young composer appeared annoyed at being "consigned to invisibility," and perhaps this is the reason he did not wish to count the work among his oeuvre.† It would not be surprising, however, if Barber's Sonata for Violin in F minor was even more Brahmsian in character than the extant Cello Sonata, which was written four years later; for as concert programs indicate, during the time he wrote the violin sonata he was well immersed in the study of Brahms's

*Letter to Barber, 18 February 1929. The friend was Gama Gilbert, the violinist who played the first performance of Barber's sonata.

†David Freed, letter to the author, 26 July 1986. Barber's violin sonata is usually counted as Opus 4, but a works list compiled by the composer in 1978 (in a black loose-leaf notebook shown to the author by Valentin Herranz) designates Opus 4 as the two Interludes for Piano (these were later crossed off the list, however) and omits the violin sonata altogether. Although it was judged excellent enough to be prize-winning, Barber always viewed the sonata as a student work and felt it was not representative of his oeuvre. Behrend and Menotti believe that he destroyed it.

THE CURTIS INSTITUTE *of* MUSIC

Fifth Season — 1928-1929

SIXTH STUDENTS' CONCERT

Monday Evening, December 10, 1928, at 8:30 o'clock

Programme of Original Compositions by Students of Rosario Scalero in Composition

SAMUEL BARBER........Prelude and Fugue in B minor, for Organ
Played by CARL WEINRICH

MURIEL HODGE......Variations on a Scotch Theme, for Two Pianos
Played by YVONNE KRINSKY and SYLVAN LEVIN

DAVID BARNETT......Variations on a Theme of Beethoven } for
Three Interludes } Piano
Played by the COMPOSER

CARL BRICKEN..........................Four Songs for Soprano
Late, Late O Miller!
Baby Toes
Upstream
Peace, My Heart!
Sung by HELEN JEPSON
The COMPOSER at the Piano

SAMUEL BARBER..........Sonata in F minor, for Piano and Violin
Allegro moderato
Andante un poco mosso, poi più mosso, quasi scherzando
Allegro agitato
Played by the COMPOSER and GAMA GILBERT

The STEINWAY is the official piano of THE CURTIS INSTITUTE *of* MUSIC

Program of the first concert at the Curtis Institute of Music in which Barber's compositions were played. *(Curtis Institute of Music Library)*

music with Vengerova.* Gama Gilbert gave the first performance of the Violin Sonata with Barber accompanying him on 10 December 1928 at the Curtis Institute's Sixth Students' Concert (see facsimile of concert program above).

On the same program Carl Weinrich played Barber's Prelude and Fugue in B minor for organ, the piece Antheil had heard in Vienna.† Barber was apparently indecisive about how to describe the tempo of the serpentine andante theme of the prelude, for he crossed out *quasi adagio* and substituted *molto sostenuto*. The four-voice fugue—a near emulation of a Bach

* On 26 March 1928 in a recital at Curtis he played two intermezzi, Op. 118, No. 1 and Op. 76, No. 1, and the Rhapsody in B minor, Op. 79, No. 10. On a 15 May 1929 program he played Op. 116, No. 6, and the Capriccio, Op. 116, No. 7.

† A manuscript of the prelude at the Library of Congress is dated 28 October 1927.

fugue*—was finished one month after the prelude, in November 1927. By this time Barber had completed Grade V (advanced counterpoint) of the institute's "theoretic course" and had written many single and double fugues and canons; he was well into Grade VI, "Larger forms," working on chaconnes, variations, rondos, and sonata–allegro forms. A notebook of school compositions kept from February to May 1927 includes many rounds (on texts by the Romantic poets), choral preludes and partitas, and fugues.[34] The adeptness with which he could write a fugue is intimated by the dedication on one "Fuga a tre voci": "to all of us who commute, and composed while doing it myself," suggesting he did many of these assignments on the train to West Chester.[35] In this book there are also assignment notes in Scalero's handwriting for the study of vocal and instrumental fugues, in particular the Kyrie of Mozart's Requiem, a fugue in Brahms's *Motett,* Op. 25, and several from Beethoven string quartets—*Grosse Fuge,* Op. 59 [No. 3], and Op. 131.

Serenade for String Quartet or String Orchestra, Op. 1

When, early in 1929, Barber wrote to Sidney Homer that he had completed his violin sonata and the Serenade for String Quartet, the elder composer replied somewhat skeptically:

> You sound fresh as a daisy, hungry for work, and as if the day were not long enough for you. Alright! go to it but don't overdo it. If Scalero is right about four hours a day piano work being too much, listen to him. What you must guard against is overwork . . . as we don't want weary counterpoint and tired melodies.
>
> Why "Serenade" as a title for the new work? Are you really serenading and to whom? Scalero? Me? Yourself? The Public? The Girl?
>
> The paucity of titles in the musical world is alarming. It indicates a lack. Perhaps language is inadequate. If so, then young men like you must invent something and not go on serenading and suite-ing.[36]

Perhaps advice of this kind foreshadowed the titles of works soon to follow: *Music for a Scene from Shelley* and *Essay for Orchestra.* Serenade, composed during Barber's eighteenth year, was jocularly singled out by Gian Carlo Menotti as being "the only one [of Barber's works] . . . that *never* bores him—perhaps because it's so short."[37] Barber finished it in December 1928 after less than two years of study with Scalero. For a student work, it reveals a refined technique: its three short movements

*Perhaps for this reason Carl Weinrich, when asked about the work in 1986, had no recollection of what it was like.

already show elements of the well-honed form and clear lyrical profile that are found in Barber's mature works.

The romantic harmonies and dance rhythms are as unselfconsciously expressed in Barber's Serenade as those in the young Hugo Wolf's quartet (later transcribed into the *Italienische Serenade*).* Even Sidney Homer recognized similarities to Wolf's work when he examined his nephew's score in the spring of 1929. His earlier reluctance to cater to Barber's self-doubts was now completely put aside as he unreservedly expressed pleasure over the younger composer's progress:

> I have been thinking about the work you showed me. I am amazed at what you have accomplished; I would not have thought it possible. The energy, strength, virility, mastery of form, definite message, clear thought-out intention, taste, freedom from commonplace, all this is astonishing. I do not feel so good about the almost too apparent maturity. It seems as if you are going to skip "youth" and jump into the Maelstrom and complexities of a mature man.
>
> Your technique has ripened with phenomenal quickness and seems to be carrying you with it. This is what happened to Richard Strauss. I knew him in Munich when we were both twenty-two. He produced his *Suite Aus dem Italien,* an astounding work for a young man. It always seemed that he had no youth and was old before his time. . . . Mozart and Schubert, on the other hand, kept the spirit of youth throughout their entire lives in spite of their highly developed powers.
>
> In your studies you are in the atmosphere of the works of mature men, but there is something to life besides that. There is a simple Joy in early life with which we can saturate ourselves. It is the Spring with its freshness, dew, green, budding hope, simplicity, tenderness, beauty, care-free innocence. It is a time for absorption, drinking in, self-saturation. Summer and Autumn come soon enough, parched and brown, and it is then that the stored-up Spring comes as the freshest and most beautiful influence in Life. What I mean is make the *most* of your youth.[38]

It was some time before a performance of Serenade was given, perhaps because the score was misplaced in the flurry of Barber's and Menotti's departure for Europe at the end of May 1929. That summer, Barber wrote from Gressoney, where he was studying with Scalero:

> Gama wrote that no-one can find the score of my "Serenade." I left it for him the day before sailing at the Curtis, they gave it to Gian Carlo by

* Both Broder (*Samuel Barber,* p. 100) and Russell E. Friedewald (*A Formal and Stylistic Analysis of the Published Music of Samuel Barber,* Ph.D. diss., Iowa State University, 1957; p. 157) remark upon parallels between the harmonic language of Barber's Serenade and Wolf's *Italian Serenade,* especially with regard to chord progressions and chromatic tendencies. Of the five analytic dissertations written from 1957 to 1989 that focus exclusively on Barber's music, Friedewald's is the earliest and still broadest in scope.

mistake, and as he didn't have time to return it, told his landlady to do so at once. At any rate it has never been heard of since, and naturally they haven't been able to study it this summer, as I had hoped. But perhaps they will perform it in Arden without studying! That is doubtless to be its fate—[39]

The score was found, but not until the following spring, two years after it was written, was the work played by the Swastika String Quartet (Gama Gilbert and Benjamin Sharlip, violins, Max Aronoff, viola, and Orlando Cole, violoncello). The Twenty-Fifth Students' Concert on 5 May 1930 included only compositions by Scalero's students—works by Alice Noonan, Eleanor Meredith, Jeanne Behrend, Gian Carlo Menotti,* Berenice Robinson, and Edith Evans Braun. The prominent position given to his Serenade—at the end of the concert—suggests Barber was considered then to be the most accomplished of Scalero's students.

The concert program indicates that the Serenade was originally composed in four movements (Adagio—Allegro con spirito; Andante; Dance; and Finale: Allegro moderato). The holograph score at the Library of Congress and programs of performances in 1936 and 1937 do not include the Finale but list only the three movements that were published by G. Schirmer in 1942.

The germinal idea for the whole work is found at the outset of the sonata-allegro first movement in the brief, languorous introductory theme (Example 3.1), which peaks in a chromatically rising series of suspensions.

The jaunty allegro that follows turns on a diminution of the introductory motive leading to a contrasting, slightly more expansive second theme. The development, so short it almost goes unnoticed, leads to the return of a truncated variation of the opening material.† In the second movement, a descending B-major scale of "sighing motives" introduces a long-lined melody spanning two octaves. The third movement, a sprightly allegro giocoso dance in a sonata-rondo form, was used by Barber in 1935 as incidental music in a play at Rollins College (see chapter 5, *One Day of Spring*).‡ Two tendencies characteristic of Barber's mature style are strong in the Serenade: a fondness for combining duple and triple rhythms (as hemiolas or as two beats against three) and expressive modal shifts between major and minor.

The Serenade of 1929 was the earliest composed of three chamber music pieces that were frequently featured during the thirties in order to advance Barber's career. With *Dover Beach* and the Sonata for Violoncello and Piano, it was presented in 1934 to Carl Engel, president of G. Schirmer

*This was "Eleven Variations for Piano on a Theme by Robert Schumann," which was played by Jeanne Behrend.

†Friedewald calls this middle section a bridge rather than development (*A Formal and Stylistic Analysis*, p. 157).

‡Orlando Cole, interview with the author, 21 April 1982. Cole was the cellist who played both the first performance of the Serenade and the music for the play.

SAMUEL BARBER

Serenade for String Quartet

or String Orchestra

Samuel Barber, Op. 1

I

Example 3.1 Serenade for String Orchestra, Op. 1, mm. 1–15.

publishers, at a hearing arranged by Mary Bok; its national broadcast on a radio program of all-Barber music was sponsored by the NBC Music Guild in 1935; and a year later, in November 1936, it was performed at a concert at the American Academy in Rome where Barber was a fellow. All three performances were played by the Curtis Quartet.

Almost a decade after he had composed the piece, Barber conveyed his pleasure at rehearing the Music Guild performance to the cellist Orlando Cole:

> I must tell you that I played the "Serenade" the other day—taken down from that Music Guild broadcast—and thought what a good double-face record it would make. How well you played it! It seemed to me a perfect performance. And it is not a bad piece at all, if I must say so myself! . . . I really was greatly surprised, and hope it will be recorded some day. Carl Engel arrives here in a few days, and I think I shall ask him to publish it now that everything else is out.[40]

When the Curtis Quartet toured Europe during fall 1936 they presented Barber's Serenade along with standard repertoire. Shortly before a performance in Vienna in October 1936 Barber wrote to Cole advising him what to do about the second violin part that had been misplaced by Charles Jaffe and about arrangements for the concert they would play at the American Academy. Of particular interest were his comments about the expected audience:

> Good luck for the Vienna concert! . . . I have told some friends in Vienna about [it], but most of the people I know there are more amusing than musical. We'll be listening to you on the radio tonight. I am glad you are playing the "Serenade," but doggone Charlie! I have the score here, but honestly have no time to copy the part and all the copyists in Salzburg are working full-time on G. C.'s opera. However I could either have the part copied as soon as I arrive in Rome, Nov. 1st, and hold or send it to you, or send you the score from here to any address you say, and if you are staying a couple of days someplace, your manager can surely find a copyist who can do it in a day. You had better wire me from Vienna what to do, as mails are slow, and I leave here early October 28th. The Princess of Lichtenstein says she will go to your London concert. . . .
>
> Oh yes, for Rome Academy, do not do a long program as it will probably be afternoon with tea afterward and they do not like long programs—Haydn, Mozart, and the Serenade, or Haydn—Serenade—Beethoven. But Wagenaar sounds a bit heavy, although I do not know it.* Remember they are mostly society people and a few musicians. An hour of a quartette is *plenty*. Thanks for suggesting "Dover Beach," but I do not want to sing—I'll be too busy to get in voice.[41]

Following Barber's suggestion, the quartet performed only three works at their concert: Haydn's Op. 54, No. 2, Barber's Serenade, Op. 1, and Beethoven's Op. 59, No. 2. The concert, at the Villa Aurelia on 16 November 1936, was played at no fee by the Curtis Quartet as a contribution to the Department of Music of the American Academy in Rome.

Eight years later, in 1944, G. Schirmer published the Serenade for String Quartet at the same time as Barber's Violin Concerto. At this time Barber, correcting proofs while serving in the United States Army, arranged the Serenade for string orchestra by adding a bass part; he also added sixteen measures of new music at the end of the first movement. This version, called Serenade for Strings, was conducted for the first time by Alfred Wallenstein in 1943 over Mutual Network. Although the critic Charles Mills found the arrangement "woefully conventional and romantic in a lukewarm way" and preferred the string quartet version, the string orchestra arrangement has been played more often since then.[42]

*The American composer Bernard Wagenaar (1894–1971) was on the faculty at the Juilliard School. He composed three string quartets.

The Unpublished Piano Concerto; Barber and Menotti in Europe

A list of Barber's compositions published in *Overtones,* the newsletter of the Curtis Institute of Music, included a "Concerto for Piano and Orchestra (1930)."[43] The work was begun in 1929 during Barber's second summer in Europe, one of the happiest times of his life. He worked on it through the autumn and the following summer, finally completing it in the autumn of 1930.* He labored painfully over this work, which was to that time the largest he had composed, and his correspondence from this period suggests that he was seldom satisfied with its progress.

Late in May 1929 Barber and Menotti sailed to Europe as third-class passengers on the *Conte Grande.* On board too, but in first class, were Scalero and his daughter, the "tall, unconvincingly soprano, loving and unloved" Maria Teresa—as Barber affectionately described her—and their school friend Jeanne Behrend.[44] Because Scalero had been unable to obtain permission for Barber and Menotti to enter first class "en visite," the young men had to be consoled by reports from the young women that, anyway, the first-class swimming pool was "too gloomy for pleasantness." "Gian Carlo says, 'it is better to be king of second class than the dogs of first!' " Barber wrote. "Besides, our deck space is the best on the boat, our cabin delightfully well-ventilated, even though the porthole can't be opened because it is three feet from the sea." Unlike the crossing the previous year, this one held "perfect weather every day, the sea like a lake, and no-one sick!"[45]

This was, he seemed to feel, an extraordinary voyage. Although his and Menotti's friendship by then was well established, now it was enriched by shared experiences and adventures, apparently moving to a new level of intensity. The young men had been raised in radically different cultures, yet their intellectual interests were unusually compatible. Whereas a year earlier, when traveling with David Freed, Barber had welcomed meeting other passengers, now he found them intrusive. In letters to his parents, he cast the trip in a spiritual, even romantic, light:

> It has been more than a dream-like voyage, because every moment of happiness has been too real for fantasy. And yet, only in books and romances does one believe that such days and nights exist—noons of blinding suns and chilling winds, and grave midnights of washing seas and many stars. And Gian Carlo and I drink it all gaily together, be it liquid spaghetti or bad white wine.
>
> We have spoken to no one on the ship and are only interrupted in our

* Numerous letters to his parents written during these summers mention the concerto. Broder, too, mentions a piano concerto that was in progress during the summer of 1929, when Barber first visited the Menotti villa in Cadegliano.

interminable séances on deck chairs by a pleasantly occasional visit from Maria Teresa Scalero.[46]

Now, in addition to music, they shared literature; language presented no barrier. Barber worked his way through Dostoyevsky's *Poor People* and d'Annunzio's *Trionfo della morte;* together they read aloud in French—Barbusse's *L'Enfer,* Bordeaux, and Alphonse Daudet's *Lettres de mon moulin.* Every day Barber read to Menotti in Italian, and Menotti in turn practiced his English. Barber was sympathetic toward his friend's slower pace:

> He is much impressed because I can read so fast, and almost without mistakes, even when I don't understand. I am sorry I can't say so much for his English, but it is delightful to hear him struggling through Cabell's "Cream of the Jest." Of course, I have the advantage, because pronunciation of Italian is so much more simple and regular.*

Apologizing to his parents for the brevity of his first letter home (a mere six pages!), he revealed his state of mind:

> I cannot bear to think of the end of the voyage, and yet it is near, I have been living without time, in immeasurable content. . . . Forgive me for making this so short and stupid. Perfect happiness breeds neither great deeds nor good letters. . . . There is so little to tell now, and so much to feel. Perhaps it is the monotony of our daily life which makes me find it so beautiful. At any rate, I am happy. HAPPY! Pranzo and Pastina! All known species of love!
>
> *Saluti,*
> *Gian Carlo and Sam*[47]

As they traveled together, Barber was profoundly aware of the reasons for his exhilaration:

> I suppose you can tell from the sincerity of my letters how much more Europe means to me this year. Every moment is a joy. Perhaps it is because one must go one time first to really enjoy the second. Or perhaps it is Gian Carlo. He is quite perfect; at close range, the defects become delights.[48]

They had landed in Naples ("stretching out her beautiful arms, as she basks careless, carefree, wanton—all that Neapolitan means—in the sun"[49]). From there they took a day trip to explore the ruins of Pompeii, followed by dinner in Sorrento. Returning to Naples, they witnessed an eruption of Mount Vesuvius beyond their powers of description, "my vocabulary al-

*Letter, Barber to his family, 31 May 1929, "a bordo del 'Conte Grande.'" James Branch Cabell (1879–1958) was a popular and controversial American novelist, who came under fire for "immorality"; *The Cream of the Jest* (1917) was considered to be one of his better novels.

ready quite worn out," wrote Barber, "nor could I paint it with harmony."[50]

Whereas in Philadelphia Barber had initiated the young Italian in American customs, in Europe their roles were reversed and it was now Menotti who guided Barber through the treasures of his native country. They were joined in Rome by Scalero, and since he had been a friend of the great Boni (the leader of excavations of the Forum), he was able to give his students a vivid presentation of the strata of Roman civilization with a clarity that Barber would never forget. They made visits to the Colosseum at night and to the exquisite gardens of the Villa d'Este and the Villa Borghese; and Barber experienced "real exultation" at seeing the little chapel of Lippi and the genius of Michelangelo in the Sistine Chapel. "Neither the works nor my reactions are possible to describe," he wrote; "I still feel the grip of Gian Carlo's hand on my shoulder as he pulled me away to see the 'Discus Thrower' and the 'Apollo Belvedere' before closing time."[51]

Before proceeding to Gressoney with Scalero, Barber and Menotti toured first to Milan, then Florence. In Milan they were "engulfed in a whirlwind of teas and dinners of Gian Carlo's relatives": his sister Amalita and her young children, aunts and uncles. Barber observed that "two years in America lend enchantment to the popularity and importance which [Menotti] seems to have always enjoyed." Such "demonstrations and kissing" must have seemed exotic behavior to the young American, who had been raised within a more emotionally restrained, even puritanical, family and was impressed with the aristocratic Italian family and their friends.[52]

Florence seemed "bewildering" in its wealth of paintings, which Barber had known before only from reproductions. In mid-June they arrived in Cadegliano, a village on the Italian side of Lake Lugano, where Gian Carlo's home was opened especially for the two young men and where virtually all of the surrounding villas were owned and inhabited by members of his family. From the moment he arrived Barber was enchanted with the little settlement and moved deeply enough to write about it:

> I am enthusiastic about Cadegliano; it seems to me the first spot in Europe where I can claim a foot-hold and which I can truly love. Hidden away in mountains of extreme natural beauty, almost unpastured, and overlooking a magnificent valley with parts of three lakes, dividing new mountain ranges which in turn form a background for the vistas of Switzerland—hidden away here, little known, not caring to be known—is this settlement of quaint villas of all styles, of diverse degrees of luxury, and most all of them owned and inhabited by relatives or members of Gian Carlo's family. There are no hotels, hence not strangers but guests. This feeling of intimacy is developed by the perpetual intercourse of the families. Gardens overlap; here a little chalet for tea built from the plans of Cousin A and with the designs of Cousin B, painted by Cousin C; children from all families come here for

> tea at five, and their mammas also, to chat. There are exquisite formal gardens, immaculately kept; and the woodsy gardens of Pellini—artificial and made with the tremendous expense necessary for the illusion of naturalness—a lake in a forest, long, overgrown walks by a rushing mountain stream, fragrant with the perfume of rhododendra, an abandoned mill and water-wheel, here and there unobtrusive little retreats for reading or tea.[53]

They spent two weeks at the Menotti villa at Cadegliano, their solitude broken only by family dinners and excursions into the countryside: "nocturnal trampings when the full moon makes each angle of the humblest peasant's cottage an artist's insomnia; mass in a country church and a visit to the preacher," whose services were "a dilemma, but always interesting." Their lives had been "flowing so smoothly, so withdrawn from the rest of the world," that they had no sense of the fleeting time; suddenly, June was almost at an end and it was time to descend to Gressoney—"to be up and doing" (Barber quoted Longfellow). "I am beginning to wish to work," he announced to his parents, "I began to write the Concerto the other day; and one cannot feel happy until it is finished."[54]

Toward the end of June, at Gressoney, he returned to "the same Monte Rosa, the same narrow valley, the same little room in the hotel, by the noisy river, but this time with a piano." There were no distractions to prevent settling down to work "more or less conscientiously." Jeanne Behrend, who had arrived two weeks earlier, joined Menotti and Barber for "rollicking meals and sedate walks with the Scaleros in the afternoons, after tea."[55] A turn in the weather, with freezing temperatures and snows, made it difficult to practice the piano without soaking one's hands in hot water beforehand. Barber and Menotti always took their lessons with Scalero in the morning and in the afternoons retreated to a favorite rock where they might read undisturbed. Barber's Italian, with much practice, was getting better and better, as was Menotti's English. The two continued to exchange books after they had read them. Their tastes were eclectic: *Pricò,* Federico Tozzi's *Gli egoisti,* d'Annunzio's *La città morta,* Joseph Hergesheimer's *Cytherea,* Anita Loos's *Gentlemen Prefer Blondes,* Claude McKay's *Home to Harlem,* Shakespeare's *Othello,* Eugene O'Neill's "The Great God Brown," and Henry James's *Daisy Miller* ("it really is a lesson for me" Barber wrote to his parents[56]).

Evidently, work on the concerto was not without snags: "Today I have been erasing all the parts of my Concerto that I composed yesterday!" he had written from Cadegliano in mid-June.[57] If the models he selected were any indication of the character of his own concerto, he had set himself an ambitious task:

> The Concerto has spells of going extremely well and terribly badly. Today, happily, is of the former quota, and I am beginning to get very much interested in it. I am making a thorough study of Beethoven's "Emperor" and

The Scalero family and students in Gressoney, 1929. Left to right: Liliana, the Behrends, Jeanne Behrend, Rosario Scalero, Barber, Menotti, Mrs. Scalero, and Sandra.

the Brahms Second, the similarity in form is amazing, yet the contrast in spirit equally so.[58]

His routine was somewhat handicapped by a neighbor who would not let him practice from two to four in the morning, his "dearest working hours." As the work progressed slowly, he realized that "at best, it is a formidable task to write a concerto."[59] By the end of July, the pressure mounted as the time with Scalero neared its end. He had hoped to finish the first movement before leaving Gressoney, but by the second week in August, although the sketch was finished, the piano score was not, and he realized the rest would have to be done in Philadelphia that winter.*

As the summer drew to a close, having bought "enough orchestration paper to write eleven symphonies and a ballet," Barber wrote his last letter of the summer to his parents; in the eloquent style that characterized all of his letters, he expressed his appreciation: "So it is almost finished, my summer, with all the finality of a memorable adventure. How can I thank you enough for letting me have it, or it for giving me a friend long-awaited, or Europe itself for opening my eyes to its fingers of beauty!"† In this

*By 11 August he wrote to his parents: "I had my last lesson on Thursday because the piano sketch for the first movement is now ready—and I am now waiting for Gian Carlo to finish a three-voice fugue and for my money to come, and then we'll make our departure."

†Letter, 18 August 1929, from Splendido Hotel, Portofino Mare. Barber's gratitude to his parents for having given him the opportunity to go to Europe was expressed frequently in letters sent from abroad in this and subsequent summers. Furthermore, he wanted them to share his experiences. A letter written the following summer, for example, urges them, "O please, please travel through Europe now while you are young, and not when you are old and ricketty like so many of the rich old dowagers at Villa d'Este!!!" (12 June 1930, from Cadegliano).

telling last sentence are the seeds that would become the emotional core of Barber's adult life.

During the winter of 1930, Barber finished the orchestra score of the first movement—or at least he thought he had finished it—and the second also.[60] He continued to work on the concerto during the next summer when he and Menotti again studied with Scalero in Italy. This time, however, their teacher and his family were ensconced in an ancient castle in Montestrutto, whose charm was exceeded only by its general condition of disrepair. The two students stayed in nearby Andrate at the Hotel Belvedere, where their room on the top floor—with an expansive view, a balcony, and hot and cold running water—far surpassed their accommodations in Gressoney the year before. Because there was only one piano in their room, Barber worked in a nearby house in a small room adjacent to a wine cellar and therefore very cool. Every Saturday morning the young men took their lessons from Scalero in his studio in the tower of the castle, spartanly furnished with a few Renaissance pieces, a suit of armor, and a grand piano.[61] After his lesson, Barber usually dined with the Scaleros—"the week's best meal"—and in the afternoons he and his teacher took long walks as they had done in previous summers.*

Once again, however, progress on the concerto was torturous—"I tore up ten pages of the concerto today and will start again tomorrow," he wrote to his family; "Scalero has the orchestral score of the second movement to look over for corrections."[62] Although his lessons were scheduled to last until the eleventh of August, whether he would remain until then would depend entirely on how his concerto progressed.[63]

Barber "destroyed to ashes" the last movement of the piano concerto because he felt it was unsatisfactory.† In mid-July Scalero had made him rewrite parts of the first movement, thus delaying the orchestration. Evidently he felt his parents needed an explanation of why this composition—his longest and most complicated work—was still unfinished after more than a year of work:

> So that if I come back to America with two movements entirely ready, you must be satisfied. If I had stayed in America with its "hurry up and get rich" spirit, I should have probably finished the last movement whether I liked it or not, presentably no doubt, so that I might play it next year. But

* Later Barber would remember their walks and talks with affection and nostalgia. On 5 August 1936 from St. Wolfgang, Austria, for example, at an especially joyful time in his life, he wrote to Scalero:

> I often think of you . . . especially when on my solitary walks through the forest (I do almost all my work walking . . .) and it seems such a shame that such distances must separate people whose thoughts about music have so much in common. . . . I see you walking there in the Val d'Aosta, or having tea on the terrace, and wish I could break into the conversation!

† Letter to his parents, 13 July 1930, from Andrate. He had begun the movement in Philadelphia during the winter.

(Left) Gressoney, 1929. First row, Eleanor Moffit, Barber, Jeanne Behrend; second row, Carl Bricken, Maestro Scalero, Menotti. *(Curtis Institute of Music Library)* *(Right)* The Scaleros, Nino Rota, Barber, and Menotti at Castello di Montestrutto, 1930.

> here it is different—one sees at every side how long it takes to make a really beautiful thing—and in Europe time is not held in such great, great esteem—time in the American sense I mean.[64]

Only three days later he lightheartedly wrote:

> I am deep at work in the orchestration of the first movement and find it great fun, but difficult to know what to do with the clarinets and oboes. Couldn't someone suggest something?[65]

The first week in August, Menotti left to join his ailing mother in South America. For him, it was "goodbye to Italy for three years," for he could not set foot on Italian soil until he was twenty-one or he would be drafted into the army. Barber's attention was now directed toward returning home and the possibility of spending the rest of August with his family in the Poconos. Shortly before he left, Scalero's newest student, Nino Rota, arrived and added more, but welcome, distractions from Barber's work. Rota, a prodigy who at eleven had composed an oratorio and an opera that had public performances, was a year younger than Barber and would enter the Curtis Institute in the fall.* With "all-knowing" candor about this slightly younger peer, Barber wrote his parents:

> Nino is unassuming though precocious. He knows many languages (English so-so), has just finished an opera, plays piano very well. . . . A little conceited, not big enough for his age, spoiled, but going to America will probably be the best thing for him. . . . He *hates* Brahms—and his opera, which he played over this morning, is very much Puccini.[66]

The summer came to an end and Barber returned to Philadelphia. Even after his piano concerto was in its final stages, Scalero was dissatisfied with it, and Barber was so discouraged he began to doubt his ability to compose anything at all. When he expressed his despair to his uncle, Homer attempted to buoy his dispirited nephew with the wisdom of experience:

> The course of true love never did run smoothly; it wouldn't be much fun if it did. It would be monotonous like a river without a ripple on it. Only, rocks have to be negotiated with care and judgment; they mustn't upset the boat. I can imagine how Beethoven felt when they stormed at him for writing the third symphony. If he believed all they said he could feel like a criminal, a debaser of public taste. I do not know a single man who hasn't had rocks in his life. Brahms had plenty. A good deal depends on how we handle them. They may not be so serious in themselves, but if we get flustered and lose our heads we can force them to do us considerable harm. . . . Poise, equanimity, philosophy, sense of proportion, gratitude for what we have, a "calm center," fixed determination and an inflexible purpose are all to the good.
>
> Resentment, impatience, self-pity, exaggerated self-deprecation, an intense consciousness of the need of making good in the *eyes of others,* a lack of grit in meeting emergencies, a general complaining spirit and weak sporting blood are all to the bad.
>
> I know how hard it is for you, but you have to make a definite choice of the spirit in which you will meet the present crisis. You can't avoid it. As a help I would suggest the following: Take some boy you know and put him in your place. He wrote your sonata, and your serenade, and struggled with your concerto. How do you regard him, dispassionately? Do you congratulate him on his gifts and what he has achieved and feel that, with good sense and intelligent self-control, he can carry his powers to a high state of development, or do you feel that he is a broken reed, a cracked canoe, smashed on the rocks of a difficult concerto, a hopeless wreck because his teacher does not agree with his opinion of his latest work? Take a sincere, objective view of your friend and make up your mind how you

*Rota's opera was a lyric comedy, *Il principe porcaro,* after Hans Christian Andersen. He eventually became director of the Liceo Musicale in Bari and wrote numerous film scores for Fellini *(La dolce vita)* and Zeffirelli *(Romeo e Giulietta).*

wish him to feel and proceed. Then act accordingly. Don't dodge. Be as strict with yourself as you would be with him.

Affectionately,
Uncle Sid[67]

At the end of this letter Barber's handwritten words *St. turned down my piano concerto* suggest that as early as the summer of 1930 he had shown the manuscript to Stokowski. Probably, though, it was not until after summer 1931, upon returning from Europe, that he submitted a bound edition of the concerto to the conductor.* While in Italy, he had taken the concerto to Varese to be bound—"I shall have it done very simply, not for looks, but because it is getting wrinkled," he wrote.[68] At the same time, he was preparing his application for a Guggenheim fellowship for six months of study in Europe. It is possible that he planned to submit the concerto as a sample of his work.

Apparently, even though Stokowski did not wish to consider performing the concerto with the Philadelphia Orchestra, he did, nevertheless, take the twenty-year-old composer's talent seriously enough to give the work a reading.† That Barber was bitterly angered by the conductor's rejection is suggested by the tone of the following letter from Homer:

Dear Sam,
Well, that's that! I am glad I wasn't there. In trying to understand Stokowski's letter you must keep in mind the actual sounds he heard and think what you would have said under the same circumstances of another man's work of which you knew nothing. As to why these circumstances had to be—that is another matter. The chances are that S. expected a much simpler and easier work and honestly thought his orchestra could read it readily. Even now, not knowing the work, he probably does not realize the "omissions and commissions." His letter shows that he had a deep respect for you and that is enough for the present.

There is one thing that I want to make clear to you and that is that resentment does not get us anywhere. It only eats the heart out of the *resenter,* and what is there to that?

I often think that a good friend could have saved Bizet's life at the time *Carmen* was produced. Patience and a sense of humor are wonderful lifesavers. I wonder what part resentment has played in S——'s life. Things

*Homer's correspondence quoted here represents only selections from the many letters he wrote to Barber between 1922 and 1953. They were originally handwritten, and after Homer's death Barber had excerpts typed and numbered in sequence. The letter (VII) that includes the inscription about Stokowski precedes a letter written more than a year later that explicitly refers to Stokowski's opinion of the concerto (10 November 1931).

†During this time Stokowski was interested in looking at new and "unusual" scores. On 22 April 1930 he presented Schoenberg's *Die glückliche Hand;* on 19 March 1931 students from the Curtis Institute participated in the American premiere of Alban Berg's *Wozzeck,* underwritten by Mary Bok (Oliver Daniel, *Stokowski: A Counterpoint of View* [New York: Dodd Mead, 1982], pp. 251, 260, 265).

happen, they always have and they always will. But, also, things change. Through it all, a rhinoceros hide is a good thing; the bigger the talent the tougher the hide, say I. Wagner had a good one, so did Beethoven. When Richard sold his book for the "Dutchman" for a Frenchman to set to music and be produced at the Paris Opera, he must have chuckled in his big strong heart. Resentment eats the heart, but philosophy is an armor that protects the source of future work which is the one thing that must be kept inviolate.

Affectionately,
Uncle Sid[69]

The score for Barber's first piano concerto is lost—probably withdrawn by the composer himself—even though during the thirties it had gained some attention. In 1931 Deems Taylor, interviewed on the subject of Americans who write music, said: "We have plenty of able young Americans. The big thing is to get their stuff a hearing. . . . In West Chester you have a very young man, Samuel Barber, who has all the earmarks of greatness. . . . He has to his credit a piano concerto that I believe is a musical triumph."[70] A piano concerto by Barber is cited also by Carl Engel in program notes for the New York Philharmonic-Symphony Orchestra's concert of 24 March 1935 (the premiere of *Music for a Scene from Shelley*).*

Several years later, however, when Jeanne Behrend requested a copy of the concerto for her husband, the pianist Alexander Kelberine, Barber answered that it was "*ausgeschlossen*—I might loot a theme sometime, but the whole thing is not worth resurrecting. I appreciate Sascha's wanting it. Sorry."† It is likely that the concerto's fate was similar to other works that did not measure up to Barber's stringent standards and were buried in the wastebasket.

Two Interludes for Piano (1931–32)

"Sam has written something wonderful, a new piece—very beautiful, very original," Scalero told Jeanne Behrend.‡ The piece, as yet untitled, was the first of two interludes that Barber wrote in December 1931 and January

* Also included on this works list was the missing violin sonata (1928) and a Motet for Double Chorus (1930), probably the Motetto on words from the Book of Job (see also chapter 7 below).

† Letter to Jeanne Behrend, 1 October 1938, from Nimaha, Camden, Maine. Sascha was the nickname of Behrend's husband.

‡ Told to the author by Jeanne Behrend, 21 September 1982, Philadelphia. The comments from Scalero followed Behrend's showing him some compositions of her own—intermezzi, written as exercises. She considered it a compliment that her teacher compared her pieces to Barber's for she knew Scalero was very impressed with her friend's music.

1932 as an assignment for Scalero. At the top of one of the manuscripts, in the bold, clearly formed letters of his teacher's hand, is written *Intermezzo.* A second piece, "Interlude II," was completed by Barber within the same month.*

Barber seemed to prefer to use the anglicized title "Interludes" for these two works; with the exception of their first performance at the institute, when they were listed as "Two Intermezzi for Piano" (possibly Scalero's preference), they are called Interludes on all subsequent concert programs and on the holographs.

Brahms's intermezzi are the models for these two pieces, but more striking than mere similarity of form are the references to pianistic patterns idiomatic of Brahms's keyboard style in general: polyrhythmic passages (two against three), hemiola rhythms, syncopated chordal passages divided with wide separation between two hands, pedal points on broken octaves and tenths, and exploration of the extreme registers of the piano. Yet in spite of these backward-looking gestures there is a thrust of melancholy characteristic of Barber's personal voice. This is especially true of the first interlude, an adagio that begins and ends in B♭ minor and has a middle section in C minor. Over a slow tremolo pedal on a thirteenth the right hand unfolds widely spaced intervals in contrary motion to the inner voice (see mm. 1–7, Example 3.2a). The chords of the middle section reshape the notated 6/8 meter into triple (mm. 39–57), beginning low in the bass clef and expanding to the high register (Example 3.2b). A false return to the opening material is accomplished by way of a passage in F minor, in which the pedal-point motive is placed in the right hand and three octaves higher.

Interlude II (Example 3.3) is tempestuous, also in an ABA form, and similar in spirit to Brahms's two rhapsodies. Beginning and ending in G minor, it is monothematic, the B section recalling and developing material from A. Section B (Example 3.3b), even with its key signature of D major, is tonally ambiguous, exploring arpeggiated seventh chords in a style that foreshadows sections of the piano sonata Barber wrote almost twenty years later.

The interludes were performed for the first time by Barber himself at the Twenty-Fifth Students' Concert of the Curtis Institute of Music on 12 May 1932, the same evening *Dover Beach* was premiered. Afterwards he gave the holographs to Jeanne Behrend, who played the first one on 1 March 1934 in the foyer of the Philadelphia Academy of Music.

Behrend's and Barber's warm correspondence through the 1940s reflects their mutual promotion of each other's careers well beyond their

*Holographs of the Interludes are in the Estate of the late Jeanne Behrend and at the Library of Congress. Variants between the manuscripts—there are two for each interlude—will be discussed in my thematic catalogue in progress. Holographs in Behrend's collection are dated 15 December 1931 on No. I and January 1932 on No. II (6 January, on the manuscript at the Library of Congress).

a.

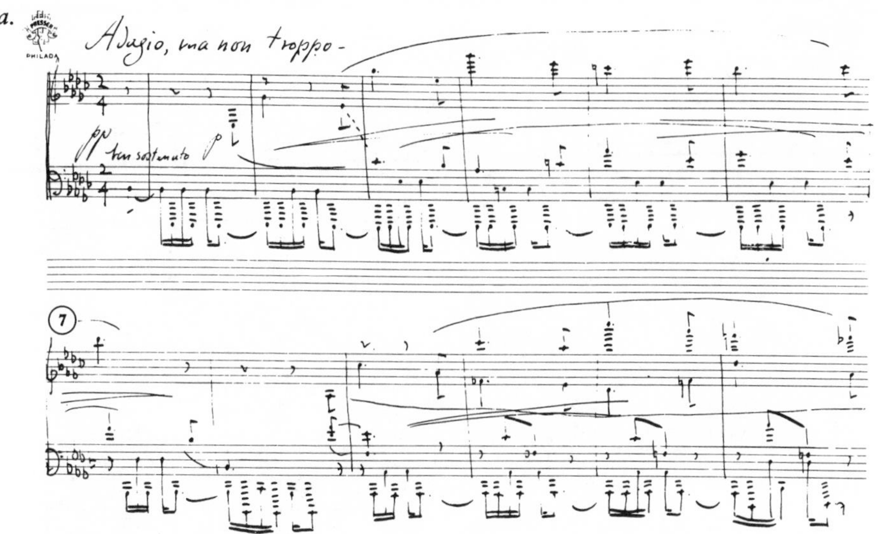

b.

Example 3.2 Interlude I, holograph, 1931. *(Library of Congress) a.* Mm. 1–12. *b.* Mm. 33–48.

student years. Through Behrend and her husband Alexander Kelberine came Barber's introduction in the summer of 1936 to the conductor Bernardino Molinari, which resulted in the premiere of his Symphony in One Movement. Behrend's loyalty to Barber was demonstrated, too, by her contin-

a.

b.

Example 3.3 Interlude II, holograph, 1932. *(Estate of Jeanne Behrend)*
a. Mm. 1–13. *b.* Mm. 36–51.

ued performance of his music, sometimes even against his protestations. Early on he had written to her from Cadegliano:

> I wish you would not even bother about fighting to play my things in New York; I really don't think it is worth your trouble, and you may be sure I'll always appreciate your interest if you play it to yourself sometimes, I'll be quite satisfied (but not to Henry Pleasants!*). It is rare to find a fellow composer who acts as you have; I shan't forget it.†

The pianist did continue to "fight" to play Barber's pieces, however, as well as to encourage him to write more for the piano. When in 1938 she announced her plans for a series of recitals of "Music for the Piano by American Composers," she asked him for a new piece to include on one of her programs. Barber, in Camden, Maine, for the summer and more interested in composing songs, wrote to her from Nimaha, a house that formerly belonged to Mary Bok and that was gratefully "far away from the madding Rockport crowd":

> I'll do my best about a piano piece, but all those black and white keys in a row staring at me from across the room give me no encouragement whatever. Your idea of a longish piece is good, though. Are you really having 3 concerts of Amuhrican music . . . ?????????! . . . ! . . . !![71]

In the end, he did not produce anything new for her series, and so Behrend played the Interludes on the last of the three programs presented at Casimir Hall in Philadelphia on 15 and 22 February and 1 March 1939. They were repeated soon afterwards at the Barbizon Plaza Hotel in New York.‡

Two Interludes for Piano are listed as Opus 4 on a works list Barber compiled in 1978 in one of his journals.[72] That they are crossed off the list is a sign that he did not wish these pieces to be counted in his oeuvre, probably because he viewed them—even more in his later years—as student works, not worthy of representing the composer he had become.

* Henry Pleasants, who graduated from the Curtis Institute in voice in 1929, was a music critic. Barber did not agree with his opinions about music in general.

† Letter to Behrend, 3 October 1933. Barber helped Behrend on several occasions: in 1933 he made an effort to obtain opportunities for her to perform in Europe through the conductor Victor de Sabata. His letter to her that summer reflects a general disenchantment with Philadelphia: "Stay away from the Curtis! They are non-musicians." In 1935 from New York, shortly before the first publication of his music, he wrote, "I wish I could help you get your music published, but being in the same boat myself (I've heard nothing definite from Schirmer) means that there is very little I could do. Do come some time. I am sure you are in New York occasionally, and I am never in Philadelphia. Thank God!"

‡ On this series were included such composers as Mrs. H. H. A. Beach, Leo Sowerby, Charles Ives, John Alden Carpenter, Edward MacDowell, Daniel Gregory Mason, George Gershwin, Ernest Bloch, Charles Griffes, and Aaron Copland; others are less well known: Frances McCollin, Ulric Cole, Charles Haubiel, Marion Bauer, and Emerson Whithorne.

Pieces for Carillon (1931–32)

In 1929 Edward Bok built a huge pink marble carillon—called the Bok Singing Tower—at the Mountain Lakes bird sanctuary in Lake Wales, Florida. At the suggestion of Leopold Stokowski, the Curtis Institute of Music added courses in campanology to its curriculum. The carillonneur Anton Brees had been brought from Belgium by Bok specifically for the purpose of teaching Curtis Institute students, who came to Florida for lessons between 1929 and 1933. Barber, Menotti, Nino Rota, Carl Weinrich, and Alexander McCurdy, Jr., among others, all spent part of their school years studying at the Singing Tower.

Barber made three visits to Florida to study with Brees, the first during the winter of 1931, when he was to spend only two weeks writing music.[73] The Boks were so pleased with his work, however, that they asked him to stay on for a third and commissioned him to write a composition for the giant carillon.[74] Much later Barber would be reluctant to speak about this work to his publisher, perhaps because, as Broder suggests, it was "tossed off" before he left Philadelphia and in Florida he spent most of his time swimming and playing tennis.*

During his second winter in Florida, Barber took ten hours, "more or less," of lessons from Brees, who said about the student, "the work done this year has been most gratifying."[75] (It is questionable whether Barber would have agreed with this report.) The third winter he visited Lake Wales for another two weeks, 30 December 1932 to 13 January 1933. During this time he "devoted himself to research into the tonal possibilities of the bells"[76] and produced the Suite for Carillon (signed "Sam" Barber), a set of four pieces published in the autumn of 1934 by Schirmer as part of the Curtis Institute of Music Carillon Series.†

Barber's suite, in four movements, appears to have only sporadically explored the idiomatic language of the instrument, primarily in the third movement, which has the melody in the lower bells and fast-moving flourishes in the treble (Example 3.4). The second movement, "Scherzetto," sounds quite different from its look on the printed page, since the very nature of the instrument precludes the possibility of crispness or silences during rests. A typescript program of an impromptu carillon recital in 1931 shows that Anton Brees played a Prelude and Toccata by Barber—probably the first and last movements of the Suite—although, according to Mil-

*Broder, *Samuel Barber*, p. 20. Barber's involvement with tennis was so great by the time he arrived in Italy for the summer of 1931 that he announced to his parents he much preferred the sport to his musical studies (see chapter 4).

†Other works included Gian Carlo Menotti's *Six Compositions for Carillon* and Nino Rota's *Campane a Sera* and *Campane a Festa*. What is significant about these pieces is that not only do they represent the first concrete results of the institute's undertaking—"to create a more extensive and better literature for the carillon"—but they were the first works of students of the Curtis Institute ever to be published (*Overtones*, 1933–34, p. 15).

III

Example 3.4 Suite for Carillon, third movement (G. Schirmer, 1934).

ford Myhre, the present-day carillonneur at Bok Tower Gardens, neither of these movements is especially idiomatic for the instrument.[77] In fact, the Finale—presenting an exciting climax with its cascades of thirds—although reportedly well received by carillon audiences, seems more appropriate for organ, since the hand stretches needed to negotiate the toccata figure are very difficult to achieve on the carillon at the indicated *allegro molto* tempo.

Four additional extant manuscripts of Barber's are in the Anton Brees Carillon Library at the Bok Tower Gardens. "Legend," dated "II, 1931," is of great interest only because it is probably the earliest of the four and most closely resembles the Belgian approach to composition for carillon. "Round" is considered to be the least idiomatic for the instrument; in contrast, the other two pieces—"Dirge" and "Allegro"—are well suited for performance and are occasionally played by Myhre in concert. "Dirge"

is monothematic, based on a motive of three descending stepwise notes that expand to seventh chords and octaves. "Allegro," in 6/4 meter, with a brilliant climax, is, of the four pieces, best received by present-day audiences. After this period, Barber showed no further interest in writing for carillon and was adamantly explicit about not wanting any of his "student carillon pieces played, much less published."*

*Shortly before Barber died, Curtis Bok, Mary Bok's son, asked the composer for, and was denied, permission to publish these pieces. Letter to the author from Milford Myhre, 19 October 1983.

4

UNCERTAINTIES

Now I only hear its melancholy . . .

Overture to *The School for Scandal,* Op. 5 (1931–32)

For his academic work at the Curtis Institute after he had graduated from high school, Barber concentrated on foreign languages and literature. Within two years, between 1926 and 1928, he had taken a total of ninety-two hours of courses in general English literature, the English novel, and French literature.[1] He also studied German for four years, supplementing his classes with private lessons, and took one semester of Spanish. His personal reading lists suggest that his education did not stop with formal courses; on the last pages of his sketchbook from the 1930s, for example, are long lists of "books to buy," and the titles and catalogue numbers suggest he might have intended to read the entire Modern Library collection: titles by Dickens, Carlyle, Marlowe, Sterne, Smollett, Swift, Turgenev, Chesterton, Mansfield, Pope, Edmund Wilson, Burton, Chekhov, Montaigne, Virginia Woolf, Yeats, and Whistler are interspersed among titles of books about music—Riemann, F. T. Arnold *(The Art of Accompaniment from a Thorough Bass),* Tovey, Cecil Gray, and Philip Heseltine (*Carlo Gesualdo, Prince of Venosa,* London, 1926). In addition there are such vital *aides-mémoires* as "Philharmonic strings 9-9-7-6-5."[2]

That literature was a strong source of musical inspiration for Barber, even in purely instrumental compositions, is obvious from the titles of two early orchestral works—the Overture to *The School for Scandal* and *Music for a Scene from Shelley.* Moreover, an overview of his total oeuvre shows that virtually all of his large-scale orchestral works, with the exception of the two symphonies, carry literary allusions; yet he would not admit to programmatic intentions even in those cases where he assigned specific literary titles.* Such was the case with his first composition for full or-

*The ballets are, of course, exceptions. One of the most openly programmatic of his

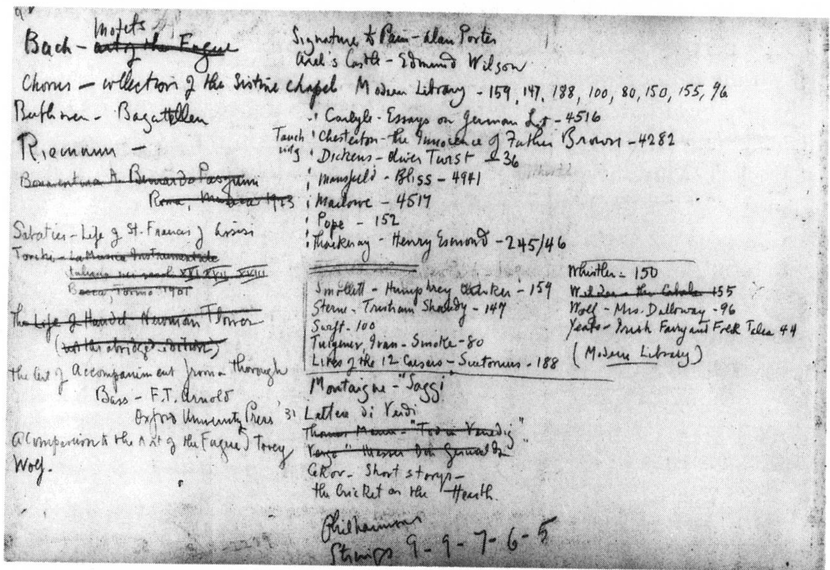

Last page of Barber's sketchbook kept during the 1930s. *(Library of Congress)*

chestra, the Overture to *The School for Scandal.* Although the title refers to the eighteenth-century drawing-room comedy of manners by Richard Brinsley Sheridan, the composer avowed it was not intended as a prelude to the play but "as a musical reflection of the play's *spirit.*"[3]

That spirit of merriment and wily intrigue is distinctively established from the outset by seven electrifying polychordal measures—a D-major triad in the strings against an E♭-minor triad in the trumpets over the bright color of the triangle. The mood is sustained by vivacious rhythms and orchestral color, the brilliance of which results from as large a score as Barber was to use in some of his later pieces for orchestra: paired woodwinds, four horns, three trumpets, three trombones, tuba, timpani, triangle, bass drum, cymbals, bells, celesta, harp, and strings. Described by Nicolas Slonimsky as a "miniature tone poem requiring a catharsis,"[4] the overture is characterized by sudden shifts in dynamics and tempo: starting at twelve measures after rehearsal letter *B,* for example, there are as many as seven changes within the next thirty measures: *marcato* to *poco allargando,* to *quasi tempo,* to *a tempo semplice,* to *molto ritardando,* to *pochissimo ritardando,* to *a tempo.* Nevertheless, the motion presses with sureness toward the climax. Characteristic of Barber's melodic style is the engaging, pastoral second theme played by the solo oboe. This theme bears

---

abstract orchestral works was the Second Symphony, or "Flight Symphony," from which, however, he ultimately went to great lengths to remove any extramusical elements (see chapter 9, below).

an English folk-song flavor, which reinforces the striking contrast between Barber's perspective and that of some of his contemporaries, who sought at this time to incorporate American folk idioms into their music.*

Barber began work on the overture in 1931 during his third summer in Cadegliano with Menotti. Crossing the Atlantic on the SS *Augustus* the last week in May, he and Menotti amused themselves by playing rolls of Italian operas on the player piano in the ship's saloon—"Gian Carlo hard at work working the expression levers."[5] As in the past they shared reading material, in particular a book on art history; and Barber, though professing to be "sick of novels," was immersed in Galsworthy's *Forsyte Saga,* a series that had been "haunting [him] uncomfortably for several years," he said, as it always "pops up in ships' libraries."[6]

Even though by this time Barber had spent three summers in Europe, he experienced the sight of Naples with renewed pleasure, conveyed in this affectionate letter to his family:

> I more or less lived the arrival at Naples in the person of one of you three: I saw Vesuvius first with your eyes, Mamma, then the city with Daddy's, the port with Sara's. So strong was the impression that we were all there on deck together! I seemed to be seeing Europe for the first time. Stepping into a carriage and up that quaint avenue of cobblestones and green trees, with the thousand noises and colors of Naples, certain times I wanted to run to the post office and cable "take the next steamer and step into a new life!"[7]

Landing in Genoa on 9 June, the two men sent their luggage ahead to Milan, for they had decided to make their way to Volterra on foot with rucksacks on their backs. Although they started their hiking tour at a rapid walking pace—"in three hours, we had made fourteen kilometers," Barber wrote home—several days later, as they trudged through the dungeons of a Florentine castle, he was plagued with one of the worst hay-fever attacks he could remember, making the final ten miles to Volterra quite unbearable.[8] His misery and the record heat wave in Italy forced the two students to curtail their walking tour and instead head directly toward Cadegliano by way of Milan.

A steady stream of visitors, mostly Menotti's relatives, came to visit that summer. While waiting for Menotti's piano to arrive from Milan, the two composers were fortunate to have at their disposal the house and fine piano of Menotti's Aunt Emma. They inaugurated the summer by playing Beethoven string quartets arranged for four hands. "It is a fine way to study them, and they are sublime music," wrote Barber.[9] With the arrival of the piano from Milan, though, the situation somewhat changed:

*Barber's overture received its premiere in 1933, about the same time as Copland was beginning *El Salón México*.

> We are having a feast of music. The grand piano arrived at last; it has a fine tone, though the transportation knocked it sadly out of tune, and the upright is in our bedroom, which by day becomes my studio. So we are finally free for working. . . . The two pianos are at opposite ends of the house so we cannot hear each other. Domenico* comes from Milan over the week-ends and brings his cello. We just finished playing Brahms and Beethoven cello sonatas, and although his technique is hardly impeccable, we enjoy ourselves immensely. He plays in a string quartette in Milan which is at present studying Gian Carlo's recently completed variations which we hope to hear later in the summer.[10]

Although Cadegliano was their home for the summer, every two weeks they traveled by car to Montestrutto for their lessons with Scalero. That Barber's interest in composition flagged as the summer progressed is evident by the disproportionate space allocated to tennis over music in his letters: "This afternoon we are forced to get to work and go to Scalero's for our lessons," he wrote to his parents early in the summer. "We surely have been lazy—nothing but swimming and tennis all day long. . . . I am getting so fond of it that I don't want to work at all."[11]

Little mention was made in his letters of exactly what music he was working on, but presumably it was the Overture to *The School for Scandal* that he referred to in the casual reports to his parents after his first lessons with Scalero: "Our lessons went well and my idea for a new piece for orchestra got by."[12] "My new piece for orchestra goes well, but it is an effort to work at it! The day seems to go fast without any music. Generally we work from one until five of the afternoon, playing tennis in the morning when there are no shadows on the court."[13]

That summer, he decided to discontinue his singing lessons:

> I have just written de Gogorza saying farewell as his pupil. . . . How soon one forgets singing; I haven't opened my mouth; I never really liked it anyway.† Instead I am eagerly looking forward to teaching next year. I should be perfectly happy to be a piano teacher the rest of my life, and play tennis a little on the side.‡

And in fact he acquired a piano student, Menotti's cousin Rosalina, who, in return for piano lessons, agreed to make him a tea service of heavily ornamented napkins. "She has considerable finger technique and loves fast things without pedal," he wrote about her,

* Menotti's older brother.

† This is a curious admission on Barber's part, for only a few years later he seriously thought of pursuing a singing career (see below in this chapter) and gave many radio concerts up to the early 1940s.

‡ Compare this letter written to his family 3 July 1931 with one written two years later: "I am always preparing, in the back of my mind, for the day when I will teach at Mudlevel College, Ark." (Broder, *Samuel Barber*, p. 23).

> so I am trying to infuse some passion into her timid frame, by one means or another, and selected Rachmaninoff's "Prelude" and the Moonlight Sonata to help me do the dirty work. If only she wouldn't tremble during the lessons! . . . But this kind of teaching I find not at all tedious.*

Before his second lesson with Scalero, Barber wrote to his parents, "Today is the day of frantic working to get things in shape for the lesson tomorrow. I must scrape something together to make it look as if the two-hundred-mile drive were worth the trouble."[14] Apparently the Barbers were not too happy about what must have seemed to them a cavalier attitude on the part of their son and began to pressure him about coming home earlier than he had planned, ostensibly so that he might spend time with his sister before she departed for her freshman year at Vassar College. Early in August, Barber protested:

> Your letter speaking of when I should come home put me in a quandary. First of all, I do not think I can ask Scalero to give me the two lessons which I am supposed to have in August before the twenty-first; he is already doing me a favor in letting us have a long lesson every two weeks instead of eight weekly ones, as he gave last year, and if I crowded two lessons in between August 6th and 20th, it would hardly be fair to the Curtis, who after all have sent me here to work. I have as yet accomplished so little.[15]

Other references to his work with Scalero, with whom he had two more lessons, were cursory: "My work is going rather well, and the piece is well on its way,"[16] and finally, "Yesterday, the last lesson—Scalero seems satisfied with our work."[17]

It is ironic that the Overture to *The School for Scandal,* tossed off between tennis matches, swimming, bicycle trips, reading, and shopping excursions, gained greater approval from Barber's teacher and brought him more recognition than the belabored and abandoned piano concerto, which had more fully—even obsessively—consumed his attention during his two prior summers in Europe.†

When he returned to the institute in the fall, Barber copied out the parts of the overture and made every effort to have the work tried out at Curtis, but evidently Fritz Reiner, conductor of the Curtis Orchestra at the

*Letter to his parents, 31 July 1931. Rosalina seems to have been Barber's first student. The lessons lasted briefly, however, because Sra. Menotti and her sister had a row about financial matters, and the daughter was, Barber wrote, "never again allowed to cross our door step" (letter, 6 August 1931). When Barber returned to Philadelphia in fall 1931, he was hired by the Curtis Institute as an instructor of Piano B, which he taught through two academic years (1931–1933) until losing his job because of Depression-era cutbacks in faculty (Faculty Record Card of Samuel Barber, Curtis Institute of Music).

†Near the end of the summer he wrote home: "I hate to tell you how lazy I've been all this week; not a note since my last lesson. . . . I bought a collection of short stories in German by Stefan Zweig, and I can hardly put them down. It is very strange, for as a rule, I am never very keen on short stories" (22 August 1931).

time, was not interested in doing it.[18] It would not be played until 1933, two years after its completion. Even then, because he was in Italy the young composer did not get to hear it.

By the spring of 1933, Barber had begun to feel restless at the institute. Perhaps he had spent too many years as a student or needed to break away from Philadelphia, which he felt to be intellectually and socially constrictive, but mostly he was eager to spend more time composing and traveling. In addition, he knew Scalero would not be rehired for the fall of 1933 because Curtis Institute was caught in a financial depression and was forced to cut back on the number of faculty members; Barber's parents, too, had suffered financial losses in the crash of 1929.[19] He wanted to leave school at the end of the semester, and, fortuitously, in April 1933 the Overture to *The School for Scandal* won Barber a second Joseph H. Bearns Prize (the violin sonata had won an earlier one; see chapter 3).[20] The $1,200 award for musical composition in the larger forms would allow him to spend another summer studying with Scalero and extend his stay in Europe through the winter of 1934.

Apparently Barber wrote to Homer of his irritation over Reiner's unwillingness to perform the overture and of his disappointment in having to miss the premiere of his first major orchestral piece since he would have to depart earlier for Italy. Homer counseled patience and trust, urging his nephew to focus on the work ahead rather than what he had accomplished thus far:

> You will have to give up speculating as to why men like R—— act as they do. You will never know why, so you may as well ignore it and forget it. Things have a way of righting themselves if (a big if!) we do the work. A good composition wins many battles, as you have found. You say you can't go abroad, and the Overture says you can! The next work may say you can be heard in Paris or Vienna, and so on ad infinitum. . . . What is a man without his works? Great, perhaps, but puerile. . . . Beethoven and Brahms planned their works years ahead. They heard few performances and this affected them just not at all.[21]

But missing the premiere was something Barber would remember for many years. "Toscanini gave me hell for that," the composer wrote in a notebook kept during the 1960s; the conductor had admonished, "Puccini always heard the first three performances of his operas in different places."*

The Overture to *The School for Scandal* was given its "first reading" on 30 August 1933 at the last concert of the Robin Hood Dell summer series before a massive audience of nearly eight thousand listeners. It was apparently upstaged, however, by a "resounding performance" of "The Star-Spangled Banner," after which the conductor Alexander Smallens, the

*In his journal (ca. 1970s) Barber commented on Toscanini's tirade: "I was not used to such treatment."

hero of the evening, was recalled again and again by a cheering audience. Nevertheless, Barber's overture made a reasonable impression. Linton Martin's review confirms a stylistic integrity between this and future compositions of Barber's:

> a work robustly scored—indeed, almost excessive in instrumentation at times—marked by a certain melodic facility and a sure sense of design, neither purely freakish in effect in the modern manner, nor complacently old-fashioned.[22]

Perhaps it was the overture's triadic themes—especially the broadly lyrical second theme—the economical and fluid development process, and the hemiola rhythms that influenced another critic to remark in the *Philadelphia Evening Bulletin* that Barber "looks at his Sheridan through Brahmsian eyes."[23]

Although not until the 1950s would the overture become established as a "regular" in the repertoire of major American orchestras, in 1938 it was presented to New York audiences twice within one week—on 31 March by the New York Philharmonic conducted by Barbirolli, and on 6 April by the Cleveland Orchestra under the baton of Rodzinski.* Olin Downes's review was not as kind as those offered by Barber's native city five years earlier, when the composer was less well known; his appraisal of the twenty-eight-year-old Barber's overture introduces some of the critical pejoratives that followed the composer throughout his career:

> The overture, well and gracefully written, is highly creditable for a first orchestral work by a young American. But here is the curious thing: it is no more American in flavor than Wolf-Ferrari. It is in essence an Italian comedy overture, slight in material, clearly composed, transparently orchestrated, conceived in the humorous vein.
>
> What influence was responsible for this? Could it have been the teachings of that admirable theorist and teacher of the Curtis School of Music, Rosario Scalero, with whom Barber studied before he went to Rome? It is hardly likely. Nor was the music written in Rome. . . .
>
> What then? We do not agree with the sort of musical patrioteer who attempts to prove that the accident of birth entitles an individual of otherwise modest claims to recognition as an American composer. On the other hand, music that lives and says something seldom if ever fails to suggest race and environment. This overture is evidently a formative work by a young artist of talent who has yet to discover his metier.[24]

The musical climate was such at this time that if a young American composer had achieved as much recognition as Barber—he had by then

*By this time Rodzinski had conducted the American premiere and numerous performances of the Symphony in One Movement (*Newsweek* [11 April 1938]: 24). See also chapter 6.

won two Pulitzer traveling fellowships and a Prix de Rome—but was not part of the mainstream's quest for a national identity, he was considered an anomaly and thus not representative of "American" music. Nevertheless, some conductors did, and still do, consider the overture a good choice for representing native music to international audiences: Walter Damrosch conducted it at the New York World's Fair in 1939; and in 1950 Barber wrote from Copenhagen that it was the only work of his other than the *Adagio for Strings* that was known to the Danish Opera Orchestra and its conductor John Frandsen.* In 1940 it was the first work of Barber's that Koussevitzky performed with the Boston Symphony.†

The Overture to *The School for Scandal* continues to have frequent performances, not only because of its popular appeal but because conductors covet good "curtain raisers" as well.‡ The earliest recording of the overture was made in 1944 by Werner Janssen with the Symphony Orchestra of Los Angeles.§ Barber's criticism of the tempos informs us about how he wanted the work performed:

> Janssen's performance of S. for S. is wrong because the end of each rhythmic section should go faster (stretto) and he takes a "sempre più mosso" just before the end slower—inexplicably. It spoils the drive. Also the performance is not as light or elegant as some I've heard.[25]

An arrangement for concert band was made by Frank M. Hudson, who as a music student at Ohio State University in the mid-1960s became enamored of Barber's music. Although Barber never commented about the arrangement when he and Hudson crossed paths in the late 1970s, he evidently gave it his approval, for it was published by G. Schirmer in 1972.‖

Dover Beach, Op. 3 (1931)

The poet Robert Horan observed once that almost everywhere in Barber's work is the sensitive and penetrating design of melancholy.[26] Perhaps, of his songs, the most compelling example is his setting of Matthew Arnold's

*Letters, Barber to Walter Damrosch, 3 April 1939, 7 East 79 Street, New York City; and to Sidney Homer, 1 December 1950, from Copenhagen. Of recent interest was its playing by the Niedersächsische Staatsorchester Hannover, under Peter Tiboris, on its first American tour in 1990.

†A letter from Koussevitzky to Barber, 10 November 1940, invited the composer to come to rehearsals and performances of his overture on 15 and 16 November 1940, confirming at the same time his "anticipation of the symphony" Barber had promised to give him.

‡Performance records of both the New York Philharmonic and the Philadelphia Orchestra, for example, show that the overture is frequently performed at free, summer outdoor concerts.

§The original recording on 78-rpm by Victor (11-8591) was reissued in 1955 on 33-rpm by Camden (CAL-205) and deleted in 1957.

‖Letter to the author from Frank M. Hudson, 17 September 1986. Hudson also did an arrangement for band of *Medea's Meditation and Dance of Vengeance*.

poem "Dover Beach."[27] Barber's chamber work for voice and string quartet epitomizes "the high serious tone" toward which Arnold—more than any other Victorian poet—strove in his poetry.* Composed during the winter of 1931, it foreshadows the restlessness and distraction that the young composer experienced during his Italian summer of 1931, a time when he wrestled with self-doubts about previously unquestioned career goals. The dark side of Barber's personality, in contrast to the charming affability known to his friends at the Curtis Institute, finds eloquent expression in *Dover Beach.* What appeal such lines as these must have held musically and emotionally for the young man: "The sea of faith / Was once, too, at the full. . . . But now I only hear / Its melancholy, long withdrawing roar." Arnold's text professes deep despair and disillusionment with a world "so various, so beautiful, so new," but where there is "neither joy, nor love, nor light, nor certitude, nor peace, nor help for pain" except through the fidelity of two human beings for one another. For Barber the song may well have represented a personal statement about his vulnerability as he emerged from the protective cocoon of childhood into the adult world.

In his seventieth year, after having endured personal and professional disappointments in the latter part of his life, Barber recalled his fascination with the poem when he was twenty-one and professed that it still held validity for him: "It's extremely pessimistic—the emotions seem contemporary. 'Dover Beach' is one of the few Victorian poems which continue to hold its stature; it is a great poem, in fact."[28]

Dover Beach gained recognition from Ralph Vaughan Williams, who heard it in 1931 when he lectured at Bryn Mawr College. Shortly after Barber completed the final version of the work, he visited the British composer and sang the song to his own piano accompaniment. "He seemed delighted," Barber reflected almost fifty years later. "He congratulated me and said, 'I tried several times to set "Dover Beach," but you really *got* it!' That was a great boost to me, since praise for my music was not overflowing in those Philadelphia days."[29]

The idea of using a string ensemble with solo voice was not completely unfamiliar to Barber. By the time he wrote *Dover Beach,* he may have heard Vaughan Williams's 1909 song cycle for voice, string quartet, and piano, *On Wenlock Edge,* a setting of poems from *A Shropshire Lad* by A. E. Housman. At the institute the Curtis Quartet had performed on numerous occasions Ildebrando Pizzetti's Three Songs for Soprano and String Quartet, based on Italian folk songs.† Respighi, too, wrote for this medium—*Il Tramonto,* a setting of Shelley's poem "Sunset," for mezzo-so-

*Louis Untermeyer, in *A Treasure of Great Poems: English and American* (New York: Simon and Schuster, 1942), p. 921, describes Arnold's poetry as "ethical, earnest, and melancholy in tone," words that could apply as well to Barber's musical setting.

†A performance at the Curtis Institute of Music on 8 November 1931, although postdating Barber's *Dover Beach,* does not preclude his having heard the work in rehearsal for this or an earlier performance.

The prize-winning composer in his early twenties.

prano and string quartet. But more significantly for Barber, it was a combination of forces that Scalero himself enjoyed. Scalero's String Quartet with Voice, Op. 31 ("Rain in the Pinewoods"), first performed in 1922, was a setting of text from the third book of Gabriele d'Annunzio's *Laudi*, and his Seven Songs in Cyclic Form for Voice and String Quintet, Op. 32, were settings of poems by Rosegger, Gauguin, George, Rückert, Falke, and Eichendorff. The last—"The Night"—is a setting of a text that evokes imagery and sentiment strikingly similar to that of Arnold's "Dover Beach." *

Although Broder states that Barber composed *Dover Beach* in Philadelphia during the fall of 1931, a holograph score dated 7 May 1931 indicates it was completed earlier. This means Barber would have worked on the piece during the fall semester of the 1930–31 academic year, while he was studying with Scalero and before he terminated lessons with Gogorza. This is confirmed by Katharine Homer Fryer's recollection that when Barber came to visit her father in Palm Beach in January 1931 he showed Homer some of *Dover Beach* and sang it for him.

Originally Barber did not plan to set the entire poem, and he only added the lines about Sophocles when prodded by Marina Wister, sister

* "The night is a silent sea. Joy and love, sorrow and pain, are blended as the soft beating of the waves.

"My desire is like a cloud, floating through the sky in the soft night wind. I cannot tell if it is a dream or a thought. I long to tell the sky of my pain, which lies deep in my heart, like the soft beating of the waves" (translation from program notes for a recital of compositions by Scalero, Curtis Institute of Music, 4 May 1939).

of novelist Owen Wister.* In an interview with Phillip Ramey in 1978, he told about the musical soirée at the Wister house when he sang *Dover Beach:*

> Marina Wister exclaimed, "But where's the wonderful part about Sophocles?" (Conversation was at a high level at those Grand Philadelphia Houses—if you said Sophocles when you meant Aeschylus, you simply didn't get another drink.) She was quite right, and so I wrote a contrasting middle section. The piece was better for it."[30]

By the time he wrote *Dover Beach,* Barber had had nearly six years of compositional studies with Scalero, with a heavy emphasis on exercises in counterpoint. He was well practiced in writing for as many as eight voices and had composed, as his notebooks from this period show, canons, fugues, variations, partitas, and chorale preludes. But *Dover Beach* is far from an academic exercise; so thoroughly has technique been absorbed by Barber that the expressive nuance of the poem is conveyed spontaneously and unselfconsciously, and with surprising maturity for a composer of twenty-one years. His interest in late sixteenth-century Italian vocal music (Gesualdo, among others, is mentioned in his sketchbook from the 1930s) seems to find a voice in *Dover Beach;* the relationship between voice and instruments, points of imitation that coincide with beginnings of text lines, the alternating contrapuntal and homophonic fabric are all suggestive of a quasi-motet style. In the middle stanza, for example, where the text leans towards the narrative ("Sophocles long ago / Heard it on the Aegean . . ."), the voice exhibits a *recitar cantando* over sustained chords (mm. 54–63). But when the persona of the poet reemerges at measure 65—"But now I only hear its melancholy longing"—the voice assumes a more lyrical shape.

A striking feature of the song is its pictorialism. Musical imagery is especially effective in the miraculous opening—"The sea is calm tonight"—where the voice and violin float languorously over a shimmering, slow tremolo of bare open fifths and fourths suggesting gently lapping waves (Example 4.1).

Such poignant lines as "With tremulous cadence slow, and bring / The eternal note of sadness in" lend themselves compellingly to tone painting, and Barber fulfills the expectation in the shape of the melisma on "tremulous," followed by a *poco ritardando* on "slow" and a fermata at the cadence (mm. 40–50). In the central section the text's mood of restlessness is musically heightened through abrupt chromatic and enharmonic modulations to keys remote from the D-minor tonality.[31]

Although *Dover Beach* is usually sung by a male voice and was origi-

* Accounts in several issues of *Overtones* inform us that it was not uncommon for Curtis students to play private concerts in the homes of prominent Philadelphia families. The Wister family were important benefactors of the musical institutions in Philadelphia, especially with regard to the Philadelphia Orchestra.

Example 4.1 *Dover Beach*, first page of holograph, 1931. *(Library of Congress)*

Example 4.2 *Dover Beach,* Op. 3, mm. 78–83.

nally notated for baritone (the range of Barber's own voice), Rose Bampton was the only singer during the thirties whom Barber asked to sing *Dover Beach* when he chose not to sing it himself. Her manuscript vocal part that was used for the early performances is subtitled for "Baritone *or* Contralto" and notated on a G clef. For the most part, the voice is presented in a lyrical declamatory style, rarely leaving a comfortable range of an octave (d to d′ for baritone). Exceptions are in two passages where Barber deliberately shaped the melodic line to reflect the intensity of an impassioned text: the f′ at measure 89, on the word *joy;* and the e′ at measure 75, for the wrenching supplication "Ah Love, let us be true to one another," set against agitated throbbing syncopated chords (Example 4.2). Barber indicates in his personal score that after the word *Love* the singer should take a "quick breath."

Four manuscripts of *Dover Beach* (all of which date from no later than 1932–33) and a photograph of the original holograph score of 1931 show that the song underwent several stages before arriving at the final version published in 1936.* The earliest manuscripts lack the short instrumental postlude that recalls the accompaniment figure from the beginning of the

*The earliest version, dated 7 May 1931, is at the Library of Congress but exists only as a photograph that Barber sent to Elizabeth Sprague Coolidge in 1933 and that she gave to the library in 1934. The holograph from which the photograph was made is also at the Library of Congress but has erasures (by ink eradicator) over which Barber entered his revisions in 1932 after the first performance. This score was probably used for the early performances as it contains a few practical instructions in Barber's hand (for example, "don't drop" is written over the melisma on the word *long* in the phrase "But now I only hear / Its melancholy, long, withdrawing roar."). Other manuscripts are copies that have autograph

piece. This five-measure instrumental coda, which as a symmetrical closure seems so natural—even necessary—to the integrity of the one-movement work, was, according to the cellist Orlando Cole, added after the first performance. Cole's copy of the cello part and a score at the Library of Congress that Barber used for his own performances show the addition of the coda in the composer's hand.

The manuscripts also reveal the care Barber administered in shaping the vocal line into its final version. At measure 19 ("on the French coast the light gleams"), for example, there was an alteration to avoid an abrupt descent through the interval of a diminished seventh (B♭ to C♯), by extending the B♭ for a longer duration, then moving to its lower neighbor, A, thus approaching the C♯ from a sixth. Example 4.3 shows the earliest version and the revisions Barber made to the holograph score (using ink eradicant) after the first performance.

Similarly, at measure 66 ("and round earth's shore / Lay like the folds of a bright girdle furled"), where disjunct intervals had presented a rather shapeless melodic line in the original version, the change to a chromatically ascending line provides stronger direction and a sharper melodic profile (Example 4.4). That these changes were made after the first performance is also corroborated by copyist manuscripts belonging to Rose Bampton and Orlando Cole, which show crossouts and erasures of notes with the new versions written over them.

A few corrections—perhaps relating to notation—may have been recommended by Scalero shortly before the score was engraved for publication. Barber wrote to his former teacher on 2 July 1935:

> I took the liberty of sending you today, dear Maestro—for there is not time enough to ask your permission—scores of the songs [opus 2], *Dover Beach,* and the [Cello] Sonata—and am asking if you would be so kind as to look them over to see if they are all in order, and write any suggestions you may have into the scores—margins, etc. I send them to you as your pupil, with the unchanged goal of receiving your blessing. . . . I am sorry to bother you with this, but there is no one in America to whom to show them whose o.k. I would respect.

Scalero's corrections arrived as *Dover Beach* was about to go to press but in time to be entered in the score. We can guess at the nature of the changes from a passage in Barber's letter of 19 August: "Many thanks for looking over my scores and returning them so promptly. I appreciate the trouble you took and will try to improve my enharmonic weakness in the future."

---

corrections or notations by Barber. These include Rose Bampton's vocal part, with a cover inscription by Barber; Cole's cello part (at the Curtis Institute of Music Library), copied by Strasser, who did much work for students at the institute; and another score (at the Curtis Institute of Music) copied by Ella Saile that includes expressive instructions in Barber's hand.

a.

b.

Example 4.3 *Dover Beach,* before and after revisions at m. 19. *a.* Original version, photograph of holograph score, 1931. *(Library of Congress, Elizabeth Sprague Coolidge Collection) b.* Revised version, 1932.

Dover Beach was performed for the first time at the Curtis Institute of Music on 12 May 1932 by Rose Bampton and students of Louis Bailly's chamber music class—James Bloom and Frances Weiner, violins; Arthur Granick, viola; and Samuel Geschichter, cello. The composition had its first public performance at a League of Composers concert on Sunday evening, 5 March 1933, at the French Institute, 22 East 60th Street, New York City. The program included works by graduates of the three most prestigious music conservatories in the United States at the time—the Curtis Institute, the Eastman, and the Juilliard schools—and Barber had the distinction of being the only composer to have two compositions performed. Rose Bampton (who was then with the Metropolitan Opera) sang *Dover Beach* with the New York Art Quartet, and Cole and Barber played the Cello Sonata.

Barber, incorrectly believing there were no music critics present, considered this performance "a horribly scholastic affair . . . and really no

a.

b.

Example 4.4 *Dover Beach,* before and after revisions at m. 66. *a.* Original version, photograph of holograph score, 1931. *(Library of Congress, Elizabeth Sprague Coolidge Collection) b.* Revised version, 1932.

début at all."[32] Hubbard Hutchinson, writing for the *New York Times,* viewed the program in general as "gratifyingly free from music of the type that slavishly copies the most advanced idioms of Central Europe with technical skill and usually a complete absence of anything to say."[33] About *Dover Beach* in particular, he wrote:

> The opening of Mr. Barber's song, if one may guess from a first performance, would have gained much by a quieter more sensitive quartet accompaniment. It had moments of considerable poetic beauty of mood, but an initial hearing, at least, did not reveal enough cohesion, unity or salience of line.[34]

Barber might have been thinking along these lines himself when he revised the voice part and added the postlude, but he never conceived the quartet part merely as an accompaniment: "The difficulty with 'Dover

Beach,' " he said some fifty years later, "is that nobody is boss—not the singer, not the string quartet. It's chamber music."[35] An accommodation to the balance between voice and strings was made after the New York performance, however, and appears in Cole's manuscript of the cello part: over the first measure of music are the boldly written words *Mute on*. The caution made its way also into the published score, in a footnote on the first page: "If mutes are used, they should be removed at *G* and restored at *L*."[36]

Composer as Singer

Barber spent the winter of 1934 in Vienna studying voice and independently practicing conducting. "Vienna has been more than kind to me," Barber wrote to Scalero on 5 January 1934. He reported in detail about his work in a letter to the Curtis Institute:

> The rest of the winter has been ideal. I found an atelier in Brahmsplatz, which looks out over the city. . . . I have a studio in the Theresianum, a convent built by Empress Maria-Theresa and now a sort of school. The place is so full of winding corridors that no one can ever find me—first good point!—and, second, the studio is so uncomfortable, with only a piano and a desk, that there is no possibility for anything but work.
>
> Shortly after getting settled here I had the idea of having a little orchestra come to play in my atelier every week so that I could learn to conduct. I was able to get sixteen of the best young strings in Vienna—all members of the Konzertorchester—for a total sum of $9 weekly. Unbelievable! These Wednesday afternoons have been my greatest fun, and what better way is there to learn to conduct?
>
> The atelier is very attractive—grand for music—and the acoustics make it often sound like a whole symphony. I play exactly what *I* want. . . . I have done much unplayed music from MSS of Vivaldi, Caldara, etc., lent to me by libraries here. The size of the orchestra is against modern music, but I did do a Sibelius premiere* and a Menotti. . . . I played the piano solo part in the Bach D minor Concerto, and sang the scene from *Orfeo*.†

Even though by that time he had discontinued his lessons with Gogorza, his interest in singing was still strong enough that he pursued further study with John Braun. On 20 April, from Cadegliano, he wrote to

*The work by Sibelius was *Rakastava*. The piece by Menotti was Pastoral and Dance for string orchestra and piano.

†Letter quoted in *Overtones*, 1933–34, pp. 77–78. Barber's and Menotti's apartment at Brahmsplatz 4 was in a house owned by a Czechoslovakian baroness, whose ornate dressing table provided the inspiration for Menotti's first opera, *Amelia al Ballo* (Gruen, *Menotti*, p. 25). He wrote to Scalero on 5 January 1934 that he had arranged the scene from *Orfeo* for strings and cembalo himself. The manuscript is at the Library of Congress.

Scalero, "After the concert, which I conducted, I threw myself into studying singing with a very good teacher . . . two lessons every day, and have made much progress." While in Vienna, he told the maestro, he had become "interested in the first German Lieder—Schmügel, André, Schulz, and so on, and copied many manuscripts of charming and gemütlich things." He had gained access to early music collections at the Vienna libraries through the help of the musicologist Karl Geiringer.

At a time when other American composers were drawn to native sources, Barber could write:

> All this time, besides my composing, I was studying a great deal of old Italian music which we should know better . . . for in the Italian primitives, where tonality is not so taken for granted as in the early Germans, there is much which our too-complicated contemporary composers might learn.[37]

We can surmise which "primitives" Barber planned to study from pages of his sketchbook from this time. On the first page is written "*Orfeo—con organo di legno e un chitarrone / Nagel archiv* No. 58—Purcell. No. 3232 AC-Peters—Monteverdi *Madrigali.*" At the back of the book is a healthy and diverse list of "music to buy," including Cavalieri's *Rappresentazione di Anima e di Corpo;* Italian folk songs; Monteverdi's *Combattimento di Tancredi e Clorinda;* Francesco Cavalli's twenty-three *Arie; Vecchi Arie Italiano:* Benvenuto, Parisotti, Torchi, and Barbi; G. Gabrieli's *Beata es, virgo Maria,* and *O Domine Jesu Christe.*[38] He wrote to Scalero that he planned to continue singing when he returned to the United States:

> I am hoping to support myself with my voice, for there is a field in small concerts in America. . . . I expect to do a group of German and early Italian things, playing my own accompaniments on a spinet which I am taking back to America with me. Do you think I am completely cracked? I shall have two or three lessons on Caccini, Falconieri and others with Giacomo Benvenuti* in Milan before I sail. Why should someone not resurrect these marvellous things for the voice as Landowska did for cembalo music?†

On Barber's return to the United States in the spring of 1934, he was invited by Mrs. Bok to spend the summer in Rockport, Maine, where a colony of Curtis faculty, students, and graduates convened.‡ Cole verifies

*Giacomo Benvenuti (1885–1943), an Italian musicologist, had published an edition of seventeenth-century songs (*35 Arie di vari autori del secolo XVII,* 1922).

†Letter, 20 April 1934, Cadegliano. Eventually Barber would build an extensive nineteenth-century vocal repertoire as well; a notebook of his (in the collection of Valentin Herranz) lists songs he sang by Brahms, Schubert, Fauré, Strauss, and Mendelssohn. Evidently he found it easy to commit songs to memory. In 1935, for example, while he was at the American Academy in Rome, the Curtis Institute's newsletter reported that he had "memorized all the *Dichterliebe* of Schumann, both words and accompaniments, as a sort of recreation" (*Overtones,* 1936, p. 24).

‡During the Depression, towns in the Camden harbor area were economically impover-

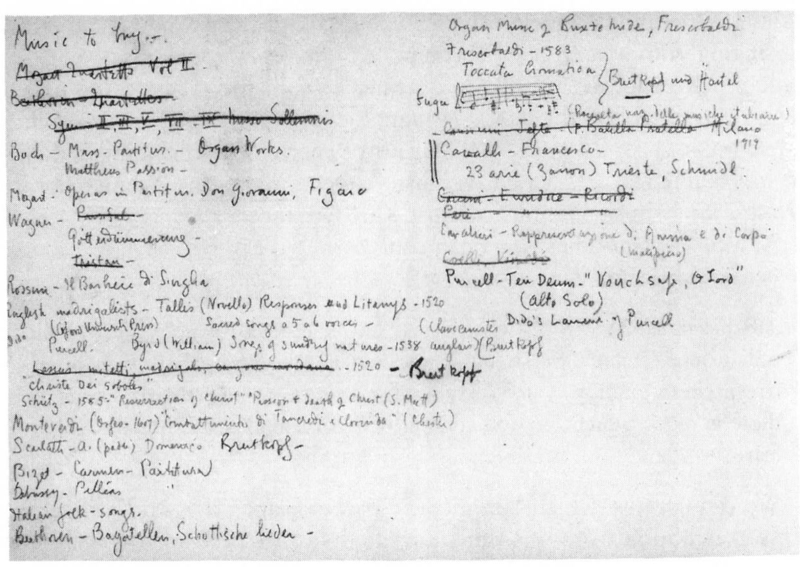
Music to buy.—
Bach — Mass-Partitur. — Organ Works.
Matthews Passion —
Mozart · Operas in Partitur. Don Giovanni, Figaro
Wagner —
Götterdämmerung —
Rossini — Il Barbiere di Siviglia
English madrigalists — Tallis (Novello) Responses and Litanys - 1520
(Oxford University Press) Sacred songs a 5 a 6 voices —
Purcell. Byrd (William) Songs of sundry natures - 1538 anglais) (Breitkopf
- 1520 — Breitkopf
"Christe Dei soboles"
Schütz - 1585 - "Resurrection of Christ" "Passion & Death of Christ (S. Matt)
Monteverdi (Orfeo - 1607) "Combattimento di Tancredi e Clorinda" (Chester)
Scarlatti - A. (pets) Domenico Breitkopf —
Bizet — Carmen - Partitura)
Debussy - Pelléas
Italian folk-songs.
Beethoven — Bagatellen, Schottische lieder —
Organ Music of Buxtehude, Frescobaldi
Frescobaldi - 1583
Toccata Cromatica } Breitkopf und Härtel
Fuga
(Raccolta naz. delle musiche italiane)
Milano 1919
Cavalli — Francesco —
23 arie (Zanon) Trieste, Schmidl
Cavalieri — Rappresentazione di Anima e di Corpo
(Malipiero)
Purcell - Te Deum — "Vouchsafe, O Lord"
(alto Solo)
(Clavecinists Dido's Lament of Purcell

Barber's sketchbook from the 1930s, pp. [90] and 91. *(Library of Congress)*

that Barber did indeed bring with him a small spinet on which he accompanied himself in concerts of songs by Monteverdi and Caccini, and Italian and American folk music.[39] Victor Gomez, reviewing one of Barber's recitals, praised him as "an artist in every sense, for he combines a beautiful voice with remarkable ease of style, and a musicality which never fails to 'cross the t's and dot the i's.' " Gomez continued:

> Mr. Barber has learned the invaluable art of voice modulation, and wisely believes that an ounce of singing is worth a ton of shouting. He held his audience in rapt silence as he modestly trod the alternate paths of humor and pathos, and created an impression which can only be established by an artist of first rank.*

ished and physically run down because many local industries folded—shipbuilding, ice-cutting, quarrying for lime. Edward and Mary Bok were able to buy considerable real estate during this time and engaged the townspeople in rebuilding houses and planting gardens. The twenty-six houses owned by the Boks in various sections of the Camden area usually took the whole month of June for Mary Bok to outfit in preparation for faculty members, who were billeted there for the summer with their families and their most talented students. The Boks also built a concert barn in which there were weekly performances. Thus a summer musical community was established that predated such festivals as Tanglewood and Saratoga. Many prominent musicians—Josef Hofmann, Lea Luboschutz, Gregor Piatigorsky, Anna Lehmann, and the Curtis Quartet—spent summers in Maine under the auspices of the Boks. Barber and Menotti each had his own studio. (*Overtones,* 1 October 1974, pp. 16–17; and author's interviews with Cole, 21 April 1982, and Nellie Lee Bok, 21 September 1982).

*Review of the Curtis Series from an unidentified Maine newspaper the week of 26 August 1934 (Annie Russell clipping file, New York Public Library, Theatre Division). Gomez was solo cellist with the Cleveland Concert Orchestra.

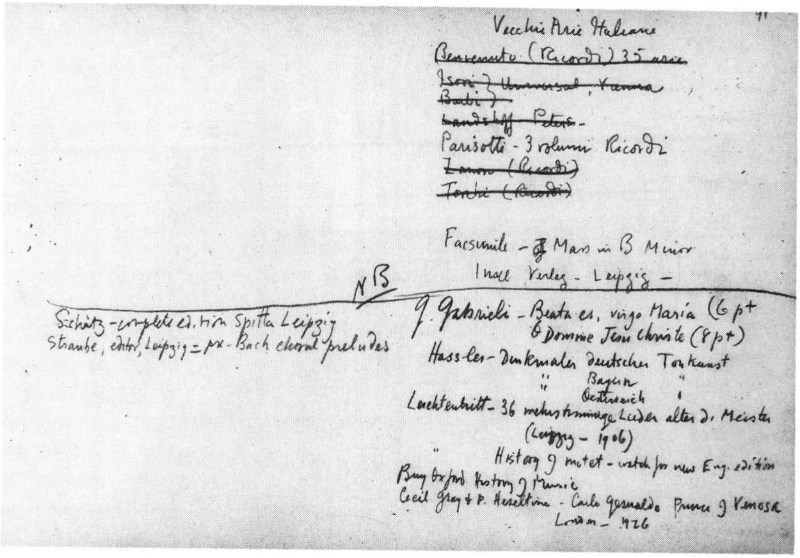

Barber planned to arrive in New York the second week in October 1934 and spend the winter singing on the radio.* Before he settled in New York, he gave a recital on 23 October 1934 at the New Century Club in West Chester. The program informs us that, "accompanying himself on a spinet from Munich," he sang "old songs . . . many still unpublished . . . sung from the original manuscripts." Those with spinet accompaniment included songs by Dowland, Rathgeber, C. P. E. Bach, Hassler, Hiller, and Schubart and eighteenth-century Italian, French, German, and Scottish folk songs. Accompanied by Yvonne Biser at the piano, Barber sang songs by Sidney Homer, Roland Leich, and Handel and three of his own songs—"The Daisies," "Bessie Bobtail," and "There's nae lark."[40]

On 4 February 1935 he made his nationwide debut as a singer on the NBC Music Guild series; he was featured again as soloist in the series on 26 March. His vocal ability during these two appearances won him a contract for a series of weekly song broadcasts. The first, on 24 April, consisted of eighteenth-century songs for which Barber again accompanied himself on the spinet, presumably repeating his New Century Club program of October.

In March 1935 Charles O'Connell, head of the artist and repertory division of the RCA Victor Record Company, expressed an interest in re-

*This is confirmed in a letter to Mme Carlos Salzedo, 17 September 1934. Broder writes that Barber's first broadcast, for which he received a fee of $25, was as a member of the chorus in a radio adaptation of *Aïda* (*Samuel Barber*, p. 27).

PROGRAM

I

Old Songs With Spinet Accompaniment.

(Many of the songs are still unpublished and are sung from the original manuscripts.)

1. Flow, My Tears..........*John Dowland, 1599*
   (Written at the Court of the King of Denmark at Elsinore)
2. Con Stizza Pizzica ....(Love Stings Me).....
   Sicilian, 18th century)
3. Stanco di Pascolar.............................
   Shepherd Song, 18th Century
   He asks a beautiful young shepherdess why she is crying; she cries "Traitor," and with a sigh, faints into his arms.)
4. German Drinking Song......*Rathgeber*, 1733
   (A Benedictine Monk)
5. Aus einem Kloster (from a Cloister).........
   C. P. E.Bach, 1789
   (Oh Love, What Have I Done !)
6. Viens dans ces Bocages
   Old French Bergerette

II

With Piano :

1. Requiem.......................... } *Sidney Homer*
2. April, April...................... }
3. Seal Lullaby.........................*Roland Leich*

"Ombra mai fu" from "Xerxes".......*Haendel*

INTERMISSION

III

With Piano :

1. There's Nae Lark.................. } *Sam Barber*
2. The Daisies...................... }
3. Bessie Bobtail................... }

(A homeless old woman wambles down the street, saying over and over to herself: "Oh God," He knows !)

IV

Old Songs with Spinet :

1. Tanzlied; Nachtanz (Dance Song; After Dance)..........................*Hasler, 1601*
2. Das Maedchen und die Hasel (The Maiden and the Hare). *From "The Wanderhorn."*
   (The maiden says : "I am beautiful, because I eat white bread and drink cool wine." The hare answers : "If you wish to remain beautiful, stay home from dances ! "
3. Lied des Zauberers (Magician's Song)
   ....*Hiller, 1770*
   (Come, evil spirits, and carry out my secret commands.)
4. Turn Ye to Me.................Old Highland
5. The Hen (translated from the German)
   ....*C. F. Schubart, 1786*

(A satire on the creative artists who used to write and publish criticisms of their own works)

Miss Yvonne Eiser at the piano.

The Spinet is from Munich.

Program of song recital Barber gave at the New Century Club on 23 October 1934.

cording *Dover Beach.* Although an early recording was made in 1933 by Rose Bampton, it was never released.* As pleased as Barber was with the prospect of another recording, he was, nevertheless, reluctant to go along with O'Connell's choice of Conrad Thibault as the soloist. Thibault had trained at the Curtis Institute, had a good voice, and was an experienced performer with some popularity in the Philadelphia area, but Barber felt it would have been very difficult to teach him *Dover Beach* without numerous rehearsals with the quartet. Thibault, as well as the young musicians in the Curtis Quartet, had so full a professional schedule by this time that it would have been virtually impossible to coordinate rehearsals.

It is more likely, however, that Barber wanted to record the song himself, as he admitted to Cole, "I am secretly delighted to be able to do my own interpretation."[41] His vocal experience gave him a considerable degree of confidence in exerting pressure on RCA to change its mind about Thibault's recording *Dover Beach,* but it was hearing Barber sing on the NBC 4 February broadcast that convinced O'Connell to ask the composer to do the recording himself. Moreover, the executive managed to obtain the more prestigious Red Seal label usually reserved for distinguished performers—"a stroke of luck," Barber recalled later, because "it was nearly impossible to get *any*thing recorded in those days." The recording session, on 13 May 1935 in Camden, New Jersey, was "nervewracking," as it was recorded on 78-rpm and the whole song had to fit on two sides. There could be no splicing, so that if someone made a mistake the performers were required to go back to the beginning of the song. Barber recalled: "We did each side twice, but that was it. . . . We had rehearsed a lot, and I was in pretty good voice that day, so it went well."[42]

Almost fifty years later he still remembered vividly the recording session:

> Not being a trained singer, I ran out of voice after the third time. When we finally got a good performance, the second violinist hit his music stand with his bow. So you hear this little 'ting,' like a triangle. But I wasn't about to sing the piece again, so that 'clink' is still on the record. Maybe it helps.[43]

There were numerous delays in production of the recording of *Dover Beach,*[44] but when it was released in June 1936 (selling for two dollars), it was hailed as a piece of "singular charm and beauty," "an outstanding recording of modern American music of true musical worth," and as "intelligent music intelligently sung—and with a naturally beautiful voice."[45] Barber's voice, though revealing "consistent sonority," was nevertheless found wanting with regard to its "blurred" diction.† Yet his voice so ex-

*Cole believes the record was not released because Bampton's diction lacked clarity. Bampton said her disappointment in not making the 1935 recording was offset by Barber's beautiful interpretation of the song.

†"W. K.," *American Music Lover,* June 1936. Student records from the Curtis Institute,

cited the admiration of Francis Poulenc when he heard the recording in the 1950s that the French composer offered to write some songs for Barber to sing.[46]

Barber heard about the release of his recording during the summer of 1936 in a little cottage in St. Wolfgang, Austria, "high up the mountain by the forest," where he and Menotti were settled for the summer. He greeted the news with a degree of modest disbelief that the recording came out well at all (recording technology was, of course, at this time relatively crude). He wrote to Cole:

> I . . . could not believe it was really released. Mother sent me a copy of the words which they put with the record with the rot about me on it—and a little criticism from Roger Smith's record news; but otherwise I've seen no reviews, so if you read any in the record columns of the New York papers, or the "American Mercury," I should appreciate no end your sending them on to me, as mother herself will not be able to see any more. I feel as you do about the record—it still makes me nervous to play it, remembering that day in Camden—but on the whole I find it good enough—especially on a good electric machine, such as Mr. Green's [William Hatton] or the one Gian Carlo brought here with him. On a portable non-electric, the quartet is too far away and the voice terrifyingly loud: but we must remember that most people who will buy such a record have good electric machines.[47]

A curiosity is an arrangement of *Dover Beach* reported by Barber in 1938 to a friend, the Italian filmwriter Suso Cecchi d'Amico:

> The conductor . . . said it sounded very well arranged for string orchestra, but that as he could find no baritone soloist, he had arranged the voice part for. . . . *trombone!* As I almost fainted at this, he reassured me that it sounded splendidly, he "picked up the tempo and the people loved it." When I asked how the line "Sophocles long ago heard it on the Aegean," sounded on the trombone, he said, "oh *fine,* the trombone player had marvelous slides!"—Bello, no?[48]

Barber continued to take singing engagements through 1939 partly as a means of financial support. The activity was worrisome to Sidney Homer: "It seems to me that from the point of view of doing great service with

---

1927–28, show embarrassingly low marks in "Diction." That Barber had to work hard to achieve the refined diction necessary for execution of *Dover Beach* is supported by the fact that he wrote portions of the text in oversized handwriting in the margins of the score, undoubtedly to remind himself to give special attention to certain phrases. A present-day comment about Barber's singing comes from composer Ned Rorem, who cites Barber as one of two exceptions that "most singers sabotage themselves" by singing their own songs; he believes Barber reveals a true, gentle baritone of professional class, albeit with the "rolled R's of uppercrust Philadelphia." The other, he claims, is Reynaldo Hahn, whose dictaphone recordings of *Les Chansons grises* show a "clean affecting tenor" (*Stagebill–Carnegie,* February 1983).

the works of the masters, you have a perfect opportunity here," he wrote to his nephew, "but if it interferes seriously with composing, that is something else again."[49] Long after his ideas of a career as a singer were abandoned, however, Barber delighted his friends at parties with impromptu renditions of Schubert, Brahms, and Schumann Lieder, an Italian folk song—"Batti, batti"—that he first heard sung in a Tuscan field, and songs by Sidney Homer, his favorite being "The Sick Rose."*

* Menotti, Turner, and Rohini Coomara in ongoing conversations with the author; Ned Rorem, "Looking for Sam," *Stagebill–Carnegie* (February 1983). A recording of one of Barber's recitals is at the Library of Congress in the Motion Picture, Broadcasting, and Recorded Sound Division. It was made on 26 December 1938 from a CBS broadcast of one of the Curtis Institute of Music's weekly Monday afternoon concerts and included the following songs, for which Barber played his own piano accompaniment: "O waly, waly" (English folk song), "The deaf woman's courtship" and "Brother Greene, or, The Dying Soldier" (Kentucky folk songs), "Zu dir" (Tyrolean folk song), "Batti Batti" and "Chi ti ci fa venir" (Tuscan folk songs), and a selection of Lieder—"In der Fremde" (Schumann), "Ist es wahr?" (Mendelssohn), "Nonnelied" (C. P. E. Bach), "Der Gang zum Liebchen" and "Der Tod, das ist die kühle Nacht" (Brahms), and "Der Jüngling am Bache: An der Quelle" (Schubert). In spite of some of the flaws in this early recording, Barber's voice comes through as warmly resonant and with good intonation.

5

INDEPENDENCE

Skyscrapers, subways, and train lights play no part in the music I write

Sonata for Violoncello and Piano, Op. 6 (1932)

Although the Cello Sonata is dedicated to Rosario Scalero and is the last work Barber composed under his tutelage, a copy of the published edition bears the inscription "to Orlando / physician at the birth of this Sonata / in appreciation of his help and interest / Samuel Barber / New York seven years late."[1] This informal inscription suggests the importance of the relationship between the composer and Orlando Cole, the cellist who premiered it.

The Cello Sonata, which involved Cole almost from its beginning, established a pattern that Barber would repeat throughout his career—that of enlisting the cooperation of the performer in order to familiarize himself with idioms and the scope of virtuosic possibilities of a particular instrument. An early critic's observation about the strengths of the sonata confirms the success of this kind of collaboration: "The composer places to his credit that he never forgets that the instrument he is writing for was intended to sing and he gives it ample opportunity to do so."[2] Cole himself said of the Cello Sonata, some fifty years after its composition: "It's very cellistic, very singing. . . . It takes advantage of the best qualities of the instrument."[3] He recalled further, at this distance, that at the time he played the early performances of the Cello Sonata many of his friends were impressed with the "new" music of what he called the "more avant-garde composers, like Copland and the whole Boulanger school, next to whom Barber's music seemed 'old-fashioned,' passé."[4]

Barber began the Cello Sonata in Cadegliano during the summer of 1932, after he and Menotti had hiked from Innsbruck to the Italian frontier near Lake Como. From there, they went by boat to the Lake of Lugano and climbed the hills to the Menotti family villa, where they arrived at the end of June. Within two weeks Barber had completed the first movement of the sonata and was working on the scherzo section of the second.[5] On 30 July he wrote to his parents from Castle Montestrutto:

> Maestro [Scalero] looked over my cello sonata and thinks I am always making progress. I wrote it entirely without piano, and next Sunday Domenico is bringing the first cellist of La Scala Orchestra to Cadegliano to play it.

When he returned to school in the fall, Barber showed the partially completed sonata to Cole, and as he continued working on the piece the two met weekly to go over new material, with Cole playing and offering suggestions, usually about notation, that were incorporated into the score. Evidently there were numerous changes at this stage, for Cole's manuscript of the cello part has passages that are written over, pasted over, and even pinned over.

The cellist's manuscript cello part suggests that the two adagios embracing the allegro section of the second movement were probably written by Barber as "an afterthought": they are appended at the bottom of the page with instructions at the end of the first adagio—"*vide scherzo.*" Another substantial change was made in the third movement, where Barber expanded a quasi-cadenza for the piano at measure 36 and again in the recapitulation at measure 128 (see Example 5.1a and b).

Barber's admiration for Brahms at this time is as apparent in this work as it was in the earlier Two Interludes for Piano. The affinity between the turbulent opening of the Cello Sonata and the F-major sonata of Brahms is unmistakable. As was mentioned before, by the time Barber wrote Op. 6 he was thoroughly familiar with the two cello sonatas of Brahms and had performed many of his piano works in recital.* The thematic material of the first movement, especially the lyrical second theme, betrays this influence, although Barber's personal style is not by any means submerged. Yet, while the sonata is Romantic in spirit, it is generally viewed as having some contemporary features, especially with regard to its rhythm and the dynamic balance of key relations in the last movement.[6]

Moreover, it has been observed that the Cello Sonata is "largely built on one striking concatenation of tones set forth in the very first measures and constantly thereafter . . . a familiar augmented-sixth chord . . . [treated] utterly unlike the older conception of this chord's function."† The exposition of the first movement presents the notes of the chord—C, A♭, G♭ (enharmonic F♯), d—in the form of a melody for the cello (Example 5.2a); at measure 16 the cello plays a rhythmically augmented

*Barber's letters written to his family document that he and David Freed played Brahms's cello sonatas while crossing the Atlantic in June 1928 (see chapter 3).

†Edward Tatnall Canby, liner notes for recording by Raya Garbousova and Erich Itor Kahn, Concert Hall B1, 1947. Canby refers to "a strange and twisted altered chord, as melody and (taking the tones separately or in groups) as whole centers of tonality."

Example 5.1a Cello Sonata, original version, holograph, 1932. *(Library of Congress)* *m. 128 in 1936 edition **m. 136 in 1936 edition

version as accompaniment to *marcato* figurations in the piano part (Example 5.2b); and in the closing theme of the movement the chord plays a prominent role in the piano part.*

Complex rhythmic structures also give the sonata a foothold in the twentieth-century literature for cello. The *presto* section of the second movement is challenging to the performer because there are many shifts between duple and triple meter as well as conflicting rhythms between piano and cello that occur at brutally rapid tempos (see mm. 10–17 in Example 5.3a).† Cole's manuscript of the cello part and the holograph score at the Library of Congress (Example 5.3b) show that these passages of the scherzo were originally notated as quarter-note triplets with a time signature of 12/4.‡ Because the cellist found the configuration unconventional and "hard to read," he urged Barber to write the part as eighth notes, temporarily penciling flags in his part in order to facilitate perfor-

*Friedewald (*A Formal and Stylistic Analysis,* pp. 165–77) points to the role of this chord in the third movement, where the augmented fourth figures prominently in the exposition with C and F♯ as tonal centers; in the recapitulation, however, there is a reversal of roles: the principal theme, originally stated in C minor, is restated in F♯ minor, and what was formerly in F♯ minor is in C minor.

†The cellist Marion Feldman finds the sonata an excellent teaching piece precisely because it combines Romantic and modern features.

‡Three other manuscripts at the Library of Congress document this as well: a dated holograph score and a photograph of the copyist Strasser's piano score and cello part.

Example 5.1b Revision with expanded piano part, mm. 127–140 (G. Schirmer, 1936).

mance (Example 5.3c).[7] At first Barber resisted changing his "pretty chains of quarter notes" and instructed the copyist Strasser to preserve them. On 2 July 1935, however, when the score was being prepared for publication, Barber wrote to Scalero asking if he thought that it was "a good idea to follow Schirmer's suggestion and change the scherzo of the Cello Sonata into 12/8 as it goes so fast." Evidently Scalero advised him to make the change, for in the 1936 edition the passage is notated in eighth notes. All three versions are shown in Example 5.3.

The holograph score at the Library of Congress indicates the sonata was completed on 9 December 1932.* Less than a month after it was

* The date is on the last page of the manuscript. A works list compiled by Barber in the 1970s (in a journal shown to the author by Valentin Herranz) lists the sonata's date of completion as November 1932, but this was probably an inaccurate recollection.

a.

b.

Example 5.2 Cello Sonata, first movement. *a.* Mm. 1–4. *b.* Mm. 16–19.

completed Cole and Barber played it at the Art Alliance in Philadelphia.[8] The first official public performance of the Cello Sonata, however, was at a League of Composers' concert on 5 March 1933 in New York, when Cole again played it with Barber.* The *New York Times* music critic H[ubbard] H[utchinson] heard only a small part of the first movement of the sonata "owing to the League's almost invariable habit of beginning its concerts fifteen to twenty minutes late" and his departure for another engagement. He indicated, however, that his opinion about *Dover Beach*—as having "poetic beauty of mood" but insufficient "cohesion, unity or salience of line"—embraced the sonata as well.[9]

While a full hearing of the sonata by Hutchinson might have produced a better understanding, the work was apparently not easily comprehended even by Sidney Homer. Barber was aware of Homer's reaction to the sonata after he played it for him ("just with piano") in the autumn of 1934:

* *Overtones*, 1934. The following year Cole and Barber played together again in Philadelphia at the Mellon Galleries, sponsored by the Society for Contemporary Music.

> At last he "got" it—and has said such fine things about it. Strange how many hearings it takes for people to really understand it, even when they are *favorably* disposed![10]

The Cello Sonata never wanted for audiences within the first decade of its birth. It was played by Cole and Ralph Berkowitz in the fall of 1934 at the Mellon Galleries in Philadelphia; by Cole and Barber on NBC radio in 1935; by Luigi Silva with Barber at the American Academy in Rome on 22 April 1936; and by Felix Salmond and Ralph Berkowitz on 7 March 1937 at a surprise party arranged by Mary Curtis Bok for Barber's twenty-seventh birthday.*

Barber especially favored Salmond's interpretation. During the summer of 1935, at the Bok summer colony in Camden, Maine, while correcting proofs of the Cello Sonata for the planned Schirmer edition, he had heard him practicing the sonata. "It sounds like a different work," he wrote to Behrend, "I had forgotten I wanted it to sound that way—dramatic. And he plays with fire."[11] Salmond's first playing of the sonata was at Town Hall, New York, on 7 February 1937, with Ralph Berkowitz at the piano; he played it with Barber two weeks later in London at Wigmore Hall.†

What is apparent from the review of Salmond's Town Hall recital is that although the musical establishment was not sure where to peg Barber's style, they were certain that he was writing from a perspective quite independent of the trends of his generation. An unnamed critic wrote:

> . . . a most heartening work in a time when an unaffectedly romantic outlook is considered in some quarters tantamount to retrogression. Those who approve of the neoclassicism of Stravinsky and the "Gebrauchsmusik" of Hindemith will hardly find this sonata to their liking.
>
> But Mr. Barber need not be disturbed by their disapproval. For while his work, as is to be expected in a composer still in his formative years, shows influences as those of Debussy in parts of the first movement, of Elgar in parts of both the first and the second, and of Sibelius in the third, it none the less reveals an individual approach throughout all three movements, without any of the intellectual striving after originality which is characteristic of most of the efforts of our younger moderns.[12]

Even after the sonata's popularity secured it a permanent place in the repertoire, Barber never seemed confident about how it would be received. When Silva played it at the American Academy in 1936 the composer wrote to Cole:

*Later concerts at the institute marked the last decades of Barber's life—his fiftieth, sixtieth, and seventieth birthdays—when the Cello Sonata became, as it were, a family reunion piece, with Cole and Sokoloff doing the honors.

†A program of this concert on 21 June, which included works by Bach, Paradis, Eccles, Brahms, Beethoven, Fauré, Ravel, Saint-Saëns, and Bridge, is at the Curtis Institute of Music Library.

a.

10 Presto ♩. = 160

p

mf

pp sempre stacc.

86674

b.

Example 5.3 Cello Sonata, second movement. *a.* G. Schirmer, 1936. *b.* Original version, holograph score, 1932. *(Library of Congress) c.* Interim version, manuscript of cello part used for first performance. The flags were added in pencil by Orlando Cole. *(Personal collection of Orlando Cole)*

c.

> I was agreeably surprised at the performance of the cello Sonata by Luigi Silva, and also at the reception by the audience. I had doubts about how that piece would go over. But Silva is a fine musician, and put it across.[13]

Some fifteen years later, in 1947, he was pleased to learn that it was going to be played in New York twice within one week—by Piatigorsky at Carnegie Hall and by a student of Pablo Casals at Town Hall. The sonata's continuing popularity with cellists is not surprising, not only because of its stature but probably also because until 1948 it was the only cello sonata in the repertoire written by an American composer.*

* * *

Dover Beach, the Serenade for String Quartet, and the Sonata for Violoncello and Piano were a triumvirate showcased frequently by Cole and the Curtis Quartet. Since these were small-scale works that required modest performance forces, they could easily be used to advance Barber's career.

In 1933 Barber sent copies of the Cello Sonata and *Dover Beach* to the benefactress Elizabeth Sprague Coolidge with the hope that she might use them in her chamber music concerts. With the scores he sent a letter: "Per-

* Elliott Carter's monumental Cello Sonata (1948) marks a radical departure from the neo-Romantic style of Barber's sonata.

haps the fact that I am an American composer is sufficient introduction in itself for you who have done so much for our music; if not, I hope you will forgive my audacity."* The conclusion of his letter tells as much about her patronage as it does about Barber's cynical view of the Curtis Institute's attitude toward composers:

> No matter what you think of the music, Mrs. Coolidge, may I assure you what a pleasure it is for me to write you at all. I have spent so much time at the Curtis Institute, where anyone who tries to create music is looked on as an inferior creature occasionally of service to virtuosi, that merely to write to one who understands the importance of a composer, and who has encouraged so many, is a privilege.[14]

His resentment, Menotti believes, was rooted in the neglectful attitude of the school toward composition students. This was especially true of the director of the Curtis Institute, Josef Hofmann, who was reported to espouse the idea that nothing of worth could be composed by Americans. A remarkable exception, of course, was the school's founder, Mrs. Bok, who ardently encouraged composers and who began to take an active part in promoting Barber's career after his graduation. Late in 1934 she engineered an audition for Barber and Menotti by inviting Carl Engel, president of G. Schirmer, Inc., to hear some of their works. Hearing about the forthcoming audition, Homer prepared Barber for the meeting with Engel:

> It is fine that you and Gian Carlo want to publish some of your works. You will find that Carl Engel is a frank and honest man who says what he thinks and has a high standard of appreciation. Have no fear. Your main task is to satisfy yourselves and even in this I hope you won't be morbidly finicky and self-conscious. Be fair to your own work even if it is not as perfect as you would wish. In the heyday, years ago, I was told of an annual appropriation by the house of G. Schirmer for the publication of works of artistic value, without expectation of financial return and I knew of some of the orchestral scores they published. In Germany, Simrock was quoted as saying: "I printed Bohm to pay for Brahms." If he said it, I don't believe him. He printed Bohm to pay Simrock, or because he had a sneaking love for his music and was afraid to say so.[15]

So important was the audition to Barber that he urgently wrote to Cole from Bolton—where he and Menotti were hard at work—to arrange rehearsals.

> I hope that the quartette will be able to cooperate and give good performances of our things. We shall appreciate it immensely—and it might not

*Undated letter to Mrs. Coolidge, probably written ca. September or October 1933, from Cadegliano (in the Elizabeth Sprague Coolidge Collection, Library of Congress, Music Division). The score of *Dover Beach* that he sent was a photoreproduction of the earliest version of the holograph score which, as was discussed earlier, was changed considerably after the first performance.

> be a wholly worthless thing from your point of view—as Engel arranges all the quartette concerts at the Library of Congress. I should like him to hear "Dover Beach" (of which I have a cello part, I think), the Serenade and Sonata for Cello, and Gian Carlo's Dance and Pastorale (Pensiero and Danza—I shall play the piano part in that).
>
> We . . . are at your service for all the rehearsals you are willing to have. Needless to say, I hope we can do the things *well*. . . . Perhaps you will be so good as to arrange with the boys well in advance about the rehearsals so that there will be no slip-ups . . . any hour or minute after the 14th will suit me. . . . I am tickled you will play the cello sonata for him. . . . Please keep this in the dark—about Engel, I mean, except to the quartette.[16]

Engel's positive response to Barber's music led to the publication of three of his songs, Op. 2: "The Daisies," "Bessie Bobtail," and "With rue my heart is laden." "Bessie Bobtail," according to a letter Barber wrote to Scalero on 2 July 1935, was picked by Schirmer's as the "most saleable" of all his songs. But as for the other works Engel had heard, only after Mary Bok provided funds from the Mary Curtis Bok Foundation to cover production costs—$325 for the Cello Sonata, and $295 for *Dover Beach*—were they published by G. Schirmer.[17]

Barber was probably not aware of his patron's intervention, or if he was, he did not wish to share the information with his uncle.* Because of the uncertainty of his financial situation, he had auditioned for a singing job with a professional chorus. Apparently, when he wrote to Homer of his plans, he mentioned only that Engel had "rescued" him by offering him a loan so that he might compose full time.† Homer chided his nephew for even considering work that would detract from his ultimate mission:

> Glorious news, including the Divine intervention which prevented you from singing successfully!!
>
> Why should you sing in a chorus? You delight in humiliating yourself.

*Menotti is confident that Barber was not aware of the arrangement and, if he had known, would probably not have accepted it.

†In 1943 Barber had the opportunity to express his appreciation of Engel's generosity by contributing to a "Birthday Offering" in honor of the publisher's sixtieth birthday. Included were canons and fugues by such distinguished composers as Arnold Schoenberg, Carl Deis, and William Schuman. Barber wrote a four-voice *a cappella* choral piece—"Ad Bibinem cum me rogaret ad cenam"—based on a Latin text by Venantius Fortunatus, which he had read in Helen Waddell's *Mediaeval Latin Lyrics* (the same source as for "The Virgin Martyrs" written eight years earlier). Omitting the eighth and ninth lines, he substituted the word *Bibi* (Engel's nickname) for the Latin *Gogo*. Set in a variety of musical textures, the text focuses on Engel's attributes and predilections: "Nectar, wine, wit, and learning, such is your fashion, Bibi; / but even beyond these plentiful gifts you charm us. / You are Cicero and Apicius reborn, / You overwhelm us with words and food. / But no more, please! / Bursting with ragout, I succumb: for there is war in my stomach when mixed foods growl at each other. / Already my eyes begin to droop and slowly my songs go to sleep." A holograph is at the Library of Congress, Music Division.

> It probably appeals to your sense of the ridiculous and gives you a proper sense of virtue. A nice feeling, but not practical at this price. Without being swell-headed you have had enough encouragement in your composing to justify your making a small loan from someone who believes in you, in order to gain the time and peace of mind necessary for good work. A good composition will be worth much to you at the present moment. Mozart and Beethoven were in the same position in Vienna, at your age, and wrote as fast as they could. They were jealous of their time and didn't sing in choruses or do any servile work, but they *wrote*, in practical forms, (Beethoven's string trios) and won out. You ought to be inspired by such appreciation from a man like Engel. Only a few men can write; but they've got to *write* and *write*, in many forms, in order to satisfy people who believe in them.
>
> Time and peace of mind are their principal requirements; so see that you get them and then get busy! It takes very little time to write music, as you know. Donizetti wrote an opera, words and music, and produced it, all within nine days and saved the company from bankruptcy. Beat that! *

Engel also brought the young composer to the attention of Werner Janssen, conductor of the New York Philharmonic Symphony Orchestra for part of the 1934–35 season. He planned to present a program entirely of Barber's music for the National Broadcasting Company's Music Guild series,[18] a project conceived by Mme Carlos Salzedo, wife of the harpist and composer. Barber was, of course, very interested in the idea and wrote to her on 17 September 1934:

> Many thanks for your letter with its project which interested me very much; I shall be glad to cooperate in every way. Unfortunately, just at the present moment, I am completely without copies of my compositions. They are all to be published, and with the exception of works for full orchestra, all my MSS are at present at the publishers. The list is as follows:
>
> "Dover Beach" . . . 9 minutes
> 8 songs for voice and piano
> Sonata for cello and piano 15 minutes
> Serenade for string quartet 10 minutes
> Two Interludes for Piano
>
> The vocal things I sing myself, and I rather imagine that they (together with the Serenade) would be the best for radio. I shall be in N.Y. for the winter, singing on the radio, and arrive the second week in October; I can have

* Homer's letter, although incorrectly dated 2 January 1934, would have to have been written at the beginning of 1935, after Barber had met Engel. This is supported by Homer's earlier letter of 8 September 1934 (in which he speaks of the forthcoming audition), by correspondence from Barber to Cole during this period, and by Broder's account. Probably Homer fell into the common mistake of misdating a letter written so close to the start of the new year.

the MS then, or could send you a copy of "Dover Beach" after October 4th—when I am singing it. I could also cooperate in the performance as far as singing goes, should you desire it.*

For the Curtis Quartet's participation, they would receive approximately one hundred dollars divided among the four players. "Sorry the fee isn't better," Barber wrote to Cole, "but they say the Musical Art plays for that. . . . However, it is the coming thing in radio, and a good thing for you to get on. . . . Later they will have more money. . . . They are a tough crowd altogether."[19] Negotiations were made for the Cello Sonata to be played by Cole rather than the French cellist Hubert, who had booked in advance a certain number of appearances with the network. Barber implored Cole:

> I did not want to upset his plan, but now it has all come out in the wash, and I hope you will do me the honor of playing my Sonata with me. Don't get nervous, I promise to practice a great deal, and I hope we can have some rehearsals in Winter Park, if I can get you away from the Rollins peaches. For this they will pay you $25 extra.[20]

On 4 February 1935 a full hour program of Barber's music was broadcast throughout the United States on radio station WJZ. He sang "The Daisies" and *Dover Beach* with the Curtis Quartet, who also played the Serenade. The composer accompanied Cole in the Cello Sonata. The broadcast began with an impassioned introduction by Carl Engel:

> I have a feeling that I am taking no undue chances in declaring that the occasion of this broadcast might easily turn out to have been . . . an event of considerable musical importance.
>
> There is nothing more calamitous for youth than to be tagged with prophecies of future greatness. I am not going to indulge in anything like the resounding flourish with which Robert Schumann so justly hailed the publication of Chopin's Opus 2, or—some years later—acclaimed the advent of the young Johannes Brahms. I should deem it a disservice to the composer this afternoon, if I were to pose as heralding unheard-of-deeds. I should merely like to say—very simply, very earnestly—that it affords me

*Letter, 17 September (1934), from Camden, Maine (Lehman Engel Collection, Yale University). From this letter, it would appear that Engel had considered publishing more than just the several works that appeared in print in 1936.

Barber's letter to Salzedo continued:

> I should like to recommend very highly the works of two of my colleagues: Mr. Gian Carlo Menotti, a young Italian who came to America at the age of 16, but who is a product of an American school. His "Pastorale and Dance" for String Orchestra and Piano was performed with great success on the Vienna "Ravag" radio, and in Italy. Perhaps you would be so kind as to let him know whether or not you can use compositions of other than American citizens. Secondly, the songs of Roland Leich [another graduate of the Curtis Institute of Music], who can be reached at Dartmouth College.

great satisfaction to have the privilege of prefacing with a few remarks the first broadcast—the first public presentation anywhere, for that matter—of a whole program of musical compositions by Mr. Samuel Barber.[21]

Thus through modern technology Samuel Barber's music was introduced to the nation, winning him virtually "instant recognition as a triple-fold musician—composer, singer, and pianist."* An NBC news release carried his comments:

I am glad of this opportunity to perform my music on the radio when all types of people from different parts of the country are listening, for to such an audience I address my work. Too many composers today write with one or both eyes on small snobbish audiences in the larger cities, and then wonder why their music spreads no further.[22]

This statement strongly suggests that Barber cared very much about audience response to his music. His ecstatic letter to Cole indicates that interest in the broadcast was widespread:

Fine reports from the broadcast. Toscanini liked the cello sonata and the Daisies—can you beat it!!—AND my voice. Everyone tells me how much I have improved!! Don't laugh! No wonder, the way I sounded in those records [of Curtis performances]! About 15 telegrams, fine reception in Florida, California, etc. Haven't seen [Olin] Downes yet, and the NBC is keeping all the mail to look through it for comments before passing it on to me. I am terribly grateful to you all, and especially to you.[23]

Shortly afterwards, Barber urgently wrote to Cole about another audition arranged by Daniel Gregory Mason, who wanted John Powell to hear the Cello Sonata. Barber had submitted the score for the Prix de Rome award, but Mason felt he could not make sense of the form of the work by merely looking at the score and wanted to hear it played. With Cole, Barber was circumspect about the reason for this audition and would only write, "This is T-E-R-R-I-B-L-Y important for me, much more so than you think. I'll tell you when you arrive."[24]

Mason, a proponent of an American national style but staunchly conservative in his leanings toward German Romanticism, reacted strongly to his two hearings of the sonata and called Barber the following morning to say he was "so excited he could not sleep that night."[25] It was soon after this audition that Charles O'Connell of RCA Victor began to negotiate arrangements with Barber for recording *Dover Beach.*

Spring of 1935, then, was a time of windfalls for Barber. Crowning his successes were the announcements, coming but three days apart, of two

* *Overtones,* May 1936, p. 22. A month later, on 19 March, Barber again sang his songs on the Music Guild Hour.

major awards: the Pulitzer traveling scholarship of $1,500—allowing him to continue his musical studies in Europe—and the Prix de Rome.*

In June 1935, as part of a celebration of the Jubilee of George the Fifth, a group of young musicians from the Curtis Institute of Music—Rose Bampton, the Curtis String Quartet, the pianists Elizabeth Westmoreland and Martha Halbwachs Masséna, the singers Agnes Davis and Benjamin de Loache, and the violinist Philip Frank—were sent to London under the sponsorship of the Philadelphia branch of the English-Speaking Union. The union had as their mission the promotion of British and American cultural exchange in music, theater, and literature. Arrangements had been made by a committee that included Edith Evans Braun and Mary Curtis Bok, whose financial support was the backbone of the venture. Two concerts were given in London, the first at the house of Lady Astor in St. James Square on the evening of 25 June; the second, at the American Embassy on the afternoon of 28 June, was followed two days later by a program of music by Bampton and the Curtis String Quartet that was broadcast over the BBC. All three programs presented music by contemporary American composers: Sidney Homer, Deems Taylor, Albert Spalding, Samuel Gardner, Harold Morris, Ernest Bloch, Edward MacDowell, Charles Griffes, Harl McDonald, George Gershwin, John Alden Carpenter, Richard Hageman, Edward Horsman, Marian Coryell, and Mrs. H. H. A. Beach. But the program at Lady Astor's featured primarily Barber's music: the songs "Dance," "The Daisies," "With rue my heart is laden," and "Bessie Bobtail," the Serenade for String Quartet, and *Dover Beach*. Also on this program was Menotti's "Italian Dance" (for string quartet), a song by Edith Evans Braun, works by Deems Taylor and Charles Griffes, and four spirituals.[26]

A distinguished audience attended the concert at Lady Astor's home. The British royal family was represented by Prince Arthur of Connaught, who apparently startled the serious Curtis students with his offhand suggestion that "the next time you fellows come, we'd like to hear you play something American, like the New World Symphony."[27] The audience was most enthusiastic about Barber's works and curious as to whether or not he was still alive. More significantly, a brief report of the musical event in the *New York Times* mentioned *only* Barber's music. This was probably because it dominated the program and also because by then he had received some national recognition with his radio broadcasts and as the winner of the Pulitzer fellowship and the Prix de Rome. His alma mater proudly boasted of his rising stature: "Who can say what future glories will cover this disciple of The Curtis Institute?"[28]

Sidney Homer had a more circumspect view of Barber's future. When Barber wrote to him in February 1937 that the London audience had re-

* *Musical America*, 25 May 1935. The Pulitzer was announced on 6 May; the Prix de Rome was announced on 9 May on an NBC broadcast of Barber's music.

sponded well to his and Salmond's performance of the Cello Sonata, Homer told him it was "well worth the trip and the sacrifice." "You had an intelligent audience that was willing and ready to appreciate," he wrote to his nephew, "and you had an honest chance to test the vitality and strength of your Sonata."[29] Homer, pleased with the public approbation of his nephew's work, nevertheless cautioned him against the seduction of fame:

> Public life has its value and often lifts a man to great efforts and inspires great conceptions, but production is done in the dark, underground, as it were, and an honest acquaintance with himself and an understanding of his own convictions is the hardest but most necessary job a composer has, if he wants to do anything but artificial work. . . .[30]

Music for a Scene from Shelley, Op. 7 (1933)

" 'Prometheus' has made you think I'm a softie, Jeannesky! We shall see," Barber wrote to Jeanne Behrend in October 1933.[31] *Music for a Scene from Shelley,* composed by Barber in Cadegliano during the summer of 1933, is a tone poem, although he insisted it was not programmatic. He wrote about the work:

> In the summer of 1933, I was reading Shelley's Prometheus Unbound. The lines in Act II, Scene V, where Shelley indicates music (quoted on the title page of the score), suggested the composition. It is really incidental music for this scene, and has nothing at all to do with the figure of Prometheus. The orchestra merely supplies the off-stage chorus of entreating voices, which call "Asia, Asia."[32]

In mid-August 1933, he wrote to Scalero that despite his sister's extended visit to Cadegliano and numerous excursions, he had finished the orchestra piece. "A sort of renewal of spring and brotherhood fills everything," he wrote about the passage from Shelley's play, "I have been so happy writing it."

Act 2, scene 5 of *Prometheus Unbound* begins with the following stage directions: "*The Car Pauses within a Cloud on the top of a snowy Mountain; Asia, Panthea, and the Spirit of the Hour.*" Panthea had described the chariot and its driver at the end of the preceding scene:

> See, near the verge, another chariot stays;
> An ivory shell inlaid with crimson fire,
> Which comes and goes within its sculptured rim
> Of delicate strange tracery; the young spirit
> That guides it has the dove-like eyes of hope;
> How its soft smiles attract the soul! as light
> Lures winged insects through the lampless air.

The Spirit's answer concludes scene 4:

> We encircle the earth and the moon:
> We shall rest from long labors at noon:
> Then ascend with me, daughter of the Ocean.

The lines that inspired Barber's music are in the next scene:

> [*Panthea to Asia*]
> . . . nor is it I alone,
> Thy sister, thy companion, thine own chosen one,
> But the whole world which seeks thy sympathy.
> Hearest thou not sounds i' the air which speak the love
> Of all articulate beings? Feelest thou not
> The inanimate winds enamoured of thee?
> List! [*Music*]

Lawrence Gilman, in his program notes for the premiere and in the preface to the published score, contended that Barber's music "seeks to convey something of Shelley's pantheistic rapture, his sense of the ideal love of all created spirits in a world too radiant for human eyes."[33] Barber insisted Gilman misinterpreted what his music was about and wrote to Mrs. Bok on 25 July that he intended

> to describe the "voices in the air" *imploring* Asia (goddess of love) to bring back sympathy and love to mankind (through Prometheus's release): not "the sounds i' the air which speak the love of all articulate beings"; and the first theme of descending harmonies is perhaps composed of the voices calling "Asia, Asia" from the distance: it is their entreaty that they may *hear* this wonderful music, rather than the music itself, which obviously should come at the end of the drama.[34]

The subtle difference lies in whether Barber's music represents, as Gilman incorrectly implies, suggested music for the end of the passage, or, as the composer professed, the voices in the air imploring Asia to let them listen to the music.

"Most beautiful and poetic," Homer telegraphed his nephew after he heard *Shelley* on the radio.* Another letter written six months later was more explicit:

> The new piece sounds like Prometheus struggling against his bonds. Not like Shelley, but still like Prometheus. . . . Why not? I believe in subjects that have an international appeal: Homer, Greek plays, Pilgrim's Progress,

*Telegram, from Palm Beach, Florida, 24 March 1935. News that the work would be performed by the New York Philharmonic so inspired Homer that he began to write a piece for orchestra himself. In a true reversal of roles, he attributed his motivation to Barber: "This is entirely your fault," he wrote to his nephew. "You will help to set the whole world singing and composing, whether you wish to or not" (21 March 1935).

Dante, Shakespeare. . . . The bigger the thought, the deeper the impression. The best part of the world is ready to consider serious and vital subjects.[35]

Barber's *Shelley,* as he called it, is the second of his large-scale orchestral works and shows him still in search of an orchestral style, now moving away from Brahms and toward Debussy. The transparent score embraces numerous passages of *divisi* strings, muted brass and strings, parallel thirds, fourths, and fifths, and occasional chords of sevenths and ninths—all suggesting the harmonic language and orchestral palette of the French school.

Music for a Scene from Shelley is cast in one movement in an AB form with a coda.* What is striking about the work is the way Barber has supported tone painting through orchestral color. A mysterious aura is cast from the beginning by undulating triplets (within the narrow focus of a fifth) in second violins and violas, *divisi* and *con sordini.* Against this veiled background, four muted horns (then three muted trumpets) announce the first theme—based on a four-note motive that descends chromatically through a major third (Example 5.4), recalling the opening of Debussy's *Nuages.* The theme gains intensity through crescendo and increased rhythmic activity, denser orchestration, and the removal of mutes; a second theme (Example 5.5, beginning at m. 34) of strong melodic profile was so distinctive it gained notice in Olin Downes's review of the premiere (see below).[36]

In Barber's sketchbook from the 1930s there is extensive material from *Shelley,* including mm. 1–82 and trumpet parts from mm. 34–42.[37] On the top of the page with the trumpet parts the composer has written "Go through Don Giovanni studying horn parts."[38] In the sketchbook, also, there are several metronome markings that do not appear in the published score: Barber calls for a metronome marking of "MM 60" (to the dotted quarter note) for the trumpet solo at m. 51, which precedes the actual tempo change by nine measures; he also suggests that from m. 68, beginning with the *rinforzando e sempre animando,* the tempo should "build up to MM 92 at climax." The poem's climax, at m. 80, is dramatically heightened by a grand pause followed by ten measures of boldly stated, chromatically descending parallel ninth chords, *pesante* and *fortissimo.* This remarkable passage was heard by Walter Henderson as "suggesting some sort of catastrophe."† A timpani solo, *diminuendo,* prepares for the coda, *Più calmo e molto espressivo,* which is a reflection upon the opening motive and concludes with a sustained B-major chord by muted horns.

Werner Janssen was reported to have examined some 150 manuscripts

* Friedewald's reference to an "arch form" seems inappropriate for this work (*A Formal and Stylistic Analysis,* pp. 280–86).

† W. J. Henderson, "Janssen Presents a Novelty: Includes George Barber's 'Music for a Scene from Shelley' in Philharmonic Program," *New York Sun,* 25 March 1935. Although misnamed in the headline, Barber is identified as Samuel in the body of the review; the "novelty" was A. Dubensky's Fugue for Eighteen Violins.

Example 5.4 *Music for a Scene from Shelley*, mm. 1–17 (G. Schirmer, 1934).

Example 5.5 *Music for a Scene from Shelley,* mm. 32–36.

of music by American composers before selecting Barber's *Music for a Scene from Shelley* for a premiere at Carnegie Hall on 24 March 1935.[39] More than thirty years later Barber recalled that this was the first time he ever heard an orchestral piece of his performed. As no one was allowed to observe rehearsals, he and Menotti hid between the rows of seats at Carnegie Hall to eavesdrop.[40] In an interview in 1949 he still remembered his frustration that *Shelley* was given only one rehearsal, during which only the first half of the piece was played.[41]

"On the impression of a first hearing," wrote Francis Perkins of the *New York Herald Tribune* about *Music for a Scene from Shelley,* "the score deserves to be rated as one of the most appealing new works by a native American that have been heard here during the last five or ten years."[42] A review in *Musical America* was more moderate:

> Mr. Barber's piece commanded the most attention on the list.* . . . investing a broad melody with shimmering color and tender mood. Great originality is not apparent, but great promise is.[43]

In contrast, Olin Downes's review, while focusing on the strengths that ultimately were consistently associated with Barber's mature works—"poetical feeling, an instinct for form, and a theme"—was more astute in appraising what the work signified to Barber's progress at the moment:

> The style is experimental and so is the development. Polytonal effects thrown about the principal theme do not appear to be those most natural to it. But what young composer would not wish, in the modern manner, thus to try his wings? This composer seeks the special color and the evocation of mood that he wants in a genuinely musical way. Furthermore there is a logic of statement and a main melody of considerable length and arch and feeling. . . . In other words, a young composer is seeking his characteristic impression and style.[44]

The successful reception of *Music for a Scene from Shelley,* as well as Barber's newly acquired status as a Prix de Rome winner, undoubtedly contributed to G. Schirmer's quick decision to publish that work and the Overture to *The School for Scandal* along with the Opus 2 songs, *Dover Beach,* and the Cello Sonata. When, on 2 July 1935, Barber sent the small-scale works to Scalero for suggestions prior to their publication, he wrote to his former teacher, "I regret that I am unable to send the orchestral works, as their decision about this was very sudden, and they began photoengraving from my score the same day." The score of *Music for a Scene from Shelley* was never engraved but was photographed from an autographer's copy, which apparently Barber did not have time to proofread before the printing. On 5 August 1936, shortly after its publication, Barber sent Scalero a score, about which he wrote:

> By the way, the copy of this "Music for a Scene from Shelley" (which I do not believe you know) is a faulty one which I have corrected: you see the whole edition had to be recalled and corrected, but I have not received the correct copies and did not want to wait.

It is questionable whether the score was ever recalled, and it is more likely that Barber's corrections found their way into the rental parts only.†

Music for a Scene from Shelley received numerous performances in the next few years after its premiere. In October 1935, during the first season

* Other works on the program were the Sinfonie from Bach's cantata *Geist und Seele;* Schumann's Overture, Scherzo, and Finale; and Beethoven's Symphony No. 2.

† Even as this book is in press, librarians David Gruender, of the Baltimore Symphony Orchestra, and Clinton Nieweg, of the Philadelphia Orchestra, have brought to my attention that there are still numerous discrepancies between the score of *Music for a Scene from Shelley* and the G. Schirmer rental parts. Barber's corrections, as they were conveyed to Scalero, will be discussed in detail in my forthcoming thematic catalog.

of its premiere, Janssen conducted it in Helsinki. Although Janssen had invited Barber to sail with him to Finland and meet Sibelius, who would be at the concert, Barber was expected to begin his residency at the American Academy in Rome then. Earlier he had written to Scalero, "It remains to be seen whether the Rome people will allow it. I should like to meet Sibelius."* Janssen conducted *Shelley* again the following summer at Ravinia. He conducted the London premiere on 6 February 1937 and afterwards in numerous American cities. When *Shelley* was played in April 1939 by the Helsinki Municipal Orchestra under the baton of Martti Simila, it was, according to Finnish sources, "the first American work to be played in a regular symphony concert in Finland."[45] The same sources reported that the work "aroused much favorable comment in Finnish music circles and probably significantly weakened the prejudice against American musical talent common throughout Europe."[46] Yet before Molinari conducted *Shelley* in Rome on 23 April 1939, Barber himself suggested that he do "a bit more recent work, 'Adagio for Strings' or 'Essay'."† Similarly, when Walter Damrosch asked for a copy of the score to consider it for the World's Fair of 1939, the composer wrote about *Shelley:*

> Appropriately enough, it is written for a place in "Prometheus Unbound," where voices implore the goddess Asia to give peace to the world! . . . "School for Scandal," however, might be a better opening.‡

The Chicago music critic Eugene Stinson remarked about *Music for a Scene from Shelley* that it was interesting "because a composer of the present day reads Shelley," and although the methods were not new, Barber "speaks with his own voice."[47] On the eve of the premiere of his "Prometheus," as he called it, Barber did speak about his music to his friend Gama Gilbert, then music critic for the Philadelphia *Bulletin:*

> Skyscrapers, subways, and train lights play no part in the music I write. Neither am I at all concerned with the musical values inherent in geometric cerebrations. My aim is to write good music that will be comprehensible to as many people as possible, instead of music heard only by small, snobbish musical societies in the large cities. Radio makes this aim entirely possible of achievement. The universal basis of artistic spiritual communication by means of art is through the emotions.§

*Letter, Barber to Scalero, 19 August 1935, Camden, Maine. They never did meet. It was not until 1937, after Barber sent scores of the *Adagio for Strings* and *Essay,* that the older composer wrote enthusiastically to Barber about his music (RCA press release, 1943, Barber clipping file, New York Public Library, Music Division).

†Letter, Barber to Suso Cecchi d'Amico, March 1939. A program of the concert in Rome indicates it took place at the Teatro Adriano and included works by Vitali, Vivaldi, Alderighi, and Max Bruch.

‡Letter, 3 April 1939, New York Public Library, Music Division, Damrosch Collection. Evidently Damrosch followed Barber's suggestion.

§Gama Gilbert, "Philharmonic Plays Youth's Work Today," *Philadelphia Bulletin,* 24 March 1935. One of the works Barber probably had in mind here was John Alden Car-

Incidental Music for *One Day of Spring* (1934)

In January 1935 *One Day of Spring,* a play by Mary Kennedy, was presented at the Annie Russell Theater at Rollins College in Winter Park, Florida.* Barber had been asked to write the music for the "fantasy" directed by Russell because, in her words, "he gives promise of becoming one of the country's outstanding composers."[48] "The music," Russell told the press, "will be presented as an integral part of the play to illuminate the sentiment of the story. It is not to be confused as an opera or musical play. . . . It is an interesting experiment, with the music forming a part of the play itself."[49]

Shortly before Christmas 1934 the score for string quartet and chorus was completed, and Barber attempted to arrange rehearsals with the Curtis Quartet in Philadelphia prior to their going to Florida. The music was still being copied when he wrote from New York to Cole of his plan to bring the quartet parts to Mrs. Bok's box at the Academy of Music, where he was invited for a Saturday evening performance of the Philadelphia Orchestra. His letter provides the only written description—albeit a meager one—of the lost score:

> There are 19 pages of score, and some of it is not easy. Only the first and last pieces are with voice, so you can work on the rest without me. . . . Any chance of a rehearsal any time Wednesday? Sorry to interrupt your holidays, but when can we do it? I also wish that you could go over it once before doing it with me, but this is probably impossible. . . . N. B. I have not put in many bowing marks, as I am not sure enough. The first phrase of the music, and all that piece, for example, is very legato. Very fast at the end of it. I will change any doubtful double stops—especially in the Gypsy dance, I think there are a few. Maybe not.
>
> *Be careful of the score please, it is my only copy.*[50]

Orlando Cole believes the Gypsy Dance was adapted from the finale ("Dance") of the Serenade for String Quartet.[51]

The composer arrived in Winter Park only a few days ahead of the performance to "take charge of musical rehearsals and to train a Gypsy mixed chorus of 12 Rollins students."[52] As a prelude to the play, on 24

penter's monumental ballet *Skyscrapers* (1923–24), which incorporated popular elements meant to depict "modern American life." Its instrumentation included two red traffic lights, and the music suggests the cacophony of a bustling city.

*Russell, one of America's foremost actresses, returned to the stage in 1932 after a fourteen-year retirement. The $100,000 theater was a gift from Mary Bok, a lifelong friend of Russell. Designed in the Spanish-Mediterranean style, the theater's construction avoided conventional boxlike architecture and had, instead, a triple-arched lobby above which was an arcaded porch. The auditorium and stage sections were flanked by loggias, patios, tiled roofs, and ornamental travertine stone columns and trim. Kennedy, a prominent New York actress, author, and producer, took the leading role in her own play.

and 25 January 1935 the Curtis Quartet, which had played previous concerts at Rollins, performed Brahms's B♭-major string quartet, Op. 67. After an eight-minute break, the two-act play was presented without intermission. The cast included six characters—the Man, the Woman (played by Mary Kennedy), the Gypsy, a Countryman, a Muffin Man, and the Shadow. The action took place in a garden. The program read: "The closing curtains and musical interludes denote a lapse of time. Music by Sam Barber. / Played by The Curtis String Quartet. / Voice, Sam Barber. / The Gypsy chorus is under the direction of Christopher Honaas."[53]

6

THE AMERICAN ACADEMY

> I am now at the point where many pleasant things are going to happen to me soon, both as a composer and singer. It is very pleasant, like being on the verge of vomiting. . . .
>
> *Yours in dyspepsia.*[1]

No matter how unsavory the metaphor Barber used in his Christmas greeting to Orlando Cole in 1934, the next three months proved the composer's intuition correct: the two NBC broadcasts early in 1935 had been followed by the announcement of forthcoming publications of three of his songs and two orchestral works, the premiere of *Music for a Scene from Shelley,* and the RCA recording of *Dover Beach.* All occurred within weeks of Barber's twenty-fifth birthday.

Barber's appraisal of his good fortune was conveyed in a letter of 5 July 1935 to Scalero:

> I have passed an exciting winter, about which, however, I have no illusions. I was simply able to "market," so to speak, a stock of already-prepared wares—most of them concocted under your supervision. Now I must start on a new tack with my same boat—to switch metaphors!—and must work harder and study more in order to navigate deeper waters. Hearing my music played encouraged me from the point of view of instrumentation; but I am still unable to do what I wish with the orchestra.

Calling the year "the end of a chapter," with characteristic insight he continued, "I am letting Schirmers publish my music. . . . It is better not to keep these things for revision any longer, for I am much too apt to keep on correcting old works of mine *ad nauseam* when at my point of the game, I should be working on fresh ones."

The Prix de Rome was awarded to Barber in the spring of 1935 as "the most talented and deserving student of music in America" and granted him two years of study at the American Academy in Rome with an annual stipend of $1,400, a free studio, and residence at the academy.[2] Only a year earlier he had submitted the Cello Sonata and *Music for a Scene from Shelley* for the same prize and was turned down. During the summer of 1934, while working at the Bok colony in Maine, he was invited by the American Academy to apply again, and on 31 January 1935, under the pseudonym "John Brandywine," he submitted the same works as he had before. This time he was granted the award, ironically by the same jury that had previously rejected his application: Deems Taylor, Carl Engel, Leo Sowerby, and Walter Damrosch. Barber attributed this reversal of fortune in part to the successful premiere of *Shelley* by the New York Philharmonic; it does seem unlikely that the mere formality of submitting his works under a pseudonym would have disguised his identity from the jury that had heard his works earlier.[3]

After a summer in Maine, followed by a week in the Poconos, Barber departed for Rome on 5 October 1935.[4] Soon after he arrived he wrote to Menotti of his reaction to what he called "the somewhat expatriated Harvard Club atmosphere" at the academy:

> I feel somewhat settled here, that is, as settled as I let myself be. (Do you know that I have not yet unpacked my trunk, out of sheer perversity, because I do not wish to feel at home in this room? My half-full trunk stands open, in complete disorder, the scandal of the Academy. And I *shall* not unpack it. I will never call this room mine!)[5]

Reportedly, he did not unpack for the two years of his stay.[6] About his studio, however, he felt differently. It was situated apart from the academy, a little yellow house approached from the garden by a winding stair—a renovation of the stables of the old Villa Aurelia and "full of charm." He especially loved to stroll around the gardens with "the pines by moonlight, Rome in the distance." Twice a week he took lessons in Dante—"my teacher comes to my studio," he wrote, "and we read aloud by the fire. . . . We finished the *Inferno* today." Two weeks later he wrote, "Next week . . . Dante and I arrive in Paradise."[7] His letters home mention the names Pirandello, Casella,* Moravia, Malipiero, Luca, Serafin, and Cecchi.[8] He wrote in detail of a visit to the Sistine Chapel that had been arranged by the academy. He and a few painters were given special permission by the Vatican to go up on the temporary scaffolding erected for the purpose of studying why the frescoes of Michelangelo in the Sistine Chapel were cracking. As an artist himself, Barber was bowled over by what he saw:

* Alfredo Casella, a champion of the music of Debussy, Stravinsky, and Bartók, was one of the leading figures of the Italian avant-garde.

> To be able to touch with your hand all the outlines, often cut in the fresco with his stylus. To see the guidelines which he made to keep the giant perspective. And then, most wonderful of all, to lie on your back for three hours in the plaster and dust and stare up at this magnificent conception . . . the two most beautiful figures of the Sybil. . . . We stared at them as long as we were allowed, the painters could not understand how the softness of the face could be done in fresco; the fine modeling of the flesh, then the impetuous sweep of the brush-strokes in the details. . . . And then there are so many things which he seemed to have painted for his own pleasure. . . . It was as if someone discovered some beautiful new work of Beethoven, after knowing every note of his for a lifetime, and seeing all of a sudden some of his most intimate secrets.[9]

Appreciation of the experience overwhelmed him:

> I cannot tell the impression it made on me, for these sensations are like secrets to be guarded jealously all one's life-time, great and magnificent secrets.[10]

Though he was bombarded with aesthetic stimuli, Barber's frame of mind was in these years never completely without its dark side. During a brief visit home in February 1936, when his parents inquired if he were happy, he responded:

> Yes and no. In fact no different from any place else. My great satisfaction and consolation is that I am not a bother to anyone for two years, and this means a great deal: and that I am able to do the work that interests me to my heart's content (or discontent).[11]

Having started work on his first symphony in Maine during the summer before he arrived at the academy, Barber intended to continue work on it in Rome.* His first months at the academy, however, saw little progress on the symphony, but the period was unusually prolific for composing songs. Barber usually wrote songs in short bursts, for—unlike instrumental music, which required sustained concentration and conscious labor—they "just seemed a natural thing to do."† By 5 January 1936 he had composed seven new songs, six of which were written within four weeks, between 7 November and 5 December.

* He had mentioned its beginnings in a letter to Behrend:

> We are working hard—the opera [Menotti's *Amelia Goes to the Ball*] is coming along beautifully, and I am well ahead with an orchestra piece of ambitious tendencies. . . . The colony is not exciting, but we do not see much of them, or anybody. . . . Janssen and Carl Engel are coming up here this week-end . . . Roy Harris is coming later. So things will be stirring. (14 August 1935, Camden, Maine)

† Perhaps his facility with this genre explains their rare mention in his letters. Many years later, Barber confessed: "Songs are small forms determined largely by text. . . . If I start a song in, say, the afternoon, I generally finish it in a day or two" (quoted by Ramey, liner notes, "Songs of Samuel Barber," 1978).

Fritz Reiner and Sam Barber aboard the SS *Paris*, April 1936. *(The Curtis Institute of Music Library)*

Three songs set to texts by the "professional hobo" W. H. Davies*—"Night Wanderers," "Love's Caution," and "Beggar's Song"—have not been published even though the last received numerous performances in the thirties. Barber himself first sang "Beggar's Song" (Example 6.1) on 5 January 1936, the day it was completed, at an evening devoted to new music at the academy.† An all-Barber concert presented at Villa Aurelia on 22 April comprised "Beggar's Song" and four others sung by the composer—"With rue my heart is laden," "The Daisies," "Rain has fallen," and "Sleep now."‡ Felix Lamond, who was in charge of musical composition at the academy, reported that these songs "proved that the composer had the gift of lyrical expression."[12] It is ironic that of the group "Beggar's

*The author of *Autobiography of a Super-Tramp,* Davies (1871–1940) at the age of twenty-two went to America, where he led a vagrant life. His collected poems were published in England in 1929.

†The holograph is in the Library of Congress, Music Division. A nearly identical draft appears on pp. 58–62 of Barber's sketchbook from the 1930s, verifying his certainty about the song from its earliest concept.

‡*Overtones,* May 1936, p. 20. On this program, also, his Cello Sonata was played by Luigi Silva.

Song," edged with cynicism, was so well received by the elite audience that Barber was asked for an encore and invited to sing again at a luncheon for young Roman painters and composers given a few days later at the home of Prince Bassiano.[13] The words should be sung "with mock solemnity":

> Good people keep their holy day, they rest from labour on a
> Sunday.
> But we keep holy every day, and rest from Monday until Monday
> And yet the noblest work on earth is done when beggars do
> their part:
> They work, dear ladies, on the soft and tender feelings in
> your heart.

In the United States "Beggar's Song" was sung many times by Benjamin de Loache on programs during the 1930s. At a surprise birthday party for Barber on 7 March 1937 at the Curtis Institute of Music, de Loache sang it accompanied at the piano by Edith Evans Braun. Although it was apparently popular with audiences and even recorded by de Loache on the noncommercial YADDO label in 1937, there seem to be no other performances reported after then.

While at the academy, Barber also set to music four poems from James Joyce's *Chamber Music*. The earliest, "Of that so sweet imprisonment," was completed on 17 November 1935.[14] "Rain has fallen," "Sleep now," and "Strings in the earth and air" were composed within a week of each other on 21 and 29 November and 5 December respectively.* Two more Joyce poems were set later during a period of great happiness in St. Wolfgang, Austria—"I hear an army," completed on 13 July 1936, and "In the dark pinewood" in 1937.†

Of the six Joyce songs, "Rain has fallen," "Sleep now," and "I hear an army" were published by G. Schirmer in 1939 as Opus 10.[15] Although it is not known on what basis Barber selected these three songs for publication, the choice seems logical since they form an interesting and unified cycle: they are tonally related—the first and last are in the same key (A minor for the low-voice edition, C minor for high voice), and the second song lies a minor third below; and the texts of the three songs provide a strong unity of theme and image—Barber mirrors the course of a love affair in settings that progress from lyrical to dramatic.‡ "Rain has fallen"

*There are dated holographs for all of these songs at the Library of Congress, Music Division. An earlier sketch of the last, undated, appears in Barber's sketchbook from the 1930s.

†Dated holographs for these songs are at the Library of Congress, Music Division.

‡Jean Kreiling, in *The Songs of Samuel Barber: A Study in Literary Taste and Text-Setting* (Ph.D. dissertation, University of North Carolina, 1986), suggests that Barber may have envisioned a less happy set of songs (p. 80). Although Kreiling's work was done with knowledge of only one of the unpublished Joyce songs, "Strings in the earth," her theory is supported by the remaining two songs that Barber put aside—"Of that so sweet imprison-

Example 6.1 "Beggar's Song," mm. 1–20, holograph, 1936. *(Library of Congress)*

and "Sleep now" were dedicated respectively to Dario Cecchi and his sister Susanna, two Italian friends of Barber's with whom he shared the plea-

ment" and "In the dark pinewood," which have certain features in common: a strong swing between major and minor modes, and rhythmic shifts from duple to triple meter. The somber hymn-like mood that penetrates "Of that so sweet imprisonment" is especially reinforced by the plagal cadence at the end; the through-composed song "In the dark pinewood" uses themes formed on major and minor scales of C.

sures of Joyce's poetry.* Suso Cecchi d'Amico said that at the time these songs were written James Joyce was their "discovery of the moment." "We were all very young," d'Amico recalled, "and we were very fond of Sam's compositions. We didn't discuss the poems together, they were a shared love."[16] For Barber, however, the reading was probably exploratory as well, for he always had in the back of his mind the feeling that he might come across a usable song text.[17] His attraction to Joyce's lyrics was undoubtedly determined more by the inherent lyricism and imagery of the poetry and its potential for translation into rhythmic and melodic language than by its popularity. Even though Barber's songs were published before Joyce's death in 1943, there is no evidence in either Joyce's or Barber's writings that the poet ever heard the songs.†

Joyce's prose was to inspire three more works of Barber's: "Solitary Hotel" (in the cycle Op. 41, written in 1968) and an orchestral work, *Fadograph of a Yestern Scene* (1971), both of which are discussed in chapter 18; and *Nuvoletta,* which was finished 17 October 1947 while Barber was working with Eleanor Steber in preparation for the premiere of *Knoxville: Summer of 1915* (see chapter 10). For *Nuvoletta* Barber drew excerpts from one of the most moving passages in *Finnegans Wake,* where the daughter (Nuvoletta-Isabel-Issy) plays one of her several death scenes. Her reflections are in typically multilayered Joycean language: invented words, double entendres, and puns that fuse conscious and unconscious meanings.[18] The song was viewed as "for sophisticates only" by a British music critic,[19] and even Barber confessed that he did not entirely understand the text:

> What can you do when you get lines like "Nuvoletta reflected for the last time on her little long life, and she made up all her myriads of drifting minds in one. She cancelled all her engauzements. She climbed over the bannistars; she gave a chilly, childly, cloudy cry," except to set them instinctively, as abstract music, almost as a vocalise?[20]

Nevertheless, Joyce's colorful prose prompted a kaleidoscope of musical imagery and puns: a monotonal plainsong incants *From Vallee Maraia to Grasyaplaina, dormimust, echo!;* a "Tristan chord" supports *as were she born to bride with Tristis—Tristior;* metric groupings correspond to *the*

* Susanna Cecchi, called Suso by her friends, was the writer of the film *The Bicycle Thief* and the daughter of Emilio Cecchi, the eminent Italian writer and literary critic noted for his work on nineteenth-century English literature. Barber's frequent teatime conversations at the Cecchis' had a literary bent. Susanna Cecchi's husband, Fedele d'Amico, is an important music critic in Italy.

† The thirty-six poems in *Chamber Music* were first published in 1907. Myra Russell reports (in "Setting Joyce's Poems to Music," manuscript loaned to author) that as many as thirty to forty composers set Joyce's poems to music during his lifetime, among them Arnold Bax, Arthur Bliss, Karol Szymanowski, and John Ireland. Twelve songs appeared before 1935, the year Barber wrote his first.

tears of night began to fall, first by ones and twos, then by threes and fours, at last by fives and sixes of sevens. The song, one of Barber's longest and most capricious in mood, has a wide-range tessitura of two octaves (b♯ to b♯″). Its rondolike form is interrupted with an elaborate vocal cadenza.

Steber sang the first performance of *Nuvoletta,* although the date is undocumented.* In 1963 she recorded the song on a historic program of American songs sponsored by the Alice M. Ditson Fund and Columbia University. The recording, which included works by Bergsma, Chanler, Copland, Griffes, Rorem, Persichetti, Moore, Thomson, Luening, and Fine, was called "treasurable" by Alan Rich, who cited Barber's song for its wit and high art.[21] *Nuvoletta* has been seldom performed, probably because the song demands from the singer a certain kind of endurance—that is, continued attention to exactly what mood is being projected—and a sustained balance between dramatic wit and gentle lyricism. Roberta Alexander's recent recording is a welcome interpretation of this enigmatic song.[22]

Symphony in One Movement, Op. 9 (1936)

The Symphony in One Movement, which Barber began in August 1935, was completed on 24 February 1936 during a two-week stay at the Anabel Taylor Foundation in the French Alpine village of Roquebrune.† He dedicated his first effort in this genre to Gian Carlo Menotti. The symphony is—in the composer's words—"a synthetic treatment of the four-movement classical symphony." Program notes for the New York premiere include Barber's own description of his work:

> It is based on the three themes of the initial *Allegro ma non troppo,* which retain throughout the work their fundamental character. The *Allegro ma non troppo* opens with the usual exposition of a main theme, a more lyrical second theme, and a closing theme. After a brief development of the three themes, instead of the customary recapitulation, the first theme in diminution forms the basis of a scherzo section *(vivace).* The second theme (oboe over muted strings) then appears in augmentation, in an extended *Andante tranquillo.* An intense crescendo introduces the finale, which is a short passacaglia based on the first theme (introduced by violoncelli and contrabassi), over which, together with figures from other themes, the closing theme is woven, thus serving as a recapitulation for the entire symphony.[23]

The work is a condensed version of the conventional four-movement symphony, but it differs in significant ways: first, the opening exposition

* Within a year of its publication by G. Schirmer, *Nuvoletta* was sung by Gayle Pierce on 20 November 1953 at the Juilliard Concert Hall.

† The roster at the American Academy in Rome's New York office records Barber's stay at the foundation from 15 February to 1 March. The date of completion of the symphony is on the holograph score at the Library of Congress, Music Division.

Example 6.2 Analysis of Sibelius's Seventh Symphony in Barber's sketchbook, p. 37 verso. *(Library of Congress)*

is never repeated; second, the sections that follow are more compact than complete symphonic movements—there is no trio in the scherzo, for example, nor are there subsections in the adagio movement. In that the entire progress of the symphony is generated from themes presented at the onset, it shares a similarity with Sibelius's one-movement Symphony No. 7, which is in fact the model Barber used for this work. Among the sketches for the Symphony in One Movement in his sketchbook from the 1930s is a chart that traces themes and the course of their development in the Sibelius symphony (see Example 6.2).*

Yet there are vast differences between these two works written a little more than a decade apart: Barber's symphony has a stronger profile—divisions between the four sections are more clearly marked; sections contrast more fully with each other in tempo, in thematic definition, and in form; and Barber's long-lined themes bear the mark of his personal style, exemplified by the romantic oboe solo in the *andante tranquillo* section. Unity is provided by tonal relationships between the sections of the symphony—the first and last sections are in E minor, the two middle sections in E♭ major and E♭ minor respectively.

In May 1936, only a few months after completion of his symphony,

*The symphony is not labeled in Barber's sketchbook. I am indebted to Samuel Baron for identifying it.

Barber learned that he had won a second Pulitzer award, enabling him to extend his stay in Europe for another year.* By this time a commitment for a first performance of his symphony had been made by the conductor Bernardino Molinari, who first learned of Barber from Jeanne Behrend and her husband. Barber, in acknowledging "the multitude of things" Behrend had done for him, wrote to her of his meeting with Molinari:

> He is enthusiastic about my Symphony, which I played for him, and is going to perform it next season at the Augusteo. He finds it "moderna ma seria" and said at once he wanted it for his programs. He promises me two weeks of rehearsals before, so I am delighted; and all the young Italians tell me he is very good at working out new things. I particularly thank you two, because . . . what Sascha told him seemed to have impressed him more than what anyone else in Philadelphia said. I noticed this at once and appreciate it—and thank you from my heart. Now if you could only be present at the premiere! It will be such fun (or maybe no fun at all!) to see the reactions of a foreign audience—rather ill-disposed, if anything—towards Americans.†

After a splendid summer in St. Wolfgang (see below in this chapter), Menotti sailed back to the United States on the SS *Normandie* and Barber was off to Rome with less than a month to correct parts of the symphony for Molinari's rehearsals.‡ The premiere was played on 13 December by

*Letter, Barber to Orlando Cole, 6 May 1936. His letter to Jeanne Behrend in May 1936 (from "Le Cottage," Hotel-Restaurant Georges Bise, Talloires, Lac d'Annecy) announces:

> Mason had made me promise not to tell anyone as there was about a 60 percent chance I would get it—I had not even tried, you know; they just decided of their own accord to renew it, because the other works were not up to qualification. . . . He was afraid it would not go through, as they had never given it twice to the same person.

†Letter, written from "Le Cottage," Hotel-Restaurant Georges Bise, Talloires, Lac d'Annecy, May 1936. The news, somewhat distorted, traveled back to Philadelphia that Barber himself was conducting the premiere of the symphony. He corrected this impression in a letter to Orlando Cole, 19 September 1936. "Not true," he wrote, "Molinari is. Mistaken report. Did you know Rodzinski has taken it for the Philharmonic in February?" Artur Rodzinski, who had heard Barber play his score in Salzburg, was so impressed he immediately planned a United States premiere in Cleveland in January and another performance with the New York Philharmonic for February of 1937 (*Newsweek* [3 April 1937]: 28). This was not their first meeting, however, as Rodzinski was the conductor of the Curtis Symphony Orchestra in 1927–28.

‡Letter, Barber to Orlando Cole, written from St. Wolfgang, 24 October 1936. After one of the rehearsals, a tuba player was so appreciative of the active role of his instrument and the solo passage in the last section that he thanked Barber and told him, "I've been waiting fifteen years for a part like that" (Barber, interviewed by James Fassett, CBS, 19 June 1949).

The holograph indicates the parts were copied by a Professor Carbonara, at Via Terenzio 7. On the front of the pencil holograph, Barber wrote the message: "Mi faccia una bella copia, per piacere. / Molinari la vuol / eseguire in Novembre—per adesso *una* copia—distinti

Rome's Philharmonic Augusteo Orchestra at the Adriano Theater the day before the first performance of Barber's newly composed string quartet at the American Academy.

The symphony was given a mixed reception. It was found "appealing for its well-defined theme, robustly developed in a classical form," yet recalling the "modern German school" and "representative of our epoch for its nervous, tormented style."[24] Loosely translated—Barber explained when interviewed thirteen years later—this meant that of the Italian audience, typically "not shy about their feelings, . . 50% applauded and 50% were hissing."[25] He recalled that even though the symphony was played quite well, it was received coldly, perhaps because "at the time it was thought too dark-toned, too Nordic and Sibelian," a comment that intimates the model for the symphony. Italian audiences, he believed, were not experienced with "new music," and the members of the orchestra were surprised that *any* American was composing music at all.*

The United States premiere was given by the Cleveland Orchestra under the baton of Rudolf Ringwall on 21 and 23 January 1937 in Cleveland.† Two months later, on 24 March 1937, Rodzinski conducted the New York Philharmonic–Symphony Orchestra in three performances of the symphony at Carnegie Hall. Barber, who had returned to the United States for the occasion, was "recalled again and again" for bows.[26] American critics were more forthcoming with praise than their Roman counterparts. Francis D. Perkins, music critic for the *Herald Tribune,* for example, declared that the symphony

> reinforced the impression of marked ability and promise made by the composer's earlier orchestral work . . . displaying clearly defined musical ideas of considerable cogency in an instrumental garb wrought with unusual mastery . . . and exceptionally well-developed knowledge of the orchestral palette . . . with a definite idea of what he wants . . . and how to attain it. . . .
>
> The andante, with the poetic song of a solo oboe, is the most imaginative part. . . . Passages elsewhere suggest that the composer has not yet fully integrated his individual musical style. Yet . . . immediately identifiable derivations are few—a hint or two of Brahms here, a reminder of Sibelius there, but such hints seemed not important.[27]

---

saluti / Sam Barber" (Please make me a beautiful copy. Molinari wants to conduct it in November—for now, one copy . . .).

* Barber, interviewed by Fassett, CBS, 19 June 1949. On this broadcast, Barber reported that a friend of his (an Italian princess, who heard a performance at the Salzburg Festival) noted that the Salzburg people were more appreciative of Barber's symphony than the Italian aristocracy who attended its premiere in Rome.

† Rodzinski was supposed to conduct the premiere but was ill. The symphony, played after intermission, shared the program with Respighi's *Pines of Rome,* Dvořák's Violin Concerto, Op. 53, and William Walton's Suite from *Façade.*

Olin Downes offered the following appraisal of the young composer:

> It is to be seen what Mr. Barber will evolve into. It is evident that he is seeking, and is not writing in a merely imitative manner. His orchestration is clear, if needing now and again a little more body and richness of texture.[28]

Sidney Homer, who read reviews from Cleveland papers, savored his nephew's success with pleasure:

> How I did long to be in Cleveland! Rarely in my life have I had such a strong desire. Your letter tells me everything. You heard a complete realization of the music you wrote—a rare occurrence and one for which you are devoutly grateful. I wonder how often it happened to Bach, Beethoven, and others. . . . I like Leedy's words: "One of the finest examples of American music this reviewer has been privileged to hear." He did not need the word *American*. I feel that the language you talk must be clear. That audience understood and *felt*. If one audience does it, others will do it, in other cities and other countries.[29]

Rodzinski considered the twenty-seven-year-old composer "a leading musical hope."[30] Indeed, Barber's "musical godfather," as the conductor was called,[31] became a zealous missionary during the symphony's first season in bringing it to audiences around the world—London (24 June 1937), Vienna, Prague, and Paris. When he conducted Barber's symphony with the Vienna Philharmonic at the opening concert of the 1937 Salzburg Festival on 25 July he was the first American, though not native-born, conductor to direct one of the concerts at the festival and it was the first time in the history of the festival that a symphonic work by an American composer was performed. Perhaps to pave the way for acceptance of a work by an American, the Austrian press and program notes for the concert gave repeated emphasis to the training Barber had received with Scalero in the "classical tradition of the Vienna School" and in particular emphasized the Mandyczewski connection: it was pointed out that Barber's "firm handling of the theme, the strict adherence to form, his constancy to the basic principles of tone can all be traced to Vienna."[32] Called "ultra-modern," the symphony was declared by the Austrian press to have been warmly received (Barber was called to the stage three times) only because there were many Americans in the audience.[33]

Although Barber was born within thirty miles of Philadelphia, the work was only finally performed there on 2 December 1938 by the Philadelphia Orchestra under Ormandy. "It is hard to believe that a composition so much discussed," remarked Henry Pleasants, "has not been played at least once by every orchestra in the land."[34]

Late in 1938, aware of Serge Koussevitzky's reputation as a champion of American music, Barber wrote to him with the hope that he would schedule the symphony on one of the programs of the Boston Symphony for the following season.

My dear Dr. Koussevitzky:
I am wondering whether you might be interested in looking at a score of mine. I have never sent you any scores because I have given my music to conductors whom I knew personally, also because I once read an interview in which you said that you could hardly take care of all American composers and that they must go to conductors in their own cities.

But I admire you and your orchestra so much, and hope that someday you will play something of mine. At present I can, unfortunately, offer you no first performance, as I have nothing new. But I could send for your examination my "Symphony in one movement" (18 minutes) which has been played by Molinari, Rodzinski, and Ormandy, or two new pieces "Adagio for Strings" (8 min.) and "Essay for Orchestra" (8½ min.) recently performed by Toscanini.

Will you please tell me frankly if you care to see any of these scores at all, or prefer that I submit something new to you.

Thanking you for your attention,

Sincerely
*Samuel Barber**

This letter—a rare example of Barber directly promoting his own music—only points up his naïveté in assuming that dropping the names of other esteemed conductors would help his cause. Undoubtedly, like most conductors, Koussevitzky preferred to do first performances of new works, as this prompt reply suggests:

Dear Mr. Barber,
Thank you for your letter.

I would much rather present a new and larger score of yours in Boston and possibly in New York during the season 1939–40.

Although my programmes for the actual season are completed, I would be interested to examine the score of your "Adagio for Strings" and would appreciate your sending it to me.

With best wishes.[35]

Although over the next few years Koussevitzky played other works of Barber's, it was not until early in 1943, when he was planning performances

*Letter, 16 December 1938. This letter and all subsequent correspondence between Barber and Koussevitzky quoted here are in the Serge Koussevitzky Collection at the Library of Congress, Music Division. Although this letter is the first Barber wrote to Koussevitzky, it is not the first time the conductor had heard about him. An undated letter from Mary H. Coolidge, a patron of the orchestra, mentioned the young composer as someone she had known "since he was a child . . . filled with musical talent." She told Koussevitzky of Mrs. Bok's sponsorship of Barber and enclosed two of his programs in the hope that "you may see a chance next season and want to use one of his compositions in your Boston Symphony concerts" (Serge Koussevitzky Collection, Library of Congress).

of Barber's Essays (see below), that the subject of the Symphony in One Movement came up again.

In 1942 Barber began revisions on the symphony, honing the structure into a more focused unity. He made minor changes that mostly involved condensing and tightening the Allegro, the Andante, and the passacaglia. The scherzo was replaced with an entirely new one built on a diminution of a figure of the chief subject of the first movement. Olin Downes, who heard both versions of the work, reported that the new scherzo—in a quasi-fugal style, filled with "sardonic humor and imaginatively orchestrated"—provided a more vivid contrast to the rest of the symphony than the original one.[36] Because Barber removed the original scherzo from the holograph score (which is at the Library of Congress) and replaced it with the new one, there remains scant evidence of what the first version was like.* We can assume from the numbering of the pages in the holograph, where the new scherzo is laid in between the Allegro and Andante tranquillo sections, that the original scherzo was only thirteen pages in length—that is, twenty-three pages shorter than the new scherzo. The page preceding the substituted pages includes eleven measures, crossed over, of the beginning of the original scherzo, with the main theme played by oboes. The last four measures of the original version appear on page 38 of the holograph.†

The principal themes of the symphony, with the original scherzo theme, were printed in program notes for a performance that occurred sometime after 1937 but before the 1942 revisions‡ as follows:

*The holograph consists of twenty-one numbered pages on orchestral score paper (the brand is Alberto De Santis, Rome) and four unnumbered pages for the Allegro section; thirty-six laid-in pages (on G. Schirmer twenty-stave paper) for the new scherzo (1942–43); and twenty-seven pages, numbered 38 to 55 (on Alberto De Santis paper) for the Andante and passacaglia sections.

†A sketch of four measures of the new scherzo is also in Barber's student sketchbook on p. 76, which corresponds to p. 37, mm. 2–8 in the 1943 edition.

‡The date is deduced from the fact that mention is made of the 1937 Salzburg performance.

Example 6.3 Principal themes of Symphony in One Movement, including original version of scherzo from 1937.

Also in the notes was a brief description of the original scherzo that tells something about the character of the discarded movement:

> *Vivace.* E-flat Major. A theme . . . recognizable as a quickened version of one of the phrases of the main theme is bandied about by various instruments. A climax for full orchestra develops, ending with a heavily accented two-note phrase which is repeated immediately by kettledrums alone—as if in afterthought.[37]

Revisions of the symphony were finished by the end of January 1943.* Correspondence between Barber and Koussevitzky about that time suggests that the conductor had expressed an interest in performing the revised symphony. In January, while serving in the United States Army, Barber reported to the conductor that, in spite of his working under duress, the revised symphony would soon be ready for performance:

> The hours in the Army are so long that I can only work at night. This is discouraging and has retarded all my work. But the symphony is just about ready to go to the copyist and is, I hope, a better work now. A great deal of it is entirely new. You shall have the score the minute it is ready.[38]

In February he wrote again:

> The copyist is taking such a long time with the score and parts of my symphony, and I am very impatient! But a score will be sent to you next week. Parts are being copied simultaneously by another copyist. I hope you will like it and that it is not too late for this season.[39]

Not waiting for a commitment from Koussevitzky, Barber cabled him that he planned to ask Bruno Walter to play the revised symphony in November. Walter agreed. Meanwhile, Koussevitzky decided to include the symphony in the 1944 spring season, writing the composer a conciliatory letter:

*Letters to Koussevitzky from Barber (4 January and 24 February 1943) confirm that the revisions were completed during this period.

> After we had talked, I looked at my schedule very carefully, and find to my great regret that it is impossible to include your symphony in the programs of the first half of the season. You see, my dear, it is quite a problem to readjust programs when one has to consider the timing of broadcasts, the proposed list of compositions, etc.
>
> However, let me assure you that, no matter how many times your symphony will be performed before March, it remains on my list for the latter part of the season, and I am looking forward eagerly to doing it then.[40]

Barber was disappointed, for the spring was exactly when he planned to "offer" the conductor his new "Flight Symphony" commissioned by the U.S. Air Force. Confessing his greediness, he wrote to Koussevitzky:

> But should you accept Symphony No. 2 for March or April, when can you play Symphony No. 1? It would be wonderful to have you play No. 1 earlier in the season, and No. 2 at the end. Perhaps I am being a gourmand in wanting you to play two works of mine in one season. But it is like 'les cocktail Koussevitzky': one cannot resist the temptation. . . . Anything you decide to do is agreeable to me, and I am always and honored at your continued interest in my work. . . . Aaron [Copland], Bill [Schuman], and I were photoed for March of Time the other day, and we were told how it came about. "Once more," we said, "we must thank Koussevitzky for everything."[41]

Thus Bruno Walter was the first to conduct the revised Symphony No. 1. The Philadelphia Orchestra gave the premiere on 18 February 1944, and Walter's enthusiasm for the music resulted in a performance that gained enormous approval from Barber. He reported to Homer:

> I had a wonderful week with Bruno Walter and the Philadelphia Orchestra, one of the best performances I've ever had. The symphony sounds much better in its revision. Walter conducted superbly (by memory, every note)* and the men came to life as never under Ormandy. Big public success, but I was more pleased with Walter's comments. He said: "an astonishing work, no-one is composing today who handles form that way." Kept saying, Kolossal, etc. Told me he would come out of his retirement next year to make records of it as soon as the Petrillo feud is over (he is taking a year off). . . . He is not usually very nice to composers.[42]

On 9 March 1944, three weeks after its Philadelphia performance, Walter performed the symphony again in New York. Here too, as reviews make clear, the maestro conducted Barber's score "con amore." But especially interesting was the canniness with which he programmed Barber's work with Schumann's Fourth Symphony. There are striking similarities be-

*In the 1960s Barber recalled Walter's playing his "whole first symphony at the piano by memory . . . the only time besides Toscanini that *that* happened!" (Barber's journal, collection of Valentin Herranz).

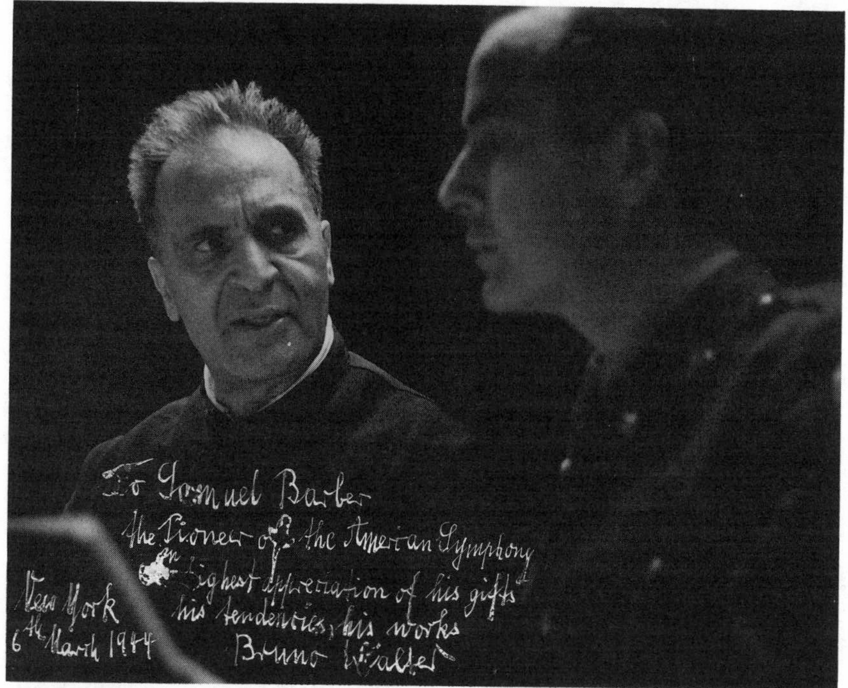

Bruno Walter and Corporal Barber. Walter's inscription: "To the Pioneer of the American Symphony . . . highest appreciation of his gifts, his tendencies, his works . . . 6th March 1944." *(Courtesy of Gian Carlo Menotti)*

tween the two works written a century apart: both are in cyclical form; in both, the four divisions are played without pause; both begin with an allegro, followed by a lengthy development without any recapitulation; and in both works there is a dramatic crescendo that leads from the third division to the finale. The juxtaposition was not overlooked by *New York Times* music critic Noel Straus:

> That Mr. Barber's revised symphony was able to hold its ground and not appear anticlimactic after the Schumann masterpiece spoke worlds in its favor. If it lacked the melodic invention, simplicity and freshness of that opus, it nevertheless was so skilled in its craftmanship, so knowingly orchestrated and filled with character that it scored heavily with its hearers, even if it was forced to bear comparison with the Schumann creation.[43]

Within a year of its premiere Walter made the first commercial recording of the symphony on the Columbia Records label.* Because the record-

* Rodzinski's recording of the 2 April 1938 broadcast with the NBC Symphony is at the Library of Congress, Recorded Sound Division.

ing was made at a time when tempos were dictated by the economics of available space on 78-rpm discs, there were, according to Barber's report, distortions of tempos: "Walter . . . loses breadth in the slow part of my symphony to squeeze it on four sides. But he does the beginning and scherzo very well."[44] This recording was a landmark, however, because Barber's symphony was one of the few works by an American composer Walter ever chose to record.

String Quartet in B minor, Op. 11 (1936–38)

In May 1936, at the same time that Barber heard about the extension of his Pulitzer fellowship, he was already thinking about a string quartet. "I have vague quartettish rumblings in my innards," he declared to Orlando Cole, "and need a bit of celestial Ex Lax to restore my equilibrium; there is nothing to do but get at it, and I will send the excrements to you by registered mail by August, so that . . . . . but no, I could continue with this figure into the realm of indecency, and I am afraid that Ossie is peeping."*

Barber knew that Cole had been planning a European tour for the Curtis Quartet and had promoted the group to Lamond, who arranged concerts at the American Academy. Lamond had been pressing Barber to write a quartet while he was in residence at the academy, and the composer believed that if it was finished about the time the Curtis Quartet would be in Europe, they would be invited to come to Rome to play it. Barber promised Cole he would work on the quartet and send it to him by August.[45]

In May Barber left the academy and went to Milan to pick up Menotti's Fiat roadster; the two composers planned to meet in France and "raise hell for a month" before settling down in the Tyrol for the summer "for a siege of work."[46] From 15 May to 1 November they lived in a cottage belonging to the game-warden of a big estate owned by a Dutch baron in the little village of St. Wolfgang, high up in the mountains near a forest and overlooking a lake.[47] This time was described by Barber as "perfection" and by Menotti as the kind of summer where "you have to stop in the middle of the day to say to yourself: 'this is *too* wonderful.' "[48] Barber wrote in detail about their situation to Orlando Cole:

> The game-warden leaves his wife to cook for us and roams the mountains looking for Lady Chatterley! Mrs. Benkard and Rudolf Schirmer† have taken a home ten minutes away and there is much going on there—but we

*Letter to Cole, 6 May 1936, written from the American Academy, Rome. Ossie is Cole's wife.

†Mrs. Benkard was the wife of the publisher Rudolph Edward Schirmer (1859–1919); the Rudolph mentioned here is her son.

Barber and Menotti in St. Wolfgang, summer of 1936.

are very inaccessible and able to work in peace. Toscanini arrives in Salzburg tomorrow, and the festival begins. We are an hour's drive from Salzburg and will go in once a week to hear the doings. I have heard no music all winter, and am hungry for some.[49]

The following letter from Sidney Homer was in response to questions Barber asked about the Schirmer family and the news that he was planning a string quartet:

> Your wonderful letter sounds like an impossible dream come true! I want to hear it all expressed in musical tones—the only language that can tell the whole truth! You ask about Rudolph Schirmer.* He was one of the noblest men that ever spread protecting care over musicians. I think he thought very little about himself. His one absorbing desire was to make the house of Schirmer one of genuine service to musicians and, of course, to Art. His brother Gustave was also an idealist and regarded music from a lofty, impersonal point of view. Some day the story of music in America will be written and the influence of these two men will be understood and appreciated. . . .
>
> I am happy you are writing a string quartet. Never was there such a day of quartet playing. . . . There is just one thing that counts and that is finished work, and by finished I mean of a quality beyond dispute. . . .

* Rudolph Edward Schirmer, one of two sons of Gustav Schirmer (1829–1893), the founder of the music publishing house G. Schirmer, Inc. From 1907 he was in sole control of the firm. He founded the *Musical Quarterly* and was a director of the New York Oratorio Society and the New York Symphony Society as well as a trustee of the Institute of Musical Art.

(left) The composer and the Curtis String Quartet at the Colosseum, Rome, 1936. Left to right: Orlando Cole, Jascha Brodsky, Barber, Max Aronoff, Charles Jaffe. *(The Curtis Institute of Music Library).* (right) The game-warden's cottage, St. Wolfgang, 1936. Barber is at window on second floor.

> Send me a few bars of the movements of the Quartet. They will make me hungry for the rest.[50]

In mid-July, even though Barber had not heard from Lamond about engagements for the Curtis Quartet, he encouraged Cole to plan a concert at the Filarmonica and also in Milan. A concert could always be arranged at the academy in Rome, but to come to Italy just for an academy concert would be "rather impractical," he advised the cellist. On the other hand, a concert in Milan—especially if it included Menotti's Italian Dance—would draw Gian Carlo's friends and his whole family, because they would see his name on the program, and that would be "enough to fill up the room."[51]

Perhaps partly because he was haunted by the ghosts of past masters, Barber made painfully slow progress on the quartet. In a letter of 5 August 1936 he told Scalero that he was studying a lot and the place was "ideal for working":

> I finished copying the Siegfried "Idyll" the other day, a sort of joyful penitence for certain orchestral indiscretions which I committed this winter. How beautiful the instrumentation of the "Idyll" is! . . .

> And of course I am composing. . . . I have started a string quartet: but how difficult it is! It seems to me that because we have so assiduously forced our personalities on Music—on Music, who never asked for them!—we have lost elegance; and if we cannot recapture elegance, the quartet-form has escaped us forever. It is a struggle.

As the summer came to a close and the quartet was still not finished, Barber had to write to Cole the disappointing news that he would not be able to send him the music in time for their European tour:

> It is coming along slowly, but will not be ready in time. The best thing will probably be for me to have it tried out by the Rome quartet in rehearsal, and then I can send it over to you from Rome.*

On 19 September, with uncanny prescience about a work that in its orchestral arrangement would be considered one of the sublime masterpieces of the twentieth century, Barber announced to Cole:

> I have just finished the slow movement of my quartet today—it is a knock-out! Now for a Finale.[52]

His high spirits did not go unnoticed by Menotti: "Sam has been in a holy humor all summer," he wrote to Cole; he "fought with very few people and insulted only one or two of them."[53] By the end of October, Barber—admittedly enjoying "playing truant" from the American Academy—was "working very hard" on the last movement of the quartet, which he hoped to finish "in a day or two."[54] Most of the time, however, the studio was too cold to work in—for the snows were already beginning—so that all he wanted to do was "to sit lazily by the stove reading Thackeray."[55] The weather forced the two composers to head for Lugano, with a detour through southern Germany in order to avoid the many Swiss passes that were closed because of snow. Pressure mounted to finish the quartet before Barber arrived in Rome on 1 November for rehearsals of his symphony.[56]

The composer's efforts to give the first performance of the quartet to the Curtis group failed; by September the Pro Arte Quartet was engaged by Lamond to play it and was already rehearsing the first two movements.[57] Nevertheless, Barber still wanted the Curtis Quartet to read through his quartet even before it was finished; he wrote to Cole that if the group had time in between rehearsals and sightseeing, he would arrange to have a second set of parts copied out for them.

*Letter, 31 August 1936, from St. Wolfgang. Barber referred here to the Pro Arte Quartet; Barber did not think too highly of them, as this earlier letter suggests: "I heard some surprisingly bad records of the beautiful Schubert C major Quintette by the Pro Arte quartet—how little they felt it, how dry it sounds!" Remembering the fine performance played by the Curtis Quartet with Felix Salmond one night at the Boks', Barber told the cellist he "scarcely had the patience to listen to this one" (letter, 15 July 1936, from St. Wolfgang).

The premiere on 14 December at the Villa Aurelia followed the first performance of the Symphony in One Movement given in Rome a day earlier. Although the last movement of the quartet had been completed in time to be on the program, Barber was so uneasy about it that he withdrew it immediately after the concert for revision. A visit to the United States from 15 January to 24 April 1937 to attend rehearsals for the American premiere of his symphony caused him to put the quartet aside temporarily. Homer pressured his nephew not to allow the flush of success over the symphony to interrupt his work; early in February he counseled him:

> In the midst of this excitement write down your musical thoughts. You never know when the next work (or works) will start. . . . Don't scorn ideas; they are precious and, sometimes, so rare that it seems as if "there ain't no such thing!"[58]

Prodding him further about the quartet, Homer urged Barber not to let anything stop his work in this form—"You make the four instruments sound gigantic," he wrote; "I also want from you the greatest intimacy in spirit. If Mozart could trust and love his listener, so can you."*

Subsequently the Curtis Quartet performed only the first two movements at a private concert at the Curtis Institute of Music on 7 March 1937 in honor of Barber's birthday. The two movements of the "unfinished quartet," wrote a Philadelphia critic, seemed "unduly pretentious, and in the opening allegro, Mr. Barber seemed to be seeking effects better suited to orchestral expression. The slow movement succeeded in evoking mood, but suffered from repetitiousness."[59] Ironically, it was, of course, the second movement that ultimately achieved the greatest recognition.

Plans for the first performance of the complete quartet in the United States by the Gordon Quartet on 20 April 1937 at the Library of Congress are chronicled in letters between Barber and Oliver Strunk, chief of the library's Music Division.† Strunk initiated the correspondence on 3 March 1937:

> *My dear Mr. Barber:*
> As Mr. Engel may have told you already, it is just possible that your new string quartet can be presented here at the library or elsewhere in Washington, on April 20, when Jacques Gordon is to play here for the "Friends of Music in the Library of Congress." Several other quartets have been put forward for this program, and, for obvious reasons, Mr. Gordon is somewhat reluctant to make the choice himself. Miss Daniels—Mr. Engel's sec-

*Letter, 6 February 1937, from Palm Beach. Barber's letter to Orlando Cole on 15 July 1936 suggests, however, that Schubert, not Mozart, was on his mind while he was working on the string quartet.

†Members of the Gordon Quartet were Jacques Gordon and David Sackson, violins; William Lincer, viola; and Naoum Benditzky, violoncello.

retary—has just written to me whether you are to send the score and parts to me or to Mr. Gordon in New York. I think it will be best if you send the material here as soon as you have finished with it. I can then make an effort to "sell" it to the "Friends" program committee, relieving Mr. Gordon of the necessity of making embarrassing decisions.[60]

Barber responded March 16:

Dear Mr. Strunk:
I am sending the score and parts of the first two movements of my new string quartet. The third movement, which I have been revising, is almost ready, but I have not had time to copy score and parts in ink. I have been unusually busy with revisions for the Philadelphia Orchestra performance this week and the Philharmonic performance next week.* Would two movements suffice for your program committee to decide about the work? If not, do you need score or parts to judge the third movement? Or both? Please tell me frankly. I could send the score in a week, parts a few days later. But perhaps it is not necessary to rush the third movement if you decide from the other two not to do the work at all.

Thank you for bothering about this, and for asking me to submit the quartet.

Three days later Strunk acknowledged receipt of the manuscript score and parts and told Barber of his eagerness to have the quartet performed even if not immediately:

My dear Mr. Barber:
This will acknowledge the safe receipt of the manuscript score and parts of your new string quartet.

I see no special reason why you should rush to work on the last movement. What you have already sent me will, I think, be sufficient for my immediate needs. If the "Friends" decide to do the work, I shall let you know in plenty of time. And if they decide not to do it, this will simply mean a postponement until next season, for I am most anxious to see the work presented here, and shall try to find another opportunity if this one does not work out.

Since the committee decided affirmatively, Barber's next letter provided a list of guests who were to be invited to the concert:

Dear Mr. Strunk:
I was very glad to hear that you are doing my quartet at the Library of Congress April twentieth and hope to be present. This is the first American performance of my quartet, which is my most recent composition. . . .

Would you kindly send invitations to:

* He was referring to the performance of the Symphony in One Movement.

Mrs. Edward Bok—Merion Pa.
" John Braun— " "
Miss Phyllis Byrne—Sutton Place, N.Y.C.
Mr. Gama Gilbert—c/o "New York Times", N.Y.
Mr. Rosario Scalero—c/o Curtis Institute
Mr. Curtin Winsor—Ardmore, Penna.
The Curtis Quartet—c/o Curtis Institute, Phila.
Ralph Berkowitz—c/o Curtis Institute, Phila.
Mr. and Mrs. Alexander Kelberine—18th and Pine St., Phila.
Mr. Thomas Brockman—c/o Curtis Institute, Phila.

I should not send you such a long list, but feel sure that few of these people will be able to come.

Looking forward to the pleasure of meeting you. . . .

The tempi of my quartet are . . . 1. Allegro appassionato 2. Adagio 3. Andante mosso, un poco agitato. Allegro molto.

The Gordon Quartet already have the third movement.[61]

A week before the concert, Strunk gave Barber his favorable response:

> Invitations to the concert have been sent as you suggested to the ten or twenty friends whom you listed for me. Needless to say, you are yourself invited, and, since I presume that you will not want to be bothered with formalities, I shall simply hold a card for you at the door.
>
> Tomorrow afternoon (Tuesday) I leave for New York, where I shall probably be until the day before the concert next week. I expect, of course, to hear the quartet in rehearsal and would naturally be delighted to see you there if you are in town at all. My New York address will be Hotel St. Moritz.

The program on 20 April began with Barber's quartet, followed by three early songs of Debussy, Virgil Thomson's *Stabat mater* (sung by Olga Averino), and Schoenberg's Quartet No. 2, Op. 10.

The third movement of Barber's quartet continued to be thorny for the composer. After the Washington concert, he was still dissatisfied with it and decided to completely rewrite the finale. The Curtis Quartet wanted to play the new movement for their Town Hall concert in March 1938, but when by January 1938 the problem of the finale still had not been solved, once again Barber had to disappoint his friends. He wrote to Cole:

> I cannot safely promise a new last movement in time for you to learn it by March 15th. The first movement also needs rewriting—in spots. In fact, I would keep only the first page or so, the entire development  etc. and the coda. It is too late to do this in time—I have been rushing—day and night—an orchestra piece and a chorus . . . and should not like to have to spend February in the same manner—feverishly rewriting the quartet.* It is a question of playing the quartet as is, or waiting until next

season. The Gordons the other day played the first movement miserably, and the hit of the concert, believe it or not, after the adagio, was the last movement!! which sounded quite brilliant, although I myself do not like most of it. Mason and Douglas Moore wrote me letters afterwards saying they much preferred the last to the first! Can you beat it? Do you play it fast enough?

Question: do you wish to play it as is, or do you prefer to wait for another later occasion, after it has been rewritten?†

The Curtis Quartet played three movements on 15 March in Town Hall. Howard Taubman, hearing it for the first time, remarked the work "combines sincerity of purpose, freshness of feeling, and a capacity to realize one's ideas," the first movement in particular displaying "virility and dramatic impact" and the second movement, "the finest of the work," being "deeply felt and written with economy, resourcefulness and distinction."[62] Like Barber, he believed the shortcomings were in the last movement, "a scrappy working out of unexciting ideas"; and perhaps it was this lackluster appraisal that convinced Barber to withdraw the finale once more and rewrite it altogether.

The Curtis Quartet wanted to play the piece on tour in California and at Bowdoin College in April 1939. Cole pressed Barber again about the new last movement—would it be ready in time? During the summer of 1938 they had played the first two movements over the radio; Barber and Menotti heard it en route from Maine to Lake George:

> Bravo for the quartet for the broadcast on Monday and many apologies for not having wired you at once. I tried to in two towns in Vermont, but the wires were still down from the storm . . . I certainly heard it in most picturesque surroundings. . . . We had no radio in the car: and, of course, about 3 o'clock we were in the most deserted stretch of Vermont woods. So we stopped in a small town of three stores, the grocery store was the only house that boasted a radio, and there, surrounded by hams, sausages, and flour I heard your fine performance and very clearly. A couple of Green Mountain boys were hanging around, listened with some curiosity and launched a few well-aimed shots during the Adagio, at a corner spittoon. All very rural! . . . Look out in future broadcasts to keep the 2 violins nearer the mike. You doubtless had records made—wasn't there a preponderance of viola and cello? That is the engineer's fault.[63]

About the last movement, however, Barber could still make no "rash" promises to Cole: "There seems to be a hoodoo over it—but have written

* The orchestral piece mentioned here is the *First Essay,* the chorus is "God's Grandeur" (see below).

† Undated letter, probably 29 January 1938, the day before the date of completion indicated on the holograph of "God's Grandeur."

about a third of it and will send it as soon as it is finished. Certainly you should have it for Bowdoin if not for your California tour, and I *hope* to finish it quickly."[64] This time he did.

The three movements of the original version of Barber's Quartet in B minor are in conventional forms: the first a sonata, the second a song, and the third a sonata-rondo, each based on different material and contrasting in character. The Allegro movement's energetic presentation of the primary theme in unison at the outset seems to evoke the spirit—if not the shape—of Beethoven's early Op. 18, No. 1 or Op. 95; a second choralelike theme is followed by a more lyrical section. The development process is continuous, not limited to the development section but pervading all parts of the movement.

A comparison between manuscript parts used by the Curtis Quartet and the G. Schirmer 1943 edition verifies the changes in the first movement that Barber wrote about in his January 1938 letter to Cole. New material was added to the section from rehearsal nos. 3 to 5; the development section was left intact. In the 1943 edition, however, Barber went a step further and substituted new material for the last fifty-two measures (beginning 8 mm. after rehearsal no. 13), transferring this original passage to the end of the quartet as the basis for the "new" third movement and thereby creating a cyclical form. This "finale," however, is not labeled as such, nor is it called "III" in the G. Schirmer score; it follows without pause the Adagio, which concludes with the instruction *attacca,* suggesting that Barber intended that the quartet be considered a two-movement work.* The second movement of the quartet, the adagio, in its later arrangement for string orchestra, would become the most well known of Barber's works (see below, *Adagio for Strings*).

The discarded third movement centered on a cheerful rondo theme in F♯ major—in 6/8, *alla breve*—introduced by an *andante mosso, un poco agitato* section in B minor, in 12/8 (see Example 6.4). The manuscript parts are at the Curtis Institute of Music. Sprightly in character and more than four times as long as the new movement, Barber's original version seems an unbalanced conclusion to the dramatically taut first movement and the elegiac second.† The revisions provide a cohesiveness and integrity of design that strengthen the work.

For a January 1943 performance of the quartet with its new "third movement" by the Budapest Quartet at the Library of Congress, Barber advised Alexander Schneider: "Acting on your suggestion of contrary motion, I am sending a change for the end of the quartet which may be an

*Broder reports that Barber considered the work to consist of two movements and thus the indication *III* that appeared in the 1943 edition was deleted from later editions (*Samuel Barber,* n. 74). Friedewald incorrectly interpreted the Broder footnote as meaning that Barber intended the *molto allegro* section to be omitted from performance (*A Formal and Stylistic Analysis,* p. 178).

†The parts, belonging to cellist Orlando Cole, are now on deposit at the Curtis Institute of Music Library.

Example 6.4 First page of violin I part of discarded finale of the String Quartet, Op. 11. Ozalid print of copyist's manuscript, 1938. *(Orlando Cole Collection, Curtis Institute of Music Library)*

improvement."[65] These final touches, all minor, direct the second violin and viola parts to approach the cadence (after no. 11) from a lower neighbor, in "contrary motion" to, rather than in unison with, the first violin part.

Toward the end of 1947, while finishing the first movement of his piano sonata, Barber accepted a commission from Mrs. Coolidge to write an-

Example 6.5 Unfinished string quartet, second movement, holograph, ca. 1948. *(Library of Congress)*

other string quartet to be completed by October 1948. His comments on the problems of writing the new quartet, while illuminating his concept of the form in general, seem to hint as well at his disappointment in his B-minor quartet despite its success: "I look forward to this with delight and some trepitude," he wrote to Homer about the new commission.

> I've never been able to manage string quartet writing very well, but will make a study of Haydn and Beethoven Op. 18. I want to try not to push the limits of the string quartet, which even Beethoven did toward the end, so everyone else pushed them still more![66]

Although he planned to work on the new quartet in Italy from February to June 1949, his piano sonata took so much longer to complete than he expected that he worked on nothing else; and a year later he wrote to Homer, "I was not in a good composing mood this summer and finally had to crawl out of the quartet commission."* Evidence that he began work on the quartet is suggested by seven pages of manuscript (numbered 13 to 19) of a single movement at the Library of Congress (Example 6.5).

*Letters to Homer, 8 February 1948 and 29 September 1950. A letter to Koussevitzky dated 1 April 1948 says he is working on a string quartet; but a letter to Homer written two years later, on 29 April 1950, states, "I am meditating on a string quartet—or maybe a piano quartet, but don't know yet, and would like to talk to you about it." Although Barber wrote to his uncle in the letter of 29 September 1950 that there was "not a note forthcoming," he may have in fact begun work on the piece.

7

RECOGNITION

Listen to the inner voice that is working with you

The Toscanini premieres: *Essay for Orchestra,* Op. 12 (1938), and the *Adagio for Strings,* Op. 11

Like so many of his contemporaries', Barber's imagination was captured by the legendary Italian conductor, Arturo Toscanini. In early spring of 1933 he wrote to Sidney Homer of his ecstatic reaction to hearing Toscanini conduct Beethoven. Homer responded from a perspective shared by Americans raised in the European tradition:

> Yes, I too have been to Heaven with Toscanini and Beethoven. This surge of greatness has set America thinking deeply. Something new is born in our country—more power to it! When Toscanini first came to the Philharmonic, after the Ninth Symphony, when Aunt Louise sang with him, I told him I thought he would be a Messiah to American musical life and I think I was right. The fight is one of greatness and true music against silliness, boorishness, and vacuity. It is a one-sided fight but it must have leaders! You can supply some of the ammunition![1]

Fortified with Homer's advice and buoyed with the news that his first orchestral piece, the Overture to *The School for Scandal,* had been warmly received in Philadelphia, in August 1933 Barber, with Menotti, visited Toscanini on Isola di San Giovanni, one of the four islands in Lago Maggiore. The Toscanini villa, atop a cliff and built around an old church of the Principe Borromeo, was surrounded by exquisite gardens, "all around, the waves of Maggiore lapping at the foot of the island's cliffs—and tiny lights on all the distant mountains."[2] Barber described this initial contact with the conductor in a lengthy, detailed letter to his parents:

> It is the most romantic place you could imagine . . . they have the whole island to themselves, and their villa is up on the crest of the rocks; all around are great trees and gardens, which are arranged in the most natural

way so that no gardener seems to have laid foot there. The house is white with rose-colored awnings, and stretching away from it on all sides is the blue lake with the purple mountains in the distance. . . .

We got out of our boat and trembled up the footpath to the house, not having the slightest idea whether they would receive us or not, for we had not written or phoned that we were coming. We asked if Mme Toscanini was at home, saying we were friends of Max Smith;* and then a *long* nervewracking wait, while the servant seemed to be hunting in the garden for her and our hearts sank; and then he returned saying, "*Madame* Toscanini is too busy to see you now, but the Maestro is coming to receive you." My heart still beats faster at the thought! Soon he appeared, coming up the path with Zirato, the manager of the Philharmonic [then assistant manager, later manager of the New York Philharmonic–Symphony Society], and greeted us. He was the nicest thing you could imagine, took us around to a terrace with a heavenly view, and there we sat and talked. . . . Our wildest thoughts were that we would have a formal, brief visit, but here he was telling us how glad he was we came, and treating us like old friends. . . . He spoke in glowing terms of Aunt Louise's *Orfeo*. . . . After a while his two daughters arrived . . . and we made a tour of the island, up and down through the gardens. Much of the time I was walking alone with him, tickled as a cat. Back at the house he took G-C and me into his studio and showed us some of his treasures—the last thing Wagner wrote, never published, a most beautiful couple of lines for the piano which he stuck in the score of *Parsifal* when he gave it to his wife on completion. Frau Wagner gave it to Toscanini, and he played it for us. . . . He has a portrait of Beethoven in his youth, the only one in the world. He picked up two volumes which he said he was never without—Beethoven's string quartets. (Owing to his extreme myopia, the poor Maestro did not realize that one of the cherished volumes he was showing us happened to be an "English Grammar Simplified for Beginners.") Then . . . we had tea and talked some more, and left in a daze of enthusiasm for him and his house.[3]

More visits followed, for Toscanini went out of his way to be hospitable to the two young composers. He usually sent his motor boat to bring them to his house for dinner or tea, and inevitably the evenings ended in music:

Once, after dinner we went through Monteverdi's *Orfeo*. I had never known this Renaissance opera before, with its amazing contemporaneousness. Toscanini played . . . and sang Eurydice . . . full of feeling. I sang Orfeo and was in the Seventh Heaven of delight. The wonderful lament—Tu sei morta. . . . Afterwards we sat on the terrace and talked half the night. Wagner's oldest daughter, Liszt's granddaughter . . . was there.†

* A New York music critic and friend of Toscanini.

† *Overtones*, 1933–34, p. 75. There is, at the Library of Congress, a transcription by Barber of "Addio di Orfeo," scored for voice, strings, and cembalo. The music paper, a German brand (J. E. & Co., Protokoll Schutzmarke), suggests the score was probably copied by Barber in Vienna sometime in 1934 when he was beginning to be interested in old music.

Apparently about this time Toscanini told Barber he would like to perform one of his works. This was a groundbreaking invitation; Toscanini, who was famous for his avoidance of contemporary international composers (Bartók, Berg, and Schoenberg, for example), up until the early 1940s had all but completely neglected music by American composers; rare exceptions were Howard Hanson's Symphony No. 2 (which he conducted in 1933) and two works by Abram Chasins.[4] Learning of his nephew's good fortune, Homer communicated his enthusiasm and compassion in a lengthy letter that must have indeed been a source of inspiration and encouragement to the young composer.

> It all sounds too good to be true, and you have it because you earned it and deserve it, and that's the best part of it! The thing now is to write something for Toscanini that expresses the depth and sincerity of your nature, and perhaps your gratitude at being able to live and work. You know as well as I do that the Maestro loves sincere straight-forward stuff, with genuine feeling in it and no artificial pretense and padding. It ought to be an inspiration to you to know a man like that.
>
> So often we begin to compose in a spirit of fearfulness. We are fearful of our listener. Will he understand? Will he be impressed? Will he be moved? Must I dazzle him, or write down to his comprehension?
>
> This consciousness of listener, publisher, or conductor can be a real impediment to profound, spontaneous work. I am sure you will agree with me. . . . Sometimes meeting a really great man can release much power in a man's soul. Think what Joachim and Schumann meant to the young Brahms, at just your age. In the same way Toscanini may mean much to you, if you keep his simplicity and real responsiveness clearly in your mind.
>
> The very distractions of the ideal way in which you are living will make it hard for you to compose. (Sounds Irish!) Try to concentrate on your composing and set aside certain hours when you are accessible to no one. The subconscious fear of interruption and the sense of limited time are both nuisances. The technique of overcoming all obstacles is one of the distinguishing marks of all the great composers, and they had plenty! I don't mean that hot-house conditions are necessary, but a certain freedom and repose are. . . . Your work will depend, in a measure, on the men you know, on the taste and perception you encounter, on your own selection of influence.*

More than three years passed before Barber produced a work for Toscanini that he felt was worthy of the conductor's attention. At the Salzburg festival in 1937, as principal conductor Toscanini had heard Rodzinski

*Letter, 15 January 1934, Palm Beach, Florida. Katharine Homer believes that the tone of this letter was part of an ongoing effort of her father to remind Barber that his recognition was in fact earned and well deserved and that his access to great conductors was not gained merely because he was a nephew of Louise and Sidney Homer.

conduct Barber's Symphony in One Movement. At this time he was thinking about including a work by an American composer on his winter programs for the newly formed National Broadcasting Company Symphony Orchestra created especially for him. Rodzinski strongly urged that he play something by Barber, whose traditionally styled music could hardly have seemed heretical to the conservative conductor, and Toscanini therefore showed renewed interest in seeing a new short piece.[5]

At the end of January 1938 Barber wrote to Cole that he was "rushing—day and night—to finish an orchestra piece,"* which was probably the *Essay* he presented to Toscanini during late spring of that year. Dedicated to C. E. (Carl Engel), this work inspired Sidney Homer to write to his nephew: "You have no idea how many people look to you for guidance in refinement, taste, and poetic insight. . . . It is a responsibility and you will have to live up to it. The longing for the highest must be satisfied."[6]

Robert Horan, the brilliant poet who befriended Menotti and Barber in the early forties and lived with them at Capricorn, believed that Barber had for some time felt the necessity for a short orchestrated form, abstract rather than descriptive in character, a form that would correspond in length and organization to the literary essay.† It was Barber's intention, Horan said, "to avoid that overworked department of modern composition, the three-part form, by fashioning . . . a subtle two-part form, in the two sections of which, although completely contrasting in mood and color, there is reciprocal interplay of thematic material."[7]

The literary analogy sparked one music critic to observe that *Essay* has a "brevity and conciseness, an almost epigrammatic neatness, that might have been derived from Addison and Steele."[8] Horan, too, wrote of the work as "terse and epigrammatic," but more provocatively—considering the poet's close knowledge of Barber—suggested this was "music of disenchantment," like the writing of André Gide, but taking "less risks with propriety."‡ Barber himself seemed to view his work in less intellectual terms, however, for in 1939, when asked by conductor Walter Damrosch to recommend a work for performance at the World's Fair, the composer replied: "The 'Essay for Orchestra' seems to me too intimate and tenuous for a program of such character and does not stand alone very well."[9]

*Broder incorrectly states that Barber had completed the *Essay* by the time he returned to the United States in October 1937. A later date of completion is suggested by Barber's letters and an announcement in the March 1938 issue of *Overtones* that "Samuel Barber has just completed a symphonic piece which he calls 'Essay.' It has been accepted by Eugene Ormandy for performance by the Philadelphia Orchestra, concert dates to be announced" (p. 48). Although announcement of a forthcoming premiere of *Essay* by the Philadelphia Orchestra on 25, 26, and 29 March 1938 did appear in a Philadelphia paper, apparently the performance never took place—probably because the piece was not finished in time.

†As was mentioned in chapter 2 of this book, Barber had explored this literary form as a musical genre as early as 1926 with the three Essays for piano.

‡Robert Horan, "American Composers 19: Samuel Barber," *Modern Music* 20 (March-April 1943):164. Horan was speaking here of Barber's *Second Essay* also.

The composer, holding a manuscript of the *Essay for Orchestra,* 1938. *(The Bettmann Archive)*

In contrast to his earlier orchestral works that integrate literary subjects with instrumental music—for example, the Overture to *The School for Scandal* and *Music for a Scene from Shelley*—in *Essay* Barber places little emphasis on orchestral sensuousness. The *First Essay*—as it came to be called after Barber wrote a second one in 1942—is similar but not exactly equivalent to the first movement of a symphony. As its title implies, the substance of the work derives from the exploration of a single subject, but in this case the discourse is unfolded in two contrasting sections: the first, a somber postulation of the principal theme; the second, a scherzo based on a rhythmic diminution of the principal theme and in which the first theme surfaces again to ultimately provide material for a brief coda. This seems to realize to some extent a design that Barber had in mind, which he described to Menotti: a two-part form, the first section containing two themes (in this case, the second derived from the first), each stated and developed, and a second section in which the two themes are combined.[10]

With his *Essay,* Barber also sent to Toscanini the *Adagio for Strings,* a five-part arrangement of the second movement of his String Quartet in B minor.* Shortly before he departed for Italy for the summer, Toscanini

* According to Brunetta Bernard, the widow of Gama Gilbert, the arrangement was suggested by her late husband (letter to the author, 11 September 1982). There exists one holograph of the work with the curious title "Essay for Strings." It is inscribed "To my friend

Mary Louise Curtis Bok and Sam Barber at the Curtis Institute Christmas party, 1938. *(The Curtis Institute of Music Library)*

returned the scores to Barber without comment. Although Barber had intended to visit the conductor at his home later that summer, he was so "annoyed" by Toscanini's lack of response to his works that he sent Menotti on without him.[11] The composer later reported an interchange that presumably occurred between Menotti and Toscanini while Barber sat in Pallanza waiting for the boat to come back:

> At the end Toscanini said to Menotti, "Well, where's your friend Barber?" "Well, he's not feeling very well," said Gian Carlo. And Toscanini said, "I don't believe that. He's mad at me. Tell him not to be mad. I'm not going to play one of his pieces, I'm going to play both."[12]

The extremely good news that Toscanini had decided to present *Essay* and *Adagio for Strings* was a major triumph for Barber.* It was reported that the conductor had committed the scores to memory and did not look at them again until the day before the performance. At the last rehearsal on the day of the broadcast, Toscanini decided that the ending of *Essay* would be "improved" by the addition of a trumpet to reinforce the strings near the end. His frantic attempts to reach Barber by telephone to secure

Henry-Louis de La Grange / Souvenir of Capricorn, April 7, 1947" and is at the Pierpont Morgan Library, New York.

*Many years later, in 1978, Barber reflected upon his career: "I think I've been very, very lucky, in general, and especially for symphonic and concert pieces. I've had perfectly marvelous conductors" (Barber, interviewed by Robert Sherman, WQXR, 30 September 1978).

permission to make the change were unsuccessful. So confident was he of the validity of his alteration that at the performance the septuagenarian conductor incorporated the trumpet part anyway, afterwards apologizing to Barber for "taking liberties with his score."[13] Toscanini's suggestion was not retained in the published score of *Essay*. A holograph at the Library of Congress with notes added in Toscanini's hand suggests that he also tampered with the *Adagio for Strings* at measures 31–32 (see Example 7.1).*

Toscanini's broadcasts were generally regarded with almost religious reverence, but the ten o'clock broadcast on the evening of 5 November 1938 held additional significance, for it marked recognition by the Italian conductor that there was enough merit in works by an American composer to bring them to the attention of a national audience. Curtis Institute considered the occasion so important that an entire script of the broadcast was printed in the newsletter *Overtones*.[14] A review by Olin Downes gives attention to the ritual aspects of the broadcast as well as the beauty of Barber's music:

> The audience assembled last night . . . with the same eagerness, and listened and applauded with the same intensity which is customary at this series of events. There was the same almost laughable silence and solemnity as the orchestra ceased tuning and the gathering waited for seconds for the conductor to step silently through the door that opens on the stage. And there was the same highly privileged sensation of listening to performances which had almost the clarity and purity of chamber music, and finally, of hearing some interesting new scores. . . .
>
> . . . It goes without saying that Toscanini conducted the scores as if his reputation rested upon the results. He does that with whatever he undertakes.
>
> Mr. Barber had reason for thankfulness for a premiere under such leadership. And the music proved eminently worth playing. The Adagio . . . is not pretentious music. Its author does not pose and posture in his score. He writes with a definite purpose, a clear objective and a sense of structure. . . .
>
> A long line, in the Adagio, is well sustained. There is an arch of melody and form. The composition is most simple at the climaxes when it develops that the simplest chord or figure is the one most significant. . . . This is the product of a musically creative nature . . . who leaves nothing undone to achieve something as perfect in mass and detail as his craftsmanship permits.[15]

* When Barber sent the holograph to the Library of Congress, he wrote to Harold Spivacke: "It might interest you to know that it was used by Toscanini at the first performance of the work and some of the red markings inside are his" (letter, 28 July 1943, Library of Congress, Music Division, Old Correspondence Collection).

Example 7.1 *Adagio for Strings,* mm. 26–42, holograph score used for first performance, 1938. Toscanini's additions appear faintly in the upper three voices of the second system. *(Library of Congress)*

Barber was astute enough to appreciate his good fortune, and he never forgot that performance, which he felt far surpassed the commercial recording made of the *Adagio* in Carnegie Hall in 1942.

> To me the Carnegie recording seems to have less surge of powerful crescendo, as Toscanini had to repeat it several times in order to get the crescendo on one side of a 78-record. . . . [Then, playing the NBC radio broadcast of the premiere] Listen to the violas here. . . . Imagine! Primrose was the first violist then, and Alfred Wallenstein was the principal cellist. Wallenstein has always said to me that he felt this was one of Toscanini's greatest performances. What luck for a young composer to have such a first performance! *

Sidney Homer, on the other hand, seemed to feel his nephew unduly exaggerated his debt to the conductor:

> I understand your feeling about Toscanini and rejoice with you, but in my opinion, you conveyed as much honor on him as he on you, and you are quits—except for the photograph and the tribute written on it. This demands a new piece that he can play next year, one worthy of him and the grandeur of his interpretations.[16]

Toscanini took the *Adagio for Strings* on tour to England† and to South America, where it was the first work of a North American composer to be presented to Latin American audiences. His selection of Barber's music as representative American works sparked an intense debate—or more accurately, *refueled* an existing controversy—over "traditional" music versus music in "the modern idiom." The past two decades had seen a conscious effort on the part of native composers to write music that could be identified as American, and Toscanini's choice of a composer who was not a participant in this trend was seen by many as regression.

The forum took place in a series of letters in the *New York Times* between 13 November and 25 December 1938, and the torch was lit by Ashley Pettis, who believed that Toscanini's "rare gesture" of performing two works by a contemporary American composer might have had potentially enormous significance to our musical life "both in acquainting a wide public with the fact that there are serious, contemporary works and in

*John Ardoin, "Samuel Barber at Capricorn," *Musical America* (March 1960). Toscanini recorded the *Adagio for Strings* on 21 March 1942 in an empty Carnegie Hall. It was his first recording of an American work, and, appropriate to wartime, he also made records of "The Star-Spangled Banner," for which the whole orchestra, including the cellists, had to play standing up as if it were a public performance (letter from Barber to Katherine Chapin Biddle, 22 March 1942, Georgetown University Library).

†A concert program from London, however, cites the "first performance in England" of the *Essay* as conducted by Sir Henry Wood, at a London Promenade Concert on 24 August 1939.

providing a fresh impetus and incentive to our musical craftsmen." In a biting expression of sarcasm about Barber and Toscanini, he wrote:

> One listened in vain for evidence of youthful vigor, freshness or fire, for use of a contemporary idiom (which was characteristic of every composer whose works have withstood the vicissitudes of time). Mr. Barber's was "authentic," dull, "serious" music—utterly anachronistic as the utterance of a young man of 28, A.D. 1938!
>
> Such a choice by the great musical Messiah in our midst can only have a retarding influence on the advance of our creative musicians. They realize only too well that they have small chance of performance by the greatest musical organizations and conductors . . . unless they write music for people who listen with ears of the nineteenth and early twentieth centuries at the latest—whose criteria are that "new" music shall have the familiar melodic, harmonic and rhythmic characteristics of the past, that it be a hodgepodge of clichés, that it presupposes no spirit or musical adventure on the part of either performer or public.[17]

Pettis asserted further that we had music by Americans "legitimately redolent of other days"—MacDowell, Griffes, and "our own living youngster, the octogenarian Edgar Stillman-Kelley of the New England Symphony," as well as living composers—Aaron Copland, Roy Harris, Roger Sessions, and the "always mentioned, but never played, Charles Ives." "What chance, if any," he cried, "have they and many others one should mention in the forward march of the followers of David against the Philistines?"

The gauntlet thus thrown, the advocates of Barber's music voiced their defense of the venerable Toscanini's choice. Among them were, predictably, Menotti and Alexander Kelberine, as well as J. L. Bawden, Verna Arvey, the conductor Franco Autori, and—representing an ecumenical viewpoint—Roy Harris.

In the name of diversity, Menotti impassionedly defended his friend: "Must there be in art one 'modern idiom'?" he asked. "Because there is a Gertrude Stein, must we condemn a Thomas Mann?" Calling Pettis "very passé" in that he still accepted as the modern idiom the Parisian style of twenty years earlier, Menotti presented Barber in a postmodernist light:

> If Mr. Barber dares to defy the servile imitation of that style (which has been called American music) and experiments successfully with melodic line and new form, is he not to be praised for his courage?
>
> . . . It is time for some one to make a reaction against a school of composition that has bored concert audiences for twenty years. All through Europe there are signs of this healthy reaction among the younger generation. . . .
>
> If Mr. Barber's music is not startlingly original, surely that is not to his discredit. He is young. The early Michelangelo accepted the influence of

> Signorelli, Beethoven that of Mozart, and some of Leonardo's early work is scarcely distinguishable from Verrocchio.
>
> It was very amusing for Mr. Pettis' generation to be revolutionists. But now let them recognize that the younger generation is left with the thankless job of building on their ruins.[18]

Responding to Pettis's biblical metaphor, Menotti concluded: "Isn't it high time that a young David appeared and struck on the forehead that inflated monster which still parades under the anachronistic name of modern music?"

Others wrote in a similar vein. Alexander Kelberine: "Must a work be cacophonous in order to be of today? How can one be all-fired sure that Messrs. Aaron Copland, Roy Harris, Roger Sessions will withstand the vicissitudes of time?"[19] Franco Autori: "The real issue is whether the composer has a message to deliver, whether he is competent to deliver it, and whether, in delivering it, he is sincere and true to his purpose."* From Verna Arvey came "the West Coast point of view": "The important fact to remember is that Toscanini did play an American composition and that he may be prevailed upon to play more of these in the future."[20]

The controversy was but a ripple compared to that of earlier historical quarrels, where the "old" versus the "new" had generated considerable fervor. It seems ironic that a composer who was hardly a radical and who was representative of the "establishment" should be the critical issue, when musical invectives are traditionally hurled against the avant-garde by conservatives. It appears that it was not enough for Toscanini to play, at last, works by an American composer if the music could not be identified as "American." Barber's music—as Menotti's letter suggests—was pitted against a trend of "modernism," experimentalism that was prominent during the twenties and thirties but no longer seemed adequate expression even to such "rebels" as Copland, for example.

Homer, with predictable loyalty, could be depended upon to put the controversy into perspective for his nephew:

> You have the convictions that created your works and you can only listen to the inner voice that is working with you. Stick by yourself and your convictions and back yourself up, to the limit. That is what every man has had to do who has ever written anything worthwhile. . . . Opinions are like the wind and blow from all quarters, and, even when sincere, can arise from inability to understand.†

The final word in the *New York Times*, however, came from Roy Harris, who Barber was later to call, with admiration, the father of the Amer-

* "From the Mail Pouch," *New York Times*, 27 November 1938. Autori, then conductor of the Buffalo Philharmonic, became associate conductor of the New York Philharmonic in 1945.

† Letter; though dated 31 January 1938, the correct date would have to be 1939.

ican symphony. Harris's letter summarized the challenge of American composers as they approached the end of the decade:

> For years there has been a cultural storm gathering in our land. The old and the new are digging up the time-worn battle-axe again. The old was ever venerable—the new ever vulnerable. The venerable dwell on their solid Parnassus, secure in the well-being of having done the right thing by us. In the spirit of good citizenship, they contributed to our cultural perspective by patronizing the best of European traditions and bringing them into our midst. They built our halls, stocked our libraries, imported the finest European musicians to play for, and teach, us.
>
> The vulnerable? A handful of improvidents with nothing but their talents, energies and ambitions. They have everything to win. A whole new world is theirs for the taking—if they can serve it. Young America's savage vitality and profound searching hopes wait their articulate expression. Thousands of young musicians who memorized the standard repertory are looking for something new; radio, recording, choruses, orchestras, wearing the proved past thin with repetition; the public—many and various publics—waiting.
>
> What can the venerable do? They can only continue to offer the past. The vulnerable contemporary composer will have to create whatever is added. And Time, who is no respecter of persons, will call his own court of appraisal to order and render final judgment on what is offered. No amount of wish-thinking on the part of either party will alter the real stature of what we do.[21]

Barber's *Adagio for Strings*—like many other of his works—has withstood the test of time and earned permanent stature. Its undisputed place in American, and in fact international, repertoire is unchallenged. There are some who may never have heard or recall the name of the composer of the *Adagio* yet who recognize the music even without knowing its title. It is the most frequently performed of Barber's works; a count of its playings by the Philadelphia Orchestra alone, for example, shows that between 1943, the year of its first performance, and 1985 it was played at a total of eighty-five concerts, rarely skipping a season.[22]

Ned Rorem believes the *Adagio for Strings* to dispel two myths about music: "that what is popular is necessarily junk, and the late improves upon the early." "If Barber later aimed higher," Rorem claims, "he never reached deeper into the heart, and he is still held most dearly for works composed before his fortieth birthday."[23]

Because the *Adagio for Strings* has been associated so often with the death of a prominent person, it has been called our "national funeral music."[24] It was played at the funerals of such diverse figures as President Franklin Delano Roosevelt, Albert Einstein, and Princess Grace of Monaco; it was broadcast in South Africa upon the death of Jan Christian Smuts, in the United States when John F. Kennedy died, and in Ohio when

Senator Robert A. Taft died.* The appearance of *Adagio for Strings* in unexpected contexts has ranged from the mundane—in a romantic advertisement for French perfume[25]—to the profound—as background music for the 1986 Academy Award-winning antiwar film *Platoon,* where it served with surprising effectiveness as the only relief from tension provoked by brutal war scenes.† Menotti believes Barber would not have been amused by its success in this film and might not even have allowed the *Adagio* to be used.‡

On a 1982 BBC retrospective broadcast about Barber, a group of prominent musicians were asked to analyze why the *Adagio* was such a "perfect piece of music." They were hard-pressed to come up with technical justifications and focused instead on the emotional response it elicits from listeners. That Barber had absorbed Sidney Homer's wise advice—to write something for Toscanini that "expresses the depth and sincerity of your nature . . . straight-forward stuff, with genuine feeling in it and no artificial pretense and padding"[26]—is confirmed by Aaron Copland's appraisal of the *Adagio for Strings:*

> It's really well felt, it's believable you see, it's not phoney. He's not just making it up because he thinks that would sound well. It comes straight from the heart, to use old-fashioned terms. The sense of continuity, the steadiness of the flow, the satisfaction of the arch that it creates from beginning to end. They're all very gratifying, satisfying, and it makes you believe in the sincerity which he obviously put into it.§

Even William Schuman, in attempting to define the *Adagio* in stylistic terms, had to admit its success lies in the fact that "you are not aware of any technique at all. . . . It seems quite effortless and quite natural"; he ultimately attributed the source of its strength to emotional expression:

*When Eugene Ormandy and the Philadelphia Orchestra played the *Adagio* on tour in Russia in the late fifties, they were approached by several Russians who wanted to choreograph it. Ormandy agreed to loan them the score if they would return it the next morning. They took it and spent the whole night copying the score (Ardoin, "Samuel Barber at Capricorn," p. 5).

†There were only a few measures of original music integrated in the film track, but they so resembled the *Adagio* in character, it was hard to differentiate them from Barber's music. The *Adagio for Strings* was used also for the films *Elephant Man* and *El norte.*

‡Menotti, telephone discussion with the author on 21 March 1990. The music was so successful in the film that in 1987 G. Schirmer published a simple piano version of the *Adagio for Strings* arranged by Larry Rosen.

§BBC broadcast, 23 January 1982. Compare Copland's statement with Homer's advice to Barber at the onset of his career:

> Everyone who joins the society in this place pledges himself to just one thing, sincerity. He tries to put into form his real feelings, not feelings he wishes he had. Pretense has no place here, and any dust thrown in the eyes of others settles very quickly. The beautiful thing about art is that it tells the truth and reveals the exact state of its origin. (letter, 9 July 1926, Bolton, New York)

> If the *Adagio for Strings* makes the effect that it does, it's because it's a perfect piece of music in the sense that the Mendelssohn Violin Concerto is a perfect piece of music. It wasn't the deepest piece of music that Sam ever wrote, but it was an early piece and had within it all the gestures and all the rhetoric and all the characteristics which would be later so fully and gloriously developed by him. But I think it works because it's so precise emotionally. The emotional climate is never left in doubt. It begins, it reaches its climax, it makes its point, and it goes away. For me it's never a war-horse; when I hear it played I'm always moved by it.[27]

On an iconoclastic note, Virgil Thomson remarked candidly: "I think it's a love scene . . . a detailed love scene . . . a smooth successful love scene. Not a dramatic one, but a very satisfactory one."[28]

It seems certain that Barber himself intuitively knew he had written something special when he finished the second movement of his quartet: recall his declaration, "It's a knockout!"[29] Yet, to a certain extent, he later believed it was to his detriment to be so identified with the piece almost to the exclusion of his other works. There is a certain frustration, for example, in his acerbic response to James Fassett's comment that the *Adagio for Strings* was the first composition of Barber's he had ever heard; "I wish you'd hear some new ones," Barber retorted, "everybody always plays that!"[30]

There are several arrangements of the *Adagio for Strings*, all published by G. Schirmer. One for chorus, *Agnus Dei*, was made by Barber himself in 1967 (the English version is "Lamb of God"). Arrangements exist for clarinet choir by Lucien Caillet (1964) and for woodwinds by John O'Reilly (1967). An arrangement for organ was made by William Strickland. He had been "bowled over" by Toscanini's broadcast of the *Adagio* and the *First Essay* and finally met Barber in 1939 at a private musicale in New York.[31] Strickland was then assistant organist at St. Bartholomew's Church; his arrangement of the *Adagio* received at first a noncommittal response from Barber. The two kept in contact throughout World War II, when Strickland, as head of the Army Music School at Fort Myer, Virginia, conducted the premiere of Barber's *A Stopwatch and an Ordnance Map*. At the end of the war, Barber expressed renewed interest in the organ arrangement of the *Adagio for Strings:*

> Schirmers have had several organ arrangements submitted of my "Adagio for Strings" and many inquiries as to whether it exists for organ. I have always turned them down, as, although I know little about the organ, I am sure your arrangement would be best. Have you got the one you did before, if not, would you be willing to make it anew? If so, will you ever be in N.Y. on leave, so I could discuss it with you and hear it? If it is done at all, I should like it done as well as possible, and this by you. They would pay you a flat fee for the arrangement, although I don't suppose it will be

> very much. However, that is their affair. Let me know what you think about it. It does not have to be done immediately, although they are rather insistent.[32]

Strickland, fortunately, had kept his arrangement, which was eventually published by G. Schirmer in 1949.

The Unaccompanied Choral Works (1930–41)

Some of Barber's most beautiful and expressive music is found in choral works composed between 1930 and 1940. With the exception of several poems of James Stephens and Stephen Spender's "A Stopwatch and an Ordnance Map," his taste leaned during this time toward religious subjects—biblical texts or nineteenth-century poetry with a religious bent. The earliest of these was composed in 1930, a four-movement piece called "Motetto on words from the Book of Job" that exists only in manuscript at the Library of Congress.* There are three extant movements (I, II, and IV) based on passages in Job: the first movement, Job 3:17 (incorrectly labeled 4:17 by Barber); the second, Job 5:1, 11:7–8, and 5:7–8; and a fourth movement, on Job 11:16, 18 and 17.† Movements I and II (both in G minor; II, ending in D major) are for four-part mixed chorus; movement IV, in F major, is for double chorus. The alternating homophonic and contrapuntal texture, the somber harmonies, imitative entrances, and antiphonal double-chorus passages all reflect Barber's interest in early Baroque choral music, in particular the motets of Schütz, which are listed in his sketchbook of the 1930s as works he intended to study. Laid in between II and IV is a pencil sketch of "God's Grandeur," on a poem of Gerard Manley Hopkins (discussed below), which may have been intended as a substitute for the motet's missing third movement.‡

The earliest published choral works by Barber are "The Virgin Martyrs," written in 1935 on Helen Waddell's translation from the Latin of

*This is probably the Motet for Double Chorus, mentioned in *Musical America* as a work soon to be published by G. Schirmer (M.L.S., "Prix de Rome Winner Prepared for Work as a Composer with Wide Musical Curriculum," 7 December 1935). A Motet for Double Chorus is also referred to in New York Philharmonic Society program notes, 24 March 1935. Both documents cite the date of composition as 1930.

†The fact that the lines were deliberately selected out of sequence but are compatible with each other confirms the meticulous care that Barber exercised in selecting his texts.

‡Several facts suggest that the two works were written almost eight years apart: the motet is on unlabeled paper, whereas "God's Grandeur" is on G. Schirmer Imperial, eighteen-stave paper, a brand used by the composer for other works composed in the late 1930s; the motet has clefs for each stave in a system; on the holograph of "God's Grandeur," Barber indicates clefs for the first system only. A copy of "God's Grandeur"—a photocopy of which was given to the author by Phillip Ramey—is dated 20 January 1938, which corresponds to the date Barber mentions in a letter of that same year in which he wrote about finishing a piece for a commission for the Westminster Choir Spring Festival. It is listed on a program for the festival.

Sigebert of Gembloux; and "Let down the bars, O Death," a setting of Emily Dickinson's poem completed by Barber 25 June 1936.* "The Virgin Martyrs," for women's chorus, was sung for the first time on a CBS radio broadcast on 1 May 1939 by students from the Curtis Institute of Music under Barber's direction when he was hired by the institute to organize a Madrigal Chorus (see below).

Lines scrawled at the bottom of the holograph sketch of "Let down the bars, O Death" suggest a curiously mixed mindset at the time Barber wrote this choral work, another child of his Austrian summer—a telling quote from Rilke: "L'oeuvre d'art a besoin de temps et de silence"; † lines that suggest things may not have been as idyllic as his letters had professed: "I could recover if I shrieked my heart's agony, yet am dumb from human dignity"; and a passage from *Billy Budd:* "Their honesty prescribes to them directness, sometimes far-reaching like that of a migratory fowl that in flight never heeds when it crosses a frontier."

Although "Let down the bars, O Death" may also have been written with the Madrigal Chorus in mind and even performed by the group, the earliest documented performance is one conducted by Barber himself on 17 October 1950 at an all-Barber concert at West Chester State Teachers' College.‡ The Dickinson text is presented with direct simplicity in a chorale like setting for SATB. Certain features—shifting modality, motto rhythmic patterns, paired imitative entrances, stretto, and well-placed dissonances to underscore textual expression—are characteristic of Barber's later choral music.[33] The swing between major and minor, for example, seems appropriate to a poem that alludes ambivalently to death. Moreover, a variant between the G. Schirmer edition and the holograph score at measures 2–3 (see Example 7.2) and repeated at measures 23–24 is an example of how Barber redistributed voices to strengthen the textual associations. The major seventh between soprano and tenor voices in the original setting is assigned to soprano and bass in the G. Schirmer edition, retaining the pungent dissonance on the phrase "O Death." A more sonorous chord is achieved by relocating the bass and tenor voices up a third (see Example 7.2c at asterisks); the resolution in similar motion to an open-fifth in the lower voices supports the somber character of the text.

About this work, Barber wrote prophetically to his parents: "I wrote a little chorus the other morning, quite good, it will be all right for some-

* A holograph and pencil sketches of "The Virgin Martyrs" are at the Library of Congress, Music Division. The text was published in Waddell's *Mediaeval Latin Lyrics* (New York: Richard R. Smith, 1930, first American edition). A pencil close-score holograph of "Let down the bars, O Death" is at the Library of Congress; a manuscript is at the Chester County Historical Society, West Chester, Pennsylvania.

† "A work of art needs time and silence."

‡ "Sam Barber Night at College Is a Big Success," *West Chester Daily Local News*, 17 October 1950. It seems unlikely that this would have been the first performance, since Op. 8 was published by G. Schirmer in 1939 and undoubtedly circulated throughout the choral community.

a.

b.

Let down the bars, O Death

For Four-Part Chorus of Mixed Voices
a cappella

Emily Dickinson — Samuel Barber, Op. 8, No. 2

c.

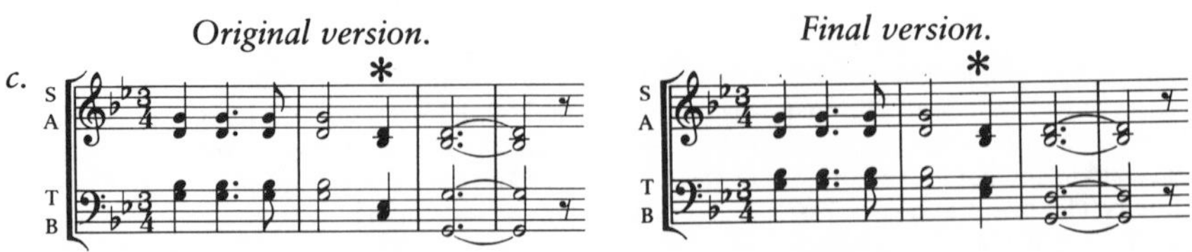

Example 7.2 "Let down the bars, O Death." *a.* Holograph, 25 June 1936. *(Chester County Historical Society, West Chester, Pennsylvania)* *b.* G. Schirmer, 1942. *c.* Reduction of mm. 1–4.

one's funeral."[34] "Let down the bars, O Death," composed during the happiest period of Barber's youth, was performed at memorial services for Barber when he died in 1981.

Similar in style to the "Motetto on words from the Book of Job," but harmonically more interesting, is another unpublished work for double chorus—"God's Grandeur," a poem by Gerard Manley Hopkins—composed by Barber for the Westminster Choir School's Festival of Contemporary American Music in the spring of 1938.* Working in haste during January of 1938, at the same time he was being pressed by Cole to provide a new last movement of the string quartet in time for a March concert, Barber wrote to Cole that he would not meet the deadline: "I have been rushing—day and night—an orchestra piece and a chorus I promised the Westminster Choir (which I finished last night)."[35] It is likely that the choral piece he mentioned was "God's Grandeur" since a manuscript copy of the score is dated January 20, 1938.†

"God's Grandeur" was performed on 31 January 1938, at the opening concerts of the Westminster Choir's annual winter tour of seven states and twenty cities; an afternoon concert was presented at the State Teachers' College in Shippensburg, Pennsylvania, and an evening performance at Mercersburg Academy. The program also included Harl McDonald's "Songs of Conquest" as representative of the younger composers.‡ Subsequent performances were given at Carnegie Hall on 2 March and at the Philadelphia Academy of Music on 22 February.

There is evidence that Barber had planned another choral work on an obscure poem of Hopkins. In the front of his sketchbook from the 1930s is written:

> O the mind, mind has mountains; cliffs of fall
> Frightful, sheer, no-man-fathomed. Hold them cheap
> May who ne'er hung there. Nor does long our small
> Durance deal with that steep or deep. Here! creep,
> Wretch, under a comfort serves in a whirlwind: all
> Life death does end and each day dies with sleep.[36]

* *Westminster Choir School Bulletin,* Vol. 3, No. 3, January 1938. According to the announcement in the bulletin, out of eight programs of chamber and choral music planned for successive afternoons and evenings, 23 to 28 May 1938, six were made up of compositions of "established American composers," divided into three groups: the "older and better established," including Arthur Farwell, Arthur Shepherd, Charles Ives, and Edgar Stillman Kelley; a second, including Aaron Copland, Roger Sessions, Walter Piston, Quincy Porter, Randall Thompson, and Roy Harris; and a third "more recently acclaimed group" that included Barber, as well as "Robert [William] Schuman, Norman [d] Lockwood, Robert MacBride [McBride], Robert Delaney [Delany], and Gardiner [Gardner] Read." Barber had the distinction of being the only composer in the last group whose name was spelled correctly.

†The score was given to Aaron Copland.

‡Incorrectly listed in *Westminster Choir School Bulletin,* Vol. 3, No. 3, January 1938, as "Songs of Concert."

Barber set the first two lines of the poem and half of the third line—a pencil sketch of eight staves of music is found on the cover of a draft of *A Stopwatch and an Ordnance Map,* written in 1940[37]—but the music is interrupted by a sketch for Spender's lines "Who lives on wears in his heart forever the space split open by the bullet"; there seems to be no evidence that he ever finished the setting of the Hopkins poem.

In 1938 Randall Thompson invited Barber to form the Madrigal Chorus at the Curtis Institute of Music, which he conducted through three academic years (1939–41) and for which he produced an especially rich group of choral works.* The composer commuted from New York every Monday to direct the group of twenty-five singers in their weekly two-hour rehearsals. During the 1939–40 school year they met twenty-two times and gave two radio performances and a concert as part of the institute's "Historical Series."[38]

For the Madrigal Chorus, Barber wrote "The Virgin Martyrs" (1938), the last two pieces of *Reincarnations*—"Anthony O'Daly" and "The Coolin"—and *A Stopwatch and an Ordnance Map,* all published by G. Schirmer in 1942. An unpublished edition of Josquin's *Ave Maria,* although undated, was undoubtedly transcribed by Barber himself for this group in 1940.† On the cover of the holograph are lists of programs of choral music with estimated durations for each work; among them is *Stopwatch.*‡ The timing of these programs was especially important because the Madrigal Chorus's concerts were broadcast over CBS radio; Gama Gilbert provided commentary for them, of which there are recordings at the Library of Congress.

The choral group provided an artistic and creative challenge for Barber at a time when he seemed somewhat disillusioned about the prospects for his career as a composer. He apparently perceived himself—although somewhat tongue-in-cheek—as a young Werther, as this letter to Suso Cecchi suggests:

> The fact is there has been so little to write about and life in New York has been rather flat. I have very few friends, and I can think of no social gaiety

*In 1939 Randall Thompson assumed directorship of the institute, and, in the interest of remedying the neglect choral training had suffered under prior administrations, he established an institute chorus, which all voice students were required to attend.

†Alfred Mann, a student at the institute during this time and a member of the Madrigal Chorus, recalled a performance of Monteverdi's "Ecco mormorar l'onde," which was sung from hand-copied parts as there were no printed editions available in the United States at that time (Alfred Mann, "Madrigal Awards," *American Choral Review* 29 [Winter 1987]: 25).

‡The titles give an idea of the music Barber preferred and therefore performed; the numbers preceding each work refer to minutes of duration: 2, "Now is the month of Maying," by Morley; 5½, "Ave Maria" (Josquin), 2½, "Adieu, sweet Amarillis" (Wilbye); 2, "Il est bel et bon (Passereau); 4¼, "Nightingale" (by Philips, a translation of Petrarch's *Quel rossignol,* from Morley's selected Italian *Madrigals,* 1598). These works represent a program of 16¼ minutes. To the list Barber appended additional selections: 4, "era l'anima mia"; 6, Elegy; making the program 26¼ minutes. Apparently if time permitted, he planned to add *A Stopwatch and an Ordnance Map,* which he estimated at a duration of 8 minutes.

to make you stick out your tongue in envy. The artistic world seems to be yawning in sheer boredom, even much of the spirit of adventure is gone. There are no more "enfants terribles" even, if there were they would inspire only a sallow smile. (A concert manager actually told me that he *adds* two years to the age of any child prodigy, instead of subtracting two, as in the good old days! This is of great significance.) In other words, *vecchia amica,* we are becoming serious and dull, and for several months I have been surveying life with scorn and taciturnity. My Miltonic humor has brought me to West Chester, Pa. for a fortnight from whence I have been roaming the Chester hills with my cocker spaniel dog Sandro. I have an idea I am a rather romantic figure as I crash through the underbrush of the fields, holding Sandro sternly on the leash, now and then issuing bitter commands to that unheeding cur, but here again it is wasted effort, as there is absolutely no-one to admire me. Not one, mind you! This could not conceivably happen in Italy, you can only *try* to imagine my stormy soul. Ahem. [here Barber marks an asterisk with a footnote "Questo à Yeats."]. . .

The only amusing thing has been my chorus, started last month. . . . At first I was frightened of them and came into the first rehearsal with trembling hands. Until I saw that they were afraid of me and that the accompanist's hands were trembling; so this put me in a splendid humour and pleased me immensely. Now I have them in *my* hands, and in case my hands betray me and I beat wrong, have learned the right tone of gentle arrogance with which to blame it on them. I am told—*uniche conquiste dell'inverno*—that most of the 1st and 2nd sopranos are overfond of me: but could you see their pinched and stupid faces out of which such lovely voices issue, you would realize that, alas, the fruits of these barren and futile amours can be only musical. (This sounds terribly conceited, but I have a rehearsal today at 4 P.M. and am trying to encourage myself: as you see I am still rather scared of them.) For sake of record, and because you have a serious and musical husband named Lele d. (and show alarming signs of growing serious yourself, God forbid!) I shall tell you, that we are singing:

Monteverdi: 1. Lasciatemi morire, con sei archi sordina; 2. Hor che'l ciel e la terra, con 2 violini e cembalo (scritto così) *bellissimo;* 3. Amor: lamento della ninfa, soprano and chorus of men's voices commenting, cembalo, violoncello, and contra b.

Pièces de resistance: 4. A un giro sol a cappella, and 5. Si, ch'io vorrei morire.

di Lasso: Echo song (2 cori);

Ravel: Trois beaux oiseaux de Paradis (carino);

Haydn: Armonia nel matrimonio, Eloquence, divertente;

Barber: Virgin Martyrs (women's voices), and Mary Hynes (full chorus, a capp).*

*Letter, March 1939. The program was broadcast on 17 April 1939 and again on 1 May, when Morley's "Now is the month of Maying" was substituted for "Mary Hynes."

Between 1936 and 1940 Barber composed five contemporary madrigals on poems from *Reincarnations,* James Stephens's collection based on verses of earlier Irish poets David O'Bruadair, Egan O'Rahilly, and Antoine O'Reachtaire (c. 1784–1835), better known as Raftery. Three of Barber's pieces—"Mary Hynes," "The Coolin," and "Anthony O'Daly"—were published in 1942 by G. Schirmer as *Reincarnations,* Op. 16. Dated holograph scores indicate that "Mary Hynes," the first of the cycle, was composed by Barber during the summer of 1937 (completed 8 August) in St. Wolfgang, Austria; and "Anthony O'Daly" and "The Coolin" were completed 17 December and 10 November 1940, respectively. These last two, although specifically composed for the Curtis Madrigal Chorus, were probably begun several years earlier, for fragments of their themes appear in Barber's student sketchbook from the 1930s (p. 63, verso) in between sketches of the first and second movements of his string quartet (completed in September 1936) and material from the *First Essay* and the Violin Concerto (completed in 1939). The location of these sketches suggests that, in anticipation of conducting the chorus, he probably began composing for the group before he officially assumed duties as conductor.

As mentioned earlier, the poetry of Stephens (1882–1950) was used by Sidney Homer and had long held attraction for Barber, bearing fruit in his earliest published songs ("The Daisies," 1927, and "Bessie Bobtail," 1934). In contrast to the earlier texts, however, most of the verses in *Reincarnations* are lyrical love poems celebrating female beauty. According to Patricia McFate, as late as the seventeenth century Irish bards complied with strict metrical rules for writing poetry, and the Stephens verses, while metrically more experimental, still follow the Gaelic poetic tradition of richness in description, wit, moods of exuberance and melancholy, and "lyricism which suggests music in words."[39] These are qualities that would hold special appeal for Barber.

The title *Reincarnations* alludes to Stephens's technique of writing new forms of the original works. Although the poet could speak Gaelic, he was not fluent enough to read the language without the aid of a dictionary and often needed to rely on the expertise of friends and acquaintances. He read "The Cooleen or, Coolun" in *Love Songs of Connacht,* a translation by his friend Douglas Hyde, who was a scholar of Gaelic literature and the author of *Songs Ascribed to Raftery,* which also includes "Mary Hynes" and "Anthony O'Daly."*

At least one chorister's recollection suggests that his disdainful attitude toward the chorus was not disguised, nor did it endear him to the group; in addition to recalling the high E's in "Anthony O'Daly," Muriel Robertson remembers the young conductor as "petulant" (telephone interview with the author, 30 October 1986). On the other hand, Katherine Harris van Hogendorp recalls "the inspiration Barber created in his classes," portraying the young conductor as "serious and very demanding of excellence" (letter to the author, 26 November 1986).

*Stephens—confessing his poetic techniques might have better been labeled "Loot or Plunder"—wrote that his "re-created" verses often "owe no more than a phrase, a line, half

Although the G. Schirmer edition (1942) cites Barber's source as Stephens's *Collected Poems* (New York: Macmillan, 1926), the spelling of the title on a holograph score—"The Coolun"—strongly suggests that he first read the poem in Stephens's 1918 edition of *Reincarnations* (both Stephens's *Collected Poems* and the Schirmer score read "The Coolin"). There is no evidence that Barber had read Hyde's translation, which also uses the earlier spelling.* The 1918 edition is further substantiated as Barber's source by the fact that in it the poems appear as a unit and chronologically, whereas in the *Collected Poems* they are regrouped in "subject sequence" with individual poems interspersed throughout Books II and IV of the collection. Therefore, a person unfamiliar with the 1918 edition would gain no clue from Stephens's preface to the *Collected Poems* about which poems were published earlier under the title *Reincarnations*.

Barber's settings show "a distinct and happy influence of the freedom of the Monteverdian madrigals."[40] "Mary Hynes," described by Stephens himself as "a poem to lift a man's heart,"[41] is based on Hyde's transcription of Raftery's six-verse song. Called "Posy Bright," the legendary Mary Hynes was reportedly the "handsomest maiden . . . born for a hundred years in the West of Ireland."[42] Stephens's verses are a distillation of Hyde's translations and contain perhaps no more than six allusions to actual phrases in Raftery's original poem. Barber fulfills the exuberant spirit of the Stephens verses through rapid parlando rhythms that trip easily off the tongue in a Parisian madrigal style that is infused nevertheless with sweeping lyrical gesture; the occasional longer note values on the word *she* (see Example 7.3a: *She—is the sky of the sun. . . . She—is a rune* [literally "secret," used here as "sweetheart"]) fasten attention on the magnetism of the song's vibrant subject; in contrast, the setting of *lovely and airy the view from the hill* projects tenderness (Example 7.3b).

The second song in the set, "Anthony O'Daly," is based on the true story of a captain of the rebel Whiteboys,† who was unfairly condemned and sentenced to hanging but went submissively and heroically to his death without betraying the other rebels.[43] Raftery's song, Hyde's translation, and Stephens's poem focus metaphorically on the martyr as a tree: Stephens's lines begin "Since your limbs were laid out. . ." and continue with "Not a tree have a leaf!" Barber's musical setting, while using the same words, places more emphasis on the finality of O'Daly's death; this is accomplished by a chilling, dirgelike setting, which is heightened by a pedal on E, beginning with bass voices intoning forty-one measures of

a line, to the Irish, and around these scraps I have blown a bubble of verse and made my poem" (*Reincarnations* [New York: Macmillan, 1918], p. 71).

*The choral director and scholar Ron Jeffers suspects that Barber knew the prose of Douglas Hyde, which is even more infused with "ecstatic lyricism" than Stephens's verses and to which Barber's setting of "Mary Hynes" seems closer in spirit.

†A secret agrarian peasant organization, active in Ireland during the early 1760s, whose members wore white shirts of recognition on their night raids on the property of landlords in redressing grievances and in protest of tithes.

a.

Example 7.3 "Mary Hynes," Op. 16, No. 1. *a.* Mm. 1–9. *b.* Mm. 34–45.

b.

"Anthony, Anthony" over and over again in an irregular, dragging rhythmic pattern. Transferred to sopranos, the pedal unrelentingly increases tension amid a stretto of overlapping phrases, each part now rhythmically independent. The archaic sound of open-fifths closes the piece. Robert Horan found this work, with *A Stopwatch and an Ordnance Map,* "unique in its cumulative and elegiac desperation."[44]

Of the three Stephens poems Barber used in his *Reincarnations,* the third, "The Coolin," is the only one in regular stanzaic form.* There are many versions of the Connacht song about "the Cooleen" or "Coolun," literally the *Cúl Fhionn,* or *fair-haired cool;*† indeed, Hyde professes "there is no song in Erin more famous than the Cooleen."[45] Barber's setting is tenderly lyrical, mimicking the gentle, lilting rhythm of Stephens's poetry.

* Stephens confesses that for the "Coolun" he "pinched from Raftery, that is, I hooked one line out of the decent man's Irish, and I played on that line the way Pan plays on his pipes, only better" (letter to James Quinn, in *The Letters of James Stephens,* pp. 223–24).

† The curl at the nape of a young woman's neck, which came to be the term for one's sweetheart.

A holograph score of this work at the Curtis Institute of Music is marked "24 copies," an indication of the choral forces Barber used for performance by the Madrigal Chorus. Two holograph versions at the Library of Congress show that Barber reworked measures 14–20 to achieve a more even distribution of voices and denser texture (Example 7.4).*

At the Library of Congress are holograph sketches showing that Barber intended to set two other poems from *Reincarnations*. One, "Peggy Mitchell" ("fair after fair . . . sweet after sweet . . . she is our torment without end"), exists as a partially finished sketch for four-voice mixed chorus. Voices are grouped in pairs (SA and TB) with imitative entrances in sprightly rhythms. Although the holograph is undated, the brand of music paper (Alberto de Santis, Rome) is the same as that Barber used when he was in residence at the American Academy, suggesting that it was probably written in Salzburg in the summer of 1936 during the same time he worked on his string quartet and "Let down the bars, O Death." Further substantiation of this date is a setting of "Mary Ruane," another of Stephens's *Reincarnations* (beginning "The sky-like girl that we knew"), on the verso side of the sketch of "Let down the bars, O Death."

A Stopwatch and an Ordnance Map, Op. 15

"A Stopwatch and an Ordnance Map," Stephen Spender's poem about the death of a soldier in the Spanish Civil War, was written in 1939, shortly before the poet was introduced to Barber in London. In a gesture of friendship Spender gave the poem to Barber in June 1939;† six months later, on 28 January 1940, the composer completed a setting of the poem for male chorus and three kettledrums.[46] *Stopwatch* was sung for the first time by a chorus of twenty-two men from the Curtis Institute Madrigal Chorus on 23 April 1940 at one of the institute's Historical Series concerts.‡ The following evening it was aired over CBS radio. At both performances David Stephens was the timpanist and Barber conducted.§

In November 1942 Barber wrote to Katherine Chapin Biddle about an expected performance of *A Stopwatch and an Ordnance Map* by the Army

*The later version matches a second holograph at the Sibley Library, Eastman School of Music, which is the score from which the Schirmer edition was made.

†In 1955, when it was published in his *Collected Poems, 1928–53* (Random House), Spender added a dedication to Barber (letter from Spender to the author, 29 November 1983).

‡*Overtones*, April 1940, p. 58, states that the seventh concert—featuring contemporary American composers—was of "exceeding interest" to the institute because of Barber's new madrigal and Randall Thompson's *Americana*.

§Although the work was listed on an earlier program (19 February 1940), the fact that the title is crossed out suggests it was rescheduled for the later date. A program of the April 23rd broadcast indicates "first performance." These programs are at the Curtis Institute of Music Library.

a.

b.

Example 7.4 "The Coolin," Op. 16, No. 3, mm. 14–20, holographs, 1940. *(Library of Congress) a.* Early version. *b.* Final version.

Music School Choir in Washington, with plans for repeating it at the National Gallery of Art on 13 December.[47] Apparently the concerts were postponed until 21 February 1943 when William Strickland directed the mixed choir of seventy-five voices in a performance in the east garden of the National Gallery. A review by Glenn Dillard Gunn called the piece "the most important native work offered on the program":

> This is a strange and moving echo from the Spanish Civil War in which kettle drums provide the major support for the chorus. The effect is grimly dramatic. It is sinister music, with a threat of disaster in every measure; but like most of Barber's works, it is also a fine page of choral technique that is modern, original, and expert.*

As much as he would have liked to attend the concert, Barber, then serving in the United States Army, could not be there because he had been assigned "non-transferable guard duty" and was required to remain on base in New York from 1 to 8 A.M.† A rehearsal at Fort Meyers, Virginia, a few days before the performance, was heard, however, by Nadia Boulanger; she was "profondément émue" by *Stopwatch*. It was "very well sung," she told him later, and made a "grande impression."‡ Barber, too, was "deeply impressed" when he heard a recording of Strickland's performance, even though it had been sung to a piano accompaniment because a truck could not be obtained to transport the timpani to the studio. The composer wrote to Strickland:

> I had no idea you could make an Army chorus sing like that. In fact, we were all surprised. I played it at Schirmers one day for Engel, B. [William] Schuman, etc., and there were nothing but compliments for you. It is such a shame that you couldn't get drums for the recording—that, naturally, is my only reservation. In the future, also, I would try to find any solo voice that could sing the tenor solo in falsetto (even a baritone could do it falsetto), as the Waacs don't quite give the same effect. Sex rears its ugly head here!§

* *Washington Times Herald,* 22 February 1943. The newspaper account incorrectly reports that the "gifted choirmaster" Strickland led a chorus of "seventy-five men." In an interview with the author (31 July 1986) Strickland recalled, however, that he used female voices (WAACs) also; this is also corroborated by Barber's letter to Strickland after the concert (see below) and a recording of the performance.

† Letter, Barber to Strickland, 18 February 1943. Unless otherwise indicated, this letter and all other correspondence between Barber and Strickland quoted here are in Strickland's private collection. On the same Sunday as the concert, Barber also had a crucial appointment (arranged by Walter Damrosch) with General Terry that resulted in a commission for his Second Symphony.

‡ The date of the concert coincided with the twentieth anniversary of the death of Boulanger's sister, Lili, in whose honor the choir sang her Psalm XXIV, "a Gaelic parallel to this brilliant example of contemporary art . . . splendid and strong" (Glenn Dillard Gunn, *Washington Times Herald,* 22 February 1943). Boulanger's comments on Barber's work are reported in a letter the composer wrote to Strickland, ca. March 1943.

§ Letter, spring 1943. Because Barber held Strickland's choral conducting in high esteem,

A Stopwatch and an Ordnance Map, like other madrigals composed by Barber during the late thirties and early forties, contains a mixture of homophony and imitative counterpoint. The form of the poem—organized into three seven-line stanzas, each beginning with the refrain "A stopwatch and an ordnance map" and ending with "All under the olive trees"—determined the form of Barber's setting: he used a double refrain—a motto starts each verse and a second refrain concludes it.

Stopwatch presents technical challenges to performance:* aside from the fact that it may be impractical to gather the required instrumental forces, intonation in particular is complicated by the juxtaposition of voices against numerous glissandi played by the timpani, which are, in any case, almost no help in obtaining or maintaining pitch. Various solutions have been attempted: Stokowski, for example, wanted to play it on NBC radio using brass instruments to support the chorus, and although Barber told Strickland that "with a good chorus and conductor like you and yours, that isn't necessary,"[48] reportedly he had difficulties himself in preparing the Curtis Madrigal Chorus for the studio recording used for the radio broadcast in 1940 and resorted to adding bassoons to support the vocal lines. Alfred Mann, who sang in the chorus then, remembered that the practice was "deemed a subterfuge to be handled with some discretion. But voices and instruments blended well indeed." During the rehearsal, Barber called to Scalero and Menotti, who were sitting in the back of the auditorium, "Si sentono troppo i fagotti?" (Are the bassoons too loud?); Mann recalled, "the maestro shook his head, then nodded approvingly."[49]

G. Schirmer's 1942 edition of *A Stopwatch and an Ordnance Map* recommends "the Kettledrums may be doubled by a Piano in octaves . . . if and where necessary to support the chorus."[50] But several years later, apparently with Stokowski's suggestion in mind, Barber made an arrangement for male chorus and timpani, plus four horns, three trombones, and tuba ad lib. A manuscript in the Library of Congress informs us how the composer constructed the new version: the original printed score was cut and mounted line by line on larger score paper, above which—in pencil and ink—Barber wrote new music for horns, trombones, and tuba.

---

he planned to write other pieces for him, in particular a setting of lines from the *Bacchae.* The notable scholar and translator of classical literature Edith Hamilton gave Barber a translation of the very lines from the *Bacchae* Strickland had marked for possible setting. "I had told her to take anything from any tragedy, and it is curious that she selected those," Barber wrote to his friend; "someday I shall compose them." The lines, eventually set for chorus by Sir Granville Bantock on Gilbert Murray's translation, begin: "Oh, feet of a fawn to the greenwood fled, alone in the grass and the loveliness" (Strickland, letter to the author, 12 April 1988).

*Even so, the work was performed quite often in the forties, probably because of the timeliness of its subject. Although he hoped Koussevitzky would perform *Stopwatch* at Tanglewood, summer 1942, and recommended it as "appropriate to the times" (letter from Barber to Serge Koussevitzky, 20 March 1942), apparently the conductor chose not to include it that season.

The new version of *Stopwatch* was performed for the first time by the Collegiate Chorale under the direction of Robert Shaw on 17 December 1945.* Barber wrote to Homer about it:

> Tonight Robert Shaw's Collegiate Chorus—a very inspiring young chorus who sings with Toscanini—are singing my "Stopwatch" chorus in Carnegie Hall, with brass and drums from the Philharmonic, and that will be fun to hear.[51]

It is puzzling, however, that a review of the performance makes no mention at all of brass instrumental accompaniment:

> Mr. Barber has made a notable contribution to choral literature with this masterly setting of Stephen Spender's poem. Here is an opus most knowingly devised for the voices, expertly constructed and profoundly moving. Music so sincerely and deeply felt is extremely uncommon today and it possessed such appeal that its success was immediate and unequivocal.
>
> In the unusually expressive and convincing creation, Mr. Barber showed a fertile imagination in regard to vocal sonorities and in the treatment of the solo timpani accompaniment, which was so perfectly adjusted to the voice parts that it provided a completely satisfying support, adding greatly to the impressiveness of the work as a whole.[52]

*The G. Schirmer 1954 edition of this version incorrectly notes that it was performed for the first time on 16 December 1945.

8

PRELUDE TO WAR

To me all great music is a protest against artificiality

Concerto for Violin and Orchestra, Op. 14 (1939)

The Concerto for Violin, Barber's first major commission,* was sponsored by Samuel Fels, manufacturer of Fels Naptha soap and a member of the board of trustees of the Curtis Institute of Music.† The concerto was commissioned for Iso Briselli, a child prodigy and the adopted son of Fels.‡

Composer and patron were brought together by Gama Gilbert, violinist turned music critic, who, because of his enthusiasm for Barber's music and their longstanding friendship, was a natural catalyst for the commission. Like Briselli, Gilbert had been a student of Carl Flesch at the institute. After graduating from Curtis, he encountered Briselli again in New York, where they simultaneously pursued careers in music. Both frequently

*The Suite for Carillon, commissioned earlier by Edward Bok, had been a student project; two works commissioned by major orchestras had remained unfulfilled—one, offered by Eugene Ormandy, for a symphonic work to be performed in 1938 by the Philadelphia Orchestra and a second work, requested by the New York Philharmonic Symphony Society, for performance in 1938 under the direction of John Barbirolli (*Overtones*, May 1937, p. 66). From 1939 on, Barber was almost never without a commission; according to Virgil Thomson in 1961, only five "standard composers in America [could] live on their take from commissions and performances" (*The State of Music*, 1939; second edition, revised [New York: Random House, 1962], p. 9).

†His wife, Jennie Fels, was a friend of Cyrus Curtis. With Curtis's encouragement, she arranged for Mary Louise Curtis to become active in the Settlement Music School in Philadelphia, initiating the young woman's involvement with musical philanthropy (*Overtones*, 1 October 1974).

‡Born in Odessa, Briselli came to the United States when he was twelve as the youngest student of the celebrated violin teacher Carl Flesch, who had contracted with Mary Curtis Bok to join the faculty of the Curtis Institute of Music from its charter year (1924) to 1929. Samuel Fels, childless, became Briselli's patron and surrogate father, eventually legally adopting him and making him heir to his estate (Iso Briselli, interview with the author, 20 April 1982, Philadelphia).

sat with Barber at concerts. During this time Barber and Menotti lived in a rented apartment on the top floor of a house at 8 East 79th Street—dubbed by them "the Water Tank."

In the early spring of 1939, Fels, at Gilbert's suggestion, offered Barber $1,000 to write a violin concerto for Briselli. The commission provided for $500 to be given to the composer in advance, the balance to be paid upon completion of the concerto.*

Barber began work on the concerto during the summer of 1939 in Sils-Maria, Switzerland.† It progressed slowly, but by the end of the summer he sent two movements to Briselli, who was reported to have appraised them as "too simple and not brilliant enough for a concerto."[1] Planning to provide a finale with "ample opportunity to display the artist's technical powers," Barber continued work on the concerto in Paris with the expectation of completing the last movement there during the fall.[2] His plans were interrupted, however, when at the end of August all Americans were warned to leave Europe because of the impending invasion of Poland by the Nazis.

Barber took the night train to Paris and stayed at the Hotel Pont-Royal. His cable to his parents (August 1939) reads, "Both sailing Brittanic September first . . . not worried." But, in fact, at the last minute the sailing was canceled; as many foreigners attempted frantically to leave Europe, pandemonium was the norm. With the aid of Rudolf Schirmer and his mother, whom Barber met quite by chance while waiting on line for a Dutch boat, he was able to obtain reservations on the *Champlain*, which sailed the next morning. These notes were jotted down by Barber at the time of the hasty departure:

> increasing war anxiety . . . giving up fall in Paris. Closing frontiers of neutral countries dangerous for G.C., phone call about German-Russian pact—difficulty with French visa for G.C., Americans warned to leave Paris. Black nights, Panthéon by moonlight. Surprise of Rudi, Ann, Rose, Navarro, Barbirolli, on board. Black nights. . . .

When Barber returned home, he brought with him a partially composed finale. After spending a few days with his family, he worked on the "concertino"—as he referred to the concerto—for three and a half weeks in the

*Broder (*Samuel Barber*, p. 34) writes that Barber began the concerto during summer 1939. Briselli, however, reports the arrangements were made earlier (interview with author, 21 April 1982).

†His notes—jotted on the reverse side of a cable sent from Paris, August 1939—inform us about some of the highlights of his trip: "Tea with Erika Mann—to Lucerne, Toscanini and Busch in Beethoven, substituting for Walter, dinner afterwards at Zum Wilden Manor with Tos., Busch, Serkin, and Molinaris—Wagner's granddaughter—until 3:30 A.M., breakfast with Chotzinoff." Busch's performance was remembered by Barber many years later as "the most beautiful performance of the Beethoven Concerto" (letter to Irene Serkin, 1 September 1952).

Poconos, until called back to West Chester because his father had taken ill.*

Even before it was finished, the third movement was a subject of controversy that placed the commission in jeopardy. Broder's account is probably the version Barber presented to his publisher:

> When the movement was submitted, the violinist declared it too difficult. The sponsor demanded his money back, and Barber, who had already spent it in Europe, called in another violinist . . . who performed the work for the merchant and his protege, to prove that the finale was not unplayable.[3]

It seems unlikely that Briselli would in fact have found the work too difficult to play, for he was, by all accounts, an accomplished violinist who had played much of the challenging nineteenth-century repertoire.† Many years later, Briselli offered another explanation in which he professes that although he believed the first two movements of the concerto were beautiful and eagerly awaited the finale, he was disappointed with the third movement as "too lightweight" compared to the rest of the concerto. He suggested that the middle section be expanded to develop the movement into a sonata–rondo form, but Barber would not consider it.[4]

In order to convince Fels that the concerto could be played, Herbert Baumel, a student of Léa Luboshutz, was recruited for a demonstration. One afternoon during the autumn of 1939, while Baumel was sitting in the commons room of the Curtis Institute of Music, Ralph Berkowitz walked into the room and handed him a pencil manuscript of a violin part without telling him the name of the composer. He was told only that he had two hours in which to learn the music, that the "piece should be played very fast," and to return "dressed up" and ready to play before a few people.‡ The private performance took place in the studio of Josef Hofmann, where the tension and solemnity of the occasion, as recalled by Baumel, suggested much was at stake for Barber besides the financial aspects of the commission. Mary Bok, Edith Braun, and Menotti were present; Ralph Berkowitz accompanied Baumel, who produced dazzling evidence that the concerto was indeed playable at any tempo. There were "bravos" and the ritualistic tea and cookies. The verdict was that Barber was to be paid the full com-

*Barber's notes on cable, August 1939: "To W. C. for a few days, then to Pocono with Alonzo Jones to work on concertino for Briselli—from September 11–Oct 5. While Mrs. Bok and Braun were visiting us Dad taken sick. Rush to W. Chester."

†For his debuts in New York and Philadelphia he played Paganini's Violin Concerto No. 2 and Beethoven's Violin Concerto. His concert repertoire included virtuoso works by such composers as Tartini, Sarasate, Wieniawski, and Ysaÿe. Reviews of Briselli's concerts praise his immaculate, facile technique, poetic expressiveness, and rich tone (concert programs and press review, Briselli clipping file, New York Public Library, Music Division).

‡Herbert Baumel, interview with the author, 18 May 1984, New York. Broder (*Samuel Barber*, p. 35) incorrectly reports Oscar Shumsky as the violinist who rescued the commission.

Example 8.1 Violin Concerto, third movement, mm. 85–94, solo violin, photograph of holograph, 1939. *(Personal collection of Herbert Baumel)*

mission and Briselli had to relinquish his right to the first performance of the work.* The trial was based on a performance of the incomplete third movement through rehearsal no. 6, ending abruptly at measure 94 (see Example 8.1, a facsimile of the holograph from which Baumel played).

While Barber continued work on the concerto, other projects also drew his attention. In January 1940 he had written enthusiastically to his uncle about a WPA-sponsored performance of his music and received much encouragement. The idea sounded "divine," Homer said, "no manager, no pull, no press." His letter to Barber presents a point of view that was prevalent then:

> Your description of the audience was great, I know these people, hungry for anything that will do them artistic good; used to being barred out of anything that costs money. We have done everything we could to put music beyond their reach, not only to one percent. When all people demand it they'll get it, just as they got cathedrals, art galleries, pure water and cheap subways. The music will *count!* You may see the day and had better prepare some music on big lines just in case.†

Even after completing the violin concerto, Barber still had reservations about the technical feasibility of the final movement. There were several trial runs prior to rehearsals for the premiere by the Philadelphia Orchestra. Baumel played the concerto with the Curtis Institute Orchestra under

*Baumel, interview with the author, 18 May 1984. After the incident, Barber referred to the work as *concerto del sapone* (Letter to Katherine Garrison Chapin Biddle, 20 September 1940; all letters from Barber to Biddle cited in this book are in the Francis and Katherine Biddle Papers, Special Collections Division, Georgetown University Library).

†Letter to Barber, 15 January 1940. But what Homer had in mind for a new work was "another dramatic overture." "I am struck by the need for Coriolan, Egmont, etc.," he wrote. "There is no doubt the drama is a universal instinct. Life is drama; we are fed on drama from the moment we are born."

the direction of Fritz Reiner.* He recalls that Barber was especially concerned about rhythmic execution—that long-note values be played with precision and dotted half notes held for their entire duration.

Early in March 1940, Oscar Shumsky, learning that Barber was anxious to have some comments and reactions to the concerto, consented to sight-read the piece from manuscript. The reading, with Barber at the piano, took place in New York at the home of Gama Gilbert six months prior to his death.[5] Shumsky "read from the piano part, peering over Barber's shoulder. All seemed pleased with the result, especially Barber, who was generous with compliments."[6]

In August 1940 Barber visited Albert Spalding in Stockbridge, Massachusetts, with the intention of showing him the violin concerto. He had heard that the celebrated violinist was eager to find an American work that he liked and could play on his concert tours. Spalding "took [the concerto] on the spot."†

Announcement of the forthcoming premiere as Barber's first effort in this form appeared in the *New York Times* two months prior to the performance.[7] The concerto was played in Philadelphia at the Academy of Music at Friday afternoon and Saturday evening subscription concerts on 7 and 8 February 1941.‡ The following notes were provided by Barber for the program:

> The Concerto for Violin and Orchestra was completed in July, 1940, at Pocono Lake Preserve, Pennsylvania, and is Mr. Barber's most recent work for orchestra. It is lyric and rather intimate in character and a moderate-sized orchestra is used: eight woodwinds, two horns, two trumpets, percussion, piano and strings.
>
> The first movement—allegro molto moderato—begins with a lyrical first subject announced at once by the solo violin, without any orchestral introduction. This movement as a whole has perhaps more the character of a sonata than concerto form. The second movement—andante sostenuto—is introduced by an extended oboe solo. The violin enters with a contrasting and rhapsodic theme, after which it repeats the oboe melody of the begin-

* Even though he would not be the one to give the first performance, he was invited to stand in at rehearsals with Ormandy and the Philadelphia Orchestra. This opportunity, which Barber arranged for him, led to Baumel's appointment to the orchestra after he graduated from Curtis Institute (Baumel, interview with the author, 18 May 1984).

† Letter, Barber to William Strickland, 14 August 1940. In this letter Barber expressed concern about Spalding's presenting the concerto to its advantage: "He's no Heifetz," he wrote, "but we shall see."

‡ Program, Philadelphia Orchestra, 7 and 8 February 1941. Barber's concerto was next to last on the program. Other works included the *Academic Festival Overture* by Brahms, the Violin Concerto in D major by Mozart, *La Mer* by Debussy, and "Dance of the Seven Veils" from *Salome* by Strauss. Other performances followed in New York (11 February), Boston, and Washington, D.C. (Arthur Bronson, "Spalding in Concerto by Barber," *Philadelphia Record*, 8 February 1941, p. 11). On a keepsake program belonging to Katharine Homer Fryer is written, "This is a most exquisite composition, but it takes a man of refinement like Spalding to play it."

ning. The last movement, a perpetual motion, exploits the more brilliant and virtuoso characteristics of the violin.[8]

Newspaper accounts report that the concerto scored an "exceptional popular success" with a "storm of applause showered on both soloist and composer."[9] Philadelphia critics concurred that Spalding's performance on his 1755 Guarnerius was brilliant and sympathetic, and they gave recognition to Barber's strength in composing with "unfaltering facility" a concerto "refreshingly free from arbitrary tricks and musical mannerisms," a work in which "straight-forwardness and sincerity are among its most engaging qualities." The conservative critic Henry Pleasants, who considered Barber one of the "ablest of what might be called the right wing of American composers," faulted the concerto on the texture of the orchestration as "insufficiently contrasted" to the violin tone; he viewed Barber's aesthetic as a nineteenth-century one, in which the solo instrument is "an integral part of the whole."[10] About the last movement, opinion was divided, one critic finding it "most effective,"[11] another, "thin and not too brilliantly orchestrated . . . the only weak movement."[12]

Those who would criticize the imbalance between movements often fail to take into account that the vitality of Barber's violin concerto lies in the spare but poignant lyricism of its first movement and the poetry of the second movement, those very qualities that are intrinsic to Barber's strength as a composer. Though predominantly diatonic music, more stringent harmonies are introduced to heighten expressiveness or dramatic tension. Virgil Thomson, in writing about the New York premiere (11 February 1941), viewed the motivating forces behind the Romantic characteristics of Barber's style in the tradition of nineteenth-century American music. He wrote that, although the concerto "cannot fail to charm by its gracious lyrical plenitude and its complete absence of tawdry swank . . . the only reason Barber gets away with elementary musical methods is that his heart is pure." He continued:

> Barber cannot legitimately be considered a neo-Romantic composer, as that term has been understood to represent the dominant Parisian school of the past ten years. . . . His abstention from ostentatious dissonance and his cult of the poetic are based on no . . . penetrative esthetic reflection. . . . He is simply an academic. . . . Not the storming, dissonance-mongering, fancily orchestrating academic we have been used to for some years . . . but the gentle sweet-singing sort . . . we used to have in Edward MacDowell and the brothers Nevin.[13]

Homer responded to reviews Barber had sent him with an impassioned letter:

> You are the only one in my narrow life with whom I see eye to eye. . . . I have the notices of the concerts and I like the line in the "Telegram": "a

sense of drama inheres in the unfolding scheme." That's what I feel in all your music, a sense of drama.

There is so much to music! It is building up an influence which no one can measure. To me all great music is a protest (a revolution) against all the artificiality which surrounds it. When greatness bursts its fetters, then the world sees something! It may look like a cataclysm, but it may be a destruction of a hypocrisy which binds creativeness and stifles the honest voice.

. . . I, myself, look at your press notices differently. To me they are tributes to your importance. The more they analyze and quibble and docket and define, the more I see recognition, mystery, and bafflement. You will always keep them guessing, because you write that kind of music. You really have no right to expect anything but good and bad guesses: it is the price you pay! Others have paid it too.[14]

The Violin Concerto is clearly tonal music, with major-minor elements integrated into the harmonic support. Cadences are often on octaves or chords with missing thirds, lending a modal character to the music; and swings between major and minor are, in general, a feature of the concerto—the first movement is in G major–G minor, for example. The aria-like second movement (in C♯ minor, E minor, and E major) turns from a tender narrative style—a *legende*—to passages suggestive of a lament, a recitative of widely spaced, drooping intervals (ninths, tenths, and elevenths).

The controversial perpetual-motion third movement has a rondo theme that rarely returns verbatim, more often digressing into virtuosic excursions. This is one of the few virtually nonstop concerto movements in the violin literature (the solo instrument plays for 110 measures without interruption). The rondo theme, played by the violin at so breathless a tempo it almost resembles a technical etude, is supported merely by terse orchestral chords. The movement abruptly climaxes in the penultimate measure with two simultaneously sounded arpeggiated seventh-chords built on E♭ and F. This polychordal cadence seems to foreshadow Barber's tendency toward bolder, dissonant harmonies, which increasingly mark his works throughout the following decade (beginning with Symphony No. 2 and *Medea,* for example, and reaching a peak with the Piano Sonata). Robert Horan remarked astutely about this movement, "Critics, in general, have naively labelled the last movement as 'more modern,' disassociating it in design from the rest of the work and failing to apprehend the fact that the dissonance involved is merely more necessary."[15]

The Mozartian purity of the opening theme spun out in the first movement—leading one critic to observe that there was "no violent wrench of mood between Barber's concerto and Mozart's"[16]—is no accident, for it was carefully wrought from the embryo version that appears in Barber's sketchbook (see Example 8.2). This fragment, in pencil, is most likely Bar-

a.

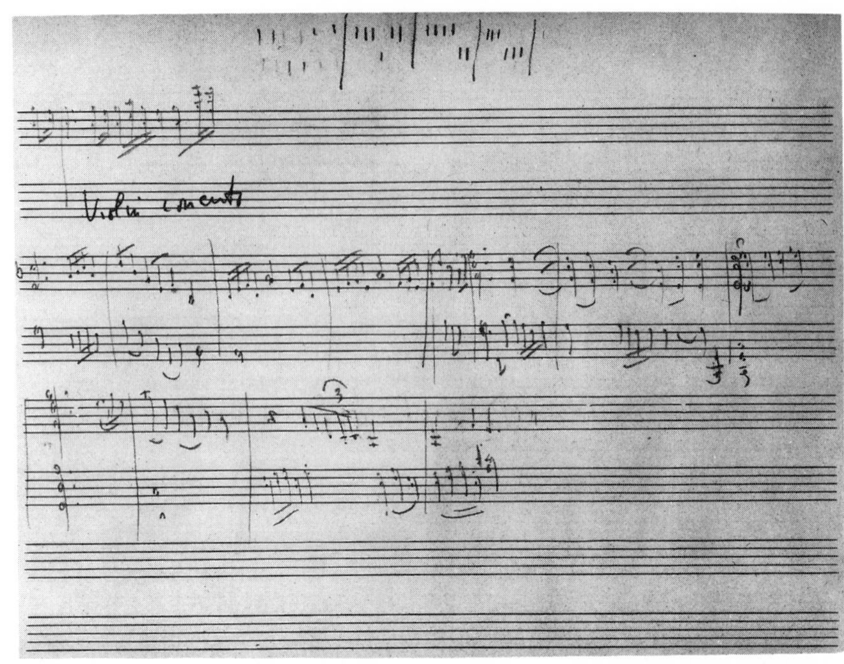

b.

Concerto for Violin and Orchestra

Example 8.2 Violin Concerto, first movement, solo violin, mm. 1–9. *a.* Barber's sketchbook from 1930s, page 55 verso. *(Library of Congress) b.* Final version (G. Schirmer, 1949).

ber's earliest conception of the theme. It appears in F major rather than in its final version of G major, a key more sympathetic to the violin (because it is brighter in sound). Later manuscripts and published editions reflect that subtle alterations were made to the melodic line: in the holograph, for example, the sixteenth-note figure in the first measure begins on the lower third rather than the lower neighbor as in the published score. Barber adds an ornamental turn that more gracefully fills in the space between the first note and its upper neighbor in measure 2, replacing the ascending fourth with a conjunct motion. It is questionable whether the rhythmic notation on the last beat of measure 4 in the sketch is an error or intentional: why three eighth notes in measure 3 and three sixteenth notes for the triplet in measure 4? Barber was usually meticulous about rhythmic notation; therefore, changes appearing in the later version—in manuscripts and published scores—suggest that he wanted to achieve greater regularity in rhythm as well as in melodic contour.

Barber's concerto is likely to be chosen by a performer who wishes to display the idiomatic lyrical attributes of the violin rather than to dazzle his audience with virtuoso brilliance. For, despite the frantic pace of the last movement and some double stops that were added to the second movement in the revised version (mm. 79–80), there are no major technical challenges or innovations that an experienced violinist would find difficult to execute.* Even the conventional virtuoso cadenza is absent from the first and last movements; Barber was reported to have had an aversion to cadenzas in concertos.† Thus the unaccompanied passages in the first movement at measure 181 and at the end of the second movement are more akin to vocal ornamentations than bona fide cadenzas. The addition of a cadenza in the revision seems less a compromise with convention than an effort to accomplish a "satisfactory climax" and a gracefully balanced descent from the apex to the conclusion of the movement.[17]

Barber himself considered the weaknesses of the concerto to be "an unsatisfactory climax in the adagio and some muddy orchestration in the finale."[18] This led him in November 1948 to make some revisions ("at long last") in anticipation of a forthcoming performance of the concerto by Ruth Posselt with the Boston Symphony Orchestra (6 January 1949). The revisions were also the prelude to a new edition. In a pattern he was to continue throughout his career when he wished to offset a period of sparse creativity, Barber turned his attention to the details of preparing parts, correcting proofs, and revising. In late winter 1949 he told Sidney

*This evaluation is based on a consensus of such violin teachers and performers as Margaret Pardee, Herbert Baumel, Oscar Shumsky, and the late Carroll Glenn.

†Both Charles Turner and Herbert Baumel spoke of this to me; but either Barber restricted this predilection to the violin concerto or had a change of heart by the time he wrote the cello and piano concertos, for in both works one cannot help but remark upon the unusual placement of cadenza-like passages at the beginning of the first movements—effecting a soliloquy or rhapsodic recitative (especially in the piano concerto). These are in addition to the traditionally placed cadenzas within the movement.

Homer that his work on his piano sonata had reached an impasse and that he hoped spring would bring new ideas. Recalling Homer's advice not to let "fallow periods" upset him, he wrote:

> I did set my house in order so to speak. A new edition of the violin concerto is being published, also "Knoxville," also "Medea."[19]

Earlier he had written about the revisions of the concerto:

> All this took a good deal of time, and it is no pleasure to fix up old things—also new parts, copyists, etc. Anyway, I did it, and it is much improved. I just returned from Boston and the performance was beautiful and a great success.[20]

Comparison between the holograph score (at the Library of Congress) and the edition Schirmer published in 1949, which incorporates Barber's revisions, indicates that there were only a few alterations in the first movement and that none involved the violin part. Subtle changes in orchestration—in the interest of clarifying the texture and tightening the formal structure—are the kind of revisions Barber typically concerned himself with in many of his other orchestral works. This was accomplished in the concerto, for example, by removal of woodwind doublings at measures 9, 11, 41, and 119–20 and by compressing some of the transition passages at measures 60, 68 (before the entrance of the second theme), and 130, thus reducing by six the number of measures in the body of the movement. Four measures added near the conclusion of the movement (mm. 182–86) prepare for the brief cadenza. A florid *ossia* passage for the solo violin that appeared in the holograph (mm. 153–55) was removed in the revision.

In the second movement, also, some woodwind doublings were deleted (at mm. 21–22, for example, bassoon and flute doublings have been removed) or woodwind activity was reduced (as at mm. 41–43 and mm. 60–64) to achieve a less dense orchestral texture. The solo violin part underwent minor changes: at measures 73–79, for example, a brighter sound is elicited from the violin by raising the passage an octave higher and by removing oboe and clarinet octave doublings, instead placing octave double stops in the violin part.

Barber's "more satisfactory climax" in this movement was accomplished by a rewriting of the last twenty measures, in which he transferred material from the solo violin to violin I and deleted woodwind doublings, thus freeing the solo instrument to play a counterpoint against strings. The passage culminates in a new, short lyrical cadenza—a cascade of triplets that descend gracefully to close the movement.

Revisions of the third movement involved merely small changes in the balance of instrumentation but considerable alteration of the violin part, especially measures 94–104, after which ten bars of solo are cut. In addition, a noticeable reworking of the piano part in the second half of the movement preserves its role as a percussion instrument—almost all woodwind doublings are removed, and the piano is used only sparingly, playing accented chords either alone or in conjunction with the tambour militaire. The addition of a glissando for piano, flute, and piccolo at measure 153 enhances the brilliance of the orchestration and effectively prepares for the finale climax of the movement.

In January 1949 Ruth Posselt and the Boston Symphony performed the concerto on a program of American music that included Leo Sowerby's Symphony No. 4, Roy Harris's Third Symphony, *Music for English Horn* by Edward Burlingame Hill, and *A Lincoln Portrait* by Aaron Copland. Barber's comments about the program, which he attended, provide an insightful illumination of his creative motivations and taste:

> Koussevitzky did a whole American program, an idea which I have always disapproved of, and I must say the lyric and simple style of the concerto rather saved the program, which was full of brass, noise, excesses of every description. . . . At least it offered a small note of contemplation, a quality conspicuously absent from the other pieces.*

Two years later, Barber conducted the Violin Concerto in Berlin and Frankfurt with his friend Charles Turner as soloist. For these performances they had rehearsed in Paris with Pierre Boulez, then a young pianist; Turner was coached by violinist Georges Enesco, who highly praised both the concerto and Turner's performance of it (see chapter 11).[21]

The concerto has been, and still is, one of Barber's most frequently performed works; the Philadelphia Orchestra, for example, lists it second in number of performances, surpassed only by the *Adagio for Strings*.[22]

Four Songs, Op. 13 (1937–40)

Four songs of Barber's written between 1937 and February 1940 represent a diverse group of poets and themes. Published by G. Schirmer in 1940 as Op. 13, these songs do not share the strong musical or textual connections of the earlier Op. 10; yet their texts all have the clarity of imagery and musicality of meter that held special attraction for Barber. In addition, their subjects were significant to the composer's personal life.

"Heaven Haven: A Nun Takes the Veil," by the Victorian poet Gerard Manley Hopkins (1844–89), deals with the quest for solitude in nature, a subject close to Barber's heart and one that he would turn to many times

*Letter to Sidney Homer, 7 January 1949. One is reminded here of Mary Bok's credo that appears in the catalogue of the Curtis Institute of Music in 1925: "They shall learn to think and express their thoughts against a background of quiet culture. . . . The aim is for quality of the work rather than quick showy results."

in future works.* Hopkins's poetry was published in 1918, almost forty years after his death, but it is likely that Barber may have seen the poem in an Oxford University Press edition of 1930. His Op. 13, No. 1, "A Nun Takes the Veil: Heaven Haven" (Barber reversed the title of the poem), was completed in 1937 and dedicated to Rohini Coomara, an English cellist whom Barber had met in Vienna in 1934 and with whom he shared the enjoyment of Hopkins's poetry.†

Called a "half-musician writing a poetry half-music," Hopkins was a skillful innovator of rhythmic techniques[23] and a self-taught musician who eventually turned completely toward composition.[24] Barber matches the poet's musicality of the text by using a freely lyrical recitative style supported by rolled chords.‡

"Secrets of the Old," by the Irish poet W. B. Yeats (1865–1939) and first published in 1928 in a collection titled *The Tower,* was added to Yeats's *Collected Poems* in 1933. The poem affirms everlasting friendship among three aged women whose bond is perpetuated by the sharing of secrets of their youth. The symmetrical form of Barber's song, Op. 13, No. 2, completed in September 1938, corresponds to the three verses of the poem; a lighthearted, witty interpretation of the text is underscored by the flexibly alternating duple and triple meters.

"Sure on this shining night," Op. 13, No. 3, completed during the same period as the Yeats song, is the first of two texts by the contemporary American poet James Agee that Barber set to music. Although the two artists eventually formed a lasting friendship, they did not meet until after Barber composed *Knoxville: Summer of 1915,* in 1948. "Sure on this shining night" is one of the untitled lyrics in Agee's first published collection of poems, *Permit Me Voyage* (1934). Barber's setting is modeled on the songs of Schumann and Brahms: this is suggested not only in the long, lyrical melodic line and by the two-voice canon—where first the voice leads, then the piano—but more specifically in similarities between Barber's pulsating chordal-style accompaniment and that of Schumann's *Ich grolle nicht* or *Liebestreu.*§ This may explain why this is one of the most frequently

* On more than one occasion, Barber spoke of his preference for working in the country. See, for example, Allan Kozinn, "Samuel Barber: The Last Interview and the Legacy," part 1, *High Fidelity* (June 1981): 43–46, 65–68; John Gruen, "And Where Has Samuel Barber Been. . . ?" *New York Times,* 3 October 1971, sec. 2, p. 15.

† Barber had great admiration for Coomara's brother, Narada Coomaraswami, whom he met through John Bitter in 1930 in Andrate. Coomaraswami's grandfather was the first East Indian to be knighted by the King of England, but Barber was more impressed by the fact that the boy had walked from Geneva to Andrate and planned to return to his starting point by way of the Breithorn and Castor (letter from Barber to his parents, 21 July 1930).

‡ Within the year, Barber set another text of Hopkins—"God's Grandeur"—for unaccompanied chorus (see chapter 7).

§ Ruth Friedberg, in *American Art Song and American Poetry,* vol. 1 (Metuchen and London: Scarecrow Press, 1981) cites "Sure on this shining night" for its effective musical support of poetic alliteration through such elements as metrical accent and contour of melodic line. She cites, as a specific example, Barber's stress of the initial *h* sounds in the lines "All is healed, / all is health, / High summer holds the earth. / Hearts all whole" (pp. 13–14).

programmed of Barber's songs both in the United States and Europe. It is a personal favorite of the singer Martina Arroyo, whose teacher Marinka Gurewich used it to teach the technique of handling a *pianissimo cantilena* vocal line. Eager to include songs by American composers in her repertoire, Arroyo frequently sang "Sure on this shining night" on European tours during the fifties and early sixties.[25] The song's popularity is suggested, also, by an anecdote that Barber enjoyed telling after he took an apartment in New York City in 1979, about a telephone operator who withheld his new telephone number until he could prove his identity by singing the opening phrase of "Sure on this shining night," a song for which she confessed "a weakness."[26]

The successful reception of "Sure on this shining night" and "A Nun Takes the Veil" led Barber to make choral arrangements of both songs some thirty years after their composition. According to Heinsheimer, they sold more than a hundred thousand copies.[27]

Frederic Prokosch's love poem "Nocturne" appeared in the poet's 1938 collection, *The Carnival.* Of the five verses published, Barber selected the four that are most unified in their focus on the theme of love, omitting the middle one.* It is probable that he set this somewhat enigmatic poem because Prokosch was a friend; Barber confessed to another poet, Katherine Garrison Chapin, that he was "not very keen" about the text, but "the music just popped out for it."[28]

The Opus 13 songs were performed for the first time on 4 April 1941 by the soprano Barbara Troxell, accompanied by Eugene Bossart. The program of "Modern American Music" was part of the Curtis Institute of Music's Historical Series. Three days later in New York, Povla Frijch performed "A Nun Takes the Veil" at Town Hall on a program of predominantly French songs.[29] On her 1942 tour, Marian Anderson sang both "Nocturne" and "A Nun Takes the Veil."

* * *

In the spring of 1940, Barber and Menotti moved to 166 East 96 Street. Earlier that year Homer had advised his nephew that he considered New York "the hardest place in the world in which to write." "One grows cynical there," he warned, "and music becomes an accomplishment. Willy-nilly you become an ornament in the 'life of New York.' "[30]

Soon after Barber moved, his sister, Sara, married Peter Beatty, a second cousin on her mother's side. For the wedding, which took place in Barber's apartment on May 4, the composer wrote a trio for violin, cello, and piano. The holograph, which is catalogued as "Commemorative March" at the Library of Congress, is titled in Barber's hand: "Composed for Susie's (my sister's) wedding in my New York apartment." As a processional,

*In his memoir, *Voices* (Farrar Straus, 1983), Prokosch refers to his pleasure in hearing Sir Thomas Beecham informally singing, to his own accompaniment, "my good friend Samuel Barber's setting of my poem 'Nocturne.' "

the march is rhythmically unusual with its alternating meters of two, three, and five, perhaps a further example of Barber's gentle teasing of his beloved sister.

On 7 June 1940 Barber was nominated by Walter Damrosch for membership in the National Institute of Arts and Letters. He was, at the time of his election, the youngest member ever to be admitted to the institute.* His nomination was seconded by Deems Taylor and Daniel Gregory Mason.[31] After his induction on 18 November 1941, he donated a manuscript and printed score of the *Adagio for Strings* to the institute's museum. In the years that followed he served on various committees, one of which was the Grant Committee.

The continuation of his appointment at the Curtis Institute of Music required that Barber commute weekly to Philadelphia to conduct the Madrigal Chorus. In 1941–42 he taught orchestration as well. When Homer read of the appointment at the institute, he worried that Barber would be teaching composition: "Nothing is more deadening than looking at manuscripts, and trying to be fair," he wrote to his nephew. "Your letter relieved me. Orchestration is the most innocuous branch!"†

In January 1941 Edith Braun submitted Barber's name as a candidate for the Bok Award. Referring to "work that is quietly being done in our city," she pointed out to the judges that "all of the commissions and performances of [Barber's] music have come without solicitation or wirepulling on the part of anyone."[32] In April of the same year, Barber wrote a commemorative trio that he presented to Mary Curtis Bok on the occasion of her move to a residence at 1816 Delancey Street in Philadelphia. "Song for a New House," for voice, flute, and piano, is in five sections: Allegro molto (for piano and flute, with an *ad libitum* cadenza), Andante con moto, Allegro giocoso, Andante sostenuto, and Allegro. The text, though unnamed by Barber, is from act 5, scene 2 of William Shakespeare's *A Midsummer Night's Dream:* "Not a mouse shall disturb this hallowed house. I am sent with broom before, To sweep the dust behind the door. Through the house give glimm'ring light, By the dead and drowsy fire Ev'ry elf and fairy sprite, Hop as light as bird from brier. . . ." The parts and score

* "Samuel Barber in Honorary Society," *West Chester Local Daily News,* 18 November 1941; Donal Henahan, "I've Been Composing All My Life," *New York Times,* 28 January 1979. In November 1958, at the age of forty-eight, Barber was elected to the American Academy of Arts and Letters.

†Letter, 4 March 1941, Winter Park, Florida. During the course of his career Barber was invited to teach at various music schools, and he usually declined. In 1946, however, he taught at the Berkshire Music Center, stepping in to take Arthur Honegger's students when the French composer suffered a heart attack. A few years later he turned down William Schuman's invitation to teach at the Juilliard Summer School (letter, 18 January 1950, from Schuman to Barber, Papers and Records of William Schuman, New York Public Library, Music Division). When Quincy Porter asked if he would be Visiting Professor of Composition at Yale University, Barber replied: "The idea you propose does not interest me. If I ever taught, I should like to start the pupils myself and then 'see them through' " (letter to Porter, 19 May 1962, Yale Music Library).

are at the Curtis Institute of Music Library and at the Music Division of the Library of Congress.

Second Essay for Orchestra, Op. 17 (1942)

Barber's sketchbook from the 1930s contains the principal themes and a part of the coda of the *Second Essay* interspersed among fragments of the Violin Concerto. It seems probable, therefore, that although the *Essay* was not completed until 1942, the thematic ideas were conceived at least three, if not more, years earlier.* The back cover of a holograph draft of the piece shows numerous versions of the principal theme. Many crossouts and several cuts on the short score and on a polished draft suggest that the piece was molded with great care into its final version.[33]

After returning from a two-week visit to Maine in late August 1940, Barber wrote to Strickland about a "new piece" he was "supposed to be working on":

> While in Stockbridge, I saw Koussevitzky, who wants a new work by October, for performances in November.† So I shall get to work at once, although I doubt if I shall be able to finish it so quickly.[34]

No new piece was forthcoming for that season, however, and with the world in turmoil during the spring before the entry of the United States into World War II, Homer advised his nephew:

> I wonder if, like Beethoven, you will soon write a music drama. I listened to *Fidelio* under Walter, ten days ago, and felt in this work music had reached heights never realized by any other operatic work I had ever heard. Even the spoken dialogue added *realism* to the experience! How do you account for this? There is something in the music far beyond the conventions of writing. . . .
>
> I assure you a music drama on the lines of *Fidelio,* built on sympathy for suffering and with a voice of true eloquence, would be a moving experience today. It would help rebuild faith in the *composer*. . . . Everyone seems to feel that after the struggle the world is going through there will be, eventually, a New World. No one seems to know what kind of a world it will be. There are prophecies, but they are half-hearted.
>
> We have at present, a new art—music—built up in the past three hundred years. It may be that music will be a powerful factor in forming the character of that New World. Music represents the contribution of the individ-

*When the sketchbook was donated to the Library of Congress in 1966, Barber added notations that identify many of his fragmented sketches. There are three excerpts of the *Second Essay,* but only one is labeled "for Essay II" (which in the final version is a passage for violas at rehearsal no. 4); below it lies another theme marked "in quartet allegro."

†Barber was in Stockbridge to talk to Albert Spalding about the Violin Concerto.

> ual to the welfare of the whole. . . . It may be that in this New World music may help to destroy that distrust in the individual that has been so carefully built up during the past fifty years. . . . It is the age of mediocrity and mediocrity so fears greatness, genius, that it resorts to cruelty and treachery to maintain itself. They say insects could destroy the world if they were unchecked. Something like that is going on in civilization. Write the greatest things you *possibly can!*[35]

The *Second Essay* was completed a year and a half later, on Sunday, 15 March 1942.[36] Barber, like everyone, was very much aware of the war and the imminent possibility of being called to service for his country. "I have been composing very hard," he wrote to Chapin, "and my music has been going so well that it seems incongruous for times such as these. But I've taken the attitude that it is better to continue in one's job *tutta forza* until one's draft board decides otherwise."[37] Later he was to say about the *Second Essay,* "Although it has no program, one perhaps hears that it was written in war-time."[38]

The morning after the *Second Essay* was completed Barber showed it to Bruno Walter, who had asked him for a piece for the centennial of the New York Philharmonic–Symphony Orchestra. It had its premiere performance at Carnegie Hall on 16–19 April 1942 at the last concerts of the season and was broadcast on the radio. Eugene Ormandy conducted the Philadelphia Orchestra in performances of the *Second Essay* on 23–24 October, which Barber thought were good and "better than Walter's."[39]

Like Barber's earlier *Essay,* but broader in scope and for a larger orchestra, this work is based on a literary form in which ideas—three themes in this case—are developed with conciseness of expression. This work, too, could also serve logically as the first movement of a symphony. The angular opening theme notated in F minor, but in the Dorian mode, is presented in an andante tempo by solo flutes against a G♭ pedal in low brasses and a *pianissimo* bass drum roll (Example 8.3). The restless and sweeping lyrical second theme, introduced by the violas, grows organically out of the first and is developed (Example 8.4). In this first section, brasses hint at a fragment of the theme that ultimately becomes the full-blown chorale of the coda. A sharp tutti chord ushers a fugue, which is based on a motive of the first theme and played by chattering woodwinds *molto allegro ed energico.* A lull in the music precedes a dramatic return of the second theme juxtaposed over motives from the first.

One of the most striking aspects of the *Second Essay* is its sophisticated use of orchestral color. The abundant solos for timpani, for choirs of brass instruments, and for individual woodwinds are cast vividly against—and indeed flow out of—the contrapuntal texture.

Howard Taubman, reviewing the premiere performance, declared Barber was "not merely flexing his muscles in a bit of harmless exercise" but attempting to say something in a "concise form." "In a short space,"

Example 8.3 *Second Essay for Orchestra*, Op. 15, mm. 1–5 (G. Schirmer, 1942).

Example 8.4 *Second Essay for Orchestra*, mm. 26–35, entrance of second theme in violas, followed by oboe.

Taubman wrote, "he creates and sustains a mood . . . worked out with economy of knowledge and assurance . . . perhaps a shade too solemn, but a composer is entitled to his own thesis."[40] Donald Fuller pointed to the *Second Essay* as Barber's best work to that time; he remarked on the composer's capacity for "real thematic invention" and compared the score to those of Copland and Harris.[41] A West Coast critic labeled Barber a "musical American Shelley."[42]

Shortly before the premiere in the spring of 1942, Barber had written to Koussevitzky advising him that Schirmers was forwarding him two scores, the *Second Essay* and *A Stopwatch and an Ordnance Map*. Koussevitzky had played the *First Essay* on tour in the fall of 1941, and it was received with "great success . . . wherever it was played."[43] Although most of Barber's letter concerned the choral work, yet to be given a public performance even though it seemed very "appropriate to the times," he reminded the conductor that the *First Essay* had never been played in a live concert in New York but had only been heard on the radio. "Perhaps sometime you will find a place for it," he told Koussevitzky. "But you have already been more than generous to my music!"[44]

On the eve of his entry into the United States Army, in September, he wrote again to Koussevitzky, informing him of his induction into the military and reminding him, "Please let me know if you ever play anything of mine, perhaps I shall be able to hear it. I hope you will do the Second Essay sometime."[45] The conductor answered promptly:

> I have missed seeing you in the Berkshires this summer—you would have shared my enthusiasm in the extraordinary achievement of the youthful musicians with whom it is a joy to work.
>
> I am performing your Overture to the "School for Scandal" at the second concert October 16–17 in Boston and am looking forward to introducing your "Essays" in the programs in New York this season.
>
> *With warm wishes and warm greetings.*[46]

On 3 April 1943 Koussevitzky performed *First Essay* in New York but apparently chose not to play the second, perhaps because it was no longer a "first" in New York. A few months before the concerts, Barber had sent him corrections for the *Second Essay:*

> I enclose a list of minor corrections which are in the parts of "Second Essay," but not in your score. You cannot imagine how eagerly I look forward to your performance of both Essays.[47]

Second Essay soon had readings by many major orchestras. Barber wrote to Koussevitzky in November 1944: "Both Szell and Ormandy have scheduled my *Second Essay* for the same week in December in New York, and I shall probably be blamed once more by the latter!" He thought Szell was an "excellent man" and his performance with the New York Philharmonic a "fine" one. Strangely enough—considering his opinion of Ormandy's earlier performance—his anticipation of that conductor's concert with the NBC Symphony Orchestra was not as optimistic; "I doubt if it will be as good," he wrote to Homer, "but let's hope."[48] With the publication of the score by G. Schirmer, Barber's *Second Essay* became a staple of the repertoire of major orchestras. With the Philadelphia Orchestra alone, it is the third most popular work of Barber's, following the *Adagio for Strings* and the Violin Concerto.[49]

9

WORLD CATACLYSM

1942-1945

How to put this in music

Commando March (1943); Funeral March (1943)

In 1942 Howard Hughes invited Barber to write music for an experimental movie he wanted to produce "with the sky as the limit." The composer liked the idea: "Music was to be a full partner, not something scuffed up at the end," he told a reporter. "The plan was to meet for several weeks of discussion and planning before a foot of film was shot, and then to build it all together like a house."[1] Barber was supposed to begin work on the project in Hollywood on 15 September 1942, but his participation in the venture was aborted by a call to report for service in the United States Army on the sixteenth.* A letter to Koussevitzky written on the eve of his departure mentioned an opera that had been commissioned by the Koussevitzky Foundation earlier that year but which he would not be able to finish. He explained:

> I am a private in the Army, and leave tomorrow for service—I have no idea where I shall be stationed. . . .
>
> It has been with the greatest satisfaction that I have followed the success of this summer's Berkshire Festival, and I have admired your courage and conviction in carrying it through. Such things are so important in times like these, and there are few people who, like you, think so clearly and so actively. . . . My next new piece will be for you, dear Maestro.†

*John Selby, "West Chester Composer Is in the Army Now," *Coatesville Record*, 1942. According to military records provided by the National Personnel Records Center (Military Personnel Records), St. Louis, Missouri, Barber was inducted into the U.S. Army on 2 September 1942 and reported for service on 16 September 1942.

†Letter, 14 September 1942, from 166 East 96 Street. Koussevitzky had told Barber that, in spite of the war, the government wanted such things as the Berkshire Festival to continue. The opera was to be a chamber opera, which would be taken on tour that year.

Earlier in the year, Barber had thought about enlisting for Special Services, but he was told that there was a chance his bad eyes might categorize him 1B, in which case he would be called for service only if the supply of eligible draftees was exhausted.[2] When he learned that his eyes were good enough for noncombatant service, he made efforts to obtain some kind of job where he might be useful to the war effort and still compose. Just before the war broke out, he had been asked to go to Italy as an unofficial observer, recommended because of his knowledge of the Italian language and Italians in general.[3] The entry of the United States into the war curtailed that.

Barber's low appetite for military duty was not for lack of patriotism but rather out of a desire to continue writing music. He had written to Katherine Garrison Chapin, "It is strange that they do not use us composers more than they do for propaganda, or perhaps I overestimate our potential usefulness and influence."[4] At the time, his career was ascending, evident from the rating of his music on a survey of orchestral concert programs that included American music in the New York area during the 1941–42 season: out of eighty-six performances of sixty-eight works by fifty American composers, Barber, Aaron Copland, and William Schuman were the most represented.* Moreover, Barber's music was in demand internationally; and not only in Western Europe—scores and parts of his orchestra pieces were being flown to Russia at the request of Shostakovich.[5]

Barber's situation was, of course, typical of the dilemma of many American musicians whose careers were interrupted by the onset of World War II. In the spring 1942 issue of *Modern Music*, Robert Ward advised musicians who were called to service that they "will do well to make their abilities known as early as possible in their Army careers and, during training, to be as good soldiers as possible."[6] There were three fields of musical activity in the military, he observed: two "authorized" activities—for which a soldier was listed on the government payroll as a musician and had few other duties except as such—involved glee clubs and military bands (which, although numerous, were not always authorized); "unauthorized" activities were limited to "free time."[7] During Barber's military career from September 1942 to 1945 he participated in both unauthorized and authorized musical activities.

On 23 September he was assigned to the Second Service Command of Special Services, where he spent four hours a day in basic training at Battery Park and worked the rest of the day at office activities at 165 Broadway, New York. At night he returned to his apartment and continued to

* Francis D. Perkins, "The American List," *New York Herald Tribune*, undated, in the Barber file at the American Academy in Rome, New York office. The list was compiled from the records of the American Composers' Alliance. Barber had five performances of three works—*Adagio for Strings, Second Essay*, and the Violin Concerto; Copland had three works played six times; and Schuman, three works played four times.

compose. After finishing basic training his hours were increased so that evening work dwindled to almost nothing. Because his office responsibilities were trivial and there was much unoccupied time, he asked his superior officer if, when he had no other work to do, he might go to a vacant room in the building for a couple of hours each day to write music for army use. His request was turned down, however, as a "dangerous military precedent."[8]

In November Barber was promoted to private first class. To Strickland's persistent pressure for a choral work, the composer replied: "I cannot see how it could be possible for me to write one—I have less and less time here, more evening guard duty and almost no access to a piano during hours—or any privacy."[9] During this time, however, he set to music "Between Dark and Dark," a lyrical poem by Katherine Garrison Chapin.* The sympathetic stance of his letter to her affirms the value of poetry at a time when the world was on the brink of chaos:

> I feel that at this moment just such an emotion should "walk": one cannot live endlessly on poetry of desolation. The mood of exaltation which you strike, is difficult to sustain and seems to me to require immense control: perhaps I felt it controlled more successfully, more tightly, in earlier things of yours—but this is a little personal opinion of a musician.[10]

It is unfortunate that the music is lost for this song that Barber acknowledged was "beautiful to do,"[11] and one can understand what pleasure he might have found in lines beginning "Beside a tranquil pool where the winds are still and the water is unbroken, where the last light stays, we have stood together" and concluding "There is ancient thunder gathering on the hill. There is flame and spark. That is tomorrow. This is our love's hour. We have been together beyond sorrow, between dark and dark."

Barber's efforts then were primarily directed toward writing music for the army. "I have been asked by the Philharmonic and other orchestras for war music," he wrote to Chapin.[12] Two works written during this time received national attention and remained in the repertoire—*Commando March* and the Second Symphony. In the spring of 1943, he wrote to Strickland:

> I've finished a march for band and think I shall ask Thor Johnson to try it out for me. I wonder how his band is. It must be played in this Service Command first. It was a nuisance to score—millions of euphoniums, alto clarinets and D-flat piccolos to encumber my score page.[13]

Commando March was completed in February 1943 and scored for D♭ piccolo; C flute; oboe; E♭ clarinet; B♭ clarinets I, II, and III; alto clarinet; bass clarinet; bassoons I and II; E♭ alto saxophones I, II, and III; B♭ tenor

* "Between Dark and Dark" is in a collection of poems and ballads, *Plain-Chant for America* (Harper and Brothers, 1942).

saxophone; E♭ baritone saxophone; B♭ cornets I, II and III; horns I, II, III, and IV; trombones I, II, and III; bass trombone; euphonium; tubas; string bass; xylophone; snare drum; triangle; cymbals; bass drums; and timpani.[14] A three-minute work in E♭ major, it is in three sections with introduction and coda and is modeled largely on marches of the late nineteenth century.*

Described by critic Fredric V. Grunfeld as "an old-fashioned quickstep sporting a crew cut," *Commando March* was played quite frequently during World War II and gained a permanent place in band repertoire after its publication by G. Schirmer in 1943.† It was viewed as representative of "a new kind of soldier, one who did not march in straight lines across parade grounds" but "struck in stealth with speed, disappearing as quickly as he came," inspiring a different kind of music that departed from tradition.[15] It has all the characteristics necessary to its function—jaunty rhythms, plentiful woodwind and percussion flourishes, and an easily remembered theme that incorporates a triplet figure from the introduction.

The first performance of *Commando March* was given on 23 May 1943 by the Army Air Force Technical Training Command Band at one of their weekly Sunday concerts at Convention Hall, Atlantic City, New Jersey.[16] Correspondence from Barber to Koussevitzky suggests that the premiere was conducted by the composer himself; in mid-August Barber responded to a request from the conductor for an orchestral arrangement of the march:

> Due to your encouragement my début as a band conductor was quite successful and I had a re-engagement in Central Park! I orchestrated the "Commando March" and will send it to you as soon as it is copied.[17]

The band in Central Park he referred to was the Edwin Franko Goldman Band, which later Barber conducted in a recording for the Office of War Information. The recording was used in American short-wave broadcasts throughout the world.[18] Koussevitzky gave the first performance of the orchestral version of *Commando March* in Boston at Symphony Hall at a Friday afternoon concert of the Boston Symphony Orchestra on 29 October 1943.‡ The concert version was scored for three flutes, piccolo, three oboes, English horn, three B♭ clarinets, E♭ clarinet, bass clarinet, three bassoons and contrabassoon, four horns, three trumpets, three

* It lacks the usual trio in the subdominant key, substituting instead a series of sequential patterns based on a triplet figure from the introduction. Friedewald points out in his analysis that the march is an example of Barber's tendency to substitute submediant harmony for the tonic (*A Formal and Stylistic Analysis,* p. 307).

† Fredric V. Grunfeld, "It Ain't Necessarily Oompah: The Concert Band," *High Fidelity* 4 (October 1954): 82. James Lyons, in a review of a 1954 Mercury recording (MG 50079) of the march in *American Record Guide* ([February 1954]: 200), wrote, "I must say, I never expected to hear Barber's *Commando March* again; we were importuned with it too many times during the late war."

‡ The program included the first concert performance of Piston's Prelude and Allegro for Organ and Strings and the Boston premiere of Khachaturian's Piano Concerto.

trombones and tuba, snare drum, bass drum, cymbals, triangle, xylophone, wood block, and strings. In spite of the large forces, Barber was in the habit of calling the work his "little march."*

After Barber heard the performance on the radio, he wrote almost immediately to Richard Burgin, concertmaster and associate conductor of the orchestra, about two corrections he wanted to make:†

> If you play the little march again, I have a couple of changes to suggest and ask you to be so kind as to tell the players and Dr. K. They are very small:
>
> 1. When the five trumpets come in, in the measure just before the recapitulation, they play flutter-tongue on a written "c"—I don't like this and would prefer the following (no double tonguing)
>
> 
>
>
> 2. on the last note of the trombones' glissando, both times, please add a ♩ *sf* for the bass-drum. . . . Many thanks for bothering with this.[19]

A review in *Modern Music* of the orchestral version of *Commando March* declared the new arrangement "lavish, but quite appropriate" and commended the music as "good and fast-spirited, as a march should be."[20]

Another march composed by Barber early in 1943, which exists only in manuscript at the Library of Congress, is titled "Funeral March (based on the Army Air Corps Song)." It is scored for woodwinds, trumpet, cornet, saxophone, horn, trombone, baritone, snare drum, and bass drum, and requires that a solo trumpet (or horn) play "Taps" from the distance. The march was performed a number of times both as a concert piece and as a funeral march but was never published.‡

The Second Symphony, Op. 19 (1944), and *Night Flight*, Op. 19a

Shortly after his induction into the army, Barber began to discuss the possibility of composing a symphonic work about flyers for the air corps.

*In a letter to Sidney Homer, who must have heard one of the Goldman Band performances, Barber wrote (27 September 1943): "It was grand to have your letter and know that you heard my little march." To Koussevitzky, after hearing the radio performance of the march, he wrote, "The little March sounded very well indeed over the radio" (letter, 11 November 1943, from Mount Kisco).

†A letter from Koussevitzky to Barber, 11 November 1943, tells of the audience's enthusiasm.

‡Colonel George Howard, who was conductor of the Army Air Force Band early in 1943, reported that the march "brought tears to the eyes of many who heard it" (letter to the author, 3 August 1985). No evidence so far has revealed whether the march was composed for a specific funeral.

"This subject is of great fascination to the public and is being celebrated in all the arts," he informed his uncle.* The composition he planned was to become the Second Symphony, a work that would consume his attention for almost ten years with composition, revisions, and promotion, only to be withdrawn by the composer twenty years later.

After submitting a descriptive brief of his project, on 30 August 1943 Barber was officially transferred to the army air corps and notified by telegram to report without delay to Fort Worth, Texas, air force headquarters for the entire country.[21] At Fort Worth, his contact was General Barton K. Yount, whose wife was interested in music and had supported the idea from the start.† Barber described his experiences in a letter to Homer:

> I arrived in Texas on a hot Sunday, temperature 105, and went out to the camp, which is almost entirely an enormous Air Field, stretched out with thousands of humming aeroplanes, under an intolerant sun. No one had the faintest idea why I was there. They didn't believe I was to be attached to the General, wouldn't allow me to telephone him—nor would they, and seemed to treat the whole idea of writing music as a bit fantastic and presumptuous on my part. After a few days of this, I began to feel the same way myself. I wandered about the camp and the miserable city of Fort Worth, packed with soldiers, and almost highest on the list of cities notable for venereal diseases. In barracks I slept with ten Chinese cooks, who woke me every morning at four with their cheery language. We could hardly sleep anyway through the pounding and hammering and glaring lights that went on all night. The third day I met a Lieutenant Holden, who turned out to be a movie star,‡ and to whom I explained my predicament. He said he would do what he could do. That night I couldn't sleep at all, so I got up before dawn and went out on the dark field and asked a pilot to take me up in the Liberator Bomber. They were going on a six-hour flight and I thought we would fly over Texas, possibly lunching somewhere and returning in style. They allowed me to come with them, strapped me into a parachute and I sat by the bomb-sight, or crouched rather, for there were no seats. We took off with two young pilots, nervous and sweating, and a gruff instructor. I kept remembering an irritating phrase in Kinch's article about me in which he said I had a "false sense of security"; it rather amused me, in my somewhat discouraged mood to go along on a flight that was

*Letter to Sidney Homer, 11 September 1943. By this time, Barber may have already heard about Marc Blitzstein's orchestral tone poem *Freedom Morning*, composed while he was a member of the U.S. 8th Army Air Force. (Blitzstein's *Airborne Symphony*, commissioned by the army, was not premiered until 1946.)

†Letter, Samuel Barber to Sidney Homer, 11 September 1943. Yount was a lieutenant general by rank. His title was that of Commanding General of Headquarters, Army Air Forces Training Command, Fort Worth, Texas. The meeting with Mrs. Yount was arranged by Albert Kohn, a young violinist, conductor, and arranger of "some reputation," whom Barber helped obtain assignment to the Army Music School through William Strickland (correspondence between Barber and Strickland, October–November 1942).

‡William Holden.

> rather dangerous and not at all a pleasure jaunt.* We banked, we twisted and twisted and turned, dived, then the young pilots, who seemed almost too young and small for the huge machine—they were only twenty-five—flew blindfolded. It was exciting to be up front with them and roam about the bomber at will. At the end of the fifth hour we began to "shoot landings," the most difficult part; land, go up again; over and over, but never stopping and there was no question of getting out. It was fun in a raucous sort of way, and I did not get sick.[22]

Armed with recordings of his works should Mrs. Yount not be familiar with his music, Barber outlined his plans for a symphony to the general's wife and was received so warmly that he was immediately given an audience with the general. Yount—described by Barber as "one of those lonely men who one meets so often, who longs to have a good talk"—met at length with the composer about his preparations for the symphony.

> I even told him that I had been in the Psychopathic Ward to talk to flyers back from combat, and about their various mental problems and fears. The statistics about men who are going through all this are terribly alarming. . . . It is hard to imagine what they are going through. Many pilots talked to me of the sensations of flying, the lack of musical climax in flying, the unrelieved tension, the crescendo of descent rather than mounting, and the discovery of a new dimension. How to put this in music, I do not know, but the talks I had were wonderful. In some way I shall try to express some of their emotions. I flew several times again in smaller planes where the sensations are more acute.[23]

Although Barber hoped that at the most he would be allowed to work in Fort Worth, his luck surpassed his "wildest dreams": Yount took the matter with such seriousness that he encouraged Barber to have the "best working conditions possible," assigned him, pro forma, to West Point, and allowed him to work at home in Mount Kisco.† He was given four months or longer, if necessary, to write the piece. The army would receive all the royalties forever.‡

During the autumn of 1943, intoxicated with the pleasures of working at home, Barber wrote to Homer:

* "Kinch" is the poet Robert Horan, who lived with Barber and Menotti at Capricorn during the early 1940s. When in 1946 Barber submitted his name to the Committee on Grants for Literature of the National Institute of Arts and Letters, he wrote about the poet: "I consider him—and Jacques Barzun and Frederic Prokosch and others back me up on this (in case a composer's opinion is considered illiterate)—extraordinarily talented. Indeed I have seen no lyric poetry of such calibre since the first poems of Auden and Spender" (letter to Felicia Geffen, 10 February 1946, National Institute of Arts and Letters). Barber wrote only one song on a text by Horan, "The queen's face on the summery coin" (November 1942), published as Op. 18 with a setting of José Garcia Villa's "Monks and Raisins."

† Letter to Homer, 11 September 1943. Barber wrote to Homer that Yount apparently believed the commission was a mandate from some "higher-up" source in Washington.

‡ Letter, Barber to Homer, 24 February 1944. Barber's expenses for rehearsals in Boston—the train fare and hotel bill—were paid for by himself.

> I can scarcely believe that I have arrived here and will be able to pass the autumn in my new studio. We hope to produce the work with a major orchestra this season, so I must work very hard. I love this atmosphere of work and we scarcely see each other until late afternoon.[24]

His housemates were Menotti, who had completed a play and was embarking on the scoring of his piano concerto, and the poet Robert Horan, who was writing a novel. Two weeks later, optimistic over the progress of the ultimately doomed symphony, Barber wrote again to Homer:

> Yes, life in the house is just as you said, and I rarely leave it. It's not easy to compose a large work knowing it must be ready for performance in March. The full orchestra sketch of the first two movements is finished and I am casting about for the last. So far, I'm sure it's my best work. I hadn't written for so long that it just bust out!
>
> . . . I wish you could look out the window of my studio and see the hemlock woods all covered with snow! Who would ever want to live in New York again! In December we may split up the week between the apartment in New York and here—but mostly here . . . from January on it doesn't matter where I am, for I'll be orchestrating. I shan't budge until I finish the sketch of the last movement.[25]

A month later, after learning that Koussevitzky planned to include his revised Symphony No. 1 in the last part of the Boston Symphony Orchestra's 1943–44 season, Barber wrote to the conductor:

> I am disappointed and this is why: just at that time (March or April), I wanted to offer you my new Flight Symphony commissioned by the Air Force, which will not be ready until March 1st. The Air Force wishes this work performed this season, and our hopes are that you will accept the premiere.
>
> I have had a couple of requests from your colleagues for this work, but you, of course, are our first choice. . . . I have already finished the full sketch of the first two movements, and am very happy about the work. I can offer you the finished score the last of February, definitely. . . . I should like you to keep the matter of the new Symphony completely confidential until you reach some understanding with General Yount as to when an announcement should be made. I have to be a little careful in my double life of composer-corporal.[26]

Yount, meanwhile, asked Koussevitzky for confirmation of his willingness to premiere the work:

> Corporal Sam Barber . . . informs me that he is getting along very nicely and feels that he is going to produce his very best work.
>
> He informs me that you are interested in giving the symphony its premiere, and that it is hoped that you will agree to introduce it in Boston, New York, and on the radio.

I have taken up the matter with the Office of the Commanding General of the Army Air Forces, and it is felt that you are best prepared to give this work its introduction to the public.[27]

Koussevitzky agreed to a spring 1944 premiere of the symphony in Boston and New York, followed by a radio broadcast.*

Every two weeks during the winter Barber reported to a colonel at West Point to demonstrate the progress of the symphony. Many years later he said about these meetings:

As it was one of my most complicated works, I had no idea what he expected to hear. I rather thought it might be something like "You're in the Army Now," so I was a little nervous when I reported to play for him on a battered up old piano in the back of an army theater. All he said was, "Well, corporal, it's not quite what we expected from you. Since the Air Force uses all sorts of the most modern devices, I'd hoped you'd write this symphony in quarter-tones. But do what you can, do what you can, corporal."[28]

To accommodate the colonel's request for "modern devices" Barber used an electronic tone-generator built by the Bell Telephone Laboratories to simulate the sound of a radio beam.†

In those days it was easy to requisition anything. We were on the phone to Bell Labs in a minute. I remember trips to Princeton to study the thing. In the end, it never did work right. I remember Koussevitzky having a fit at rehearsals and shouting, "Throw the damn thing out!"[29]

Used in the second movement and integrated into the orchestral texture, the tone-generator produces the pitch a‴. Its sound resembles that made when the rim of a crystal wine goblet is rubbed rapidly with a finger.‡ Barber said he intended the tone to symbolize the beam used to guide flyers: "It's a different world up there, in more ways than one," he said. "At night and in blind flying, the radio beam is the only connection with civilization down below."[30]

At the end of January 1944, he wrote to Koussevitzky:

* It happened that the broadcast coincided with Bruno Walter's performance of Barber's revised Symphony in One Movement (letter from Barber to Strickland, 7 February 1944).

† The instrument, called a tone synthesizer, was invented in 1923 by Harvey Fletcher of Bell Laboratories, where he worked from 1916–1949 on various acoustical problems of transmitting sound stereophonically. His research in the 1930s, conducted with the cooperation of the Philadelphia Orchestra, allowed concerts to be transmitted to Washington, D.C., by a three-channel stereo system and permitted Stokowski to raise the stereo loudspeaker levels to 10 db above the normal orchestral sound. The tone-generator used for Barber's symphony consisted of 100 acoustic discs side-by-side and rotating together. Its signals were picked up at the rims and fed through to amplifiers and attentuators to a loudspeaker that projected a musical sound with various harmonics. The author is indebted to Floyd K. Harvey, formerly of Bell Telephone Laboratories, for this information.

‡ Phillip Ramey provided me with a tape cassette of the premiere performance. A recording of the premiere, the only one of this version of the symphony, is at the Library of Congress, Motion Picture, Broadcasting, and Recorded Sound Division.

> The symphony is finished and orchestrated and I am happy about it. I hope it will not disappoint you. The copyist's score of the first two movements is ready and the copied score of the last movement will be ready in about ten days. . . . The timing of the whole work is between 28 and 30 minutes.
>
> . . . In Washington, every officer has a different idea about the title, the last word to be General Arnold's. The composer seems to have nothing to do with it! I believe they will make the newspaper announcement from A.F. Headquarters in Washington.
>
> Should you wish to look over the third movement in New York when you come, I should be delighted, but realize how busy you are on these trips.
>
> At any rate, I look forward with greatest anticipation to the Boston rehearsals, and repeat how happy I am to have the premiere in your hands.[31]

Koussevitzky and Barber met at the conductor's apartment at the Savoy Plaza on the morning of 10 February.[32] There is no evidence, however, that Koussevitzky suggested any changes in the score during that meeting.

With the orchestration completed and corrections being made up to the last minute, Barber was notified by the orchestral manager one day before rehearsals were scheduled to begin that he would have to bring the parts to Boston himself.* Without a hotel reservation, he took the night train and arrived in Boston at 1:30 A.M., carrying "the heavy parts" from hotel to hotel and finally "falling into bed someplace." So intent was he on the first rehearsal that he rushed off in the morning without noticing where he had spent the night, and the orchestra manager had to phone all the hotels in Boston to locate where he had registered.[33]

Upon his return to Mount Kisco, Barber wrote to Koussevitzky, "It was a great joy to leave the symphony in your hands; now I await the magic you will bring to it next week."[34] He returned to Boston for a week of rehearsals prior to the premiere.

Announcement in the newspapers of the symphony's forthcoming premiere on 3 March 1944 came from Air Force Headquarters in Washington. Although General Arnold had named the work "Flight Symphony," it was listed on the program as "Second Symphony (Dedicated to the Army Air Forces)."† The day of the premiere the *Christian Science Monitor* reported Barber's comments on his music:

* He had wired Koussevitzky he would arrive with the electrical instrument for rehearsal on February 28 (telegram, 15 February 1944).

† Program of the Boston Symphony Orchestra, 3 March 1944, p. 1047. The title "Flight Symphony" appears in a letter from Matthew Arnold to Samuel Barber, 31 March 1944. This title must have been commonly used by others in the armed forces as well, for it appears in a letter to Koussevitzky from Howard C. Bronson, Chief of the Music Section of the Armed Forces (24 March 1944), in which he inquires whether or not the "Flight Symphony" could be recorded by the Boston Symphony under Koussevitzky's direction so that Barber's composition could be carried to the many soldiers who could not attend the concert.

> "I have not been confined in any limitations of techniques, but have felt free to use any devices which I considered would best express the mood, the adventure, the vivid action of the individual Army flying man." In the Second Symphony, he said, he had not tried to depict anything as tremendous as the whole Air Force or heat of battle, but had applied himself solely to the story of the pilot himself.[35]

Barber's symphony was played before intermission on the Friday afternoon program and flanked by Mozart's Symphony in A major (K. 201) and Rachmaninoff's Third Piano Concerto. Plans were already under way for broadcasting the symphony by the Office of War Information over short-wave stations throughout the world and for scores to be sent to London and Moscow.[36] The composer wrote his own program notes for the premiere:

> The first of the three movements, which is in sonata form, begins with repeated chords of seconds at the interval of a seventh, and the first theme, based on them, is announced by the strings. Later a second figure in sixteenths . . . leads into a lyric theme, played first in the oboe. A crescendo closes the exposition. The development opens with a contrapuntal section beginning with the seconds and works up to a stretto for full orchestra based on the agitato figure in sixteenths. Woodblocks and drums join the percussion in augmentation and diminution of this figure. . . . The second movement, of nocturnal character, is based on a slow ostinato 5-4 rhythm, first played by muted slow cellos and basses. . . . Over this accompaniment an English horn sings a lonely melody in 4-4 time, which gives a curious oscillating rhythmic counterpoint. . . . The third movement begins presto, with a spiral figure for strings and interruptions by brass, in free rhythm. This introduction leads into a set of variations and short fugato . . . on a relentless bass. . . . The spiral string figure reappears in augmentation in the brass, and also in the coda, bringing the work to a dynamic close.*

The large score is identical in forces to Barber's first symphony, except for the omission of a harp and the addition of a piano. The use of piano as an orchestral instrument, while viewed as somewhat unconventional at the time, was not new for Barber, who had included it in earlier works—*Essay for Orchestra* and the Violin Concerto.† In the symphony it serves

*Boston Symphony Orchestra program, 3 March 1944. His draft of the notes are included in a letter to Homer, written on 24 February 1944. The description is perhaps the longest and most explicit Barber ever permitted to appear in concert notes. Compare these notes, for example, to the spare notes he submitted for the revised version of the symphony six years later (see below in this chapter). In subsequent years he avoided commentary on his music altogether.

†He was to use the piano again as an orchestral instrument in the ballet *Medea* (1946) and the opera *Antony and Cleopatra* (1966).

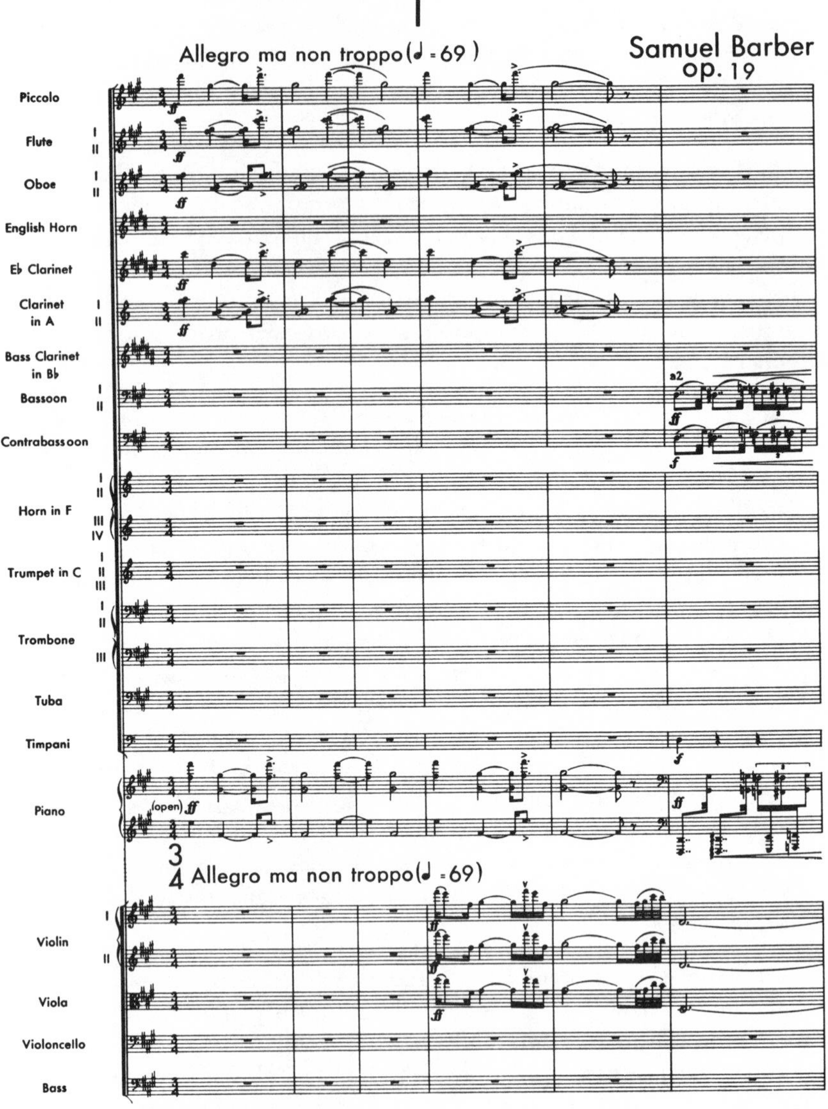

Example 9.1 Second Symphony, first movement, mm. 1–6 (G. Schirmer, 1950).

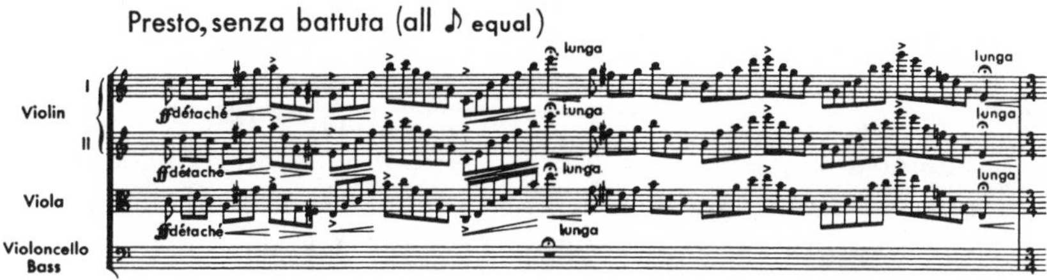

Example 9.2 Second Symphony, opening of third movement.

either to underscore passages in the lower strings or to emphasize upper woodwind passages.

The Second Symphony marks a departure from Barber's earlier style, however, for in this work there is an emotional climate of greater tension and energy. This is accomplished by the use of persistent ostinato dotted rhythms, more dissonant intervals, and angular lines: the first few measures of the symphony, for example, concentrate on sevenths and clusters of seconds, which in their linear form combine to become the jagged first theme (see Example 9.1).

The thematic material of the symphony, stated Barber, was designed to express the sensation of flying.[37] The last movement, for example, begins very fast with no barlines. Barber is reported to have wanted to express a spiral and believed the way to go about it was to have the music flow very freely with no definite accents (Example 9.2).[38]

Barber seemed particularly concerned that the Second Symphony not be considered program music in the conventional sense. Yet, upon completion of the first two movements, he provided Homer with a description of the symphony that suggests he did have at least an emotional program in mind:

> The first movement tries to express the dynamism and excitement of flying—and ends way up 50,000 feet! The second is a lonely sort of folk-song melody for English horn, against backgrounds of string-clouds. It might be called solo flight at night. Otherwise there is no program.*

Notes for the Boston premiere, though, stoutly denied programmatic intentions in the music: "The composer has made no attempt to describe a scene or tell a story, since the emphasis in this work is on the emotional rather than the narrative factor. . . . It is in no sense program music." Yet, although we are told that the use of the electrical tone-generator is "primarily musical not descriptive," literal representations are not com-

*Letter, 27 September 1943. The note seems to foreshadow *Night Flight,* Op. 19a, an independent orchestral piece derived from the second movement (see below).

pletely discounted: "Various instruments in the orchestra imitate the rhythmic code signal. . . . The muted trumpets echo the fading radio beam."*

Reviews of the premiere in Boston placed greater emphasis on the symphony's value as propaganda than on its musical worth. Boston music critics pointed to the work as "the first serious music written about Uncle Sam's present Army by a man in uniform"; it was expected that it would be recognized that "first-class American music is good American propaganda in the best sense of the word" because it would have a "good effect upon morale in our own ranks" and would "introduce fittingly the American spirit and the American musical genius to peoples of other lands."[39] The hope was that other gifted composers who were in uniform would be given similar commissions by the Army.[40] Viewed as Barber's most ambitious work to that time, the symphony was described as "lean and muscular," with "stringent dissonance," and as "sophisticated music."[41]

Of the New York performance a week later, Olin Downes (calling the symphony "program music") commented on the "modernity" of the score, "if modernity is assumed to be absent unless typified by dissonance." He declared the work to be the "most closeknit and concise" of Barber's he had heard thus far.[42] A review in the *New York Herald Tribune* cited the third movement as a "tour de force" toward which the entire symphony cumulatively builds.[43] Only Virgil Thomson found the work lacking in striking melody and contrapuntal life (ironically, two characteristics most often attributed to Barber's music). Thomson's observation that the "constant abuse of instrumental doublings for purposes of emphasis has produced a muddiness of texture" may have influenced the nature of Barber's revisions made six years later. He viewed Barber's "new" style as not really new:

> I admit some uncertainty as to what it is all about. If his First, which we heard on Wednesday at the Philharmonic, represents, as I think it does, a Hamlet-like backward yearning toward the womb of German Romanticism, this one may well be Hamlet in modern dress. I've a suspicion they are really the same piece. The new one is modernistic on the surface; at

*John N. Burk, program, Boston Symphony Orchestra, 3 March 1944, pp. 1016–66. The search for extramusical events in a titled work seems irresistible, especially if one is aware of the circumstances surrounding its composition. *Newsweek* magazine, for example, maintained that the "screaming trumpet and crashing percussion in the third and final movement suggest the blockbusters of an air raid" ("The Case of Samuel Barber," 13 March 1944, p. 94). Even Nathan Broder, when writing about the revised symphony almost a decade later, could not resist pictorial language, treading a fine line between the emotional expressiveness and programmatic aspects of the music:

> An imaginative listener . . . could easily find in it the reaction of a poet thrust into a world of war machines. The pervasive dissonance, the wide angular leaps in some of the melodies . . . the throbbing ostinati . . . the whirring of strings . . . readily summon to mind the deadly serious atmosphere of preparations for battle, the sense of great distances, the roar of airplane engines, the whirling of propellers. (Broder, *Samuel Barber*, p. 81)

least an effort has been made to write in a dissonant style. But the melodic material would have been set off just as well, and probably better, by a less angular harmonic texture.[44]

But more importantly, Thomson perceived that what other critics glorified was not necessarily in the composer's best interest: "I am inclined to think the commission to write a work glorifying the Army Air Forces has led him to try his hand at a publicity task for which he has little taste and less preparation," he wrote.[45]

Barber, however, tried to turn the propaganda effort to his advantage, hoping the success of the symphony would lead to a more lenient military assignment that would allow him to continue composing at home. In February, after the orchestration for the symphony was finished, he was in such a good working streak that the thought of having to return to army life and stop composing made him desperate. This motivated him, even before the premiere, to press Koussevitzky to perform the work more than once in New York:

I heard that many Air Force officers wish to come from Washington to the New York performance—the Commandant from West Point, General Yount, General Spaatz's wife, General Doolittle's wife, and Mrs. Arnold, so it would be wonderful if you could play it twice in New York so they all could hear it. Many officers might have to miss it if it were a single performance. But I understand your problem perfectly.[46]

After the New York performance, Barber expressed his gratitude to Koussevitzky:

Doubtless for conductors one exciting week succeeds another, but it is not so for composers. Certainly I shall never forget the fortnight in Boston and New York. No composer could have asked for a more inspired interpretation or kinder cooperation. It is quite impossible to express my gratitude.

Sometime I shall send you parts of some of the letters I have received from various sections of the country—the comments of pilots and A.F. men were particularly touching. Now I am awaiting orders from Washington as to my future—if only I am allowed to continue to work in my art! It is a great deal to ask in these times.

To you and your niece my affectionate greetings,

Always sincerely,
Sam Barber[47]

Koussevitzky appealed to General Yount and General Arnold on Barber's behalf:

My dear General Yount:
I am writing this letter with a feeling of deep appreciation. For it is to the Army Air Forces that musical art of America owes a composition of real significance and magnitude.

> I am speaking of the Symphony commissioned by the Army Air Forces to Samuel Barber, which has just had its first performance by the Boston Symphony Orchestra. Not only is this a work of lasting importance and creative value but it also reveals the amazing growth of the creative powers of a young American. Samuel Barber is now, without exaggeration, the most outstanding and exceptionally endowed composer in this country. Only a man of genius could have so brilliantly fulfilled his task, stirring the soul of thousands of listeners, bringing close to reality the mission of our hero flyers.
>
> This is the reason why I take the liberty of appealing to you to protect this young talent for the sake of American musical art and afford Samuel Barber a further opportunity of developing and creating, which is essential for the cultural welfare of the nation. Believe me.*

Yount did not attend either the Boston or New York performances, but he did hear the symphony on the radio. He responded to Koussevitzky's "fine letter . . . concerning Corporal Samuel Barber and his fine symphony":

> I am sorry I could not get to Boston for the opening, but I did have the pleasure of listening, with several of our friends, to the first radio performance. I am sure this symphony lost a great deal via the radio, but even at that, we all thought it was magnificent.
>
> I have taken steps to be certain that Corporal Barber obtains a suitable assignment. Mrs. Yount and I enjoyed meeting him, and I am most appreciative of the fine spirit he has shown. No matter what his success, nor how busy he has been in the completion of this symphony, he has never failed to remember that he is a soldier and has always been ready to do his duty, no matter what it might be. He is a great musician and, in addition, a fine, patriotic citizen.[48]

General Arnold, too, responded to Koussevitzky with a report that he had heard from both "layman and musician . . . that the 'Flight Symphony' is one of the most outstanding contributions to musical literature that has come out of this war era. . . . The enlisted man of the Army Air Forces will take great pride in knowing that one of his own fellow soldiers is responsible for this fine work."[49] He told the conductor that since Yount had been responsible for "placing Corporal Barber on detached service in order to complete his symphony," he was referring the letter to him "for such action as he may deem appropriate."[50]

Several weeks later, after Barber learned of Koussevitzky's efforts on his behalf, he wrote to him again:

*Letter, 6 March 1944. Koussevitzky sent an identical letter to General Arnold, Commanding General of the Army Air Forces Headquarters, Washington, D.C., 4 March 1944. Both letters are in the Serge Koussevitzky Collection, Library of Congress, Music Division.

> I've been here several weeks waiting for the military minds to be made up as to my future: but I'm hopeful, due to your wonderful letter. May they decide soon, for I am anxious to compose again![51]

The army was so eager to promote Barber's symphony that they immediately began negotiations for recording the work. Howard C. Bronson, chief of the Music Section of the Special Services Division, wrote to Koussevitzky requesting his cooperation:

> We all take a great deal of pride in having as a fellow soldier a man of Corporal Barber's attainments.
>
> Of necessity, relatively few of Corporal Barber's fellow soldiers have been privileged to hear his new work and the only means whereby his composition may be carried to the Army is through the medium of a phonograph recording.
>
> It is felt that if the "Flight Symphony" is to be recorded, it should be played by your Orchestra under your Direction. I am therefore taking the liberty of inquiring whether it will be agreeable to you and the members of the Boston Symphony Orchestra to permit us to record the "Flight Symphony" for distribution to the Army on V-DISCs. In case this proposal meets with your approval, I will arrange to have our Recording Officer, Captain Vincent, come to Boston at your convenience.
>
> It is my personal opinion that the "Flight Symphony" marks another milestone for the music of the Army of the United States. Likewise, it has been a matter of international consequence. From informal sources, I have been informed that one of the allies of our country has asked for the score to Corporal Barber's Symphony.
>
> Trusting that you and your great Orchestra may find it possible to be the medium for carrying the "Flight Symphony" to our soldiers throughout the world and with kindest personal regards, I am. . . .[52]

OWI reportedly planned recordings of the symphony that would be broadcast in Moscow, London, and other cities of the Allied countries.[53]

* * *

Shortly before Christmas 1946 Barber wrote to Sidney Homer about revisions he was making on the Second Symphony.[54] By February he considered them complete and wrote: "My Second Symphony is all revised and improved and I hope someone will play it."[55] Several months later, probably late spring of 1947, he wrote to Koussevitzky: "I am taking the liberty of having the new score of revised Symphony II sent to you at the hotel, in case you would like to look it over during your vacation. It seems to me much better, and I hope you will like the new lyric string coda in the last movement."*

*Letter, undated. However, the stationery and the familiar salutation ("Dear Sergei Al-

A letter of 5 September to Scalero tells that he had "taken out some of the unsuccessful programmatic elements which were in the work," but to Homer he was more specific about the changes he had made:

> It now seems satisfactory to me: a long, quiet coda I inserted in the somewhat nervous last movement, and the electrical instrument in the second movement . . . replaced by E-flat clarinet, trombones deleted, etc.[56]

Comparison of the 1950 edition and the 1944 holograph score (at the Library of Congress) shows other revisions that were extensive and that consisted either of redistributing woodwind parts—to clarify melodic lines—or of tightening the score by condensing and telescoping passages into fewer measures. The first movement, for example, is twenty-three measures shorter in its revised version. The last movement, too, underwent cuts that resulted in more succinct transitions, a reduction of scoring that produced a more transparent texture, or—as in the case of the recapitulation's *allegro molto* (at rehearsal no. 29)—an increase in orchestral forces that heightened dramatic tension.

Not until 1949, however, did Barber hear the symphony played in its new version.* The American premiere of the revised Symphony No. 2 (sans its subtitle and original dedication) took place on 5 January 1949 before an invited audience at the Philadelphia Academy of Music, in celebration of the twenty-fifth anniversary of the Curtis Institute of Music. Alexander Hilsberg conducted the Curtis Symphony Orchestra. Barber wrote to Homer about the performance:

> It was very inspiring. Hilsberg is a fine conductor, and the orchestra of young people, many in knee-breeches, gave a moving and dedicated performance of my Second Symphony. You know how difficult that work is: I am remembering the Boston Symphony sweating over many parts! Well, the Curtis Orchestra had rehearsed for three months, in sections (with their teachers, all Philadelphia Orchestra men) and then together, and it was a wonderful performance, with a quality of enthusiasm which professionals rarely have, and a surprisingly high technical standard. It was the first time I had heard the symphony in its revised form.[57]

Hilsberg repeated the symphony on 21 January with the Philadelphia Orchestra. About this performance Barber wrote, "At last it is right, one of those rare moments which are never forgotten by the composer."[58] For

exandrovich"), as well as the subject of the text, would suggest it was written sometime after the close of the Boston Symphony Orchestra's 1946–47 season.

*There were several performances before then that he could not attend: Barber's friend John Bitter conducted a performance with the Berlin Philharmonic the week of 14 December 1947, when Barber was involved in preparations for simultaneous performances of his Cello Concerto and *Medea* (the premiere) in Philadelphia and New York. Barber reported that Charles Münch heard these performances and was so enthusiastic about the symphony that he asked for a score. Although he planned to play it in France, at the Edinburgh Festival, and in New York the following season, these performances never materialized.

these concerts, as for earlier ones, Barber wrote his own program notes, presenting the revision as independent of any extramusical interpretation:

> In this revised work there are no programmatic intentions; the emphasis is entirely on the Symphony's appeal as absolute music rather than the descriptive implications read into the original score. The composer offers the following terse comments on his Symphony in its present form, which henceforth will be the definitive version.
>
> The work is in three movements. The first, *Allegro ma non troppo,* is in sonata form. The second, *Andante un poco mosso,* is a slow movement of nocturnal character. The concluding movement begins with introductory spiral-like figures, *Presto,* leading to variations and fugato on a theme, *Allegro risoluto.* The whole is scored for large orchestra.
>
> . . . The composer prefers that his Symphony stand on its own merits without further elaboration on his part.[59]

Reviews of the revised symphony, like those of the earlier version, recognized its significance as a turning point in Barber's style. However, it was Barber's adherence to convention that still gained the most critical praise. Max de Schauensee, writing for the *Philadelphia Evening Bulletin,* said of the symphony:

> Like all important music, Mr. Barber's symphony speaks; it has plenty to say. Though conceived in the modern idiom, it is in the grand symphonic tradition and its architecture and scope are correspondingly impressive.
>
> The intensely emotional opening movement with its smashing climaxes has a feeling of protest throughout its span. The affecting song of the strings and woodwinds, which constitutes the second movement, bears the imprint of resignation. The last bars of the opening movement are arresting, unexpected, and thoroughly original. Furthermore they are singularly right.
>
> . . . It is rare to hear in this age of slick commercialism and smart-aleckism a composer who has so sincere an utterance.[60]

A visiting British music critic who reviewed a performance of the symphony on 6 April 1951 by the Boston Symphony Orchestra likened the work to Vaughan Williams's Sixth Symphony in that it "harnesses modern discords to basically nineteenth-century modes of construction."[61]

In 1950 the symphony was one of three works by Barber selected for recording by the New Symphony Orchestra on Decca of London, conducted by the composer himself (see chapter 11). He prepared for the recording sessions by contracting for a series of rigorous conducting lessons with Nicolai Malko in Copenhagen and practicing with the Danish Opera Orchestra. After the London recording sessions were finished, Barber conducted the symphony again in Frankfurt and Berlin.

But his own evaluation of the symphony took an ironic twist. It is clear, as his letters demonstrate, that Barber had been enthusiastic about the work while in the throes of its composition. Moreover, his satisfaction with the revised version is documented by the letters to Homer quoted above and a letter he wrote to Koussevitzky in 1949:

> I have asked Schirmers to send you the new version of my Second Symphony, which I thought you might like to see. Hilsberg did it with the Philadelphia Orchestra and most musicians and press seemed to think it was my best work. I myself am happy over the improvements.[62]

Almost twenty years later, however, in 1964, he was to reverse his position and withdraw the work from circulation. Though well reviewed at its onset, the symphony had been infrequently performed, and Barber attributed its lack of popularity to the "simple reason" that it was "not a good work."[63] Much to Hans Heinsheimer's consternation, but with his assistance, Barber destroyed all the scores of the Second Symphony in the Schirmer library, "tearing up page after page of the beautifully and expensively copied materials."[64]

That same year Barber salvaged the second movement of the symphony as a seven-and-a-half minute tone poem, *Night Flight,* Op. 19a. The scores are identical with only a few exceptions. From measure 61 to the end, in *Night Flight* the E♭ clarinet is supported in unison by the piano; an asterisk at 61 indicates that the clarinet, imitating an electric signal or radio beam, may be played instead by an electrical instrument at the pitch *a''*, in which case the piano is *tacet.* In addition, a rhythmic alteration to the "radio signal" imbues the E♭ clarinet part with a crisper, more active rhythm.

Night Flight was performed for the first time by the Cleveland Orchestra under George Szell, 8–10 October 1964 at Severance Hall in Cleveland. For the program notes, Barber provided an explanation of the relationship of the work to the Second Symphony:

> This is a revised version, twenty years later, of a movement from my Second Symphony, the rest of which is now withdrawn. It was composed during the years of the Second World War. Such times of cataclysm are rarely conducive to the creation of good music, especially when the composer tries to say too much. But the lyrical voice, expressing the dilemma of the individual, may still be of relevance.
>
> So I have kept this second movement, suggested by the feelings of a lonely flier at night, whose only human contact is through a radio-beam. St. Exupéry, of course, has expressed this better than anyone else and in admiration I have used his title.[65]

He suggested that the following excerpt from Saint-Exupéry's book *Night Flight* be included in the program as appropriate to the music:

> The pilot could mark night coming in by certain signs that called to mind the craters of a harbor—a calm expanse beneath, faintly rippled by the lazy clouds. . . . A single radio post still heard him. The only link between him and the world was a wave of music, a minor modulation. Not a lament, no cry, yet purest of sounds that ever spoke despair.[66]

Barber seemed not to want to put to rest the first movement of the Second Symphony either, for its opening themes (in particular, the "turn motive") were incorporated into works composed toward the latter part of his career—the opera *Antony and Cleopatra* in 1966 and *Fadograph of a Yestern Scene* in 1971.

In 1984 a set of orchestra parts that somehow were overlooked and had escaped ruin turned up in the warehouse of a G. Schirmer agency in England. They were returned to New York and used for a recording of the symphony by the New Zealand Symphony Orchestra under the direction of the American conductor Andrew Schenck.[67] Renewed interest in Barber's music in general led G. Schirmer in 1990 to reprint the 1950 edition.

Four Excursions, Op. 20 (1942–44)

As early as 1938 Jeanne Behrend had pressed Barber to write a "longish piece" for piano, something that would be appropriate to perform on one of her programs of American music.[68] With nothing forthcoming, she continued to play his Two Interludes of 1929–31 on her recitals. By this time, Behrend had established a reputation for promoting piano music of American composers to international audiences. "You certainly merit a decoration for all the missionary work you have done for American music down there," Barber wrote about her concerts in South America, "that is, if you have done it for the right people. For heaven's sake, don't be democratic. Why don't you publish your book about American music in this country? I should like to see a good one for once."[69]

For Barber the "right people" probably meant the "right composers." His ideas about which American composers were representative are revealed in a letter he wrote several years later in response to a request from Laurence Roberts, director of the American Academy in Rome, for a "small list of contemporary American music on records" and a library of contemporary American scores.[70] Barber suggested the following list of scores: Schirmer's Study Scores for all the orchestral works of Harris, Schuman, Piston, Bloch, and himself; in addition, his own *Capricorn Concerto*, Violin Concerto, and *Excursions;* Aaron Copland's *Appalachian Spring*, Piano Sonata, *El Salón México*, and *Billy the Kid;* and Randall Thompson's choruses and Second Symphony. For recordings he recommended the three works by Copland mentioned above; Roy Harris's Third Symphony; Schuman's *American Festival Overture;* Virgil Thomson's *The Plow that Broke the Plains* and *Four Portraits;* and Barber's own *Adagio for Strings, First Essay*, Overture to *The School for Scandal*, and First Symphony. Significantly, missing from the list are Ives, Sessions, and Carter. Interviewed in 1979, Barber expressed himself strongly on one: "I can't bear Ives," he said. "It is now unfashionable to say this, but in my opinion he was an amateur, a hack, who didn't put pieces together well. . . ."*

A works list compiled by Barber around 1970 reports June 1942 as the date of completion for the first of *Four Excursions,* solo piano pieces based on native folk genres.[71] *Excursion I,* in the style of a boogie-woogie, was not performed until almost two years later in May 1944, when Behrend played it on WQXR radio.

Barber wrote about this performance:

> G. C. told me you played Excursion extremely well over WQXR—I was in West Point at the time and couldn't hear it. He thinks I should publish it but I would like to hear what you do with it before I decide. Is there any chance of making a record sometime, that is if our paths do not cross?[72]

Although almost a week earlier he had completed two more *Excursions* (II and IV), he made no mention of these to Behrend in his May letter.† Later he wrote, "I am very anxious to have your copy of Excursion for a peek, not only to discuss markings but for the cuts, which are not marked on the copy I have."‡ Several weeks later, after receiving her copies, he wrote again to the pianist; his note suggests that he may have incorporated her suggestions into his final version of No. I: "Many, many thanks for sending your remarks so promptly—most of them I agreed with, strange to say! I've written two more pieces to go with that one and will show them to you sometime."§ Behrend's manuscript indicates that the cuts she suggested were few and were made to avoid redundancies.‖

By the end of July, however, Barber had given three *Excursions* (I, II, and IV of the final set) to Vladimir Horowitz, who agreed to play them the following season.# Horowitz had long wanted to perform a work by

*Phillip Ramey, "Samuel Barber at Seventy," *Ovation* (March 1980):19. His opinion of Gershwin is revealed in a letter of 8 March 1951 to Sidney Homer, in which he wrote that while in Vienna he was invited to the Musikvereinsaal to hear "an entire evening arranged by the American government of Gershwin—a highly overrated composer who only sounded childish in these surroundings" (letter, 8 March 1951, Paris).

†Behrend showed me manuscripts Barber had given her; manuscripts also exist at the Library of Congress, Music Division. No. IV is dated at the end 16 June 1944.

‡Letter, 22 June 1944, from the United States Office of War Information, 224 West 57th Street, New York. Barber commuted daily to the office from his home in Mount Kisco. He told Behrend, "I keep weekends religiously for my own work and don't come into N. Y. unless forced to: I'm here so much during the week, and it's the only method to get any composing done."

§Letter, 6 July 1944, from Capricorn. Perhaps Barber did not tell his friend about these two pieces in his earlier letter because he anticipated Vladimir Horowitz would do the first performance of the set.

‖Comparison of her manuscript of No. I and the G. Schirmer edition, 1945, shows variants at mm. 34, 35, and 81, where deletions of one or two measures were made to shorten a sequential pattern or avoid a repetition. Behrend's manuscript of No. IV shows several rhythmic variants from the G. Schirmer 1945 edition (at mm. 17, 37, 44–45, and 48) where, curiously, the original version seems more imitative of banjo playing.

#Horowitz and Barber had met in the early 1930s through Toscanini.

an American composer, and although he had considered some pieces by George Antheil, it was Barber's music that held the most appeal for him.[73] On 4 January 1945 at the Philadelphia Academy of Music he played three *Excursions* (published by G. Schirmer as I, II, and IV), which were received with a "great ovation" and cited by critics as being "made with delicacy, affectionate good humor, and in the modern mood of the times."* Max de Schauensee found the "slow blues" a particularly attractive section of the "three charmingly wistful and quasi-humorous pieces."†

The three *Excursions* were given their New York premiere by Horowitz on 28 March at Carnegie Hall.‡ Sandwiched in between Liszt, Rachmaninoff, and Czerny, Barber's suite was recognized by the press as a first for Horowitz:

> Last night was an unusual occasion for Mr. Horowitz, since neither Beethoven sonatas nor contemporary American works figure normally on his program. . . . Samuel Barber's "Excursions," which were given a masterly first New York reading, suffer from a drab blues. The outer movements are, however, agreeable enough, and their native folk dance material lends them a cheerful note to the program. The deliberate, repeated "wrong note" of the first piece, and the facetious close of the third, are a bit obvious. But this was a fine gesture for Mr. Horowitz to have made, and it is to be hoped that he will favor other Americans as well in the future.[74]

The tepid reception of the blues may have been due more to an unconvincing performance than the fault of the music itself. Although Barber liked the way Horowitz played his pieces, a curious letter to Behrend suggests that the blues had been problematic for the Russian pianist, whose repertoire before then had almost exclusively featured nineteenth-century European music and who apparently was handicapped by his unfamiliarity with American genres: §

* Quoted in "Horowitz Plays New Composition by Samuel Barber," *West Chester Daily Local News,* 5 January 1945. In referring to the second movement, it was pointed out that Barber "says 'hello' to syncopated rhythms without borrowing ideas from Gershwin." The review reads: "The Russian pianist never plays the works of a living composer if he is in the audience, however, Corporal Barber . . . attended the concert . . . but the soloist was not aware until after the performance."

† "Recital by Vladimir Horowitz Is Heard by Capacity Audience," *Philadelphia Evening Bulletin,* 5 January 1945. The capacity audience included at least four hundred persons sitting on the stage.

‡ An article in the *West Chester Daily Local News,* 5 January 1945, states that *Excursions* (incorrectly called a five-movement piece) was first played by Horowitz in Brooklyn and then in Washington, D.C., before the Philadelphia performance.

§ A letter from Barber to Koussevitzky, 27 November 1944, states, "Horowitz is playing my 'Excursions' beautifully." Koussevitzky's letter to Barber on 8 December 1944 indicates that apparently the conductor agreed: "Vlodia Horowitz 'came to town' and I heard him play your 'Excursions' last Sunday. He does play them beautifully and it is altogether a charming composition," he wrote. Regarding II, Behrend, on the other hand, believed that Horowitz never really understood the sultry "lazy" quality that was inherent to the blues style (Behrend, interview with the author, 1 September 1982, Philadelphia).

> I had Schirmers send [Horowitz] a copy to New Hampshire, as he was leaving that afternoon. He says he can't figure out how to play the blues, prefers the last one![75]

Excursion III was the last composed of the set, and although it was completed by September 1944, it was not played by Horowitz on his programs in 1945. It remained for Behrend to play all four *Excursions* for the first time in her monumental Concert of American Piano Music, which took place on 22 December 1948 at the New York Times Hall, 240 West 44th Street.* Behrend organized the event around a notable roster of performers: John Cage, John Kirkpatrick, Ralph Kirkpatrick, Arthur Loesser, and Leo Smit. Barber's *Excursions* shared the program with works by Reinagle, MacDowell, Ives, Gottschalk, Copland, Harris, Cage, and Gershwin. When Behrend played the *Excursions* again at the Blue and White Series at University of New Hampshire on 8 March 1950, her notes recognized the pieces as "admittedly, excursions into a style not typical of Barber."[76]

Barber once remarked lightly that he wrote *Excursions* just to prove he could write "American" music.[77] As discussed in earlier chapters of this book, his interest in folk music was intense during the thirties but seems to have been exclusively focused on European sources; a change of perspective, however, was expressed in 1943 to Harold D. Spivacke, chief librarian of the Music Division of the Library of Congress:

> Would it be possible for you to send me the seven record albums of American folk music from the Archive of American Folk Song? I am very eager to have them and have no idea whether they are available gratis or for sale.[78]

Barber knew about these recordings from a recent visit he had made to the library, but the extent of his familiarity with the music is not clear. Spivacke informed the composer:

> It is with great regret that I must tell you that we cannot send you the seven albums of recordings of American folk song recently issued by the Library of Congress. They were prepared on a completely self-sustaining basis and we do not have one single record to give away. For your information I am enclosing a catalog describing the contents of the albums, listing the prices, and giving ordering information. Since these are rather expensive, it occurred to me that you might arrange for the Army to purchase them for you if they have any connection at all with your army work.[79]

There is no information about which, if any, recordings Barber ordered or whether there was any relationship between his inquiry and the three *Excursions* written after his inquiry to Spivacke.

* The concert was a benefit for the purchase of manuscripts of Louis Moreau Gottschalk for the Americana Music Collection in the New York Public Library.

With these pieces, however, he seemed to be following the trend of American composers, in the years surrounding World War II, to write piano music reflecting popular influence.* Evidence that music based on regional American idioms was received warmly in Europe after the war is supported by the gratifying reception *Excursions* had when Rudolf Firkusny played them in Prague in 1946 (see below in this chapter).†

But whereas European audiences did not question the authenticity of *Excursions,* some American composers and scholars perceive them as unconvincing: Virgil Thomson, for example, while declaring them as "sonorously agreeable . . . charming and high class, both in style and sentiment," nevertheless pointed out "they do not travel much farther in subject matter than a New York night club. The one about a mouth organ is the gayest and the freest, the one about boogie-woogie, the most interesting in thought";[80] Ned Rorem suggests that the boogie-woogie and blues could have been extemporized by any jazz pianist;[81] and H. Wiley Hitchcock believes "the models are misheard, not really felt deeply," and are lacking the "amused side-long glance" inherent in parody.[82] Yet, judging from the frequency of performances and the number of available recordings, pianists and audiences have continued enthusiasm for *Excursions.* This may be due in part to the fact that Barber's published works for piano are few and these affable short pieces are a welcome representation on programs that do not want the length and breadth of his Piano Sonata; they are not, however, as easy to perform as the direct simplicity of their style suggests.

Barber's opinion about his *Excursions* was that "they are, of course, nothing but bagatelles."[83]

> These are "Excursions" in small classical forms into regional American idioms. Their rhythmic characteristics, as well as their source in folk material and their scoring, reminiscent of local instruments are easily recognized.[84]

The words "classical forms" and "rhythmic characteristics" that are "reminiscent" illuminate his intentions here. For, rather than parody, he seems to have had in mind stylized concert pieces, somewhat "refined" and elaborated versions that compare to their sources in much the same way as Stravinsky's *Piano-Rag-Music* does to the popular prototypes. No. I, for example, the boogie-woogie, contains 4/4 ostinato "walking bass" figurations in eight-bar phrases, interrupted by five-, three-, or seven-beat measures; "blue notes" are incorporated into melodic patterns; syncopations and unexpected dissonances result from juxtaposition of right- and

* Maurice Hinson and H. Wiley Hitchcock, in their article "Piano Music" (*Grove Dictionary of American Music,* p. 564), mention *Excursions* as one of several examples that include also Copland's *Four Piano Blues* (1926–48), Harris's *American Ballads* (1942–45), Schuman's *Three-Score Set* (1943), and Thomson's *Ragtime Blues* (1943).

†Letter, Barber to Schirmer, 11 June 1946, Hotel de la Ville, Rome. This was the last concert Firkusny played in his native country until 1990.

left-hand parts—the "crushed notes" that occur when "adjacent notes are struck together in rapid succession" are evident, but these are polite discords, as it were, compared to the real thing. That Barber intended to formalize the popular style is supported by Behrend's recollection that he advised her to play the sweeping scale passage at measure 24 articulated rather than as a glissando.[85]

Excursion II, "in slow blues tempo," uses the conventional harmonic progressions and melodic and rhythmic features associated with blues.* *Excursion* III, Allegretto, is a set of variations over an ostinato harmonic bass progression. The theme's similarity to "The Streets of Laredo" and the rhythmic similarities to Latin American popular music—especially dance music—have been observed by some.† *Excursion* IV, with its opening block chords and exclusive use of tonic and subdominant harmonies, suggests to Sifferman "the limited vocabulary of the mouth organ or harmonica" and melodic patterns indigenous to fiddle playing in a barn dance.[86]

Capricorn Concerto, Op. 21 (1944)

The initial success of his Second Symphony made it possible for Barber to realize a goal that had become almost an obsession with him during the first years of his service in the army—the freedom to continue composing without the restrictions of military obligations. To return to a schedule where he could work only at night seemed unthinkable to him; he wrote to Homer: "I can't compose in this regimentation, you can lecture me all you want, but it doesn't work!"[87] Moreover, in 1944 there were too many opportunities for Barber that would have to be postponed should that be the case: Rodzinski had asked him to compose a work for the New York Philharmonic and the Westminster Choir; and Koussevitzky had offered $1,000 for another symphony for the following season.[88] A report of Barber's situation in the spring 1944 issue of *Newsweek* suggests that his status was not without wrinkles:

> Since Barber is probably the most outstanding American serious composer in uniform, the question of how best to use his talent has been controver-

* Although the second *Excursion* has no key signature, James Sifferman (*Samuel Barber's Works for Solo Piano,* D.M.A. treatise, University of Texas, 1982, pp. 5–21), in agreement with Broder and in contrast to Friedewald, presents a compelling case for analyzing the piece in G, which is "undeniably clear to the ear" as a tonal center (p. 13).

† See, for example, Allan Kozinn, "Samuel Barber: The Last Interview and the Legacy," part 2, *High Fidelity* (July 1981):47; and Sifferman, *Samuel Barber's Works for Solo Piano,* pp. 15–18. Sifferman isolates the specific features that give this work "a Latin flavor": the prevalence of the "tresillo" rhythm popular with Latin American dances, dotted-rhythmic figures, and syncopations both in the melodic line and accompaniment, as well as the rhythmic juxtaposition of seven against eight.

> sial ever since he was inducted in September of 1942. At a Town Hall symposium on music for the armed forces in January last year, an unnamed "distinguished young composer" became a mild cause célèbre when Laurence Tibbett stated that the Army had refused the composer permission to write a special American musical greeting to the Russian people and, because of his limited-service classification, had kept him doing a clerk's work instead.
>
> Barber was never named as the composer in question, but the facts fitted him because of his own limited service and because his music is extremely popular in Russia. Sometime thereafter Barber was transferred to the Air Force and was assigned to write the new symphony. He now says that he is "very happy that America is beginning to use composers in the same way Russia is using Shostakovich."*

One of the people to whom Barber expressed his frustrations then was Daniel Saidenberg, head of the Music Department of the Office of War Information.† His job involved producing musical recordings into which propaganda material was later inserted. In an effort to show the "Allied, neutral, and enemy nations that the United States was not lacking in culture," Saidenberg selected and recorded live performances of concert music—European as well as American—to be broadcast overseas.[89] To help Barber, he approached Louis Cowen, director of OWI, and impressed upon him the importance of having "a world-famous composer" on the staff.‡

Meanwhile Barber waged an aggressive campaign of his own to obtain the assignment to this desirable post. In addition to his requests to Koussevitzky to write on his behalf to General Matthew Arnold and Barton K.

*"The Case of Sam Barber," *Newsweek,* 13 March 1944. He probably referred here to the *Leningrad Symphony* of 1942, which became a national symbol of the defense of Russia and was used to build morale during the war. It was smuggled into the United States, where several conductors fought for the right to give the first performance (Barber heard Toscanini's performance on the radio on 19 July 1942). In 1949 when Shostakovich came to New York for a so-called Congress in Defence of Peace, Barber protested to Sidney Homer:

> I never met Shostakovich at all! It seems a shame that conflicting ideologies, which have always existed, are regimented now to such an extent that artists are guarded, not allowed to meet their colleagues in a normal way, nor indeed to converse at all freely. . . . I also found Shostakovich's attack on Strawinsky unnecessary and unworthy of him. (letter, week of 7 April 1949)

†A former cellist with the Philadelphia Orchestra, and later the Chicago Symphony Orchestra, Saidenberg was founder and conductor of the Saidenberg Sinfonietta, with which he toured the country playing neglected works by Sowerby, Arthur Foote, Shostakovich, Roussel, Milhaud, Hindemith, and Miaskovsky. In 1940, the publishing house Boosey and Hawkes established the orchestra's headquarters in New York under the name of the Saidenberg Little Symphony, whose aim would be "to introduce as many contemporary works as possible as well as perform the more rarely played works of the old masters." The conductor was convinced that such an organization would be "an incentive to native composers" (Daniel Saidenberg, "New Little Symphony," *New York Times,* 29 December 1940).

‡Saidenberg, interview with author, 7 June 1985, New York. Cowen's office was allowed to employ two servicemen without having to pay their salaries.

Yount (mentioned above), he wrote to Walter Damrosch about the forthcoming performance of the Second Symphony and prevailed upon him for help:

> It is the first time the Army has allowed any serious creative music—until now everything has been jazz—and they are waiting for public reaction. Should you approve, it would mean a great deal if you would wire General Arnold . . . after the performance.
>
> What happens next to me, I don't know, but I hope very much to be allowed to compose.[90]

Barber's attitude that jazz did not fall into the category of "serious creative music" was not unusual among classical musicians during the 1940s. His position is illuminated further in an orchestration notebook kept during that period, in which he wrote, "Jazz is really not supposed to be edifying. You listen to jazz with feet or snapping fingers, not so much the ear." *

The request for help was undoubtedly received sympathetically by traditionalist Damrosch, who, after hearing both of Barber's symphonies, telegraphed General Arnold:

> I heard performance of new symphony by Corporal Sam Barber, received with great enthusiasm and immense audience. I consider Barber one of most gifted American composers. I hope he may be permitted by Army authorities to continue his creative work.[91]

Grateful for Damrosch's support, Barber wrote to him:

> I was delighted to see you that day in Carnegie Hall for Symphony I and to know that you heard Symphony II. Thank you for your kindness in wiring General Arnold.
>
> I am awaiting their decision, having suggested to them an assignment to the Music Department of the O.W.I. in New York. I feel that I would be of some use there and a job is open: at the same time I should be able to continue some composing of my own. It seems to me I am just getting into stride as a composer and I don't want to slip! All it needs is the army O.K., but I am hopeful. At any rate, many thanks to you for your continued encouragement.[92]

Sidney Homer, too, was ready to exert influence to obtain a post for his nephew in Florida. But Barber clearly preferred the OWI job and cautioned his uncle to hold off on his plan:

* This orchestration notebook, Music Division, Library of Congress, seems to have been prepared by Barber for teaching. His metaphorical description of the relation between the parts of a jazz ensemble is psychologically oriented:

> In Jazz the soloist is like a feather; bass and drums give him a blast of air and push him up, curiously feminine, leaving soloist alone, to work with or against. Not to play square! symph. musician takes the beat with him. Dialectic is the struggle between two opposite poles—continuo versus passivity of soloist.

> Please do me a favor. I am trying very hard to get transferred into the OWI music department in N.Y., a very interesting job writing music for broadcasts, and must be assigned by the General. If they request me in Florida, it will *can the works*. Much as I'd like to be near you, I feel this job would be better. I'm planning to write something for the Florida group anyway, and they should send me the instrumentation required. But please phone them and tell them not to do anything official about a transfer until I see what happens about this other thing. Gosh, I hope they haven't already asked for me![93]

By 1 May 1944—a month before the Anglo-American invasion of Western Europe on 6 June 1944—Barber's assignment to the New York Office of War Information was confirmed. He was, according to Saidenberg, the only composer employed in that office and evidently given special status, because he was not required to punch a time clock.[94] Although he was reassured by Saidenberg that he could retreat to Mount Kisco most of the time to write music and return to the office only when music was completed, letters to Strickland document that Barber was kept busy with the office's recording sessions for overseas broadcasts.*

On 8 September 1944 Barber completed *Capricorn Concerto*, a chamber piece for flute, oboe, trumpet, and strings, which he presented to Saidenberg almost immediately.[95] The title, though enigmatic to those who were unaware of its source, was chosen as a tribute to Barber's and Menotti's home, Capricorn, which Mary Curtis Bok had helped them purchase in 1943. The composers had named the house Capricorn because it received maximum sunshine in the winter. Designed earlier by the Swiss architect William Lescaze (possibly his first in America), the house met the special requirements of two composers—"demanding a studio apiece, each large enough for a grand piano, and far enough away from each other so that they would not be hearing double when both were at work."[96] The poet Robert Horan, who shared the house with Barber and Menotti in the early years, provided a lengthy description of the house in a popular magazine:

> We preferred it quiet, somewhat isolated in beautiful country, but near New York, not too difficult to clean or maintain, and not ornamented with many antique and breakable objects. It seems to me one of those rare gratuities of fate that we found, on a beautiful uninhabited hill outside of Mount Kisco, this particular house.
>
> [It] resembles, from the outside, a modern but not "moderne" chalet set into the side of a mountain and overlooking Croton Lake and the far hills. . . . There is a small, raised, stone terrace at the front of the house

* For example, a letter Barber wrote on 15 June 1944 reads: "We had a recording session the other afternoon and I got tied up. . . . We have a recording session of the Philharmonic this week, Golschmann conducting, which keeps us busy."

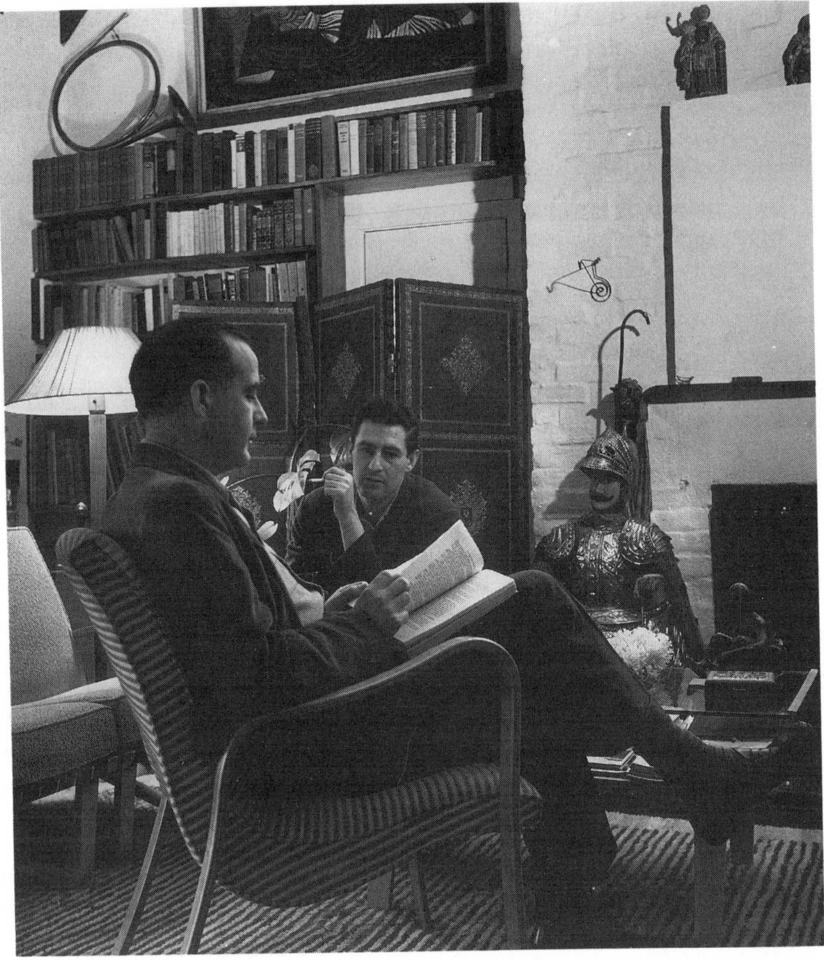

Barber and Menotti at Capricorn, 1946. *(Courtesy of Gian Carlo Menotti)*

bordered with flowers or weeds, depending on our industry and the mysteries of the weather. At the back of the house, leading from the living room by half-doors . . . is a large flagged terrace built around a white birch tree. . . . Here . . . one can eat in the summertime. . . . There is a roof deck over one of the studios reached from this terrace by an outside staircase, and this makes possible long, indolent sun baths.

Inside, it is a private house and a triple workshop simultaneously. All built on one floor in wings from a central, two-storied living room. . . . There are slightly raised levels going into the bedrooms, separating them from the main room. The living room . . . is a general refuge when work is going badly, serving intermittently as a dining room and a library. . . . In the winter, we migrate to the fireplace side.[97]

Capricorn, Mount Kisco, New York. *(Courtesy of Gian Carlo Menotti)*

Barber's private quarters contained modern furniture and a pale old Chinese rug. His studio looked out into the wooded side of the hill and was built around a piano and music desk, with storage especially built for books and music manuscripts. On the bookshelves were signs of the music Barber loved and studied—the complete works of Bach, Mozart, Palestrina, Vivaldi, and Monteverdi, together with numerous volumes of Brahms, German Lieder, and opera scores.[98]

In 1944 Capricorn provided for Barber a sanctuary from both military schedules and public life. Many years afterwards, in 1979, when interviewed by Allan Kozinn, he revealed how important a rural setting was to his work:

> I think I'm a country person. Most everything I've composed, I've composed in the country, and the pieces I've written in the city have generally been started in the country. . . . Like Messiaen, I like birds. And I need the absolute silence of the country. I need places to walk.[99]

Capricorn Concerto was premiered by the Saidenberg Little Symphony at Town Hall on 8 October 1944, one month after its completion. The soloists were flutist John Wummer, oboist Mitchell Miller, and trumpeter Harry Freistadt. The program was divided between eighteenth-century music—Bach, Cimarosa, and Geminiani—and three contemporary works by Barber, Cowell, and Miaskovsky.

Barber's concerto, composed with Saidenberg's orchestra in mind, is in three movements and designed like a Baroque concerto grosso, with the same instrumentation as Bach's Brandenburg Concerto No. 2: three solo instruments (trumpet, oboe, and flute) and strings. Certain Baroque techniques abound—contrasting *ripieno* and *concertante* episodes, the returning rondo theme, alternation of contrapuntal and homophonic styles, fugue, "walking-bass" pizzicato accompaniments, and figurations of triadic patterns and measured trills.

Barber viewed the style of *Capricorn Concerto* as different from his earlier works, as this note to Henry de La Grange suggests: "It is hard to explain, and you may find this music rather new for me, but it is in a sense decorative, slightly baroque à la Brandenburg Concerto, less romantic."[100] Sidney Homer described the concerto as "an abstract conversation of angels, who seem to understand each other."[101] Their tonal language, however, is contemporary: Friedewald's observation is well placed in pointing out that, although *Capricorn Concerto* is not atonal or polytonal, the use of chords with added tones and other coloristic devices (polychords, for example) often obscures the harmony at any given moment.[102]

Rhythmically, too, the piece represents a new direction for Barber. Seldom does any regularity of the underlying meter continue for long: frequent and sudden shifts from divisions of two to three (in the first and third movements) and between eight, twelve, five, and nine (in the second movement), which provide rhythmic vigor and suggest—especially in the first and third movements—the nervous, dance-generated rhythmic syncopations of Copland's orchestral music.*

The first movement, a rondo form, has five shifts of tempo between allegro and andante con moto. Like earlier works of Barber's (the Serenade for String Quartet and the *Essays,* for example), material from the introduction (four motives, in this case) dominates the progress of the movement. A slow-moving, lyrical three-voice fugue is derived from a rhythmic diminution of a tripartite subject of the introduction. In the second movement (an allegretto ABA form), oboe and trumpet or flute and oboe cheerfully march in dotted rhythms over a pizzicato viola continuo, which is interrupted only briefly by the lyrical *tranquillo* section. The third movement features a trumpet fanfare, which seems to allude to the final movement of Brandenburg Concerto No. 2 and the rhythm of the opening motive of Stravinsky's *Ebony Concerto*. The spirit of *L'Histoire du Soldat*'s trumpet march is evoked here as well.

The premiere of *Capricorn Concerto* earned from the large audience "the chief applause of the newer works" on the program. Saidenberg, commended for "displaying the music for its own sake rather than the

*The resemblance was sharply pointed up by Charles Mills, who reviewed a CBS radio broadcast of *Capricorn Concerto*. He wrote: "It exemplifies what a productive study of Copland will do for a young musician who has been brought up in the tradition of big, fat sounds and pompous effects" ("Over the Air," *Modern Music* 23 [Winter 1946]:74).

qualities of the virtuoso ensemble," evidently gave the piece a sterling performance.[103] Nevertheless, Barber's *Capricorn Concerto* elicited a mixed reception from music critics. Curiously, some reviews seem to suggest a misunderstanding of the composer's intentions to derive his model from the Baroque concerto grosso. The critic Noel Straus, for example, comparing *Capricorn Concerto* to Cowell's *Hymn and Fuguing Tune* (on the same program), pointed to Barber's work as lighter, "modernistic in its method of treatment," with "nothing particularly original to import" and "largely episodic and fragmentary in its three divisions," yet serving its purpose "well enough in rather inconsequential but clever fashion."[104] In contrast, Lou Harrison's warm review of *Capricorn Concerto* in *Modern Music* presents a promising appraisal of Barber at midcareer:

> Samuel Barber's new *Capricorn Concerto* is a brilliant work, and takes the cake for orchestration this month. The charming combinations he achieves with the wind concertino are very telling indeed and produce a bubbling opalescence. The music is well worked, although very Stravinskian, and makes intentional and persistent use of that old academic bugaboo, the general pause. Actually Barber has done an obvious but seldom thought of thing. When he comes to the end of a section of material, instead of making the fluid and highly professional transition into the next idea, he simply stops. Dead silence for a fraction of a second, and then everything begins at once with the new material already in full action. The device is effective and frank. It is used over and over again and becomes an integral stylistic feature. Except for this, though, the piece might have been signed by Stravinsky of a few years back. Barber has tremendous technical grasp and an essential urge to expression, but seems fascinated in turn by each of the famous masks and mantles. If he ever catches up with himself, he certainly will be a composer of power and interest.[105]

One cannot fail to take into account the strong influence of Stravinsky in *Capricorn Concerto,* and this is especially true with regard to the timbres and textures, the rhythmic freedom, and the treatment of the solo woodwind instruments. But beyond surface influences, the treatment of musical ideas and the ideas themselves always retain the stamp of Barber's personality, an aspect that has always been recognized in later critical reviews of the work.[106] When, soon after the premiere, Barber was invited to conduct *Capricorn Concerto* at the University of Chicago, there were supposedly concerns that the concerto would be damaged by comparison with Stravinsky's *Dumbarton Oaks Concerto,* which was scheduled to precede it on the program.* But the Chicago concert was an unqualified success, according to critic Cecil M. Smith, and fears were "laid to rest":

*Cecil M. Smith, "Big Names in Chicago," *Modern Music* 22 (January–February 1945):2. To prepare for the concert, Barber took a few conducting lessons from George Szell. Afterwards, he confessed to Koussevitzky that he regretted he had not had the opportunity to

> While there can be no doubt that Barber has observed much that Stravinsky had to show younger composers, he nevertheless invents his own themes, maintains them by his own special kind of rhythmic urgency, and orchestrates them with his own pointed economy. More than most of his contemporaries, Mr. Barber understands the difference between beginning, middle, and end. He evolves movements out of new material, which are reasonable, consecutive, and emulative, and he does not disdain to be friendly or communicative along the way.[107]

That the Stravinsky association was canonized is exemplified by the choice of *Capricorn Concerto* in 1966 on the opening concerts of "A Festival of Stravinsky: His Heritage and His Legacy." The New York Philharmonic under Leonard Bernstein played Barber's work on a program titled "Stravinsky and American Music" that included also Copland's *Dance Symphony,* Revueltas's *Sensemayá,* and Stravinsky's *Le Sacre du printemps.**

Barber, however, had viewed Stravinsky's music with reservation. In 1948, after hearing what he thought was a "very good performance" of *Capricorn,* conducted by Ernest Ansermet, the composer wrote:

> One of the foremost protagonists of Strawinsky, in the old days, he [Ansermet] is one of the few musicians I know who seems to realize Strawinsky's value *and very definite limitations:* in other words, why Strawinsky is not a great composer. With all Strawinsky's talent and imagination, his lack of lyricism and utter inability to work in more than small periods weigh heavily against him.†

This bald assessment seems to tell as much about Barber's own compositional strengths and predilections as his perception of Stravinsky.

The title of the concerto led some to seek extramusical events in the score. Before the New York premiere, Barber had given a typically cryptic response to a newspaper critic who asked him about the implications of the title: "Nothing at all—it is just a word, but perhaps its meaning will get across when you hear the music."[108] Several years later, to Sidney Homer's query whether there was a program, Barber wrote, "There is *no* program for *Capricorn Concerto.* Just cheerful noises!"[109] A curious article in a Philadelphia newspaper, however, announced that residents of Capricorn were represented in the concerto and offered as proof facsimiles of the copyist's score with programmatic captions:

> In the concerto—which receives its Philadelphia premiere by the New Chamber Orchestra, Ifor Jones conducting, at the Academy of Music to-

---

study conducting with him at the Berkshire Music School. Letters from Barber to Koussevitzky, 20 October 1944 and 21 April 1945.

*The concert on 30 June, which was repeated on 5 July, was the first of the series and was followed by "Stravinsky and Russian Music," "Stravinsky and the Eighteenth Century," and "Stravinsky and Recent Years."

†Letter, Barber to Sidney Homer, 8 February 1948.

morrow—the string section represents the house proper, while the solo flute, oboe and trumpet represents the two wings and a guest room, or, in that order, Barber, Menotti, and Horan.*

There followed pictures of the house and musical examples in which *ripieno* passages in the first movement were said to represent the house; themes in the second and third movements to be associated with Menotti, Horan, and Barber; and the coda to suggest "Sunday afternoon on the terrace" (Example 9.3).

In December 1945, three months after the war had ended, Barber wrote to La Grange that he had sent the score and parts of *Capricorn Concerto* to the cultural attaché of the American Embassy in Paris, "in case anyone would like to perform it." Apologizing for being "a deplorable correspondent," he explained: "There were months this summer waiting for demobilization (and in camp I do nothing but exist) and then the appalling amount of work already promised which I found here on my return, uncompleted." About *Capricorn Concerto* he cautioned:

> It must be very well performed or not at all. Are the Serenade Concerts still going? It can be for small body of strings (25 circa) or complete symphonic strings, and an excellent trumpet is necessary. *And* a good *French* conductor: no American soldier-conductor, please. . . . It was very successful when played here and is to be played in London next month: of course I should love it played in Paris, but would prefer to have it in a really French concert: I dislike those official American ones. . . . The only other people whom I am telling about its being played in Paris are Gian-Carlo's cousin, who has a group of young composers and artists interested in new works—Mme Virginie-Bianchini Schils (sp?) . . . and Duchamel (celui de "Musique consolatrice") who seems interested in my music, whom I met here recently.
>
> Chappell (Bond St.) London has all my music—scores and parts, and there are many performances in England, but Paris——nothing.[110]

Six months later Barber was invited to participate in a meeting of international musicians and composers in Prague. While there, he conducted the Czech Radio Orchestra in some of his works: *Capricorn Concerto*, the *Adagio for Strings*, and the suite from *Medea* (see chapter 10). The letter Barber wrote to his publisher presents a view of the emerging interest in American music in postwar Europe:

> It was a very good idea to go there. The best Russian, French, and English musicians had come, the first real meeting of artists since the war, and one got to know them quickly and well. It was the first time the Russian mu-

*"Musical Architecture," *Philadelphia Evening Bulletin*, 18 January 1947. The source of the manuscript is not revealed. Holographs at the Library of Congress present no evidence of such titles.

I. Orchestra—House

Example 9.3 Principal themes of *Capricorn Concerto* as represented in the *Philadelphia Evening Bulletin,* 18 January 1947.

sicians had met an American composer—indeed any foreign composer at all—and we had three weeks together, seeing each other constantly and without any supervision. An amazing violinist, Oistrakh, certainly in the Heifetz class, the pianist Obonn, and their best conductor Mravinsky to whom Shostakovich dedicated his 7th symphony.

Especially with Mravinsky, the conductor, I was able to talk very often and quite frankly (in German—none of them speak English or French).

They are crazy to know about American music, want more of it, and I found their reactions to Bernstein's American concert quite interesting. Indeed, I wish all the American composers represented on that program could have heard their music in such unusual surroundings—in an old concert hall dominated by a 15th century castle and to a foreign audience, for some of the shortcomings of the American school were more apparent than in Carnegie Hall—much more! Nevertheless they were deeply interested in our music in Prague, and after Firkusny played my "Excursions" at his piano concert I could have sold a hundred copies on the spot! Of course they *all* want the Schirmer agency. I must say also that the American concert here was much more impressive than the British in the general opinion. Here in Rome, too, there is much interest, but neither Italy or Czechoslovakia is the right place for distribution and as yet one cannot make contracts with private publishers in these two countries due to currency complications. I shall go into this more extensively in Paris and Switzerland.

Paris is very active musically. Dozens of concerts, and they all ask where they can get our scores and material. Münch, the very best French conductor (who is to conduct the Philharmonic next season), whom I met in Prague and Paris, is especially interested. And this at a time when the State Department is taking a 75 percent cut and all the cultural attachés are leaving their posts right and left. One cannot count on the State Department at all, unless its funds are considerably increased. But I have a better idea, which I'll explain later.[111]

About the concert he conducted, he wrote:

All the Russians, BBC representatives, Kubelík (conductor of the Prague Philharmonic), etc. etc. came to the concert, which was very successful. The Russians invited me to Leningrad where they are going to perform some of my things, but of course this must be for another time and another trip. We exchanged presents, vodka, and went back to our separate worlds. The Embassy people in Prague described it as "the closest contact yet made in Prague with the Russians." But there is nothing surprising in this. Diplomats are always suspicious and artists quickly bridge frontiers. Music brought us together.[112]

10

MIDDLE YEARS

The clear status of a master

Concerto for Violoncello and Orchestra, Op. 22 (1945)

"I've accepted a commission from Koussevitzky to write a cello concerto—which Raya Garbousova will play with him next year," Barber wrote to Homer in early spring of 1945.[1] The Concerto for Violoncello and Orchestra was, in fact, paid for by John Nicholas Brown, a Providence philanthropist, whose enthusiasm for music led him to support a broad range of activities.*

The idea of commissioning a concerto came from Koussevitzky, who had encouraged Garbousova's career since her American debut in 1935.† Until the early 1940s she had played almost annually with the Boston

* An amateur cellist himself, Brown had the distinction of being the first non-Bostonian trustee of the Boston Symphony. He founded St. Dunstan's College for Sacred Music and with his wife, Anne, instituted an annual festival of chamber music in Providence; they often invited artists to their home on Fisher Island: the Musical Arts Quartet, Koussevitzky, Garbousova, Menotti, and Rostropovich were all part of his circle. A longtime patron and friend of Garbousova, he gave her one of the great Stradivarius violoncellos—the "Archinto," 1689 (J. Carter Brown, "John Nicholas Brown and Music," *Newsletter of the Violoncello Society*, June 1982, p. 5; and correspondence from Anne S. K. Brown to the author, 11 October 1983).

† Raya Garbousova, interview with the author, 28 October 1983, New York City. All quotations or information attributed to Garbousova, unless otherwise indicated, are from this interview or one conducted on 30 October 1983. Up to 1945 there were a handful of cello concertos written by contemporary composers—Ibert (1926), Honegger (1930), Milhaud (1935), Hindemith, and Martinů (1930)—and concert programs virtually excluded performances of these pieces beyond their premieres, relying instead on the few popular works by Dvořák, Schumann, and Saint-Saëns. Programs of the New York Philharmonic–Symphony Society for the seasons 1940–42 list, for example, Dvořák, Op. 104; Brahms's Double Concerto; Beethoven's Triple Concerto; Richard Strauss's *Don Quixote;* and an arrangement for cello of Mozart's Concerto for Horn, K. 447, by Gasparo Cassado.

Symphony Orchestra, but as her engagements dwindled Koussevitzky suggested she commission a work for herself by Bohuslav Martinů.* By the time Garbousova had entered preliminary arrangements with Martinů, Barber called to inform her he had already been commissioned by Koussevitzky to write a concerto for her for the forthcoming season of the Boston Symphony.†

In January 1945 Barber wrote to Koussevitzky, "I have started work on the cello concerto and discussed technical possibilities with Garbousova."‡ As he was to do later with Vladimir Horowitz before writing the Piano Sonata and with John Browning before embarking on composition of the Piano Concerto, Barber had the cellist play through her repertoire to demonstrate her particular technical resources and the potential of the instrument. The meeting lasted for hours, during which time she played for him a concerto by Davidov,§ etudes by Duport and Popper, and twelve caprices of Piatti—works in which the whole range of the fingerboard was explored—and she lent him much music to study at home. Garbousova had a reputation for enjoying the high registers of the violoncello; and she departed from the traditional notion that "the only way to break somebody's heart was to vibrate on the C-string."[2] Barber recognized and appreciated the freedom he would have in composing for an artist with virtually limitless technique.

But the work went slowly. In March, he first mentioned the cello concerto to his uncle: "A very difficult job and it hasn't progressed at all. Perhaps spring weather will do the trick." Although during this time his army responsibilities with OWI continued, Barber was still able to continue to live and work at home. He heard little music that winter of 1945 but read a great deal of French literature and attended weekly philosophical lectures in New York. There were occasional visitors from France at Capricorn; everyone, including Barber, was focused on the Russian victories reported on the radio.[3]

Garbousova was visiting a friend in nearby Ossining, the pianist Nadia Reisenberg, and stayed in close communication with Barber. As he completed passages of music—even if only a few measures at a time—he sent

*Garbousova, in her interview with the author on 28 October 1983, recalled Koussevitzky's words: "There are no more Esterhazys or Rasoumoffskys. Artists are earning good money now; you must commission works yourself from composers."

†Evidently Koussevitzky either forgot his earlier suggestion or changed his mind after he realized John Brown preferred Barber for the commission.

‡Letter, 28 January 1945, from Mount Kisco. A month later Garbousova wrote to Koussevitzky that she expected the concerto would be ready in May so that she could learn the music during the summer in time to play it the following season. She anticipated it would help her career enormously by stimulating invitations to play with other orchestras (letter, 5 March 1945). The schedule was delayed, however, because of Barber's difficulties in beginning the work.

§Carl Davidov (1838–1889) was an outstanding Russian violoncellist and reputable composer who wrote four concertos for cello and orchestra.

them to her to try out; she worked out fingerings and bowings, occasionally suggesting alternatives to allow for better articulation and more idiomatic technique. Up to the last minute there were changes designed to eliminate awkward passages. Frequently, as Garbousova mastered a portion of music, Barber would send her a message to disregard specific measures and substitute new ones as the final version.[4]

The cellist reported this collaboration to be one of the most creative and happiest times of her life. But there was frustration and quarreling as well. Barber seemed ambivalent—his friends chided him—about yielding to the influence of a performer. Garbousova persuasively countered with "Stravinsky never wrote a note for the violin without consulting Dushkin."* The effectiveness of Barber's and Garbousova's work is corroborated by Ross Lee Finney's appraisal of the concerto as "one of the finest concertos for the instrument composed during this century . . . written with complete understanding and sympathy for the technique of the instrument."[5]

On 28 July 1945 Barber wrote to Olga Koussevitzky: "Two movements of the concerto are done—one more to go—and Garbousova seemed enthusiastic."[6] At this time, also, he suggested to her that he might possibly gain an early discharge from the army if a "strong letter" of justification were written by Koussevitzky:

> It would be well to emphasize that only as a civilian can whatever gifts I have to offer be fully exploited for the cultural propaganda of this country.
>
> It is so kind of you both to bother with this, but it is my last chance! Under the point system of discharge I shall be in the Army for two more years, and I never know from month to month whether I shall be permitted to remain in New York.[7]

On 28 September, Barber was discharged from the army and wrote to the conductor:

> I wanted to send you the happy news and thank you for your very real help in some of my military difficulties of the last three years. Your letters have been of invaluable aid—the last one speeded up most definitely my

* Garbousova, interview with the author. The precedent for such collaborations, of course, goes back to the nineteenth century: that between Brahms and Joachim is richly documented in Boris Schwarz's "Joseph Joachim and the Genesis of Brahms's Violin Concerto," *Musical Quarterly* 69 (Fall 1983):503–26. Tchaikovsky and William Fitzhagen had a noteworthy collaboration for the *Variations on a Rococo Theme*. Moreover, when this kind of cooperation did not take place, the finished product often reflected the omission of idiomatic virtuosity: for example, the cello part in Dvořák's concerto is considered more symphonic in style; Schumann's finale "betrays its pianistic origins and presents technical difficulties in terms of tone production" (Marx, "Violoncello," *The New Grove Dictionary of Music and Musicians* [London: Macmillan, 1980], p. 862, col. 1). A contemporary example of a working relationship between composer and cellist is that of Robert Starer and Janos Starker (see Starer, "Composing with the Soloist in Mind," *New York Times*, 1 May 1988, sec. 2, p. 23).

> demobilization—and I cannot tell you how much I appreciate your kindness and understanding. It is wonderful to be completely free to work at my music again!
>
> The cello concerto is finished, and I shall begin instrumentation immediately: it should not take too long.[8]

Even before Barber finished the orchestration, he wrote to John Brown:

> Perhaps you and Mrs. Brown may be interested to know that the cello concerto is just about ready and goes to the copyist in a fortnight. I shall send you a score, of course, but after the first performance, in case there are any changes. Garbousova already plays the work very well indeed: she returns to New York December 7th and should you and your husband be in New York sometime after then, we should be glad to play it for you.
>
> I would appreciate receiving the commission fee at your earliest convenience. I am sorry to bother you with this, but having devoted myself exclusively to this work for the past eight months, I find myself suddenly forced to consider the non-musical side! I hope so much you will like the concerto.[9]

If Barber had any fears that this commission would repeat the course of the threatened Violin Concerto, his worries surely were laid to rest by the prompt and warm reply from his sponsor:

> It is indeed a pleasure to receive your letter addressed to Mrs. Brown . . . and to learn that the great cello concerto is so nearly completed. As a matter of fact Raya Garbousova stayed with us when she gave her recital here last week and told us a little about the new work.
>
> Of course I am more than eager to hear the concerto and accept immediately your kind suggestion. . . .
>
> Ever since my return from Europe, I have been meaning to tell you how deeply interested I am in this whole affair. I look back upon the day, now almost a year ago, when I first had the inspiration of asking you to compose a concerto and now await with impatience the plan's fruition. Of all the composers I considered asking to write a cello concerto, I feel sure that you are the one most fitted for the task.
>
> I take pleasure in sending you my cheque to your order for one thousand dollars in payment of your commission fee. The monetary compensation for great artistic creation seems always an untrue measure and yet some measure must be determined upon.*

*Letter, 17 November 1945, in private collection of Anne S. K. Brown. Barber met Brown for the first time at the end of the summer of 1945, when Olga Koussevitzky suggested that Barber come to Tanglewood at a time when Mrs. Brown, "who is interested in your new cello concerto," was sure to be at the festival (letter from Olga Koussevitzky to Barber, 31 July 1945).

Orchestrating the concerto did not go according to schedule, however; two trips to Boston (for performances of Menotti's piano concerto and intermezzi from *The Island God*) and a trip to Philadelphia to hear Ormandy conduct the *Second Essay* interrupted Barber's work. A holograph score at the Library of Congress is dated at the end 27 November 1945, in Barber's hand. A day earlier, he had written to Homer:

> 1000 apologies for never writing, but I'm *so* busy. Almost finished the orchestration of the cello concerto (over 100 pages of score already), it has taken longer than I thought and must be done next week: came out very well, I think.[10]

He described his new work as "lyric and romantic, with, however, some of the vivacity and rhythmic tension of 'Capricorn.'"[11] At the end of November, Menotti, ebullient over the recent triumph of his own piano concerto, wrote to Sidney Homer, "Sam has just finished a wow of a cello concerto which will make the cellist's hair stand."*

On 4 December 1945, Barber wrote to thank Brown for his cheque: "I only got the concerto off to the copyist last night," he explained. "I am delighted you are so interested in the work, and will come to New York sometime for a preview—bearing in mind, of course, that the piano often gives a very inadequate idea of the orchestra."[12] The Browns heard a reading in January in New York at the home of Anne Benkard, and a month later Barber and Garbousova played it for Koussevitzky in his suite at the Savoy Plaza Hotel. Although, according to Barber, "he seemed to like it—en déshabillé," evidently at this hearing it was apparent to the conductor that Garbousova had not had enough time to learn the concerto thoroughly.[13] To help her meet the deadline, the cellist engaged Frederic Waldman to work with her and within one week she had memorized both the difficult cello part and the score, so that by the time rehearsals began in Boston she was thoroughly at ease with the music.[14]

On 5 April 1946 the Boston Symphony Orchestra premiered the concerto in Symphony Hall, followed by more performances at the Brooklyn Academy of Music on 12 and 13 April. The Boston program featured an all-Romantic program—Strauss's tone poem *Don Juan*, the prelude to Moussorgsky's *Khovanshchina*, and Tchaikovsky's orchestral fantasy *Francesca da Rimini*, as well as the first Boston performance of David Diamond's *Rounds for String Orchestra*. Barber submitted his concerto on "its own musical terms, which do not call for verbal description or analysis."[15] Similarly, five years later when the concerto was recorded on the London label, the company "bowed to the wishes of the composer that no musical analysis be printed."[16]

Nevertheless, the Concerto for Violoncello and Orchestra can be de-

* Letter, 26 November 1945 (collection of Katharine Homer Fryer). Indeed, the work is still considered to be one of the most challenging in cello literature.

Barber and Raya Garbousova with Serge Koussevitzky (center) after he first heard the Cello Concerto at his suite at the Savoy Plaza, February 1946. *(Courtesy of Raya Garbousova)*

scribed as in three movements—Allegro, in D minor; Andante, in C♯ minor; and Allegro, centering around A minor. The first movement is a loosely structured sonata form with a double exposition, but divisions between sections are diffused because of a continuous developmental texture. With the succinctness that is characteristic of Barber, within the first twenty-five measures all the material that forms the basis for the whole movement is presented by the orchestra (see Example 10.1). After an introductory rhythmic exclamation, the lyrical main theme is presented (mm. 3–11); a transition passage based on a tricky, syncopated triplet motive (mm. 13–17) leads to an expansively melodic second theme (mm. 18–22).* The solo cello begins its exposition with a cadenzalike solo discourse—a warm-up soliloquy as it were—based on the transition passage's triplet motive from the earlier orchestral exposition. This cadenza, placed so early in the movement, may seem out of character with Barber's professed aversion to cadenzas, but here it serves a musical function rather than merely providing a display of virtuosity for the soloist. In this sense it foreshadows the

*Although, according to Garbousova's recollection, Barber off-handedly remarked that American Indian music influenced thematic material in the concerto, there is no evidence that any themes were derived from authentic folk music.

Example 10.1 Cello Concerto, Op. 22, first movement, mm. 1–31 (G. Schirmer, 1950).

opening soliloquy of Barber's Piano Concerto written two decades later.

The second movement of the Cello Concerto spins a sad and romantically tender siciliana in canon between the cello and orchestra in a set of free variations. A long, descending cantilena is cast against the siciliana theme; both themes are worked out imitatively by cello and orchestra.

The third movement, a kind of rondo-fantasy, has a restless theme characterized by a persistently reiterated descending semitone and an arpeggiated seventh chord. There are many discursive cello passages based on thematic or, in some cases, new material. Twice, the mood is contrasted by interjections of a somber, dirgelike theme (in C minor) over a ground bass.* The dramatic tension of the finale is accentuated by the argumentative nature of dialogues between solo instrument and orchestra.

Boston critics who reviewed the premiere seemed uneasy about the concerto. Warren Storey Smith, for example, claimed the first movement to be "nervous and jittery"—bringing to mind Bernard Shaw's comparison of a "cello with a bee buzzing in a stone jug."[17] Cyrus Durgin compared Barber's concerto to its program companion, Diamond's *Rounds*, and pointed to certain elements they shared: "light in weight . . . strictly contemporary and very nervous music." He saw a triumph for Barber, however, in the "brilliant and probably idiomatic treatment of the solo instrument," wherein he provided Garbousova with "a showy but exacting role."[18] Garbousova's performance was unanimously declared brilliant—L. A. Sloper commended her style, "a distaff version of Piatigorsky, with emotional fervidity, pure tone, wonderful technique," but perceived it as overshadowing the concerto, which was "spotty," its themes "fragmentary, and the structure vague." Sloper wondered whether it was "Raya Garbousova's Russian temperament that made Mr. Barber's music sound Russian, or had his score taken on a Russian flavor because she was to play it?"†

In New York, Virgil Thomson's generous review praised the concerto as "the most ample this composer has yet produced":

> It is full of thought about musical expression in general and about the possibility for musical expression of the violoncello in particular. It is full of ingenious orchestral devices for accompanying the instrument without drowning it. And it is full of reasonably good tunes. . . . The working up of these into a richly romantic, well-sustained structure is musical, masterful, thoughtful, and not without a certain Brahms-like grandeur.
>
> The work has the feel of serious repertory about it and it is most advantageous for the cello, which has a lot to do all the time. . . . It keeps the more powerful orchestra sounds pretty constantly on leash. Perhaps if Mr. Barber had dramatized more the functional contrasts between orchestra and soloist, instead of letting these two always express the same sentiments, they might have together a little less than they do the aspect of a lion lying down with a lamb. . . .
>
> And for all its occasional modernity of texture, it has the formal solemnity of Late Romanticism and an expansive melancholy of mood that makes

* According to Anne S. K. Brown (letter to the author, 11 October 1983) and her son J. Carter Brown (in "John Nicholas Brown," cited in the first footnote to this chapter), Barber said the third movement was jettisoned and rewritten on the day the first atomic bomb was exploded over Hiroshima on 5 August. Although Garbousova summarily rejects the idea and there is no evidence to support it in Barber's correspondence, the emotional context of these funereal passages gives some credibility to the Browns' account.

† *Christian Science Monitor*, 6 April 1946. In fact, the Cello Concerto's popularity with Russian audiences led to publication of a Russian edition in 1972. Barber reported that when Rostropovich first came to the United States in 1960, "he embraced me warmly and sang the theme of my Cello Concerto in my ear" (quoted by Ardoin, "Samuel Barber at Capricorn," p. 5).

it both adequate and suitable to a permanent place on the standard symphony orchestra programs.[19]

Olin Downes commended Barber's "unprecedented directness and confidence of manner" and Koussevitzky's skill in revealing every detail and facet of the score to the service of the composer. He especially showered praise on the middle movement:

> It grows in melodic interest and in intensity of mood, and for its coda, a young American dares to express himself poetically. . . . The last movement is remarkable for its structure, even tragical.[20]

Subsequently, that same year the Fifth Annual Award of the Music Critics Circle of New York was awarded to Barber for the concerto, "exceptional among orchestra compositions performed for the first time in New York City during the concert season."* Ironically, a year and a half later Downes, who earlier had extolled the concerto, reversed his position. He wrote:

> Mr. Barber's concerto, heard for a second time, let us down, or better said, confused us.
>
> Was it a different treatment of the score or a different degree of receptivity in ourselves from the time when the concerto was first presented here in 1946 by the Boston Symphony Orchestra under Koussevitzky? Mr. Mitropoulos, who conducted with the greatest care, and his customary authority, gave Miss Garbousova every possible cooperation. She played with the warmth and distinction, the technical resource and musical intelligence, which have given her her present high position among colleagues of the concert platform. Nevertheless, with all these favorable circumstances, the concerto, at the second hearing, felt overlong for its contents, with many good melodic ideas, but not enough physiognomy.†

Barber, brooding over this review, believed the inadequate performance was due, at least in part, to a sluggish tempo. He wrote to Homer after the concert:

> The rehearsals . . . were a great joy. I was there in Carnegie Hall all alone and it was so beautifully played: ovations for Garbousova after each move-

* *New York Times,* 28 June 1946, p. 16, col. 5; *New York Times,* 11 April 1946. That same year an award was given to Diamond for *Rounds for String Orchestra,* and a special citation was bestowed on Charles Ives's Third Symphony, written forty-two years earlier (but performed for the first time that season). These awards were bestowed after a conservative spring concert season during which, according to Olin Downes, the "most modern music" on one program presented by the Boston Symphony Orchestra was Aaron Copland's *Appalachian Spring.*

†*New York Times,* 2 December 1947. The performance, on 4 December 1947, was by the New York Philharmonic–Symphony Society conducted by Dimitri Mitropoulos with Raya Garbousova as soloist.

a.

Example 10.2 Cello Concerto, first movement 5 mm. after [15], before and after revisions. *a.* Copyist's score used for first performance, 1946. *(Personal collection of Raya Garbousova) b.* G. Schirmer, 1950, p. 24.

ment at all three rehearsals! The eyes of the entire cello section on her every instant. . . .

. . . I think she and Mitropoulos sinned somewhat through excess of devotion at the Thursday night performance and it went rather flat for some reason: too much attention to details and some of the initial excitement went out, and the big line; but these things can happen. In Friday p.m. they picked it up, and Sunday was good again. But it is *such* a difficult problem to balance solo cello (with all its limitations of sonority) and orchestra! One or the other always seems too loud, dependent on the hall too: I think if I had realized the difficulties involved I should never have attempted it! *

Sometime during or after 1947, he addressed these problems by revising the concerto to improve the balance between cello and orchestra, thus affecting the overall sonority of the ensemble. A comparison of the holograph score and manuscript with the 1950 edition shows that these revisions almost exclusively involved the first movement and were of several

* Letter, 21 December 1947. In this letter, also, Barber mentions that Charles Münch, who came especially to hear the concerto and followed the score behind stage, kept repeating "quel beau concert, magnifique."

b.

kinds: telescoping of passages into a more focused structure and reworking instrumental doublings or reducing the accompaniment activity in order to obtain a more transparent orchestral texture and lessen competition between orchestra and cello.* A dramatic change was made, for example, seven measures after no. 15, where the deletion of active figuration in strings and woodwinds allows the solo cello to emerge more clearly (see Example 10.2). A similar change seems designed also to reduce the "busyness" of the texture: at no. 6, for example, hocketlike figurations in bas-

*Two holographs exist: an orchestral score is at the Library of Congress, Music Division; and a piano-cello arrangement (with inserted pasteovers of a copy) is at the University of Oregon Library. Three manuscripts—copies of the orchestral score and the cello part that were used for the premiere and a copy of the piano-cello arrangement—and an engraver's proof of the violoncello part (with Barber's holograph corrections) are in the private collection of Raya Garbousova.

soon and flute parts were replaced by a clarinet part playing evenly pulsating, staccato eighth notes (see Example 10.3).

An important change affecting the overall design was made at the beginning of the development section (m. 168 in the 1950 edition), where Barber added twelve measures that reintroduce thematic material from the beginning of the movement. This repetition adds unity to the formal structure, perhaps the composer's remedy to the amorphous physiognomy that Downes pointed to in his review.[21]

When the concerto was in the page-proof stage but not yet published, Barber reassessed the ending of the third movement, which, according to Garbousova, had been problematic in the original version because the cello and orchestra played the concluding chords in rapid alternation. The new ending adds thirteen measures of orchestra to the original score, with the cello playing the last four measures in unison with the orchestra. Barber felt so strongly about the change that he was willing to pay G. Schirmer the additional cost of making new plates for the last two pages of the score.[22]

The revised score was published in 1950 and recorded by Zara Nelsova in London the same year. In preparation for conducting the recording himself, Barber contracted with Nicolai Malko for a series of rigorous lessons in Denmark (see chapter 11). After the recording sessions, he wrote to Homer that at last the orchestration was to his satisfaction, making the concerto "an altogether different work." Apparently the problem of tempo, too, was resolved, for after hearing Nelsova, Barber said, "for the first time . . . I heard the first movement fast enough."[23]

The Cello Concerto is acknowledged as one of the most challenging works in contemporary cello literature. Leonard Rose said it was the most difficult concerto he had ever played.[24] Astonishing ascents to the extreme registers of the instrument (b♭'''' in the third movement, for example), sudden wide descending leaps, sweeping runs and arpeggios, interspersed with pizzicati and harmonics, multiple stops, and complicated rhythmic patterns contribute to the technical demands of the work.

Later attempts made by Barber to remove some of the more awkward passages in the concerto did not seem to help secure more frequent performances. Garbousova performed the concerto many times during its first decade and recorded it in 1966. Even after Nelsova's recording and performances by Leonard Rose and the New York Philharmonic (under Leonard Bernstein) in 1959, performances were infrequent until the 1980s. Sometime during the seventies Orlando Cole asked Barber if he would decrease some of the technical hurdles in the concerto for one of his students—specifically, change some of the thirds in the first movement to more easily executed sixths and adjust the *agitato* section to a slower tempo.[25] Barber was amenable to the idea, hoping there would be more performances, but by then he was so ill with cancer that he never had the opportunity to fulfill his plan.[26]

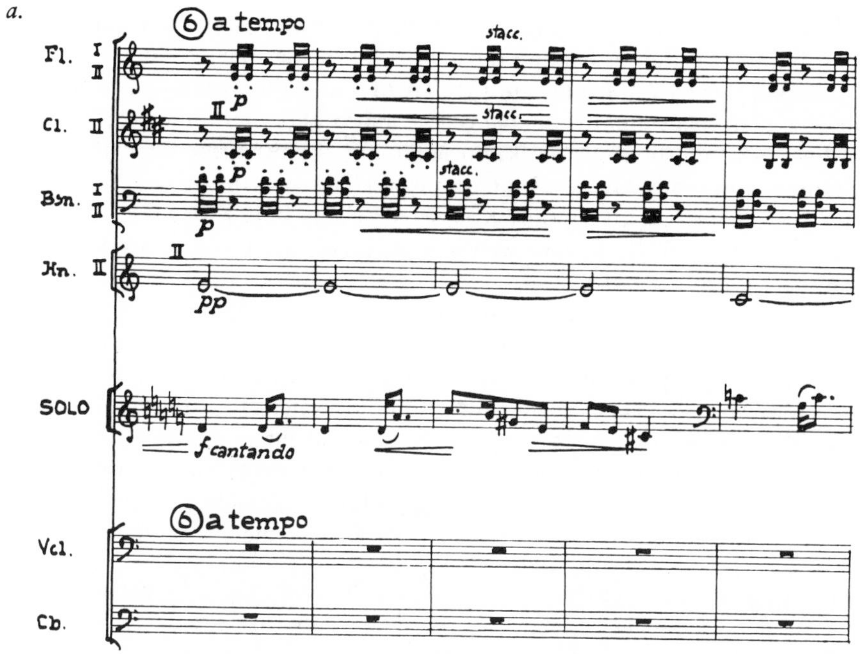

a.
6 a tempo
Fl. I II
Cl. II
Bsn. I II
Hn. II
stacc.
p
pp
SOLO
f cantando
6 a tempo
Vcl.
Cb.

b.
6 Tempo I
Ob.
I
Cl.
II
Hn. II
staccato
p
pp
Tempo I
cantando
Solo
f
6 Tempo I
pizz.
Vcl.
p

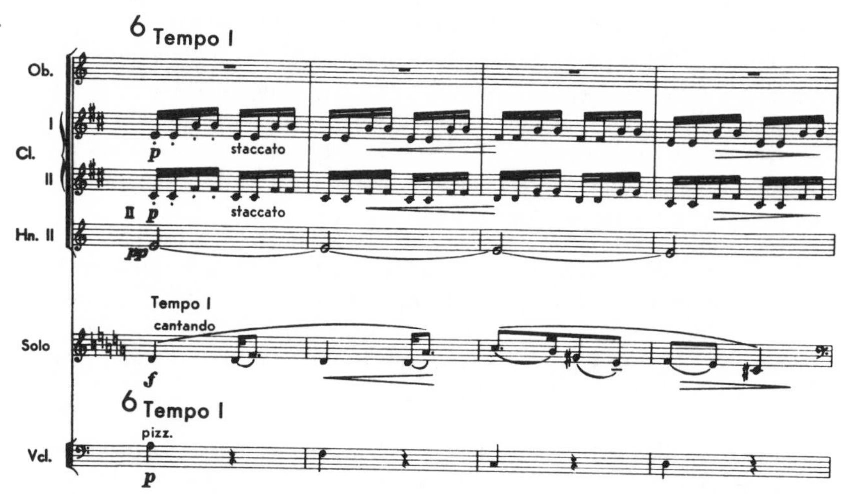

Example 10.3 Cello Concerto, first movement, mm. 67–70, before and after revisions. *a.* Copyist's score, 1946. *(Personal collection of Raya Garbousova)* *b.* G. Schirmer, 1950, p. 6.

In spite of its fierce challenges, however, the concerto has had its champions and increasingly is gaining the interest of the new generation of cellists, among them Paul Tobias and Yo Yo Ma. In 1988, it was a required work for performance in the annual cello competition at the Juilliard School of Music. During the same week, on March 7, Ma performed it with the Baltimore Symphony Orchestra at Carnegie Hall; subsequently he has recorded it. This seems to support Koussevitzky's appraisal that the Barber Cello Concerto will be to the twentieth century what the Brahms Violin Concerto was to the nineteenth.[27]

* * *

By 1945 Barber's growing international reputation led him to be viewed by his publishers as one of their most promising American composers. The financial implications of his new stature enabled him to arrange to his advantage "many practical things" with G. Schirmer.[28] The composer's negotiations suggest the position of strength he had already achieved with the firm that would continue as his sole publisher for the rest of his career:

> I threatened to give certain pieces to other publishers who had requested them unless S. pay me a retaining fee for the exclusive rights to my music. So they finally agreed to pay me $2000 a year (for three years) besides the usual royalties and no compunction to produce what they want, etc.* In fact, no strings at all. It was a sort of minor triumph. . . . But it helps me financially a good deal. Also there have been many requests from England for my music. (H.M.V. have released my records there). So the R.A.F., if you please, is flying all my scores and parts over to London. I am publishing Second Essay and Capricorn Concerto now—much proofreading of parts. . . . Also, I'm pushing Schirmer into opening their own small agency in Switzerland and I think they will. All these things interest me in the abstract, but I'm glad not to be employed by them, for the working out of details doesn't interest me at all.[29]

Moreover, as American music in general gained greater popularity in Europe in the wake of World War II, Barber became aware of the potential for more performances of his own works (particularly in England) and began to assume a more active role in self-promotion. This letter to Anne Brown is an example of his assertiveness:

> Something has happened which I shall pass on to you, and as I remember your saying that you are entertaining Sir Adrian Boult, perhaps you might mention it to him, if you think it auspicious.
>
> Schirmers have asked me to go to Europe this summer to look over the field on the continent for a possible agency: there is at present no way to

* Entries in Barber's date book indicate that from 1966 to 1969 he received an annual retainer of $10,000 from G. Schirmer in addition to his royalties.

> meet the demand for American music there, and our music should be on hand. Louis Dreyfuss, owner of Chappell's in London, who represents Schirmers in England, was present at the meeting; according to him, my music is meeting with some favor in England, and he wants me to stop off there during this trip and do some more conducting of my own works. . . .
>
> This interests me very much indeed, and also Raya. She said she would be eager to go to England to play the first performance of the cello concerto with me, and of course I would love to introduce it there with her. I plan to go about the middle of May. . . . Sir Adrian, who I believe knows some of my music, might or might not be interested . . . it would be very kind of you, if the occasion presents itself, to sound him out. I should be very grateful.[30]

Barber had always yearned to do more conducting. It would be four years, however, before that wish was realized.

Medea, Op. 23: Ballet, *Cave of the Heart* (1946); Suite, (1947); *Medea's Meditation and Dance of Vengeance* (1955)

One of the frequent visitors to Capricorn during the early forties was Martha Graham. The dancer was introduced to Barber and Menotti by the poet Robert Horan, who was a member of Graham's company.[31] Invited by the Alice M. Ditson Fund of Columbia University to premiere a new work for the Second Annual Festival of Contemporary Music, which would be held in May 1946, Graham asked Barber to compose the score.* Dancer and composer agreed upon Euripides' *Medea* for the subject of a ballet. The music Barber composed was to undergo two transformations before he was satisfied with the score as an expression of the myth.

It was not the first time Graham had been interested in the *Medea*, for in November 1942 she had given Carlos Chávez a script, "The Daughter of Colchis," for ballet music commissioned by Elizabeth Sprague Coolidge. But Graham was dissatisfied with the partially completed score Chávez presented to her more than a year later (and two weeks past the scheduled first performance) and wrote to her patron, "It seems to be music as such and seems to bear no relation to the script we had agreed on."† In January

*Beginning in 1932 Graham decided to choreograph only commissioned scores, thus providing many composers (mostly American) an opportunity to advance their careers through active collaboration with her—Copland, Cowell, Menotti, Schuman, for example. See Don McDonagh, *Martha Graham: A Biography* (New York: Praeger, 1973), p. 90.

†This letter to Elizabeth Sprague Coolidge, 16 January 1944, and all subsequent correspondence cited here between Graham and Coolidge is quoted from Wayne D. Shirley's article "Ballets for Martha," *Performing Arts Annual* 1988 (Library of Congress), pp. 40–73. Chávez's abstract score was ultimately used for Graham's *Dark Meadow*, premiered on 23 January 1946.

1944 Coolidge suggested that Graham offer the commission to someone else, her preferences being Hindemith, Toch, or Stravinsky.[32] Graham, who had begun work on a new script and was also immersed in choreographing a score by Aaron Copland (that would become *Appalachian Spring*), was uncertain if any of the three composers Mrs. Coolidge suggested would be interested in providing music for her. If not, "I do not know who to suggest," she wrote to Coolidge; "I like Samuel Barber, but he is in the army and now is at work on a commission from the army, I believe."[33] Shortly before Barber was discharged from the air force in 1945, Graham recommended him to the Alice M. Ditson Committee of Columbia University for the ballet score for the contemporary music festival. Otto Luening and Douglas Moore approved Graham's suggestion and offered Barber a commission of $1,000 for the score, twice as much as Graham received for the choreography.[34]

It seems unlikely that the script Graham presented to Barber in July 1945 was exactly the same one she had given to Chávez earlier, for there is little resemblance between the resulting ballet *Cave of the Heart* and "Daughter of Colchis." The earlier script, which is at the Library of Congress, Music Division, revolves around five characters—the Passerby (the spectator, corresponding to the Greek chorus), the Man (the poet, "the free masculine spirit"), the Woman (of the Medea tradition), the Muse ("the dream of the Man" and sorceress), and the Fury ("the sinister aspect of the Woman"). The ballet *Cave of the Heart* centers on four roles—Choros, Medea (seemingly a fusion of Graham's earlier Woman and Fury), Jason, and the Princess (perhaps like the Muse of the earlier script)—and focuses on events leading up to Medea's murder of the Princess (the ballet substitutes a poisoned crown for the gown of the legend). Graham and Barber agreed that they did not want to present a literal portrayal of the legend in the ballet; in their words, "These mythical figures served rather to project psychological states of jealousy and vengeance which are timeless."* Much later, in a television interview Graham described the story as dealing with "a passion that we all understand, because we all possess the impulse: it's envy, it's covetousness, it's maliciousness. It's the unnamable thing of fire that dominates when the laws of the heart and the body are interfered with."[35]

Graham's usual method of working with composers has been described by Menotti:

> To work with Martha was both very exciting and very frustrating. . . . She begins by giving you a very detailed scenario of what the dance is going

* Preface in G. Schirmer Study Score (No. 53, 1949) *Medea* and liner notes, London LPS 333, Ballet Suite *Medea*, New Symphony Orchestra, cond. Barber. The awakening of Graham's interest in classical Greek mythology, beginning in 1945, coincided with her treatment with a Jungian psychotherapist, Dr. Frances Wickes, who had a profound influence on Graham's work (McDonagh, *Martha Graham*, p. 187) as well as James Agee's at the time he wrote "Knoxville: Summer of 1915" (see below).

> to be. She gives vivid descriptions of the general mood. Martha has the extraordinary gift of inspiring her composers by throwing them all sorts of visual images. Often she does this in a rather inarticulate way, but somehow through her great effort to express herself, the ideas become even more expressive.*

That this mirrors Graham's collaboration with Barber—and that it is likely that even after she gave him a script she continued to provide images for the ballet—is suggested by the composer's somewhat cryptic notes scrawled on one of his musical sketches:

> Jason coming from a festival (from which she is excluded) from his external life — Jason enters at end of music, callous, aloof, ambitious — Medea comes in drunk with blood — He dances while she moves detachedly like a spider in a web — he goes out dancing while she continues — then both enter the robes.[36]

Barber began work on the ballet late November 1945, as soon as he had finished orchestrating the Cello Concerto. The urgency of a February deadline completely consumed him, and his letters were filled with reports on the progress of the work for Graham. To Homer, in November, he wrote: "Now I begin the ballet for Graham (Medea) which must be done in February. . . . After that, no more commissions and pressures for awhile."[37] In December he complained to his uncle: "Art takes so long, one never allows enough time. But the cello concerto was finished three weeks ago and I am on the ballet for Graham now."[38] A letter to La Grange reads: "Now I must do a ballet score for Martha Graham for small orchestra of twelve instruments. She is our greatest dancer and it will be interesting to do—but it must be ready by February, alas!"[39]

In mid-January he was still "sunk" in the music for *Medea,* knowing that Graham expected to dance it in May and needed the score well before then.[40] Attempting to exclude all pleasantries from his mind, he wrote to Anne Brown at this time: "I must force myself to remain in a deep Medea-gloom for the Martha Graham score, and dare not think of that very good afternoon when you and your husband were so kind to the little cello concerto!"[41] Early in March he wrote to John Brown: "I am still not through with Medea's troubles."[42]

One month before the premiere Barber presented Graham with what was to become the first of three versions of the score.† Scored for a chamber orchestra of thirteen instruments (flute, piccolo, oboe, clarinet, bassoon, horn, piano, violins I and II, viola, cello I and II, and contrabass), the ballet is in nine sections.

*Gruen, *Menotti,* p. 84. Menotti and Graham collaborated in 1947 on *Errand into the Maze,* a ballet suggested by the myth of Theseus and Ariadne.

†A holograph sketch (a short score) of this original version of the ballet is at the Library of Congress and contains indications of scenes and notes on the action.

Medea's world premiere was on 10 May 1946 at Columbia University's McMillin Academic Theater on the opening program of the festival.* The ballet was titled "Pain and Wrath are the Singers" (a line from Robinson Jeffers's translation of *Medea*); the characters—listed in a program printed for the first performance, but apparently not used—were the Barbarian, a Hero, a King's Daughter, and the Choragos. A note explained:

> This dance is a re-telling of the myth of the jealous act. Within the cave of the heart is a place of darkness, plunging far into the earth of the past. This cave is peopled with shadows of acts of violence, terror, and magic.
>
> Try as we might to escape this monstrous heritage, we are caught up into its surge, and the past is alive.[43]

At the last minute before the first performance, Graham changed the name of the ballet to "Serpent Heart" and renamed the characters as follows: "One like Medea; One like Jason; Daughter of the King; and the Chorus." The new program more explicitly connected the psychological plot to the Medea legend:

> This is a dance of possessive and destroying love, a love which feeds upon itself, like the serpent heart, and when it is overthrown, is fulfilled only in revenge.
>
> It is a chronicle much like the myth of Jason, the warrior hero, and Medea, granddaughter of the Sun.
>
> The one like Medea destroys that which she has been unable to possess and brings upon herself and her beloved the inhuman wrath of one who has been betrayed.[44]

The dancers included Yuriko as the young princess (in her first leading role), May O'Donnell as the Chorus, Erick Hawkins as "One like Jason," and Graham, who, as the Medea character, was reported to have created "one of the most venomous parts in her repertory."[45] In his biography of Graham, McDonagh described the electrifying climax of the ballet, "Medea's Dance of Vengeance":

> Her solo, in which she extracted a long red ribbon from herself, simulated the spewing up of a vile liquid having the corrosive power of acid. For décor, Noguchi prepared a rough gray, textured block for the chorus to stand on and a brass harness with quivering brass rays emanating from it, which Medea took upon herself after the murder. Moving about the stage in it, she was like a glittering, malevolent presence. The piece was the incarnation of jealousy and signalled a turn on Graham's part to another examination of the role and effects of passion.†

* On the same program was Copland's *Appalachian Spring*.

† McDonagh, *Martha Graham*, p. 190. Graham's choreography for her two solos is in *The Notebooks of Martha Graham* (New York: Harcourt Brace Jovanovich, 1973), pp. 162–63.

The dance critic Robert Sabin viewed this as one of Graham's profoundest studies, "doubtful if expressionism could go any farther than she has carried it in this portrait of a desperate soul."[46] Sabin declared Barber's score "an excellent dance score which sustains the atmosphere of the piece from its earliest measures. There are patches which sound a bit thin, owing to their peculiar scoring, but the music is imaginative and rhythmically alive."[47]

Irving Kolodin, on the other hand, found Graham's "dance of possessive and destroying love" less engaging than Barber's music:

> There were some valid musical ideas audible in the score, and the climax, particularly, was a good deal more suggestive of the tortured misgivings of the principal character than Miss Graham's action, but the meager instrumentation and the halting performance futilized any final estimate of its qualities. . . . If the distance that separates Barber's conception from what was heard was similar to the disparity between audible results in Copland's "Appalachian Spring," and what one knows to be in that score, Barber could well have a brilliant work here.[48]

Robert Horan viewed the performance as "somewhat the victim of circumstances," given in an "overcrowded, airless lecture hall instead of a theater, and a work rushed headlong into production a little too early." He continued, "Both its title and many of its parts are now in revision, and if this adds clarity to its other virtues it should be one of Graham's finest works."* He claimed:

> Barber's score is brilliant, bitter and full of amazing energy. The alternation of parts, like the swing of a pendulum, between relaxed lyrical flow and tense angularity, make a wonderful scaffolding for the tragedy. Its very real beauties were muffled . . . by an initial performance that lacked accuracy and spirit on the part of the orchestra.[49]

Although there was general agreement that Barber's music had vividly portrayed the anguished, tormented Medea, what seemed lacking was the usual "sense of long line and the broad period" associated with Barber—"his lyrical gift"—for which were substituted "an interminable series of nervous, gasping phrases, which strive for no real goal and seem to insinuate but unconstructively."[50] These comments, however, suggest that Barber's music embodied Graham's choreographic philosophy at that time: "Life today is nervous, sharp and zigzag. It often stops in midair. It is what I aim for in my dances."†

* Robert Horan, "The Recent Theater of Martha Graham," *Dance Index* 6 (1947): 14. Horan knew that because Graham's winter season ended in Chicago in April 1946, the dancer had only a month to prepare the new work (McDonagh, *Martha Graham*, p. 189).

† Selma Jean Cohen, "The Achievement of Martha Graham," *Chrysalis* 10 (1958): 6. Menotti's account of his first rehearsals with Graham—where he began to realize that the dances she was weaving over his score had "nothing or very little to do with what she had

Graham revised the ballet for the following season. Renamed *Cave of the Heart,* it was performed in New York on 27 February 1947 at the Ziegfeld Theater and remains in her repertoire under that title to the present time. The following description of the final version—with the characters taken directly from the myth—illuminates the intention of Graham's and Barber's collaboration:

> Choreography and music were conceived, as it were, on two time levels, the ancient-mythical and the contemporary. . . . In both the dancing and music, archaic and contemporary idioms are used . . .
>
> Besides Medea and Jason, there are two other characters in the ballet, the Young Princess whom Jason marries out of ambition and for whom he betrays Medea, and an attendant who assumes the part of the onlooking chorus of the Greek tragedy, sympathizing, consoling and interpreting the actions of the major characters.*

Although there have been other choreographies of Barber's Medea music, mostly in classical styles, it is Graham's that continues to be performed.† Early in 1947 Barber rearranged the ballet score into a twenty-three-minute, seven-movement suite for full orchestra. On 10 February 1947, the very day he completed the score, he wrote to Homer about his productive winter, which had seen the completion of the suite, revisions of the Second Symphony, and a piano reduction of the Cello Concerto:[51]

> We are covered with two feet of snow, but I feel light as a feather for I finished a full orchestral suite of music for Graham's ballet of last year. It makes a very nice 23 min. suite, but had to be all re-arranged from the original chamber orchestral version. I think it will be better this way: the music was too dramatic for small orchestra. That is why I haven't written—it was sort of an idée fixe to get it finished.[52]

Whereas Graham had entitled her ballet "Serpent Heart," and the revision *Cave of the Heart,* Barber preferred to call the seven-movement dance suite for full orchestra simply *Medea.* Rehearsals for the premiere with the Philadelphia Orchestra and Eugene Ormandy coincided with the New York Philharmonic's performance of the Cello Concerto, requiring the composer to commute between the two cities almost daily. After the performance 5 December 1947, he wrote to Homer:

---

planned originally . . . but instead enriches it with her own highly evocative personality"—seems to support a pattern of discrepancy between her choreography and the composer's music (Gruen, *Menotti,* pp. 84–85).

* "Note for 'Medea,' " in G. Schirmer Study Score No. 53, *Medea,* 1949.

†In 1967 the Estonian Ballet Theatre danced *Medea* choreographed by Mai Murdmaa. It was the first ballet to Barber's music performed in the Soviet Union (*Dance News* 50, no. 2, [February 1967]:6). Another version, choreographed by John Butler and danced by Mikhail Baryshnikov and Carla Fracci at the Spoleto Festival of 1975, received accolades from the dance critic Clive Barnes ("Spoleto's Heart Belongs to Dance," *New York Times,* 13 July 1975). It was repeated in New York by the American Ballet Theater on 13 January 1976.

> Next came "Medea" with the Phila. Orchestra and that was even more exciting: for some reason I hadn't counted on it particularly. . . . The first rehearsals were a bit of a struggle: (Ormandy announced to me the 1st day that it was going to be a flop, and he wished it had never been put at the end of the program: very encouraging!), but little by little enthusiasm began to grow with understanding, and the performance was *superb*. It is infinitely better, of course, with a subject of such scope, in full orchestra. Medea's big dance was wildly exciting and I was thrilled. About 200 Friday afternoon old ladies walked out on it (one by one, shaking their umbrellas and grumbling) to Mother's intense annoyance! It really isn't *that* violent. But Saturday night's audience got it and there was cheering, and I had to come out 3 or 4 times. Ditto in N.Y.—G.C. thinks it is one of my very best. I hope so. They play it in Washington and Baltimore the 29th and 30th and I may go. I wish they would do it on the radio: let us hope.[53]

The new (second) version of *Medea,* while using much the same musical content of the ballet, merges the original nine sections into seven and uses a greatly expanded orchestra, maintaining the piano, doubling woodwinds and strings of the original score, and adding an English horn, two trumpets, two trombones, timpani, harp, cymbals, side drum, tom-tom, bass drum, and xylophone. Dedicated to Martha Graham, the score was published by G. Schirmer in 1949. For the edition Barber provided the following preface:

> The suite follows roughly the form of a Greek tragedy. In the *Parados* the characters first appear. The *Choros,* lyric and reflective, comments on the action which is to unfold. The Young Princess appears in a dance of freshness and innocence, followed by a heroic dance of Jason. Another plaintive *Choros* leads to Medea's dance of obsessive and diabolical vengeance. The *Kantikos Agonias,* an interlude of menace and foreboding, follows. Medea's terrible crime, the murder of the princess and her own children, has been committed, announced at the beginning of the *Exodus* by a violent fanfare of trumpets. In this final section the various themes of the chief characters of the work are blended together; little by little the music subsides and Medea and Jason recede into the legendary past.[54]

Hearing New York performances, Charles Münch was as enthusiastic about *Medea* as he had been about the Cello Concerto.[55] But critical reactions were of two minds, representing the extreme viewpoints of Barber's audiences. Those of conservative taste, who had always been drawn to Barber's music because of its lyricism, found the work "disappointing . . . heavily orchestrated, stiff in rhythm"; one Philadelphia critic, for example, claimed it "could have been culled from a study of Stravinsky's 'Rites of Spring' [*sic*] and the latest Shostakovich" because "in it, the composer has definitely forsaken his earlier melodic and poetic style. Several parquet sitters left during the performance."[56] Critic Linton Martin, on the other hand, embraced the work as bringing to Barber "new musical stature and distinction" and claimed *Medea* should be added to the limited list of works that "survive the tonal test" as concert works—for example, *Daphnis and Chloe, Firebird,* and *Petrouchka.*[57] There are indeed passages in Barber's *Medea* that keenly reflect the profound influence Stravinsky had upon the ballet scores of the generation of composers that followed him, even those of such lyrical tendencies as Barber (and, one might add, Copland).

Virgil Thomson, after hearing the first New York performance of the suite, recommended "a little tightening up might be of advantage to it, since the extended alternations of very loud and very soft, very active and very static, lose some of their force by the time the suite is half over." But more importantly, in *Medea* he viewed "a Samuel Barber freed at last from the well-bred attitudinizing and mincing respectabilities of his concert manner":

> Long known as the most conventional among America's stronger musical spirits, his frank violence in the rendering of a subject that demands violence was rewarded last night by a not considerable number of departures during the course of the work's execution. This is all to the good. Once more the theater has made a man out of an American composer who had passed his early years as a genteel musical essayist. The public at large will, from now on, be aware of his real power. . . .
>
> Its style, which is broadly eclectic modernism not at all clumsily amalgamated, is in its favor. So is its expressivity, which is intense all through. So, also, is its instrumentation, which is varied and piquant, with plenty of brutality added and not inappropriately. Whatever reserves your reporter cherishes are a matter of the work's loose (for concert listening) form and perhaps a certain weakness in the tune content, due to Mr. Barber's facile melodic chromaticism. . . . The work has, in any case, a high expressive power and a far from inconsiderable interest as musical invention. It brings its author suspiciously close to the clear status of a master.[58]

Thomson's favorable reaction meant a lot to Barber; he sent the review to both Sidney Homer and Henry-Louis de La Grange.[59] It is not surprising—given Thomson's observation that the suite had "all the sonorous amplitude of a Strauss symphonic poem"—that when Barber conducted a program of his music in Frankfurt in 1951, the German musicians favored *Medea* over the Second Symphony, the Violin Concerto (played by Charles Turner), and the *Adagio for Strings.*[60] Barber, however, found their preference astonishing:

> The concert was very successful. Strange to see here, as later in Berlin, the orchestra and much of the audience preferred "Medea". (Mother, please take notice.) In fact, in Berlin the German newsreel people asked to film a

few minutes of my music which we had to replay after the concert, and after listening to the whole program, it was Medea's dance they chose! So, after the audience left we played it over, with cameras and lights clicking away. (I wonder how it looked). . . . In Frankfurt . . . the whole concert created plenty of enthusiasm. I started with 3 numbers from Medea (I, IV, V), then the Violin Concerto, which made a pleasantly serene contrast after the violence of Medea's dance, intermission, Adagio for Strings, and then the Second Symphony, which closes the program with plenty of noise![61]

In 1955 Barber rescored the suite into one continuous movement, renaming it *Medea's Meditation and Dance of Vengeance* (Op. 23a). Selecting the excerpts he had conducted in 1951 in Germany, he based almost all of the new version on material that is related to the central character—I. *Parados,* IV. *Choros,* and V. *Medea.* He reduced the length to fourteen minutes (nine minutes shorter than the suite) and considerably expanded the orchestra—adding a third flute, clarinets in E♭ and A, bass clarinet, a third trumpet, a third trombone, tuba, and extra percussion (triangle, tam-tam, and whip). The preface to the published score (dedicated, like the ballet, to Martha Graham) includes the following "program":

> Tracing her emotions from her tender feelings towards her children, through her mounting suspicions and anguish at her husband's betrayal and her decision to avenge herself, the piece increases in intensity to close in the frenzied Dance of Vengeance of Medea, the Sorceress descended from the Sun God.[62]

A quotation from Euripides' *Medea* is an epigraph to the score and the emotional key to the music:

> *Look, my soft eyes have suddenly filled with tears:*
> *O children, how ready to cry I am, how full of foreboding!*
> *Jason wrongs me, though I have never injured him.*
> *He has taken a wife to his house, supplanting me. . .*
> *Now I am in the full force of the storm of hate.*
> *I will make dead bodies of three of my enemies—*
> *father, the girl and my husband!*
> *Come, Medea, whose father was noble,*
> *Whose grandfather God of the sun,*
> *Go forward to the dreadful act.*[63]

For the "meditation" music (the first 101 measures of the work), Barber retained material from four movements of the earlier suite: *Parados* (I), *Choros* (II and IV), and *Kantikos Agonias* (VI). The "dance of vengeance" (rehearsal nos. 16 to 33) is virtually a literal statement of the earlier suite's movement V ("Medea"), supplemented with forty measures of completely new material for a frenzied, climactic coda.

Example 10.4 Comparison of opening measures of the ballet *Cave of the Heart* (1946), the *Medea* Suite (1947), and *Medea's Meditation and Dance of Vengeance* (1956). *a. Cave of the Heart* (G. Schirmer, 1946). *b. Medea* Suite, Op. 23 (G. Schirmer, 1949). *c. Medea's Meditation and Dance of Vengeance,* Op. 23a (G. Schirmer, 1956).

As an orchestral piece, *Medea's Meditation and Dance of Vengeance* is more cohesive than its earlier counterpart: in reducing the seven movements to one, the most defined lyrical material from the suite is reworked into a logically developed structure. Especially striking is the reorchestrated opening material from *Parados,* which in its transformation has acquired a mysterious aura—the opening figure on the xylophone and two flutes "appear to bump and separate like a pair of slow motion dancers."[64]

b.

To Martha Graham

MEDEA

Marked *broadly and from the distance* (as opposed to the earlier suite's *maestoso and forte* or the ballet score's *maestoso*), the xylophone's eerie, jagged motive is no longer doubled by piano and woodwinds (in *Cave of the Heart* there is no xylophone); instead, it is set in relief against a *pianissimo* double pedal (G♯ and A) in harp, piano, and strings—with violins, violas, and cellos playing harmonics. Examples 10.4a, b, and c show all three versions.

c.

Dedicated to Martha Graham

Medea's Dance of Vengeance

Samuel Barber, Op. 23-A

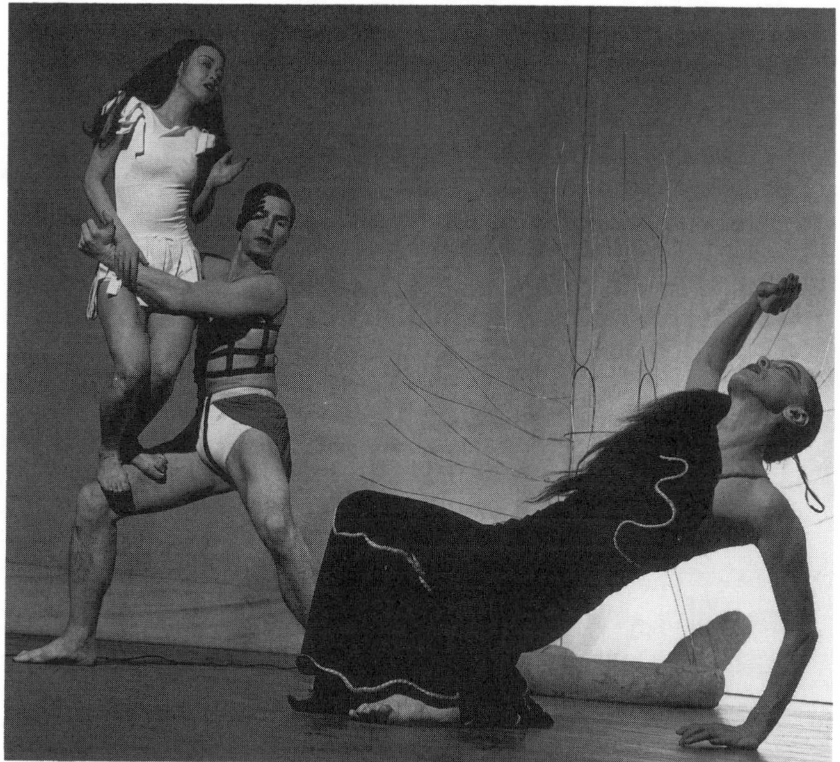

Yuriko, Erick Hawkins, and Martha Graham in *Cave of the Heart*, 1947. *(Photograph by Philippe Halsman. © Yvonne Halsman)*

As with earlier works, where Barber's method of revision usually involved rescoring to eliminate muddy orchestration and telescoping material to shorten passages, with *Medea* he applies similar procedures: at rehearsal nos. 7–8, for example, a woodwind passage is reworked for stringed instruments, then repeated in thirds by paired flutes and clarinets; the triple meter is adjusted to duple through a hemiola, resulting in a passage half the length of the original.

In the new version, more than in the two earlier ones, expressive tempo indications mirror the psychological states of the central character's meditation: *mysterious, moving ahead, anguished, sombre, with dignity, biting, with mounting frenzy*. It is as if the more independent of the ballet the music became—that is, as the corporal representation of emotion was removed—the more Barber was compelled to explicitly designate psychologically oriented expression markings in the score.

In general, in *Medea's Meditation and Dance of Vengeance* climaxes are more intense, more intricately and dramatically prepared. Compare,

Example 10.5a *Medea* Suite, Op. 23, [46]–[47] (G. Schirmer, 1947, p. 62).

for example, the lushly orchestrated transition passage to the ending of the "Dance of Vengeance" with the earlier version in movement V of *Medea* (see Examples 10.5a and b). The addition of repeated glissandi in the strings more forcefully prepares for restatement of the theme, which is now accompanied by tremolos.

The completed third version, entitled *Medea's Meditation and Dance*

Example 10.5b *Medea's Meditation and Dance of Vengeance,* Op. 23a 31–32 (G. Schirmer, 1956, p. 44).

of Vengeance, Op. 23a, was first performed on 2 February 1956 by the New York Philharmonic under Dimitri Mitropoulos.* The New York Philharmonic played it on nine programs in South America in 1958 and the following year played it in Greece, Russia, Germany, and Belgium. In 1966, Skrowaczewski conducted it with the Philadelphia Orchestra throughout South America. The emotional impact of the music, where brashness dissolves into lush harmonies, the obsessive ostinato rhythmic underpinning of the piano in Medea's dance (reminiscent of the propulsive rhythms of *Le Sacre du printemps*), and the drive to the climax are met consistently with ovations.† The revision, more focused and strident in tone, suggests that Barber may have been eager to break away from his image as a lyricist with appeal only for conservative audiences. It is a very modern, compelling, twentieth-century piece of music. The distance traveled between this *Medea* and the first suggests that perhaps the Piano Sonata, written in the interim, permitted Barber to make a major stylistic leap.

Knoxville: Summer of 1915, Op. 24 (1947)

"We have been through some difficult times in West Chester," Barber wrote to Sidney Homer in the spring of 1947.[65] On his mind as he wrote this letter was his father's deteriorating health and the strain it placed on his mother; at this time, also, he knew Louise Homer was gravely ill.‡ During the previous week, on 4 April, he had finished *Knoxville: Summer of 1915*, on a nostalgic text by James Agee.

> I enclose the text of a new work, just finished, for lyric soprano and orchestra. The text moved me very much. It is by the same man who did "Sure on This Shining Night"—James Agee. He also did a wonderful book on Southern share-croppers, with whom he lived in a spirit of humility and compassion (not the usual spirit of "social investigator"); it was called "Let Us Now Praise Famous Men". I met him last week and admired him. This was actually prose, but I put it into lines to make the rhythmic pattern

*The program included the music of Chausson (Symphony in B♭), Chabrier (*Fête Polonaise*), and Rachmaninoff (*Rhapsody on a Theme of Paganini*). At this concert John Browning made his debut with the Philharmonic and was introduced to Barber (see chapter 15).

†The St. Louis Symphony Orchestra's performance under Leonard Slatkin on 8 July 1988 at the New York Festival of the Arts was met with exuberant applause and cheers that far surpassed the polite reception of the other works on the program—Joseph Schwantner's Piano Concerto (world premiere) and Aaron Copland's *Appalachian Spring*.

‡Louise Homer died on 6 May 1947, Barber's father on 12 August.

clear. It reminded me so much of summer evenings in West Chester, now very far away, and all of you are in it!

Eleanor Steber will probably do it with Koussevitzky, if she likes it.[66]

Barber had read Agee's prose-poem, "Knoxville: Summer of 1915," in *The Partisan Reader: Ten Years of* Partisan Review, *1934–1944: An Anthology.** He was arrested as much by its lyrical prose style—which broke easily into poetic fragments, with persistent alliterations and word repetitions—as by the impressionistic but faithful reverie of childhood Agee had portrayed:

> I had always admired Mr. Agee's writing and this prose–poem particularly struck me because the summer evening he describes in his native southern town reminded me so much of similar evenings when I was a child at home. I found out, after setting this, that Mr. Agee and I are the same age, and the year he described was 1915 when we were both five. You see, it expresses a child's feeling of loneliness, wonder, and lack of identity in that marginal world between twilight and sleep.[67]

When they met after Barber had written the music, he and the writer discovered that they had many "odd coincidences" about their lives:

> We both had back yards where our families used to lie in the long summer evenings, we each had an aunt who was a musician. I remember well my parents sitting on the porch, talking quietly as they rocked. And there was a trolley car with straw seats and a clanging bell called "The Dinky" that traveled up and down the main street. . . . Agee's poem was vivid and moved me deeply, and my musical response that summer of 1947 was immediate and intense. I think I must have composed *Knoxville* within a few days.†

The intensity of Barber's identification with Agee's reverie coincided with Roy Barber's impending death and may be the reason he dedicated *Knoxville* to his father. The genesis of Agee's poem reveals a parallel to Barber's experience: Agee, too, was so overwhelmed with nostalgia that the writing was rapidly accomplished:

> I was sketching around, vaguely, on a possible autobiographical novel (about 1937), and was so much involved and interested in early childhood memories. I was greatly interested in improvisatory writing, as against carefully composed, multiple-draft writing: i.e., with a kind of parallel to improvi-

*Eds. William Phillips and Philip Rahv (New York: Dial Press, 1946), pp. 30–31. The text had first appeared in *Partisan Review* 5 (August–September 1938): 22–25. After Agee's death in 1955, his editors added the piece as a prologue to his posthumously published autobiographical novel, *A Death in the Family* (New York: McDowell, Obolensky, 1956).

†Ramey, "Samuel Barber at Seventy," p. 20. Inconsistent with this report is his statement in an earlier interview with Ramey when he claimed to have had difficulty setting the text because of its complexity (liner notes, "Songs of Samuel Barber and Ned Rorem," New World Records, 1978).

sation in jazz, to a certain kind of "genuine" lyric which I thought should be purely improvised. This text turned up more out of both states of mind, than anything else: specifically, remembrance of the way water from garden hoses looked and sounded at twilight. This brought nostalgia for much that I remembered very accurately; all I had to do was write it; so the writing was easier than most I have managed. It took possibly an hour and a half; on revision, I stayed about 98 per cent faithful to my rule, for these "improvised" experiments, against any revision whatever. There is little if anything consciously invented in it, it is strictly autobiographical.*

Agee could not attend the premiere of Barber's piece because he was recovering from an appendix operation; when he eventually did hear it, his only comment seems to have been, "Barber's music is self-sufficient."†

Describing *Knoxville* as a "lyric rhapsody," in a letter of 5 September 1947 Barber told his former teacher Scalero that he viewed the new work as "perhaps in some ways going back to the old days of 'Dover Beach,' " although he hoped it was better. His association is valid in that *Knoxville: Summer of 1915* is completely lyrical and displays the same predilection for instrumental tone painting. It is, however, a mature expression of Barber's artistry in setting texts, bringing into focus his strongest creative powers as a musical poet and master of orchestral color.

The work is in one movement (eighteen minutes long), and moves naturally through three major tempo changes without abrupt breaks—adagio ma non troppo, allegro agitato, and tempo primo. It is in a rondolike form with a thrice-recurring refrain.‡ The music is characterized by shifting major-minor modes and hints of blues (especially in the use of the flatted seventh when the lilting refrain recurs its second and third times). The middle section has frequent metrical shifts—three to four to five—and hemiola rhythms, increasingly intrinsic to Barber's style.

* Agee's words are quoted in program notes of the Boston Symphony Orchestra, 9 April 1948, p. 1244. The piece was in fact drafted in 1935 when Agee, in a state of great unrest and self-analysis, was living in Florida. His marriage strained, brooding over an autobiographical novel, he was inundated with "large doses" of the works of Proust, Sigmund Freud, and Frances Wickes. His mind was flooded with memories of his father and childhood in Knoxville. Concurrently, he had "discovered" the process of improvisation in jazz (Laurence Bergreen, *James Agee: A Life* [New York: Dutton, 1984], p. 153).

†Bergreen, *James Agee*, p. 313. Agee's reaction to the music is quoted, too, in David Diamond's review in *Notes* (March 1950): 309. Afterwards, when Barber and Agee became good friends and the writer was a frequent visitor at Capricorn, the composer pressed him for another text for a choral piece, but Agee never came through with one (see Ramey, "Samuel Barber at Seventy," p. 20).

‡Three dissertations address themselves to *Knoxville*. Friedewald (pp. 61–73) views *Knoxville* as approximating a five-part rondo form with an introduction and coda. In addition to the cohesive nature of the form, he sees the work as another example of Barber's propensity for using chordal constructions as the basis for melodies. Kreiling (pp. 173–201) views *Knoxville* as Barber's most "Americanist" song text and provides an extensive critical analysis of the relationship of Barber's formal design, textual revisions, and use of harmonic, melodic, and rhythmic devices to support the imagery and emotional climate of Agee's text. Eugene Lickey provides an extensive melodic and motivic analysis in *An Analysis of Samuel Barber's* Knoxville: Summer of 1915 (D.M.A., Indiana University, 1969).

Example 10.6 *Knoxville: Summer of 1915*, Op. 24, mm. 6–8.

Agee's text, understood as poetry by Barber, was translated musically into a quasi-pastoral setting that is pictorially, as well as emotionally, expressive. The choice of a declamatory style—like a lyric recitative with a freely varied metrical beat—mimics (especially in the refrain) the swinging rhythms that haunt the chants of childhood (see Example 10.6).

The imagery of Agee's text provides abundant opportunity for musical word painting: "Talking casually" (mm. 23–24); the "increasing moan" of the trolley car (mm. 65–66); "the bleak spark crackling and cursing . . . the iron whine rises on rising speed; still risen;—faints;—halts" (mm. 72–78, pizzicato glissando in the strings).* Alliterations create an irresistible rhythmic momentum: "the faint swinging bell rises again,—still fainter; fainting,—lifting;—lifts," (mm. 79–86). The contrasting allegro agitato section evaporates on a high *a''* on "Now is the night one blue dew" (mm. 99–107).

*These and all future measure numbers refer to both G. Schirmer editions (piano-vocal score, 1949; orchestral score, 1952).

The letter Barber sent to Sidney Homer with the excerpts of Agee's prose rearranged into "lines to make the rhythm clear"[68] appeared as the following typescript:

> We are talking now of summer evenings in Knoxville Tennessee in the time that I lived there so successfully disguised to myself as a child.
>
> it has become that time of evening
> when people sit on their porches,
> rocking gently and talking gently
> and watching the street and the standing up into their sphere
> of possession
> of the trees, of birds' hung havens, hangars.
>
> People go by; things go by.
> A horse, drawing a buggy,
> breaking his hollow iron music on the asphalt;
> a loud auto; a quiet auto;
> people in pairs, not in a hurry,
> scuffling, switching their weight of aestival body,
> talking casually, the taste hovering over them
> of vanilla, strawberry, pasteboard and starched milk,
> the image upon them of lovers and horsemen,
> squared with clowns in hueless amber.
>
> A streetcar raising its iron moan;
> stopping; belling and starting, stertorous;
> rousing and raising again its iron increasing moan
> and swimming its gold windows and straw seats
> on past and past and past,
> the bleak spark crackling and cursing above it
> like a small malignant spirit set to dog its tracks;
> the iron whine rises on rising speed;
> still risen, faints; halts;
> the faint stinging bell;
> rises again, still fainter;
> fainting, lifting, lifts, faints foregone:
> forgotten.
>
> Now is the night one blue dew.
>
> Now is the night one blue dew, my father has drained, he has coiled
> the hose.
> Low on the length of lawns, a frailing of fire who breathes.
> Parents on porches; rock and rock. From damp strings morning
> glories hang their ancient faces.
> The dry and exalted noise of the locusts from all the air at once
> enchants my eardrums.

*On the rouch wet grass of the back yard
my father and mother have spread quilts.
We all lie there,
my mother, my father, my uncle, my aunt,
and I too am lying there.
†First we were sitting up,
then one of us lay down,
and then we all lay down,
on our stomachs, or on our sides, or on our backs,
and they have kept on talking.

They are not talking much, and the talk is quiet,
of nothing in particular,
of nothing at all in particular,
of nothing at all.

The stars are wide and alive,
they seem each like a smile of great sweetness,
‡and they seem very clear.

All my people are larger bodies than mine,
quiet, with voices gentle and meaningless
like the voices of sleeping birds.

One is an artist, he is living at home.
One is a musician, she is living at home.
One is my mother who is good to me.
One is my father who is good to me.

By some chance, here they are, all on this earth;
and who shall ever tell the sorrow
of being on this earth,
lying, on quilts, on the grass, in a summer evening,
among the sounds of the night.

May God bless my people, my uncle, my aunt, my mother my good father,
oh, remember them kindly in their time of trouble;
and in the hour of their taking away.

After a little I am taken in and put to bed.
Sleep, soft smiling, draws me unto her;
and those receive me, who quietly treat me,
as one familiar and well-beloved in that home:
but will not, oh, will not,
not now, not ever;
but will not ever tell me who I am.

* *rouch* is a typographical error.

†This paragraph appears only in the 1947 holograph; Barber did not retain these lines in his chamber setting of 1949.

‡*clear* found in *The Partisan Reader* (1946) and in Barber holograph sources only.

The excerpt below from Agee's original prose reveals the context from which Barber selected lines for his earliest musical setting (1947). Agee's opening sentence—"We are talking now of summer evenings in Knoxville . . ."—became an epigraph to the musical score. Barber set to music the last third of Agee's text, omitting only five lines within that section (see bracketed lines in the excerpt below).* The typescript of the text and existing holographs present evidence that *The Partisan Reader* (1946) was Barber's source but also that before the work was published the text was brought into conformity with the earliest version as it appeared in the *Partisan Review* (1938). In the 1946 source, the lines beginning "The stars are wide and alive . . ." conclude with "and they seem very *clear*" (italics mine). Both the 1938 source, however, and the posthumously published prologue to *A Death in the Family* read "and they seem very *near.*" Both of Barber's holographs use the word *clear* (see circled word in the Agee excerpt and in Barber's typescript); his piano-vocal score (1947) shows an erasure of a letter *n,* with *cl* written boldly over it at measure 146. A copy of the 1949 piano-vocal score prepared for engraving, which is at the Sibley Library in Rochester (on loan from G. Schirmer), also shows the word *clear,* and although there are many musical corrections in Barber's hand on the proofs, no textual change was indicated. Both Schirmer editions, however, have substituted *near* (see m. 164 in the piano-vocal score, 1949, and Study Score No. 153, 1952).† This suggests that *clear* was a typographical error in *The Partisan Reader* and that Barber's original impulse may have been to retain the more poetic image for his early effort.

Barber's source for "Knoxville: Summer of 1915" appeared on pages 30–31 of *The Partisan Reader* (Dial Press, 1946) as follows:

[*page* 30]

> of at least a thousand. The noise of each locust is pitched in some classic locust range out of which none of them varies more than two full tones: and yet you seem to hear each locust discrete from all the rest, and there is a long, slow, pulse in their noise, like the scarcely defined arch of a long and high set bridge. They are all around in every tree, so that the noise seems to come from nowhere and everywhere at once, from the whole shell heaven, shivering in your flesh and teasing your eardrums, the boldest of all the sounds of night. And yet it is habitual to summer nights, and is of the great order of noises, like the noises of the sea and of the blood her precocious grandchild, which you realize you are hearing only when you catch yourself listen-

* Holographs of the piano-vocal score with text and the original orchestral score without text, both dated 9 April 1947, are at the Library of Congress, Music Division. A holograph of the later chamber version, 1953, is also at the Library of Congress.

† It is interesting to note that on the earliest recording of *Knoxville: Summer of 1915* (Columbia ML-2174, 1951) Steber sings the word *clear.*

ing. Meantime from low in the dark, just outside the swaying horizons of the hoses, conveying always grass in the damp of dew and its strong green-black smear of smell, the regular yet spaced noises of the crickets, each a sweet cold silver noise three-noted, like the slipping each time of three matched links of a small chain.

But the men by now, one by one, have silenced their hoses and drained and coiled them. Now only two, and now only one, is left, and you see only ghostlike shirt with the sleeve garters, and sober mystery of his mild face like the lifted face of large cattle enquiring of your presence in a pitchdark pool of meadow; and now he too is gone; and* it has become that time of evening when people sit on their porches, rocking gently and talking gently and watching the street and the standing up into their sphere of possession of the trees, of birds' hung havens, hangars. People go by; things go by. A horse, drawing a buggy, breaking his hollow iron music on the asphalt: a loud auto: a quiet auto: people in pairs, not in a hurry, scuffling, switching their weight of aestival body, talking casually, the taste hovering over them of vanilla, strawberry, pasteboard, and starched milk, the image upon them of lovers and horsemen, squared with clowns in hueless amber. A streetcar raising its iron moan; stopping; belling and starting, stertorous; rousing and raising again its iron increasing moan and swimming its gold windows and straw seats on past and past and past, the bleak spark crackling and cursing above it like a small malignant spirit set to dog its tracks; the iron whine rises on rising speed; still risen, faints; halts; the faint stinging bell; rises again, still fainter; fainting, lifting, lifts, faints foregone: forgotten. Now is the night one blue dew.

Now is the night one blue dew, my father has drained, he has coiled the hose.
Low on the length of lawns, a frailing of fire who breathes.

[*page* 31]

†[Content, silver, like peeps of light, each cricket makes his comment over and over in the drowned grass.
A cold toad thumpily flounders.
Within the edges of damp shadows of side yards are hovering children nearly sick with joy of fear, who watch the unguarding of a telephone pole.
Around white carbon corner lamps bugs of all sizes are lifted elliptic, solar systems. Big hardshells bruise themselves, assailant: he is fallen on his back, legs squiggling.]

* Barber's setting begins here.
† Lines in brackets are omitted from all Barber sources.

Parents on porches: rock and rock. From damp strings morning glories hang their ancient faces.
The dry and exalted noise of the locusts from all the air at once enchants my eardrums.

On the rough wet grass of the back yard my father and mother have spread quilts. We all lie there, my mother, my father, my uncle, my aunt, and I too am lying there. *First we were sitting up, then one of us lay down, and then we all lay down, on our stomachs, or on our sides, or on our backs, and they have kept on talking. They are not talking much, and the talk is quiet, of nothing in particular, of nothing at all in particular, of nothing at all. The stars are wide and alive, they seem each like a smile of great sweetness, and they seem very (clear)† All my people are larger bodies than mine, [quiet,]‡ with voices gentle and meaningless like the voices of sleeping birds. One is an artist, he is living at home. One is a musician, she is living at home. One is my mother who is good to me. One is my father who is good to me. By some chance, here they are, all on this earth; and who shall ever tell the sorrow of being on this earth, lying, on quilts, on the grass, in a summer evening, among the sounds of the night. May God bless my people, my uncle, my aunt, my mother, my good father, oh, remember them kindly in their time of trouble; and in the hour of their taking away.

After a little I am taken in and put to bed. Sleep, soft smiling, draws me unto her: and those receive me, who quietly treat me, as one familiar and well-beloved in that home: but will not, oh, will not, not now, not ever; but will not ever tell me who I am.

1938

As early as February 1947, Barber wrote to Homer, "Eleanor Steber asked me to write something for her voice and orchestra." He confided to his uncle:

> Do you like her? Her voice seems very small to me, but she is intelligent. There seem to be no young singers (or old!) with enough voice to stand up against a symphony orchestra and I don't want Traubel.§

*Underlined sentence is found in Barber's letter to Sidney Homer, 15 April 1947, and the 1947 holograph (Library of Congress). It is omitted from the 1949 holograph.

†*Clear* (in circle) appears in this source and Barber holographs only.

‡*Quiet* (in brackets) is omitted from all Barber sources.

§Letter, 10 February 1947. Barber's confidence in Steber was to strengthen. A year later, after they had worked together, he wrote about her to Homer: "I have had some excellent rehearsals with Eleanor Steber . . . who sings 'Knoxville' better and better" (letter, 8 February 1948).

Steber's interest in commissioning an orchestral work had been encouraged by her manager, David Hocker, as part of a campaign to promote her career. "They were doing everything and anything to get some kind of publicity through the news media," she recalled.[69] Up to that time no American singer had ever commissioned an orchestral work for voice, and the idea of promoting a singer's career through performance of American music was unusual during the 1940s. Even Steber, for example, included few American songs on her programs, and most were songs her mother had taught her—those by Charles Griffes and Arthur Foote.*

When Serge Koussevitzky first broached the subject of a piece for voice and orchestra to Barber, he apparently had in mind a three-movement symphony.[70] Barber, however, who began work on *Knoxville* before Steber confirmed her commission and with no particular singer in mind, said his conception of the piece involved a more intimate orchestration. Once he realized Steber might sing it, he continued with a more expansive version:

> I suspected that what she really wanted was a big, whooping thing to do with Koussevitzky and the Boston Symphony, but of course, *Knoxville* is not that kind of piece. I also knew Koussevitzky preferred the full orchestra, so I continued with the original scoring, and it was premiered that way.[71]

He completed the work on 4 April 1947 and five days later wired Koussevitzky:

> Have completed work for soprano and orchestra and would love to play it for you from the piano score this week if you ever have a moment please wire me Capricorn, Mt. Kisco, NY if possible for you. Affectionate Greetings. Sam Barber.[72]

Koussevitzky responded immediately that he "would be delighted" to meet with Barber at his New York apartment in the Savoy Plaza.[73] Evidently, after this reading the conductor suggested other possible singers for the premiere. Steber had not yet heard the score, but Barber expected her to sing it if she liked it. He confided in Homer: "I didn't like Carol Brice, so got out of that."[74] When Steber's managers heard the piece, they believed

*Steber, interview with the author, 2 September 1983. David Diamond, in his 1950 review of the piano-vocal edition of *Knoxville,* mentioned that vocalists were more inclined to include in their programs short groups of one or two American songs for "sure-fire effect"; but short of some of Ives's or Aaron Copland's music, which achieved a refreshing simplicity and intellectual honesty, Diamond maintained, more often American songs were characterized by folk-tunes, "emotional vulgarities," or a kind of "cuteness" and "affected modalities with polytonal cliches" ("Samuel Barber: 'Knoxville: Summer of 1915,' New York: G. Schirmer, Inc., 1949," *Notes* [March 1950]: 309). Compare this to Martina Arroyo's later account of her training during the fifties, when American singers were virtually expected to include American works on their programs, especially for European audiences (see chapter 13).

it to be right for the American singer, that it would bring much attention to her.[75] Two weeks later Barber wrote to Koussevitzky:

> *Dear Sergei Alexandrovich,*
> Eleanor Steber is happy to commission "Knoxville: Summer of 1915" and I am glad, for I think she is the best possible choice. Of course we both count on you to give the first performance! She returns from tour to New York May 15th, and I will work on it with her. Then, whenever you have time, I want her to sing it for you.
>
> Thank you for the time you gave me the other day, and for the valued suggestions—it is always wonderful to spend time with you.*

From the beginning of their rehearsals, Barber was pleased with the progress and the way Steber worked. Only a few changes were required, primarily adjustments that allowed the voice to be heard over the orchestra. At Steber's suggestion, for example, one of the most difficult passages, beginning "Now is the night one blue dew," was moved to a higher register. The difficulty of this passage lies in the placement of the tessitura—b♭″ to a high a″. Steber also urged that Barber change to a higher register the substantial passage at the end, "May God bless my people . . . ." She pointed out to him that it was too low for a singer's voice to be heard above an orchestral accompaniment.[76]

A commitment to work at the American Academy in Rome threatened to prevent Barber from attending the first performance of *Knoxville,* which was scheduled for 9 April 1948 in Boston. In October 1947, because he was aware of the conflict and wanted to hear the premiere, he attempted to persuade Koussevitzky to reschedule the performance. Enclosing a lengthy list of alternate dates for Steber's availability from November to February, Barber wrote to Olga Koussevitzky:

> Will you be an angel and get out S. A.'s mysterious little book which can break the hearts or decide the fate of artists, dynasties, and poor composers? . . . I do hope S. A. can work a miracle and advance the performance.[77]

Koussevitzky's telegram made it clear what the alternatives were:

> Consider most important your presence at first performance—unfortunately cannot arrange later dates. Suggest postponing to next season, or if you prefer—would have no objection your giving first performance to another organization this season. Warm greetings. Serge.[78]

Barber answered:

*Letter, 22 April 1947, in Serge Koussevitzky Collection, Library of Congress, Music Division. Barber's letters from 1946 on address Koussevitzky as "Sergei Alexandrovitch," reflecting the shift from formality to a warmer relationship.

Thank you for your telegram. It is too bad the performance date cannot be advanced, but I well understand such complications.

Both Eleanor Steber and I are so anxious that *you* do the 1st performance of "Knoxville: Summer of 1915" that it would be a great disappointment to offer it to another organization. And postponing it to next season makes it so very late.

So I suggest that we let it stand as it is now scheduled—for next April. I shall train Steber letter perfect in the part and will do everything in my power to come back to America for the performance.

Affectionate greetings to you and Olga.

Sincerely,
Sam[79]

Nevertheless, although Barber went through with his original plan to sail on the *Vulcania* for Naples on 13 February 1948, he remained uneasy about his absence from the premiere. Before he left, at his insistence, arrangements were made for the complete text of "Knoxville" to be printed in the program—"not in tiny italics which they always do, but so that people can *follow* the words."[80] He still hoped that he might plan an early return in time to hear *Knoxville,* but early in April he wrote to Koussevitzky from Rome:

I am heartbroken to be unable to return for the premiere of "Knoxville." Until the last minute I thought it might be possible and that I could fulfill my contract here later: in that case I could have returned to America in order to hear my work. But the entire future of the Academy here depends on the outcome of the forthcoming elections: if it is anti-American we shall all have to leave the end of April, so it is really impossible for me to leave now. You must know that I am bitterly disappointed: a premiere in your hands is a composer's dream; and then this is a work which is particularly dear to me. I shall be thinking of it and of you next Friday. Please let me know how it goes, my address is American Academy, Rome.[81]

The premiere of *Knoxville: Summer of 1915,* on 9 April, was upstaged by the unexpected announcement of Koussevitzky's retirement at the end of the 1948–49 season and the naming of Charles Münch as his successor. Some claimed that after this news any premiere would fall into the category of the "also-rans."[82]

In fact, the work was received with a mixture of sentiments. There was agreement among critics that Barber had successfully captured "with honest sentiment and feeling" the wistful nostalgia associated with memories of childhood. Steber's performance received uniformly high marks, the part believed to be "perfectly suited to [her] extraordinary legato and impeccable musicianship."[83] Agee's words were considered by some unsympathetic to a musical setting and therefore a challenge to the composer:

> They do not lend themselves to dramatic interpretation [and] . . . do not suggest the tension of an emotional climax. . . . In his workmanlike fashion [Barber] has deliberately designed music to mirror the mood of the text. Its texture is soft and pretty like a Monet landscape. . . . Although Mr. Barber's music seems to lack character on first hearing . . . it would grow on one in repeated hearings.[84]

News of the premiere was transmitted by friends to Barber across the ocean: Koussevitzky wired that the performance was "an outstanding success and made a deep impression on all."[85] Hearing about the conductor's forthcoming retirement, Barber sent a message:

> How happy I was to have your kind cable and to know you liked "Knoxville." Cables from Steber and Menotti told me what a wonderful performance and atmosphere you created. . . . Yesterday Menotti phoned me from London; I besieged him with questions about my work, made him talk for one hour and now I feel very au courant. . . . A thousand thanks from my heart for the interest you have taken in this work of mine; I am delighted. . . . The brilliance and importance of the twenty-five years you have given to the Boston Symphony, and to America and its composers, are unequalled and not to be repeated. We are eternally your debtors.[86]

If this expression of appreciation seems effusive in the light of his later recollections, it is no less sincere, for at this time Barber probably had more reason to be grateful to Koussevitzky than to any other conductor.* He had gone out of his way to promote Barber's music and—as the correspondence to army brass has shown—to enable him to have the freedom to compose. Koussevitzky's aid to many American composers was generous not only because he was convinced of their artistic worth but because, as a naturalized citizen, he was fiercely loyal to all things American.

Koussevitzky never performed *Knoxville* again, and Barber first heard it sung by Steber in Minneapolis in December 1948. Dimitri Mitropoulos conducted a "fine performance," he thought: "The orchestration was very good which made me happy after all the revisions I've had to do on other things: nothing to be changed."[87]

For practical reasons he was to change his mind about that a year later. In the winter of 1949, while attending a rehearsal of a forthcoming summer broadcast by Eileen Farrell and the CBS Orchestra, conducted by Bernard Herrmann, Barber and Strickland discussed the possibility of a chamber orchestra version of *Knoxville* for an all-Barber concert Strick-

*Much later, Barber's recollection of the premiere was of "terrible reviews." Perhaps unfairly, he laid the responsibility on the conductor: "Koussevitzky hadn't the faintest idea of what the words meant, at least not unless someone sat down with him and carefully translated the words into Russian. With *Knoxville* you *have* to know the words, and even so, I'm not sure that they would mean to a foreigner what they mean to an American" (Ramey, "Samuel Barber at Seventy," p. 20).

land was planning at Dumbarton Oaks. Barber wrote to Sidney Homer about the idea:

> As so few singers sing with symphony orchestra these days, I am thinking of making an arrangement of "Knoxville" for small orchestra (say 10 or 12 players) which could be used all over: they tell me there is great activity in the colleges for this sort of thing. (I heard "Stopwatch and an Ordnance Map" for men's chorus and drums sung by the Bowdoin Glee Club and was amazed at how they do it!)[88]

A comparison of the 1947 holograph scores at the Library of Congress and the G. Schirmer editions of 1949 and 1952 reveals that Barber made the following changes in the score of *Knoxville: Summer of 1915:* woodwinds and trumpets were reduced to *primo* parts only; timpani and bass clarinet parts were deleted altogether; and the oboe and flute parts were alternated with English horn and piccolo respectively. The number of horns was increased from one to two (in F), and the triangle, harp, and stringed instrument parts were kept intact. The score for smaller ensemble has, for the most part, preserved all the voices of the original version through a redistribution of *secondo* parts: the oboe or clarinet plays what was formerly flute II; and the flute plays what was formerly clarinet I.

Further cuts were made to Agee's text—several lines that do not affect continuity of the prose (see above, Barber's letter to Sidney Homer, 15 April 1947, at †). Nor does the ten-measure cut at measure 147 present a problem musically. The accompaniment material from the phrase that was cut is maintained for the phrase that follows (beginning at m. 148), with necessary minor rhythmic adjustments and overlapping of arpeggios. Thus the transition is effected smoothly. This is shown below in Examples 10.7a and 10.7b, which compare the holograph of the piano-vocal score (at the Library of Congress) with the G. Schirmer 1949 edition.*

The chamber version of *Knoxville: Summer of 1915* had its debut on 1 April 1950 at Dumbarton Oaks in Washington, D.C., in the ornately frescoed music room of the former home of Robert Woods Bliss. Farrell and a small orchestra of about twenty players were conducted by William Strickland. Barber described the performance to Sidney Homer:

> I really think it sounded much better in this intimate version. Bill Strickland conducted and made it move all the time: the performance you heard dragged so. It seemed to move the audience greatly, although as I saw them sitting there in their furs and pearls, I wondered how many had ever "lain in the back-yards on quilts."!!
>
> How I wish I had a recording of "Knoxville" to send you: I would like you to know that better.[89]

* A comparison between the holograph orchestral score at the Library of Congress with the G. Schirmer 1952 edition (Score No. 153) shows a similar change in the same location.

a.

Example 10.7 *Knoxville: Summer of 1915*, revisions at m. 146. *a*. Holograph piano-vocal score, 1947. Cuts are shown in brackets. *(Library of Congress) b*. G. Schirmer, piano–vocal score, 1949. Cut was made before m. 147.

Homer was deeply moved when he heard *Knoxville* for the first time:

> *Dear Sam,*
>
> I have been through a wringer! I am still hearing that tremendous downward final passage, enough to break your heart; and am asking the question: who am I? I wonder if I will ever know this work intimately so that I can grasp all the beautiful subtleties of sympathy and understanding.

b.

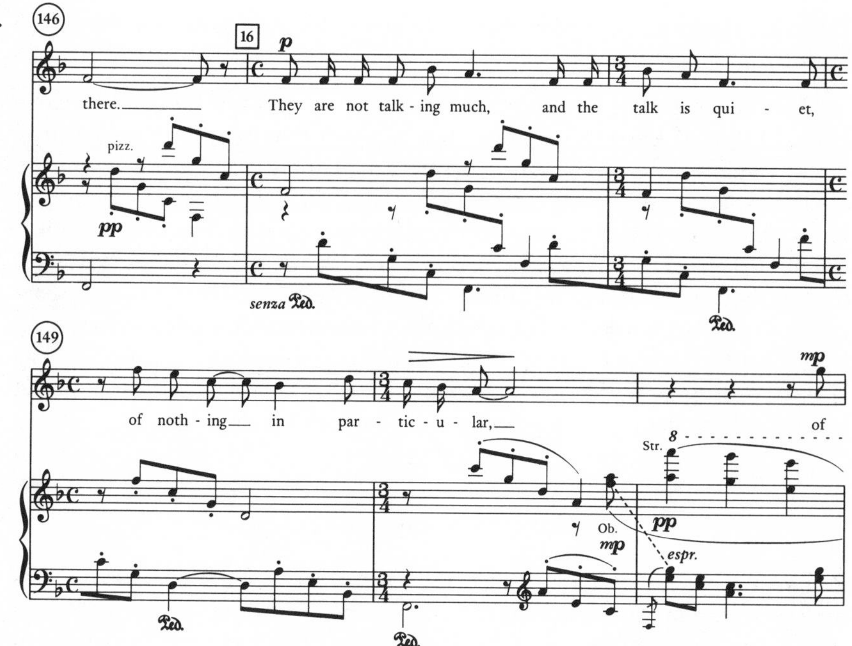

> Perhaps you will be blest with a great recording. I hope so, I want to know every treatment of every word. It sounds like a masterpiece, but my hearing does not get all the words and I long for the *real thing*. How about a one-act music drama? Voice parts like that would be sweeping, thrilling, and convincing.
>
> There is so much to be expressed. The world is not yet convinced! Not yet! Perhaps nothing short of crucifixion will teach them.
>
> *Love,*
> *Uncle*[90]

Knoxville: Summer of 1915 is considered to be the most "American" of Barber's works, not only because of the text—wherein Agee's nostalgic reflections identify with the folklore of growing up in America—but also because the music so accurately evokes the emotions of these reflections. That this is true is confirmed again and again by the personal response of performers who sing it. Eleanor Steber and Leontyne Price, for example—each of whom has recorded and frequently sung *Knoxville: Summer of 1915*—speak of the perfect correspondence between Barber's music, Agee's introspection, and their own experience. "That was *exactly* my childhood!" declared Steber, recalling growing up in Wheeling, West Virginia.[91] Leontyne Price said:

> As a southerner, it expresses everything I know about my roots and about my mama and father . . . my home town. . . . There's no cataloguing a

great artist, it's just delving into the beauty of the Agee poem and setting it right to music. You can *smell* the South in it.[92]

The musical style of *Knoxville: Summer of 1915* is sometimes compared to that of Aaron Copland. There is a hint that even Barber measured himself against the paradigmatic American composer. Shortly before he died, Barber listened from his hospital bed to a radio performance of *Knoxville,* after which he was reported to have said to Turner: "I think I did almost as well as Aaron here, don't you?"[93] Menotti claims, however, that Barber meant this ironically and that he rejected any serious comparison of his own works with Copland's.* Comparisons aside, other critics have viewed Barber's setting of the quintessentially American text as "as clear and original and American as anything yet written . . . the pinnacle beyond which many a composer will find it impossible to go."[94]

Piano Sonata, Op. 26 (1949)

Perhaps no other of Barber's works, except the *Adagio for Strings,* has had as stunning an impact on the American musical world as his Sonata for Piano. Its premiere was a landmark event, the first time an American piano piece of major importance was played by an internationally renowned virtuoso—Vladimir Horowitz. No doubt the sonata's critical reception was enhanced by the monarch pianist's claim that it was "the first truly great native work in the form."[95] The enthusiasm with which both young and seasoned pianists—in Europe as well as in the United States—programmed Barber's Piano Sonata in the fifties and sixties suggests that it was not only a tour de force for the performer but filled a gap in the repertoire as well.†

Prophetically, Olin Downes said of the sonata after Horowitz gave the New York premiere on 23 January 1950, "Many pianists will now attempt its performance, but few can expect to approach the authority and imagination, the power and the delicacy, on occasion, as also the rather incredible virtuosity which went into its performance yesterday evening."‡

*Telephone conversation with the author, September 1985. The deeper irony lies in Copland's remark that he wished he had found the text of *Knoxville* first. "It's just as well it happened the way it did," Copland confessed, "or we wouldn't have Sam's beautiful score" (Phillip Ramey, "Aaron Copland at Eighty," *Ovation* 1 [November 1980]: 14).

†See Nathan Broder, "Current Chronicle," *Musical Quarterly* 36 (April 1950): 279, in which he reports that although at least "thirty to forty full-length piano sonatas by American composers were published in the last thirty years . . . less than a half-dozen were performed in public enough to be said to have established a place for themselves in the repertory."

‡"Horowitz Offers Barber's Sonata," *New York Times*, 25 January 1950. Many years later, recalling Downes's observation, Barber said: "Well, the joke is that now the sonata is a required work at just about every piano competition and young people have no trouble with it at all. I get letters all the time saying, 'Please, please, write something else for the piano: we're sick of that fugue' " (Kozinn, "Samuel Barber: The Last Interview and the Legacy," part 2, p. 45).

Vladimir Horowitz and Barber, 1950. *(Courtesy of Gian Carlo Menotti)*

He was right about the tide of interest that followed in the wake of the sonata's arrival on the scene. Although there was no contractual agreement, it was understood Horowitz would have the first performance rights for the 1949–50 concert season, and he programmed it on twenty-one concerts within the first year of its New York premiere.[96] But even before the premiere, special permission had been sought from Barber and Horowitz so that Rudolph Firkusny could play the sonata in the spring of 1950 at an all-Barber concert at Dumbarton Oaks in Washington, D.C.* After its first year, the sonata had many performances in the United States and in Europe: Thomas Brockman premiered it in Philadelphia in the autumn of 1950; Robert Goldsand, Frank Sheridan, Samuel Lipman, Daniel Pollack, Marjorie Mitchell, Ruth Meckler (later Laredo), Jeffrey Siegel, Abbott Ruskin, Van Cliburn, Michael Block all played it.† John Browning recalled working on it as a student at the Juilliard School, and afterwards he performed it many times and recorded it.‡ Robert Wallenborn and Moura Lympany performed it in England in 1950. Its popularity extended to the Soviet Union; a Russian edition was published in 1960, and the last movement was orchestrated.[97]

Although Horowitz had played Barber's *Excursions* in 1945, his repertoire since then continued to favor nineteenth-century European Romantic music with only occasional ventures into the twentieth-century literature—Prokofiev and Kabalevsky.§ As early as the 1930s, he had asserted:

*Barber, writing from Rome, 25 October 1949, outlined to Strickland what he must do:

> I have written to Horowitz first to be sure it is O.K., he will then tell Gian-Carlo who will advise Heinsheimer to let Firkusny have a score: complicated procedure, but I want to avoid any trouble with Horowitz. Keep in touch with G.C. about this, as Horowitz will let him know directly. Schirmers have master sheets of the Sonata and will make a copy for F. and you.

Firkusny played the sonata, 1 April 1950, with "tremendous power and beauty," as Paul Hume *(Washington Post)* reported, "on a piano no artist should have been asked to touch. . . . Out of tune, with a bad tone and a twanging string."

†"City Premiere of Barber Sonata Heard in Weiss Concert Here," *Philadelphia Evening Bulletin,* 24 October 1950. Barber was at this concert and stood to applaud Brockman. Meckler's dazzling performance at her graduation recital and at Barber's fiftieth birthday celebration at Curtis Institute inspired the composer to inscribe on the young pianist's copy of the sonata, "Brava! Bravissima! Samuel Barber, March 9, 1960." Barber never forgot her performance and some twenty years later requested that she be invited to play the sonata in honor of his seventieth birthday celebration (*New York Times,* 1 March 1980).

‡John Browning, "Samuel Barber's Nocturne, Op. 33," *Clavier* (January 1986): 21. Browning performed the sonata in Pasadena, California, and Town Hall in New York in 1958.

§By 1949, Horowitz had introduced New York audiences to the Sixth, Seventh, and Eighth Sonatas of Prokofiev. When he premiered the Seventh Piano Sonata, 13 January 1944, at a private concert at the Soviet Consulate in New York, Barber was among the two hundred musicians who were present; the audience, according to Horowitz's recollection, included the "quintessence of all musicians"—among them, Toscanini, Stokowski, Koussevitzky, Walter, Bernstein, Copland, Thomson, Varèse, and Rodzinski (interview with David Dubal, cited in Plaskin, *Horowitz*). Critics clamored for more contemporary programming from Horowitz; Howard Taubman, for example, wrote: "One would like to hear Mr. Horowitz do a program of big contemporary works some day—perhaps sonatas by Prokofiev, Stravinsky, and

"I would like to find a good large work by an American composer."[98] His attraction to Barber's music was explained many years later:

> Barber is one of the few American composers who knows how to write for the piano. Copland has some good things, but they are not pianistic. I like pianistic music. Somehow American composers don't understand the piano too well. Either they write music that is very pianistic, but has no substance, or write music that has substance, but isn't pianistic.[99]

Barber's sonata was commissioned in the fall of 1947 by Irving Berlin and Richard Rodgers in honor of the twenty-fifth anniversary of the League of Composers.* Although beginning it was relatively easy for him, it was almost two years before the work was completed in June 1949.† Early in December 1947, he told Sidney Homer he had finished the first movement.[100] But progress was interrupted by a whirlwind schedule that claimed his attention: rehearsals for *Medea,* the Cello Concerto, and plans for *Knoxville: Summer of 1915*. "In between all of this, I have finished the 1st movement of the piano sonata," he wrote to Homer, "good, I think."[101] Homer had sent his nephew recordings of his own violin-piano sonatas, and these made a deep impression on Barber. He wrote about them:

> We love the records of your Sonatas and have played them often. It is so much better to have an actual performance of them than a printed score. I wish those records were available to the public at large. I would love to steal that scherzo . . . as it is just what I want for the scherzo of my sonata. Why did you get it first? It is wonderful.‡

Copland. He could get away with it, since his audience buys without seeing the program" (*New York Times,* 18 January 1949). Similarly, Arthur Berger complained: "One wonders why he does not attempt more twentieth-century music. . . . Mr. Horowitz's ventures in this direction have been all too few and timid" (*New York Herald Tribune,* 18 January 1949).

*As a "tribute to the League's pioneering efforts in behalf of living composers," commissions were given by orchestras, publishers, artists, and musical groups: BMI, Carl Fischer, Boosey and Hawkes, the National Federation of Music Clubs, Lucy Rosen. The festival began in November 1947 and took place in different locations, including Carnegie Hall, Times Hall, the Museum of Modern Art, and WQXR, NBC, CBS, WMCA, and WNYC radio stations. Among the composers commissioned besides "Sam Barber" were Robert Ward, William Bergsma, Peter Mennin, Wallingford Riegger, Harold Shapero, and Nicolai Berezowsky (*Composer's News-Record* 3, Fall 1947). Announcement of Berlin and Rodgers's commission to Barber (at the suggestion of the League of Composers) was in the *New York Times* on 24 September 1947.

†The date is at the end of the holograph at the Library of Congress. In addition to this pencil score and a holograph page of corrections submitted to Schirmer's copyist, Weissleder, there are also two blueprint copies with holograph corrections at the library.

‡Letter to Homer, 21 December 1947, from Capricorn. The scherzo to which he was referring was the third movement of Homer's Sonata for Violin and Piano in F minor, Op. 65 (1948). There is some suggestion of the melodic and rhythmic shape of Homer's theme in the *scherzando* second movement of Barber's sonata, but the form, harmony, and evanescent character of the latter place it in a different world from Homer's. Homer's sonatas were recorded about a week after Louise Homer's death by Alphonse Carlo, then head of the string department at Rollins College, and Katharine Fryer.

He planned to finish the sonata in Rome at the American Academy, where he would be from the middle of February until July. He wrote of these plans to Homer:

> I look forward to this trip and the change of scene. Reports from the Academy itself are not too encouraging: crowded working conditions, disgruntled wives (who have been allowed to come for the first time), and the usual artificial condition of throwing twenty men, supposedly artists, together under one roof in Italy. But I shall live in a separate house away from it and keep to my own work for the most part. . . . I have passage back early in July, and may even return sooner, so it won't be long before I see you again . . . and I have a feeling I shall write you more often when there is a little ocean between us. It will be good to start working over there, to finish my sonata, then the quartet, far from our "musical life" here, of which, by the way, I see less and less.*

But when Barber arrived in Rome, he was beset with immobility. He wrote to Homer:

> It is terribly hard, the first months here, not to fall into a "dolce far niente" state. . . . The change from America is rather violent, and about all one can seem to do for awhile is drink in impressions. The climate, in general, is heavenly (even the Italians say it is impossible to organize politically under such a sun!), the beauty of the surroundings so profligate and excessive, the people, no matter from what class, generally so charming that I find it terribly difficult to focus my thoughts, use any except an innate critical sense which I may or may not have, and above all, "produce." Perhaps it is well at times only to drift, and silence one's New England conscience which sees empty MS. paper as a sign of eternal damnation![102]

The postwar flux of Italian politics and society diverted Barber:

> Certainly I've met many people—the nicest are the intellectual young communists, who have a strong sense of personal Italian dignity and are not overjoyed that Italy is being used as a pawn in the international game of chess . . . but I am also interested in the lost aristocracy, coasting along in their extraordinary houses, towards they know not what, incapable, surfeited with tradition as they are, of facing a new reality: and this goes, in most cases, for their charming younger generation, as well. Then I have met some outlandish figures high in Vatican circles, cynical and brilliant, Baroque and worldly, playing power games as corrupt as Wall Street: Rome has rarely been the place to feel the spiritual side of the church. Then a host of artists and, least interesting as they have always been here—the

*Letter, 8 February 1948. The quartet he referred to was the one commissioned by Elizabeth Sprague Coolidge, but which he never completed (see chapter 6).

musicians. I have even become interested in a friend of mine's excavations on the coast near Cosa: he is looking for the lost key to the Etruscan language.

And so it goes: there were two wonderful concerts of newly discovered music of Vivaldi, which makes me think that this composer deserves a more important rank than posterity has given him. Bach had good taste!*

In this manner went the rest of his stay at the academy; the work he had enthusiastically looked forward to did not get done, and he returned to Capricorn earlier than he might have. "There were so many distractions in Rome that I accomplished precisely nothing," he confessed to Homer:

> This is the real reason I came back to America this summer—to sit here, not to move, and work. . . . The Sonata had started off so well here in January. 1st movement finished—but then Italy seemed to stop the progress: so I came back here, and with the exception of visiting mother and Sue for several days, have not budged off the place. I can't say it has been very amusing, especially as I have no servant and am a lousy cook and hate the inside of a kitchen! . . . For a month nothing happened: not an idea worth jotting down. I bought the 46 volumes of the Bach Gesellschaft and found them here on my return from Europe—a great temptation to peruse for hours and hours. But I didn't allow myself to play any music at all and left all possible room for my own to appear. Last week, at last, an idea, and I've just finished the second movement—a scherzo. So now I don't want to move again until it is finished. (Horowitz is furious at me, as he had programmed it for this season, and it is probably already too late—he learns everything in the summer. However, I don't think about that: only about the sonata.) I'll just continue my hermit-like existence until the Sonata is finished. I don't force things, but six months without writing a note is disarming, and makes me feel I have no reason to exist. Anyway, it moves ahead now, and I shall first plug away. The first two movements are good, I think. Now a slow movement-finale.†

*Letter to Sidney Homer, 14 April 1948, from the American Academy, Porta San Pancrazio, Rome. Barber's attitude towards the milieu at the academy seemed to become more disdainful in the next few years: in 1951, a lunch there, "at the insistence of some of the inmates," provoked the wry comment, "Sunday dinner with the Laird Bible Class would have been wilder and more festive" (letter to his family, 10 January 1951).

†Letter, 20 August 1948, Capricorn. Despite what Barber says about stoically resisting opening the pages of the newly acquired Bach Gesellschaft while he was writing the piano sonata, his friends report it was rare that a day went by without his playing an hour of Bach (John Browning and Phillip Ramey, interviews with the author). That his study of Bach continued well beyond this time is indicated by Manfred Ibel, who, in describing Barber's routine during the late 1950s and afterwards, said: "Often he would play Bach fugues for me and explain how masterfully they were constructed" (Ibel, interview with the author, 10 April 1987).

Sketches of the third movement of the Piano Sonata given to Henry-Louis de La Grange confirm that Barber was working on the third movement at La Grange's home in Sachem's

Because the association between Horowitz and Barber's sonata was so firmly established, many assumed the piece was written especially for the pianist.* Although afterwards both stated publicly this was not so, the above letter strongly indicates that Barber was indeed writing the sonata for Horowitz.† Afterwards, he was candid about the enormous impact of hearing Horowitz play the piano:

> Of course he had a great influence on me for writing for piano. Good God! He taught me so much about piano. He used to play Scriabin for me all night in Mount Kisco. . . . My piano teacher, Vengerova, was a great teacher, but hearing Horowitz play was for me a great experience. I learned so much.[103]

John Browning has pointed to Barber's predilection for the "old Russian style of pianism . . . the big tone, broad romantic style, ample but intelligent use of the pedal, lush sonorities, strong voicings—in short, all the best attributes of Horowitz."[104] Moreover, as Barber's letter to Homer suggests, after finishing the first two movements in August 1948, he had in mind a three-movement work, but when Horowitz heard these movements, he suggested that Barber write a fourth.[105] The pianist claimed:

> I saw three movements and told him the sonata would sound better if he made a very flashy last movement, but with content. So he did that fugue, which is the best thing in the sonata.[106]

It was not, however, as simple as that. Early in 1949, Barber reported to Sidney Homer that—as had happened before—he was beset by many interruptions involving performances of his works: revisions on the Violin Concerto for a forthcoming performance by Ruth Posselt with the Boston Symphony, arrangements for new parts, copyists, and rehearsals in Boston; a two-day festival in honor of the twenty-fifth anniversary of the Curtis Institute; a trip to Minneapolis to hear Steber and Mitropoulos do *Knoxville,* which he was obligated to reorchestrate for chamber orchestra before the summer. "No progress on the sonata with all this running around," he wrote, "but in a fortnight things will be quiet, and I shall be able to work."[107] But at the end of January he ground to a halt:

> I am in one of those "lying fallow" states which you warned me years ago not to let upset me. No ideas at all most of the winter. I hope with the spring this will change.[108]

Head, Connecticut, in August 1948: inscription on the first page reads, "pour H. L. / Souvenir de Sachem's Head / August 1948." The manuscript is at the Pierpont Morgan Library.

* Olin Downes's review of the premiere (*New York Times,* 25 January 1950), says precisely this: "One would think, indeed, that the sonata had been conceived with Mr. Horowitz in mind."

† Barber claimed to Robert Sherman that he did not have the pianist in mind when he set out to write it: "No, I think I just started to write a sonata" (WQXR Great Artists Series, 30 September 1978).

Barber made good use of this dry period by "putting his house in order"—correcting proofs and revising his violin concerto for a new edition. The eighty-four-year-old Homer, however, interpreted his nephew's impasse as a lack of confidence:

> I guess we expect too much of "ideas." They must be distinguished, original, profound, yet be as putty in our hands. It is a great deal to expect. Sometimes ideas are stronger than we are and we should be as putty in *their* hands, but we refuse and an impasse results. Sometimes the answer may be short forms, lyricism, but we expand. We know best. There is a certain cooperation and acceptance that is the true technique of creative men, even in "fallow" periods when ideas germinate. Resistance, impatience, discontent may prevent just what we look for. If so, away with them!
>
> I believe confidence is the watchword and receptivity the objective. . . . Anything that interferes with these two things is wrong. . . . If we surround ideas with a sense of mysticism and chance we may not even recognize them when they float through our noble brows.
>
> I say trust the ideas and be receptive, on the lookout, keen, quick. When I hear of a vacant spot in the lives of the great composers, I wonder how they felt. Did they know they were going to write late quartets, the Magic Flute, the E-minor Symphony, Parsifal?[109]

Barber recounted how he finally dealt with the finale:

> And then came a period when I couldn't think of what to do with the fourth movement, and Mrs. Horowitz called me up and said "the trouble with you is you're *stitico*"—it means constipated—"that's what you are, a constipated composer." That made me so mad that I ran out to my studio and wrote that [fugue] in the next day. And that has kept plenty of pianists busy since.[110]

Horowitz claims also to have suggested other changes in the sonata.[111] At least one of those changes involved the penultimate measure of the scherzo, turning it from a spare arpeggio of eighth notes to a sweeping three octaves of thirty-second notes (compare holograph, manuscript copy, and G. Schirmer 1950 edition in Example 10.8).* Idiosyncratic graphic details of the last system of the published score—marked but incomplete

*This is confirmed by John Browning. Also, a comparison between the several manuscript versions at the Library of Congress and the published edition shows this change. Given Horowitz's propensity for spontaneous "embellishment," it is conceivable, as Browning suggests, that the flourish was added during performance and later made its way into the score (Browning, interview with the author, 22 April 1986). Horowitz's reputation for departing from the printed page is well documented: Harold Schonberg, for example, observed that the pianist substituted alternating octaves at a *prestissimo* for unison scales in the coda of Chopin's B-minor scherzo, "causing the faces of the many pianists in the audience to turn positively green" (*New York Times,* 18 April 1966).

a.

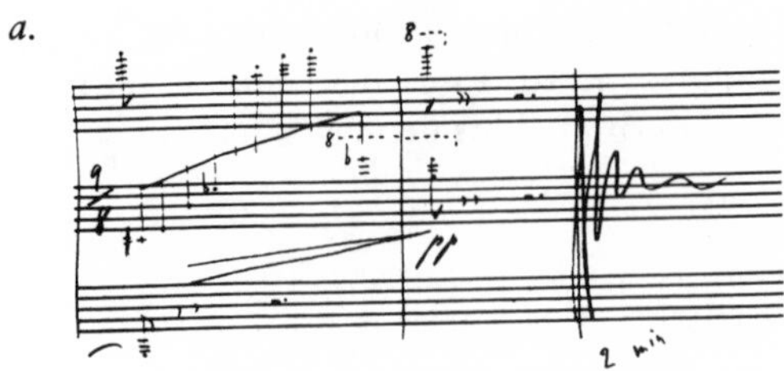

b.

c.

Example 10.8 Piano Sonata, Op. 26, end of second movement, showing progress to final version. *a.* Holograph, August 1949. *(Library of Congress) b.* Blackline print of copyist's manuscript, 1949. *(Library of Congress) c.* G. Schirmer, 1950.

ledger lines above the staff and unextended stems of bass notes—tend to support the notion that these final measures were reengraved late in the printing process.

Other variants between the holograph and the published edition—al-

Example 10.9 Piano Sonata, opening of fourth movement, blackline print of copyist's manuscript. *(Library of Congress)*

terations to tempo and metronome markings, for example; penciled duration markings for each movement; and certain pedal indications (such as the words *con molto pedale* penciled over measure 3 in the third movement)—seem also to correspond with Horowitz's style of performance and may have been added at his suggestion. Horowitz's diminutive, "Volodya," is inscribed on the first page of the blackline proofs of the fourth movement (Example 10.9).

Barber's statement that he wrote the fugue for Horowitz offers a compelling case for the possibility that certain details may have been added specifically at the pianist's suggestion after he played through the fugue. Such an example might be the instructions Barber gave to the copyist Weissleder to insert two measures of cadenza after measure 97 (see Example 10.10a). Example 10.10b shows the holograph before the insertion, and Example 10.10c, the final version.

In June 1949 Barber wrote to Henry-Louis de La Grange: "I've just finished the sonata and feel years younger and happy. The last movement is quite a big fugue."* A month later he wrote again to La Grange about Horowitz's preparations:

> I have been having a wonderful time with Horowitz, who has spent much time out here practising 5 hours a day on the sonata, and then playing it for me. He has only had it a month, but already does it superbly: and with a surprising emotional rapproachement which I had not expected. He left for California yesterday, but I made a tape recording which I can play for you.[112]

With faith in the critical success of the sonata and in anticipation of healthy sales, G. Schirmer planned for publication to precede the premiere. Before the first performances in Washington, D.C., and New York (Horowitz had already played the sonata in Havana, Cuba, on 9 December 1949†), a private hearing was scheduled for 4 January 1950 in the director's room on the seventh floor of the old G. Schirmer building at 3 East 43rd Street. Horowitz insisted upon playing his own piano, but evidently the mammoth instrument would not fit inside the old and creaky elevator, because a notice in the recital program advises "For technical reasons, Mr. Horowitz will play a Music Room Grand Piano Model B."‡ The audience

*Inscription on a prepublication announcement of the complete works of Brahms sent from Barber to La Grange.

†So important a premiere may have taken place in Cuba only because Horowitz happened to be playing a concert there; Barber, however, considered it "silly of them [in Broder's book] to give the Havana [date]" (letter to Claire Reis, 31 December 1965, League of Composers Collection, New York Public Library).

‡Hans Heinsheimer, in an interview with the author on 21 November 1985 in New York, told of the attempt to transport Horowitz's piano to the seventh floor: it had to be precariously balanced on top of the elevator and slowly, steadied by many hands, raised. Katharine Homer's letter to her father (8 January 1950) announced, "Horowitz was having a fit because he had to play on a 'small' piano." She recalled further that a day earlier he

a.

b.

c.

Example 10.10 Revision of fourth movement of Piano Sonata at m. 97. *a.* Barber's instructions to the copyist Weissleder appended to holograph: "insert the following at p. 29 of my M.S., brace 4, after the first measure of 3/8." *(Library of Congress)* *b.* Piano Sonata, fourth movement, before cadenza was inserted (at arrow), holograph, 1949. *(Library of Congress)* *c.* Final version with inserted cadenza (G. Schirmer, 1950).

Barber, aboard the SS *Nieuw Amsterdam,* returns to New York in December 1949 for the premiere of his Piano Sonata. *(UPI/Bettmann)*

included many important musicians, among them Gian Carlo Menotti, Virgil Thomson, Douglas Moore, William Schuman, Thomas Schippers, Aaron Copland, Lukas Foss, Myra Hess, and Samuel Chotzinoff. Sidney Homer could not attend but received a full report from his daughter Katharine Fryer.[113]

After its first public performance at Constitution Hall in Washington, D.C., on 11 January 1950, Barber's Piano Sonata was declared a milestone by local music critics: "The sound of the instrument has not been exploited in like manner by any twentieth-century composer," wrote Glenn Gunn.[114] Richard Keith called the last movement "one of the most musically exciting and technically brilliant pieces of writing yet turned out by an American."[115] Homer—who had read notices in the Washington papers but not yet heard the sonata—responded with pride and vicarious pleasure in his nephew's success:

> Three cheers for Washington! Top of the world! America is waking up. There is a deep note in those notices that I have never seen before, a feeling

had threatened not to play unless he had his own piano, and that during the concert he "behaved most ungraciously . . . scowling and shaking his head."

of awe or complete surprise. You are now repaid for all the intensity and complete abandonment you put into this work. Now—sing from the heart.[116]

After hearing a radio performance by Horowitz, he wrote again to Barber:

The Sonata was a great experience for me. What must it have been for you! To me it was a national event, landmark, an artistic outpouring of deep emotion.[117]

The New York premiere on 23 January at Carnegie Hall gained unqualified praise from Olin Downes:

We consider it the first sonata really come of age by an American composer of this period. It has intense feeling as well as constructive power and intellectual maturity. It is stated naturally and convincingly in the language of modern music.[118]

Touring the country, Horowitz became the sonata's most active promoter and made no secret of his admiration for Barber and his music. In Cleveland he said:

It is romantic, subjective, and written in the modern idiom. The first movement is difficult to understand perhaps. But Barber has put warmth and a heart into the work that the ultra-modern compositions, with their mechanical pyrotechnics, lack. I don't, for instance, play Bartók because I don't like his percussive use of the piano. Barber is very brilliant and very different.[119]

In Atlanta:

This sonata is terrific. . . . [Barber's] music is like him: aristocratic and full of taste, and also very American. That is why I am proud to present it.[120]

By April 1950 arrangements had already been made for Horowitz to record the sonata so that it would be released by Christmas of that year. Barber thought the first issue was "stunning," and he received mischievous pleasure from the fact that on the reverse side would be the Chopin Sonata in B♭, so that "anyone who wants to hear Horowitz play the funeral march—and many will—will be forced to buy my sonata as well." * This recording of the sonata on the RCA Victor label was to remain Barber's favorite for at least ten years.[121]

As frequently happens with new works, music critics and historians alike seek its ancestors; Barber's sonata was seen as the progeny of, variously, Liszt, Schumann, Chopin, Prokofiev, Rachmaninoff, and Scriabin;

* Letter, Barber to Sidney Homer, 29 September 1950. The pressings were made on long-playing records, a relatively new procedure that made Barber ask Sidney Homer if he had a long-playing attachment that could fit on any gramophone or victrola.

its "highly original harmonic sense" and approach to fugue were compared to Max Reger's; the lyricism and hint of waltz rhythm in the middle of the scherzo movement evoked allusions to the music of Brahms or to the ghostly waltz rhythm in Busoni's *Nächtlichen,* from the *Elegies* (1910).[122] The dirgelike third movement has been described by Hans Tischler as a twentieth-century reinterpretation of the archaic passacaglia and reminiscent of the Baroque lament.* But the cantilena's rhythmic pattern and melodic focus on the half-step over an arpeggio bass seem to lie even more strongly in the shadow of Liszt's *Les Funérailles* (compare, for example, Liszt, mm. 23–26, with Barber, third movement, mm. 3–4).

Barber's Piano Sonata in E minor, though not revolutionary in its formal structure—it adheres to traditional designs for each movement—is a monumental masterpiece of its time. Its strength lies in the remarkable alliance between long sweeping melodic ideas that are distinctive to Barber's musical imprint and the modern harmonic language and structural techniques that are idiomatic to the eclectic musical style of the twentieth century.† The first movement is generated from an extraordinary economy of thematic material, and the sonata form is more aptly delineated by melodic design than by harmonic structure (the home key of E minor is not fully ascertained until the coda‡). In this movement, as in II and III, the half-step features prominently as an organizing interval. Twelve-tone rows appear in three movements, not as a rigid technique of organization but as one of many agents of, in Tischler's words, "logical patterning." They exist in melodic lines as part of themes (for example, see I, m. 20) or accompaniment patterns (for example, see III, mm. 1–7), over which a lyrical melody is fused but never in conflict with, sometimes even con-

*"Barber's Piano Sonata, Op. 26," *Music and Letters* 33 (October 1952): 353. Sifferman, however, sees neither the dotted-rhythm characteristics of a dirge, nor the variation aspect of a true passacaglia (pp. 51–52).

†The sonata has elicited more analytical writings than any other of Barber's works. Of particular interest is James P. Fairleigh's article "Serialism in Barber's Solo Piano Works" (*Piano Quarterly* [Summer 1970]: pp. 13–17), which focuses on the fusion of tonal and serial procedures in the sonata and Nocturne, Op. 33. James Sifferman's *Samuel Barber's Works for Solo Piano* focuses on formal design and harmonic structure and traces motivic development and Barber's particular way of incorporating twelve-tone rows into the first and third movements. Sifferman evaluates and sometimes refutes earlier analytic writings (Nathan Broder, "Current Chronicle," *Musical Quarterly* 36 [April 1950]: 276–79; Fairleigh; and Friedewald, *A Formal and Stylistic Analysis*). Hans Tischler's article, cited in the preceding footnote, compares the sonata's fugue to its Italian precursors, Handel's Concerto Grosso No. 9 in F and post-Baroque fugues. Also useful is his abstract "Some Remarks on the Use of Twelve-Tone and Fugue Techniques in Samuel Barber's Piano Sonata" (*Journal of the American Musicological Society* [Summer 1952]:145–46). More recently, with fresh insight Douglas R. Heist examines how *harmonic* procedures of the first movement differ from those used in traditional sonata forms ("Harmonic Organization and Sonata Form: The First Movement of Barber's Sonata, Op. 26," *Journal of the American Liszt Society* 27 [January–June 1990]:25–31).

‡Heist ("Harmonic Organization and Sonata Form") demonstrates that the tonal ambiguity between C♭ major and E♭ minor contributes as much to the movement's "intense restlessness" as does the chromatic character of the work.

tributing to, the tonal structure of the movement.* Some of the twelve-tone melodic patterns in the first three movements coincide with specific examples in Nicolas Slonimsky's *Thesaurus of Scales and Melodic Patterns* (New York: Scribner's, 1947), a book that lay on Barber's piano about the time he was writing the sonata.†

The second movement is an evanescent, scherzolike dance movement in a rondo form. In the third movement an ostinato bass comprising six dyads (a vertical statement of twelve tones) is transformed in measures 3–4 to an arpeggio and then repeated in a half-step transposition.

The four-voice fugue of the fourth movement may well be the most brilliant twentieth-century example of the genre. Barber uses the traditional structure—an exposition with subject in E♭ minor and the answer in the dominant, progressing through developmental and episodic sections to an electrifying coda. There are conventional fugal devices—augmentation, retrograde, inversion, and stretto—but in no sense is this an academic exercise or a fossilized resurrection of the form. Syncopated rhythms and "blue-note" harmonies associated with American jazz are integrated into the fabric of the music.

The fugue in the Piano Sonata is not merely an imitation of the Baroque prototype. Its contemporary authenticity is so convincing that it evoked accolades from composer Francis Poulenc, who, after he heard Horowitz play the sonata at Capricorn (5 February 1950), wrote:

> It [the sonata] pleases me without reserve. It is a remarkable work from both the musical and instrumental point of view. In turn, tragical, joyous and songful, it ends up with a fantastically difficult to play fugue. This is a long way from the sad and scholastic fugues of the Hindemith pupils (the pupils, I say).‡ Bursting with energy, this finale knocks you out ('Vous-met knock-out') in (something less than) five minutes.[123]

In a sense, Barber viewed this work as a further step away from his conservatory training. Before the premiere, in anticipation of an early pub-

*This observation—with regard to I and III—is corroborated by James Sifferman, p. 108.

†Charles Turner, interview with the author. The correlations are as follows: in the first movement, m. 9 = Slonimsky 415 (a sesquitone progression, that is, the equal division of one octave into four parts, with an "ultrapolation" of two notes); m. 20 = Slonimsky, 1233a (a twelve-tone spiral); mm. 23–26 (the ostinato accompaniment to the second theme) = Slonimsky 1214a, while the right-hand part of m. 25 is an augmentation of its retrograde (Slonimsky 1214b). In the second movement, Barber draws from Slonimsky's examples of "ditone progressions with the ultrapolation of one note," specifically nos. 187 and 188. In the third movement, the tone row in the left hand of mm. 4 and 5 correlates to Slonimsky 1242a ("twelve-tone spiral with mutually exclusive augmented triads").

‡Poulenc was candid in his displeasure over the double fugue in the last movement of Hindemith's third piano sonata: "trop Reger." Felix Aprahamian was reminded of this commentary when, halfway through a performance of *Ludus Tonalis,* Poulenc passed him a folded scrap of paper, which read "Dieu sauvez-nous des fugues. Amen!" (*The Listener,* 2 November 1950, p. 474).

lication of the sonata by Schirmer, he wrote to his school friend Jeanne Behrend, "Maybe you won't like it; it is not at all like that 'lovely' sonata you love so. But do try to, for the sake of your old friend."[124]

When Barber traveled to Italy early in 1951, Scalero had opportunity to scrutinize the sonata; he appraised his former pupil's progress through nineteenth-century eyes, just as he might have done more than two decades earlier. In fact his criticisms confirm Barber's emancipation from his teacher.

> Among other things he told me he had taken the time to carefully correct all the mistakes throughout my piano sonata and that it sounds much better now. I felt just as I did twenty years ago, making a violent effort not to show the annoyance coming through every nook and cranny of my face, even though I saw the funny side. He ended the session, dear old Maestro, with a typically tactful remark. . . . "You are talented—why do you write such bad music? You can do better. Go on, keep working. Goodbye." And he vanished into the Milanese fog looking very old and very far away from the joys of our atomic world, erect, unbending, dissatisfied.[125]

Sidney Homer, after hearing a recording of the sonata, wrote to Barber: "How about a sonata right now full of peace and happiness, while the iron is hot? Don't you feel the urge?"[126] What little he could hear of his nephew's piano sonata gave him the desire to "get the full message" of the sonata, "to have time to discuss it." He said, "I say all art is born of sympathy. Do you agree? I hear it constantly in your works."*

*Letter, ca. 4 October 1950, from Winter Park, Florida. Homer's health was failing, and because he was confined at home, the only hope he had of hearing live music was when one of two pianists came regularly to visit him.

11

COMPOSER AS CONDUCTOR

Through the baptism of fire

In the early autumn of 1950, Barber announced to Homer, "I have suddenly had an offer to go to London and conduct and record three of my works—*Medea,* the Second Symphony, and the Cello Concerto."[1] He continued:

> This would be for a company—London FFRR (Decca)—which is supposed to make the best records today, and I must say the records I have heard made by them are superior to ours in sound. All of these would be long playing, so Medea would be on one side, Symph. II on the reverse; and the cello concerto a whole record to itself.* Zara Nelsova, an English cellist whom Piatigorsky highly recommended to me when she introduced my concerto in England, will play. And she has already made a stunning record of "Schelomo," of Bloch for this same company. We are waiting to see about dates, but I think of leaving the second week in November and doing the recordings at once.[2]

As much as Barber viewed the recordings as a promotional mission, they were also an opportunity for him to explore the possibility of a career in conducting, to which he had periodically been drawn. At the Curtis Institute of Music in 1932 he had studied conducting with Fritz Reiner, but his student records indicate he was "dropped"; his "progress did not warrant retaining," according to Reiner, because he "would never make a conductor."[3] In spite of so dismal a prognosis, Barber was not discouraged. While in Vienna in the winter of 1933–34, at the suggestion of Karl Geiringer, director of the Gesellschaft der Musikfreunde, he conducted a

*In fact, each work was cut on its own ten-inch disk: Ballet Suite *Medea,* LPS 333; Concerto for Cello and Orchestra, LPS 332; and Symphony No. 2, LPS 334.

concert at the Volkshochschule Wien Volksheim.* His debut was received warmly by the critic Anne Holden, whose review in the *Vienna Herald* stated:

> Mr. Barber's advent in the field of conducting reveals a technique naturally not yet flawless, but firmly grounded on creative musicianship. . . . The orchestra under his direction gave smooth performances thoroughly interpretive of the varying musical styles.[4]

In subsequent years, however, any interest he had in conducting was eclipsed by his work as a composer. Apparently Koussevitzky encouraged him to think about conducting his own music, and so in October 1944, when Barber was invited to lead members of the Chicago Symphony Orchestra in a performance of *Capricorn Concerto,* he wrote to the maestro about his good fortune:

> You must be psychic! The day after you asked me why I never conducted, I was invited to conduct my little "Capricorn Concerto," for flute, oboe, and strings in Chicago, so this will be my debut. George Szell gave me a few conducting lessons, and we shall see what happens.[5]

Koussevitzky answered, "I was very glad to receive your letter and delighted with the news that you have started to conduct. All good wishes at the start of a new venture!"[6] After his debut, Barber reported:

> I appreciated your good wishes for my conducting venture and it went well, I think. The best men from the Chicago Symphony—not enough rehearsal time, but a success with public and press.[7]

The following spring he was invited to conduct a half-hour of his music on a CBS broadcast of "Invitation to Music" on 5 May 1945 at 11:30 P.M.[8] The program included *Capricorn Concerto* and four songs he had arranged for orchestra sung by Jennie Tourel.† He wrote again to Koussevitzky before the concert, "I wish that I had worked with you at the school."[9]

In September 1950, when the London recording offer came through, Barber had been through a creatively dry summer in the aftermath of his

*The program took place on Sunday, 4 February 1934, and included works by Vivaldi, Corelli, Haydn, Schumann, Hugo Wolf, and Richard Strauss, and two premieres, Sibelius's *Rakastava* and Menotti's *Pastorale (Pensiero e danza)* for piano and strings, which was written "in the space of a few days" especially for the concert and met with such enthusiasm it had to be repeated (*Overtones,* 1933–34, p. 79). The author is indebted to John Bitter, the soloist in Vivaldi's Flute Concerto, for providing a copy of the program; other artists who participated were the pianists Helen Perkin and Dr. Paul A. Pisk, and Georg Maikl, a singer with the Vienna State Opera Company.

†These were "Nocturne," Op. 13, No. 4, "Sure on this shining night," Op. 13, No. 3, "I hear an army," Op. 10, No. 3, "Monks and Raisins," Op. 18, No. 2. Holographs of all four of these orchestrated songs, without the words, are at the Library of Congress, Music Division.

Piano Sonata, and he welcomed a diversion and a new challenge. He told Homer:

> I'm rather glad to have something difficult and *active* to do: I was not in a good composing mood this summer. . . . So I shall be a conductor for a couple of months, as well as I possibly can. It is rather a year of records for me, and I am so glad, for I can send them to you, and you will get to know the new music I've written.[10]

His mentor could offer nothing but encouragement: "Think of well-nigh perfect recordings of your profound and beautiful works," he wrote to Barber:

> They open every door and bring you close to very many of those who understand and love your works, and to many others who *want* to hear and know them. Don't think of this as a sacrifice. Every great composer had his periods of silence and germination, and grew greater. Let your creative mind work in its own creative way. . . . The conducting will be a great experience and will prepare you for many important occasions in the future. Works like these require finished conducting.[11]

Barber had told Homer: "As these works are difficult, I have thrown myself into learning how to conduct them. Bill Strickland is coaching me, and I shall have a week of daily lessons with (I am told) a very fine teacher, Nicolai Malko, when he passes through New York en route to Europe."[12] Evidently the few sessions in New York were not enough, so he arranged with Malko to continue study in Denmark before going to London.

On the evening of his arrival in Copenhagen, Barber was invited to dinner at the home of the Danish millionaire Alfred Olesen, where he was introduced to some of the musical community and sang for them. There he met one of Denmark's leading composers, Knudage Riisager; the most prominent conductor of the opera, John Frandsen; and a piano merchant named Müller, who put his store at Barber's disposal.*

Staying in a hotel bordered by the old city, he looked down the square to the Royal Opera House and Theatre:

> A few blocks away by the King's palace, very handsome with its French architecture, is the Odd Fellows Hall, a sort of diminutive Rococo Musikvereinsaal as in Vienna. Here the concerts take place; and down the bustling street from that is the piano shop where Mr. Müller, the owner, allows me to have my lessons every day. My life is somewhat bounded by

*Barber's letters home on this trip—as detailed as those he wrote when he traveled to Europe for the first time in his teens—were addressed to "Dearests" or "Hello Everybody" and intended to be circulated to his whole family. All letters written by Barber to his family between November 1950 and March 1951 that are cited in this chapter were mailed to his housekeeper Agnes Moynihan, forwarded to Sidney Homer, and are now in the collection of Katharine Homer Fryer.

> these four corners, which gives the city for me a circumscribed and almost cozy terrain. . . . Malko, my teacher, who seems to me better and better as a conducting coach, is very famous here, so that I have had a fine introduction to the leading musicians. . . . Even today—Sunday—I had my lesson, working hard for this week. . . . I'm very happy at all of this and feel young and studentish again.[13]

Malko had made arrangements for the hire of an orchestra from the Danish Opera for Barber's practice sessions. After his first rehearsal, Barber wrote:

> I have gone through the baptism of fire, enjoyed it, and feel that the worst is over. It really was the most wonderful idea to come here with my coach; for no matter how many pointers a teacher can give about conducting theoretically, the real test can only take place in front of the orchestra; and here, too, the ever-present Malko was on hand, sitting far back in the balcony and jotting down remarks like "No petulance in voice; the first smile was observed only after 40 minutes; say 'please' to the orchestra occasionally; shoulders too tense."
>
> The orchestra is really excellent, and I was somewhat unprepared for their high standard. Together with the orchestra of La Scala, they were the hit of the Edinburgh Festival last summer and have been invited to America by Columbia Concerts. This also means that they are rather proud with an esprit de corps not always justified technically. Remember also that I was in the peculiar position—very unpleasant for me to think about—of not having been invited by them but rather of having engaged them to play for me. Such situations are never too happy, and I'm glad to say, if I may, that my music won them over poco a poco whether or not my conducting did. The latter felt easy enough; Malko said that I relaxed considerably as the rehearsal progressed and with the exception of one or two frightfully difficult places in *Medea*, I felt happy conducting them; occasionally even *conducting*, that is, making music as opposed to mere time-beating.[14]

Barber thought Malko was an unrelenting but first-rate teacher:

> It is difficult to write you about these rehearsals, but together with the conducting lessons, my life has been little more than that; in fact, I had a small upright piano sent to my room so I could work at will. You know how difficult it is for a teacher not to repeat himself to a pupil; I must say that my interest in Malko's lessons is unflagging and I consider him a teacher in the great line of Scalero and Vengerova. . . . I do not see him much in between lessons as he can become tiresome, and I'm sick of hearing what Glazounov or Rimsky-Korsakov said or didn't say. The main problem has been shortness of time, four two-hour rehearsals to prepare three such difficult works of mine.[15]

Though praise from Malko lifted his spirits, even more buoying was an unexpected message from Mary Bok Zimbalist, who heard news of Barber's progress. Barber wrote:

> I was waiting to go out on the stage. It was that fateful and exciting moment when the orchestra is tuning up, each man for himself. I stood there feeling rather lonely, listening to themes from my symphony being tossed about haphazardly by the indifferent orchestra, when an attendant handed me a cable. It was addressed to Samuel Barber, American Composer and Orchestra Conductor . . . Copenhagen. No more address than that! I couldn't imagine who would have risked sending a wire to so ethereal a destination. I opened it and found it was from Mary, with congratulations on the conducting progress.* I went out on the stage illuminated as if by a half bottle of brandy.[16]

That rehearsal was spent entirely on the Second Symphony. "Malko congratulated me," wrote Barber to his family; "he said that for every minute of the rehearsal I knew exactly what I wanted and so did the orchestra."[17] Frandsen sat in on one of the rehearsals of *Medea* and the Second Symphony and remarked afterwards what a "different and bigger composer" Barber was now than the one of *Adagio for Strings* and *School for Scandal,* those being the only works of his known in Denmark.[18] He was a devotee of the *Adagio for Strings,* which he had heard at the Edinburgh Festival and immediately purchased; he told Barber he considered it the "Fifth Gospel." Frandsen talked of having *Medea* done by the Royal Ballet. "I was pleased that my little music had traveled so far and more than ever am convinced of the efficacy of records and my present mission," Barber wrote home.[19]

Barber's goal was to be secure with the three works, but not go over his budget. Because he knew that there would not be enough time in Denmark to work out some of the more difficult passages, he engaged Malko to come to the London recording sessions and continue coaching him for a fee of $25 a lesson per day.[20] He had been engaged to conduct the same pieces in Berlin and Frankfurt after the first of the year. "No more Malko then," he wrote, "and I shall be on my own."[21]

On December 7, arriving in London with "ninety pounds of orchestral parts," he was joined by Charles Turner, who proved to be a great asset playing the scores on the piano while Barber practiced conducting. As guests

*Barber's affection for his patron was demonstrated the following spring, when he invited a group of composers—many distinguished—to harmonize variations on "Happy birthday to you," in "any shape, style, or variant which might amuse [them]," in honor of Mary Zimbalist's seventy-fifth birthday on 6 August 1951 (letter, Barber to Scalero, 12 June 1951, from Mount Kisco). In addition to his own, the album included tributes from Bax, Bloch, Chávez, Copland, Dohnányi, Harris, Hindemith, Honegger, Martinů, Menotti, Milhaud, Piston, Pizzetti, Poulenc, Scalero, Schuman, Sibelius, Stravinsky, Thomson, Vaughan Williams, Villa-Lobos, Walton, and Efrem Zimbalist.

of Dreyfuss in Hyde Park, after daily lessons with Malko they were able to see old friends—Stephen and Natasha Spender, Nicolas Nabokov, Alan Pryce-Jones (then editor of the *Times Literary Supplement*), composer Alan Rawsthorne, and Edward Sackville-West.[22] Referring to a concert performance of *Der Rosenkavalier,* conducted by Erich Kleiber, Barber wrote that it was a "gem of an opera, but gone seem to be the days . . . when the singers dominated, and the drop of a handkerchief by Lotte Lehmann on the stage almost made you choke, aside from her singing."[23]

"I do not think I will have the same battle that I had with the Danish orchestra at first, because my music is really well known here," Barber declared. "Today on B.B.C. radio they performed the First Symphony in the afternoon and Moura Lympany gave the first performance of my piano sonata on the radio while I was having a cozy dinner here in the flat, having corrected orchestral parts all afternoon."*

Even with only two days of piano rehearsals with cellist Zara Nelsova, he was nevertheless optimistic—"she did what I wanted and played beautifully indeed, with imposing tone and better intonation than Raya."[24] Two days of three-hour rehearsals were held with the Decca recording orchestra, and a third day of three sessions (nine hours of conducting) took place at Kingsway Hall, where they would make the records. "It is a very old wooden auditorium . . . now used as a sort of mission home," Barber wrote, "but they still consider it the finest hall from the point of view of acoustics and for recording." He continued:

> I went out on the stage with that queasy feeling which every artist knows so well . . . but my fears were soon dispelled by the excellence and malleability of the orchestra, carefully chosen for recording. I was told that many of the men did not regularly play in symphonies but were chamber music players of high caliber. Only the brass and the pianist—especially the latter—and I had repeatedly warned them from America of the difficulty of the piano part—left something to be desired.
>
> With this group of men I worked for four days, two three-hour sessions a day with the exception of the last day when there were three sessions (nine hours conducting). As far as I can remember not once did their attention waver . . . and I felt a real interest, on their part, in my music and in getting it recorded as well as possible, which was indeed touching.
>
> It is of course nerve-wracking work, but while we had to stick to schedule and finish all three works in four days—rather a feat since all the works were totally unknown to the orchestra and had to be learned technically

*Letter to Barber's family, 7 December 1950, Baywater Road, London. Barber's music had been well known in England even before then. In 1948, Wayne Daley, educational director for Chappell Publishers, reported in the newsletter of the League of Composers that "Sam Barber is the most played American in the British repertory . . . and remains the most familiar American name on the musical scene" (*Composer's News-Record,* Summer 1948).

> from scratch—nevertheless the English engineers, who are supposed to be the finest in their profession and were hidden with their machines in a room somewhere behind the organ pipes, managed to give a sense of calm which one does not feel making records in America. A calm British voice saying "Carry on" does much to assuage the terror engendered by that little red light which means that the tapes or disks are turning. A telephone on my music desk would give me private instructions from the engineer, and as soon as we made a record, we would go behind stage, have a sort of Salvation Army tea, and discuss the merits or demerits of the playbacks.[25]

The first three sessions were devoted to the Cello Concerto. One rehearsal took an unexpectedly humorous turn:

> Nelsova ended with such brilliance that a cello player leapt up from the cello section on to the stage, screamed something about "giving up playing the cello after playing such as hers," took his cello and smashed it in a thousand pieces on the side of the stage, in full view of us all, bridge, fingerboard and strings flying in all directions. There was a general howl from the orchestra, Nelsova had turned pale, and then we realized that it was a joke engineered by the cello section as a compliment to the difficulty of the concerto: each man contributed a crown toward buying a two-pound cello in a pawn shop in order to smash it! Who but the English would have thought of such a prank? There was unrestrained merriment until the mellifluous impersonal voice of the engineer coming seemingly out of the organ pipes stopped it all with his beautifully enunciated, "That's enough; quiet down."[26]

Malko and Turner attended all the recording sessions and offered musical criticisms. The results of the recording sessions were "beyond all my expectations," wrote Barber to his family. He continued:

> I am absolutely delighted about the whole venture. Acoustically they are superb. As you may know, London FFRR has the highest technical standard of record-making extant today, and they told me they used a new improvement for the first time on my records in order to improve them further; and that after each session the same engineers would go back to the studio and work until midnight improving my recording.
>
> When I went to hear the records they seemed enthusiastic and as delighted as I was. Mr. Olaf, the head musical director, says I am the only composer he knows—and he knows them all—who can conduct his own works and wishes me to do further work for them. . . . The records, according to the people here, should come out in America by mid-February; if this is true, it is incredibly fast, and I am so happy to think that you will know these works of mine much better.[27]

Malko, too, observed how well the orchestra responded to his student and during the recording of the finale of the Second Symphony reported to Strickland, "the hall is very cold, but Barber makes the orchestra not only very hot, but even warm, which is much more difficult."[28]

With almost two months to spend as they pleased before the concerts in Germany, and after "a bleak, sunless Sunday morning in London," Barber and Turner arrived in Rome—"teeming with life and exuberance"—in time to spend Christmas with Dario and Suso Cecchi, Princess Bassiano,* and Princess Boncompagni. "This is my beloved indifferent city," he wrote home.[29] After three days in Florence, Barber and Turner headed for Milan to watch preparations for the performance of Menotti's opera *The Consul* at La Scala. Seasonal festivities culminated with a memorable performance of *Otello,* when for the first time Barber heard Renata Tebaldi:

> I was swept off my feet by the magnificence of the performance and staging and the power of the music which had never moved me very much before. I confess I wept like a babe quite promptly from the storm scene on. It is a long time since any opera has affected me like that. Perhaps it was because the ensemble had such conviction, each costume of the huge chorus a raison d'être in the general scheme, like parts of a vision: and there was de Sabata conducting simply and passionately and a most wonderful young soprano of 26, Tebaldi, who sang the third act as I have never heard it sung before or never will, I'm sure.[30]

The manager of the forthcoming concerts in Germany had sent word that the cellist who was going to play the Cello Concerto had canceled, and it was suggested that Barber's Violin Concerto be substituted instead. Escaping to the mountains for a quiet place to work and rest, Barber found himself, coincidentally, in the town of Sils-Maria, where more than twelve years earlier he had begun the Violin Concerto. Because Turner was a violinist and "on the spot . . . knowing the concerto almost," he would play it with the German orchestras.[31]

At the Hotel Sonne im Fextal, where Barber had stayed in 1939, Turner practiced the concerto while Barber finished correcting the score of his Cello Concerto. He was reassured by Turner's playing, for, after the mediocre performance of the Cello Concerto by a Danish cellist in Copenhagen, he did "not like to look forward to the unknown quantity of some German violinist."[32]

They returned briefly to Milan and La Scala where the days before the opening of *The Consul* were, in Barber's words, "a sort of Stendhalian existence . . . for our attention was almost completely focused on La Scala, much as his was a century ago."[33] Nor did the changes in La Scala escape his notice:

*Bassiano had a salon in Rome and produced an important literary magazine, *Botteghe oscure,* in which were published first works by writers who later achieved prominence. Through her Barber met Stephen Spender and other poets.

> La Scala is a real symbol of life in Milan and is jealously guarded by its traditions, many of which are outdated, by a goodly number of boxholders and Milanese families of means. There is a liberal group at the head of the opera (among these Toscanini's daughter, Wally, and de Sabata) who believe in modernizing the performances, building up new young singers for the future, young stage designers, etc. and I was much impressed with what I saw there. Certainly we have nothing to compare in America to the performances I saw of *Otello* and a wonderful *Don Giovanni* conducted by Von Karajan with Schwarzkopf and Los Angeles in the cast. But any novelties are bitterly resented and vehemently disputed by much of the audience in the theatre which one might call a sort of citadel of Italian operatic tradition.[34]

The Consul, which had been designed for a smaller opera house, was received by the Italian audience with cheers and ovations, boos and hisses. The magician scene, which Barber considered a "stroke of genius that makes such a gloomy libretto musically digestible," caused near pandemonium. "I am told," he said, "no opera in the last twenty years has awakened such interest and excitement."*

By the time he and Turner arrived in Paris, Barber was happy to forget Milan, "fascinating, full of violent and colorful reactions, and at the same time with nervous tensions." In Paris he and Turner rigorously prepared for the concerts in Berlin and Frankfurt. Staying with Henry-Louis de La Grange, Barber worked daily in the library on the family's Steinway grand on his scores and worried that this time not only had he "to face an orchestra, but a public!"[35]

So that he would be free to practice conducting the concerto, Barber hired Pierre Boulez, then twenty-six, to accompany Turner. About these sessions he wrote to Homer, "I have been going to talk about rhythms and all possible combinations of the same with a talented young French composer, Pierre Boulez."† As the rehearsals progressed, Barber's confidence in Turner grew:

> By now he plays it very beautifully. I am glad to play it with someone as intelligent and musical as he, and with whom I worked on it daily. G. C.

*Letter to Barber's family, 28 January 1951, Paris. After the performance, Barber was invited to a party given by Puccini's daughter and had an opportunity to talk to her about her father (see chapter 14, *Vanessa*).

†Letter, 8 February 1951, Chez Henry-Louis de La Grange, Paris. In his memoir *Setting the Tone* (New York: Coward McCann, 1983, p. 264), Ned Rorem writes the following anecdote (with an incorrect date and apparent naïveté about the reason for the rehearsals):

> Paris, 1950. Samuel Barber arrives with violinist Chuck Turner. They are preparing Barber's concerto for recording. Who is the rehearsal pianist? Why, Pierre Boulez. Barber kids the stoical Frenchman about the twelve-tone system. "Is the Habanera a row?" he asks. (He loathes the imputations of the serial elite. He persists in addressing the perplexed René Leibowitz as Mr. Ztiwobiel. "Well, if a composer can't recognize his own name in retrograde, how can his listeners be expected . . .").

> stopped in for a few hours en route to London, heard him play and was surprised and delighted. The next day Chuck played it for the great violinist and musician Enesco, with me at the piano. Enesco gave him many good pointers and much encouragement.[36]

Barber had arranged for the critique of the concerto by requesting a master class with Georges Enesco.[37] At the time of the session, he was unaware that among the highly regarded composer's violin students who audited the class was Elizabeth, Queen of the Belgians, "a nice little old lady with stringy white hair," Barber noted.[38] She turned pages for him while he accompanied Turner; "she seemed to like the concerto immensely," he reported, "heard it through twice."[39] Apparently she liked it so much she invited Turner to come to Belgium to play it for her.*

One afternoon in February, Barber and Turner paid a visit to Maurice Ravel's house, "a tiny oblique house nestling on the side of a tiny hill with a lovely view and tiny walled garden." The pair coaxed Ravel's old housekeeper into showing them the unheated dimly lit house where everything remained as it had been when the composer died a decade earlier:

> His little studio full of minute objects, which he loved to collect, was touching, even in the somewhat execrable and quick-to-fade taste of "1920 Modern"; but the whole thing, including the peevish old woman who complained about the stinginess of the present Mrs. Edward Ravel and why her ex-boss got no royalties from American ASCAP ("His music is often played over there in America," she kept on saying; and I thought: as usual the royalties are going to Deems Taylor.†)—the whole scene was like something out of "L'Enfant et Les Sortilèges."[40]

* Letter, Barber to his family, 8 February 1951, Chez Henry-Louis de La Grange, Paris. Turner, however, reports that the concert in Belgium never materialized (telephone interview with the author, 14 January 1989).

† Barber's bitterness about inequitable treatment of ASCAP composers continued to build for the next year until he and other composers—Thomson, Copland, Schuman, and Menotti—met with the classification committee to protest: he wrote to Homer:

> G. C. only gets $600 a year, Deems Taylor, $12,000; Copland and I get $2000. The whole thing is so full of injustice that if something is not done about it we may all resign. We ask that 20 percent of the distributable income be divided among the standard composers, as it was before the consent-decree; in this way there would be hope for all of us and we should all advance normally to higher classes; but it is perfectly ridiculous to have Copland compete against Berlin on a strict point system. All of this, which Copland and I started, was rather unpleasant. No one likes to go in and fight for money. But it had to be done, so we formed this very small committee of symphonic composers. (3 February 1952, from Capricorn)

The resolution of all this occurred in June of that year:

> I think we have had a minor victory as far as orchestral writers are concerned [he wrote to Homer]. They have tripled the point value as works increase in length, and the result is that we will all be paid more. They simply were not taking larger works seriously. Now they have to come around. I will be paid about double, and advancement to a higher class will be more rapid under this new system. . . . I do hope it will affect you at least a little, and think it may, as the weight of *concert* points for

A Sunday night dinner was arranged with Barber as guest of honor at Marie Blanche Polignac's musical salon:

> This is all due to Poulenc, who has told so many people about my music here, so all the musicians are very charming to me and curious to hear something, but as usual no one does anything about actually arranging a *performance*. Poulenc told them about my singing—even played them the recording of "Dover Beach" which he stole from Capricorn, so there was nothing for me to do but sing. . . . Countess Polignac, Sauguet, the composer, and others insisted I go on and on until I had sung myself out.[41]

The performances of his works in Berlin and Frankfurt evoked in Barber a keen awareness of his American identity and the power of his music to bridge chasms between people who were at one time at war with each other. He described his reactions during one rehearsal in Berlin:

> The orchestra was adept without any great amount of style, but warmed up considerably as we became better acquainted, and I was no end pleased when, after the concert, several of the first-desk men came to me to express their appreciation at having worked personally with me, and to tell me of their interest in getting to know the new music which had been forbidden in the Third Reich. In fact, all through Germany, although there has sometimes been personal coldness on the part of the orchestra when I *spoke* to them, the minute the music began there was what the first cellist in Berlin called *"Kontakt"* from the first rehearsal on.
>
> I am not so naïf as not to realize the fact that several years ago these people were my "enemies" and that my personal position in conducting them was, to put it lightly, somewhat precariously "superimposed." I suddenly recalled, while conducting the Second Symphony, that this work was composed while I was nominally in that Air Force which was technically responsible for those square miles of desolation and rubble in the middle of their particular city! Nevertheless, it was true what the cellist said: there was a "Kontakt" and a valid one between us for the most part, through the music, and I felt thankful to my art that seemed, for the moment at least, to transcend racial and political barriers. Not always. There were the usual technical struggles with the older, less plastic elements of the orchestra, their will to resist, but this can happen anywhere, I am sure.[42]

After the concert in Frankfurt, Barber wrote to his family:

> I started with three numbers from *Medea,* then the Violin Concerto (which made a pleasantly serene contrast after the violence of Medea's dance), intermission, Adagio for Strings, and then the 2nd symphony, which closes

---

songs has also been tripled; however, unfortunately, this particular field has not brought in much revenue as yet (licensing concert artists—radio is still the main source of revenue) . . . I am glad it is all over and am sick of talking about $$$. Bah. (2 June 1952, from Capricorn)

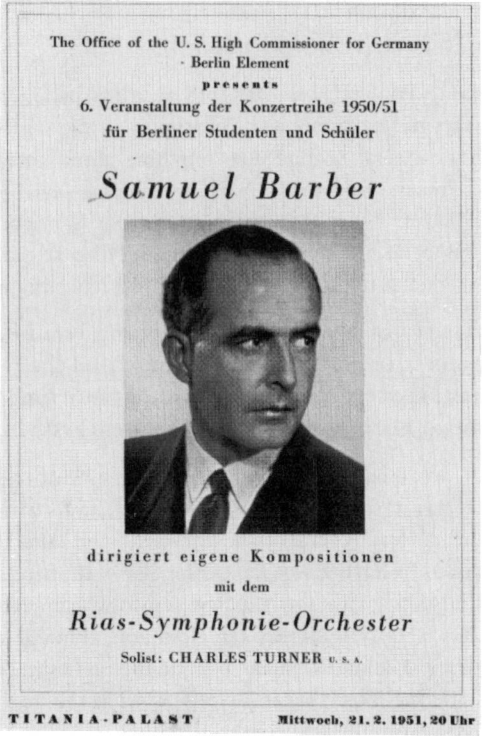

The Office of the U. S. High Commissioner for Germany
· Berlin Element
presents
6. Veranstaltung der Konzertreihe 1950/51
für Berliner Studenten und Schüler
Samuel Barber
dirigiert eigene Kompositionen
mit dem
Rias-Symphonie-Orchester
Solist: CHARLES TURNER U. S. A.
TITANIA-PALAST
Mittwoch, 21. 2. 1951, 20 Uhr

Program of concert Barber conducted in Berlin on 21 February 1951.

> the program with plenty of noise! There was no party and although there were posters all over town announcing our concert, only a half dozen out of three thousand Americans stationed in or about Frankfurt bothered to come. So that it was a real German audience, and ditto Berlin, where they were almost entirely young German students and wonderful to play for. Frankfurt was the first time I conducted a whole concert of my works and I was happy that it had gone so well.
>
> Did you know that just before leaving Paris I received a letter from Münch asking me to conduct my Second Symphony in Boston sometime in April, the date not fixed as yet? That is a wonderful beginning for conducting my own music in America and of course I accepted. And then enough of this conducting and I shall settle down at Capricorn and write some more music . . . . to conduct![43]

Upon returning to the United States Barber accepted Münch's invitation and headed for Boston the last weekend in April 1951. "Münch gave me *three* complete rehearsals for my symphony," he wrote to Homer, "I never have had so much time; and with that wonderful orchestra."[44] He continued:

> By Friday it just seemed to flow, so that at certain times I felt relaxed enough to improvise and dream with them. . . . Press good, I was told. The good thing about conducting is that without any concerts there is no fascination, one cannot play with it, like singing at home; so I have promptly forgotten the whole thing, though I hope to do some here and there next season.*

In spite of good press reviews, this was the last time he took the podium. In the fall of 1951 he wrote to Homer: "I had hoped to do some conducting here next year, but no American orchestra wanted me, so I must hold this pleasurable experience temporarily in abeyance."[45] He doubted that conducting offered a viable career for himself: "I simply don't want to get myself together as a conductor for one concert every three years. . . . I wouldn't do it well," he wrote William Strickland in late 1952 when he was asked to conduct his own works in another recording session.[46]

In the last year of his life, 1981, when Allan Kozinn asked Barber why he stopped conducting, he answered:

> Because on-stage I had about as much projection as a baby skunk. Projection, nerves—and I got bored of rehearsing my own music. Some composers just adore it, but I don't find it very interesting. There's a lack of pedagogical talent. And when you're guest conducting, either you have that talent or else you have to have an authority over the orchestra to make them do it right. Guest conductors rarely have that authority, whereas if it's your own orchestra, you can do what Toscanini did: You can scream "Stupid! Imbecile!" and throw down your watch. I've seen him do that. But he was Toscanini, and it was his orchestra; they wouldn't dare make the mistakes with him that they did with me.
>
> Oh I suppose there's something to be gained from hearing a composer conduct his own work. My tempos could be definitive. But generally, I don't believe composers make very good conductors. . . . I remember the last work of mine I conducted: my Second Symphony with the Boston Symphony. Not a bad way to end a conducting career. But by the time I got to Boston, I'd conducted it in Denmark and England, and I knew exactly where the violas were going wrong, and where I'd have to make them do it over and over, very slowly. Now how can you remain interested in doing that, whether it's your own music or not?[47]

*Letter, 29 April 1951, from Mount Kisco. A remark in this letter reveals an important facet of Barber's relationship with Menotti: "Mother came up on Friday and Mrs. Braun and Zimbalist on Saturday. But I missed G. C. to tell me how it really went, as it is hard to hear one's self."

12

SONG CYCLES

In this sphere of composing you are alone

Mélodies passagères, Op. 27 (1950–51)

About a week before the New York premiere of the Piano Sonata, Barber had written to Homer: "I am writing some songs, and happy to be doing them again."[1] Warm letters from Homer applaud his nephew's triumph: "And now the songs; what could be finer! I hope you are feeling happy, content, serene."[2] Several months later he wrote: "Tell me about the songs you are writing when you can. You promised me a really long letter, but I am patient. Nothing must interfere with those songs."[3]

Late in October 1949 Barber had been asked by William Strickland to write a song cycle and a choral work for a concert he was planning at Dumbarton Oaks for the following spring, to be performed by Eileen Farrell, Rudolf Firkusny, and chamber orchestra. Barber wrote to Strickland, "I am wildly casting about for a text for three songs, am sure I will find something. But there's not a chance of a chorus piece this year."[4] In January he wrote again to Strickland:

> I've finished two songs to Rilke French poems and they are already at the copyist's—I'm in touch with Farrell who will have copies to learn in several days. So I still have one or two more Rilke to compose and the orchestration of "Knoxville."
>
> . . .The Rilke songs are quite lovely, I think; Poulenc and Bernac were here Sunday and I played them for them to check on French prosody (o.k.) and they want the first performance in Paris.[5]

The Rilke songs to which Barber referred were "Puisque tout passe," completed in January 1950, "Départ," and "Le clocher chante" (the title page of the holograph reads "Chant du clocher"), completed 10 and 16

February 1950, respectively. The three songs were the first, fourth, and fifth of Barber's song cycle *Mélodies passagères,* settings of five texts by the great German lyric poet of the twentieth century, Rainer Maria Rilke. Four of the songs come from *Poèmes français,* an anomaly among Rilke's almost exclusively German texts written when he was secretary to the French sculptor Auguste Rodin in Paris in 1910. Barber took the words for "Le clocher chante" from *Les Quatrains Valaisans.*

The songs break away from the style of Barber's earlier songs, which follow in the path of nineteenth-century German Lieder. *Mélodies passagères* are closer instead to the style of the French art song, not merely because of the texts, but primarily because of their semi-parlando vocal lines, fluid piano accompaniments marked with gentle syncopations, and expanded tonal language. Through-composed, they are of short duration and in moderate tempos, with the exception of "Tombeau dans un parc" and "Départ," marked *lento e sereno* and *molto lento,* respectively. Only occasionally do fragments of the vocal line surface in the piano accompaniment, as in "Puisque tout passe." Textual imagery is suggested by the sonorities in "Le clocher chante," where a chiming-bell figure pervades the accompaniment. The harmonic language of the songs recalls that of Fauré and Debussy—with chords of sevenths, ninths, and elevenths, black-note arpeggiations (as in "Un cygne"), and ambiguous cadences on widely spaced triads with added notes that cloud the tonality (as at the conclusion of "Tombeau dans un parc," or the final rolled chord of "Départ").*

When Barber wrote to Strickland that he had been "wildly casting about for a text" for three songs, he was not implying that he selected his texts capriciously: "The text means a great deal to me," he told Robert Sherman in a radio interview in 1978. "I read lots and lots of poetry anyway, so I go through tons and tons of poems that could possibly be songs. It's very hard to find them. . . . They are either too wordy or they are too introverted."[6] Moreover, his enjoyment of poetry was tempered by the self-consciousness he felt in evaluating a poem's potential for a musical setting. When interviewed that same year for liner notes for a recording of *Mélodies passagères,* Barber explained:

> It's hard for me to enjoy poetry per se, as I always have in the back of my mind the feeling that I may come across a usable song text. I tend to mark things when I read a promising poem for the first time, and then go back

* Kreiling (*The Songs of Samuel Barber,* p. 290) points out that although certain details in the songs that are characteristic of the French style—declamatory vocal parts, frequent metrical changes, ambiguous tonality, and asymmetrical formal design—are traits that appear throughout Barber's songs, in *Mélodies passagères* he uses repeated notes in melodies with greater frequency than usual and the songs expand significantly on his usual use of dissonance and chromaticism. In "Départ," for example, although tonal orientation is suggested by a persistent pedal on g′ in the inner voice in mm. 1–11, the "scale"—while not corresponding fully to Kreiling's description as octatonic—tends in the direction of octatonicism.

> and try to appreciate it simply as poetry. However I do enjoy reading contemporary poetry, not only in English but in German and French, and I've made a real study of Dante and Goethe in their original language.[7]

As fluent as he was in French, however, Barber was still somewhat hesitant about writing songs in that language. "Setting French to music is ticklish," he told Robert Sherman about the songs in 1978. "The French are very, very particular about it. On the other hand, I thought, why not? So I plunged in and did these *Mélodies passagères.*"[8] Poulenc's confirmation of the correctness of his prosody was important to Barber. "He was a good friend and he was one of my only composer friends," Barber said about the French composer; "I've rarely been that close to another composer."* The two composers probably first met in 1946 in Prague, at the International Music Festival, where Barber represented the United States, and Poulenc and Arthur Honegger, France.[9] Later, Poulenc had dedicated to Barber his *Capriccio d'après "Le Bal masqué"* for two pianos; Barber reciprocated by dedicating *Mélodies passagères* to the French composer.

When asked in 1978 by Phillip Ramey, "Was Poulenc enamoured with those songs?" Barber replied, "Francis was a darling man, but he was enamoured only with his own songs." Yet we know that when Barber first played him the Rilke cycle, Poulenc liked the songs so much he immediately planned to premiere them with Bernac the following year in Paris and New York. Nor did he suggest any changes in the French prosody.[10] He did say, Barber recalled, that while there were no flaws in the French setting, he thought that a sensitive French musician would nonetheless know the songs were not written by a Frenchman, "probably because the musical style is my own," Barber said; "I certainly didn't try for a French tone."[11]

In spite of Poulenc's enthusiasm, three of the songs—"Puisque tout passe," "Le clocher chante," and "Départ"—were first sung in Washington, D.C., by Eileen Farrell for the Friends of Music of Dumbarton Oaks under the aegis of Harvard University, with Barber accompanying her at the piano. The concert on 1 April 1950 included, also, the new arrangement for chamber orchestra of *Knoxville: Summer of 1915* and *Capricorn*

*Interview, Robert Sherman, WQXR, 30 September 1978; Ramey, liner notes, "The Songs of Samuel Barber," 1978. To John Gruen (*New York Times,* 3 October 1971), Barber remarked:

> I'm not an analyzer, and I don't surround myself with composers. Aaron Copland, who lives just across the hills, is surrounded by composers. There are people like that who like to be the *Chefs d'Ecoles*. . . . It seems to me that the most practical thing is to simply write your music in the way you want to write it. Then you go out and find the interpreters who will give it voice. The point is, composers have never helped me. Performers have *always* helped me.

This is a somewhat exaggerated statement, since there were, of course, several composers who did help Barber.

Concerto, both conducted by Strickland, and the Piano Sonata, played by Rudoph Firkusny. So well received were the *Mélodies passagères* that they had to be repeated.[12]

The second and third songs of the cycle—"Un cygne" and "Tombeau dans un parc"—were finished a year later at Capricorn on 21 and 26 April 1951, almost immediately upon Barber's return from his European recording and conducting tour.[13] It is probably not a coincidence that Barber wrote the songs after a drab winter visit to Vienna—"grey, dispirited, discouraged and reactionary"—when his last stop before returning home had been Paris.[14] There his spirits lifted, for spring had set in and "it makes one happy to be here," he wrote to his family; "lovers are already strolling up and down the quais."[15] Almost a decade later, when interviewed by Robert Sherman, quite spontaneously he made a connection between Paris and his Rilke songs: "Do you know the real reason that I wrote in French? Because I was in love in Paris."[16]

When he was ready to return home he announced to Homer, "It will be spring there: I must compose some music."[17] By the end of April—with Paris still fresh in his mind—Barber was back at Mount Kisco, and he wrote again:

> Perhaps when I tell you that I have just composed two more songs this week, and was quite sunk in them, you will forgive me for not having written to you before. . . . The songs . . . are two more to add to that group of three from the French poems of Rilke which were sung at Dumbarton Oaks last year, and Poulenc and Bernac, who will sing them in Paris next year, and in New York too, asked me to throw in some more, as the group was too short. I plan to be here for the whole summer and hope to have some larger works to report to you as finished![18]

Poulenc and Bernac performed the complete cycle for the first time in Paris early in February 1952. Barber, attending a meeting of the International Music Council, heard their performance; they repeated it a week later in New York. Reviewing the concert for *Musical Quarterly,* Richard Goldman spoke of the "feeling of rightness" about Barber's music—"neither startling nor novel, but far beyond mere competence." He praised the songs' lack of pretentious mannerism, their consistent delicacy, and the ease with which they fit into the French repertoire.[19] Carter Harman, music critic for the *New York Times,* found *Mélodies passagères*

> a truly beautiful setting of the Rilke texts, a dark, yet delicate, romanticism pervades and the prosody adds that sense of detail and emphasis that fine prosody can. So poetic was the performance, so exactly suited to these artists that piece, that one feels the instrumentation must read "for Bernac and Poulenc" rather than merely for baritone and piano.[20]

"Bernac and Poulenc did the Rilke songs so well, especially in New York," Barber wrote to Bill Strickland in February 1952, "I was very much

Gian Carlo Menotti, Daisy Barber, and Samuel Barber dine at the Plaza Hotel, early 1950s.

touched. They are making a Columbia LP record of them this week."[21] With Barber turning pages, the French musicians made what he called "fine recordings" of the songs.[22] The record was not released until twenty-six years later. Barber never knew why the release was held up. "Bernac had a voice then, but not much of a one, and I kept wondering how we were going to get through," he reflected in 1979. "Somehow, though, they came out rather well on the recording."[23] The cycle was published by G. Schirmer in 1952. In a letter to Sidney Homer, 11 July 1952, Barber remarked about "all the care Mrs. [Edgard] Varèse had taken for the translation for Schirmers"; but the G. Schirmer edition does not attribute the translation to anyone.

Souvenirs, Op. 28 (1952)

In 1952 I was writing some duets for one piano to play with a friend, and Lincoln Kirstein suggested I orchestrate them for a ballet. Commissioned by Ballet Society, the suite consists of a waltz, schottische, pas de deux, two-step, hesitation tango, and galop. One might imagine a divertissement in a setting of the Palm Court of the Hotel Plaza in New York, the year about 1914, epoch of the first tangos; "Souvenirs"—remembered with affection, not in irony or with tongue in cheek, but in amused tenderness.*

The Palm Court held sentimental significance for Barber because it reminded him of his childhood trips to New York, when his mother would take him to the Plaza for tea.† The unnamed friend mentioned in this preface to Barber's four-hand piano edition of *Souvenirs* is Charles Turner, who was introduced to Barber by Gore Vidal at the Palm Court in 1950. One of Barber's and Turner's favorite New York haunts was the bar at the Blue Angel club. There they would often listen to a two-piano team, Edie and Rack, play sophisticated arrangements of popular and Broadway show music. Encouraged by Turner to write something in a similarly light vein, Barber wrote a four-hand piano suite and dedicated it to Turner. They often played it at parties given by their friends in New York and Europe.[24]

Although early in 1952 Lincoln Kirstein had suggested that Barber orchestrate the suite for a ballet, it was three years before the ballet was performed. Early in February 1952 Barber was appointed to the executive board of the International Music Council.‡ As he prepared to leave for meetings in Paris, he wrote to Sidney Homer his disappointment at not being able to visit him since he was hard pressed to finish his new ballet before leaving the country. He explained:

> I have taken your advice to do something *enjoyable* and have just finished a ballet score for Balanchine (the best choreographer) which gave me great pleasure to compose. *Very* light. A waltz, schottische, galoppe, tango, pas de deux, and two-step. Think of that coming out of your seriousminded Westchester Presbyterian nephew. . . . . . It will be for the whole company, sets by Cecil Beaton § and will be done by the City Center Ballet next season. It will take place circa 1910, but neither story nor title is set yet, I shall do the scoring now in Europe, for that is something that can be done in hotels.[25]

* Preface, *Souvenirs* for piano, four hands, G. Schirmer, 1954. Barber's memory may not have been correct about the year he began the suite, for he and Charles Turner had been playing it together during their European travels in 1951.

† Menotti, telephone interview with the author, 11 March 1990. Barber's fondness for the ambiance of grand hotels was constant into his later years and once led him to suggest to Menotti—probably not entirely in jest—that he should plan a concert at Spoleto of "all those silly pieces we used to hear in grand hotels throughout Europe."

‡ The International Music Council, a nongovernmental organization attached to UNESCO, was founded in 1949. At the time Barber served on the council, its membership comprised more than forty countries and numerous international music organizations. Its mission was to further the cause of music on an international scale, to resolve copyright problems, and to encourage young performers and composers. The request for Barber's appointment came from his European colleagues Honegger and Roland-Manuel.

§ Although ultimately Beaton did not design the sets for the ballet, he did design costumes and sets for *Vanessa* (see chapter 14).

In mid-May, still rushing to finish the ballet before he left for a summer in Europe, he wrote to La Grange, "I write in haste and briefly to save my eyes, for I am orchestrating the ballet and want to get it off my hands before I leave."[26] But in July, in Paris for another series of UNESCO–IMC meetings, Barber still had not finished the score. While in Paris, even with no immediate plans for a performance he spent time with dancers of the company that would eventually perform *Souvenirs*: Balanchine, Nora Kaye, Jerome Robbins, and Tanaquil LeClercq.[27]

At the IMC meeting, Barber was appointed vice-president of the council. He wrote home about the endless discussion over the wording of a proposal for a new program:

> "to discover unpublished compositions of young composers. . . ." The representative from Austria objected to this because he said it would have excluded Alban Berg's "Wozzeck," for instance, as he was over forty-five before it was produced; it should be worded differently: "to discover works, possibly unpublished, of not necessarily young (preferably, however) composers. . . ." This went on so long that I couldn't resist suggesting "YOUNG works of UNPUBLISHED composers"—oeuvres jeunes de compositeurs inédits—it was wonderful, what a mess the translators got into and everyone was happy for a moment![28]

The incomplete orchestral score of *Souvenirs* was taken by Barber to Ireland, where he was a guest of Henry McIlhenny. At Glenveagh Castle—on the side of a grey lake flanked by mountains—he wrote that the weather was rainy and icy cold, but "joy of joys, peat fires are burning in every room . . . they call it turf . . . and burning it has an ineffable perfume, at least for me." Barber buried himself happily in work on the ballet.

> There are two towers in the castle, six drawing rooms, with fires always burning; so I confiscated one at once and messed it up p.d.q. with orchestration, paper, and pencils, et al, announcing that I would see no one until lunch time; and I worked very well every day and almost finished two numbers of the ballet; lots of fun working at it. There was really no one to see for almost a week.[29]

Returning to Paris and a fine performance of *Pelléas,* which fascinated him always more, he wrote, "The old 1910 sets were used. Very pleasant lunch with Roland-Manuel, president of our council. . . . His reminiscences of Debussy and Ravel entranced me."[30]

A few weeks later, at La Casarella, La Grange's home in Calvi, Corsica—besieged by an exceptional heat wave that flattened an appetite for work—Barber announced to Homer that he had at last finished the orchestration of the tango, "but that is mechanical work; anything more speculative would be impossible in this heat."[31] He depicted the setting in which the score was completed on 17 July 1952:

> I am sitting looking out on certainly one of the most lovely and dramatic views imaginable in this strange, wild, savage, recalcitrant and irritating country, the sea is a shameless blue, offered only by the Mediterranean. . . . The house, which belonged to Prince Youssoupoff, the murderer of Rasputin, from whom H. L. bought it last year, nestles in a ruined citadel of imposing dimensions, built by Genovese conquerors in the 11th century . . . and it is a long walk up from the sea to the house; we do it twice a day and sometimes the heat is almost slaughtering. . . . But the sea itself, who could describe that? Warm, coquettish, limpid (one can see down as if forever), classic, neo-romantic, salty, healing, taunting.[32]

At La Casarella Barber found the most inviting diversion was playing duets on an out-of-tune Erard concert grand:

> After lunch there is a great burst of four-hand music which I enjoy, for for some years I have only frequented the silent houses of famous "tired" musicians such as Menotti and Horowitz where never a note of music is heard and only the shuffle of cards brings solace; chamber music being banished to the legendary days when there was no income tax. . . . How beautiful music is, even though badly played, how much Schubert, even in a four-hand arrangement, can say to us, wrong notes and all! There should be no summer vacation from great music! Not one day![33]

Afterwards he spent a week in Salzburg, where he attended rehearsals of *The Marriage of Figaro,* an opera he was "only just beginning to know," he confessed to Homer:

> It takes a good deal of listening to grasp the ensembles completely with all their counterpoint. It was wonderfully sung by the three women, Schwarzkopf, Seefried, and Gueden; curious how the German-Viennese sing better than anyone today; I have never heard it sung so well.[34]

His quest for a quiet place with a piano—"a corner of my own, so to speak, after hotels and other people's houses, where I could gather in my thoughts"—simply had not worked out, and as summer came to a close Barber thought only of finding a place to work. Noisy and crowded Salzburg did not offer a retreat, but there he happened upon the composer Nicolas Nabokov, who invited him to join him in Gstaad, Switzerland, where he was staying at the home of Hansi Lambert, an Austrian-Belgian countess and widow of a Belgian Rothschild. Barber had known her slightly during the war years in New York—"a birdlike creature, tragic and wistful, and enormously wealthy, yet very unpretentious, and with a great love for things intellectual."[35] Stephen Spender and his family were there also. Barber's description of the visit was as follows:

> It has worked out beautifully and made such a charming and restful end to the summer. The chalet where she lives is chock-full and something is always up; the conversation is wonderful! Nabokoff is somewhat older

> than I and is quite brilliant, a very witty talker and what I haven't learned about politics! He is a good composer and was a great friend of the Koussevitzkys, Strawinskys, and Diaghileff; in fact, there seems to be no one he doesn't know and no book he has not read. . . . His talks with Stephen are fascinating.
>
> Hansi has found us places (of sorts) to work, there being a piano shortage, and off we go to peasant houses in various meadows, where in the living room filled with pictures of grandpa, hair-wreathes from grandma, dried flowers, a tinkly piano and a superb view of distant peaks, I try each morning to work (but nothing happens to the blank music paper). . . . It is a happy household and a pleasure to be in. Late afternoons we walk through the woods and in the evening listen to the talk. Nicky has begun to read aloud to us (my suggestion—to get him off politics sometimes) and last night it turned cold for the first time in summer; we lit the fire and he read us "First Love" by Turgeniev, almost acting out the parts of the various characters. Occasionally we would hear a squeal out of Elizabeth Spender, aged two.[36]

In this warm household Barber completed the orchestration of *Souvenirs* by the end of the summer. Its production was to be delayed, however, for three years. In November 1952 he was told the performance was being put off until the following spring because the City Center lacked funds for scenery.[37] But at that time the ballet had not even been choreographed.[38]

In 1952 Barber arranged the four-hand version of *Souvenirs* for solo piano. That same year, Arthur Gold and Robert Fizdale had recorded a two-piano version for Columbia Records. Reviews of the two-piano version suggest that *Souvenirs* was recognized as salon music: "an exceedingly lightweight score . . . but it never resorts to the cute: it is almost a pure re-creation of the past with the crudities and vulgarities lost in a happily sentimental haze";[39] "the six sections of the new Barber work . . . show no lack of inventiveness";[40] "airy, gracious, inventive, and lighthearted";[41] and "a facile trifle."[42] The two-piano team played it for the first time on a program of contemporary works on 11 March 1953 at the Museum of Modern Art.

Todd Bolender of the City Center Ballet heard the Gold and Fizdale recording of *Souvenirs* and was so fond of the music he requested and received approval from Balanchine to choreograph the score.[43] He presented the tango to Balanchine and Lincoln Kirstein, and although they liked what had been done and planned to try it out within six months, there always seemed to be reasons for more delays: the company's tour to Europe interfered with its production; Balanchine was ill and the repertoire had already been set for the following season. Bolender recalled that although he continued working with the dancers for the ensemble parts, by the time he finished the variations for the last movement he was still never sure when it might be produced.[44]

When William Strickland asked if he could perform *Souvenirs* in its orchestrated version, Barber was reluctant to allow it. He wrote:

> Alas, the ballet score cannot be played until the ballet itself has been produced and that is indefinite—perhaps in the spring season if they raise enough money, perhaps not. I think I told you they have no money for the necessary sets or costumes. . . . Anyway, much as I would be pleased to have you do it, it cannot be. . . . Money is so tight here and all the orchestras, opera etc. are moaning; perhaps it will change after the elections.[45]

Finally, in May 1953 Barber wrote to Strickland, "It keeps being postponed—but Heinsheimer* has become impatient and has given the first orchestral performance to Reiner in Chicago in November."[46] Nevertheless, even with plans in sight for a premiere of *Souvenirs* by Reiner on 12 November, Barber withheld future concert performances; to another request from Strickland, for one in December, he answered, "I am not absolutely decided, but my feeling is that the work should be known first with the ballet and later in orchestra concerts."†

Similarly, even after the Chicago performance he discouraged Virgil Thomson's interest in conducting the New York premiere of the orchestral suite:

> Dear Virgilio—No one is going to play "Souvenirs" now, so H. H. [Hans Heinsheimer] and I think it better to hold off for a next winter premiere—I've written so little in the orchestral field of late. Thanks for wanting it!‡

In August 1954, after a London performance of the orchestral version, a review in *Musical Opinion* proclaimed *Souvenirs* "likely to rival the *Adagio for Strings* in popularity even if it is not one of the composer's finest works,

* Hans Heinsheimer, who was then head of G. Schirmer's symphonic and operatic divisions.

† Letter, 25 July 1953, from Capricorn. Another request came from a conductor who wanted to omit the pas de deux, "A Corner of the Ballroom," because he thought it made the piece too long. Barber, irate, wrote an icy reply:

> As much as I am in favor of brevity, I cannot agree with your conviction that the pas de deux be cut. For purely musical reasons, it is the only cantabile piece in the suite, the *only* one with a long melodic line, and if you speak of a public success, I have never noticed the public to object to that! . . .
>
> Believe me, I admire your musicianship and vast experience, but your statement [that dance music cannot be longer than 14½ minutes in a symphony concert] seems arbitrary and untenable. What if Maestro Eugene should say that 15½ minutes were the maximum duration, or Maestro Wilhelm 22, or Maestro Arturo 3? The thought is too terrifying to pursue. . . . If you do not have my complete blessings, you do have my very best wishes. (Paul Hume, "The Musical Legacy of Samuel Barber," *Washington Post*, 1 February 1981)

‡ Postcard from Barber to Thomson, probably February 1954, Virgil Thomson Papers, Yale University Music Library. After relinquishing his post as music critic of the *New York Herald Tribune*, Thomson made his debut as a conductor in Town Hall in New York on 15 November 1954 at 5:30 P.M. (two and a half hours before Leontyne Price's first performance of Barber's *Hermit Songs* in the same hall).

nor truly representative of his style," concluding, "I suggest that here is a first-rate work for ballet companies."[47]

By then, finally, preparations for production of the ballet were well under way. As Bolender developed the dance scheme, he and Barber consulted frequently, dining together almost every evening.[48] The dancer's original concept of the ballet shifted from a classical orientation to that of a theater piece in the comedy vein.[49] In a small antiquarian book store in New York, he found fashion magazines from the turn of the century in which there were detailed drawings of haute couture for men and women. The pictures were, Bolender said, "a gold mine of inspiration" for costume designer Rouben Ter-Arutunian, who also designed the set—a resort hotel in about 1914.* Balanchine, too, became involved with the costumes.

On 15 November 1955, at last the ballet was performed, with Bolender dancing one of the leading roles, Jillana as prima ballerina, and Irene Larsson as the "Vamp." *Souvenirs* was greeted as one of the funniest and most perceptive ballets of the season. Francis Herridge's review in the *New York Post* praised its satirical flair:

> a thoroughly engaging potpourri of Mack Sennett bathing girls, thin-mustached Lotharios and bloodthirsty vampires. . . . A series of brief sketches includes a spoof on the Irene Castle dance styles, a hotel hallway farce, three wall flowers at a dance, a bedroom seduction, and an afternoon on the beach. Bolender has etched them with a fine inventive wit and a nice balance between pantomime and dance. The result is likely to be his most popular ballet to date.[50]

The music was cited by the critic Robert Sabin as serving "excellently as background for Mr. Bolender's madcap work."[51]

Hermit Songs, Op. 29

In November 1952, with the score of his ballet *Souvenirs* finished but with no performance in sight, Barber wrote Sidney Homer that he was working on some songs:

> I have come across some poems of the 10th century, translated into modern English by various people, and am making a song cycle of them, to be called, perhaps "Hermit Songs." These were extraordinary men, monks or hermits or what not, and they wrote these little poems on the corners of MSS they were illuminating or just copying. I find them very direct, unspoiled and often curiously contemporaneous in feeling. [Barber added a

* Bolender, interview with the author. A later version, produced on television in 1959 for the Bell Telephone Hour and performed by the two-piano team Gold and Fizdale, set the ballet in the Palm Court of the Plaza Hotel, in accordance with Barber's original concept.

note: much like the Fioretti of St. Francis of Assisi] I am copying the texts of those already done to see if you like them.*

There followed the texts for four songs of the ten-song cycle *Hermit Songs:* "The Crucifixion," "The Heavenly Banquet," "At St. Patrick's Purgatory" ("awfully hard rhythms," Barber wrote in the margin of the page), and "The Church Bell at Night." The only line in his letter that varies from the final versions of text is in "The Heavenly Banquet": "I would like to have Jesus, too, here among them" became "I would like to have Jesus sitting here among them." Following the text of "The Church Bell at Night" ("Sweet little bell, struck on a windy night, / I would liefer keep tryst with thee / Than be / With a light and foolish woman"), Barber added a postscript that betrays, in spite of his denial, a personal orientation to the texts:

> Dear Uncle, do not take the last one literally; I am not that much of a Hermit, for I have just rented a little apartment in New York, having decided that there is some life in the old dog yet.[52]

Notwithstanding his protestation to Homer, the subject of reclusion seems a compelling and recurring theme throughout Barber's life, wherein he was inevitably pulled between the quest for solitude—so necessary for his work—and the need for stimulating companionship.† His family's cottage in the Pocono Lake Preserve—a retreat for Barber in the late 1930s and early 1940s—was named The Hermit. He considered the ideal setting for composing to be the country, for only there could he write undisturbed. Mount Kisco, when not beset with visitors, was his own hermitage; much later, after the crises of the first performances of his opera *Antony and Cleopatra* in 1966 and the sale of Capricorn in 1972, his sanctuary was a home in Santa Cristina.

Barber's love of Irish literature and poetry, as discussed earlier, had been established in his youth and produced, for example, the songs on texts by Stephens and Joyce in the 1930s. The logical fulfillment of his interest in Irish culture was a trip to Donegal during the summer of 1952, which preceded his composition of *Hermit Songs*. In anticipation of this

*Letter, 18 November 1952, from Capricorn. In the introduction to the G. Schirmer edition (1954), Barber amplifies his description of the poems: "They are small poems, thoughts or observations, some very short, and speak in straightforward, droll, and often surprisingly modern terms of the simple life these men led, close to nature, to animals and to God." He quotes from Robin Flower's *The Irish Tradition*:

> It was not only that these scribes and anchorites lived by the destiny of their dedication in an environment of wood and sea; it was because they brought into that environment an eye washed miraculously clear by a continual spiritual exercise that they, first in Europe, had that strange vision of natural things in an almost unnatural piety.

†His cycle *Despite and Still*, Op. 41 (1968), for example, is also marked by a preoccupation with the theme of solitude.

trip, he wrote to Henry-Louis de La Grange that he was "much excited, for I don't know Ireland."[53] A long stay at Glenveagh, Henry McIlhenny's castle in Donegal, reawakened with fervor his interest in Gaelic lore. His letter to Sidney Homer reveals how enchanted he was by the world of Yeats and Joyce:

> We left [Glenveagh] after a week of candlelight . . . and peat and Gaelic twilight. I sank rather easily into the latter and began to read a lot of Yeats again; A.E. himself had stayed in the castle and there are many people around who have seen wee folk, leprechauns and other such. Driving down to Dublin we stopped at Yeats' grave. I had been immensely moved rereading him and wanted to see if they had really marked his grave with the bitter words of Ben Bulben in a country church-yard where his grandfather, I think, was parson. I do not remember this poem line by line and do not have it before me, but I think his family and friends took him too literally when they used this poem on his tombstone. There the words are, on a very plain tombstone in this little country church-yard, far off from nowhere; there was not a sound, only swallows darting; it could have been any country church in Chester County, Birmingham, for instance. It was dusk and there was one farmer pausing in the field, leaning over a fence and smoking while he stared over the graves towards Ben Bulben and over the fields where Yeats had so often walked as a child. Silence. On the stone W. B. Yeats, the dates, and these words:
>
> "Cast a cold eye
> On life, on death:
> Horseman, ride on."*

His love affair with Ireland was strengthened by the discovery that "lo and behold, Yeats was surrounded, nay, he lay in the very bosom of a family—tombstones of uncles, cousins, brothers, sisters on every side of him—of Barbers." The composer's sense of destiny at being linked to one of his favorite poets provoked a wry description of the sight of "one lonely Mr. Yeats lying solitary amidst this display of marble on the part of the family Barber."

> Nor were there any doubts in *their* minds: "Safe in the arms of Jesus" was carved on every one of their stones. They almost grinned with confidence, such was their aplomb. Now faith is never excessive and never to be censured, but there are limits of good taste in displaying one's optimism. Maybe the Barbers got there first (I did not think to check the dates), and did not know how very lonely Mr. Yeats might be feeling in such good company.[54]

Arriving in Dublin, the romance of Barber's literary journey sobered when he realized there was no marker on either Joyce's or Yeats's house. He wrote:

* "Horseman, *pass by*," is the correct quote. Letter, 4 July 1952, from Cannes.

> Most of the poetry seemed to me to come from the glory of an immediate past to which Dublin itself is quite indifferent. Indeed it probably was then as well. . . . The young people are not interested in writers. Mrs. Yeats lives on, forgotten, and Maud Gonne, the flashing beautiful one, is an old lady now, and it bores people when she is mentioned. "The sorrows of your changing face . . ." The Abbey Theatre burned down, Joyce but a man who wrote dirty books, and Yeats . . . . a Protestant. I walked through St. Stephen's Green and the court at Trinity College and thought about all this, and how beautiful the first chapter of *Ulysses* is, and the Tower scene by the sea (so many towers—which one was it?) and was glad to hop on my little plane again and leave this strangely dead city. Sic transit.[55]

This disillusionment may explain why Barber never experienced a resurgence of interest in setting more poetry by Yeats.*

The impressions of his first trip to Ireland undoubtedly were still on his mind, however; upon returning to the United States, he began work on *Hermit Songs,* to texts written on the margins of manuscripts by monks and scholars during the eighth to thirteenth centuries—"perhaps not always meant to be seen by their Father Superiors." The four songs to which he referred in his November 1952 letter to Sidney Homer were composed quickly—within three weeks—in the following order: V. "The Crucifixion," October 26; II. "Church Bell at Night," November 3; IV. "The Heavenly Banquet," November 13; I. "At Saint Patrick's Purgatory," November 17.[56]

The remaining six songs of the cycle were composed within the first three weeks of the new year and in the following order: VI, "Sea-Snatch," January 6; III, "St. Ita's Vision," January 9; X, "The Desire for Hermitage" and VII, "Promiscuity," both finished on January 15; IX, "The Praises of God," January 27 (inserted in the holograph under an erasure "January 26"); and VIII, "The Monk and His Cat," February 16.

Barber used texts from three different literary sources for the songs. For V and II (the earliest composed) he used Howard Mumford Jones's translation of "The Speckled Book" (twelfth century), published in *Romanesque Lyric.*[57] Kenneth Jackson's *A Celtic Miscellany*[58] provided poems for two of the songs, VI and VII. Although six of the poems are found in *The Silver Branch,*[59] Barber used only three of Sean O'Faolain's translations from that book—for "The Heavenly Banquet" (attributed to St. Brigid, tenth century), "At St. Patrick's Purgatory" (anonymous, thirteenth century), and "The Desire for Hermitage." Not finding O'Faolain's translations of "The Monk and His Cat," "The Praises of God," and "St. Ita's Vision" to be adequate, he commissioned W. H. Auden to provide him with translations for the first two and Chester Kallman, for the last.†

*Almost two decades would pass before Barber would set another text of Joyce's—"Solitary Hotel," from *Ulysses*—and make his final musical reference to that poet in an orchestral setting of "Fadograph of a Yestern Scene" from *Finnegans Wake.*

†Barber first met Auden in New York in 1940 and had discussed a possible text for an aria, which never came to fruition.

The ten *Hermit Songs* in their diversity seem to represent a summary of Barber's stylistic development with regard to his songs at midcareer. They are in a variety of forms and styles, predetermined by the text—through-composed, binary, ternary, strophic, recitative and aria (the aria in "St. Ita's Vision" is a strophic variation). Although most of the songs favor a declamatory setting and with only a few exceptions are syllabic ("The Praises of God," for example, appropriately has a melismatic section), there is still an infusion of lyricism even in the songs with shorter texts and narrower tessituras—"Church Bell at Night" and "Promiscuity," for example.

In this cycle, Barber's prosody acquires unusual suppleness by omitting metrical signatures throughout, thus allowing the performer to project flexibly the rhythmic irregularities of the poems. The cycle is marked by a prevalence of quasi-archaic open fourths and fifths. An omnipresent three-note motive is found in at least eight of the ten songs (a descending whole tone followed by a descending fourth, or a retrograde of this configuration).*

A variety of contrasting moods and subjects coexists within the songs themselves as well as within the cycle: the drama of the recitative introduction, followed by a tender lullaby in "St. Ita's Vision"; wit and avarice mingled in "Heavenly Banquet"; the "surging" outrage in "Sea-Snatch"; and the sultry, philosophical swing of "The Monk and His Cat."

There are at the Library of Congress numerous pencil sketches of *Hermit Songs,* as well as Barber's notes about the texts of the songs, which give particular insight into his compositional process with regard to the handling of melody and text and suggest that his early conception of a song most frequently centered upon the union of the two.† The extensive

---

Two studies trace Barber's literary sources for *Hermit Songs* and his manipulation of the poetic forms for his vocal settings: Alycia Kathleann Davis ("Samuel Barber's 'Hermit Songs', Op. 29: An Analytical Study," M. A. thesis, Webster University, St. Louis, 1983) and Kreiling, *The Songs of Samuel Barber.* Kreiling's study benefits from Barber's notes and sketches at the Library of Congress, which clearly enumerate his sources and other references he may have consulted for his transcriptions.

*Davis's study, cited in the preceding footnote, confirms the frequency of this pattern in each song.

†Kreiling cites twenty-five separate musical sketches (including entire songs and fragments of varying lengths). There are, in addition to these, a pencil holograph, a black-line print from the copyist's manuscript, and an isolated sketch in a notebook mostly related to the choral work *Prayers of Kierkegaard.* In addition, there are items that concern text only or consist mainly of text that include Barber's notes about the sources, which suggest the broad scope of his reading of old Irish literature.

Of the three dissertations and one master's thesis on *Hermit Songs,* only Kreiling's *The Songs of Samuel Barber* (pp. 245–71) is based on the materials at the Library of Congress, and it offers the most penetrating discussion. The following studies are analytical; Friedewald, *A Formal and Stylistic Analysis,* which provides for each song a description of formal design and tonal structure (pp. 83–104); Davis, "Samuel Barber's 'Hermit Songs,' Op. 29," which identifies the group as a "modern song cycle" through an interesting survey of elements of rhythm, meter, tempo, form, motivic patterns, and the melodic range of the vocal

revisions of the melodic lines in several of these songs, in particular "The Heavenly Banquet" and "The Desire for Hermitage," suggest that Barber used a more deliberate compositional method for this cycle than for his other songs, which were often produced with more spontaneous facility in short periods of time.* His extensive notes on these texts offer still another example of his meticulous care in shaping texts, where attention to details led him to cross-check sources, use texts from more than one translation, or rework passages from a single source in order to produce a refined composite that would offer the fullest opportunity for musical expressivity.†

Included among Barber's sketches for the *Hermit Songs* is also a transcription of another Irish text that he attempted to rework from prose into poetic form but never set: "Look before you to the northeast at the glorious sea, home of creatures, dwelling of seals; wanton and splendid, it has taken on flood-tide."‡

Hermit Songs were commissioned by the Elizabeth Sprague Coolidge Foundation, some twelve months after Barber began writing them, for the annual Founder's Day concert celebrating the benefactress's birthday. Two of the songs in the cycle are dedicated to other individuals: "The Praises of God" is in memory of Mary Evans Scott; and "The Monk and His Cat," completed a week before Isabelle Vengerova's seventy-sixth birthday, was dedicated to her.

Barber's relationship with Mrs. Coolidge had begun some thirty years earlier, when he first wrote to her about himself and sent her scores of *Dover Beach* and the Cello Sonata. In 1947 he had received a commission from the Coolidge Foundation to compose a string quartet, which he did not fulfill apparently because of his inhibitions about the genre—despite the success of his earlier string quartet—and also because of difficulties he had in completing the Piano Sonata, which took longer to compose than he had anticipated.

---

part as well as the textural, tone painting, and harmonic vocabulary of the piano accompaniment; and John Albertson, *A Study of Stylistic Elements of Samuel Barber's "Hermit Songs" and Franz Schubert's "Die Winterreise"* (D.M.A., University of Missouri, Kansas City, 1969).

* Kreiling reports that measures 14–16 of "The Heavenly Banquet," for example, underwent five melodic transformations before the final version, and that only two of Barber's sketches, "Church Bell at Night" and "St. Ita's Vision," appear in versions closely resembling the finished songs (p. 252).

† Other examples that come to mind are Barber's handling of the texts for *Knoxville: Summer of 1915* and *Prayers of Kierkegaard* (chapter 13), the several translations he worked with for *The Lovers* (chapter 18), his collaboration with Patrick Creagh in fashioning the text for *Andromache's Farewell* (chapter 16), and his work with Zeffirelli in selecting and rearranging Shakespeare's text for the opera *Antony and Cleopatra* (chapter 17).

‡ Kreiling traces the text to an epigram called "Flood-tide" in Jackson's *A Celtic Miscellany* (p. 128). But as Barber's transcription differs considerably from Jackson's text, I suspect he used another source and did not, as Kreiling suggests, attempt to rework Jackson's. My experience with Barber's text transcriptions is that where only one or two words differ from a source he might have substituted a word of his own (as he did with Graves's "A Last Poem," see chapter 18), but more often, when there are numerous variants, it means he used a second or third source.

The earliest mention by Barber of the new Coolidge commission is his letter to Strickland of May 1953, in which he deplores the delays in production of *Souvenirs* but continues:

> In the meantime, I have finished an eighteen-minute song cycle called "Hermit Songs" to texts translated from the tenth-century Irish, and fascinating poems they are. It was commissioned by Mrs. Coolidge and I shall play it in Washington in October, but haven't found the ideal singer yet. I am dying to play them for you.[60]

The search for the "ideal singer" for the *Hermit Songs* led him to consider several voices. Leontyne Price, who by then was known for her role of Bess in *Porgy and Bess* but as yet had not made a recital debut, was introduced to Barber through her teacher Florence Kimball. As late as July 1953, even after Price had been given the songs and was learning them, letters to Strickland indicate Barber still had not found what he considered the right voice:

> Do you know the soprano Seefried? I have sent her my Hermit Songs to look over; they are to be sung by someone in October at the Library of Congress. I do not know whether Seefried is the right one or not, I love her singing but have never met her and do not know how good her English is. She is supposed to be a delightful person. Maybe you would meet her and play them with her, although I am sure she is very busy with the Salzburg season. The negro soprano, Leontyne Price—very talented—is learning them here and I shall hear them next week. Do you know the baritone Fischer-Dieskau?[61]

Apparently Strickland suggested Eleanor Steber as a possible choice. However, Barber by then had heard Price sing his songs—"she does them beautifully; it is a beautiful voice."* She sang the songs in the Coolidge Auditorium at the Library of Congress on 30 October 1953, the eighty-ninth birthday of Mrs. Coolidge. Accompanied by Barber at the piano, Price also sang his songs "Sleep now," "The Daisies," "Nocturne," and *Nuvoletta*. On the program, too, were Francis Poulenc's *Four Songs to Poems by Paul Eluard* and Sauguet's *La Voyante*.

This concert inaugurated Barber's long professional collaboration and friendship with Price. In Rome, April 1954, they repeated the songs on a program of "Chamber Music for Voice and Instruments" at the Twentieth-Century Music Conference.† Price was the only American vocalist to

*In a letter from Barber to Strickland, 25 July 1953, from Capricorn, he wrote of his hesitations about using Steber: "I was really interested in what you said about Steber being a really serious artist; I should like to believe this and will if she ever cuts out the Firestone-hour-glamour-girl act: one Lieder recital in a black dress and no makeup would convince me!!" Probably the soonest Barber would be convinced of Steber's professionalism would be in 1958, when prior to the opening of *Vanessa* Sena Jurinac backed out of her contract and Steber stepped in to learn the entire leading role in only six weeks.

†These concerts were organized by Nicolas Nabokov for the Congress of Cultural Freedom. Barber and Virgil Thomson planned some of the programs and recommended which

appear in the festival. Ned Rorem, in his *Paris Diary* ("England, Germany, and Italy, 1953–54") wrote about her splendid performance of Barber's songs: "beautiful, in a gown of blue sequins, sopranoing by heart and tonally (after hours of villainous bearded dodecaphonists) Price sang Sam Barber's *Hermit Songs* perfectly, but with a trace of Southern accent."[62]

Barber and Price were invited to perform *Hermit Songs* again on 17 July at Mrs. Coolidge's summer music festival at South Mountain, Pittsfield, Massachusetts. Each received a fee of $500 from the Coolidge Foundation, for which negotiations were handled by Harold Spivacke, then Chief of the Music Division of the Library of Congress.[63]

For Price's New York recital debut at Town Hall on 14 November 1954, she sang *Hermit Songs* with Barber at the piano. Jay Harrison toasted her "enormous capacity for projecting a personality that literally spills charm over the footlights," predicting that "when the day arrives that Miss Price is able to bring into parallel lines her huge vivacity and vocal disposition, we shall have a goddess performing for us." He claimed Barber's *Hermit Songs* were "far and away the most significant" of the song cycles Price introduced to New York.[64] In fact, only one other cycle on the program was a first New York performance, Manuel Rosenthal's *Epitaphe de Thomas*: "L'Irondelle," "Epitaphe luy-mesmes," "Chanson d'amour," and "Bacchanale."*

On the basis of their successful reception Price and Barber contemplated touring together much in the manner of Bernac and Poulenc. "We announced to the world that we were available," Barber recalled somewhat poignantly, "but we received only two invitations, and that put an end to our joint-concert career."[65] Nevertheless, over the next twenty years he was to write some of his most important and beautiful music for Price—the soprano solo in *Prayers of Kierkegaard,* the opera role Cleopatra, and the song cycle *Despite and Still.* Moreover, Price became one of the most ardent proselytizers of Barber's music. Her intense feeling for him and her astute assessment of the strengths of his vocal music were candidly expressed in 1982 after his death:

> For a singer Barber's music is always a challenge; but the end product is so rewarding and so terribly vocal, you can't wait to pick up another piece of his. It also falls intellectually to the mind and beautifully on the ear, which is a rare combination.[66]

Hermit Songs are a favorite of many singers and among the most performed of Barber's works.† Like Schubert's *Die Winterreise, Hermit Songs*

---

critics should be invited. On the same trip, in Barcelona, Thomson conducted Barber's Overture to *The School for Scandal* (Virgil Thomson, letter to the author, 8 August 1988).

* *New York Times* preconcert listing, 14 November 1954. A search for a review of Price's recital in the *New York Times* revealed there was none.

† It would be expected, of course, that established singers who knew Barber personally—Price, Arroyo, and Steber, for example—would be familiar with the cycle. But it has been my experience in informal queries of younger singers during the course of this study that if they

Barber and Leontyne Price at the Piazza d'Espagna, in Rome for the Twentieth-Century Music Conference, April 1954.

create a entire world of their own, and in this sense they can be considered without reservation one of the great song cycles of the twentieth century. William Schuman was so profoundly affected when he heard *Hermit Songs* that he sent Barber a "fan letter."[67]

> As far as the songs go, I feel that you have created in an absolutely unique manner and that in this sphere of composing you are alone. There is no-one else in America and, for that matter, perhaps nowhere else, who has the particular gift that you display in these new works.*

"Adventure" (1954)

An unpublished anomaly in Barber's oeuvre is a single movement for orchestra titled "Adventure," written for a television collaboration between the Columbia Broadcasting System and the Museum of Natural History.†

know any of Barber's songs at all, *Hermit Songs*, "Sure on this shining night," and *Knoxville: Summer of 1915* are usually the first mentioned.

*Letter, 27 October 1953 (Papers and Records of William Schuman, New York Public Library, Music Division). Barber replied: "Your note was the very nicest I've ever received. . . . Having such words from a colleague one esteems is such a rare experience. . . . Thank you from the heart" (letter, 20 November 1953).

†The autograph score is at the Library of Congress.

The "Adventure" series was inaugurated by CBS in 1953 and ran for several years, during which time 125 programs were produced and directed by Perry Wolfe in consultation with Dr. Harvey Shapiro, director of the museum's Department of Anthropology and Ethnology. Each program centered around a different culture and usually included a film, with discussion and presentation of artifacts from the museum.[68]

Music for the series was drawn at first from field recordings made in Polynesian and African cultures. But because recording technology was at that time still relatively crude—requiring the transport of heavy battery packs connected by cable to tape recorders—the resulting sound tracks were often too poor for broadcast, and Wolfe conceived the idea of supplementing the sound tracks with instruments from the museum's collection.[69] He asked Herbert Harris, percussionist with the New York Philharmonic and himself an avid collector of instruments from all over the world, to provide music and musicians for the program.* Harris's knowledge of musics of non-Western societies stemmed from extensive travels to the Pacific and Africa. From his collection of conch shells, sansas (mbiras), xylophones, Yoruba drums, and gongs, he composed original music for the "Adventure" series modeled on and closely resembling the style of what he had heard in the field; this was then dubbed in as "native" music to "sweeten" the sound track of the documentary films.

Wolfe, however, was interested in doing a program focusing on the instruments themselves and wanted to commission music from a prominent composer who would utilize the museum's collection. He recalled, "I was not interested in the avant-garde, I wanted—from a viewer's point of view—music with recognizable Western instruments," a combination of forces that mixed primitive instruments with conventional orchestral instruments.[70] He liked Barber's music precisely because it was melodic and thought it would be ideal for this project.

Barber was given a two-week deadline to complete the score for the broadcast on 28 November 1954.† After accepting the challenge, he asked Harris to select an array of instruments from the museum's nearly thirty vaults based on those he thought would be most viable for performance. Harris remembers that he brought together a huge pile of predominantly woodwind and percussion instruments, expecting them to be transported to Barber's home in Mount Kisco. Instead, however, the composer suggested that Harris play and record a selected variety of instruments on tape so that he might have access to their sounds, timbres, and pitch range while he worked on the piece at home.[71]

* Harris, recommended by Alfredo Antonini, conductor of the CBS Symphony Orchestra, had worked with composers who were interested in non-Western musics—Colin McPhee, Lou Harrison, and Peggy Glanville-Hicks, with whom he had put together an orchestra for films made by the United Nations.

† "Composer's Corner," *Musical America* (December 1954):31. Both Harris and Wolfe, in interviews with the author, confirm the time period.

"Adventure" was completed on 25 November 1954, three days before the required deadline.[72] Of eight minutes' duration, it is in three sections—ABA—with coda; a key signature of B♭ major is indicated. Barber drew on the melodic characteristics and individual sonorities of the non-Western instruments, combining them with the Western instruments to achieve a unity that is essentially representative of his personal style.

Harris recalled Barber saying that he wanted to be faithful to the cultural idiosyncrasies of each instrument and therefore would write the xylophone parts to their existing tunings, believing these to be the scales used by the African musician at the time the instrument was purchased and therefore authentic. Evidently he was particularly interested, too, in the contrast between the six-hole Japanese flute[73] and the Western flute.[74] The score bears this out in the kind of music Barber wrote for the two flutes, which were to be played alternately by the same player: the Japanese instrument plays melodic phrases mostly within the range of an octave and suggesting a gapped scale; in contrast, the modern (or "ordinary" as Barber calls it) flute part is written within a wider range—more than two octaves (d′ to a‴)—and plays diatonic, though sometimes disjunct, melodies with a broader sweep. Nevertheless, the transition between the two instrumental parts does not seem awkward; the two are integrated in Barber's melodic style. Harris noticed this when he first heard the score: "There was considerable lyricism, which he wouldn't get away from," he recalled; "he most definitely was writing a Sam Barber piece with these instruments."[75]

With the exception of two instruments from Harris's own collection—specifically a conch shell and a large gong, both from the Fiji Islands—all other non-Western instruments in Barber's score came from the Museum of Natural History. These included three African sansas, a Balinese water drum, small and large African xylophones, a very small oriental bell and a medium bell, a wood block, two gourds filled with peas, small and large hollow tree trunks, a Javanese saron, three African drums, a Congo horn, large and small bamboo shakers, small and large pressure drums, and a gourd (to strike). To this group he added a Japanese flute, Western flute, piccolo, clarinet, French horn, and harp.

"Adventure" begins with the soft rattles of a sansa and a harp (on B♭) as an introduction to a slightly exotic flute melody (alternating between 5/8 and 3/4 meter), which is a recurring refrain throughout the work. Florid triplet figures in fast tempo—for horn, "ordinary" flute, and clarinet—mark a transition passage to a widely arched second theme played by the horn to the accompaniment of harp and sansa I. Barber indicates by way of a note in the score that sansa I is played at "exact pitch. Sansas II and III (two-keyboards) are at approximate pitch only."

A second section in livelier, more accelerated rhythms features glissandi for flute, clarinet, and harp. Following is a section for percussion only—each instrument playing in turn: water drums, squeeze drums, xylophones,

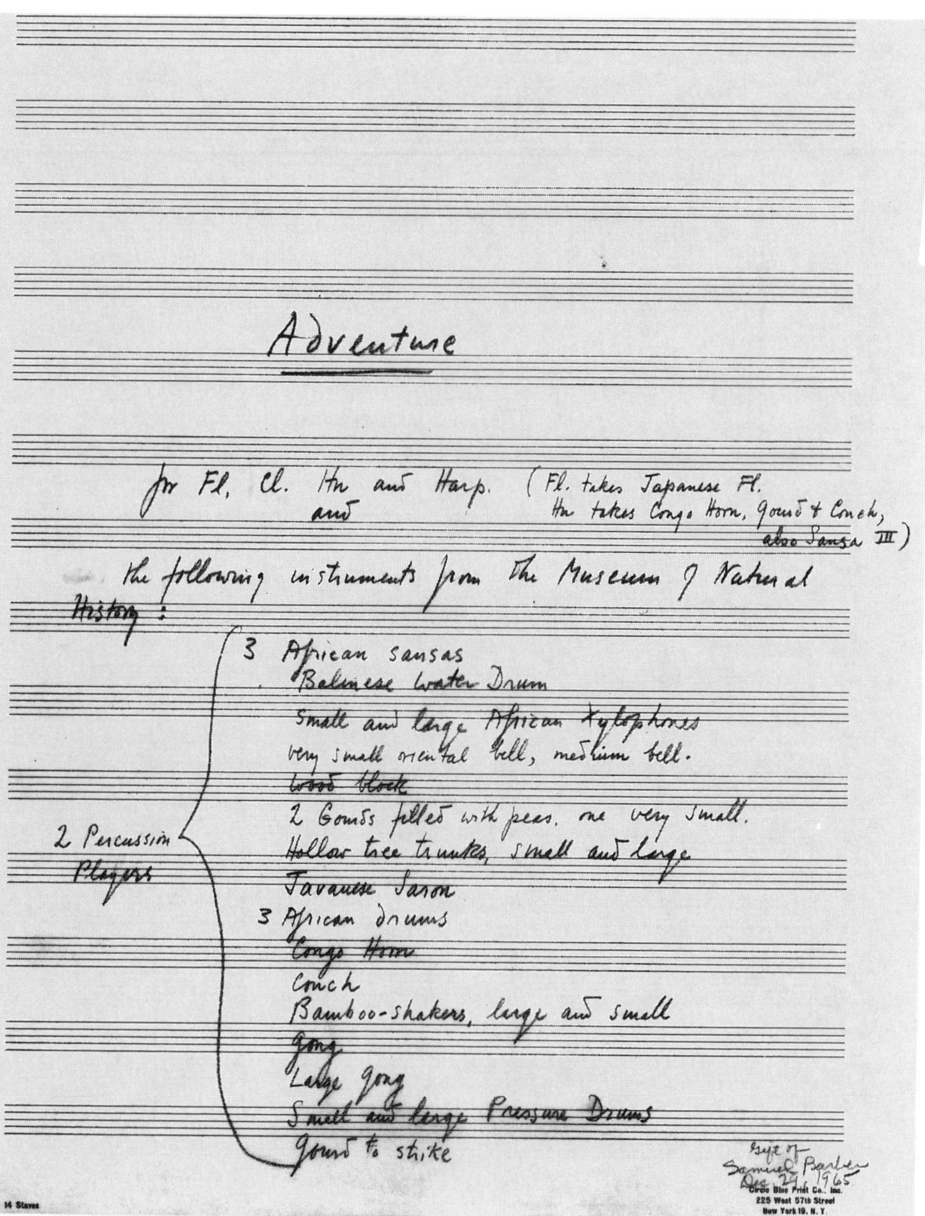

Example 12 "Adventure," cover and title page, mm. 1–14, holograph, 1954. *(Library of Congress)*

hard mallets, large tree trunk, bamboo shakers—accelerating *poco a poco* to climax in a single, freely vibrating, strike of the gong. A long gourd with peas, "like a sigh, dies away." A recapitulation of the haunting flute theme and transition passage leads directly to the coda, in which the flute theme returns again. The ring of the smallest bell closes the movement as the sansa "dies away" on B♭.

For the television broadcast the music was played by Harris and members of the New York Woodwind Quintet: Samuel Baron, flute, piccolo, and Japanese flute; John Barrows, French horn, Congo horn, gourd, conch shell, and sansa III; and David Glazer, clarinets in A and B♭. Harris played the percussion instruments. Barber rehearsed the group and conducted the live television performance, displaying, according to Harris, a compassionate attitude toward the musicians. Jac Venza had suggested to Wolfe that dance be added to the program, and although Barber had not set out to compose a score for dance, he apparently had no objections to the idea.*

* The dancers included John Butler, Glenn Tetley, and Mary Hinkson.

13

SEARCHES

A truth which is true for me

Prayers of Kierkegaard, Op. 30 (1954)

Three letters from the early fifties illuminate the spirit that guided Barber's grand-scale religious work *Prayers of Kierkegaard,* Op. 30, for orchestra, mixed chorus, soprano solo, with incidental contralto and tenor solos. In January 1951, in Rome for a performance of Menotti's Piano Concerto, he wrote home about an experience that profoundly moved him:

> Christmas eve, after a dinner party for a hundred guests at the Roberts' . . . we went . . . at midnight to . . . a little church, St. Anselmo, on the Aventine, a plain, cold little church where a choir of 60 Benedictine monks sang a Gregorian Mass to a few onlookers. The simplicity and sincere style with which they sang this overwhelming music warmed all the corners of my heart left cold and untouched by the morning's magnificent pageantry.*

The recollection of that evening remained sharp, for when he revisited the church several years later, he wrote to Turner:

> I got up early this morning and went alone to Mass at St. Anselmo's; remember? The whole Aventine hill was very quiet in the morning mist, a few birds singing and the sun coming up over snowy hills. Only a few nuns were there, one of whom showed me the text to follow, but there must have been 80 monks in the chorus and the Gregorian sounded better than ever. For me it is the only religious music possible, and it was well sung, I think; only I wish they wouldn't use organ at all.[1]

*Letter, 10 January 1951, from Hotel Sonne im Fextal, Engadin, Switzerland. The "pageantry" mentioned in this letter was a reference to a ceremony signifying the end of the year—the Closing of the Door—which Barber attended at St. Peter's Basilica.

Apparently he had written of his feelings also to Sidney Homer. The elderly mentor, near the end of his life, answered from his heart:

> I am so glad you are at home with your thoughts and your ideals. . . . I know how you feel about Gregorian chant. I have been listening to the Catholic Hour Sunday mornings on the radio and have heard some wonderful unaccompanied Gregorian chants. They satisfy something in my soul and help me to believe that "all is right with the world" and that the truth is just as simple and straightforward as a Gregorian chant. There is no place for complexity and perplexity. Away with them! The creative mind and the composing spirit have no use for them. . . .*

Gregorian chant, a preoccupation with monastic solitude, the approaching death of his uncle, and perhaps the questioning of his own religious faith—in the aftermath of *Hermit Songs*—were on Barber's mind as he began work on a new piece. "With the exception of a fortnight in Paris in June," he wrote with uncharacteristic reserve to Strickland in May 1953, "I shall stick close to home and the heat, for I am embarking on two rather big works about which I shall tell you absolutely nothing."†

One of the "big works" to which he referred was *Prayers of Kierkegaard,* a commission by the Koussevitzky Music Foundation given to Barber in 1942 and long overdue.‡ Completed in January 1954, the work was first performed on 3 December 1954 at Symphony Hall by the Boston Symphony Orchestra under Charles Münch. Leontyne Price was the soprano soloist; the supporting parts were sung by Jean Kraft, contralto, and Edward Munro, tenor; the Cecilia Society Chorus was under the direction of Hugh Ross.§ Barber undoubtedly wrote the beautiful soprano solo with Price's voice in mind since the work was begun about the time of their initial collaboration and he was enormously impressed with her voice:

*Letter dictated by Sidney Homer, to Barber, 30 April 1953, Winter Park, Florida. Homer dictated his letters because he suffered from macular degeneration, a condition that severely affected his central vision. This letter seems to mark the last known correspondence to Barber from Homer before his death on 10 July 1953.

†Letter, 5 May 1953, written from Capricorn. Barber may have been reluctant to share his plans because Strickland had been urging him to compose a work for his orchestra in Nashville.

‡The foundation was established in 1942 by Serge Koussevitzky in memory of his late wife Natalie and with the expectation that, through a permanent endowment at the Library of Congress, new works would be commissioned annually from American composers and composers from other countries of the world. A stipulation of Barber's commission was that the resulting work was to be dedicated to the memory of Serge and Natalie Koussevitzky. A holograph score of *Prayers of Kierkegaard* is in the Serge Koussevitzky Collection of the Library of Congress. Also at the library, in the Samuel Barber Collection, are holograph sketches.

§Program notes of the Boston Symphony Orchestra, 3 December 1954. Even before its premiere, however, there were requests to perform it "sight unseen"; Barber had written to Strickland, 23 June 1954, specifically mentioning a commitment from Fritz Reiner, conductor of the Chicago Symphony Orchestra. The Schola Cantorum sang the first performance in New York four days later on 8 December, with supporting solos by Mary MacMurray, contralto, and Earl Ringland, tenor.

Hermit Songs had already been performed in Washington, and they were planning recitals in Rome and New York.

Although Søren Kierkegaard's writings had been well known in Europe for almost a quarter of a century, not until the decade after 1936 did almost the entire body of his writings appear in the United States. Barber, like many of his contemporaries, perceived the Danish theologian as "a major literary figure and an exciting but enigmatic intellectual force."[2] In preparation for *Prayers,* he had delved into Kierkegaard's own writings and others' about him. In particular, his notes on reading the 1949 translation of Jean Wahl's *A Short History of Existentialism*[3] indicate fertile introspection:

> It is through intensity of feeling that one attains true existence. . . . The existing individual is one who possesses that intensity of feelings caused by the fact that he is in contact with something outside of himself. . . . The existing individual will be inspired. He will incarnate the infinite in the finite. The passion which animates him will be "the passion of liberty."*

Usually "inclined to allow his music to speak in its own voice without verbal assistance from himself," Barber's contribution to the Boston Symphony Orchestra's program seems to point even more markedly to the affinity between his own quest for truth and that of the Danish religious thinker:

> It is difficult to give a philosophic appraisal of Kierkegaard's standpoint since he elaborated no philosophy and was indeed the sworn enemy of philosophical systems. . . . The entire literary production of Kierkegaard is motivated by the intent of bringing men into a religious relationship with God, and throughout his writings one finds his three basic traits of imagination, dialectic, and religious melancholy. The truth he sought after was a "truth which is true for me," one which demanded sacrifice and personal response.[4]

For his text Barber selected four passages: two prayers interpolated in Kierkegaard's *Journals* (no. 692 from 1847; and no. 1030 from 1850);[5] one from *Christian Discourses,* 1848;[6] and one on which Kierkegaard gave his last sermon, "The Unchangeableness of God" (1855).[7] Barber arranged the prayers in reverse chronological order and took liberties in fashioning the text to his musical needs: this he did by reordering the sequence of lines, excising internal phrases, and substituting his own translation for specific words. Compare, for example, David Swenson's translation of "The Unchangeableness of God" with what Barber set to music (see Example 13.1): the words in italics are the ones Barber set; words also in brackets are his own.

*These are excerpts from several pages of notes interspersed among more than fifty pages of Barber's musical sketches for *Prayers* at the Library of Congress.

> *O Thou who art unchangeable, whom nothing changes!* Thou who art unchangeable in love, precisely for our welfare not submitting to any change: may we too will our welfare, submitting ourselves to the discipline of Thy unchangeableness, so that we may, in unconditional obedience, *[May we] find our rest and remain at rest in [Thee unchanging.]* Thy unchangeableness. Not art Thou like a man; if he is to preserve only some degree of constancy he must not permit himself too much to be moved, nor by too many things. *Thou* on the contrary *art moved, and moved in infinite love, by all things.* Even that which we human beings call an insignificant trifle, and pass by unmoved, *the need of a sparrow, even this moves Thee; and what we so often scarcely [see]* notice, *a human sigh, this moves Thee, O Infinite Love! But nothing changes Thee, O Thou who art unchangeable!* O Thou who in infinite love dost submit to be moved, may this our prayer also move Thee to add Thy blessing, in order that there may be wrought such a change in him who prays as to bring him into conformity with Thy unchangeable will, Thou who are unchangeable.[8]

Approximately twenty minutes in length, the work is in four contrasting but musically continuous sections that could be called movements. In *Prayers* Barber has combined his neo-Romantic perspective with elements of twentieth-century, Baroque, and medieval practice in a magnificent fusion. The choral texture, often polychoral, alternates blocks of sound with rich contrapuntal writing—principally canon and passacaglia—sometimes in combination; rhythmic augmentation is employed frequently. Although modal in orientation, there is a continuity of harmonic style between *Prayers* and Barber's earlier works.* The lyrical voice of the composer finds one of its most eloquent expressions in the warm soprano solo—"Lord Jesus Christ who suffer'd all life long that I, too, might be saved"—and the trio for soprano, alto, and tenor, moving transcendentally, "But when longing lays hold of us, O that we might lay hold of the longing." Nor is there a departure from Barber's usual practice with regard to the use of dissonance; polychordal passages exist, but dissonance is more often the result of voice-leading or for the sake of textual expressiveness.

In accord with Barber's acknowledged conviction that Gregorian chant should be sung without accompaniment (recall his letter to Turner), *Prayers of Kierkegaard* opens with an incantation in the Dorian mode by male chorus, *a cappella* and in unison, the tempo "grave and remote," thus establishing a liturgical mood. The chant is of Barber's invention, and, typically, this opening material is used throughout the work. An orchestral interlude introduces a full choral declamation—"But nothing changes Thee,

* William A. Dailey, for example, in his dissertation, *Techniques of Composition Used in Contemporary Works for Chorus and Orchestra on Religious Texts* (Catholic University of America, 1965), notes the prevalence of tertian and quartal chords and complex chords built on added thirds, as well as major and minor sonorities and chromatic and pandiatonic passages (pp. 193–201). He finds the work tends to derive its harmony from the melodic line; the chant motives, in particular, dictate the harmonic practice (p. 287).

Example 13.1 *Prayers of Kierkegaard,* holograph sketches, pp. [15–16]. *(Library of Congress, Serge Koussevitzky Collection)*

O Thou unchanging"—with polychordal accents by woodwinds and the xylophone. The striking symbolic setting of this text has been observed: the tonality of the work from the beginning is D major-minor; the chorus, even when countered by orchestral punctuations on D minor, remains virtually "unchanging" in adhering to its major tonality. Chorus and orchestra come together in a brilliant climax of clashing major and minor chords.*

The tempo quickens to *andante con moto*; strings and a lone oboe foreshadow the soprano solo on new material. The section concludes dramatically with a sudden drop in volume for a whispered choral recitation, "Father in Heaven."

Imitative entrances by solo tenor, alto, and, finally, soprano initiate the long passage "but when longing lays hold of us," in which the solo tenor theme is based on a ten-tone scale and simultaneously sung in augmented

* See Dailey (especially pp. 6–8), whose penetrating study considers three important representative works of the period from 1952–1962—*Prayers of Kierkegaard,* Stravinsky's *Canticum Sacrum,* and Hovhaness's *Magnificat*—analyzing each from the standpoint of text, structural design, tonal and modal organization, harmony (from a Schenkerian perspective), counterpoint, rhythm, melody, idiomatic choral characteristics, voice grouping, and accompaniment.

rhythm by the tenor section. Barber presumably was unaware of the near-dodecaphony of this striking passage until it was brought to his attention.[9] Rising waves of polyphony gradually gain in tempo and turn to antiphonal choral outbursts—"When Thou in the longing dost offer us the highest good"; a passacaglia theme for the harp and xylophone is eventually stated in almost exact retrograde. About the xylophone part Barber wrote, "Players of that curious instrument must almost always memorize passages like that because they cannot look up while playing."[10]

At the declaration "Oh, that we might hold it fast," orchestral forces press excitedly toward a symphonic climax, which begins the fourth section. The final choral section, inaugurated by an antiphonal "frenzied" outcry, "Father in Heaven!" fades gradually to a hum and continues with a quiet triple-choral passage accompanied by "very distant, if possible off-stage," bells. Finally the entire chorus, soloists, and orchestra come together for a "broad and straightforward" chorale of Barber's invention, only vaguely related to its predecessors in its modal character and asymmetrical meter.

The bells were of special concern to Barber. In the autumn of 1954, after his return from Paris and shortly before the first rehearsal, he wrote to Leonard Burkat (then artistic administrator of the Boston Symphony Orchestra and assistant to Charles Münch) specifying the effect he wished to achieve with the bells and why the incidental alto and tenor solo voices ought to be selected with care:

> I have two messages for M. Münch: I have worked with Leontyne on the solo and she does it beautifully. Tell him please that I hope the alto and tenor soloists are more than "adequate"; they come at a strategic place in the score and theoretically should have just as fine voices as Leontyne; so I hope that you have found two first-rate "church soloist" voices which can be fine in Boston, and have not just promoted a tenor eunuch or contralto Amazon from the ranks of the chorus! Ditto for New York; it would ruin it. I spoke to Perry about this last summer and he agreed.
>
> Münch mentioned the wonderful bells used for Berlioz to me. Although they are in C and G (if I recall) instead of E as in my score, I would like to suggest that we try them, placing the lower one well off-stage with an assistant conductor. It would be wonderful to have a really distant effect, like a monastery bell, an effect only approximated by tubular bells, I feel.[11]

The bells he referred to were real bells of cast iron that Münch had had built especially for his first Boston performance of *Symphonie fantastique* in 1950. Leonard Burkat reports that Barber transposed the score in order to use these bells in *Prayers of Kierkegaard.* A comparison of the sketchbook version and the Schirmer edition, however, suggests that the transposition may in fact have had nothing to do with the bell pitches since the change begins considerably before the bell passage; from after the trio solos (at no. 15) to the end of the piece everything was transposed up a whole tone, with the bell pitch remaining E in both scores. A letter from Barber to Strickland, written a year later, described the bells used for the premiere and indicates that the pitches were not of concern to Barber: *

> [At No. 27] we used two real bells, not tubulars (weight 250 lbs. each, any pitch will do) the lower in pitch should be off stage and the effect is wonderful if it can be off-stage to the opposite side of the on-stage bell (possible in Boston, not in Carnegie).[12]

The perfect fusion of musical and spiritual expression in this impassioned composition was recognized by Olin Downes in his perspicacious—even if effusive—review of the New York performance:

> The thought of the poetry, the attempt . . . of the music, is so far from dogma, so elemental, so Blake-like in conception and tonal design, that one

* Normally orchestras use tubular bells, even though they can only approximate the rich harmonies of real bells. The problem with heavy cast bells, in addition to their weight (often as much as twenty tons), is that they produce a "tap note" and a "hum note," which is about a major seventh below the tap note; such bells disturb and are disturbed by the harmonic scheme of the orchestra. The solution, according to Forsythe (*Orchestration,* 1914), is to use a heavy bell whose tap note is removed from the harmony of the orchestra. In this context, Barber's indifference to the pitch of the bells would be logical.

wonders whether many pages of the score are symbolic rather than expressive . . . of what cannot be communicated. But that quest on the part of a musician is a Research Magnificent, one to which, certainly, the composer has addressed himself, with all the sincerity and knowledge that he possesses.

. . . Free-metered recitation in carefully shaped recitative has the flavor of plainchant, reshaped, freely recast in forms of our own modern consciousness. Sometimes the music becomes nearly barbaric, and intensely dramatic in its effect. Polytonality is used freely, logically, with destination.

The instrumentation is intensely dramatic. The final chorale is no more an imitation of a Lutheran form, any more than the choral recitative comes from the Catholic direction. Universality is the suggestion, a universality that does not dismiss but includes inevitably the consciousness of the infinite mercy, the infinite tenderness, the cosmic design.[13]

Paul Henry Lang, too, found the "cantata" a "serious, moving, and convincing piece" and extolled Barber's impeccable craftsmanship, taste, good judgment, and adeptness at avoiding obvious climaxes by "landing on points of quiescence with stunning surprise." At a time when Romanticism was on the wane in America, Lang remarked about Barber's felicitous "harmonic idiom" and concluded, "He knows there is a good deal of life left in that outmoded tonal system and he uses it without fear. Yet he is ready to resort to twelve-tone writing."[14]

Lang's reservations about the performance itself—"not a distinguished one, the choral diction was often cloudy, the orchestra a bit raw, and the soloists, with the exception of Leontyne Price, timid"—suggest that Barber's cautionary note about the quality of the voices for the incidental parts was well founded. Nor was the composer especially happy about the Boston performance, and although he expected to make final corrections to the score before the New York concert, his plans were thwarted for lack of sufficient rehearsal time. In January 1955, in anticipation of a forthcoming performance of *Kierkegaard* in Vienna, Barber sent a lengthy list of remedial instructions to William Strickland:

> K. went well, but all performances were inadequate and Münch was disgusted with the chorus, inadequately rehearsed, both in Boston and N.Y. . . . In N.Y. the Schola rehearsed with the B.S.O. only at 7 p.m. the night of the performance! Therefore, I have to wait for Reiner and Chicago to make final corrections. *So* we are sending you a corrected vocal score (only pages 24, 25, 26, 27 have been changed). I removed the triplet figure before the climax, it was messy. In the orchestra, little change and you must put this in the fresh material sent to you today *yourself*. If I did not love you, I would call off your performance until after *Reiner*, so there.[15]

There followed twenty-six corrections to the score, many of which have since been incorporated into the published edition. Significantly, however, there were numerous suggestions involving performance practice:

> [13] Trombone I, muted—tempo here moves forward, rapturous. . . .
> [21] 3 after: Trb, cb, celli, the *cantus firmus* very sustained, big bows. . . .
> [24] timpani, *wild* with hard sticks (timpani part very hard, but possible). . . .
> [28] awfully tricky. Allargando molto. Münch subdivided and made it worse! From [27] to [29] should be a sort of *interior, individual* meditation. Legato, not rhythmic: they are apt to solfège it for accuracy unless they are damned sure of it. Perhaps the augmentations at [28] should predominate—no time for experiment in rehearsal here.*

Strickland canceled the Viennese performance of *Kierkegaard,* not to Barber's displeasure, for after further reflecting on the Boston and New York performances the composer had "lots more" to tell Strickland.[16] Evidently, the cancellation was related to Strickland's dissatisfaction with the quality of the performing capabilities of the group in Vienna. Barber was appreciative: "I am glad that your feelings of responsibility . . . to the work made you feel that it was better to call the whole thing off," he wrote to Strickland. "You are quite right and of course I do not want a second-class performance there."[17]

Barber, of course, did not want a second-class performance of *Prayers of Kierkegaard* anywhere. It was in Vienna, however, where *Kierkegaard* opened a three-week international festival of top-flight artists and orchestras from all over the world, that he heard finally what he considered the ultimate performance of his work.

Leaving New York on 26 April, Barber preceded the festival with five days of "tedious and disappointing" IMC meetings in Paris, about which he reported to his family:

> Gone, or going, is the aristocratic spirit and guidance of Honegger or Roland Manuel; a great deal of attention must be paid to the Philippine delegate, eager and rather shrewd; and to an Inter-Asia Conference. But all this becomes increasingly political, non-musical, and I wondered why I was here.
>
> In the evening I escaped to the theatre and saw a heart-breaking performance of Chekhov's "Three Sisters," done by the Pitoeffs, and also two evenings given by the Hamburg Opera Company, celebrated for their staging. I was impressed by "Wozzeck" done easily and effortlessly as if it were chamber music and, thus given, immensely effective; but by the second evening of Schoenberg and Dallapiccola—I was on to their stage tricks, which led all too directly back to the German 1920's, a style apparently suffocated by Hitler and now resuscitated, a little middle-aged and flaccid. On my last Sunday Chandler Cowles and Aaron Copland appeared as a surprise in my hotel room for breakfast and gossip.[18]

*Letter to Strickland, January 1955, from Capricorn. Barber also informed Strickland about the bells used for the first performances.

After the meetings he made a "dash off to Greece . . . alone, without musicians"—his bags filled with books that he had been reading about Greece since Christmas; he then understood the truth in Stephen Spender's off-hand comment, "All these books are bosh; the minute you are there you will understand Greece in a flash. It is in the air." "And it was," Barber wrote, "in that tenuous, intellectually-charged air. . . . Something of the civilizations once felt—the situation of a temple, an amphora, a verse, the light—follows one about forever after."[19]

The climax of Barber's tour was hearing *Kierkegaard* at last to his satisfaction. His vivid account of the rehearsal, sung in German under Massimo Freccia's direction, suggests what he hoped a performance would be:

> All the rest was such a wonderful experience for me that I even hesitate to report it. At the rehearsal that night, the chorus of almost two hundred sang with such fervor and impact, and Gueden . . . did the solo with such purity and perfection of style, her voice soaring and disembodied, more unearthly than Leontyne's: the orchestra fine, blending, intelligent; the German text apparently very good and convincing to the performers—all of these people performing my work moved me very deeply: I had no qualms about the performance.
>
> And Freccia, the conductor about whom I knew so little, had all the correct tempos and succeeded in creating a mystical and at the same time passionate atmosphere.[20]

He continued, poignantly:

> No more sufferings as I went through in Boston, New York, and even Chicago: here at last was my work as I meant it to be, the chorus dominating, shattering, moving: not stodgy and oratorio-like. The deep German basses and altos and the sopranos with body, like trumpets, not like Thomas Whitney Surrette recorders! I think I had never heard a work of mine in a foreign language before and that too encouraged me with a sense of power.*

The festival's ceremonial start offered much colorful fanfare. "*Our* Stokowski and Ormandy and the Philadelphia Orchestra" were participants, Barber wrote. The concert hall was resplendent with searchlights and flags of all nations, similar to a Salzburg Festival opening; the stage was decorated with flowers, and even the singers' music had been bound in black for the solemn occasion—"very Austrian," he thought.

> There was an air of great expectation and a packed house while the mayor of Vienna and two other government officials made the opening speeches.

* Barber's travel log, p. 7. The Schirmer edition of *Prayers of Kierkegaard* includes both English and German texts. While there were at this time numerous foreign editions of Barber's instrumental music, there were none of his vocal works. Plans for a French edition of *Knoxville* were eventually considered but evidently never implemented.

A little long perhaps, but it only made the audience desire the music—any music—all the more. Then a long pause, Freccia came out, and the *Prayers* began, the male chorus alone, *pianissimo* and distant, until the orchestra entered and augmented and then the whole chorus came on that D minor chord like a thunder clap: "Nichts aber wandelt Dich!" At the end of the chorale a long silence before the applause began.

I was sitting in a box with Mrs. Freccia, Mrs. Brailowsky (he [Alexander] was soloist), and [Zino] Francescatti, the violinist, and bowed several times before I was called to the stage. They said it was one of the biggest successes for a new work in a long time in Vienna. And that the audience had given so much to *Kierkegaard* that Brailowsky, a Viennese favorite, who followed in the Chopin Concerto, supposedly to "save" the program, had only a token success.

And how I wished some of you had been with me; there was no one I cared a fig about to hear it! No American friends at all.[21]

After Vienna, there was a performance in London. "Here I went to fewer rehearsals," he wrote, "for I felt I could trust Freccia and I wanted to see my friends and did; I enjoyed so much the comfy sense of British wit not unmixed with brilliance"—the Spenders, John Craxton, Cyril Connolly, and Alan Pryce-Jones.[22] But the London performance of *Prayers*, with the exception of the chorus, seemed an anticlimax to the brilliance of Vienna:

I share (with Aunt Louise—in her case, from Covent Garden days) an ingrained Yankee distrust of British music-making—by that I mean great music-making in a really ineluctable sense—so was not surprised or alarmed when a quavering hooty, high-churchy voice with an Estelle Winwood accent sang the solo I had recently heard so caressingly sung by Gueden. But the solo is short and the Philharmonic Choir, 300 strong, was stunning; the basses fine, with superb diction, and the London Philharmonic technically better than the Vienna Orchestra.

The new Festival Hall I had not seen and did not like much. There are four restaurants and five bars, and it is super-modern with great glass windows looking out on the Thames. Too exhibition-hallish; it makes you want to row, not come to listen; there is no recueillement. But it is superbly equipped and imposing. . . . The boxes jut out insolently into the space generally reserved for the music vibrations—i.e., over the audience's heads, like an archeological drawing of the various strata in the interior of a pyramid! The acoustics not as bad as contemporary architects generally devise, but my ears longed for the seasoned and yielding wooden resonance of Vienna. Such an anachronism, I thought—using warm old Italian stringed instruments on the stage, with the ultimate refinement of wood, and expecting them to sound in a hall of cold cement and steel.[23]

The hall, however, was packed, and the performance "moving, spacious, less frenzied, perhaps more Handelian than Vienna," Barber thought.[24]

The glow of the Vienna and London performances lingered with Barber for some time. From Italy—where he had settled himself for the summer with the intention of working on *Vanessa*—he wrote to Olga Koussevitzky, the conductor's widow:

> Just a line to tell you of the quite exceptional success of "Prayers of Kierkegaard" in London and Vienna (particularly the latter, where it opened the Festival). In both places the chorus was superb (Singakademie of 175 in Vienna, and Philharmonic choir of 300 in London) and had a dramatic effect it did *not* have in America. . . . I wish you had been [there] for you would have been happy! I was.
>
> I shall miss hearing the Berkshire performance: it would have pleased me to hear it sung by young people and I hope there will be many of them!*

In an almost identical letter to Münch, he added: "I am still hoping that you, who were such a wonderful 'papa' to this work at its birth, will present the work in Paris and am reserving French premiere for your performance whenever you wish. Von Karajan has programmed it for Rome and Berlin."[25] Having the benefit of the European performances behind him, Barber—writing from Capri—advised Münch, "There are still one or two minor modifications which I bring to your attention." These few alterations (see facsimile below), which have been incorporated in the published score, have to do with performance practice.

Summer Music for Woodwind Quintet, Op. 31 (1955), and "Horizon"

In 1953 Barber was commissioned by the Chamber Music Society of Detroit to write a septet for three woodwinds, three strings, and piano. It would be performed by first-desk players of the Detroit Symphony Orchestra in fall 1954 in honor of the society's tenth anniversary season.[26] The commission gained nationwide attention as the first ever to be financed by public subscription. Barber agreed to set aside his usual fee, accepting instead the proceeds of a "pay what you can" collection from audience contributions, most falling between $1 and $5, with the society acting as guarantor for $2,000. The composer recalled:

> The idea was that if this caught on, music societies around the country would take up similar collections and use the funds to commission young local composers who needed experience and exposure. I made a speech against myself, essentially, telling them it was crazy that they didn't use

*Letter, 29 June 1955, from Capri, Italy (Serge Koussevitzky Collection, Library of Congress, Music Division). In this letter, also, is a brief paragraph on musical politics: "As my term on the I.M.C. soon expires . . . I proposed the nomination of Aaron Copland as President of the Board and hope he will accept. Among other reasons, it would be a fine tie-up with your Foundation." The plan never materialized.

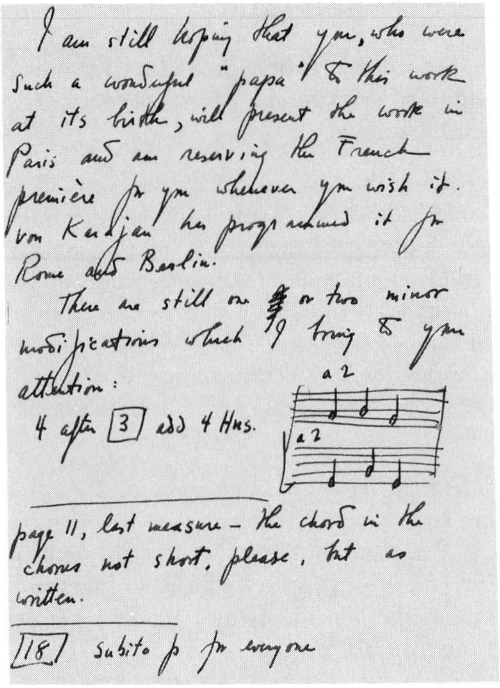

I am still hoping that you, who were such a wonderful "papa" to this work at its birth, will present the work in Paris and am reserving the French première for you whenever you wish it. von Karajan has programmed it for Rome and Berlin.

There are still one or two minor modifications which I bring to your attention:

4 after [3] add 4 Hns.

a 2

a 2

---

page 11, last measure – the chord in the chorus not short, please, but as written.

---

[18] subito *p* for everyone

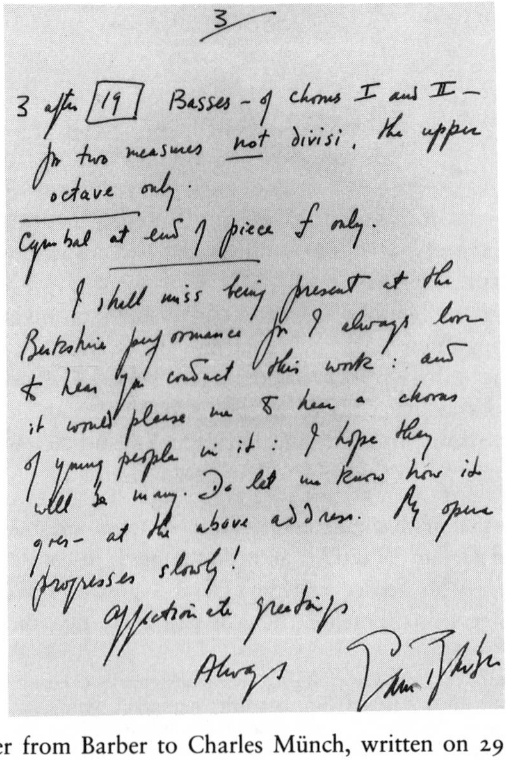

3

3 after [19] Basses – of chorus I and II – for two measures <u>not</u> divisi, the upper octave only.

Cymbal at end of piece *f* only.

I shall miss being present at the Berkshire performance for I always love to hear you conduct this work: and it would please me to hear a chorus of young people in it: I hope they will be many. Do let me know how it goes – at the above address. My opera progresses slowly!

Affectionate greetings

Always

Sam Barber

Excerpt of letter from Barber to Charles Münch, written on 29 June 1955 from Capri. *(Yale University Music Library, Leonard Burkat Papers)*

> local composers. It was certainly done in Bach's day. But they didn't like that idea. They wanted the same old tired names—Copland, Sessions, Harris, me—so it never got off the ground.*

Reportedly, Barber had accepted the commission because it involved an instrumentation for which there was virtually no available literature.[27] The composer's concept of the ensemble, however, underwent several stages, producing in the end his only quintet, *Summer Music,* Op. 31.

For *Summer Music* Barber drew on thematic material from a work he had written almost a decade earlier, "Horizon." Early in 1945 he had been asked to compose an orchestral piece based on Arabian themes for "The Standard Oil Hour," an NBC radio series broadcast during the mid-forties and the fifties. This still unpublished work was played by the San Francisco Symphony Orchestra under Efrem Kurtz and broadcast over the NBC network 17 June 1945.† "Horizon," about seven minutes in duration, is in one movement, seventy-four measures in length. It is scored for a large orchestra of woodwinds, two horns, trumpet, timpani, harp, and stringed instruments but is unusually transparent in texture compared to Barber's other orchestral music. For the Detroit Chamber Music Society commission in 1956, Barber borrowed the opening seven measures of "Horizon"—transposing the repeated tritone interval C and G♭ up a step to D and G♯. Whereas in "Horizon" these few measures had generated thematic material for the whole composition, that is not the case in *Summer Music* (see Example 13.2a and b). Another borrowing from "Horizon" was the violin solo at measure 18, which in *Summer Music* is given a contrapuntal elaboration for flute and bassoon (Example 13.3). Although the performance forces vastly differ, there are similarities between the two works: they are rhapsodic in character, modal, and somewhat French in style—"Horizon," in particular, has passages that sound vaguely like Debussy.

Barber's composition of *Summer Music* went beyond the thematic borrowings or reworkings of the earlier work, however. A stipulation of the Detroit Chamber Music Society's commission was that the published edition must bear an inscription to the Chamber Music Society of Detroit and name the musicians who performed the premiere. Although the Schirmer score credits the Detroit ensemble, in fact Barber composed *Summer Music* with the New York Woodwind Quintet in mind and with their coopera-

* Allan Kozinn, "Samuel Barber: The Last Interview and the Legacy," part 1, p. 46. Although the Chamber Music Society of Detroit, founded in 1943, had afforded Detroit audiences a first hearing of works by such local composers as Ross Lee Finney, Leslie Bassett, and Bernhard Heiden, and between 1945 and 1955 had given Detroit premieres of twenty-five works, including those by Bloch, Dohnányi, Loeffler, Milhaud, Poulenc, Prokofiev, and Villa-Lobos, the work by Barber was the first commission they ever offered.

† Letter, Dan Stehman to the author, 7 April 1988, Los Angeles Valley College, Van Nuys. On the same program, which took place at the NBC studios in San Francisco, was a new work by Roy Harris titled "Mirage." A recording of the program made on 17 December 1945 (loaned to the author by Manfred Ibel) was probably a rebroadcast. A holograph of "Horizon" is at the Library of Congress, Music Division.

Example 13.2a "Horizon," mm. 1–8, holograph, 1945. *(Library of Congress)*

tion. The omission of a dedicatee in the Schirmer edition is probably not an oversight; rather it may have been Barber's way of tacitly acknowledging the New York group's participation in the course of the compositional process, much in the same way as Orlando Cole and Raya Garbousova had, many years earlier, witnessed the birth of Barber's works for cello.*

*Much to their credit, within the first few years after its founding in 1947, the New York Woodwind Quintet—Samuel Baron (flute), Jerome Roth (oboe), David Glazer (clarinet), Bernard Garfield (bassoon), and John Barrows (French horn)—had brought to audiences an extensive repertoire of woodwind music hitherto unknown or neglected. Regarded highly by numerous composers, by 1954 the group had already been the recipient of several Coolidge Foundation commissions, and a substantial library of chamber music for woodwind instruments had been composed for their ensemble. For them Elliott Carter wrote his *Eight Etudes and a Fantasy* (1951); they premiered Meyer Kupferman's Quintet for Woodwinds and Piano and played works by such contemporary composers as Irving Fine, Hindemith, Françaix, Schuller, Riegger, Etler, and Bergsma. Villa-Lobos coached them in rehearsals of his woodwind quintet.

Summer Music

for Woodwind Quintet

Samuel Barber, Op. 31

Note: This score is written without transposition; parts, however, are transposed for B♭ Clarinet and Horn in F. Passages enclosed in [ ] to the fore.

Example 13.2b *Summer Music,* Op. 31, mm. 1–4 (G. Schirmer, 1957).

Barber first heard the New York Woodwind Quintet during the summer of 1954 at the seacoast village of Blue Hill, Maine.* Deeply engrossed in composing the music for the first scene of *Vanessa,* with only a partially finished libretto at hand, he had still not begun the Detroit commission.

* The program for this concert on 1 August 1954 included Beethoven's Quintet, Op. 71a, Milhaud's *La Cheminée du Roi René,* Vivaldi's Concerto in G minor (for flute, oboe, and bassoon), Irving Fine's Partita (1948), and an arrangement (R. Taylor) of Bartók's Suite of Children's Pieces (Samuel Baron, unpublished journal of the New York Woodwind Quintet, 1954 season, pp. 67–68, Samuel Baron Collection, Library of Congress, Music Division).

“Horizon,” mm. 18–25.

Example 13.3 *Summer Music,* 2 mm. after 18.

His work on the opera was interrupted because his librettist, Menotti, was called to New York to produce his own opera. Needing to work on the Detroit commission—and impressed with the quintet's performance at Blue Hill—Barber asked French horn player John Barrows and flutist Samuel Baron if he might sit in on their rehearsals in New York and if they would be willing to play sections of a new *sextet* he was in the process of writing. This recollection of Baron's suggests that Barber was still undecided then about the forces he planned to use for the commission.

Barber first met with the quintet on 12 January 1955 in John Barrows's apartment in Greenwich Village. The ensemble was rehearsing a work by Villa-Lobos and also played some intonation studies that Barrows had designed specifically for the group.[28] He had made an extensive chart incorporating a staff line for every pitch from the lowest to uppermost notes of each instrument; from this it was possible to see at a glance the overlapping of ranges. Each player had "characterized" every note within the range of his particular instrument: was it naturally flat or sharp on the instrument? dull or brilliant? did it behave differently if it was played loudly or softly? From their observations, Barrows composed a series of studies using the "worst" chords—those where tone production and intonation were accomplished with great difficulty but resulted in sonorities that were especially effective. The group practiced these etudes, some of which were only four or five measures long, in order to master the more difficult chords. During the rehearsal, Barber "listened avidly, made notes on Barrows's notes," and borrowed the chart to study at home.[29]

Eight months later he notified the group that he had nearly finished a woodwind quintet—not the sextet originally proposed—and asked if they would like to rehearse a portion of it the following week.[30] On 14 November at a late-evening rehearsal at CBS studios, after the quintet practiced works by Poulenc and Mozart with pianist Vera Brodsky, Barber led them through a reading of *Summer Music*. Afterwards, Baron recorded his colleagues' reactions to the music:

> We were completely gassed! What a wonderful new quintet conception. Barber has studied our charts and has written some of our favorite effects. The piece is very hard, but so far it sounds just beautiful to us.
>
> A slight pall was cast when Barber told us that we could not play the piece until after March 20, 1956, at which time it will be played in Detroit. We had hoped to do it in Washington.[31]

The "favorite effects" Baron spoke of are also the most difficult chords in *Summer Music* and do reflect the influence of Barrows's studies: for example, the passage of five choralelike measures beginning at rehearsal no. 23 (see Example 13.4*). Here, the flute's D♭ is most unsympathetic to execute (and is, perhaps not without coincidence, the enharmonic equiva-

Example 13.4 *Summer Music,* 23–24. Asterisks mark chords suggested by John Barrows's chart.

lent of the same breathy note used by Debussy for the magical opening of his Prelude to *Afternoon of a Faun*); on the oboe, D♭ tends to be squawky; similarly, G♭ is a stubborn note for the bassoon to play. This measure, followed by a *subito piano* on another difficult chord (one measure after rehearsal no. 23; see Example 13.4**), is a demanding passage and has the effect of stopping the motion almost completely.

Throughout the winter of 1956, after their initial meeting with Barber, the New York Woodwind Quintet continued to practice several passages of *Summer Music* with the hope of giving the first performance at their New York concert early in April.[32] In mid-February Baron made the following entry in his journal:

> Today we rehearsed at Music House from 10 to 12:30. We did about an hour on the Françaix (or Anthrax, as it is now called) and then started to work on the Barber.
>
> This rehearsal was distinguished by the presence of Barber and Gian-

> Carlo Menotti who drove in from Mount Kisco to hear us. We played the piece fairly well—not great, just fair—but we really learned a lot when Barber gave us the correct tempos and touched up certain little spots. It started to sound extremely good after a while.
>
> We made a tentative appointment to play the piece for Barber up at Mount Kisco March 15 or thereabouts.*

At this rehearsal Barber tended to favor generally increased tempos for the faster sections.† The rehearsal also provided an opportunity to adjust the notation in the more technically difficult passages. Comparisons between holographs of *Summer Music* (at the Library of Congress and in Baron's collection) and the published edition (1957) illuminate the progress of Barber's original conception of the work to its final version. For example, according to Baron, four measures before rehearsal no. 26 Barber had originally written the clarinet arpeggio in thirty-second notes, like the bassoon and flute parts, which both double-tongue the passage. Because this is technically impractical for the clarinet, he experimented by adding neighbor notes (Example 13.5a, holograph). He later rejected that version in favor of adding a horn part, double-tongued, the clarinet playing sixteenth notes for the first half of the measure, then tonguing very fast for the remainder of the measure (see Example 13.5b, at asterisk). Nevertheless, the passage is still difficult to play cleanly even for the most veteran performer.

The premiere of *Summer Music* took place at the Detroit Institute of Arts on 20 March 1956, during the twelfth season of the Chamber Music Society. Broad newspaper coverage was given to the event because of the precedent-breaking method of raising money for the commission, and over the several years since the work had been planned many subscribers had voiced proprietary sentiments: "When will *our* composition be played?"[33] Attention was also given to the fact that the piece would be played twice at the concert—an innovation at that time. Performed immediately after intermission and again at the conclusion of the concert by first-desk members of the Detroit Symphony Orchestra—James Pellerite, flute; Arno Mariotti, oboe; Albert Luconi, clarinet; Charles Sirard, bassoon; and Ray Alonge,

* Baron, unpublished journal, 13 February 1956. In fact this private concert did not take place until April, after the Detroit premiere of the quintet.

† In a flute part used by Baron, the tempo at rehearsal no. 5, for example, was changed from "Somewhat faster (♩=66)," to merely "faster" with a metronome marking of 80; at rehearsal no. 7 the metronome marking was increased from 92 to 96; and at rehearsal no. 19, "slightly faster (♩=72)" was changed to "faster (♩=92)." At rehearsal no. 11, where the holograph showed a metronome marking of ♩=66, the flute part was changed to ♩=80 (as it appears in the 1957 edition). In addition, Barber added tempo and expression markings as well as precise metronome markings in numerous other places. Although some of these appear in the 1957 edition, some do not and probably reflect Barber's performance practice suggestions to the New York Woodwind Quintet: at rehearsal no. 23, for example, there is a pencil inscription requesting that the chords be played "a little sustained."

a.

b.

Example 13.5 *Summer Music,* revisions of clarinet part, 4 mm. before 26. *a.* Holograph. *(Library of Congress) b.* Final version (G. Schirmer, 1957).

French horn—*Summer Music* shared a program with Beethoven's Op. 11 for clarinet, cello, and piano and Poulenc's Sextet for piano, flute, oboe, clarinet, bassoon, and horn.[34]

The Detroit critic Josef Mossman marked the warm response of the local audience, who were charmed by the new quintet's "mood of pastoral serenity" and the "highly skilled performance" and who responded even more enthusiastically to the second hearing. *Summer Music* was credited with being a "chamber work of both beauty and humor."[35]

After hearing the premiere, however, Barber reassessed the work as too long and decided to make cuts, the most substantial being one of eighteen measures near the end of the piece at rehearsal no. 13; this included a six-measure repeat of the chorale passage.* In preparation for a private con-

*Baron's journal entry of 5 April 1956 describes the cut, which had been made in two stages. These can be seen clearly from comparing the holograph at the Library of Congress with Baron's copy of the flute part and with the 1957 edition.

cert at Menotti's studio at 160 West 73rd Street, New York, on 5 April 1956, the New York Woodwind Quintet continued to rehearse *Summer Music*, timing its duration at twelve and a half minutes with the changes Barber had suggested. The consensus of the group, however, was that they preferred to play the piece without the second cut because it contained some of their favorite chords from John Barrows's etudes. Baron wrote of the musical soirée in his journal:

> Present were Barber, Menotti, David Hall and his wife, Jim Maher, Alfred Breuning, Walter Trampler, Ezra Laderman, and other people that are friends of ours, Barber's, or Menotti's.* It was an informal and friendly atmosphere, but not without tension for us. We played the "Summer Music" twice—once with the cuts Barber had asked us to do, and the second time without making one cut (31 to 33) which we preferred. Finally Barber was able to make up his mind on this cut and on other small compositional matters. I think the piece is now in its final form.†
>
> Everybody expressed great delight with the composition and most people were very impressed with the way we played it. David Hall is interested in recording it, however, he made no offers or promises.[36]

The New York Woodwind Quintet played *Summer Music* at two concerts on their Boston tour—at a member dinner-concert at the Harvard Musical Association, 27 April 1956, and at Radcliffe College two days later. By the time they played it in New York at Carnegie Recital Hall on 16 November 1956, they had performed it widely, including fifteen times on their three-month tour of South America.‡

Music critics have, from its earliest performances, found attractive *Summer Music*'s nocturnal, romantic language. The work was seen as more than a retrospective effort by Harold Schonberg, who after the first New York performance assessed the music as "very much of our day" because of "clever rhythmic shifts and sharp-sounding harmonics."[37] Oliver Daniel, in his review of the first recording of *Summer Music* by the New York Woodwind Quintet in 1959, welcomed Barber's diatonic lyricism as "a soothing contrast to the more naughty world of many of his dodecaphonic confrères."[38] Moreover, at a time when academic experimentation was in full force, Daniel heard Barber's music as a genuine case for expressiveness:

*Hall was a critic and director of Mercury Records; Jim Maher, a novelist and private collector of woodwind music; Breuning, a violinist; Trampler, a violist; and Laderman, a composer.

†The twelve-measure cut at rehearsal no. 31 was made after this meeting and prior to publication.

‡Baron's schedule of programs indicates this record was surpassed only by the number of times they had played Beethoven's Op. 71a.

a.

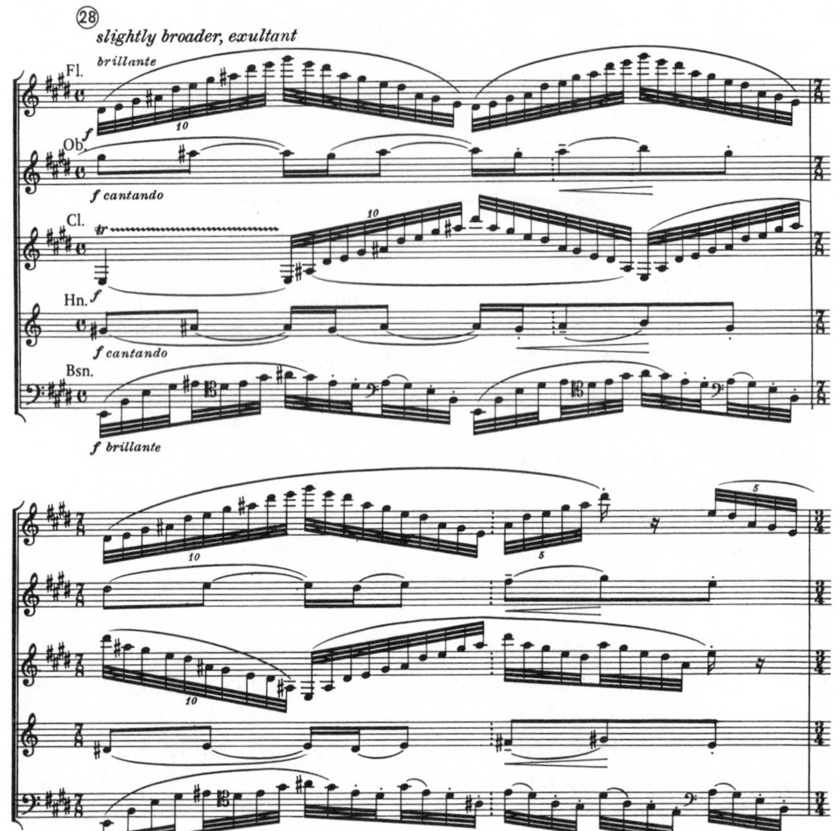

Example 13.6 Similarities between Barber's *Summer Music* and Jean Françaix's woodwind quintet. *a. Summer Music,* at 28. *b.* Jean Françaix, *Quintette,* end of first movement.

> The climate of Samuel Barber's "Summer Music" is more that of where fancy is bred. It sounds. It is not an intellectualized score, and its climax soars in a "slightly broader, exultant" passage that builds without obvious calculation. Its title is apt and the seeds of lyricism here are more those of a summer's languor than of academic agitation.[39]

Summer Music, in one continuous movement and rhapsodic in character, stands apart from other woodwind compositions of its period, which tend to be in three or four movements of traditional formal design. The music is quiet and contemplative, incorporating the wit and chatter of the French school of woodwind writing but without its stridency (see, for example, nos. 5–14). Indeed, the climactic contrary-motion arpeggios at rehearsal no. 28 may have been inspired by the woodwind quintet of Jean

b.

Fl.
Ob.
Cl.
Bsn.
Hn.

fff
f *sempre cresc.*
fff
fff
fff

8
pp *fff* *secco*
fff
pp *secco*
pp *fff* *secco*
pp *fff secco*
tr
pp *fff secco*

B·S·S 37495

a.

Paul Hindemith, *Kleine Kammermusik*, Op. 24, No. 2.

b.

Example 13.7 Similarities between Barber's *Summer Music* and Hindemith's quintet. *a.* Paul Hindemith, *Kleine Kammermusik*, Op. 24, No. 2, first movement, mm. 52–53. *b. Summer Music*, 3 mm. after [26].

Françaix that Barber heard rehearsed by the New York Woodwind Quintet at the time he was writing *Summer Music* (see Example 13.6).

The quintet's repertoire also included, during this period, Paul Hindemith's *Kleine Kammermusik*, Op. 24, No. 2, in which an arpeggiated chord of fourths is remarkably similar to a passage in *Summer Music* (see Example 13.7).

Because of the indolent mood and abrupt ending of the piece, which falls undramatically upon the ear, *Summer Music* seems best positioned in the middle of the first half of a program or as the first work after an intermission. Barber had his own ideas about its performance: "*Do not play it too slowly,*" he warned a young student clarinetist from South Wales, who asked for other pieces Barber wrote for his instrument.* He addressed himself to the subject of tempo more fully in an interview with Allan Kozinn:

> It's supposed to be *evocative* of summer—summer meaning languid, not [clapping hands loudly] killing mosquitoes. Henry Cowell once wrote a piece in which the orchestra members had to clap their hands in that fashion—"brilliant innovation," the critics called it. But all I can say about *Summer Music* is that everybody plays it too slowly. Which leads certain charming colleagues of mine to come up with real mean remarks. Two of them—one of our better-known composers and one L. F. [Lukas Foss] from Brooklyn—once told me they heard a performance that dragged so, it should have been called *Winter Music.*[40]

*Letter from Barber to Jonathan Williams, 26 October 1961. At the time most of his music—but nothing for solo clarinet—was available at Chappell's, New Bond Street, London. "Some day maybe," he wrote Williams.

14

VANESSA

At last, an American grand opera!

When it was performed on 23 January 1958, Barber's opera *Vanessa* was the first new American work produced by the Metropolitan Opera since 1947 and only the twentieth since the opening of the opera house in 1883.* The weight of its historical position caused the critic Howard Taubman to observe: "What a spot for *Vanessa*! When the Met finally gets around to an American opera, it is as if the honor of the nation as well as the health of the box office depended on the man who had the temerity to create the piece."[1]

The Met's longstanding resistance to American opera is apparent from William Schuman's letter to Barber after he learned that *Vanessa* would be produced:

> My joy goes beyond the natural pride in the work of an esteemed colleague and concerns my affiliation with the Met as a director. Attempts I have made in the past to get the management interested in contemporary opera in general and contemporary American opera in particular met with absolutely no success.[2]

A letter from Barber to Scalero written in mid-February 1952—ironically, only two months before Barber settled on Menotti as his librettist—suggests, moreover, that the Met commission was a sign of a renewed enchantment with opera in general in the United States:

> Orchestra concerts . . . are fast losing their glamour and we hardly ever go; no more great conductors, and a shrinking repertoire; and there is great interest in opera, all over the country, not to be thought of twenty years ago. I would love to find a libretto, but cannot.

* Bernard Rogers's *The Warrior* was produced on 11 January 1947 and won the Alice M. Ditson Award, but was short-lived.

With his reputation secure as a composer of absolute music, Barber had taken two decades to find a libretto before beginning his first effort for the lyric theater. When asked why he delayed so long in writing his first opera, he reflected:

> During the thirty years that I have been going to opera, all the time I have thought seriously about it. But before I wrote one, I wanted to make a long-term preparation for the job. This meant working in all concomitant techniques necessary for opera writing. That is, how to write for orchestra, how to write for chorus and ballet, how to write for solo voice and orchestra. When I had learned that, I was ready.[3]

Barber's quest for the "right" libretto began as far back as 1934, when he wrote to Scalero that he was "anxious to attempt" an opera on an American libretto. In 1942 he was offered commissions for two operas; he declined one, from the Metropolitan Opera, because they insisted on a libretto by Christopher La Farge that Barber found "uninspiring."* Serge Koussevitzky commissioned him to write a chamber opera for the Berkshire Festival with no restrictions on his choice of libretto. Dame Edith Sitwell introduced him to Dylan Thomas, a poet Barber greatly admired. The two talked at great length about opera, and Thomas agreed to write a libretto. When World War II broke out, communications between Barber in the United States and Thomas in England were interrupted.[4] Mary Bok Zimbalist offered to bring the poet to the United States so that librettist and composer might move ahead with their work, but Thomas became a fire fighter in London and Barber was drafted into the U.S. Army. On the eve of his induction, Barber wrote to Koussevitzky of the aborted plans for an opera:

> I am a private in the Army, and leave tomorrow for service—I have no idea where I shall be stationed. I was already in correspondence with a librettist [Thomas] for the opera and eager to finish it for next summer, but I am afraid that is no longer possible.[5]

After the war Bruno Walter was so taken with conducting the Symphony in One Movement that he offered to accept any opera the young composer wrote for production even before seeing the score.[6] At the same time, the management of the Metropolitan Opera began to express interest in an opera by Barber. By then his popularity with audiences and the frequency with which his music was programmed suggested that any opera he wrote would hold considerable box office appeal.†

*Letter, Barber to Katherine Garrison Chapin, 22 March 1942. La Farge (1897–1956) was an American poet who wrote novels in verse.

†In one week of December 1944 in New York, for example, the *Second Essay* was performed twice, conducted by Szell and Ormandy; Horowitz played *Excursions*. The Cello Concerto was nearly completed, and a month earlier Barber had conducted some of the best players from the Chicago Symphony in *Capricorn Concerto,* which met with success with the

Koussevitzky continued to prod the composer about his plans for an opera: "Hope the librettist you are considering will have a brilliant libretto to show you for your future opera. I am greatly interested in it as you know."* Barber answered:

> Very shortly I hope to begin setting the libretto. My librettist has seen Graf several times and he seems to like it very much. I am reserving my own decision until it is complete, but have very high hopes.†

Five months later, he wrote again to Koussevitzky: "I have had to abandon the opera, as the libretto was not to my satisfaction. I shall look for another, and it is so difficult to find anything! Most of the young writers have lost their sense of the stage."‡

A year and a half later there was still no libretto. By now Barber was busy with revisions of the Second Symphony, and Eleanor Steber had asked him to compose something for her for voice and orchestra. "The opera is still talk so far," he wrote to Homer, "but I'm negotiating a libretto."[7]

He had approached Thornton Wilder about a text, but their lengthy discussions too led nowhere. Barber told about his meetings with Wilder to Hans Heinsheimer:

> I knew him somehow better than I ever knew Dylan Thomas. I remember especially one summer in Guilford, Connecticut. We went there to visit him. He had a great deal to drink, and then he would read sections from *Finnegans Wake* and explain them to us. He was a great admirer of the work, and he also talked a lot about Lope de Vega. The next day we took a long walk—there is a kind of mountain there—we walked for hours and I tried to pin him down on an opera. "I cannot propose a plot," he kept saying, "I don't work that way." I said, "Thornton, I have to have something to go on. I cannot go on strings of words." But he was very much influenced by *Finnegan* at that time and said again and again, "No, no, I can't do it. My plays grow out of their own words." It all didn't seem very promising to me. He later did an opera with Louise Talma on a Greek subject, *Alcestis*§—at least there was a subject—but my talks with him didn't strike any fire, so it all came to nothing.[8]

---

public and the press (letter from Barber to Koussevitzky, 27 November 1944, from Capricorn).

*Letter to Barber, 30 October 1944. By this time, the commission for an opera offered by the Koussevitzky Foundation was extended from its original date of 1942; it was fulfilled in 1954 as *Prayers of Kierkegaard* (Library of Congress, Koussevitzky Collection, Box 254).

†Letter to Koussevitzky, 27 November 1944, from Capricorn. Herbert Graf was stage director at the Metropolitan Opera House from 1936 to 1949.

‡Letter, 21 April 1945, from Capricorn. The libretto he rejected may have been the one by a "socially prominent friend of an influential member of the Met board." "A composer must make his own choice," he said about turning down the $5,000 commission (Barber, "On Waiting for a Libretto," p. 6).

§*The Alcestiad*, 1955–56.

Another person with whom Barber broached the operatic subject was James Agee, whom he saw frequently during the years following the success of *Knoxville*. Barber recalled:

> He had certain ideas that were interesting, but could never get them down on paper. I used to have lunch with him once every two weeks or so and ask him, "How old are you today?" because he was then writing *A Death in the Family*. He was twelve years old, then fourteen, and finally he got to be fifteen, but he never seemed to get any older. I teased him about that, and he would laugh and say, "There is so much, Sam, so much to be written." But I never could pin him down. Then he became awfully interested in films.[9]

Also, at various times, poet Stephen Spender and Barber discussed opera subjects, and although Spender was very interested in the idea, no libretto developed.[10] Barber did not believe that an ordinary play could be put to music, and so when someone suggested making an opera out of Tennessee Williams's *A Streetcar Named Desire,* he responded:

> The play has marvelous situations—a trio in one room and a quartet in another—but the texture of the poetic language of Tennessee Williams is adequate in itself, and leaves no room for music. Music acts very quickly and can set a scene and atmosphere in a very few seconds, whereas a play needs more time and more words. With a few chords, Verdi sets a scene, with one or two *Ti amo*'s and *Amore, Amore,* we have an aria. Music makes everything move very quickly. Most librettos are entirely too wordy. That is why I say that in this day, when everyone is looking for new American librettists, there should be new relationships between writers and opera houses. . . . Writers must get the feel of the lyric stage—the real smell of the stage. One must be a habitué of the opera, like Stendhal at La Scala. It has always seemed curious to me that he never wrote an opera libretto.[11]

A logical conclusion to Barber's search culminated in his backyard, as it were, during the spring of 1952 when, upon returning from a visit to Sidney Homer, he announced to his uncle:

> Do you remember mentioning the short story of Tolstoi about the cobbler as a possible opera text? I was amused to read in last week's *Times* that Martinů, the Czech composer, is using it. Do you know what I think will finally happen? Gian Carlo has offered to write me a libretto and will submit a couple of scenes first to see if I like it; if not, no harm done and he won't mind; of course, we will discuss the story together. This may or may not be a good idea; certainly his knowledge of the stage is tremendous, and if we can hit on a subject which would interest us both, who can tell? Anyway it is a great secret, and you are the first person I have told.[12]

The following letter from Homer seems to mark a dichotomy between the older composer and his nephew:

> I heard some of Gian Carlo's opera last night. This is the kind of story I do not like. I believe the most impressive plots are those which are most true to life and could most truly and easily happen. I believe the modern mind wants truth and no deception, dust, or camouflage. I wish you would read Truman's speech to Congress in January of 1951 in which he speaks of the Point IV program and then read some articles on the subject. The librarian at the Public Library will find it for you. This subject is attracting world-wide attention. It is so simple, so needed, yet so full of infinite possibilities. Opposition has already sprung up.
>
> The idea is to lift the standard of living in all backward countries by teaching them modern methods of production. It has appealed to the general imagination. It is a magnificent conception, and there are men working on it in all parts of the world. I know great art works will come from it.*

It would seem that compared to his nephew, the eighty-eight-year-old Homer was considerably more modern and forward looking, almost prophesying operas that would be written later by John Adams and Philip Glass. While Barber's music by this time had taken on a cast of modernism in fusing twentieth-century elements with traditional harmony, his ultimate choice of a libretto—a subject of the heart rather than of contemporary history—reinforced his pattern of insulation and maintained his profile as a conservative.

Since 1938, when the Metropolitan Opera production of Menotti's youthful opera buffa, *Amelia Goes to the Ball,* thrust him brilliantly upon the operatic scene, Menotti had come to be regarded as the foremost American operatic composer.† But he had never before written a libretto for which he did not write the music, and even though Barber could not have been happier with his friend's offer, the collaboration was approached cautiously by both men. "We had the usual suspicions that very good friends have about each other," Barber remembered. "I wondered if he would really do it. He wondered if I really could do it."[13] Menotti, when asked what makes one composer write a text for another, answered:

> First of all, you must admire the composer. And that was easy enough for me; I have admired Sam Barber's music since we were students together at the Curtis Institute of Music. Secondly, you must *love* the composer, because, believe me, it is rather heartbreaking to give up a libretto to another composer, particularly if you happen to like the libretto yourself.
>
> Thirdly, you must be *pestered* by the composer, almost daily. I don't

*Letter, 6 April 1952, from Winter Park. Although *The Consul* had been recorded at this time, the content of Homer's letter suggests that he referred not to that opera (which deals with a contemporary subject) but an earlier one, perhaps *The Medium.*

†Shortly after Barber and Menotti had met at the Curtis Institute, they made a "sort of a blood pact" that neither one would ever write an opera. Menotti, of course, was the first to "betray" their agreement (Barber, "On Waiting for a Libretto," p. 5).

> know how severely Verdi harassed poor Boito, but I can assure you that Sam haunted me in my dreams until the very last words of the opera were written.*

Not being bound by the restrictions of a commission, they felt utterly free in their choice of time and place for their story. After discussing many ideas together, Barber and Menotti settled on a story that was admittedly inspired by Isak Dinesen's stories, in particular her *Seven Gothic Tales.* "I felt that the atmosphere of . . . any one of them would make a wonderful opera," Menotti recalled. "How did I happen to choose such a theme? Because I was writing a libretto for Sam, and Sam is essentially a romantic personality. Italians aren't really, you know. They act in a romantic way, but they are really skeptics at heart."[14]

Feeling that the Gothic flavor called for a European setting, Barber acknowledged "we allowed ourself the same freedom that Mozart, Verdi, and Puccini did—we picked an exotic scene."[15] Another reason Menotti chose a European setting was because his text was poetry or quasi-poetry and he felt it would be difficult for him to do it in American dialogue. When called upon to defend their choice of location for an "American" opera, Barber responded:

> Again the question of American subject matter comes up, but I don't see any reason why it always does. After all, the Puccini operas and most of Verdi's, although Italian, are located outside of Italy. . . . An opera need not have an American setting to be an American opera. Besides, art is international, and if an idea is inspired, it needs no boundaries.†

Once the plot was settled, it was decided that Menotti would write the first scene and they would evaluate it and progress from there. Barber planned to spend the summer of 1952 in Europe—with visits to Paris, Ireland, Corsica, and finally Austria, where he expected to settle down to compose. Shortly before his departure for Europe, however, he wrote to Homer: "G. C. has no time to work on the opera libretto as yet. He wants to stay here quietly this summer—says he is too tired to travel—and I hope

* Menotti, interviewed by John Gutman during intermission of a radio broadcast of *Vanessa,* 1 February 1958. Tape at New York Public Library, Rodgers and Hammerstein Archives of Recorded Sound; material reprinted here by permission of Metropolitan Opera Company. In this interview, Boito and Verdi were cited by Barber as the only other instance in which one composer wrote a text for another.

† Coleman, "Samuel Barber and *Vanessa,*" p. 87. Miles Kastendieck made the interesting observation that *Vanessa* could just as easily haven taken place in New England and that Menotti missed a great opportunity to help make a truly American opera: "Is he so unaware of New England backgrounds which have bred this kind of story?" Kastendieck says ("Some Afterthoughts on 'Vanessa,' " *New York Journal American,* 2 March 1958). When in 1961 *Vanessa* was produced in Spoleto, Italy, in fact, Barber changed the location of the story to the upper Hudson River (see below). Menotti's first opera in English, *The Old Maid and the Thief* (1939), had an American setting inspired by his numerous visits to West Chester, Pennsylvania.

he will have something for me when I return. In the meanwhile, I shall tackle an orchestral work."*

By November there was still no libretto. Menotti had been busy with the orchestration of his new violin concerto. A letter written to Homer suggests that Barber may have given up on Menotti at this time and was searching for an alternative libretto: "I have no progress to report on finding an opera libretto," Barber wrote, "but when I read some of the troubles that Puccini went through on this score, I know I must be patient."[16] In the interim he began and finished *Hermit Songs*.

Two years later, in June 1954, although Menotti had sketched the first scene, he was now hard at work on his own opera *The Saint of Bleecker Street*. Barber had begun "casting about for ideas" for the music for *Vanessa,* and for the summer the two composers worked on the seacoast in an old farmhouse in Brooklyn, Maine, on Frenchman's Bay across from Bar Harbor. Barber, following the advice of Francis Poulenc on beginning an opera—"just throw yourself in"—began work with fervor.[17] He was, he said afterwards, "immediately struck by the flexibility of the libretto, the impeccable sense of timing (people arrive and leave the stage exactly when they should) and by what I can only call air holes that leave space for musical development."[18]

At the end of the summer, he had finished the music for the first scene. By then completely engrossed in the story, Barber asked Menotti for more words so that he could press forward. "Here was the beginning of a new trial of patience!" he recalled:

> He explained that I would have to wait until January, as he must leave for New York to produce *The Saint of Bleecker Street*. This was at the point in my opera when, after Vanessa's aria, Anatol first appears, silhouetted in semi-darkness in the doorway. She turns to him and screams. He remains standing.
>
> And standing there in that drafty doorway in a northern country in deep winter, Anatol remained for four months until January. Once again my errant librettist asked for a reprieve, for now the *Saint* was to be done at La Scala. Not to mention the trials of Anatol (for no tenor must stand in a draft for even a second), and this composer was not fit to live with that winter. He fled to Greece and reorchestrated his *Medea*. And Anatol stood.[19]

This reminiscence by Barber, though colorful, is not entirely accurate—in fact he fled to Greece for a vacation on the way to Vienna and London for the performances of *Prayers of Kierkegaard,* which were so successful that promises of future European performances of *Vanessa* were held out even before the opera was completed: "Afterward, at a party given by the

*Letter, 2 June 1952, from Capricorn. He finished the orchestration of the ballet *Souvenirs* that summer.

head of the festival, I was definitely offered the premiere of my opera at the Salzburg Festival, with cast and conductor of my own choice," Barber wrote to Homer. "This is encouraging, but it is much too soon even to consider. In fact, several opera companies in Europe have already evinced definite interest in 'Vanessa.' "[20]

From June on, Barber, Menotti, and Charles Turner spent most of the summer in Italy, first in Positano and after July 1 in Capri, where Barber reshaped the *Medea* suite into its one-movement version, *Medea's Meditation and Dance of Vengeance*. From Positano he wrote, "My librettist's wishes are my wishes," continuing:

> Here we see no one and work mornings; but I rather expect we shall have more guests at Capri. I await, with my tongue hanging out of my mouth, in impatience, a word or words of my libretto; but I am not allowed to ask and do not, for I know Gian Carlo is working on it in his own inimitably distracted way. And so soothing is the atmosphere and so various my interests (for instance I have done some good temperas with fine new colors I brought from London and have also a lot of Greek to study, having remembered some of the smattering I once had) so that I do not fret.*

With his librettist at last at his disposal, Barber expected to have a complete libretto by the end of the summer and to begin to compose "in dead earnest" when he returned to Capricorn.[21] But things did not work out as he planned, for the stay in Capri—noisy and full of tourists—was a deterrent to rigorous work. Perhaps, too, the summer was too jolly with congeniality: living in nearby Ischia, the composers William Walton and Hans Werner Henze invited Barber and Turner to their villa for conversation; and their longtime friends Stephen and Natasha Spender and Cyril Connolly were guests on Hansi Lambert's yacht moored in the harbor. Then Menotti was interrupted by a sudden call to Milan for a performance of *The Medium*. Barber now employed a unique kind of pressure on Menotti: he refused to write a note until the complete libretto was finished—a technique Menotti himself did not use. He wrote:

> My tactic succeeded brilliantly: it made him so nervous that he sat on a rock by the Mediterranean every morning until, by the summer's end, what I think is perhaps the finest and most chiselled of his libretti was finished . . .[22]

Menotti's plot, originally in four acts (revised to three in 1964), is a melodrama in the grand operatic tradition. Set in an unnamed "northern country about 1905," the story unfolds about two women: Vanessa (so-

* Barber's travel log, p. 10. Barber's newly acquired interest in painting produced several landscapes. One—a scene of small fishing boats hauled up on a beach—was offered for sale at a fundraising benefit to raise scholarships for the Spoleto Festival in 1957 (*New York World Telegram*, February 1957).

prano), "a lady of great beauty," who for twenty years of winter after snowy winter has awaited the return of her only love, Anatol; and her beautiful young niece, Erika (mezzo-soprano). Upon this somber gothic dreamscape, in which chandeliers are dimmed and mirrors draped against the reflection of Vanessa's advancing age, the wizened Baroness (contralto), Vanessa's mother, through her silence condemns her daughter's withdrawal from life. Another Anatol (tenor), the errant lover's fatally charming son, a bounder and opportunist, enters the manor. Vanessa, mistaking the young man for his father, passionately inquires if he still loves her; she is devastated when she discovers the visitor is not her lover. Erika entreats the impostor to leave, but he refuses.

A month later (act 2) Erika confesses to the Baroness that she had been seduced by Anatol on the night of his arrival but has refused his offer of marriage because he cannot promise eternal love—"We have learned today that such words are lies," he told her. Her grandmother advises: "Love never bears the image that we dream of; when it seems to, beware the disguise!" Vanessa and Anatol, radiant, return from ice skating and announce to the Old Doctor (baritone) plans for a New Year's Eve ball reminiscent of earlier celebrations. When she realizes that her aunt is blindly in love with the rake, Erika confronts Anatol and bitterly rejects him.

At the New Year's Eve ball (act 3) Anatol and Vanessa declare their love and the Doctor announces their engagement. Erika, dazed and carrying Anatol's child, stumbles into the bitter cold to cause an abortion. Unaware of the reason for, and disturbed by, her beloved niece's behavior, Vanessa nevertheless marries Anatol. As they prepare to leave for Paris, they are joined by Erika, the Baroness, and the Doctor in a quintet, a canon ("To leave, to break, to find, to keep"). As her aunt had earlier, Erika resigns to withdraw from the world: "Now it is my turn to wait," she declares to the silent Baroness as the opera concludes.

The point is, Menotti stated about his creation, "Love only exists as a compromise. . . . Whomever we love, it's not the image of the person we expected."[23] "The story is one of two women, Vanessa and Erika, caught in the central dilemma which faces every human being," he wrote in the preface to the vocal score, "whether to fight for one's ideals to the point of shutting oneself off from reality, or compromise with what life has to offer, even lying to oneself for the mere sake of living."[24] Menotti's characters seem drawn from his personal experience:

> Erika is a passionate idealist. Vanessa is more human. . . . Anatol is charming; I have many friends like him. He has imagination, fantasy, even if he's not a very strong character. The one who is really strong is the Baroness. She represents the affirmation of life and order; she speaks only to those who accept life for what it is. And she values life above order; from the moment she learns that Erika succeeded in destroying her baby,

even though it is illegitimate, she will no longer speak to the girl—just as she has not spoken to Vanessa, who sacrificed her youth in a dream.[25]

As their collaboration progressed, Barber and Menotti often discussed twists and turns of plot and character, but, according to the composer—other than asking for an extra aria for the doctor—very few changes were made to Menotti's words.[26] This was because Barber appreciated that economy of words was necessary for the singing stage—"their utter simplicity (how wonderful to set!)"—and Menotti's sense of theatrical timing seemed to Barber unique.[27] On his part, Menotti suggested few changes in the music.[28] "Of course I always showed him the music once I wrote it," Barber said. "He's a wonderful critic—he has a superb sense of line."*

"I lost myself completely in the life of Gian Carlo's characters," Barber said. "It was a wonderful sort of a vacation from leading my own life; and the act of composing an opera seemed quite natural to me."[29] Menotti deliberately incorporated into the libretto references to Barber's past and his personal tastes: thus the recitation of a French menu to open the opera, a skating scene, a waltz, and a Protestant hymn. The ending—each character bidding farewell to the house, leaving Erika and Grandmother alone on the stage—is similar to that of Chekhov's *The Cherry Orchard,* one of Barber's favorite plays.[30]

During the winter of 1956 at Capricorn Barber began work in earnest on the music; a Metropolitan Opera news release announced it would take about a year to complete the music.[31] An admirer of Barber's music, Mrs. Sikey Lucas of Cleveland, gave the composer and Turner the use of one of her houses on Nantucket near the Sconset Lighthouse. Accommodating to only a few interruptions in his rigorous work schedule—visits from Leonard and Felicia Bernstein, Aaron Copland, and Nanni Ricordi—Barber finished the music for acts 2 and 3 by early autumn.[32]

At the suggestion of Heinsheimer, in October Barber arranged an audition of the three completed acts for Rudolf Bing and three other representatives of the Metropolitan Opera. In the director's room of G. Schirmer, he played the score and sang all the vocal parts himself—"this was not easy," he recalled; "fortunately the quintet in act 4 was not yet composed."[33] Immediately Bing began discussion of the problems of casting. All during the next winter, while composing the last act, Barber spent a good deal of time at the opera house listening to available singers and suggesting possibilities; many times he had to play individual roles for the various candidates, he said, "explaining, cajoling, hoping."[34]

*Allan Kozinn, "Samuel Barber: The Last Interview and the Legacy," part 2, p. 89. It was standard procedure for Barber to have Menotti evaluate his music. Manfred Ibel, who lived at Capricorn during the 1960s, observed: "Whenever Sam had an idea, or finished composing something, he turned to Menotti. . . . He was the final person who Sam trusted" (interview with the author, 10 April 1987).

Even though he was given complete freedom to choose whom he wished, the selection of singers was problematic. His first choice for the role of Vanessa was the soprano Maria Callas, whom he had heard for the first time in *La Traviata* at La Scala. Invited by Barber to Capricorn to hear the music, Callas brought with her an entourage—her husband Menenghini, Dario and Dorle Soria, a secretary, and a small dog. Barber sang and played most of the music from the opera for her, but Callas rejected the role.* Reportedly, one of the difficulties was that although Callas was born in the United States, she had never sung opera in English and was hesitant to do so.[35] Barber, however, believed there were other reasons for her reluctance to sing the role of Vanessa: "Being very astute," he said, "she noticed certain things about the libretto which gave a little bit too much importance to the mezzo-soprano, the role of Erika, which is a very strong role."[36] In fact, the role of Erika carries such weight that critics in general seem to perceive her as a more sympathetically and clearly drawn character than Vanessa.†

Sena Jurinac, a Yugoslavian soprano who had the reputation of specializing in Mozart, was eventually chosen for the role; but she was never to play it. Her English was very good; she had lived for a long time in England and was a star at Glyndebourne, yet until then she had refused to sing English translations. She agreed to sing in Barber's opera because it had been conceived in English.[37] Nicolai Gedda, the Swedish-born tenor who was new to the Metropolitan, would play Anatol, and he, too, spoke fluent English.[38] Barber had heard him sing at the Opéra Comique in Paris and was convinced he was right for the role. In March 1957, even before *Vanessa* was finished, the Metropolitan Opera announced its premiere for the 1957–58 season, with Dimitri Mitropoulos as conductor, Menotti as stage director, and sets and costumes designed by Cecil Beaton.‡

"The music is finished, the cast is chosen, and now all I have to do is fill in one thousand empty pages of orchestration," Barber wrote to Nicolai Malko late in April.[39] The opening measures of the quintet from the last act had been sketched earlier that month while Barber dined with the composer Lee Hoiby at a restaurant in Pound Ridge (see facsimile on facing page).

During the early summer in Rome, in a sun-drenched studio offering expansive views of the entire city, Barber finished act 2's simulated folk

*A letter from Barber to William Schuman on 1 December 1956 suggests that act 4 was still unfinished when Callas met with Barber and that he completed it knowing she would not sing the role (Papers and Records of William Schuman, New York Public Library, Music Division).

†The role was declared as giving Rosalind Elias the "triumph of her short career" (Harriet Johnson, *New York Post,* 16 January 1958).

‡The English designer had received accolades for his work in the musical *My Fair Lady,* but this would be his first opera.

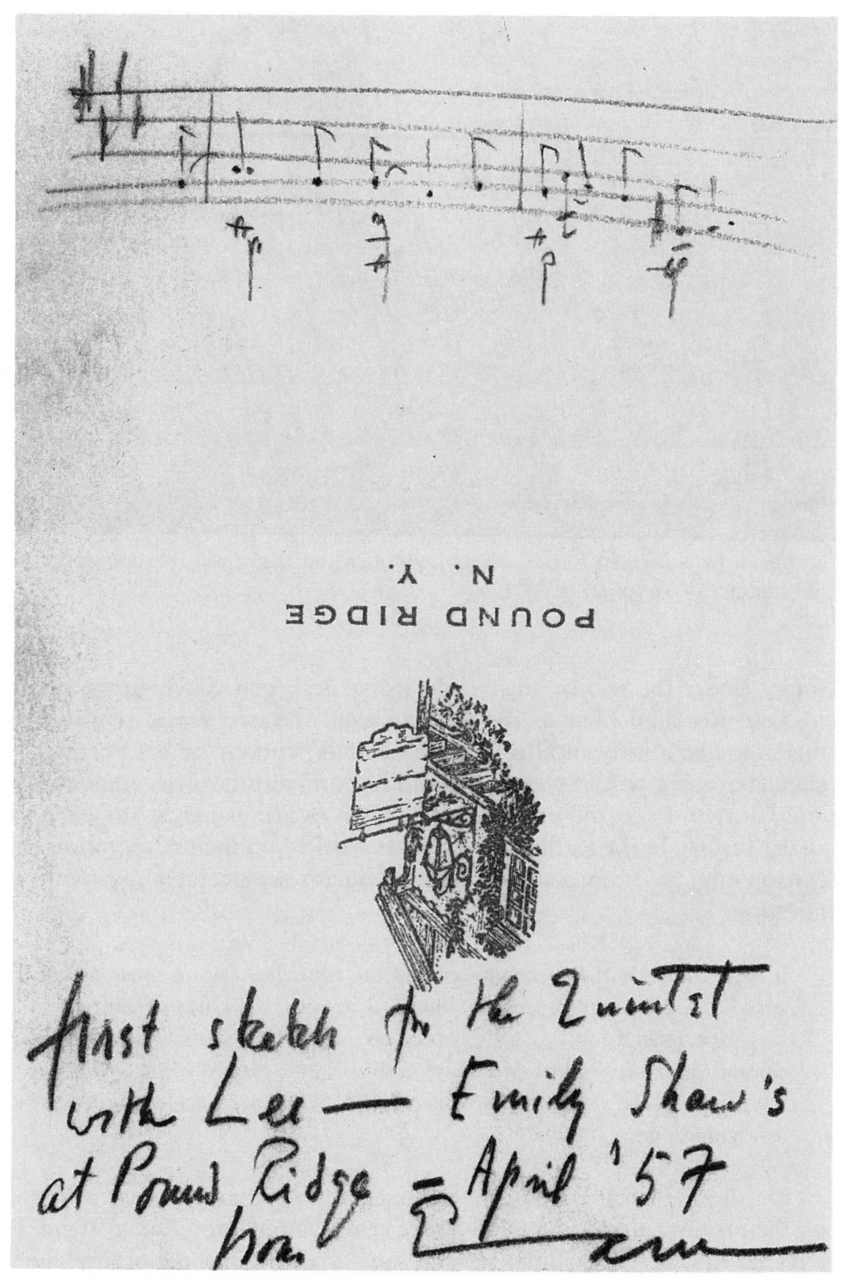

Earliest sketch of the Quintet from *Vanessa,* written on the reverse side of a wine list from Emily Shaw's restaurant in Pound Ridge, New York, April 1957. *(Courtesy of Lee Hoiby)*

Barber in his studio in Rome, where he worked on the music for *Vanessa* during the summer of 1957. *(Herbert List)*

song "Under the willow tree."[40] In Rome he began coaching the mezzo-soprano Rosalind Elias as the young Erika. The two supporting roles by this time had also been filled—Regina Resnik, known for her portrayal of character parts, would play the foreboding and mostly silent grandmother, and Giorgio Tozzi the comic doctor. With occasional trips to Vienna to coach Jurinac in the leading role, Barber worked on the orchestration with Mitropoulos at Montecatini.[41] The conductor would later say, with admiration:

> It was a miracle that a composer had the courage to write music in this style. . . . He hadn't been contaminated by different kinds of contemporary experimentation. . . . The whole texture of *Vanessa* is highly theatrical and dramatic, full of orchestral surprises and climaxes, but always at the service of the stage, as any real opera should be. . . . At last, an American grand opera![42]

During the latter part of the summer of 1957 Barber continued work on the orchestration in a rented house near Southampton, Long Island. He adhered to a strict schedule: several hours of work in the morning, lunch, an hour on the beach, a nap, a few more hours of work, dinner, and an early bedtime.[43] In the fall rehearsals began in earnest; many arduous hours were spent at the Metropolitan Opera, going over the music and the acting with an assistant conductor at the piano. On 1 November construction of the sets was begun in the Met's 40th Street shop. With a crew of fifteen carpenters, six prop men, and seven painters, they were completed within six weeks and on 20 December hauled to the Metropolitan Opera House, where stagehands could begin rehearsing their handling of them. On 23 December the first piano rehearsal was conducted on the new sets so that singers could familiarize themselves with the exits, the furniture, and props.

Everything seemed to be going smoothly when, only a little more than six weeks before opening night, Jurinac canceled her engagement (presumably because of illness) and Barber found himself without a Vanessa. Confusion followed; there was talk of a year's postponement, when two days later Bing phoned Barber to ask if he would consider Eleanor Steber.[44] "If there's one person who can do it, it's Eleanor. . . . She should have done it in the first place," her press agent Edgar Vincent assured Max Rudolf, the Met's coordinator.

Almost thirty years later Steber recalled her delight at seeing the score: "The part was made for me," she said; "it was both a singer's part and an actress's part."[45] As one of the leading rising young American sopranos in the Metropolitan Opera, she had already assumed major roles—her first Donna Anna had been done under Karl Böhm, and she was singing her first Tosca that season. Moreover, Steber felt a strong empathy for Vanessa—"it became as if my whole life was lived through that particular role," she recalled in an interview.* But more importantly, far from believing the character Vanessa to be eclipsed by the young Erika, Steber felt she could give the title role significance by making it her own; and indeed, eventually she was to become thoroughly identified with the opera.†

In what was considered a major feat, Steber learned the role of Vanessa in six weeks. Her familiarity with Barber's music, through her earlier performances of *Knoxville* and *Nuvoletta,* was an asset—"once you find the style of a composer, you have the key to him," she said.[46] The challenge was nevertheless enormous, and Barber, recognizing this, greatly appreciated her "rescue" of his heroine. "It was a meeting of old friends," he told the press; "I cannot adequately extol her gallantry in undertaking this difficult role in so short a time."[47] In comparison to other difficult operatic roles she had sung—Marie in *Wozzeck,* for example, or Butterfly—only Minnie in *The Girl of the Golden West,* Steber believed, was a challenge equal to Vanessa. *Vanessa,* with its wide vocal range and many extended phrases, is a "big opera" that requires a mature vocal technique. This, in addition to the short time Steber had in which to learn the part, taxed every skill the singer possessed, and it is understandable that for the dress rehearsal she still had to depend on a score hidden on a mantlepiece.[48]

Though Barber had coached her through the music and was present at rehearsals, Menotti took complete charge of direction. Steber recalled:

* In her interview with the author, 1 September 1983, Steber pointed to parallels in her own life: "The story ends at the point where I was married to Colonel Edgar Andrews, whom I had met in the South Pacific many years earlier and felt was the love of my life. Twenty years later, he turned out to be an Anatol."

† At the gala farewell performance in the old Metropolitan Opera House, on 16 April 1966, Steber sang her signature role in the quintet from *Vanessa,* which begins, appropriately, "Who knows when I shall see this house again?"

Barber and Menotti with Eleanor Steber in costume for *Vanessa,* January 1958. *(Mélançon, Metropolitan Opera Archives)*

> You have no idea what Gian Carlo had me doing in acting that role. He had me singing in incredible positions. It was a very difficult act. I was lying on my back, the range was difficult, it was heavily orchestrated and took a lot of riding over the orchestra to be heard. There was a skating scene with a coloratura aria that was enormously difficult. . . . I never thought about the difficulty at the time. After the premiere, the aria was cut from future performances.[49]

With candor, Barber stated his principles of vocal writing and his views of opera in general on a radio broadcast of *Vanessa* soon after its premiere:

> When the voice takes over—what I call the raptus—it dominates. As a composer, I can admire barking operas, with their emphasis entirely on the orchestra, but as an unsuccessful singer myself, these operas leave me cold. Everyone said when I was sixteen that the human ear would become accustomed to the new music. And the voice would automatically adapt itself to the new exigencies. To a great extent this has happened with the ear, but I'm afraid that over these last thirty years, the voice has remained somewhat recalcitrant. The human throat is still a human throat; a clarinet is a clarinet.[50]

Beaton's lavish period costumes and sets were designed to capture, in his words, "the evanescent, elusive atmosphere of the opera . . . mysterious and not specific." "You might call the period Edwardian Gothic," he said. "Isak Dinesen is certainly a figure behind the scenes, a vital ghost." Intending to focus an aura of "moody elegance" upon Vanessa, whom he saw as "a terrific romantic . . . a kind of Anna Karenina figure," he allowed the heroine to impose her "romantic tastes and domestic dreams completely upon the drawing room of the opera's first and second acts and its final scene."[51] As a result, the designs called for more bric-a-brac and greenery than had graced the stage of the Metropolitan Opera House for years.

In fact Beaton's sets seem remarkably like a house Barber visited in Copenhagen in 1955, a manor that reminded him, even then, of the world of Isak Dinesen. He had written about it to Sidney Homer:

> They picked me up that evening and it was like driving through the night and dark woods into the *Seven Gothic Tales* which I so love. It was a large country manor house, the host Alfred Olesen, an old Danish millionaire, welcomed us gravely in the hall before a roaring fire. . . . The house was a strange mixture of beautiful Scandinavian furniture, great chests and high-boys, and dreadful paintings; a large number of huge marble women . . . leading the way to the large salon opening out onto a shivering garden and a dark lake.[52]

It seems no mere coincidence that Vanessa's country manor is located in a northern country, the year about 1905, and is described similarly:

> A night in early winter in Vanessa's luxurious dressing room. A small table is laid for supper. All the mirrors in the room and one large painting over the mantlepiece are covered over with cloth. There is a large French window at the back which leads into a darkened *jardin d'hiver*.[53]

As in Barber's earlier account, Menotti's "dark winter garden" is framed by a snow-clad lake—although the details are reversed; Olesen's lake was dark and the garden illuminated.

Beaton's costumes were said to be influenced by a trip to Japan. Vanessa, for her six changes of costume, was sumptuously clad in velvet and fur: in act 1 she wore a ruby-red dress with gathered tulle sleeves and a stole in the same hue; for church in act 2, a violet-blue suit and toque with matching ostrich plumes; for the ice-skating scene, sober black broadcloth bordered in ermine, with matching cap and muff. The act 3 ball gown was scarlet, parting to reveal an underskirt of white and gold brocade, and worn with an abundance of diamond jewelry (a $1,500,000 collection borrowed from the prominent jeweler Harry Winston).* For the farewell in

* Steber did not think the color of the ball gown was suitable for her and asked to have a new dress designed in some blue color for the Salzburg performance. Beaton and Bing

Vanessa, act 2; at left, Steber and Nicolai Gedda (Anatol); center, Giorgio Tozzi (Doctor) sings to Regina Resnik (Baroness); on far right, Rosalind Elias (Erika). *(Mélançon, Metropolitan Opera Archives)*

act 4, Steber wore a plum-colored suit, with a high-tilted hat, and carried a sable muff pinned with violets; her negligee for this act was of saffron chiffon with mink tails. Erika's costumes, in contrast to her aunt's, were demure and conservative. The men were dressed simply but with Edwardian dash: Anatol was in grey tweed and gold-buttoned red vest for act 1 and a brown frock coat trimmed at collar and cuffs with brown velvet for act 2.[54]

Musically, the significance of *Vanessa* in Barber's development is not that it explores a new language, but rather that it is the summation of his musical powers brought together effectively in a full-length dramatic work. While the libretto provided every opportunity for him to compose forms conventional to grand opera—a glimpsed ball scene requiring a waltz, for example, a folk-dance ballet reminiscent of *Eugene Onegin,* and a colora-

---

corresponded about the costume, deciding that the extra expenditure of $1,500 was unwarranted. However, at Beaton's suggestion, Steber agreed to discard Vanessa's red wig and instead scrape back her natural hair absolutely straight in a huge knot on top of her head. Beaton wrote to Bing:

> It's a different conception, but I think it would be more distinguished and cleaner. I would agree to her having a wig of her own colour, but I think it would be better still, have more style, and be more uncompromising, for her to have her own hair taken back into a huge chignon *on the crown of her head,* not on the nape of her neck. (Letter, 12 May 1958, from Kensington, England; Metropolitan Opera Association Archives)

tura skating aria—he sought to present them in an unstylized manner. The three or four set-piece arias and the love duet ("Love has a bitter core, Vanessa") are approached seamlessly from lyrical recitatives. Even declamatory passages cannot suffer for long the restraint of narrow tessiture, but irrepressibly broaden into long expressive phrases. A simultaneous musical representation of different threads of action supports the psychological undercurrents of the drama, demonstrating that Barber learned well from Mozart. For example, a Protestant hymn sung from an offstage chapel is pitted against the orchestral background to Erika's brooding over Anatol; at the ball, dance music is strikingly juxtaposed against music expressive of her anguish.

Several arias and one orchestral interlude (the intermezzo to act 2) are well known as independent pieces: Erika's poignant aria "Must the winter come so soon"; Vanessa's dramatic aria "Do not utter a word, Anatol"; the ländler, "Under the willow tree," which, in the opera, is sung as a solo, a trio, and a chorus and finally used for a dance.* Also published was the finale's quintet ("To leave, to break, to find, to keep"), which is surely one of the most brilliant climaxes in the twentieth-century opera repertoire (Example 14).† Called by Irving Kolodin "the best realized episode I know of in native opera lore,"[55] the quintet moved William Schuman to write to Barber after he heard a broadcast of the opera in 1979, "I was struck again with its extraordinary beauty. Those last pages, especially, are among the finest of operatic literature."‡

A telling observation about the stylistic tendencies of opera at midcentury was made by the British critic Henry Brandon in his review of *Vanessa:* "Artists need daring in our time to express the courage of their romanticism, especially in America. 'Vanessa' is romantic opera in the best old traditions, not an adventure into the unknown but a fresh expression of already established taste."[56]

Indeed, *Vanessa* does epitomize the conventional lyrical style of late nineteenth- and early twentieth-century Romantic operas; but while its models derive from Verdi, Puccini, and Strauss, the musical ideas are always on Barber's own terms. "He may be inspired by good examples,"

* At the Curtis Institute of Music Library there is a pencil manuscript of "Under the willow tree" that Barber presented to Mary Zimbalist in 1956 with the inscription "For Mary—souvenir of wonderful waltzes!"

Barber affectionately referred to the music for the interlude in the final act as the "Krawitz Intermezzo," because Herman Krawitz had suggested that he publish it independent of the score. As a concert piece, Kostelanetz first performed it with the San Francisco Symphony and then again in New York with the New York Philharmonic on 15 March 1958 (*New York Times,* 17 March 1958, and letter from Barber to Herman Krawitz, Metropolitan Opera Association Archives).

† European papers compared the beauty of the quintet to that of the trio in *Rosenkavalier.*

‡ Letter to Barber, 30 May 1979. Barber reciprocated the compliment in his letter to Schuman of 2 June 1979: "You have always been so kind to my music, which I don't forget. In fact, to turn the tables, I know I will never be able to write a crescendo such as you have in your Third Symphony, about which I have been jealous for years" (both letters are in Papers and Records of William Schuman, New York Public Library, Music Division).

Example 14 *Vanessa,* act 3, scene 2, Quintet, holograph. *(Library of Congress)*

Paul Henry Lang stated, "but he never borrows."[57] In *Vanessa* Barber's musical footprints are strongly apparent—shifting modality, metric flexibility that flows out of the logical rhythm of the text, a facile use of harmonic color to underscore the bittersweet poetry, and an abundance of diatonic, accessible melody. Rich orchestral sonority and lucid counterpoint are striking in the orchestral interludes; there are generous solos for the favored oboe and the English horn and, throughout, surges of grand sweeping lyrical gestures.

Vanessa received spectacular reviews. The sold-out house to a nonsubscription audience that included many celebrities was reported to have "thundered its approbation as the final curtain fell," and Barber, brought to the stage, was greeted by "deafening delirium."* That Steber had risen to the challenge of so difficult a role on such short notice was appreciated, and if some critics pointed to her performance as uneven or said her dic-

*Paul Henry Lang, "New American Opera Is Hailed at the Met," *New York Herald Tribune,* 16 January 1958. The audience included Artur Rubinstein, Fritz Reiner, Lucrezia Bori, Katharine Cornell, and Barber loyalists Mary and Efrem Zimbalist and Rudolf Schirmer.

tion lacked clarity at times, it was recognized nevertheless that she was ideally cast and would grow into the role once she became more familiar with it.[58] Elias received brilliant notices, her portrayal of Erika considered not only a vocal but a dramatic triumph.[59] Giorgio Tozzi stopped the show in act I with his remarkable characterization of the bibulous old family doctor.

New York papers judged *Vanessa* a winner: it was declared, almost as a matter of national pride, "the best U.S. opera yet staged at the Metropolitan," "the best American opera ever presented at the stately theater on Broadway and Thirty-ninth Street,"* and "a major contribution to the international repertory."[60] Lang found it hard to believe that it was a first opera for the composer: "Barber's mastery of operatic language is remarkable and second to none on the Salzburg-Milan axis."[61] Winthrop Sargeant, music critic for *The New Yorker* magazine, extolled *Vanessa* as "the finest and most truly 'operatic' opera ever written by an American . . . one of the most impressive things . . . to appear anywhere since Richard Strauss's more vigorous days," and concluded, "Mr. Barber has demonstrated that an American composer with sufficient knowledge and feeling for the great international operatic tradition can turn out a near masterpiece in the genre, using all the wonderful vocal and dramatic potentialities of the opera-house stage."[62]

New York Times critic Taubman claimed that for Barber's first opera, he "emerged from the ordeal by fire in remarkably good shape":

> Mr. Menotti's libretto is effective theater, and by the time the composer has reached the fourth act he has conquered the problems of opera. He has educated himself en route, as it were, and the most significant lesson he has learned is that the surest way to reach the heart of the audience is to be true to his own deepest musical instincts.†

Barber himself considered this first opera an education: "Nothing could take the place of the experience I am having at the Metropolitan," he wrote, "and I know no better apprenticeship than one among professionals."[63]

The judgment of his peers led Barber to further honors: for *Vanessa* he was awarded the 1958 Pulitzer Prize.‡ In May he received the Henry Had-

* *Time Magazine*, 27 January 1958. The three most successful American operas of the nineteen produced by the Metropolitan to that time were Deems Taylor's *The King's Henchman* (1927) and *Peter Ibbetson* (1931) and Louis Gruenberg's *Emperor Jones* (1933): Howard Taubman, *New York Times*, 16 January 1958.

† " 'Vanessa' at the 'Met,' " *New York Times*, 26 January 1958, sec. 2, p. 9. In an earlier review, on 16 January, Taubman wrote that "[Barber] edged into his first attempt cautiously and self-consciously . . . and by the time he has reached the last act . . . has learned to write for the lyric theatre with perception and impact." Katharine Homer Fryer's diary entry—"The opera grew and grew on me. At first I was detached"—is a subjective, but educated, reflection that seems to mirror Taubman's analysis.

‡ Although there was some early confusion in the press, this was Barber's first Pulitzer Prize. Pulitzers awarded to Barber in the 1930s were, in fact, traveling fellowships.

ley Medal of the National Association for American Composers and Conductors, a medal awarded for exceptional services to American music. In November of the same year, he was nominated to the American Academy of Arts and Letters, the select inner circle of the National Institute of Arts and Letters of which he had been a member for eighteen years. His election to the thirtieth chair—filling the place vacated by the death of Henry D. Sedgwick—was supported by Douglas Moore, Archibald MacLeish, Gilmore Clarke, Walter Piston, and Deems Taylor. At his induction, Allan Nevins read an address written by Douglas Moore:

> Still a comparatively young man, Mr. Barber has long since won fame by his lyrical music, presented in a wide variety of compositions. Though a fundamental classicism marks his works, he has not failed to experiment in modern techniques; and he has written for the orchestra, for chamber groups, for the chorus, for voice, and for piano. His ballet *Medea,* his *Capricorn Concerto,* his Overture to *The School for Scandal,* his symphonies, and his opera *Vanessa,* performed at the Metropolitan Opera House, illustrate the freshness of his creative gift even more than his range. In its solidarity and strength, in its melodic quality, and in its union of sparkling new ideas with tested forms of expression, his music promises to outlast the fashions of the day.[64]

Such prestigious acknowledgment of Barber's stature and the favorable critical reception of his first opera would seem to promise a bright future for *Vanessa,* but in spite of its auspicious beginning, the opera was to travel a rocky terrain.

Vanessa at Salzburg

The 1958 production of *Vanessa* at the Salzburg Festival was laden with "firsts." Not since 1910 had the Metropolitan Opera been represented in Europe, in which year there was practically a "Metropolitan season" at the Paris Opera.* *Vanessa* would be the first American opera performed at Salzburg, and it was also the first time in Salzburg history that an opera was sung in English and the first time the festival's novelty took the form of a guest appearance by an outside organization. Moreover, Barber's opera was not a world premiere, as Salzburg usually preferred, but a "mere" first European performance.[65]

The production and cast duplicated the New York original performance, with a few exceptions: the roles of the Baroness and two servants were recast, the orchestra was the Vienna Philharmonic Orchestra, and the

*"Topics of the Times," *New York Times,* 21 May 1958. Major singers who participated then were Enrico Caruso, Leo Slezak, Geraldine Farrar, Frances Alda, and Louise Homer.

chorus and ballet were those of the Vienna State Opera. Cecil Beaton's costumes were loaned by the Metropolitan, and his sets were copied identically. Rudolf Bing was reported to believe the performance was even more effective in Salzburg than in New York because of the smaller size of the Festspielhaus, which was about one-third the size of the Metropolitan.[66]

The American press reported that *Vanessa* in Salzburg was heavily criticized. Everett Helm and Howard Taubman, for example, suggested that reviews were so exaggerated in their diatribes that there seemed to be almost a conspiracy on the part of the Austrian press to destroy the credibility of American opera altogether.[67] Taubman wrote perceptively about the "excessive" violence of the European reaction:

> Can it be that criticism abroad did not mete out to "Vanessa" the even-handed justice it would bring to opera by contemporary Europeans?
>
> It can be. You have to consider the quality of some of the European pieces that are hailed with pleasure to realize that a severer standard is brought to bear on the judgment of American opera. It is as if some Europeans resented our achievement in an area that has been a European province. . . .
>
> Is it so much worse than Rolf Liebermann's "School for Wives," which had an enthusiastic reception from these very Austrian critics when it was put on at Salzburg?* Not at all. In fact, it is a far better work, and, praise be, it does not go in for a busy modernism that is as vacuous as it is fashionable. How about Von Einem's "Der Prozess," Martin's "The Tempest," Orff's "Der Mond," . . . all warmly received in Europe? All inferior to "Vanessa."
>
> One of the gravest troubles of "Vanessa" apparently was its American origin. Isn't opera a European invention, and shouldn't creativity in this field by materialistic Americans be suspect?†

Taubman's position is supported by reports, months before the festival began, of passing references to the "unfortunate" choice of *Vanessa*—before anyone in Europe could even have had any inkling as to whether or not the music itself was good or bad.[68] As the date of the performance neared, "strange rumors" began to circulate, most of which were entirely groundless—Menotti's departure for Brussels in order to prepare the production of his opera *Maria Golovin* was misinterpreted as his having "left in a huff" because everybody was "at each other's throats." The singing of the opera in English was incorrectly rumored to be necessary because Steber did not have enough time to learn the role in German, when, in

* Liebermann's work was presented in Salzburg as the modern opera in the 1957 festival.

† Howard Taubman, " 'Vanessa' Again," *New York Times,* 18 January 1959, sec. 2, p. 9. Taubman pointed to *Porgy and Bess* as having had immense success in Europe earlier, but being equated with American musical theater, it was not "asked to live up to rigorous operatic requirements."

fact, the Metropolitan Opera, and Dimitri Mitropoulos in particular, had decided long before the performance at Salzburg that the opera should be given in its original language.[69]

Although *Vanessa* was received warmly by the Salzburg audience, native journalists and critics attributed this not to the success of the opera but to the preponderance of Americans and other foreign tourists in the audience. Everett Helm pointed to the reaction of the European press to *Vanessa* as symbolizing striking differences in the intellectual approach to music between America and Europe at the time.[70] The opera was judged not for what it was but for what it *ought to have been* in light of contemporary European ideas about modern opera, which in the fifties, especially in Central Europe, considered realism out of style. Thus the focus of criticism was on the libretto—at best "dated, old-fashioned, Strindbergian, Ibsenesque, 'plush'—a combination of fin de siècle realism and pseudo-psychology"; at its worst "disgusting," "wretched," and "enough to make one cry."[71] Then, too, current German ideas of staging leaned toward the abstract, which could be seen, above all, in the 1950s productions at Bayreuth.[72] In the light of this view, it is understandable that Beaton's stylishly detailed sets were called "insipidly naturalistic."[73]

A letter to the *New York Times* from Menotti rebukes the American press's reports of uniformly bad reviews from European critics:

> It seems to me the time has come to correct the erroneous impression given by many American reports on "Vanessa" 's debut in Europe that the opera was received adversely by *all* European critics. . . . "Vanessa" was reviewed favorably—often glowingly. Even when reserved, as some English critics were, no critic displayed the outrageous hostility of the Germans. Nevertheless the success of "Vanessa" with the international audience of Salzburg was as uncontested as with the American public in New York.[74]

The music was received with greater appreciation than the story. It is true that some Salzburg papers assaulted Barber's music as being eclectic—"a chromaticized Puccini, plus a few ounces of Wagner, Strauss, and Tchaikovsky and a shot of Debussy"[75]—but many found it masterly. Henrik Kralik's review in the Vienna *Presse,* while declaring *Vanessa* "eine Oper fürs Publikum und nicht für die Schriftgelehrten" (an opera for the public and not for intellectuals), nevertheless credited Barber with having made the conscious choice to stay within "old-fashioned harmonic and melodic lines" and develop the entire experience along tonal lines with remarkable skill and authenticity of expression.[76] He marked the special talent of the composer to use conventional forms and create "charming," lyrical music that carried the "mood" of the drama—"not everything was pure gold, but what he does present is with gusto and animation."[77] Hans Hauptmann, who found Menotti's libretto "longwinded" and lacking in proper dramatic excitement, nevertheless found great merit in Barber's music:

> Samuel Barber . . . is today the representative American master, an excellent craftsman, who knows how to make an interesting score, who is skilled and controlled in the orchestral medium and has good, if not exactly original, ideas. His music—rich, opulent sounding—is relatively accessible. He writes beautiful, grateful melodic passages in the grand opera style, incorporating elements of dance accents; what he has to say is best expressed in the Quintet. However, what is novel here is that he proceeds, stylistically and with respect to method, in the old track.[78]

* * *

Vanessa's first performance in 1958 had been before a sold-out, nonsubscription house.[79] Five performances followed during the 1957–58 season, all of which sold well. The following season, however, after four New York and two out-of-town performances (in Baltimore and Boston), one Met official described the box office as "disastrous."[80] Subsequently, in spite of excellent New York reviews and the fact that no other American work had scored so heavily in over a quarter of a century, it was announced that *Vanessa* would not be included in the repertory for the 1959–60 season. "It would seem that the opera had reached its audience in one season," a spokesman for the Metropolitan Opera said.[81]

There have been only sporadic performances of *Vanessa* since then. Menotti produced it at the Spoleto Festival in 1961. For this performance Fedele d'Amico translated the libretto into Italian and the setting was changed to the upper Hudson River (the Baroness was renamed "Grandmother"). Yet for all the attempts at Americanization, an Italian critic wrote:

> As to the question of whether an American opera has been created . . . we are perplexed what to say. For 50 years American musicologists and musicians have been waiting to announce its birth, but the attempts made so far—from Taylor to Hanson, from Cadman to Gruenberg, from Virgil Thomson to Antheil—all have been more or less shaped by European styles and syntax, and all have failed to produce an American opera.*

Franco Abbiati reported that Italian audiences, nevertheless, received *Vanessa* with enthusiasm:

> The measure of the production's success was indicated by the thirty or so curtain calls for the singers after the five acts were over, and by the intensity of applause during the course of the performance.[82]

In 1964 Barber revised *Vanessa*. Perhaps in response to criticism that the beginning of the opera was slowly paced and that the first act in par-

*Guido M. Gatti, "Spoleto," *La rassegna musicale* 31, no. 2 (1961):131–32. Trans. Richard Frank, cited in Hennessee, *Samuel Barber: A Bio-Bibliography* (Westport: Greenwood Press, 1985), p. 186. In contrast, when *Vanessa* was produced in Salzburg, Thomas Ernst wrote about the opera, "Despite its European setting and its European models, this work is truly American" (*Neue Zeitschrift für Musik*, October 1958, pp. 589–91).

ticular was too long, he shortened the work, consolidating four acts to three by merging acts 1 and 2. In addition, some of the vocal demands of Vanessa's role were modified by eliminating the brutally difficult skating aria, which expanded possibilities for casting.

In 1965 the "new" *Vanessa* was produced by the Metropolitan Opera with Mary Costa as Vanessa and John Alexander as Anatol. William Steinberg, who rarely conducted operas, received unusual praise for drawing clear and elegant sounds from the orchestra.

A letter from Barber to Rudolf Bing, written toward the end of 1963, suggests the kind of evasiveness the composer encountered in trying to obtain a commitment for more performances:

> *Dear Rudi—*
> Why do you tease me? The Bible says: "In the beginning was the word." You say "in the beginning is the *Date.*" Fascinating possibilities trail their evanescent perfumes across my country nostrils and disappear—to Von Karajan, La Scala, Covent Gardens, the other big Leagues; unavailable, because it is March or April!! My god! Can't you swap 5 Cherubinis for a Sciotti? Are we, as Mme Nhu says, so powerless? Are you so powerless, like the $? Am I left with a Stich-Bloomingdales? To a composer, it is never March or April, but the *right person.*
>
> Just don't give *Vanessa* and let me write for a new young minor league company—I like that idea. And tell Tony Bliss and Gutman not to lecture me, because you have no really good dramatic soprano . . . . available.[83]

After 1965 *Vanessa* disappeared from the Metropolitan repertoire entirely and was not performed again by a professional company until Menotti produced it at the Spoleto Festival in Charleston, South Carolina, on 27 May 1978.* With Johanna Meier as Vanessa, Katherine Ciesinski as Erika, and Henry Price as Anatol, this performance was videotaped and broadcast nationwide on television by Public Broadcasting Service on 31 January 1979 for the series "Great Performances."†

More recently, on 13 June 1988 the Opera Theater of St. Louis, as part of its continuing effort to revive neglected works, recast *Vanessa* in the 1950s. The production required a reduction of Barber's lavish orchestration in order to accommodate to the theater's small orchestra pit, which could seat only fifty musicians.‡ James Medwitz, a composer, created the new version, which used two flutes, two oboes, two clarinets, two trumpets, and two trombones instead of the original three of each; three horns instead of four; and a reduced number of string players. A Yamaha DX7

*There have been student productions of *Vanessa* at the Indiana University Opera Theater on 1 March 1975 and at the Juilliard School in December 1991.

†The producer was Jac Venza (see above, "Adventure"). The Kansas City Lyric Opera gave five performances of *Vanessa* in October 1979.

‡Paul Kilmer of the St. Louis Opera, in a telephone interview with the author, 4 February 1989, reported that the stage has a three-quarter thrust into the pit.

synthesizer was used for organ and accordion parts where required. Director Graham Vick's staging was criticized heavily by Michael Kimmelman:

> Dressing Anatol, the young stranger, in a James Dean–like leather jacket and chains, and having Vanessa, the baroness, in stiletto heels and a gown that seemed as if Christian Lacroix had been watching the "Jetsons," Mr. Vick evoked laughs that undercut moments of supposed seriousness.[84]

Such "updated" versions might be expected to undermine the music as well, but apparently that was not the case. "The score has passages of genuine emotion," wrote Kimmelman, "that allow Mr. Barber's music to rise somewhat above the tale it accompanies."[85]

15

INTERLUDE 1958-1960

Paying tribute

Wondrous Love: Variations on a Shape-Note Hymn, Op. 34 (1958)

A typical day at Capricorn during the late fifties was described by a close friend of Barber's as follows:

> Sam loved to have a fire in his bedside fireplace every morning. Through the Menotti-designed large picture window he would look out on the forest which he loved so much. During breakfast his large black dog, Fosca, a French briard—later a blond one called Golaud—would lie at his side. He would then move into his adjoining studio to start the day's composing. Ordinarily he did not like to be interrupted.*

During this period Barber composed *Wondrous Love: Variations on a Shape-Note Hymn* for the inauguration of a new organ at the Christ Episcopal Church in Grosse Pointe, Michigan. It was dedicated to, and performed in 1958 by, Richard Roeckelein, the organist of the church. Roeckelein met Barber in Rome during the summer of 1957 when the composer was completing the orchestration of *Vanessa*.[1] Later that year the organist asked him if he would write a piece for the dedication ceremony of a new three-manual organ of classic design that was being built by Walter Holtkamp for the Christ Church.† Barber agreed and visited Grosse Pointe during the fall of 1957 to get a feel for the sound of the

* Manfred Ibel, interview with the author, 10 April 1987, New York. Ibel lived at Capricorn in a cottage near the main house (see chapter 16).

† Walter Henry Holtkamp, Sr., was, with G. Donald Harrison, among the first builders of organs to return to classical tonal principles (*New Grove Dictionary of American Music*, vol. 2, p. 413).

building. Before the composer left for New York Roeckelein loaned him a book on the chorale preludes of J. S. Bach, which elucidated in particular how Bach used various musical motives and techniques to symbolize human emotions.[2]

For his theme Barber used the shape-note folk hymn "What wondrous love is this, oh! my soul!" The hymn was first published in 1835 in William Walker's *The Southern Harmony and Musical Companion* and reprinted in 1844 in the earliest edition of *The Sacred Harp*.[3] George Pullen Jackson reports the tune as widely sung even before 1701 when it became associated with the tale of Captain Kidd.[4] The theme Barber used includes an alto part that had been added in 1911 by S. M. Denson, and a facsimile of this version is included in the Schirmer score.* Barber's setting begins with a nearly literal statement of the four-voice shape-note harmonization that is reproduced in facsimile in the Schirmer score, but places the tenor melody in the uppermost line (soprano). Furthermore, instead of the printed D♭ that appears in his source he uses a D♮, which suggests that he was aware of the regular practice of singing the hymn in the dorian mode rather than as notated.†

There are four variations: in the first three, each phrase of the theme is varied; the first and third variations in particular display Barber's lyrical style. The tune in the second variation is reserved for the feet while the hands are doing the "fuguing," and its lively counterpoint was pointed to by Roeckelein as similar in style to that of William Billings.[5] The fourth, which is the longest and most expressive variation, makes wonderful use of a descending-fourth motive treated chromatically and imitatively, while the hymn-tune weaves its melody in the upper voice, almost unrecognizable in its freely ornamented transformation.‡

*The Schirmer score (1959) incorrectly informs the reader that the hymn was published in the "Original Sacred Harp," Atlanta, Ga., 1869. The citation is inaccurate because not until 1911 was the hymn book published under that title. Earlier publications of "Wondrous Love" are written in three parts and with a key signature of G minor.

†Jackson writes specifically about this practice with regard to "Wondrous Love":

> There is still another type of minor-sounding scale or mode met with here and there in the *Sacred Harp*. It is that scale which has the lowered third and seventh and the *perfect sixth* . . . called in olden times the "dorian mode." In its lower tones it sounds minor . . . and in its upper reaches it sounds major. . . . It has been blurred in some instances in the notation because it was confused, by those who first recorded those unwritten dorian tunes, with what they took to be "minor." But the mode comes out clearly in such beautiful tunes as "Wondrous Love" where the printed *d*-flat is sung regularly as *d*-natural. ("The Story of the Sacred Harp," p. xiv)

‡An analysis of *Wondrous Love* by Larry Lynn Rhoades in his dissertation, *Theme and Variation in Twentieth-Century Organ Literature: Analyses of Variations by Alain, Barber, Distler, Dupré, Duruflé, and Sowerby* (Ohio State University, 1973, p. 109), concludes that Barber's work, on the whole, is conservative harmonically and structurally compared to other twentieth-century organ variations, even though the highly chromatic fourth variation contains some passages that suggest a "serialist" approach. Citing measures 80–81 as his example, Rhoades bases his observation on the fact that many of the measures contain ten or

Nocturne, Op. 33 (1959)

In 1959 Barber wrote a short work for piano, *Nocturne* (Op. 33), "an homage to John Field." One of the visitors to Capricorn during this time was pianist John Browning, who saw the manuscript of *Nocturne* and expressed an interest in performing it.* Later that year Barber sent him a copy, and Browning played it in San Diego, California. The pianist's comments about *Nocturne* may provide a clue to Barber's intentions:

> I think Sam was paying tribute, not so much to John Field as to Chopin, who often spoke of his admiration for Field's nocturnes. I doubt that Sam loved Field's music the way he loved Chopin's. So, in essence, Sam honors Chopin in this small but powerful work.†

On the surface, *Nocturne* shares features with the Romantic prototypes of the genre. In the outer sections of the three-part form (ABA′) an arpeggio accompaniment supports a serpentine cantabile melody; recurrences of the nocturne theme are decorated with a feathery chromatic filigree of sixteenth-note embellishments and trills; and a brief cadenza prepares for the final section. In his performance suggestions about the cadenza, John Browning cautions:

> You can play with ringing basses, a big sound, and flamboyant style. And don't drop the intensity until the piano marking in the fourth line of this page. Don't take the thirty-second duplets within the little notes of the cadenza too seriously. Barber often did this for two reasons: to keep the groups of sixteenth notes intact, and to indicate a slight rubato or irregularity in the way it should be played. Be free with it—make it sound sumptuous and colorful, diminishing to the feathery shimmer of . . . Debussy.[6]

more notes of the chromatic scale, and one (m. 81) all twelve tones of the scale. However, since the basic harmony is stabilized in the dorian mode, this passage seems to me another example of Barber's tendency during the fifties to flirt with twelve-tone procedures in combination with tonal structures.

*John Browning, interview with the author, 22 April 1986. Browning met Barber in 1956 when the young pianist's New York debut coincided with the premiere of *Medea's Meditation and Dance of Vengeance*. As a student of Rosina Lhévinne at the Juilliard School, Browning's career had skyrocketed with his successful winning of several major piano competitions—the Steinway Centennial Award (1954), the Leventritt (1955), and second prize in the Queen Elizabeth International Competition in Brussels (1956). Blessed with one of the most brilliant techniques of his generation, Browning was well versed in nineteenth-century repertoire; his playing met with the immediate favor of Barber.

†Browning, "Samuel Barber's Nocturne, Op. 33," *Clavier*, pp. 20–21. Sifferman supports Browning's intuition that Barber turned primarily to Chopin for his model. He points out, for example, that although *Nocturne* shares in common with Field's works its compound meter of 12/8 (as in ten of the eighteen in Field's collection) and freely embellished melodic line, it bears a closer stylistic resemblance to the nocturnes of Chopin because of the widely spaced intervals in its accompaniment figuration, ternary form (relatively rare in nocturnes of Field), rhythmic freedom of the embellishments of the melodic line (Field's embellishments are "measured"), and tendency toward double-note figurations in descending thirds and fourths (*Samuel Barber's Works for Solo Piano*, pp. 78–93).

Nocturne is not an imitation of either Field or Chopin. By the fourth measure, the theme displays Barber's own melodic penchant, especially for motion by intervals of fourths. The more restless middle section contains a melodic motive that is treated imitatively in all voices and introduces a developmental function rather than merely contrast.

Moreover, in *Nocturne,* as in several other works written during the period after the Piano Sonata, Barber tentatively introduces certain twelve-tone procedures in the thoroughly tonal context. Unlike the Piano Sonata, where the rows appear in the accompaniment, in *Nocturne* two twelve-tone rows are integrated into the melodic line, which remains anchored to a harmonic, tonal accompaniment. In the middle section, segments of the second row are used but borrow their rhythmic patterns from the first row.* Here, as in the sonata and the later *Ballade,* Barber favors large-scale motion by thirds—in the first section, the music moves from the tonic A♭ to the dominant by way of the mediant; in the last, from the tonic to F and back to A♭.

A Hand of Bridge, Op. 35 (1959)

In 1958 Menotti founded the Festival dei due Mondi in Spoleto, Italy. He instituted cabaret-style presentations called *Album Leaves* for which numerous artists wrote brief works lasting from three to fifteen minutes in various genres—operas, short overtures, theater pieces, and poems. Artists who contributed to these "intellectual cabarets" produced during the early years of the festival included Jean Cocteau, Thornton Wilder, W. H. Auden, Robert Rauschenberg, Larry Rivers, Donald McKayle, Italo Calvino, Aaron Copland, and Hans Werner Henze, among others.[7]

For the 1959 season, Barber and Menotti collaborated on *A Hand of Bridge,* a bitingly witty nine-minute opera. With settings and costumes by Jac Venza and conducted by Robert Feist, it was presented on 17 June 1959 at the Teatro Caio Melisso. Scored for four soloists and chamber orchestra, including piano, the opera unfolds around a card game played by two suburban couples "acutely alienated from one another, each living in his or her own private world."[8] The characters—Sally (played at Spoleto by Ellen Miville), Bill (William Lewis), Geraldine (Patricia Neway), and David (René Miville)—play out the situation on two levels, through the conversation over the bridge table and through glimpses into each of

*For a discussion of serialist techniques in *Nocturne,* see Sifferman, *Samuel Barber's Works for Solo Piano,* pp. 89 and 118–21; and Fairleigh, "Serialism in Barber's Solo Piano Works," pp. 16–17. Both Fairleigh and Sifferman point to Barber's individual way of combining serialism with tonality; the employment of such development techniques as retrograde and transposition, and a recurring characteristic of his serialist approach—a tendency to repeat one tone at the beginning and end of the row, thereby creating a series that does not really permit equality of the twelve tones because the repeated pitch acts as a tonal anchor.

Barber at Villa Verdiana, Spoleto, 1960.

their private thoughts. For the formalities of the card game, the vocal lines assume a recitative style accompanied by a solo piano (the theme returns twice more, in rondo fashion). As the inner monologues of the players are expressed, their vocal lines become increasingly melodic, each player in turn having a solo "arietta," as it were. The opera climaxes with a counterpoint of themes representing each of the four characters' subconscious thoughts. The rhythm is occasionally touched with jazz syncopations.

"On a superficial level, I often use the names of friends in the delineations of certain of my characters," Menotti has said about biographical aspects of his librettos, "as well as certain events in my own life. And sometimes I find myself mirrored in some of my characters, quite unconsciously however."[9] In *A Hand of Bridge,* there are indeed several conscious allusions to Menotti's and Barber's circle of friends. The character Bill is modeled after a businessman neighbor of the composers' who had pretensions of being very religious. In the opera he fantasizes about his secret lover Cymbaline, enumerating a list of names of men with whom he imagines her. Only those initiated into Barber's and Menotti's personal life would recognize the names: Christopher (Barber's nephew Christopher Beatty), Manfred (Ibel), Chuck (Charles Turner), Tommy (Thomas Schippers, conductor and close friend of Menotti who helped organize the first Spoleto festival and who eventually would conduct Barber's next opera *Antony and Cleopatra*), Dominic (the son of Barber's and Menotti's Mount Kisco neighbor, Hoime Chereau), Oliver, and Mortimer. Geraldine, who fantasizes about her ailing mother, is modeled after Sara, Barber's sister, who, according to Menotti, had a problematic relationship with her mother.

Victor Yellin, reviewing the score for *Notes* in 1961, pointed to Barber's music as "jazzy, funny, sensual, psychoanalytical, and vulgar," as the drama demands.[10] *A Hand of Bridge* has been extremely popular with college and conservatory groups because it is effective without requiring large performance forces or elaborate staging, and perhaps also because it carries a well-known composer's name. Crucial to the success of a chamber opera of brief duration, however, is a cast of singers who are able to establish characterization rapidly and who are vocally adept at conveying changes of mood. In nine minutes there is little time to develop a character or grow into a role.*

Toccata Festiva, Op. 36 (1960)

While on tour with the Philadelphia Orchestra in 1960, Eugene Ormandy received a long-distance telephone call from Mary Curtis Bok Zimbalist, which was given in a newspaper account as follows: "Eugene," she said, "are you standing? Please, sit down, I'm giving you that pipe organ you've been longing for." To Ormandy's incredulous response "Do you know how much it will cost?" the Philadelphia philanthropist assured him, "Don't worry about that."[11]

Mary Zimbalist's gift was donated to the Philadelphia Academy of Music in memory of her father, Cyrus H. K. Curtis, who had played the organ himself. It seems appropriate that she invited Barber—one of her most prominent protégés and a composer whose work suited her musical tastes—to write a piece for the new organ in memory of her father. As a gesture of friendship and in appreciation of her continued patronage, Barber refused to accept a fee for the commissioned work, called *Toccata Festiva*, which was begun at Capricorn during the early spring of 1960 and finished in Munich by May of the same year.†

The new organ, built by the Aeolian-Skinner Company of Boston, cost $150,000 and was reported to be "a lordly example in the royal tradition."[12] Its construction aimed, above all, for tonal brilliance.[13] At the time it was built, the instrument was the largest movable pipe organ in the world, weighing 200,000 pounds and having 4,102 pipes, three manuals, and seventy-three stops. Except for permanent pipe installations in the two upper boxes, it could be moved on the stage for performances and then taken apart and stored until needed.

Toccata Festiva—scored for solo organ, piccolo, two flutes, two oboes, English horn, two clarinets, bass clarinet, two bassoons, four horns, three

* A comparison of two student performances I saw in 1987, for example, one at the New England Conservatory and one at Brooklyn College, pointed up this difficulty. The latter, although produced without costumes or sets, seemed more convincing because the singers demonstrated a quick grasp of their parts and the production maintained a lively momentum throughout the nine minutes.

† The amount of the commission was reported to have been $2,000.

trumpets, three trombones, tuba, timpani, percussion, and strings—was intended to exhibit the full technical possibilities of the new organ in combination with the famed virtuosity of the Philadelphia Orchestra. The music bears Barber's hallmark of expressive lyricism in combination with characteristic idioms of the Baroque toccata. In one movement, the work is organized in sections alternating rapid finger work with quieter passages. Most of the material for the work is generated from a two-measure theme that bears a strong rhythmic profile (in 5/8 meter). Its subtle transformations are interspersed with solo passages for organ—florid and virtuosic, improvisatory or developmental. A brilliant opening fanfare, with the full orchestra used as a giant keyboard, leads into the emphatic announcement of the main theme by trumpets with impassioned interjections from the organ. A virtuoso pedal cadenza for solo organ, pointed to as one of the most striking features of the work, was written with the cooperation of the composer's friend Thomas Schippers, who was an accomplished organist as well as a conductor.[14]

Paul Callaway, organist and choir director of the Cathedral in Washington, D.C., was asked by Barber to play the first performance of the piece less than a month before the concert. The organist's recollections of rehearsals with the Philadelphia Orchestra, during which Barber added suggestions about tempos, reveal that although Ormandy seemed to have viewed the work as "slight"—and clearly it is a virtuoso *pièce d'occasion*—he was determined to make it gain significance through his performance.[15]

For the organ's inauguration on 30 September 1960 at the Academy of Music, much fuss was made over the imposing instrument, its array of black and gold pipes forming a backdrop to the members of the Philadelphia Orchestra. The concert had a double significance in that it also marked the beginning of Eugene Ormandy's twenty-fifth season as conductor. Moreover, it was the first time the city had an organ in a concert hall, in addition to those in churches or, most famous of all, in Wanamaker's Department Store, where an elephantine organ had been installed in the grand court during the thirties.

Reviews of *Toccata Festiva* marked the work as "expertly written, sonorous and majestic in scope,"[16] "a display piece which set forth the possibilities of the instrument and the technical prowess of Callaway,"[17] who played the pedal cadenza "*con fuoco,* with flying feet."[18] Barber was on hand to receive the "tumultuous applause" one might expect for a native son of Philadelphia.[19]

Die Natali, Op. 37 (1960)

Following completion of *Prayers of Kierkegaard* in 1954, Barber was given a second commission by the Koussevitzky Music Foundation in conjunction with the Boston Symphony Orchestra. It was six years, however, before he got around to writing the orchestral piece, primarily because his attention was consumed with the opera *Vanessa* and the several short works discussed above. An inscription in a notebook kept by Barber in the late 1950s portends the work that fulfilled the commission: "*Die Natali carminum sequentia* (At Christmastime)/*Seguito di canti nel giorno de Natale* (a row of carols)."* *Die Natali,* dedicated to Serge and Natalie Koussevitzky, was begun in July 1960 at Santa Cristina and completed at Capricorn in November of the same year.

Die Natali is scored for full orchestra, with a percussion section that includes antique cymbals, celesta, and bells. It was first performed by the Boston Symphony Orchestra under the baton of Charles Münch on 22 and 23 December 1960 in Symphony Hall. Using Christmas carols for thematic material, Barber composed an ingenious fabric of harmonically colored contrapuntal variations, employing such devices as canon, double canon, augmentation, and diminution. The work opens with strings and brasses sounding the melody "O come, O come, Emmanuel." Next, antiphonal choirs—flutes, piccolos, and strings grouped against brasses—play the melody and three variations of "Lo, how a rose e'er blooming." "We three kings of Orient are" (with separate preludes for each of the Magi) is followed by rhythmic variations on "God rest you merry, gentlemen," interrupted by "Good King Wenceslas." "Silent night" is heard over a figuration in 7/8 meter. A return of "O come, O come, Emmanuel" is followed by two variations, pizzicato and lyrical. An ostinato based on two phrases of "Adeste fideles" crescendos to the climax with "Joy to the world." "Silent night" brings the work to a quiet close.

Correspondence about *Die Natali* between Barber and Harold Spivacke, chief librarian of the Music Division of the Library of Congress, bears on financial matters that were probably of concern to composers in general during the 1960s and to the future of historical archives specifically:

> I have just completed, at long last, a very late Koussevitzky commission which Münch will perform in Boston December 22nd. It is called "Die Natali"—chorale preludes for Christmas. As you know, Koussevitzky commissions automatically come to you so I do not suppose I could consider this my donation for this year. Or could I? Please clarify this for me.[20]

Barber referred here to a situation that existed prior to 1976, when composers were able to receive substantial tax benefits from donations of their manuscripts to a nonprofit organization. A composer of Barber's stature,

*The notebook, in the collection of Valentin Herranz, was made in Germany and was probably kept by Barber during the late 1950s after he had met Manfred Ibel (on the last pages of the notebook are summaries of German grammatical constructions and vocabulary, English idioms and their Italian translations).

for example, could declare a high figure for the gift of a holograph score, or even his sketches, as a "donation to the Library." This explains to some extent the large numbers of holographs given by prominent American composers up to that date and their decreasing numbers afterwards. The terms of the Koussevitzky commission, which stated a composer was *required to donate* his manuscript to the library, were somewhat ambiguous about whether or not composers could deduct the value of their manuscripts from their income tax. Spivacke was not able to clarify the issue and so referred Barber to his own accountant.[21]

Barber sent the manuscript of *Die Natali* to the Library of Congress in March of 1961 and asked for the remaining half of the commission fee, $1,000. A month later he wrote again to Spivacke, pressing him, "I wonder if you would be so kind as to speed up the check for payment of the Koussevitzky Commission as I am going to Europe May 9th and need to pay some bills."[22] Apparently the matter was resolved, as there is no further correspondence between them on the subject.

In 1979, when Barber learned that Eugene Ormandy was planning to perform *Die Natali* with the Philadelphia Orchestra, he made known some of his dissatisfactions with the piece and made suggestions to the conductor about its performance, in particular about the problematic beginning:

> This is a piece which has both good and bad places, and I am sure you will doctor up the bad ones to my advantage. . . .
>
> The piece might, however, be useful for Christmas, and I am going to try to come over for the performance to see how it hangs together under your magisterial hand. The beginning, for instance, simply doesn't come off. I wanted very distant string harmonics, like an echo, but I'm afraid it is a bad key for harmonics. Perhaps if you just play it sordina and forget the harmonics, it will solve the problem; or maybe you have a better idea. The rest goes along quite well and I particularly like the variations on "Silent Night".*

Ormandy responded:

> The last time I saw you I told you we would perform your "Die Natali" on December 14th and 15th and you seemed pleasantly surprised. At the same time you told me you would like to attend the performance because you have some questions in your mind.
>
> I spent yesterday on this work and not having exact tempo instructions for several parts of it, I believe I got it into my head.
>
> Would you want to come to the last rehearsal on December 14th, either at 10 o'clock or around 11, but not later, and also sit with Gretel at the 2 P.M. performance?
>
> With much affection from Gretel and myself.[23]

*Letter, 16 November 1979, Philadelphia Orchestra Archives. Barber was so fond of the variations on "Silent night" that he made a transcription of them for organ in 1961.

This warm exchange of letters—written shortly before Ormandy's eightieth birthday and his retirement, and only two years before Barber's death—seems to represent some reconciliation of what had been an uneasy relationship that had peaked between the composer and the conductor in the late 1970s.*

*Throughout their relationship, Barber's comments about the conductor suggest mistrust: for example, about the performance of his First Symphony, he wrote, "Walter conducted superbly; the men came to life as never under Ormandy" (letter to Homer, 24 February 1944); on another occasion: "Both Szell and Ormandy have scheduled my Second Essay for the same week . . . and I shall probably be blamed by the latter" (letter to Koussevitzky, 27 November 1944); about *Medea,* "Ormandy announced to me the 1st day that it was going to be a flop and he wished it had never been put at the end of the program: very encouraging!" (letter to Homer, 21 December 1947); Barber tells of "dinner at Ormandy's (an unpleasant experience which I could not avoid; Virgil Thomson was his house guest, and the amount of musical politics shamelessly exchanged between these two made one tremble for the American musical world)" (letter to Homer, 17 August 1952, from Gstaad, Switzerland). Misunderstandings were apparent, also, in the late 1970s in circumstances surrounding plans for a commission and for recordings of *The Lovers* and *Prayers of Kierkegaard* (see chapter 17).

16

LINCOLN CENTER COMMISSIONS

The Opening of Philharmonic Hall

Concerto for Piano and Orchestra, Op. 38 (1962), and *Canzone* for flute and piano, Op. 38a (1959)

The piano concerto that Barber had worked on for more than three years while a student at the Curtis Institute, and which was neither published nor performed, was his only effort in this genre for three decades.* When asked in 1964 why he thought American composers had such inhibitions about writing piano concertos, he replied:

> I think some American composers don't know the piano well enough . . . and they know the orchestra. They have a funny attitude toward the piano—they use all the possible richness in orchestral scoring, and they will cut down their palette to the point of a gray sort of a palette for piano, and I think sometimes they just don't know it.[1]

In 1959 Barber's publishers asked him to write a piano concerto in honor of the forthcoming hundredth anniversary of G. Schirmer, Inc., which would coincide with the inaugural week of performances at the new Philharmonic Hall at Lincoln Center for the Performing Arts in 1962.† When,

*In 1964, when asked by Jay Harrison if he had written a piano concerto before, Barber either forgot, or wished to forget, his earlier one: "This is my first concerto, and there seems to be a need for one in the field," he said ("Entr'acte," interviews with Barber and Browning, program notes of the Cleveland Orchestra, 24 January 1964, pp. 393–97).

†Lincoln Center had been in planning stages since 1955, but by the time the groundbreaking ceremonies took place on 14 May 1959, commissions for the opening week of twelve concerts were already being announced by many institutions and individuals. Sponsors included the New York Philharmonic, Eugene Ormandy, the Juilliard School of Music, the Ford Foundation, G. Schirmer, Inc., and the center itself, for works by Copland *(Connotations)*, Thomson *(Pange Lingua)*, Henry Cowell *(Hymns and Fuguing Tune No. 14)*, Persichetti *(Shimah B'koli*, Psalm 130), Piston *(Lincoln Center Festival Overture)*, Bergsma *(In Celebration: Toccata for Orchestra)*, and Schuman *(A Song of Orpheus)*. Barber received a $6,000 commission for the concerto.

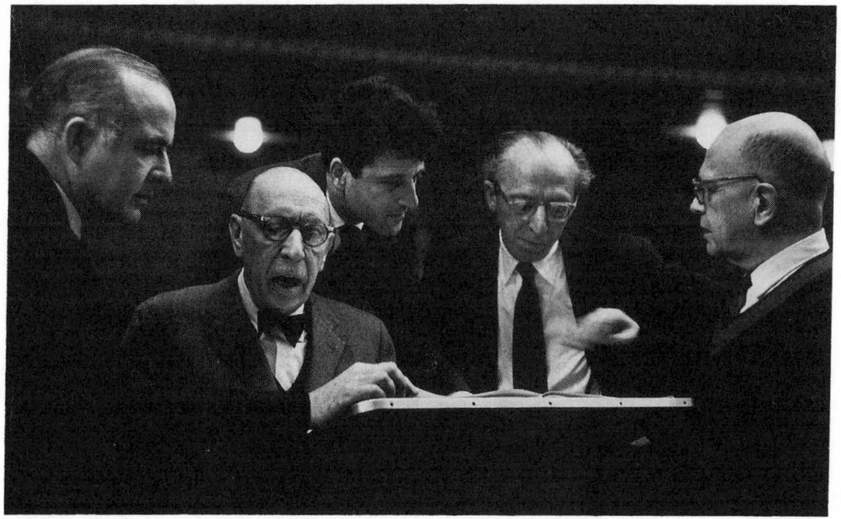

Igor Stravinsky, second from left, and pianists Barber, Lukas Foss, Aaron Copland, and Roger Sessions at rehearsal of *Les Noces,* December 1959. *(Courtesy of Gian Carlo Menotti)*

twenty-six years later, retired Schirmer executive Hans Heinsheimer was asked "Why Barber?" he emphatically declared, "There was no one else, he was our most popular composer—our best."[2]

Barber apparently had already begun work on the concerto early in March 1960, for in an interview with John Ardoin he referred to finishing a Boston Symphony commission *(Die Natali)* that was "he would not say how many years late" and in the same breath mentioned possibilities of writing works for the opening season of the Philharmonic and the new opera house at Lincoln Center.[3] When Ardoin visited Barber at Capricorn, he noticed that on the composer's work table were many contemporary scores, including some by Boulez, Copland, Webern, Berg, and Schoenberg.*

The concerto was written for John Browning for performance with the Boston Symphony Orchestra under Erich Leinsdorf. When the young pianist had made his debut with the New York Philharmonic on 2 February 1956, Barber attended all rehearsals because of the premiere of one of his own works and heard Browning prepare the Rachmaninoff *Rhapsody on a Theme by Paganini.*† He had always admired the Russian style of pian-

* Ardoin claims to have "eyed a suspicious number of scores of piano concertos, which seemed to indicate that this is a form Barber was seriously considering" ("Samuel Barber at Capricorn," p. 5). Also on his desk was a newly acquired autographed picture of Stravinsky rehearsing a recent performance of *Les Noces,* played by Barber, Copland, Foss, and Sessions at Town Hall.

† The program included *Medea's Meditation and Dance of Vengeance.* The young pian-

ism and Browning, who had studied with Rosina Lhévinne, had been rigorously trained in that style.[4] Later, Barber would express his admiration for Browning's playing:

> I'll say . . . that to have anybody who is such a musician—I am not going to throw so many bouquets—but who is so plastic in his approach for new work, who is able to change interpretations when we find out something is wrong, when something doesn't go, when something can be improved—to have an artist who can change the way Browning can with his musicianship and with his technical equipment is just wonderful.[5]

As he had done in the past for other soloists, Barber planned to tailor the concerto to Browning's individual style and technical prowess. Almost as soon as he began thinking about the work he invited the pianist to Capricorn, where for three days he had him play through virtually all of his repertoire; Barber, Browning remembered, especially loved Chopin, Scriabin, Debussy, and Rachmaninoff.[6]

Barber profited from Browning's stories of Madame Lhévinne, her insistence that he practice double sixths, her use of the term *flutter pedal*—keeping a "wet" pedal but shifting it rapidly so the sound does not become too thick—and her "old Russian trick" of effecting a brilliant sound by placing a run of parallel octaves two octaves apart.[7] Much of this technical *sagesse* came to be incorporated into the concerto.*

The second movement of the concerto—Canzone—was completed a year before the outer movements.† It had begun life independently of the concerto as Elegy for Flute and Piano, written in 1959 for Manfred Ibel, a young German art student and amateur flute player to whom Barber dedicated the piano concerto.‡ Because from the early 1950s Menotti was

---

ist, who greatly admired Barber's music and was to maintain a long friendship with the composer, introduced *Souvenirs* to Los Angeles audiences in 1957 at the Hollywood Bowl and premiered *Nocturne* in 1959 (discussed in chapter 15).

* See, for example, movement I, one measure before rehearsal no. 23.

† Browning recalls that this movement was the first to come to him, and that he began practicing it from a copy Barber gave to him (interview with the author).

‡ Barber met Ibel in Munich during the spring of 1958, before rehearsals began for *Vanessa* at Salzburg. They were introduced by the eminent photographer Herbert List, who had done portraits of many famous contemporary artists, including Picasso, Cocteau, Miro, and whose photograph of Barber appeared in several publications related to the forthcoming Salzburg production of *Vanessa*. Ibel, from Hamburg, was the son of a painter and of a well-known anthologist and interpreter of German classic and Romantic literature. He was twenty-one at the time Barber met him. In November 1960, Barber eventually helped Ibel come permanently to the United States, where he lived for several years in a stone cottage on the grounds of Capricorn. Twice, in 1965 and 1972, he expanded the cottage, and, in addition, created many miles of walking trails through the fifty-three acres of woodland so that Barber could enjoy long nature walks on his own land. Ibel's talents in design and construction were recognized and encouraged by Barber's neighbor, the architect Edward Barnes. Aided by Barber's financial support and scholarships, he earned a degree in architecture from Yale University in 1969. When Capricorn was sold in 1973, Barber and Menotti deeded the stone cottage and four acres of land to Ibel (Manfred Ibel, interview with the author, 10 April 1987, New York City).

drawn more and more into the public arena and the demands of his and Barber's professional lives limited their time together, Barber welcomed having an available companion with whom he could travel and talk about music and literature. What seemed to draw him to the charismatic Ibel was their "mutual affinity for the spirit of German Romanticism and culture."*

During the summer of 1959 they shared a house on Martha's Vineyard, and it was at this time Barber wrote the song for flute and piano, "Elegy," that in 1962 he orchestrated for the second movement of his Piano Concerto.† It is, in a sense, a wordless Lied, tenderly and mournfully romantic.‡

When Barber orchestrated the piece for the concerto, he distributed the original melodic line among solo flute, oboe, and piano.§ While some of the original piano accompaniment in "Elegy" is preserved in the piano part of the concerto, most of it is divided between harp and strings, which play the original sixteenth-note figurations in tremolos of thirty-second notes. Barber extended the original version twenty-six measures, making the second movement of the concerto nearly twice as long as "Elegy." The new material is a variation of the unadorned melody, which now is presented alternately by piano, violins, or solo wind instruments against the piano's intricate chromatic figurations, redolent of the cascading inner voices found in the piano music of Rachmaninoff.

After the first two movements of the Piano Concerto were completed in 1960, Erich Leinsdorf was invited to Mount Kisco to hear Browning play them. The conductor believed that the *pianissimo* ending Barber had written for the first movement did not offer enough contrast to the beginning of the slow movement. Within two days Barber responded to his

*Ibel, interview with the author, 10 April 1987. Ibel's observation is supported, too, by the tone of Barber's letters in the course of their friendship, which—like that with Charles Turner—long outlasted a romantic relationship and extended almost to the end of Barber's life. His correspondence to Ibel is filled with poetic references, anticipations of long country walks and conversations, confessions of nostalgia and angst (especially over the sale of Capricorn) that are not as prevalent in Barber's correspondence to other friends.

One of their activities was playing flute and piano duets, mostly Bach flute sonatas. In order to circumvent Ibel's intimidation by obscure key signatures, Barber would either facilitate his reading of the flute parts by Bach or Debussy by transposing them into easier keys or else rewriting the music without a signature, inserting accidentals throughout the score. As Manfred's skills on the flute improved, Barber on two occasions presented him with a new flute (Ibel, interview with the author, 10 April 1987).

†"Elegy" was published by Schirmer in 1962 as *Canzone* for violin and piano (also for flute and piano).

‡So that Ibel would be able to play "Elegy" with piano accompaniment in Germany after the summer, Barber made a "music-minus-one" recording with the piano part played by himself and mailed it to the young man as a Christmas present (Ibel, interview with the author, 10 April 1987).

§A photocopy of "Elegy" for flute and piano is at the Library of Congress, Music Division. The original holograph pencil score of this work, also at the Library of Congress, shows an erasure of the word *Elegy,* over which are written the words *Canzone (for Manfred).* Both pieces, identical except for title and dedication, bear the inscription "Copyright 1961 by G. Schirmer, Inc."

Barber and Dimitri Shostakovich at the Congress of Soviet Composers, Moscow, March 1962. *(Courtesy of Gian Carlo Menotti)*

suggestion with a new *fortissimo* ending so that the second movement, in contrast, could seem to "emerge from nowhere."[8]

The third movement took Barber the longest time to write. The death of his sister on 3 July 1961 put him into a depression that noticeably affected his ability to work for a long period of time.[9] Further interruptions occurred in March 1962 when Barber was invited to Russia as the first American composer ever to attend the biennial Congress of Soviet Composers, an official gathering to discuss methods and philosophies of composition. Because he was invited as an individual, not as an official representative of the United States government, he had an opportunity to speak his mind freely. He told an audience of over a thousand composers from all over Russia and other Eastern European countries that they and their American colleagues faced many of the same problems in the "search for contemporary national style"—but he warned that there could never be a five-year plan for talent and that too much interference with a composer was as unwise as too much encouragement. "I even made a plea for experimentation," he said. "They seemed to like what I said, although much of it was at variance with policies and thoughts outlined by others at the conference."[10] Over luncheon, he had an opportunity to converse about music with Nikita Khrushchev.* While in Russia, Barber found that several of his works were printed in Russian editions—the collected songs, the Piano Sonata, the *Adagio for Strings,* the Cello Concerto, and the Violin Concerto—and he was able to collect royalties on these publications, something no other American composer had ever done before.[11]

* Khrushchev, declaring "any statesman who doesn't like music is abnormal," obviously had conservative taste: he told Barber he had mistakenly believed something was wrong with his radio while it was playing music of a contemporary Russian composer; "music should be musical. . . . I don't really understand new Russian music" (Alan Rich, "Khrushchev Talks of Modern Music," *New York Times,* 14 April 1962).

After his trip to Russia, Barber continued work on the Piano Concerto. He finished the last movement on 9 September 1962, only two weeks before the premiere, thereby putting enormous pressure on Browning. The pianist not only had to commit to memory the notes, markings, and all of the orchestral score but also had to grasp the overall musical meaning of the composition and form a concept of how the work should be played in only a few days—"a process which would normally take over a year of constant playing and study to achieve," he said.*

With little time for rehearsals—there were two in Boston the week before the premiere (one of which was taken up almost totally with correcting orchestral parts) and one in New York—refinements were made up to the end. Only one day before the premiere, for example, Barber telephoned the orchestra's librarian with instructions to bring a whip for the third movement, a change that was incorporated into the Schirmer edition of 1962. A holograph score of this movement shows also that the original scoring called for a wood block and that at rehearsal no. 8 the percussion called for a xylophone with soft mallets, unlike the 1962 edition, which calls for hard ones.

The three movements of the concerto are in minor keys, related by descending minor thirds—E minor, C♯ minor, and B♭ minor. The first movement, in sonata form, begins with a quasi-cadenza for the solo piano. Uncharacteristically, Barber wrote an analysis of his music for the program notes for the premiere:†

> The Concerto opens with a solo for piano in recitative style in which three themes or figures are announced, the first declamatory, the second and third rhythmic. The orchestra interrupts, più mosso, to sing an impassioned main theme, not before stated. All this material is embroidered more quietly and occasionally whimsically by piano and orchestra until the tempo slackens (doppio meno mosso) and the oboe introduces a second lyric section. A development along symphonic lines leads to a cadenza for soloist, and a recapitulation with fortissimo ending.‡

The composer's description of the last movement is as follows:

* *New York Herald Tribune,* 16 August 1964. Barber told Jay Harrison ("Entr'acte," p. 396) that Aaron Copland visited him and declared "You cannot treat a soloist like this!" "So I suddenly thought of something the next morning," he continued. "I was terrorized into thinking of something which became the last movement."

† No doubt this was done under some duress, for his attitude about such writing was clearly stated near the end of his life to Phillip Ramey during a torturous interview (for interviewer and composer) for program notes for the first performance of the *Third Essay.* Ramey asked: "Where for instance is the first subject?" Barber responded: "Do you think anybody really reads these things?" Ramey: "Sure, I grew up on them, didn't you?" Barber: "No, I didn't read them." (I am indebted to Phillip Ramey for allowing me to listen to this recorded interview from 1978.)

‡ "Notes on the Program," *Philharmonic Hall Program* 1962–63, 24 September 1962, p. 44. A paper delivered by Paul Hayden (Louisiana State University) at the Sonneck Society Annual Meeting in March 1985 assembles evidence of twelve-tone writing throughout the first movement.

a.

b.

Example 16.1 Barber, Piano Concerto, Op. 38, third movement at 20. Debussy, *Les Fées sont d'exquises danseuses,* mm. 1–5 (Durand, 1913).

> The last movement (allegro molto in 5/8) after several fortissimo repeated chords by the orchestra, plunges headlong into an ostinato bass figure for piano, over which several themes are tossed. There are two contrasting sections (one "un pochettino meno," for clarinet solo, and one for three flutes, muted trombones and harp, "con grazia") where the fast tempo relents; but the ostinato figure keeps insistently reappearing, mostly by the piano protagonist, and the 5/8 meter is never changed.[12]

Browning recalls Barber's strong response to the Debussy he was playing at the time the concerto was being written, and he believes that passages in the third movement (beginning at rehearsal no. 20, for example) were inspired specifically by the prelude *Les Fées sont d'exquises danseuses.*[13] It is true that certain characteristics seem similar—possibly the fluidity of the rapid *pianissimo* figurations and transparent texture—though the rhythmic groupings and harmonic progressions differ (see Example 16.1).

a.

b.

Example 16.2 Piano Concerto, revisions of piano part in third movement, 3 mm. before [32]. *a.* Early version, holograph. *(Library of Congress)* *b.* Final version (G. Schirmer, 1962).

Certain influences in the third movement are traced to Vladimir Horowitz.[14] Twice prior to the premiere Barber took Browning to play the concerto for his "pianistic god," who warmly received the young pianist and made suggestions about the work and how it should be played.[15] At one of these visits, Horowitz confirmed Browning's insistence that a passage in the third movement—rising seconds in sixteenth notes—was unplayable at the required tempo or, for that matter, any tempo compatible with the movement.[16] Comparison between the passage as it appears in a partial holograph manuscript at the Library of Congress (Example 16.2a) and the final published version (Example 16.2b) reveals that in three measures before rehearsal no. 32 rising seconds of sixteenth notes were changed to eighth notes.*

Four measures before rehearsal no. 15, a major alteration to the piano part was evidently made in the final stages of publication (see Example 16.3, page proofs and published edition). According to Browning, these changes were suggested by himself and Vladimir Horowitz because rapid tempos precluded so dense a texture.[17]

* Holographs at the Library of Congress include sketches of all movements, short scores of all movements, and a full orchestral score. There are also copies of the orchestral score and a two-piano score of the second movement. John Browning has a photocopy of the holograph short-score (similar to the one at the Library of Congress, but with annotations by the pianist) and a copy of the two-piano score of the second movement.

a.

b.

Example 16.3 Piano Concerto, revision of piano part, third movement, 4 mm. before [15]. *a.* Early version, page proof. *(Library of Congress) b.* Final version (G. Schirmer, 1962).

The premiere of the concerto was on 24 September 1962 at the second concert of the opening week of performances in the new Philharmonic Hall. Presaging acoustical problems that would haunt the concert hall for many years hence, after the previous night's performance it had been necessary to make adjustments to the overhead panels in an attempt to improve the clarity of the orchestral sound. It was observed the night the concerto was played that, although there were still difficulties, the basses sounded stronger, the woodwinds more defined, the violins warmer, and,

John Browning and Barber discuss the Piano Concerto prior to its premiere on 24 September 1962.

with the exception of the overbrightness of the brasses, in general there was a more homogeneous mix of sound.[18] After the premiere, Barber wrote to William Schuman of his reaction to hearing the concerto played alternately in Boston and New York:

> I think I marked the winds up and down quite a lot according to which state I was in. But I draw no conclusion from this and was myself enthralled with the sound of the hall—a new sound perhaps: and there you are raising and lowering your clouds like Zeus, to match the orchestration.[19]

Browning's performance brought the audience to its feet shouting and applauding. The critic Harold Schonberg acknowledged the pianist as one of the "more expert technicians around" who "gave a very strong performance" that would be "even stronger when he works his way into the score." He further commented that, other than having some difficulty with the middle movement's cascades of inner voices, Browning had "stormed the work, surmounted the peaks, and proved himself to be a virtuoso with a fine sense of line."* The pianist's exhilaration and persuasiveness, Miles Kastendieck declared, conveyed his awareness of "just how good the concerto is."[20]

But more significantly, what was recognized uniformly was "the birth of an American classic."[21] "Aside from being an exciting piece rhythmically, it is unashamedly melodic," wrote Kastendieck, "undoubtedly, the latter aspect finding favor with the audience, for people even in the sixth

*Harold Schonberg, "Music: Barber Concerto," *New York Times*, 25 September 1962. Schonberg found the concerto modeled roughly on such contemporary works as Prokofiev's Third Piano Concerto, with the finale in 5/8 a "first cousin to his Seventh Sonata."

decade of the century still find a well-turned melodic line most gratifying."[22] Moreover, he claimed, Barber "has not been afraid to be himself in the midst of the whirlpool of musical currents surrounding him. The concerto is of this century but also of the mainstream of traditional music."[23]

Browning—who still considers the work to be the most important contemporary piano concerto written since Bartók's third—played the concerto fifty times within its first two seasons. In 1965, while on an international tour with George Szell and the Cleveland Orchestra through Sweden, Poland, France, Czechoslovakia, Germany, and England, he received critical acclaim for Barber's concerto in whatever city it was performed; Russian audiences found it "very Russian in flavor . . . written in the grand bravura style."[24] By 1969 Browning had played the work almost 150 times and thus had become as closely identified with it as Horowitz had been with Barber's Piano Sonata.[25]

The concerto won two awards for Barber: in 1963, his second Pulitzer Prize;[26] and in 1964, a belated Music Critics' Circle Award, the awards for the 1962–63 season having been delayed because of a newspaper strike in 1963.[27]

In his review of the concerto Paul Henry Lang offered a defense of Barber's conservatism as a demonstration of the viability of traditional form and musical language:

> Mr. Barber, though a modern composer, is not a member of the avant-garde and in some quarters will be denounced as a "traditionalist." But what is tradition? The slavish imitator of the past denies the history of progress, denies his own age, and insults the very thing he pretends to imitate by misusing it. There is considerable difference between this sort of traditionalism and a true understanding of the continuity of creative endeavor. That a work is deliberately within a somewhat older style is not a flaw unless it fails to gather impetus from the artist's temperament in the proceeding. This concerto rises everywhere above the painstaking and the ingenious; its individual elements have importance in themselves and the whole is not greater than the sum of its parts.[28]

The Piano Concerto marks the high point in Barber's career. With an arrow-straight record of consistent success, his esteem with the international musical public and his recognition from established American cultural institutions were perhaps more secure during the early sixties than those of any other living American composer.

Andromache's Farewell, Op. 39 (1963)

Greek mythology and literature had long been a source of inspiration to Barber and, as was discussed in earlier chapters of this book, had yielded

Samuel Barber in the early 1960s.

several musical works. His sketchbook from the 1930s includes a setting of lines by the Greek poet Meleager of Gadara, translated by J. A. Symonds.[29] Later, in 1943, he had considered, but did not write, a choral setting of lines from *The Bacchae.** A commission for Martha Graham in 1946 resulted in a ballet, an orchestral suite, and a one-movement work based on Euripides' *Medea* (see chapter 10).

For the second of his commissions for the opening season of Lincoln Center, 1962–63, Barber turned again to Euripides, using for this occasion a scene from *The Trojan Women.*† He composed a concert scene for soprano and orchestra, *Andromache's Farewell,* Op. 39, an intensely dramatic portrayal of the captive mother who must relinquish her son to be killed. There is no evidence that Barber expected to expand the scene into an opera, though it might have worked well as such.‡

*In a letter to William Strickland (spring 1943, on United States Army stationery) he mentions his preference for Edith Hamilton's Greek translations over Murray's "stuffy ones."

†A copybook in Barber's estate (loaned to the author by Valentin Herranz) and dating from the late 1950s includes an outline of the family tree of the Trojan Priam and Hecuba. His notes include the comment that Andromache (wife of Hector) was destined to marry Achilles' son, Neoptolemus. There are also notes on the family trees of the "House of Atreus (in Aeschylus)" and of the Theban plays of Sophocles (441 to 405 B.C.).

‡Martha Graham choreographed the scene as a ballet—*Andromache's Lament.* Dedicated to world peace, it was performed for the first time on 23 June 1982. Her ballet includes

A prefatory note in the score explains the events leading to the episode he set to music:

> Scene: an open space before Troy, which has just been captured by the Greeks. All Trojan men have been killed or have fled and the women and children are held captives. Each Trojan woman has already been allotted to a Greek warrior and the ships are now ready to take them into exile. Andromache, widow of Hector, Prince of Troy, has been given as a slave-wife to the son of Achilles. She has just been told that she cannot take her little son with her in the ship. For it has been decreed by the Greeks that a hero's son must not be allowed to live and that he is to be hurled over the battlements of Troy. She bids him farewell. . . .[30]

Barber's music begins at this point. For Andromache's anguished soliloquy he used a new translation of Euripides' text especially provided for him by the contemporary American poet John Patrick Creagh (b. 1930). The two had met in the early 1960s in Val Gardena, where Barber and Menotti had rented a chalet for the summer near the hotel where Creagh happened to be staying.[31] Barber suggested that the poet might be able to "help him with a text he wanted to set but was having trouble with because the English scripts he had in hand were simply not conducive to music in any way."[32] Creagh recalled:

> I worked away at it (and it isn't long), and when I thought I'd gotten something together I went down and we tried it out. For about three long days we tried it out, amending and suggesting this way and that between words and music.*

Barber attempted to express in his music the broad range of emotions suggested by Andromache's soliloquy: dignity, resignation, reflection, anguish, tenderness, compassion, anger, and bitterness. Scored for a large orchestra of two flutes, piccolo, two oboes, English horn, two clarinets, bass clarinet, two bassoons, three trumpets, four horns, three trombones, tuba, harp, percussion, and strings, *Andromache's Farewell* represents a masterful fusion of lyricism, inventive counterpoint, and a full palette of orchestral color, all directed toward a precise rendering of the emotional and psychological values of the poetry. Solo woodwind passages project tenderness and poignancy; choirs of brass instruments associate with anger, destruction, and acrimony.

The vocal music for *Andromache's Farewell* is in three sections—*moderato with dignity, andante un poco mosso,* and *tempo primo*—with two impassioned allegro interjections. A lengthy orchestral introduction

---

four characters—Andromache, Hector, child, Menelaus—and two choruses, one of men and one of women.

*Letter to author, 8 December 1988. Creagh, who has since written three librettos (all for works by John Eaton), said that working with Barber was his first experience of working as a "word-man with a composer" and in retrospect he was very grateful for it.

(allegro con fuoco) is based on two of the principal themes, which are presented at the outset and which obsessively permeate the vocal and orchestral texture throughout, sometimes with greatly altered character. The first theme, announced boldly by trombones and a tuba (Example 16.4, m. 1), will be mirrored at measure 46 in Andromache's opening words, "So you must die, my son." The second theme, for piccolo, flutes, and strings (mm. 1–2), will be associated with her outburst "He cannot come from the grave."

A third motive, an inner-voice counterpoint, played by oboes and violas at measure 2, is a twelve-tone set developed largely from perfect and diminished fifths and fourths. This jagged-shaped figure is woven into the fabric of the score in numerous places throughout. The aria closes with a modified recapitulation of the primary theme set against a more transparently textured accompaniment.

Musical imagery is used sparingly, for the psychologically directed text offers less opportunity for pictorialism than for emotional expression. A striking example of Barber as a skillful imagist, however, occurs on several levels with the words "falling! falling. . . . Thus will your life end." In this passage, a three-part counterpoint underlines the downward motion in different rhythmic units and melodic shapes—sustained note values for the vocal line; five-note clusters of superimposed fourths and fifths (spanning an interval of a seventeenth) for the brasses; and a jagged sixteenth-note pattern in the lowest voices. The precipitous fall is portrayed even more vividly by descending blocks of chords, the rapid tumble accelerated through rhythmic diminution (see Example 16.5).

The American soprano Martina Arroyo prepared for the premiere performance of *Andromache's Farewell* under Barber's tutelage.* She had auditioned for the part with Thomas Schippers, who would conduct the work and who had enthusiastically recommended her to Barber. Arroyo believes that the composer was attracted in particular to the warm, dark tones of her voice and her ability to spin a *pianissimo* tone, much as he had appreciated those qualities in the voice of Leontyne Price.[33]

At the time of Arroyo's audition, *Andromache* was nearly completed; only the orchestral introduction and the middle section remained to be set, the passage in which Andromache vents her anger at Helen and expresses outrage over the anticipated murder of her son Astyanax (in the score, beginning four measures after rehearsal no. 20 to the return to *tempo primo*). These dramatic passages were, according to Arroyo, composed after Barber had heard her sing and knew the particular strengths of her voice. "The finishing touches were tailored to my voice," she said, "the *pianissimo*, the *crescendo*, for example, in some of the phrases."[34] Those dy-

* Arroyo, born in New York, was a student of Marinka Gurewich. In 1958 she won the Metropolitan Opera Auditions. By the time Barber met her she had sung many minor roles at the Metropolitan and major roles in companies throughout Europe. She had also sung many of Barber's songs in recitals in Europe during the late fifties and early sixties.

Example 16.4 *Andromache's Farewell,* title page (G. Schirmer, 1963).

Example 16.5 *Andromache's Farewell,* mm. 88–99, piano-vocal score.

namic markings calling for abrupt shifts from *pianissimo* to *forte* (for example, in the section beginning "Come close—embrace me, who gave you life"), which are brutally demanding and require a vocal technique of enormous control and flexibility, were added only after Barber had begun working with Arroyo.

The role requires the experience of an opera singer, one who can establish the dramatic character within the eleven-minute scene and handle sudden shifts of mood and dynamics with technical ease.* Arroyo spoke at length about the challenges to the performer:

> Without the drama, the piece is nothing. . . . The same voice must sing tenderly and beautifully at one moment, talking to a little child directly,

* Paul Henry Lang, in fact, linked *Andromache* to an earlier genre by labeling it a "modern solo cantata" (*New York Herald Tribune,* 5 April 1963).

> and then at the next turn, curse Helen, sustaining the dramatic impact over the full orchestra, over the big orchestral sound. Shift from dramatic outburst, pull back and spin off the high note, then crescendo on it while staying in control throughout . . . that is the technical challenge . . . but, at the same time, to become deeply involved with the character—a mother saying goodbye to her son, the wrench of it—and still not lose control technically so that you can't sing. To be able to go from *piano* to *forte* and not lose control is a difficult thing for a singer to do beautifully . . . and I think Mr. Barber was very concerned with beauty.[35]

Annotations in Arroyo's score, added by herself and Barber, give some clues about the composer's performance intentions: "Hector's valiant spirit, shield of thousands" (m. 50) is indicated as a "narrative"; the passage at measure 64, beginning "He was to be lord of all Asia," called for a "free, darker" execution; the following "and not for the Greeks" should be sung "fiercely." Over the concluding passage, "Hide my head in shame, cast me in the ship as to that marriage bed across the grave of my own son," Arroyo had written the words *Now I'm a tragic princess.**

Barber's working relationship with Arroyo epitomizes the value he placed on the artistic judgment of performers in general. As the date of the premiere approached, he and Arroyo met frequently in New York or in Mount Kisco, where they worked several hours at a session, followed by a break for dinner and more rehearsing. They spent many hours discussing the psychological nuances of the mother's dilemma and probing the meaning of the words of the text. "Barber worked with me for drama from the inside," the singer reported,

> for truth and sincerity of what was said, not for external gestures—flinging the arms to the right or left, or a wild look on the face. He tended toward reaching the inner person, and that takes time you see. . . . I had a real sense that he wanted me to use my voice to service the words.[36]

That Barber conceived of the aria as a dramatic scene is indicated also by his attention to the visual impression Arroyo would convey to the audience, even to the point of helping her select the right gown from her wardrobe and escorting her to the design studio of Valentina to have it finished: "He wanted *Andromache* to have a whole look," the singer recalled, "to be a scene."[37]

Thomas Schippers conducted the New York Philharmonic in performances at the new Philharmonic Hall on 4–7 April 1963. Included on the program also were Britten's *Variations on a Theme by Frank Bridge* and Sibelius's Symphony No. 2, Op. 43. *Andromache's Farewell* was played before intermission and received a sustained ovation, calling Barber to the stage several times.

* Barber added to her note: "and a great artist and person—with admiration and appreciation. Sam Barber, April 4–63."

Reviews were uniformly appreciative of the richness, intensity, and maturity of Arroyo's performance.[38] With few exceptions, most music critics agreed that Barber had vividly captured the dramatic intensity of the tragic scene—calling it one of his most "moving and compelling" works.[39] If Harold Schonberg shot arrows at Barber's "conventional score," "conventional even in its dissonances," lacking in profile and personality, it may be less a reflection of the work's flaws than a signal that the musical winds of taste were at this time beginning to turn away from the lyrical, Romantic style inherent in Barber's music. Still, the audience expressed "genuine enthusiasm" for *Andromache's Farewell.*[40]

The orchestral texture and late-nineteenth-century harmonies—and the subject, in particular—strongly suggest the music of Richard Strauss; both Schonberg and Kolodin, for example, pointed to Strauss's *Elektra* as the stylistic progenitor of Barber's *Andromache.*[41] Winthrop Sargeant saw this influence as an indication of "sound musical judgment" on Barber's part, forecasting that the music of the "greatest of the last orchestral composers would be a logical jumping-off place for those who hope to continue in the grand manner of musical composition."[42] While it is true the brisk flourish of the opening measures does bring to mind Strauss, the chromatic harmonies, angular themes, densely constructed chords, strident military brass passages, and even certain exoticisms of *Andromache's Farewell* seem more to presage the direction Barber would take in his next major work, *Antony and Cleopatra.*

17

A NEW OPERA HOUSE

Nothing to do with what I had imagined

Antony and Cleopatra, Op. 40 (1966)

The commission that was one of the greatest tributes to Barber's whole career turned out, ironically, to be his nemesis. *Antony and Cleopatra,* written for the opening of the new Metropolitan Opera House on 16 September 1966, was the monumental misfortune of Barber's career. In the words of one German publication, "everyone in the world . . . heard this opera was not a success."[1] The immediate failure of the premiere was accentuated by a press that was overly attentive to the spectacular elements of the new opera house and celebrity watching and that offered a great deal of comment by people who had not enough professional expertise to evaluate music at all. The inflated Zeffirelli production, with its complicated and problematic paraphernalia, eclipsed for the most part any serious evaluation of the music.

Although the score contains some of the most beautiful of Barber's music, the initial performances were—in the composer's words—"strangled by a costly, confusing, overloaded production that did not even function."[2] Most of the criticism leveled at the opera as "gaudy," "vulgar," "overdressed," and "overproduced" seems directed toward Franco Zeffirelli, who wrote the libretto, directed and staged the opera, and designed the sets and costumes. This does not explain, however, why Barber—usually so decisive about aesthetic principles—seemed to abdicate his artistic assertiveness in this instance. A study of the progress of *Antony and Cleopatra,* from the forging of the libretto to its production, points to the wide chasm between Barber's and Zeffirelli's concepts of the opera as a major factor in the overwhelming failure in 1966. Fair appraisal of the music was not completely resolved until the opera was revised with the help of Menotti in 1975.

* * *

Almost immediately after the completion of *Vanessa,* Bing began pressing Barber for another opera. The 1966–67 season of the Metropolitan Opera would be the fruition of the nearly fifty years of looking for a new home for the opera. The repertory for the first season of the $45.7 million opera house at Lincoln Center had been discussed many years in advance of its opening. The eventual choice of Barber to write an opera for the inauguration of the new Metropolitan Opera house seemed inevitable: as an American composer whose metier was song as well as orchestral music, his tonal and lyrical music was the kind favored by the conservative Met audiences; moreover, he had already proven himself as a composer of opera with the Pulitzer Prize-winning opera *Vanessa.*

Although as early as 1959 Barber had tentatively agreed to write something for the first season of the new opera house, he had not chosen a libretto, nor was he even ready to commit himself to another major opera so soon after *Vanessa.* A letter from Rudolf Bing reveals that the tough-minded manager was evidently becoming impatient with the composer's indecision:

> If you are still thinking—as I do—of a new opera of yours for the first season of the new house, we—that is to say, you—must seriously get on with it. May we talk about it, because in the light of various developments I think we have to know whether or not there is any serious prospect of an important new opera by you.[3]

Bing had managed the Metropolitan Opera with an iron hand since 1950 and had made enormous improvements in the company.* After the production of *Vanessa* the Metropolitan Opera gave Barber carte blanche to attend as many rehearsals as he wished, to listen to singers, and observe conductors, with the expectation that he would be inspired to write another opera. In casting about for a libretto, the composer went often to theater, talked to playwrights, and read many scripts.[4] He approached Tennessee Williams, for example, but was not interested in working on an unsuccessful play that was the only one offered by the author.† James

*Governed by his conviction that opera is for the eye as well as the ear, he replaced the worn, tattered scenery with sparkling productions, borrowed design and directorial talent from Hollywood and Broadway, and upgraded the ballet troupe. He increased the length of the opera season from eighteen to thirty-one weeks, insisting upon iron-clad contracts with principal singers so that they might not be lured by handsome fees in the concert circuit ("Lord of the Manor," *Time* [23 September 1966]:46–61; "The New Met and its Old Master," *Newsweek* [19 September 1966]: 70–79). Most important, he made it possible for black singers to sing at the Met.

†Howard Klein, "The Birth of an Opera," *New York Times Magazine* (28 August 1966): 32. Earlier, in 1958, Barber had rejected the idea of an ordinary play as suitable for opera, especially those of Williams, feeling the texture of the playwright's poetic language left no room for music (Coleman, "Samuel Barber and Vanessa," p. 88). See above, chapter 14.

Baldwin was considered also, but "his priorities lay elsewhere."[5] On numerous occasions, as they had done before *Vanessa,* Stephen Spender and Barber discussed subjects for an opera. "I suggested Henry James's *The American* for the Lincoln Center commission," Spender recalled, "but Sam found it too close to Puccini (with the convent ending)."[6]

The Metropolitan Opera suggested *Moby-Dick* as a possibility, and there is evidence that Barber gave more than a fleeting consideration to the subject even though he ultimately rejected the idea, reflecting later that "an opera that had a lot of whales and water, but no soprano, had a doubtful future."* A transcription of passages from Melville's novel appear untitled in one of the composer's notebooks.† Barber's arrangement of the lyrical prose into poetic stanzas suggests more than a casual acquaintance with *Moby-Dick* (see facsimile below).

"The Met tells me I can have any poet in the world, Auden, Thomas—anyone, but none seems right for me," he complained to his friends.‡ The only thing he had decided upon for certain was that whatever opera he wrote would be for Leontyne Price; Bing and Barber had agreed to that three years earlier.[7] Since her debut with the Metropolitan in 1961 she had achieved the reputation of having one of the richest, most sensuous voices in the Metropolitan Opera.§ By singing in Barber's opera, she would make history by opening the new house.

Apparently pressure was mounted from all quarters.‖ For example, Thomas Schippers, who would be the conductor on the podium for the opening of the new opera house, adamantly wanted not only a new opera for the occasion but an American one, not one of the staples planned by Bing. Schippers is reported to have played a major role in convincing Barber to commit himself in 1964—two years prior to the opening of the new house—to an opera for the opening night.[8]

William Schuman wrote of his pleasure in hearing that Barber would write a new opera for the new house:

*Hans W. Heinsheimer, "Vanessa Revisited," *Opera News* (May 1978):24. This story, reworked several times by Heinsheimer, varies with each telling. In his article "An Opera Is Born," Metropolitan Opera program (17 September 1966) and in a recast version of the same article, "Birth of an Opera," *Saturday Review* (17 September 1966), Barber's retort about *Moby Dick* is quoted as "Too much water for an opera, and too much wind."

†The excerpts quoted in Barber's notebook come from several chapters of Melville's novel. See Hennig Cohen and James Cohalan, *A Concordance to Melville's* Moby Dick, 3 vols. (n.p.: Melville Society, 1978).

‡In 1960, when asked by John Ardoin about the prospects for another opera, Barber was still evasive. The Metropolitan Opera had been trying to pin him down to a commitment for the opening of the new house, he told Ardoin; "when I have a libretto that interests me," he said, "I will write another opera" (Ardoin, "Samuel Barber at Capricorn," p. 5).

§Price made her debut on 23 January 1961 as Leonora in *Il Trovatore.* She opened the following season in the starring role of *La Fanciulla del West,* only after President John F. Kennedy ordered the arbitration of a musicians' strike that threatened to cancel the whole season.

‖When asked why he did finally accept Bing's offer, Barber, more often than not, would flippantly offer a remark designed to ward off those who would probe too deeply—"I only did it because I realized none of my friends would speak to me if I didn't" (Heinsheimer, "An Opera is Born," p. 50).

What do ye do when you see a whale, men?
Sing out for him!
Good! And what do you next, men?
Lower away and after him!
And what tune is it ye pull to, men?
A dead whale or a stove boat
All ye mast headers have before now
heard me give orders about a white whale
Look ye, d'ye see this spanish ounce of gold?
D'ye see it?
Whosoever of ye raises me a white-headed whale
with a wrinkled brow and crooked jaw —
whosoever of ~~you~~ ye raises me that white
headed whale —
with three holes punctured in his starboard fluke —
look ye, whosoever of ye raises me that same white
whale
he shall have this gold ounce, my boys!

Huzza, huzza!

It's a white whale, I say, a white whale, the same
that some call Moby Dick. Moby Dick that
dismasted me
Moby Dick that brought me to this dead stump I
stand on now

Barber's transcription of lines from *Moby-Dick* in a notebook from the late 1950s.

Aye, aye, it was that accursed white whale
that razeed me —
made a poor pegging lubber for me for ever and
a day —

Aye, aye, and I'll chase him round Good Hope
and round the Horn
and round the Norway Maelstrom
and round perdition's flames
before I give <u>him</u> up!

Death to Moby Dick! God hunt us all, if we do
not hunt <u>Moby Dick</u> to his death!

God Keep me! — <u>Keep</u> us all!

All visible objects are but as pasteboard masks
If man will strike, strike through the mask!
How can the prisoner reach outside except
by thrusting through the wall?
The white whale is that wall, ~~[illegible]~~.
I see in him outrageous strength, with an
inscrutable malice sinewing it
That inscrutable thing is what I hate
and be the white whale agent
or be the white whale principal
I will wreak that hate upon him

Death to Moby Dick!

Sunset

I leave a white and turbid wake:
pale waters, paler cheeks, where'er I
sail.
The envious billows sidelong swell
to whelm my track:
let them;
but first I pass.

Harpooneers and sailors:
Dance and sing.

Ship ahoy! Have ye seen the White Whale?
Up helm, Keep her off round the world!

> I am simply overjoyed that you will be doing an opera for the new Met. You know how long I have been plugging for precisely this. It has always seemed to me that the new house must open with a new opera by an American composer, and, by all odds, you are the logical choice for the Metropolitan. They have confidence in you, as do the rest of us, to produce a magnificent singing score.[9]

Some of Barber's friends persisted in offering advice about what kind of libretto they thought he should *not* set. The libretto of *Vanessa* had been the main target of negative European reviews of the Salzburg performance; Barber was told that he would be making a mistake to continue to build his operatic reputation in collaboration with Menotti.[10] Katharine Fryer reports that when she asked him about the opera, he groaned, "I have no libretto. Don't think I haven't looked. No one can write a libretto except Gian Carlo, and his was criticized so, and besides they want an American scene and he can't do that." To Fryer's query as to what scene in American history he would consider most dramatic, Barber replied "the Civil War."[11]

Many years later, Menotti recalled the tenuous period of their relationship after the choice of Shakespeare's *Antony and Cleopatra* had been made and said he was heartsick that he had not worked with Barber from the start:

> Perhaps the only moment of bitterness that actually ever existed between Sam and me was because of *Antony and Cleopatra*. . . . I was very hurt, because I was dying to write another libretto for Sam, that would have been a joy.[12]

Antony and Cleopatra was, in fact, Barber's favorite Shakespearean play,* and many critics consider it to contain some of the poet's richest and most poetic language.† But a musical setting of *Antony* presented—as Andrew Porter was to say in a review of the revised version—"a triple hurdle," for historically the odds were against success.[13] First, of all the opera librettos using Shakespeare word for word, only one—Britten's *A Midsummer Night's Dream*—had ever been successful; second, none of the operas based on the Roman tragedies had been successful at all; and third, misfortune had usually attended large new works premiered in untried opera houses or before audiences attracted as much by the event as by the music.‡

*"Make Mingle with our Tambourines," interview with Barber in *Opera News* 31 (17 September 1966):35. The play held sentimental associations for Barber because his sister had played the part of Cleopatra in a performance at Vassar College.

†Samuel Coleridge recognized its superiority, calling it "the most wonderful" of Shakespeare's plays and citing "its strength and vigor of maturity" and "happy valiancy of style" (*Shakespearian Criticism*, vol. 1 [London: Dent, 1907; New York: Dutton, 1960], p. 77).

‡Andrew Porter cites as an example Bellini's *Zaira,* which opened the Teatro Nuovo in Parma ("Antony's Second Chance," in *Music of Three Seasons: 1974–1977* [New York: Farrar, Straus, and Giroux, 1978], pp. 97–98).

The challenge of setting Shakespeare's words—which are so full of meaning that their significance cannot be rapidly absorbed by listeners, most of whom would be ill-equipped to handle Elizabethan English—was admittedly something of a problem for Barber, whose youthful exposure to the English singing tradition was that of "distorted vowels and a high-flown pseudo-Elizabethan vocabulary."[14] But ultimately, Shakespeare's iambic pentameter seemed to him "surprisingly free and pliable."[15] Turner demonstrated to the composer that *Antony and Cleopatra* did not have to be organized only as blank verse by typing out lines from the death scene, cutting out "excessive verbiage" to show its lyrical potential.*

In the spring of 1964 Barber had already begun to write his own libretto for *Antony* when he learned at second hand that Bing had asked Franco Zeffirelli to become a partner in the collaboration.† From the start of the project, Zeffirelli's imagination was captured by the potential for extravaganza that the facilities of the new house presented. So enthusiastic was he about directing the opera for the opening of the new house that he went to New York to watch construction of the building so he would be utterly familiar with the elaborate stage equipment that was being installed under the direction of Herman Krawitz.[16] But by July Barber still had not received text from his librettist-director, who had left for Rome so hurriedly that he had not even signed a contract.‡ Determined to obtain a libretto by the end of the summer and not wanting to repeat the endless wait he had experienced with Menotti nor to jeopardize fulfillment of the commission, he followed Zeffirelli to Italy, settling himself in Tuscany near his librettist's villa to press him for a text. Each day for two weeks Zeffirelli traveled the two miles to Barber's house, where they worked with the single-minded purpose of fashioning the libretto. Zeffirelli later said about the adaptation:

> From the beginning I was concerned with shaping the whole opera. The form and conception came to me as one idea, and I simply elaborated it. We inherited a love story in which there are no real love scenes. We emphasized the disturbing elements in the relationship between Antony and Cleopatra from the outset, concentrating all the emotions of love into the second-act scene which is their last moment of happiness. . . .
>
> I wanted a big choral scene for the opening. We used only Shakespeare's lines, but we rearranged them. Sam added or dropped lines as he

*Turner, discussions with the author. In fact, this scene received uniform praise among the harsh reviews of the 1966 performance.

†John Browning, in an interview with the author; Barber was quoted by Howard Klein as having read about it in the newspaper. Zeffirelli's staging of the last opera produced in the old Metropolitan Opera House, *Falstaff,* had been so well received that Bing was eager for him to design, stage, and write the libretto for the first opera in the new house (Klein, "Birth of an Opera," p. 32).

‡Katharine Homer Fryer's undated notes on this subject (probably spring 1964) from a telephone conversation between herself and Barber mention that Bing had "weakened" and let Zeffirelli leave without the contract.

wrote the music later, but essentially the line of development of the libretto was set.[17]

A manuscript typescript of the libretto in its early stages contains Barber's handwritten notes that suggest he thought Shakespeare was concerned with "order vs. life-fulfillment" in *Antony and Cleopatra;* Cleopatra is transformed into an absolute image, Barber wrote, a "principle of life in destruction . . . a coincidence of contraries, all for love *and* the world; Antony's greatness is to have been Cleopatra's lover." *

Regarding it a challenge to sustain dramatic continuity through the sequence of so many short scenes, Zeffirelli and Barber reduced Shakespeare's play of forty-two scenes in five acts to a libretto of sixteen scenes in three acts. Fourteen characters were eliminated, and the play's six different geographical locations were reduced to two—Rome and Egypt (plus one scene aboard a Roman galley, which was omitted in the revised version). The text consists entirely of Shakespeare's words. It was honed down by rearranging and cutting material—omitting entire scenes, eliminating connecting dialogues between important speeches, and pruning lines within speeches. The choral text that opens the opera, for example, is culled from rearranged lines from speeches of Caesar (Shakespeare, I, iv, 3–9; 73–74; 55–56), Pompey (II, i, 21–27), Caesar (I, iv, 55–56); Philo (I, i, 1–2; 6 and 9); and Caesar (I, i, 12–13; and iv, 55–58). Similarly, Antony's four-line speech in the opening dialogue was derived from twenty of Shakespeare's. Single lines that slip by unnoticed in the play become significant in the opera as recurring themes—"Salt Cleopatra," "She is cunning past man's thought," "My man of men."

The outline of the story as presented in the 1966 version of the opera is as follows:

> Act 1. The Empire: There is no overture; the curtain rises on a chorus of Greeks, Romans, Persians, Jews, and soldiers, who describe the idleness of the Roman general Antony, calling on him to leave his "lascivious wassails with the Egyptian queen Cleopatra." *Scene 2,* Alexandria: Antony resolves "I must from this Egyptian Queen break off," but is warned by Enobarbus that she will resist. *Scene 3,* Roman Senate: Caesar and Antony review their grievances, and Agrippa suggests that Antony wed Octavia, Caesar's sister, to ensure peace. *Scene 4,* Alexandria: The love-smitten Cleopatra reminisces of Antony ("Bring me some music, some moody music . . . My man of men!"). *Scene 5,* Rome, Caesar's palace: Antony meets his future bride and vows to be fair to her. *Scene 6,* Alexandria: Cleopatra reviles the messenger who brings news of Antony's marriage, but is mollified by eliciting details about Octavia that offer no competition to herself. *Scene 7,* a Roman galley: During a celebration of Antony's mar-

* The manuscript of the libretto is at the Library of Congress, Music Division, in the 1984 bequest of the Estate of Samuel Barber, Box 1.

riage, Enobarbus recounts the story of the lovers: "When first she met Mark Antony, she pursed up his heart, upon the river Cydnus"; an offstage chorus sings "Cleopatra", and she gradually appears on a barge as in a vision—"Where's my serpent of old Nile? (for so he calls me). . . . My man of men." Antony is wakened from a drunken stupor, sees the image of the queen and, impassioned, vows, "I will to Egypt / In th'East my pleasure lies!"

Act 2. Rome: Caesar breaks the news to Octavia of Antony's desertion and resolves to beat Antony on the battlefield. *Scene 2*, Cleopatra's palace: Cleopatra and Antony's amorous meeting is interrupted by news from Enobarbus that Caesar is advancing. Antony leaves to mobilize his men; Cleopatra vows to accompany him and make a bold showing to the enemy. *Scene 3*, Antony's camp: Ghostly music is interpreted by Antony's soldiers as the departure of Hercules, the god he idolizes. *Scene 4*, Antony's tent: Against the advice of Enobarbus, Antony chooses to fight Caesar by sea. *Scene 5*, the Actium battlefield: Cleopatra's fleet is seen in retreat; Antony is urged to make peace with Caesar, who appears scornful of any mercy for his brother-in-law. *Scene 6*, Cleopatra's palace: Antony rages over seeing Caesar's ambassador kiss Cleopatra's hand, learns that Enobarbus has gone over to Caesar, denounces Cleopatra, and storms away. The captive queen announces her intention to hide in her monument and feign suicide, leaving a messenger to tell Antony that her last word was of him. *Scene 7*, the battlefield: Enobarbus, remorseful over his betrayal of Antony, dies of a broken heart. *Scene 7*, Antony's tent: Believing Cleopatra dead, Antony implores Eros to strike him a mortal blow; Eros takes his own life instead; Antony falls on his own sword, learning, as he dies, that Cleopatra still lives. He is carried off to her monument.

Act 3. The monument: Antony dies in a last embrace with Cleopatra. As she grieves for him, Caesar arrives, warning her not to kill herself too. Antony is borne off, and Cleopatra—realizing Caesar means to march her triumphantly as a captive puppet in Rome—resolves that she will not be separated from her lover and calls for her deadly asp to end her life—"Give me my robe, put on my crown, I have immortal longings in me."

* * *

At the end of summer 1964, Barber returned to Capricorn and dug in to the task of composing the music. Imposing upon himself a rigorous work routine that precluded virtually all social engagements, he took telephone calls only early in the morning or at lunch time, visitors were discouraged, and mail went unanswered.[18] One of the few excursions he allowed himself was a monthly visit to West Chester to see his ailing mother.[19]

He began composing the music for the beginning of the story and worked straight through, for the most part completing scenes in sequence before going back to earlier ones.[20] In the autumn of 1964, he announced to

Katharine Fryer that he had completed music for four scenes and must finish everything a year from Christmas, as the singers needed six months to learn their parts.[21] Throughout the winter of 1965 his trips to New York were limited to, at best, one day a week; every few weeks he would visit his publisher to talk "strategy" or to deliver packages of music. "He would rush in—always hatless, mostly coatless—and leave the package on a corner table of the office," Heinsheimer recalled, "almost embarrassed, not even permitting us to open and glance at it in his presence, rather talking about other things."[22] Scene after scene of music arrived at Schirmer's in this manner or delivered by "mysterious messengers."[23] Once delivered, Barber's manuscript was transcribed by Eugene Wolf (Barber's exclusive copyist at G. Schirmer), returned to Barber for proofreading, and finally sent to Arnold Arnstein, who, with his staff of seven, copied out parts for the orchestra. There were thirty-two different instrumental parts in *Antony and Cleopatra.* Unlike the Piano Concerto, however, on which Barber had worked so close to his deadline that the Boston Symphony did not obtain parts until a day before the concert, *Antony and Cleopatra* ran on schedule.*

In March 1966 he told Katharine Fryer he had finished all the music and had only five more scenes to orchestrate.[24] He expected to be finished with the orchestration by the end of April. Price had seen some of the music a year earlier and was now "singing it beautifully," he said; rehearsals in the new house would begin in August.[25] Seven months before the opening, help in producing the score was enlisted from Lee Hoiby, who came every morning to Mount Kisco to work under Barber's specific instruction. Hoiby recalled that during this period Barber was "soaring on some kind of magical energetic field, driven to finish the opera."[26] Yet Stanley Hollingsworth observed that, in spite of the pressure, there was no element of musical neglect in the score; and everyone was anticipating a successful premiere.

As rehearsals were barely under way, Barber spoke to Howard Klein about the music for act 1, scene 3, the meeting of Antony and Caesar in the Senate:

> This is difficult to sing. The rhythms and pitches of this fugal section between Antony and Caesar are quite tricky. I hope they get it right. Cleopatra's part is not easy, but every vowel was placed with Leontyne's voice in mind. She is all impassioned lyricism. I had a problem just keeping her off stage. Shakespeare's iambic pentameter had to be broken up or it would

* Klein, "Birth of an Opera," p. 109. Heinsheimer reports that Schirmer's had wanted to break a precedent by releasing the vocal-piano score to the public before the opening night. Barber protested, "Don't even talk to me about it—I can't possibly think of publication—I have to write an opera—I'll let you know when I am ready." Secretly, however, Heinsheimer gave Paul Wittke permission to prepare the reduction of the score for engraving so that when it was finally finished, with Barber's approval, they could execute the publication immediately (Heinsheimer, "Birth of an Opera," p. 57).

> have trampled right over the music. The blank verse is wonderful for the Romans; Caesar is hard, terse, and cautious.
>
> There is a split fascination between political power and almost satiated love. There was never any danger in the music's sounding Egyptian or Roman, though. The problem was avoiding an Elizabethan Purcellian sound, which is almost dictated by the sound of Shakespeare's language.[27]

Similarly, he told Eric Salzman, "There is almost no atmosphere in the conventional sense in the play, and there will be little of it in the score." That meant few coloristic or oriental touches, he said; there would be "no danger of a neo-Aïda."[28] Thus the scenes in Alexandria are sensuous, with only a slightly oriental cast—the orchestra augmented by a bell tree and antique cymbals. The drama is heightened by unusual instrumentation: eerie or exotic sounds are obtained, for example, by the use of the ondes Martenot in the "Music i' the air" episode (act 2, sc. 3, of the revised version) in combination with a series of parallel fifths and octaves scored for double bass and a brief passage for celesta; emotional drama is colored by unexpected instrumental combinations, such as the sparely orchestrated end of act 2, where only flute and timpani accompany Antony's suicide. These passages are some of the most effective in the opera.

The requirements of characterizations govern the style of the vocal music: leaping vocal lines are assigned to the Romans in scenes on the battlefield or in the senate.* Although the most defined lyrical music is tailored to Price's voice, much of the music for Cleopatra in the original version called for a throaty parlando style, what the singer referred to as her "Carmen voice, the dusky quality of the low voice."[29] In act 3, however, where Cleopatra is present almost the entire time, the music is consistently lyrical and most representative of the melodic style usually associated with Barber. Since the resolution of the drama occurs here as well, it is in this act that the strength of the opera lies. Beginning with the last two scenes of act 2 (Enobarbus's aria "I am alone the villain of the earth" and Antony's suicide) and through the end of act 3 (Antony's death and Cleopatra's suicide), the singing dominates.

Geographical locations are differentiated by the orchestral music also: angular leaps and irregular rhythms suggest brashness for the "Roman" music; syncopations characterize the argument between Antony and Caesar in act 1; in contrast, the music for the Egyptian scenes and for Cleopatra is marked by sinuous melodies, opulent, luminescent harmonies, and exotic timbres. Barber claimed that he took his musical cues from Shakespeare, who created "a counterpoint between the language and rhythms of Rome and the more fluid and imagistic language and rhythms of Egypt."[30] Although the orchestral writing in general supports and reinforces vocal

* Lee Hoiby reported that Barber was impatient with Zeffirelli's requests for additional battle scenes, having an aversion to writing military music (telephone conversation with the author, 5 May 1990).

lines, the orchestra is not always clearly the pitch source for the singers. Barber would eventually revise some passages to allow vocal and orchestral lines to double each other. Even before the premiere, an extended improvisatory passage of *Sprechgesang* to the accompaniment of sticks was cut because it was not able to be worked out in rehearsal.* According to Stanley Hollingsworth, the dance had been choreographed and was in rehearsal before Barber wrote the music. He was given the beats over which he wrote the music.[31]

Barber uses clearly defined musical structures for dramatic episodes, such as the tense meeting of Caesar and Antony in the Roman senate (act 1, scene 2) where a two-part invention over a walking bass of eighth notes is followed by a foreboding passacaglia on Agrippa's "thou hast a sister, admired Octavia," and then transformed into an orchestral interlude as the senators exit muttering to themselves.

The musical language is pervaded with parallel fourths and fifths, themes built on ascending fourths. Recurring motives reinforce dramatic associations through transformation or expansion, giving audible unity to the opera: for example, the brass fanfare of the Prologue opens the Roman scenes in acts 1 and 2; the phrase associated with Cleopatra's name and recollections of her (see Example 17.1a and b); or the striking minor-ninth motive—"My man of men!"—identified with Antony and remembrances of him (see Example 17.1c and d). Themes gain an ironic twist as they are transformed in the course of the opera; for example, the ascending fourths of the love theme that first appears in the lovers' duet in act 1 (see Example 17.1e) are presented in diminution in scene 6 to express Cleopatra's bitter outrage toward the messenger (Example 17.1f). In the 1966 version, a rhythmic distortion of the theme fugally mocks Octavia (see Example 17.1g); in the revision, Barber changed this to whispered speech but maintained the orchestral passage. The theme softens and expands into flowing lines for the lovers' duet in act 2: Cleopatra sings, "If it be love indeed, tell me how much"; Antony continues, "There's beggary in the love that can be reckoned" (Example 17.1h). A brilliant stroke in act 3 is the recurrence of the love theme as Cleopatra clasps the asp to herself and prepares

* The passage occurred in act 1, scene 6 (aboard a Roman galley), at the conclusion of a stick dance by Antony, Caesar, Lepidus, Dolabella, and Enobarbus, who are conversing at the front of the stage. While the sticks continue in ostinato rhythms that are notated in the score, the following instructions are to be executed by the characters on stage:

> They should improvise their own sung recitative, without conductor or orchestra, and pay no attention to the rhythms of the sticks behind them. They must follow the rhythms and cadences of the text, each one choosing a comfortable tessitura. It is by no means a *spoken* recitative. Dancing girls might imitate the crocodiles, etc. of the words. In no event should the stick ostinato be allowed to obscure the words. (G. Schirmer, vocal score, 1966, p. 117)

Halfway through the passage, a soprano voice sings offstage to the accompaniment of a Spanish guitar—both parts notated in the score—their music "to be performed in its own meter independent of the others" (vocal score, 1966, p. 118).

Example 17.1 *Antony and Cleopatra,* recurring motives and themes. All examples *a–i* except *g* are from the 1976 edition.

Example 17.1 *(continued)*

e. "Love" theme, act 1, scene 1.

f. "Love" theme, act 1, scene 3.

g. "Love" theme, act 1, scene 6 (G. Schirmer, 1966).

Example 17.1 *(continued)*

h. "Love" theme, act 2, scene 2.

i. "Love" theme, act 3.

to die: she sings "Does thou not see my baby at my breast, that sucks the nurse asleep?" (Example 17.11), and the theme is transferred to the orchestra in juxtaposition to her final words "O Antony! Nay, I will take thee too: What should I stay . . . In this vile world?"

In preparation for her role as Cleopatra, Price put herself in almost complete isolation for a year, accepting as few singing engagements as possible. She read every book she could find, including Plutarch, on Cleopatra, "the strongest character I have played to date," Price said, "and the most provocative."* To facilitate proper pronunciation, she went through the whole play with the British actress Irene Worth and listened to a recording of it;[32] for other members of the cast, the Metropolitan brought in Philip Burton, another leading British stage figure, to clarify and correct Americanisms. To further prepare her voice for the role, Price returned to Florence Kimball, her vocal coach of many years.[33]

Justino Díaz, the twenty-six-year-old Puerto Rican-born bass who would play Antony, was picked by Barber in 1965 for the role, and the composer lowered and adjusted what had been originally conceived as a high baritone role to suit the singer's lower voice.† For Díaz, Antony's music seemed to express "the whole gamut of emotional possibilities . . . moody, rather than very dramatic . . . not very far out by modern standards—not like *Wozzeck* by any means . . . romantic music."[34] Other members of the cast included Ezio Flagello as Antony's friend Enobarbus; Jess Thomas as Caesar; Rosalind Elias as Cleopatra's attendant Charmian; and Mary Ellen Pracht as Octavia, Caesar's sister and Antony's wife.

By the time Zeffirelli began rehearsals of *Antony and Cleopatra,* he found himself beset with crises. Bing had scheduled only twenty-five days of rehearsal for the opera since the stage had to be shared with preparations for other operas in rehearsal; Zeffirelli had hoped for twenty days to rehearse the Actium battle scene alone.[35] In addition, up to the last rehearsal the orchestra, which had been working for two and a half years without a contract, was threatening to strike, having agreed only to play for the opening night of the new opera house.‡

Zeffirelli designed symbolic sets for *Antony and Cleopatra:* a geometric fusion of metal, plastic, and wood, but no canvas. The colors were steel,

*Emily Coleman, "Leontyne Makes a Date with History," *New York Times,* 11 September 1966, sec. 2, p. 21. Price considered the honor of opening the new opera house a special mission. "I feel about this responsibility that it is the strongest way . . . I can speak for my people," she said. "I am no self-designated Joan of Arc, but I feel that I was given this privilege for a reason . . . that being given this opportunity as one of my people, may be the beginning of a certain dimension, that anyone who wants to aspire to be so completely free artistically as I have been, to be chosen . . . on one's artistic merit alone is truly an American act" (ibid.).

†In the 1966 edition, Antony is indicated as a high bass; for the 1976 revised edition, Barber changed the part to a baritone.

‡Resolution came during the second-act intermission when the members of Local 802 voted overwhelmingly to accept a new contract and returned to play the third act as the highest paid orchestra in the world. The announcement was made publicly by Bing before the third-act curtain (*Daily News,* 17 September 1966).

Leontyne Price and Barber before the opening of the new Metropolitan Opera House, 1966. *(Mélançon, Metropolitan Opera Archives)*

white, crystal blue. The form central to the overall design was the pyramid. A huge sphinx had been erected for the Egyptian scene, the figure, turning awesomely one way or the other, looming high over the stage. A naval battle scene was played out by toys, seen in the distance.[36]

Determined to design for the full capacity of the luxurious space of the new stage, which was six times as large as that of the old Met, Zeffirelli had devised a barge scene, for example, that stretched back 146 feet deep from the footlights.[37] A scaffolding of transverse and vertical metal tubing was suspended over the Roman senate scenes, but because there was no backdrop at the first performance, singers' voices were diffused in all directions rather than beamed toward the audience, thus making them difficult to understand.[38] The eighteenth-century practice of changing scenes in view of the audience was planned to be accomplished by lights and sliding mechanisms, including a fifty-seven-foot turntable.

The night of the opening on 16 September saw an audience of 3,800, while 3,000 onlookers outside of the house gaped at arriving celebrities, among whom were President Lyndon B. Johnson's wife and her guests Ferdinand Marcos, president of the Philippines, and his wife; Governor and Mrs. Nelson Rockefeller; and a host of foreign ministers, chancellors, ambassadors, and other dignitaries representing major nations of the world.[39]

Everything that could have gone wrong mechanically did. Lighting cues misfired, causing Cleopatra to make her entrance on a pitch-black stage. The revolving stage, around which Zeffirelli had designed the whole production, had gone out of order one week before the performance and had to be manually revolved by a stage crew dressed in costume. The metallic

Justino Díaz as Antony and Leontyne Price as Cleopatra, 1966. *(Mélançon, Metropolitan Opera Archives)*

scrapings of mechanical procedures for changing sets and the noise of the menagerie of live animals competed with the music. The director's grandiose plans for the battle of Actium—a vast revolving pyramid, around which were supposed to be six barges, twelve horses, four elephants, 120 Romans, and a huge crowd of other players milling around simultaneously[40]—were reduced to a mere "160 on stage, 2 small Arabian horses, 1 black horse, 2 camels, 1 elephant, 65 senators."*

Price, fifteen years later, recalled the calamities of opening night:

> With a three-minute cue, I was locked in the pyramid at the first aria because something mechanical didn't open up at the right time. But I must say, there's no business like show business, and I kept singing in the pyramid—I'll be heard no matter what—and I kept singing right through to the next cue. . . . There was no way in the world I could make that cue. I was to be dressed in the pyramid for the next scene, and I simply said "Zip this one back up, whether it fits or not, I'll keep singing, and just go out!"[41]

Price's recollections reveal only to a small degree how much the staging competed with, rather than enhanced, her musical execution of Barber's

*Katharine Fryer (notes from her telephone conversation with Barber). Evidently, the elephant was discarded, for Barber told John Gruen that although Zeffirelli wanted elephants, he was not allowed to have them (Gruen, "Where Has Samuel Barber Been?"). Fryer's diary entry of 11 September 1966 (after the dress rehearsal) paints an alarming picture: "And what have they done to Sam's beautiful, sincere music!! What a garish crude display! . . . It's all too lavish, Gian Carlo told me."

Antony and Cleopatra (1966), act 2, scene 4, Cleopatra's palace in Alexandria. *(Mélançon, Metropolitan Opera Archives)*

score.* Even her costumes—five changes, designed especially for her—worked against the execution of her role. Zeffirelli's plans for the wardrobe never wavered from his original conception, "a pastiche of Elizabethan, Roman, Egyptian, and modern . . . a baroque exuberance."[42] For Cleopatra he declared:

> I want to give the message of all civilizations. . . . She will be all black and gold. The bodice is Elizabethan, the lines around the neck are more oriental, and the headdress is modeled on the Egyptian. She will look like one of the greatest widows in the world, like a giant praying mantis.[43]

Price's costumes and hairdo were, in fact, ponderous, cumbersome, and overbearing, inhibiting her movement and dispelling any illusion of the lightness usually associated with the seductive Cleopatra.[44]

Barber, however, went beyond blaming the fiasco on mechanical difficulties, for he viewed the real problem as having to do with fundamental differences between his and Zeffirelli's concept of the opera:

> As far as I'm concerned, the production had nothing to do with what I had imagined. . . . The Met overproduced it. . . . The Shakespeare play is rather intellectual—it's one of the problem plays. Cleopatra is an older woman and Antony is going downhill. What I wrote and what I envisioned

*In her diary entry (11 September 1966), Katharine Fryer notes how "muffled" Price's voice sounded at first, the confusion of the swarms of people on stage, the abstract sets, and how "incensed Barber was at the mechanical failures."

Barber and his cousin Katharine Homer Fryer, opening night at the Metropolitan Opera House at Lincoln Center, 16 December 1966.

had nothing to do with what one saw on that stage. Zeffirelli wanted horses and goats and 200 soldiers, which he got, and he wanted elephants, which fortunately he didn't get.[45]

Zeffirelli's account in his 1986 autobiography suggests that from the very beginning he and Barber were of different minds about what kind of opera they were writing. "Given the subject and scale of the occasion," he said, he assumed that what Barber was planning to compose was something akin to *Aïda,* and he was "all set to rise to the occasion with mammoth sets, a vast cast, and sumptuous costumes," convinced that would be the sort of spectacle worthy of honoring so important an event. "This turned out to be a dangerous assumption," he said, "but for the moment I was happily planning all manner of wonders with the extraordinary machinery that I had watched being installed."* He admitted his "grandiose settings would be totally at odds with the music" but was unrelenting in his position that his was the only way to proceed—"Sam was writing a

*Franco Zeffirelli, *Zeffirelli: An Autobiography* (Great Britain and New York: Weidenfeld and Nicolson, 1966), p. 202. *Aïda* could not have been further from Barber's compositional mindset. "The real subject matter of the play has nothing to do with Egypt," he said, "but is based on Elizabethan hard politics and a kind of purification that arises out of a somewhat decadent love affair" (Eric Salzman, "Samuel Barber," *HiFi/Stereo Review* [October 1966]: 86).

pleasant chamber piece," he said, "and not at all the grand epic we had all been anticipating." He expressed his doubts about the music to Bing and evidently expected Barber to rewrite his score, but instead "arrived to find the composer had made few changes, being determined to do it in a small-scale way." To Zeffirelli anything less than grandiose seemed trivial:

> At the end of August I suggested to Bing that we move the opera to later in the season and open the House with a gala evening crammed with as many international stars as we could commandeer. . . . In any case, I argued, the opening night audience weren't coming for the opera, they were coming to flash their jewels.[46]

A completely different mindset governed Barber:

> Actually Shakespeare's *Antony and Cleopatra* is a very sophisticated play and by no means spectacular. There's a dichotomy between the struggle for political power and the great passion which blazes through to sheer poetry to the end. What I'm trying to say is that for this occasion, the opening of a new opera house, the spectacular side is being emphasized more than it has to be.[47]

Barber had worked into the score a large share of musical pageantry—fanfares, bacchanal dance scenes, and large-scale choruses—but apparently it was the excesses that bothered him. By the time he saw the opera in production, it was too late for him to do anything about that:

> The point is, I had very little control—practically none. I was not supported by the management. On the other hand, the management supported every idea of Zeffirelli's. Then, of course, there were all the major mishaps of the first night in a new house. I was simply a victim of all that.[48]

In spite of the composer's analysis of the course of events, scores of the reviews of the opera laid blame for its failure almost as much on his music as the production.* Only the third act was pointed to as brilliant, possessing the strongest emotional music and finest arias—"flashes of the old, imaginative Barber," for example, were found in the scene of Antony's suicide, Enobarbus's final lament (act 2, sc. 7 and sc. 8), or the proud, defiant, striding music that Cleopatra sings over Antony's body (act 3).[49] Harold C. Schonberg's review, for example, laced meager praise with pejoratives:

> skillfully put together, but lacking ardor and eloquence; big in sound, but stingy with arresting musical ideas. It abounds in declamation and pagean-

*It is, of course, difficult to judge the fairness of such criticism of the music without having been present at the first performances of the opera. Because newspaper coverage of the opening virtually eclipsed all other local and international news, there is an ocean of material written by journalists who focused on the construction of the new opera house itself and the social aspects of the opening, or who presented superficial musical criticisms. Only reviews that appeared in major papers, periodicals, and music journals are considered here.

> try rather than in an exploration of the subject—love between man and woman. Instead of lyric rapture, we get prose.[50]

Schonberg's observations mirror the overall criticism, which asserts that there were two major flaws in the opera. First, the music had only rare moments of the lyrical style usually associated with Barber: Price had to "push her voice up with guttural outcries . . . only in rare moments, could the shimmering gold of her voice shine through";[51] it was in general "a prosaic and spiritless exercise relieved only occasionally by a rare oasis";[52] "lyrically fine moments were more often given to the orchestra than to singers."[53] Second, the opera lacked an overall sense of dramatic purpose and musical momentum: "the music seemed a score for a great dramatic pageant"; "a piece of musical manufacture that proceeds in jerks from scene to scene"; "the opera failed to concentrate on the essential relationships between the characters"; and the ultimate blow, "How can a composer undertake to tell it without writing any love music, or even any real love scenes?"[54]

There is a taped recording of the premiere at the New York Public Library for the Performing Arts at Lincoln Center, and while it cannot permit a realistic appraisal of *Antony and Cleopatra* as a whole, it does provide some opportunity to judge the music on its own merits.[55] The recording suggests that the general criticisms of the opera in its original version legitimately derive from more than one source. Although there were love-duet passages in the 1966 version of the opera, they seemed too brief, almost always aborted by bad news or, in the end, by death, whetting the appetite for, but not fulfilling, what one critic calls "the truly rapturous melodic surge that would irresistibly envelope the listener in this tale of overwhelming passion and lust";[56] Cleopatra's aria "If this be love indeed," in act 2, for example, was too brief and became more fully realized when the opera was revised. In addition, Barber's parlando writing for Price's voice—in what she called her "Carmen voice"—resulted in abrupt transitions between throaty, even hoarse or strident, declamations and a silken singing style that is more compatible with Barber's usually mellifluous vocal writing. In this early version there is a marked dichotomy between the character of the music in the first act and much of the second as compared with the rest of the opera, where the lyrical flow is continuous and intensifies the drama of the death scenes.

Criticisms of the structure of the opera itself were a signal that even though Zeffirelli and Barber had eliminated many scenes from the original play, more pruning was required. In its 1966 version *Antony and Cleopatra* presented a complexity of locations and characters that seem to diffuse attention from the most compelling focus of the opera, the dilemma of the lovers, who are pulled between amorous and political forces.

Apparently, only two critics availed themselves of the recording of the original version in order to appraise the music independently of the production: Andrew Porter and Irving Kolodin. Porter concluded that Barber's music, though "mellifluous, fluent, and romantic in a general way," with "much able invention, simply did not rise to the size of its subject."[57] In addition, he likened Shakespeare's verses and Barber's music to "jostling bedfellows," with much of the syntax and vocabulary "jarring against the manner of the music" and inhibiting the performers from "an easy, communicative dramatic utterance," being "at odds with the natural speeds and stresses of the lines." Some of Porter's examples seem picayune, though, such as finding fault with the rising inflection on the last syllable of Antony's name, or the extension of Octavia's name to four syllables. He attributed the awkwardness and misplaced stress in part to the singers' lack of empathy with the poetry and criticized the publisher's "blunt modern manner" of tying together the tails of eighth and shorter notes, thus prompting the singers toward metrical delivery rather than "eloquent utterance."[58]

In contrast, Kolodin thought "the musical proceedings gain in interest without the distraction of the scenery and staging."[59] His discerning critique proclaimed the last scene "a stunner." Price was

> finally triumphant through the beauty of her vocal art . . . a woman (or all women) lamenting a lost lover—Iseult over Tristan, Brünnhilde over Siegfried, agony over agony. In the spirit of the poet he essentially is, Barber has embalmed this emotion in a pensive essence of elegy, with a rich intersticing of instrumental silver among the vocal gold.[60]

Barber, too, believed the strength of the opera was the third act, saying afterwards to Bing, that he would "not change one note of act III—*that* really works."[61]

The morning after the premiere of *Antony and Cleopatra,* Barber sailed for Europe on the SS *Constitution.* Although his disappearance to Italy was interpreted by his friends, publisher, and the press as a flight made out of disgust and in disgrace, it was in fact neither, for even before the premiere he had planned an extended vacation in Bolzano after the opening. Interviewed in 1971, he said, "When I left I had no idea of the enormity of the failure. It was not until I arrived when I began to get letters from friends, letters of condolence, full of pity" that he fully absorbed what had happened.[62] This public statement is somewhat ingenuous, for Katharine Fryer's diary suggests otherwise; after the problematic dress rehearsal he despaired, "I'm not going to write any more music—I'm through."[63]

The management of the Metropolitan Opera, however, was not immediately dissuaded by the bad press notices of *Antony;* three days after the premiere Anthony Bliss, president of the Metropolitan Opera, wrote a letter to Barber that suggests he was optimistic about the opera's future:

> *Dear Sam:*
> Now that I have heard your opera all in one reading instead of little snatches here and there, I want to congratulate you. It may take time for our audiences to get wholly familiar with the work, but I am sure that this opera will become one of the first contemporary works to be a regular part of our repertoire.[64]

Rudolf Bing, too, must have been interested in preserving the opera for the repertoire, for soon after the premiere, while on vacation in Bolzano, he talked with Barber about how it might be redone.*

* * *

Prompted by a conviction that, in spite of the vitriolic reviews, the opera contained some of his best work, Barber directed his energies intermittently over the next decade toward salvaging the opera. Some of the revisions he made suggest he believed there was a degree of veracity in the critical opinions of the first performances in 1966. The earliest reworking, in 1968, was of what had been considered the two best scenes in the opera, Cleopatra's arias in act 1 and act 3—"Give me some music" and her suicide monologue, "Give me my robe." By providing an introduction and an interlude that binds the arias together, Barber created a concert scene, approximately sixteen minutes in duration, that was performed for the first time by Ella Lee and the National Symphony Orchestra under Howard Mitchell at the Fourth InterAmerican Music Festival on 23 June 1968 in Columbia, Maryland.

Price's recording of these arias in 1969 prompted Kolodin to confirm his initial opinion of the opera, that "there is much music in the score of higher quality than was generally acknowledged at the time."[65] So well received, also, was Martina Arroyo's performance with the New York Philharmonic on 11 December 1971 that Donal Henahan suggested, "No doubt another try hereabouts is indicated, perhaps in a revised smaller-scale, more musically centered version."[66]

In 1972, long before any new production was in view, Barber and Menotti began talking about revising *Antony and Cleopatra*.† A hint of their plans was communicated to Turner in June when Barber wrote from Spoleto.

> The only thing I must warn you is that if I'm working, you mustn't play the other piano downstairs, for unfortunately I can hear it. . . . And G.C. and I may be working on the revision of . . . you know. Please don't tell that around as it is terribly uncertain.[67]

* To date, however, the Metropolitan Opera has never included it in another season.

† In fact, at the dress rehearsal of the premiere, Barber and Menotti were already planning changes—a quieter opening and expansion of the ballet scenes—which ultimately did not figure in the revision (Katharine Homer Fryer's diary entry, 11 September 1966).

In September 1973 Barber and Menotti listened to tapes of the opera, Menotti taking notes. They decided what to cut, what to add, and where new scenes were needed.[68] Two years passed before the opera was ready in its new version. In the winter of 1974 Peter Mennin, president of the Juilliard School, asked if the opera could be produced at the school's American Opera Center during the following season. As the deadline encroached, Barber was behind schedule, and Stanley Hollingsworth, at the request of G. Schirmer, assisted in producing the orchestral score under Barber's tutelage.[69]

A few months before the production, Barber was invited by Orlando Cole to lecture on his music at the Philadelphia Art Alliance, which was presenting a series on "Philadelphia-area composers"—Persichetti, Rochberg, Crumb, and Druckman. Unable to attend because he was involved with the preparation of the Juilliard production, Barber wrote to Cole, "Nor would I even dream of explaining my music, as you so well know!" and spoke optimistically about the forthcoming performance of the revised opera:

> I have revised "Antony" and have written a great deal of new music for it which all has to be orchestrated for performances the first week in February. . . . I shall be in full rehearsal on January 25th. Gian Carlo arrives from Europe and will be stage director. A young man named [James] Conlon will be the conductor and I hear he is very talented. . . . I am looking forward to the performance at the Juilliard since it is non-union and there is an excellent opera theatre at our disposal.[70]

Four performances of the revised version were given by the American Opera Center at the Juilliard School on 6–10 February 1975, staged by Menotti and conducted by James Conlon, with Esther Hinds as Cleopatra, a role she sang again in the 1983 Spoleto Festival performances in Italy and Charleston, South Carolina. Zeffirelli's name was discreetly dropped from the title, and, under the guidance of Menotti, the libretto was completely transformed.

Alterations were addressed to the shortcomings of Zeffirelli's libretto and overblown production, a style that Menotti believed was counter to Barber's fundamental personality:

> In a certain way, part of the trouble was that Zeffirelli . . . did not understand Sam's character at all and he filled the libretto with fanfares and big scenes and so on. Sam's always been a very intimate and introverted composer and all that was completely out of style with him.[71]

For the revision, Barber said he "tried to tighten up the two basic elements of the opera, the political and the amorous . . . in general, giving more space to the lovers. In other words, more Egypt and less Rome."[72] He cut in half the length of the opening chorus, lengthened the ensuing duet between Cleopatra and Antony, and eliminated the drunken orgy aboard the Roman galley—"all that Rotary Club talk by the Romans," he told Dorle Soria as he worked on the revision.[73]

Menotti's version shuns elements of grand opera spectacle in favor of a more intimate production: the chorus, as in Greek tragedy, was placed on the two sides of the stage; ballet—the extended "Stick Dance"—was omitted in the 1975 version almost completely; and there are fewer alternations of scenes between Rome and Egypt in act 1. The Juilliard production eliminated, also, camels, goats, horses, and pyramids and, instead of using abstract sculpted scenery, set the opera in a simpler realistic environment evocative of Egypt.*

The opera, now in three acts and fourteen scenes, is an hour shorter than the original version.† It has six fewer characters; Octavia no longer has a singing part, Caesar's role is considerably diminished, and a number of minor Roman characters are omitted.

In general, there is greater continuity of action and stronger dramatic direction: the lovers are thrown into sharper focus and the importance of the world at large is diminished. Barber accomplished this by consolidating, rearranging, and cutting material. In act 1, for example, two scenes in Cleopatra's palace (sc. 4 and 6) interrupted in the 1966 version by a scene in Caesar's palace (sc. 5) are combined in the revision as one (sc. 3), so that "Give me some music" leads directly to the queen's violent reaction over hearing news of Antony's marriage. The 1966 version's galley scene (act 1, sc. 7), greatly trimmed, has been relocated ashore in a Roman banquet hall (the final scene in act 1) and gains Caesar's aria "A sister I bequeath you," the only passage retained from scene 5 of the 1966 version. The revised death scene no longer includes Charmian's speech over the dead queen; her music is redistributed, instead, to the orchestra and to Cleopatra. The reprise of "Now I feed myself with most delicious poison," as the queen takes the snake's venom, affords an ironic reference to the erotic drug mandragora she took in act 1.

Zeffirelli's libretto for the original version of *Antony and Cleopatra* had provided Barber only rare opportunities for what Menotti called lyric meditation. There were no love scenes allowing for the obligatory lovers' duet; Cleopatra's dramatic recitative beginning "Give me some music," culminating in "my man of men"—although spine-chilling in its immediate

*In any case, there was no possibility of using any of the original sets and costumes, because in November 1973 a fire swept the Metropolitan Opera warehouse, destroying sets and costumes for forty-one productions, *Antony and Cleopatra* and *Vanessa* among them. Although Barber mourned the loss of Cecil Beaton's costumes and sets for *Vanessa*, he had no regrets about the loss of Zeffirelli's creations (Dorle J. Soria, "Artist Life," *Musical America* [September 1974]: 5).

†The tape of the opening night performance was two-and-a-half hours long. The G. Schirmer piano-vocal score was reduced by fifty-three pages for the revision (1966, 342 pp.; 1976, 289 pp.). One of the best explications on the textual structure of *Antony* and its relationship to Shakespeare's play is in Andrew Porter's article "Antony's Second Chance," in which he discusses the opera in connection with its 1974 revisions (see pp. 99–101). In particular he discusses which parts of the play were preserved by Zeffirelli and which were relocated in the libretto.

effect—had been interrupted before its development. Cleopatra's lament over her lost lover in the last act was one of the few passages in the 1966 version Barber had composed with the full lyrical magnitude that typifies his style. In contrast, the new version benefits from expansion and addition of love music. "Give me some music" is now a full-fledged aria; included also is the concert-piece close of Cleopatra's suicide monologue, "Give me my robe," Barber's earliest reworked music from the opera. The most effective addition is the luxurious and tender but erotic love duet in act 2, "Oh take, oh take those lips away," from Beaumont and Fletcher's *The Bloody Brother* (1616), which Barber preferred to the more famous one-stanza version in Shakespeare's *Measure for Measure*. It is interesting to note, however, especially in light of the general opinion that the original version of *Antony* would be improved by the addition of more lyrical music, that Porter found the most "striking scenes" in the revised production to be the two that "did not depend on full-throated lyricism": the soldier's conversation during the mysterious "music i' the air," and the last conversation of Antony and Eros, over a kettledrum ostinato.[74]

The orchestral music, which had been acknowledged as one of the strongest features of the original version, where left intact was not revised, although sometimes it was relocated; for example, the borrowing of the brooding marchlike material from the withdrawn Second Symphony remains in the new version, but as the music for Caesar's entrance to the Roman senate (see Example 17.2).

The revised *Antony and Cleopatra*—more focused dramatically, more developed musically, and with staging more sensitive to Barber's musical style—offered an opportunity to test whether the opera could critically hold its own apart from its original Zeffirelli production. Apparently it succeeded in going, as one critic suggested, "a long way toward escaping entirely from the shadow of the dismal premiere . . . with flashes of eloquence and power."[75]

* * *

In spite of improvements, *Antony and Cleopatra* has been slow to enter the repertoire of major opera houses. The lack of subsequent performances may have been in part a reflection of a growing interest in "new music" of widely divergent musical techniques and languages, music with anti-Romantic and antiexpressionist tendencies that are the antithesis of Barber's musical style.[76] Concurrently, from about 1963 to 1970 there was also a decline in the number of Barber's orchestral works on concert programs of American symphony orchestras.[77] Next to Carter, Boulez, Penderecki, Ligeti, and minimalist composers, whose music gained in popularity after 1960, Barber's music could conceivably have been perceived as reactionary and ultraconservative.

In 1980 a concert version of *Antony and Cleopatra* was performed in Paris at the Théâtre des Champs-Elysées, with Radio-France conducted by Jean-Pierre Marty. Barber, ill with cancer, was unable to attend; his phys-

16
Allegro con brio ♩ = 92
ff
Più sostenuto ♩ = 69
Cym.
Tom-tom
17
pesante
f cantando
sim.

Jeffrey Wells (Antony) and Esther Hinds (Cleopatra), Spoleto Festival U.S.A., Charleston, 1983. *(William Struhs)*

ical condition had become so critical that he had to return from Yesterhouse—Menotti's home in East Lothian, Scotland—to be hospitalized in New York. Menotti, who had seen the Paris production, brought a tape of the opera to Barber's room at University Hospital; a poster announcing the opera was pinned on the wall near his bed.*

In 1983, two years after Barber's death, *Antony and Cleopatra* was produced as a fully staged opera at the Spoleto Festivals in Charleston and Italy. Menotti directed the opera; set and costumes were designed by Zack Brown. Esther Hinds was Cleopatra, Jeffrey Wells played Antony, and Christian Badea conducted the orchestra. Four performances taped during the festivals were used for the first full-length recording of the opera.[78] Two makeup sessions of the orchestral interludes were conducted in order

*A year after Barber died a concert version by the Abbey Opera in London (at Logan Hall on 27 March 1982) was found, understandably, "more notable for individual effective episodes than for any sense of dramatic, compelling continuity." Nevertheless, Barber's "soaring Italianate manner" was called inspired; the final scene was considered to contain the most deeply moving music of the opera (undated reviews, ca. 28 March 1982, by Henry Pleasants, *International Herald Tribune;* Peter Stadlen, *Manchester Guardian;* and Max Loppert, *London Financial Times* were shown to the author by Valentin Herranz).

Example 17.2 *(facing) Antony and Cleopatra,* act 1, scene 2 (G. Schirmer, 1976). Themes borrowed from Barber's Second Symphony are in brackets.

to eliminate stage and audience noise and allow for the restoration of some of Barber's original orchestration.* The album won the 1984 Grammy Award in the category of "Best New Classical Compositions" and was chosen by the editors of *Opera News* as one of the best recordings of the year.

In Italy, appropriately, *Antony and Cleopatra* at last found its rightful appreciation and a serious critical appraisal. Much was credited to "the perfect care for the production" exercised by Menotti, who "poured all the skill and musical precision of his exceptional talents as a director, thus allowing the succession of scenes to flow smoothly, and to have an expressiveness which . . . always gave . . . respect for the music in every respect."[79]

Further changes had been made since the Juilliard production. The chorus, now dressed in black street clothes, was removed from the stage entirely and placed on the two sides of the orchestra pit, diminishing the appearance of multitudes and eliminating a crowded stage yet preserving the musical presence of the singers. It was suggested that by drawing attention entirely to the protagonists and their internal romantic tensions and separating them from the "masses," Menotti was, in a certain sense, "the reinventor of the opera."[80]

For the changes of scene, only a small number of elements were used, arranged in a very "movable" order—not as symbolic representations, however, which might have worked against the realism of the music—obtaining, in one critic's words, "a figurative precision that heightened the score and 'framed' it wonderfully." The apparition of Cleopatra on a ship as a kind of sumptuous dream, the battle depicted with a few touches, and the final death scene were considered to be "worthy of entering into the legends of melodramatic productions."[81]

The critical reviews of the Spoleto production give much attention to the musical strengths of the opera. First, there was uniform appreciation of Barber as a master of the orchestra—"his particular taste for the play of timbres," his treatment of individual instruments with an "exquisite subtlety of relief," and his ability to handle large blocks of sound that suddenly dissolve into chamber music to great dramatic effect (the kettledrums and flute passage was praised as a "living token of Barber's musical imagination").[82] "One will understand," wrote the music critic Teodoro Celli about these passages, "how right it was that this opera be produced in Italy."[83]

One of the strongest attributes to the opera was considered to be the music for the chorus—"often treated like a second orchestra"—which surrounded the drama as a "strongly suggestive vocal ribwork," and where twentieth-century models "very distant from each other like Pizzetti and

*The orchestral whip in act 1, sc. 3, and the original woodwind instrumentation of the battle scene, act 2, sc. 5.

Catherine Malfitano (Cleopatra) and Richard Cowen (Antony), Lyric Opera of Chicago, 1991.

Stravinsky" are happily united.[84] Barber's vocal writing, acknowledged Cavallotti, offers a richness of design that in a masterful way clarifies the inner movements of emotional confusion.[85]

While the Italian press found the roots of Barber's stylistic recollections in Puccini's *Turandot,* Stravinsky's *Symphony of Psalms,* Respighi's *Pines of Rome,* and even Franz Lehar's *Land of Smiles,* they still recognized his originality. In fact, his ability to bring together techniques, languages, and emotions quite dissimilar—to "savor" tradition and yet "not burn his bridges with the linguistic experiments of his own time"—was seen as a strength and, moreover, as a uniquely American asset. It was pointed out that where European composers are weighed down by a tradition "whose glory often turns into a Procrustean bed," blocking imagination and leading to a war between the romantic heritage and the avant-garde, American music, on the other hand, is not afraid of being trapped in spontaneity of Romantic expression; "in the direct transmission of the heart into the word, it sings in an open manner."[86] In this respect Barber's *Antony and Cleopatra* is exemplary:

> The work of the American composer is a perfectly crafted melodrama, following the canonical rules—the succession of love and death, the music that is molded by it and comments on it in its particular expressive vein, the great orchestra that rises from it, the vocal quality that displays itself luminously in spacious and solemn arches. The opera proceeds . . . to magnetize the hearer and to involve him in the tremor of a lyric pathos.[87]

It is promising that the Lyric Opera of Chicago included *Antony and Cleopatra* in its 1991–92 season, the first production of the opera in a major house since its premiere. Directed by Elijah Moshinsky, with Catherine Malfitano and Richard Cowen in the title roles, the three acts of the 1967 score were reorganized into two, with an intermission following the love duet ("Oh take, oh take those lips away"). Thus the pause occurred at the height of romantic tension, midway through the opera, allowing the denouement—beginning with Enobarbus's major aria—to proceed without interruption to the end of the opera. The Chicago company met the challenge of rapid scene changes with a permanent backdrop of reflecting panels on which images of Rome and Alexandria were projected for each location. The Spoleto and Chicago performances give hope that *Antony and Cleopatra,* an opera that has languished too long in the shadow of prejudicial early reviews, may find a permanent place in the repertoire of major companies.

18

THE LAST YEARS 1967-1981

Despite and Still, Op. 41 (1968)

During the last fifteen years of his life, Barber struggled with emotional depression, alcoholism, and creative blocks that profoundly affected his productivity. Menotti's perception of him, based on many years' first-hand experience, portrays Barber's internal struggle with the creative process and his drive for perfection as continual:

> He was so gifted, but actually he was a very tormented soul. He was never happy with what he had done. He was only happy while he was composing. When he finished a piece, he could not bear to look at it. When he had to correct something, it was truly agony for him to go over a piece. And he also suffered a great deal because he went through long periods of dryness. But once he'd gotten into a piece, he would work day and night without stopping.[1]

The dry periods intensified after *Antony and Cleopatra*. His publisher, Hans Heinsheimer, believed Barber had been so accustomed to—perhaps even spoiled by—easy success from the start of his early career that he was unable to cope with the vitriolic reception of the opera and fled to Europe in defeat. After Barber's death, Heinsheimer said:

> *Antony and Cleopatra* was a turning point in the life of Barber. It was a terrible catastrophe from which he never recovered. And I think—I cannot prove it, I am not a doctor—that his sickness and his physical collapse later on started at this time. The interesting thing is that Barber's life took a complete turn from that moment. He never wrote anything of importance any more.[2]

In an earlier article, Heinsheimer had written:

> I believe he, who had known nothing but success, never really recovered from that humiliating disaster, and that the long illness that took him away was only the final, logical reflection of his state of mind and soul.[3]

It is, however, an exaggeration to attribute Barber's creative blocks and physical decline entirely to one so-called musical failure. Negative opinion was not new to him, and he had more than once in the past been the subject of criticism for swimming against the tide of modernism. One has only to recall the Ashley Pettis diatribes after the Toscanini premieres in 1938 or the negative reviews of *Vanessa* by European critics after the Salzburg Festival performance.

Barber's pilgrimages to Europe—annual "escapes" as they were—had begun, in fact, as early as 1962, well before *Antony and Cleopatra*. His intention to spend more time abroad is made clear from correspondence between Barber and the National Institute of Arts and Letters regarding his participation on the Grant Committee. He wrote to Felicia Geffen, assistant secretary-treasurer, "I definitely plan to be in Europe six months a year for the next three years. In other words, I could only be of use to you Oct., Nov., December—possibly April and May. You decide."*

After 1962, Europe had become more accessible because, with money from the Metropolitan Opera commission, he was able to build a small chalet in the Dolomites at Santa Cristina. Only when his mother died in 1967 did he return to the United States, and then only for a brief visit. In April he wrote to his cousin Katharine Fryer that he would be in the States at least until July, but "[I] hardly ever come to New York and share your fascination for N.Y. less and less. Well, you see, we revert to type, and I'm just a small town kid."[4]

His letters from this period show a streak of cynicism, but the writer also, paradoxically, seems more sentimental and conscious of his own mortality than before. A letter to Orlando Cole, for example, ends:

> But I hope to . . . come and see you, for it has been much too long. There is a lot to talk about, including Gian Carlo's newly-acquired Scottish mansion. I suppose at our age we should congratulate each other for being in good health and working away as usual; and I really do want to see you and Ossie one of these days. Say hello to Max [Aronoff] for me, and Martha [Massena Halbwachs], and anyone else who remembers me.[5]

Barber's seclusion for several years following *Antony and Cleopatra* did not necessarily represent a musical withdrawal; but he made no apologies for choosing to write only what and when he wanted to. When Eugene Ormandy made plans in 1967 for Philadelphia's bicentennial celebration nine years ahead, Barber was the first composer offered the

*Letter, 22 January 1962, Santa Cristina. Other correspondence between Barber and Geffen from January 1962 to May 1963 confirms that he was out of the country more than in.

commission—"it should be a work for large orchestra, mixed chorus, and four or more soloists and the theme should be based on the history of our city," the conductor suggested.[6] Barber's refusal of the commission seemed an expression of his weariness with a means of support that had stimulated virtually all of his mature works but in the end had led to disappointment.

> I am honored by your request for a piece for Philadelphia for 1976. But after thinking this over carefully I must stick to my decision not to accept any more orchestral commissions. I have fulfilled so many of them, but now want to compose what I want on my own time, be it 48 preludes and fugues for piccolo!
>
> Fortunately my old music, in which you have played such a friendly and protecting role through the years, supports me adequately without such commitments. . . . For your faith in my music, past and future, I can only thank you and send you and Gretel my affectionate wishes.*

Ormandy responded:

> I need not tell you that your letter was quite disappointing to me as I had hoped that you would accept the commission since, de facto, you would have had five years to write it. But after our conversation, and after what you said in your letter, I bow to your decision and accept it with reluctance. . . . I sincerely hope that in 1968 you will turn over a new leaf and continue your creativity where you left off a year ago. You are young yet and you have so much to offer that I feel the best is yet to come from you.[7]

Three years later, for Ormandy's seventieth birthday, Barber—with seventeen other composers†—contributed to a set of variations on "Happy Birthday," presented to the conductor on 24 January 1970, at the 113th Anniversary Concert and Ball at the Academy of Music in Philadelphia. Barber's dissonant contrapuntal version for brass choir and timpani, which begins with a canon at the twelfth for tenor and soprano voices, includes an unexpected nostalgic reference to his own *Adagio for Strings* woven into the inner voices at the cadence (see Example 18.1). The holograph manuscript of the short score was published in a limited facsimile edition of two thousand copies by RCA Red Seal.

During the period of semi-seclusion, perhaps as a kind of self-restoration, Barber turned to what had always been the gratifying task of writing

*Letter from Barber to Ormandy, 12 December 1967. The letter suggests that he had also turned down an earlier commission (from Mrs. Alexander Hilsberg, wife of the late concertmaster of the Philadelphia Orchestra), apparently because he did not want to be bound to the pressure of a scheduled premiere.

†Theodore Berger, Leonard Bernstein, Aaron Copland, Paul Creston, Norman Dello Joio, David Diamond, Gottfried von Einem, Ross Lee Finney, Nicolas Nabokov, Carl Orff, Vincent Persichetti, Walter Piston, George Rochberg, Miklós Rózsa, William Schuman, Roger Sessions, and Virgil Thomson.

Example 18.1 Barber's contribution to *Variations on Happy Birthday,* for Eugene Ormandy on the occasion of his 70th birthday (RCA Red Seal limited edition, 24 January 1970). *(Eugene Ormandy Collection, Special Collections, Van Pelt-Dietrich Library Center, University of Pennsylvania)*

vocal music in short forms. The texts he chose for his songs and choral works seem to reflect a preoccupation with dark and quasi-religious themes—loneliness, rededication, reconciliation, and solitude. In 1968, he produced a cycle of five songs, *Despite and Still,* Op. 41; a pair of choral works, Op. 42, on texts by Louise Bogan ("To Be Sung on the Water") and Laurie Lee ("Twelfth Night"); and a set of "mutations" for brass instruments on the plainsong-based chorale melody "Christe, du Lamm Gottes."

The cycle *Despite and Still,* Op. 41, taking its name from the last song of the group, was completed in June 1968 and dedicated to Leontyne Price, who gave the first performance with pianist David Garvey on 27 April 1969 at Avery Fisher Hall.* The songs are both intellectually and vocally challenging, which may explain why they have been the most neglected of the Barber repertoire in this genre.† In their keenly dramatic rendering of enigmatic texts, the songs (especially Nos. I, III, and V) represent the duality of Barber's mature style—an affinity for late nineteenth-century German Romantic Lieder and a free use of twentieth-century harmonic language. They deserve a greater depth of analytic study than is within the scope of this book.

The diverse texts—three by Robert Graves (the poet's "A Last Poem," pointedly retitled "A Last Song"; "In the Wilderness"; and "Despite and Still"), Theodore Roethke's "My Lizard," and a paragraph from James Joyce's *Ulysses,* beginning "Solitary hotel in mountain pass"—might seem an illogical grouping, especially to those with only a casual knowledge of the composer's personal demons.[8] One critic, for example, found the thoughts "disparate, compartmented, and unrelated to each other. An enigma."[9] All the texts of the five songs, however, suggest that the cycle has profound biographical significance, perhaps even acting as a catharsis for the composer; they probe bleak themes about loneliness, lost love, and isolation—in the creative quest, in old age, in the pious mission.‡

Barber believed the texts for Op. 41 (as well those for Op. 45) asked for more dissonant music than his earlier songs.§ Characteristic of the harmonic language of the group is a tendency toward tonal ambiguity—a blurring of tonal centers—with tritones, full chromaticism, conflicting triads, and whole-tone scale segments directed toward a vivid expression of textual imagery.

Barber particularly liked the poetry of Robert Graves (1895–1985). "It sets very well," he told Phillip Ramey; "there's a real structure and a taut

* Price sang the group at a memorial service for Barber in 1981.

† Roberta Alexander's recording (Etcetera, 1988) is the first of the complete cycle.

‡ During this period, domestic tranquility at Capricorn was severely strained. Barber did not especially get along with Francis ("Chip") Phelan, a young man who was adopted by Menotti. Although Menotti says it was not unusual for the two composers to be highly critical of each other's friends and that a rift between Barber and himself had begun as early as the start of the Spoleto Festival, mounting tensions in the late sixties led to the eventual sale of Capricorn.

§ Ramey, "Samuel Barber at Seventy," p. 19. Earlier in this interview, Ramey asked Barber, "Has poetry ever dictated a change, however slight, in your musical style?" Barber responded, "I think that's happened a little, but when it did it would only last for one poem. For instance, in *Nuvoletta,* a slightly ironic song, there are quotes from Wagner's *Tristan,* that sort of thing. However, I really don't think my style has ever changed, except perhaps in details due to text." Ramey: "Are there songs where, to illustrate text, your music became more dissonant than usual?" Barber: "Yes, in some of the later ones—the cycle *Despite and Still,* written for Leontyne Price, and the *Three Songs,* Op. 45, for Dietrich Fischer-Dieskau." These answers suggest that Barber considered an increased use of dissonance uncharacteristic of his generic style.

quality that I find formally inviting."* Graves's "A Last Poem" was published in *The New Yorker* magazine, 6 June 1964; but Barber's source was probably Graves's *Complete Poems* (1965), which is the first place the three he used for Op. 41 appeared together.[10] Barber substitutes the word *song* for Graves's *poem* in the text as well as the title, strengthening the personal connection. Op. 41, No. 1—"A last song, and a very last / and yet another / O, when can I give over? / Must I drive the pen until blood bursts from my nails / And my breath fails and I shake with fever"—suggests the task of the artist, driven to continue creative activity even without affirmation from his muse: "Shall I never hear her whisper softly: / 'But this is truth—written by you only,' / and for me only; / Therefore, love, have done?" The poem was written in the wake of Graves's Oxford lectures of 1963, in which for the first time he ventured to dramatize the "vicissitudes of a poet's dealings with the White Goddess, the Muse, and the perpetual Other Woman."†

Characteristic of Barber's setting are frequent metric changes, which follow the impulse of the poetic rhythms, and layered conflicting triads, such as those in measure 2 (F♭ major/A♭ minor, see Example 18.2a). The climax of the song, at measures 28–29 (Example 18.2b), is emotionally heightened even more poignantly by conflicting triads (G♭ major/F minor); the unresolved question of the text lingers in the ambiguity of the concluding arpeggio.

"My Lizard," Op. 41, No. 2, was subtitled by its poet Theodore Roethke "Wish for a young wife." Again Barber's alteration of the subtitle, to "Wish for a young love," suggests a personal inflection. The text is metaphorical:

My lizard, my lively writher,
May your limbs never wither,
May the eyes in your face
Survive the green ice
Of envy's mean gaze;
May you live out your life

* "Samuel Barber at Seventy," p. 19. This was provoked by a comment of Ramey's that T. S. Eliot once told him that poetry should not be set to music. Barber's answer was, "That's silly. But, except for one or two of them, his own poems are not really very settable anyway, so he is relatively safe—at least from me. Another poet I cannot set, who is a great friend of mine, is Stephen Spender. His poems just don't lend themselves to my music. Robert Graves is quite a different matter."

In fact, Barber may have been considering setting one of Eliot's poems: "Eyes that last I saw in tears" appears in a black loose-leaf notebook kept by Barber during the seventies. The choral setting of "A Stopwatch and an Ordnance Map" was the only one of Spender's poems set by Barber.

† Robert Graves, *Between Moon and Moon,* ed. Paul O'Prey (London: Hutchinson, 1984), p. 231. Central to Graves's writings is the idea—first expounded in *The White Goddess: A Historical Grammar of Poetic Myth* (New York: Creative Age Press, 1948)—that the dedicated poet must fall in love with a "Muse-possessed" woman and suffer at her hands as the ancient myth is acted out, the White Goddess myth that he claims is the archetype of which all true love poems are either fragments or variations.

Without hate, without grief
And your hair ever blaze
In the sun, in the sun,
When I am undone,
When I am no one.[11]

Although the poem is a benediction of sorts—expressing the poet's wish for eternal youth for his beloved—the loving sentiments are overshadowed by his nihilistic perception of old age and its companion envy; musically, the underlying pathos is never quite offset by the cheerfulness of the recurring "fast and light" tune. The A♭ tonal orientation is blurred by a perpetually moving sixteenth-note figuration with frequent fourths and tritones, anchored alternately to A♭ and G (Example 18.3). Heard against the restless piano part is a fluid vocal line, inaugurated by a minor ninth and including many other disjunct intervals. Barber never set another of Roethke's texts, which he considered incompatible with his musical style. A decade after he wrote this song, when asked about his interest in more modern, or avant-garde, poetry, he replied:

> I wouldn't think of setting Allen Ginsberg. I did once use Theodore Roethke poems, but they were not really very near to me. I admit that I often get bored looking through modern poetry for texts, so little of it seems suitable—the wrong poetry for me.[12]

The text of "In the Wilderness," Op. 41, No. 3, about the suffering of Jesus, is based on a poem Graves wrote in 1915, at a time when his religious faith was certain; later, he rejected the poem, only to reinstate it in his 1947 collection, and it has remained as the first poem in editions ever since. The song's gentle 6/8 meter and the shape of its theme recall the *andante con moto* section of Barber's earlier song about the infant Jesus, "St. Ita's Vision." But the Graves poem, beginning "He of gentleness, thirsting and hungering, walked in the wilderness," wants a bleaker setting. Lilting outer sections in G minor frame a contrasting, tonally less stable, middle section. The piano introduces and supports the triadic lullaby with a long, decending scale, the two voices constituting a heterophonic texture over arpeggios dominated by fifths and fourths. The text of the middle section presents contrasting harsh images—"Basilisk, cocatrice / Flocked to his homilies / With mail of dread device / With monstrous barbed stings / With eager dragon eyes / Great bats on leathern wings"—and Barber set the stinging words to clashing hollow fifths and tritones.

Op. 41, No. 4, "Solitary Hotel," from a passage in the "Ithaca episode" near the end of Joyce's *Ulysses,* is a description of a scene constructed by Stephen Dedalus for Bloom. Earlier in Joyce's narrative, a question about Bloom had been presented: "What example did he adduce to induce Stephen to deduce that originality, though producing its own reward, does not invariably lead to success?"[13] The question would have

a.

SAMUEL BARBER

Despite and Still

for Voice and Piano

Samuel Barber, Op. 41

1

A Last Song *

* In the original "A Last Poem"
** Used by permission.

Example 18.2 *a.* "A Last Song," Op. 41, No. 1, mm. 1–11. *b.* "A Last Song," mm. 21–32.

been of great interest to the composer who believed his *Antony and Cleopatra* to be unappreciated. For the vocal part, Barber used a declamatory, syllabic style that mirrors the bare language of Joyce's descriptive passage, in which short phrases—sometimes consisting of only one or two words—seem analogous to a series of musical motives. A monotone recitative juxtaposed against the piano's tango creates an atmosphere of emotional dis-

tance, like a memory preserved in a faded photograph (Example 18.4a). As in Joyce's passage, the singer ends in midword, the text's inconclusiveness mirrored in the final chord (Example 18.4b).

"Despite and Still," Op. 41, No. 5—like the first of the Graves settings in the cycle—is a searing personal voice, the emotional tone indicated as "darkly impassioned." The foundation of the piece, from beginning to end,

2

My Lizard
(Wish for a Young Love)

Theodore Roethke

Example 18.3 "My Lizard," Op. 41, No. 2, mm. 1–8.

is a large-scale A-minor pedal with numerous embellishments. Two motives recur—a semitone triplet figure and a rapidly ascending scale of five thirty-second notes—which inaugurate each line of text and provide an undercurrent of uneasiness, of tension. Rubato indications, in general, dramatize the emotional thrust of the text; see for example measure 11,

a.

4

Solitary Hotel

James Joyce: *Ulysses*

Example 18.4 *a.* "Solitary Hotel," Op. 41, No. 4, mm. 1–11. *b.* "Solitary Hotel," mm. 50–52.

where the words *I of my rashness* are marked "impetuously" (Example 18.5).

In his review of the first performance of *Despite and Still,* the critic Donal Henahan remarked that "the odd emotional distance that characterized an otherwise enthralling recital made a puzzle of the first perfor-

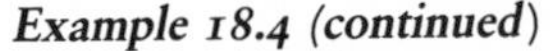

Example 18.4 (continued)

mance" of the Op. 41 songs, even though they were in Barber's "utterly singable rather impressionistic manner."[14] He believed this effect was partly accentuated by Price's delivery, which leaned, characteristically, toward "an odd distancing." Somewhat quixotically, Heinsheimer saw the songs as a gesture of defiance aimed at the detractors of Barber's recent opera, the title of the cycle meaning "despite this disaster, he will still compose."[15] The title, as well as the songs themselves, was also meant, Heinsheimer believed, as a desperate and final defense of his Romantic style: "Despite all the criticism that was leveled against his style of music, people began to wonder, can you really continue composing like that in a day and age of Berio and Stockhausen?"[16]

More likely, however, the biographical significance of these songs is not limited to the aftermath of Barber's opera. "Despite and Still," though positioned last in the group, is given prominence as the title of the cycle, and here, too, the events in Graves's life seem to have a counterpart in the composer's.* It is not a song of defiance, it is a love song—about ill-fated lovers ("you of your gentleness, I of my rashness, Both of despair") whose unity is threatened by still other loves ("loves in alternative"). The plea from the poet—"But O, refuse to choose"—concludes the poem, but Barber adds one more line, reinforcing his perspective, "to love despite and still."

It is also unlikely that Barber needed yet again to defend his Romantic style, as Heinsheimer proposes; the major criticism leveled against the music in *Antony and Cleopatra* was, after all, that the lyrical voice so inseparable from Barber's musical persona was too *meagerly* expressed in the opera.

*Graves wrote the poem at a time when he was, according to his biographer Martin Seymour-Smith, "nearer to disintegration" than at any other time of his life, his muse (poet Laura Riding) having withdrawn from him and transferred her emotional and intellectual support to another. "Despite and Still" (1942) is viewed as an emotional acknowledgment to Graves's wife Beryl that there could still be a "single mind" between them—one of serene and shared confidence—even when chance presents other loves (*Robert Graves: His Life and Work* [London: Hutchinson, 1982]). The situation seems parallel to Barber's.

Two Choral Works, Op. 42; *Mutations from Bach*

Two unaccompanied choral works, Op. 42, were composed by Barber in December 1968—"Twelfth Night" (Laurie Lee) and "To Be Sung on the Water" (Louise Bogan). They are predominantly syllabic, chordal settings of greatly contrasting texts. Central to Laurie Lee's poem is the idea of the rebirth of Christ as symbolic of the earth's awakening from its state of "utter death," essentially an optimistic outlook. Stark images characterize the opening lines of Lee's poem:

> No night could be darker than this night,
> no cold so cold,
> as the blood snaps like a wire
> and the heart's sap stills,
> and the year seems defeated.
>
> O never again, it seems, can green things run,
> or sky birds fly,
> or the grass exhale its humming breath.*

Fourths, fifths, and octaves in the lower voices and a hymnlike setting mirror the austere tone of Lee's poetry. With the description of the emergence of Christ, the musical texture becomes imitative and the melodic line moves more freely:

> Out of this utter death he's born again,
> his birth our Saviour;
> from terror's equinox, he climbs and grows,
> drawing his finger's light across our blood—
> the sun of heaven and the son of God.

The closing measures, hushed and in tempo *calmando ed allargando,* return to the opening words, "No night could be darker than this night."

The setting of Louise Bogan's "To Be Sung on the Water"† was completed on 14 December 1968. The image of gentle, lapping water is suggested by a pulsating three-note motive: A♭—B♭—A♭. Voices are grouped in pairs (SA and TB), which sing antiphonally or in imitative counterpoint

*Laurie Lee, *My Many-coated Man* (London: André Deutsch, 1955), p. 7. Although Barber wrote to Lee (b. 1914) for permission to use the poem, they never discussed the text, nor had the British poet heard or seen the score as of 1982 (letter from Laurie Lee to James Fahey, quoted in his master's thesis, "Samuel Barber, a Portrait in Poetic Voice" [California State University, Fullerton, 1983]).

†Louise Bogan (1897–1970), *Collected Poems* (New York: Farrar, Strauss & Giroux, 1954). Although in 1958 Barber and Bogan had a brief correspondence regarding his service on the Grant Committee of the National Institute of Arts and Letters, to the best of my knowledge they had no more than a professional acquaintance.

Example 18.5 "Despite and Still," Op. 41, No. 5, mm. 1–19.

of three-syllable phrases (or words) in rhythmic clusters of two sixteenth notes tied to an eighth, or eighth-note triplets tied to an eighth. Barber contemplated adding this chorus to the galley scene for the revised version of *Antony and Cleopatra* but evidently decided against it.* The choral work was performed at a memorial service for Barber on 9 February 1981 at St. Bartholomew's Church in New York.

*Andrew Porter mentions seeing the choral piece in an interim score (*Music of Three Seasons,* p. 101).

10
p sub.
cresc. (impetuously)
You of your gen - tle - ness. I of my rash - ness,
l.h.
5
p sub.
cresc.
12
poco allarg.
Both of de - spair
f
14
ff broadly
mf a tempo, with motion
Yet still might share This hap - py will: To love de - spite and
broadly
ff
marcatiss.
p
mf espr.
17
f molto allarg.
Tempo I
still, To love de - spite and still.
sf
f
appassionato
3

In deference to his long-standing favorite composer, in 1968 Barber wrote a short piece—*Mutations from Bach* (sometimes called "Meditations on a Theme of Bach")—for an ensemble of four horns, three trumpets, three trombones, tuba, and timpani. The plainsong "Christ, Thou Lamb of God" is presented in four transformations chronologically ordered, beginning with the earliest, a somber setting by the seventeenth-century composer Joachim Decker (1604). Next is Bach's brighter, richer harmonization as used in his Cantata No. 23 ("Du wahrer Gott und Davids Sohn"), then the elaborate reworked version from his prelude for organ, a canon at the twelfth. Following is Barber's own, slightly askew, arrangement of Bach's harmonization for a muted trumpet in its highest register, over a solo horn, with the melodic line given greater prominence. The set of transformations concludes with a return to Decker's version.

The Lovers, Op. 43

In spite of Barber's reluctance to bind himself to a commission for the bicentennial celebration and his intention not to accept any new commissions at all, he did, in the end, fulfill two important ones in 1971. The first of these, *The Lovers,* for the Girard Bank of Philadelphia,* is a thirty-five-minute work requiring substantial performing forces: a mixed chorus of two hundred voices, baritone, a supporting soprano, and full orchestra—three flutes, two oboes, English horn, two clarinets, bass clarinet, two bassoons, four horns, three trumpets, three trombones, tuba, timpani, percussion, celesta, harp, piano, and strings. It was performed on 22 September 1971 by the Philadelphia Orchestra with the Finnish baritone Tom Krause and the Temple University Chorus under the direction of Robert Page.

The Lovers is based on selections from *Twenty Love Poems and a Song of Despair*[17] by the Chilean poet Pablo Neruda (1904–1973), one of the strongest of the modern poets writing in Spanish; in 1971 he won the Nobel Prize in literature. Like Barber's music, Neruda's sensual poetry is a personal response to experience, which may explain why Barber loved the poems so much when he first read them in a Penguin paperback book of translations given to him by Valentin Herranz.† Neruda commented

*The source of the commission was significant as a continuation of the Girard Bank's program of "contributing constructively to socially oriented and cultural aspects of the community and the nation" ("Bank Commissions Samuel Barber Work," *Philadelphia Bulletin,* 18 January 1971). Pennsylvania's Governor Milton Shapp viewed the project as a "pilot example of what he and the state arts council hoped would become a movement among local business firms to do likewise" (*Philadelphia Bulletin,* 23 September 1971). Valentin Herranz says that by the time he came into Barber's employ as a valet in 1969, the composer had already committed himself to the new work although he had not yet decided what it would be like (Herranz, interview with the author, 16 May 1986, New York).

†Gruen, "Where Has Samuel Barber Been?" Herranz, whom Barber met at Spoleto in the summer of 1970, became his valet and companion. Born in Madrid in 1944, Herranz left

Barber and Eugene Ormandy prepare for the premiere of *The Lovers,* September 1971. *(Courtesy of Gian Carlo Menotti)*

that these poems marked a focal point of his work, a point illuminated by "memories and aromas, pierced by excruciating melancholy of youth, open to all the stars of the South."[18] Barber had a lifelong propensity for nostalgic texts, and there is clear evidence that the erotic poetry held further attraction for him as a symbol of his own romantic attachments: for example, the dedication of so highly charged a text to his companion Herranz; the inscription "To Manfred from Sam / Nov. 26—1974," written

home when he was eighteen and lived in Paris, during which time his love for music and literature ripened and he became fluent in French. Although his relationship with Barber was briefly romantic, it soon took on filial-parental overtones, and for almost twelve years Herranz was a loyal companion to Barber, seeing the composer through some of the most difficult periods of his life, including bouts of alcoholism, arid periods of creativity, episodes of bitterness and depression, and finally a losing battle with cancer. After Capricorn was sold in 1973, Herranz maintained a place of his own but came daily to care for the composer in his apartment, first at 200 East 66th Street and, from 1975, at 907 Fifth Avenue. He lent an attentive ear to new works in progress, giving reactions that Barber evidently respected. Herranz cajoled him through dark periods, encouraging him to meet with friends and arranging lavish parties in celebration of important occasions. Even though Barber's appreciation was not always shown, it was evident in his dedication of *The Lovers* to Herranz and the generous provision for the young man in his will. In an interview with the author, Herranz recalled that Barber told him, "*The Lovers* is your piece, Valentin."

on the title page of "Tonight I can write the saddest lines" (see Example 18.6c);* and numerous letters from this period that disclose Barber's grief as he became aware that the last material bond between him and Menotti would soon be dissolved.

Beginning the commission for the Philadelphia Orchestra was not easy for Barber, Herranz recalled. In preparation for the selection of poems and putting the words in order—what Barber called "shaping the words" —he worked from two published translations, Christopher Logue's and W. S. Merwin's, and with the assistance of Herranz worked out a literal translation of his own as well.[19] At the outset, as existing manuscripts of the text and a preliminary outline of the work in Barber's hand suggest, he planned to use passages from more than fourteen poems arranged in a sequence of four movements.[20] "I arranged them in a kind of scenario so that the love affair has a direction," he said about his method.[21] It is clear, if one looks at the passages under consideration and the titles designated for the third and fourth movements—III: "Beginning estrangement" and IV: "Dénouement"—he planned the work to mirror the course of a love affair, as did Neruda's cycle.

Although Barber retained the idea of a program, he discarded his original plan of a mosaic of fragments of Neruda's poems—in some cases he had planned to use only two or three lines from a poem—in favor of using more substantial passages from fewer poems. The final version includes passages from nine of the *Love Poems* and the last fourteen couplets—about half the total—of *A Song of Despair.*

The complex weaving of translations into the finished libretto is another example of the immaculate attention Barber gave to the synthesis of his vocal texts. He used five poems translated by Logue; he used Merwin's complete translation for only one (I. "Body of a Woman"); for three he used a combination of Merwin and Logue, and in two of those he substituted individual lines or words of his own translation.† Only three of Neruda's poems are used in their entirety, and their order in Barber's script does not follow the poet's sequence. Nevertheless, Barber's arrangement can be said to be more cohesive than Neruda's in its logical tracing of a love relationship from its fervent beginning to its anguished conclusion. The concordance below lists the Neruda source and translation sources for each of Barber's settings.

More than musical obstacles had to be overcome for this commission. Although the Girard Bank had given Barber plenty of creative latitude, they wanted to have some idea of what the music would be like before the performance. At a meeting that included three officers from the bank and five directors from G. Schirmer, Barber read some of the erotic poetry—

*The dedication, in Barber's handwriting, is in Manfred Ibel's personal score, p. 56.

†Program notes for the Philadelphia Orchestra (22 September 1971) attribute the translations to Christopher Logue and W. S. Merwin, but the G. Schirmer edition (1971) cites only Merwin's translation (*Twenty Love Poems and a Song of Despair*, Penguin Books, 1969).

Text and Translation Sources for *The Lovers*

	Barber's Text	*Neruda's Poem*	*Translation*
I	Body of a woman	I (entire)	Merwin: p. 9
II	Lithe girl, brown girl	XIX (entire)	Logue: p. 75
III	In the hot depth of this summer	IV (cplts. 1–3)	Logue: p. 60
IV	Close your eyes	VIII (omits cplts. 1–3)	Logue: p. 64
V	The Fortunate Isles	IX (entire)	Logue: p. 65
VI	Sometimes	XV (1 verse)	Logue: p. 71
VII	We have lost even this twilight	X (omits cplt. 3)	lines 1–9: Merwin; 10, 11, 13–15: Barber; 12, 16–17: Logue
VIII	Tonight I can write	XX (omits lines 14–16 and 34–36)	Merwin; Barber substitutes *infinite* for *endless; staring* for *still; far away* for *distant*
IX	Cemetery of kisses	A Song of Despair (last 14 cplts.)	lines 1–8: Merwin; Barber substitutes *our longing* for *my longing*

"my voice getting louder and louder in my nervousness," he recalled. At the conclusion of the reading one of the representatives from Girard Bank made a curt response, in Barber's words "a very Philadelphia comment": "Very interesting, Mr. Barber." Barber, by his own report, exclaimed, "My God! Don't you have love affairs in Philadelphia?" to which the officer responded, "That's about all we have left."[22] Governor Shapp, who spoke during intermission at the premiere, was reported to have "spoofed the sacred establishment" of Philadelphia for allowing the drawing of "naked lovers" on the program and such lines as "Your wet body wedged / Between my wet body."[23] Conservative Philadelphians raised their eyebrows a second time over the fact that Barber had chosen to use a text by a Communist poet. Evidently, the fact that Neruda was not always in favor with his party assuaged the bank's reservations.*

Most of the music was composed at Capricorn, probably started very early in the spring of 1971. Herranz reports that a songbird heard in the woods near the house inspired the motive that opens the Prelude and which

* *Philadelphia Inquirer,* 19 September 1971. Neruda joined the Communist Party of Chile in 1945 and became a senator the same year. He was prosecuted as a Communist and went underground in 1948. In 1950 he shared the World Peace Prize with Paul Robeson and Pablo Picasso (Pablo Neruda, *Selected Poems,* ed. Nathaniel Tarn [New York: Dell, 1970]).

a.

b.

Example 18.6 Transformation of motives in *The Lovers*, Op. 43.

is featured prominently throughout the work.* The motive, played by a flute and echoed by a clarinet, is an ascending fourth followed by a descending major third (Example 18.6a, mm. 1–2); a second motive, played by an oboe, is an inverted form of the first, substituting the downward leap of a tritone for the perfect fourth (see Example 18.6a, mm. 7–8). The motives pervade all movements, recurring as a basic element of more extended themes or buried in the texture of inner voices (Examples 18.6b and c).

* Herranz, interview with the author, 16 May 1986, New York. Herranz recounted how Barber asked him to listen to the birdcall and then went to the piano and played it.

c.

To Manfred

Nov. 26 – 1971

VIII. Tonight I can write.

(Baritone Solo)

In contrast to the motivic cells presented in the Prelude is a long-lined melody—a fully realized theme, *passionato* (Example 18.7a), which returns again at the climax of the penultimate movement (VIII) with the wrenching words "To think I do not have her, to feel that I have lost her" marked *desperately* (Example 18.7b).

Completed in Spoleto on 18 May, the score took two months to orchestrate, somewhat longer than Barber had anticipated.* However, it was finished well before rehearsals began on 19 September, only three days before the performance at the newly renovated Academy of Music.

The Lovers shared the program with Barber's Piano Concerto, played by John Browning, and Brahms's First Symphony. Ormandy had planned to start with the new work, followed by Barber's concerto, intermission, and the Brahms symphony. To his credit, Herranz recognized that *The Lovers*, with its delicate ending, would be eclipsed by Barber's fiery concerto and urged the composer to press Ormandy to reorder the program. As reluctant as Barber was to impose his views on the conductor, he felt strongly enough about their validity to persuade Ormandy to play the concerto first.

At intermission the governor of Pennsylvania presented Barber with a certificate for special achievement in the arts.[24] The composer was apparently so nervous about how *The Lovers*—his first large-scale orchestral work since the ill-fated opera—would be received that he asked Herranz to meander through the chatting audience during intermission to gauge their reactions, which, in the end and to his relief, were favorable.[25]

*Letters to Turner, 28 June 1971, and Manfred Ibel. The last page of the holograph orchestral score bears the date "May 18, 1971." This score was given to Valentin Herranz by Barber.

a.

Example 18.7 *a. The Lovers,* Prelude, mm. 17–21. *b. The Lovers,* VIII, mm. 26–31.

Subsequent performances followed on 4 October at the Kennedy Center in Washington, D.C., and on 5 October in New York, opening the season at Philharmonic Hall. On 18 August 1972 the Philadelphia Orchestra performed *The Lovers* at the orchestra's summer home in Saratoga, New York, with Benjamin Luxon as baritone solo and the Saratoga-Potsdam Chorus. In spite of the reported "rousing welcome" and "enthusiastic response" it received from Philadelphia and New York audiences, *The Lovers* was not performed again for two decades.[26] Harold Schonberg claimed that the cantata would "help to reestablish Mr. Barber's reputation as America's most important lyricist"; and he believed the introspective vocal music had much the same lyric, sweet quality as Barber's *Dover Beach* and *Knoxville,* while probing even deeper. He wrote:

> The third chorus, simple and lovely, and the richly sensuous fourth chorus are but two details in a score that has a variety of mood. The thing that impresses about "The Lovers" is its naturalness. Here, Mr. Barber is not forcing his talent, and he is at his very best.[27]

A longtime champion of Barber's music, Irving Kolodin heard "the overshadowing presence of Maurice Ravel (the first of the *Chansons ma-*

b.

décasses) in the intervallic pattern of the motivic kernel as well as in the coloristic use of woodwind instruments"; but he suggested that this late work of Barber's, "exemplary of his instinctive and sympathetic vocal writing . . . procreates music of identity and power."[28]

Reflecting on his career in 1979 with Donald Henahan, Barber remarked that although he had astonishingly little to complain about—he wished to write another string quartet, "a very private piece for quartet"—high up on the list was to have recordings made of the revised version of *Antony and Cleopatra* and of *The Lovers*. "I'm fond of *The Lovers,* my Neruda songs, which Tom Krause sang so well," he said.[29] In 1976, a substantial commission would be offered to make recordings of Barber's works that had never been previously recorded. But plans negotiated with Eugene Ormandy were aborted because of misunderstandings about how the money was to be allocated.* Like *Prayers of Kierkegaard* the work lies dormant, mostly because it requires large performing forces. Yet *The Lovers,* together with parts of *Antony and Cleopatra,* is one of Barber's most sen-

* Correspondence between Barber, Ormandy, and the management of the Philadelphia Orchestra indicates the amount of money to be from $40,000 to $60,000 (see discussion of *Third Essay* below).

suous musical statements and exemplifies some of his most characteristic musical strengths.

Fadograph of a Yestern Scene, Op. 44

Not long after he completed the score of *The Lovers* in May 1971, Barber told Manfred Ibel about another commission he had received. On his mind at this time was the possible sale of Capricorn:

> G.C. was delayed two days in Paris, so I didn't see him at all: but he seems more and more anxious to sell Capricorn if we can get a very high price, which may be difficult now. I think he wants to live in Europe. I am trying not to think about all of this, since I have a new piece to start (always the most difficult moment for me) and it must be ready for the copyist July 31st.[30]

To Turner he wrote, "Now up here for the summer, working like a dog on the piece for Steinberg—Pittsburgh. The copyist is coming to grab it from me July 31! First rehearsal September 6—Oh gosh!"[31]

He was referring to *Fadograph of a Yestern Scene,* commissioned by the Alcoa Foundation for William Steinberg and the Pittsburgh Symphony Orchestra in honor of the opening of the new Heinz Hall.* In mid-July he wrote again to Ibel:

> I just work away on the new piece. The Schirmer copyist, Mr. Wolf, will come to Bolzano on the 21st July to pick up what I have finished and will take it to Vienna, copy it there and then to New York himself, end of August. So this is my busy week. It only has to be 8 minutes, and 7′15″ are done and orchestrated. Dio mio![32]

Two copies of the finished score, estimated by Barber as nine minutes long, were sent to Steinberg on 29 July with the reassurance that the orchestral parts would arrive in adequate time for the first rehearsal.[33] The manager of the Pittsburgh Symphony was advised that since "Mr. Barber says he really does not want to write an 'analysis' of the piece himself . . . the ball should therefore be considered passed to Mr. Dorian."[34]

In August, liberated from the pressure of having completed two commissions within two months of each other, Barber was at ease and working his way through the sixth volume of Anthony Trollope's Barsetshire series. He requested a favor from Turner:

> The title of the Pittsburgh piece . . . is "Fadograph of a Yestern Scene"—from Joyce, natch, but which book?? It's Finnegans I think. But can't be sure as I have no books here. Ask Elizabeth [Hardwick Lowell]! And let

* Barber received a $10,000 fee for the commission.

me know soon, please, as they want to know the exact source for the program notes.*

It is not known whether the "punning line of James Joyce"—to use Barber's words[35]—from *Finnegans Wake* (p. 7, line 15) inspired *Fadograph* from the onset of its composition, or whether, when the piece was completed, he made the literary association because of the music's affinity to his earlier style. The music is reflective in several aspects: Barber returns to Joyce, a poet whose work had inspired his music since the 1930s; the harmonic language and romantic themes of *Fadograph* bespeak the old Barber; and more specifically, there are musical allusions to a work he seemed never able to completely abandon—the Second Symphony.

If he was indeed remembering Joyce's passage when he wrote this orchestral piece even without recalling which book it came from, it seems likely that his imagination would have been captured by the alliteration, onomatopoeia, and humor of the author's punning references to musical instruments:

> And all the way (a horn!) from fjord to fjell his baywinds' oboboes shall wail him rockbound (hoahoahoah!) in swimswamswum and all the livvylong night, the delldale dalppling night, the night of bluerybells, her flittaflute in tricky trochees (O carina! O carina!) wake him. . . . Only a fadograph of a yestern scene.[36]

Barber's *Fadograph of a Yestern Scene* is a single-movement work, without key signature. The orchestral texture is transparent, yet the forces are large: piccolo, two flutes, two oboes, English horn, two clarinets, bass clarinet, two bassoons, four horns, three trumpets, three trombones, tuba, timpani, percussion, antique cymbal, celesta, two harps, piano, and strings. The many solos for woodwind and brass instruments never—as do Joyce's—"wail," but they have, rather, the fluidity and grace of Barber's invention. The plucked arpeggios of harps and muted tremolos of strings intone a veiled and mysterious backdrop against which a lone oboe unfolds a diatonic primary theme in 7/4 meter (Example 18.8); the melody is echoed by a muted horn. A bassoon melody is picked up in turn by a muted French horn, an English horn, a harp supported by pizzicato violas, and, finally, muted strings. Against the song fabric is a lyrical countertheme, its profile transfigured as the piece progresses. Concurrently, a motive from the principal theme of Barber's discarded Second Symphony offers a counterpoint to the melodic lines, subtly at first, then increasingly persistent. The motive, which was ominous and plodding in the symphony and which

*Letter, 3 August 1971, from Santa Cristina in Val Gardena, Italy. The fact that Barber had to ask Turner about the source of the Joyce text—of which the language is so distinctive and which in 1947 had provided him with a passage for his song *Nuvoletta*—seems to corroborate Dr. Jack Nelson's report that Barber's memory was at this time beginning to be seriously impaired from alcohol.

for the Alcoa Foundation

Fadograph of a Yestern Scene

Samuel Barber, Op. 44

Moderato, cantando liberamente ♩ = 72

Piccolo
Flute 1 2
Oboe 1 2
1 Solo *con tenerezza*
mp espr.
English Horn
Clarinet 1 2
Bass Clarinet
Bassoon 1 2
Horn 1 2 3 4
Trumpet 1 2 3
Trombone 1 2 3
Tuba
Timpani
Percussion
Antique Cymbal
p
Celesta
Piano
Harp (a second Harp ad lib.)
p *l.v.* *l.v.* *sim.*

Moderato, cantando liberamente ♩ = 72

Violin I II
con sord.
pp
div.
con sord.
pp
Viola
div.
con sord.
pp
Violoncello
Contrabass

The title is from James Joyce's "Finnegans Wake."

Example 18.8 *Fadograph of a Yestern Scene,* title page (G. Schirmer, 1972).

was used again in *Antony and Cleopatra* for the militaristic entrance of Caesar and Antony into the Roman senate, now takes on an exotic cast in the context of the veiled harmonies of *Fadograph*.

Eerie orchestral color is promoted by special instrumental effects—*divisi* passages, tremolos placed in high registers, and bowings *sul ponticello* for stringed instruments; unusual pairings—piccolo and celesta, flute and horn; and specific performance instructions—"from the distance," "echo," "Snare drum on handkerchief, without snares," and "punta d'arco."

Fadograph of a Yestern Scene was conducted by Steinberg on 11 September 1971 during the inaugural concert of the $7-million Heinz Hall in Pittsburgh. It was not overlooked by music critics that the composer was as solidly entrenched as ever in his Romantic outlook: "a quiet impressionistic work that might have come from a musical era long since past," wrote Allen Hughes in a review in the *New York Times*. "It is pretty music, skillfully wrought, and a century from now no one will be much concerned with the fact that it seemed an anachronism at its premiere."* Such comments may be better understood in the context of Frederick Dorian's program notes, which compare *Fadograph* to other music played during the early 1970s:

> The musical spell of *Fadograph of a Yestern Scene* reaches us through a romantically inspired score. The lines are easier traced than its more subtle, secret ties to *Finnegans Wake*. Barber's music, both at its lyrical and more dramatic phases, is softly affectionate. The dynamics shun the large volume. Often, the music speaks only in a low voice. This is fortunate in a world that may prefer to listen to nothing but shouts.†

Although *Fadograph of a Yestern Scene* was played again by the Pittsburgh Symphony Orchestra in New York in November 1971, and by the Cleveland Orchestra in June 1972, it is another of those late works of Barber's that has rarely been heard since.[37]

Three Songs, Op. 45

Contributing significantly to Barber's low morale and compositional inactivity for five years between 1972 and 1977 was the forced sale of Capricorn, the home he and Menotti had shared for thirty years. The upheaval was to Barber equivalent to the dissolution of a marriage; for no matter

*"Music: Heinz Hall, Pittsburgh's Acoustical Gem," *New York Times*, 12 September 1971, p. 94. Because Pittsburgh newspapers were on strike during the opening, there were no reviews by local music critics.

†Program notes for the inaugural concert of Heinz Hall, 10 September 1971. His description recalls Barber's comment twenty years earlier about his Violin Concerto, played on a program of American music at Tanglewood: "At least it offers a small note of contemplation, a quality conspicuously absent from the other pieces" (letter to Homer, 7 January 1949).

how often the professional and personal lives of the two composers had separated them in past years, their cohabitation had consistently provided stability in their personal commitment to each other. Although Barber's and Menotti's friendship and professional admiration for each other was constant—and would remain constant up to Barber's death (their collaboration on the revision of *Antony and Cleopatra,* for example, came about after the house was sold)—by the middle 1960s their personal lives had become less and less interwoven, and Barber frequently found himself alone in their residence in Mount Kisco. In addition, the house had become expensive to maintain and in need of repairs; taxes were increasing.* Menotti, who had long recognized the inevitability of their living separately, had already taken an apartment in New York and had plans for buying a house in Europe. Barber could not afford to carry the cost of Capricorn by himself, nor would he wish to live in the house alone.[38]

In June 1971, Menotti was becoming increasingly eager to sell Capricorn, while Barber—worried that they would not be able to get their asking price—thought perhaps they might even keep it as a weekend house for the winter.† Over the next two years, the prospective sale of Capricorn was to color every aspect of Barber's life.‡

"I don't feel very musical," he wrote to Turner from Spoleto, in March 1972. He planned to remain in Europe, only coming to the United States for a month or so for an ASCAP meeting the end of March and "trying out New York."[39] In June, when Turner announced a possible visit, Barber responded, "I am not up to much; but fiddling around and feeling very rested." In a footnote, he explained: "I mean, cannot get started on any musical work. Just tear up beginnings. Not the first time!"[40] At the same time, he and Menotti were planning—though "still terribly uncertain"—revisions of *Antony and Cleopatra,* and Barber wrote to Turner, "The continued unsale of Capricorn makes winter plans so difficult and depressing for us both."[41] In July, in Santa Cristina for the summer, despondency mixed with despair colored Barber's letter to Ibel about his stay in Spoleto. He wrote:

> The Festival was not very interesting and I became depressed and hot. I liked the chamber music daily and the two German pianists from Hamburg—Eschenbach and Justus Frantz . . . G.C.'s Consul a great success. But there were just the same people. . . . [Christopher] Keene and his wife

* In September 1971, the *Philadelphia Inquirer* made reference to the possibility of high taxes as forcing the sale of Capricorn (Daniel Webster, "Samuel Barber: Reading Love Poems," 19 September 1971, p. 6).

† Letters from Barber to Ibel, 11 June 1971 and 15 July 1971, from Santa Cristina. Barber planned to keep fifty acres of land for himself (letter to Stuart Kessler, Barber's accountant, 21 August 1973).

‡ Menotti said (telephone conversation with the author) that although Barber was at the outset amenable to moving to New York himself, when faced with the reality of dividing the household possessions, he became highly emotional, seeing the closure of their years in the house as marking the end of their youth.

> were among the *real* people. I was glad to drive up here to escape the heat, with Valentino. . . . I had to go to Brussels for 5 days for ASCAP, a real bore . . . and useless. . . . There is little to recount and nothing inside of me! I work on Haydn Sonatas every day and take a walk and sleep well enough: but the idea of returning to New York in that apartment without Capricorn torments me, and Capricorn without a servant. . . . Valentin has not got his immigration visa yet. I phone the Consul every month who just says "it's being processed." And 149 E. 61 [a *pied à terre* Barber kept in New York] is giving me trouble, they want to take it away from me October 1.
>
> G.C. must be at Capricorn by now and I hope everyone will be patient. I hardly saw him at Spoleto, but this was to be expected.[42]

Yet within the context of this summer of discontent Barber produced three songs for Fischer-Dieskau, a singer he had admired ever since he first heard him in 1953, but whom he was not to meet until 1974.* He wrote to Ibel:

> I have finished three songs for Fischer-Dieskau and sent them to the copyist in New York. Worked rather hard on them, too. One is a translation from Georg Heym, one (a funny one) trans. from the Polish. Now he can get to work on them, F.D., I mean. They are for New York in January. You must get his beautiful record of Schumann's *Dichterliebe*.†

Three Songs, Op. 45, were commissioned by the Lincoln Center Chamber Music Society for the German singer. Their metaphorical texts are particularly portentous, considering the composer's anguished state of mind. The first and third song of the set suggest the act of completion: having "eaten the rose" is a symbol of the depletion of the source of creative energy; ‡ "Soon the glow / Of long hills on the skyline will be gone" seems symbolic of the eventuality of death, thus the completion of a life.

"Now have I fed and eaten up the rose," Op. 45, No. 1, from the Swiss poet Gottfried Keller's cycle *Gedanken eines Lebendig-Begrabenen* ("Thoughts of one buried alive"), is an English translation by James Joyce of an abbreviated version used for a song by composer Othmar Schoeck.[43] The holograph of Barber's setting at the Library of Congress indicates the song was completed at Spoleto in March 1972. The morbid text is intensified by obsessive repetitions in the piano part, where the unrelenting reiteration of a four-note motive introduced in the first two measures seems to gain momentum from the ornamented upbeat (see bracketed motive in Example 18.9).

*Barber's letter to William Strickland, 19 July 1953, is the first mention of Fischer-Dieskau's name.

†Letter to Ibel, 31 August 1972, from Santa Cristina.

‡Barber had a propensity for using digestive images in relation to the compositional process; recall his letters to Jeanne Behrend and Orlando Cole about the Symphony in One Movement and the string quartet.

Example 18.9 "Now have I fed and eaten up the rose," Op. 45, No. 1, mm. 1–9 (G. Schirmer, 1974).

"A Green Lowland of Pianos," translated by Czeslaw Milosz from the Polish surrealist writer Jerzy Harasymowicz, was the poem Barber cited as "funny" in his letter to Ibel. It presents a ludicrous fusion of pianos and cows: "a herd of black pianos." Exaggerated pianistic flourishes humorously support the surrealistic images of the text: glissandos in tandem on

Example 18.10 "A Green Lowland of Pianos," Op. 45, No. 2, mm. 1–16.

the word *pianos* (see Example 18.10, m. 6); double trills on the word *gurgle* (mm. 11–12); luxuriously arpeggiated seventh-chords following the phrase *chords of rapture* (m. 13); and the interruption of an ingratiating waltz rhythm by an elongated stress on the first syllable of the word *moonish,* suggesting the mooing of cows (m. 15).

"O boundless, boundless, evening," Op. 45, No. 3, translated from the German of Georg Heym by Christopher Middleton, is the most lyrical and

Example 18.10 (continued)

romantic of the cycle. The vocal line is expansive and diatonic in contrast to the chromaticism of the rippling sixteenth-note accompaniment. The piano part contains within it a heterophonous counterpoint of its own, evoking the fabric of Lizst's *Waldesrauschen*.

Although Three Songs, Op. 45, were scheduled to be performed for the first time on 23 January 1973, Fischer-Dieskau's illness resulted in the cancellation of the concert. The singer wrote to Barber of his disappointment in delaying the premiere. His words are quoted by Barber in a letter to Manfred Ibel:

> I had the following letter from Fischer-Dieskau, which I transcribe:
>
> "Dear and admired S——B——, it is more than a misfortune to me that a flu had to cross over our beautiful premiere which I was *so* looking forward to. Let me assure you that I *love* your songs and certainly will perform them as soon as it is ever possible for me.
>
> Take all my best wishes and the expression of deep regret for my cancellation.
>
> *Your ever,*
> *Dietrich FD"*
>
> So (as Herbert L.* would say it) That is the strangest premiere I've ever had.[44]

Rescheduled for performance in New York at Alice Tully Hall on 30 April 1974, the songs were programmed with two earlier songs by Barber—"I hear an army" and "Nocturne." Fischer-Dieskau received manuscripts of the songs from Charles Wadsworth, then president of the Chamber Music Society of Lincoln Center. The singer first met Barber at a rehearsal, where the composer sat alone in the back of Alice Tully Hall. Afterwards, Barber expressed his approval of Fischer-Dieskau's interpretation of his songs. Following the successful premiere, there was a reception given by Alice Tully in her home overlooking Central Park. Fischer-Dieskau spoke briefly to Barber, who again sat quietly alone and seemed ill at ease among the many guests. What seemed apparent to the German baritone was that the composer was very shy, considerably depressed, and extremely irritated by all the small talk around him.[45]

The songs received little comment in the press. They were viewed as reflecting Barber's conservatism, his lyricism, and his practiced hand as a composer. Emphasis was placed on Mr. Fischer-Dieskau's "fine diction" and "impeccable artistry" and on the fact that he rarely sang songs in English.[46]

Barber's depression, observable even to those who barely knew him, intensified as the sale of the Mount Kisco house became imminent and his health failed. In April 1973, from Spoleto, where he expected to stay until the end of June, he wrote to Ibel:

> There is little news, only much affection to send you in the confusion of this very difficult year. I have suffered and still do suffer greatly about it, it seems I have made so many mistakes (the N.Y. apt.) but the selling of Capricorn was really necessary, I could not run it alone or carry it financially alone. . . . But I really feel as if I have no home. Thank god for Sta. Cristina, but it is so far away from you all! I hope you will come over for a brief visit, and we shall take many beautiful walks.[47]

June in Santa Cristina found Barber growing increasingly lonely. "I am playing lots of Bach organ fugues arranged by Liszt for piano," he wrote

* The photographer Herbert List.

to Ibel, "and getting my fingers (if not my mind!) to work again. And I walk alone now when the weather is good."[48]

Plans for the sale of the house had solidified, and by mid-August Capricorn was being closed. "It is better to do it and finish it," Barber wrote with resignation. "Rilke wrote 'Es ist Zeit. Der Sommer war sehr gross. Wer jetzt kein Haus hat, baut sich keines mehr.' "* Although he held on to a piece of land in Mount Kisco, never considering himself a true New Yorker,[49] he was not able to fulfill his plan to build himself another house.† When he returned to New York in October 1973, he took an apartment at Manhattan House, 200 East 66th Street. The apartment was described by Dorle Soria as having a large living room, walls covered with pictures, and a smaller room, "where the composer's bed fights an unequal battle for space with the nine-foot Steinway which once belonged to Rachmaninoff":

> He needs more space, he says, and he talks nostalgically of Capricorn. He was missing the excitement of spring in the country—the early bulbs and daffodils, the dogwood, the lilacs, the new green of the leaves and the first flowering trees. The composer has said that "One of the physical nurturing components that makes my music sound as it does is that I live mostly in the country."[50]

Barber intensely disliked the apartment and during this time often drank excessively, occasionally suffering memory blackouts. A friend, Seymour Palestin, helped him find a doctor who, after a thorough diagnostic examination, put him on a strict regime in an attempt to control his drinking

*Letter to Manfred Ibel, 17 August 1973, from Santa Cristina. Barber joined excerpts from the first and third verses of Rilke's "Herbsttag" (Autumn Day) to suit his needs. His lines translate "It is time. The summer was so great. . . . He'll not build now, who has no house awaiting"; Rilke's text continues, appropriately, "Who's alone, for long will so remain / sit late, read, write long letters, and again / return to restless perambulating / the avenues of parks when leaves downrain." Trans. M. D. Herter Norton, in *Translations from the Poetry of Rainer Maria Rilke* (New York: W. W. Norton, 1938).

†Menotti, quoted by John Gruen in the *New York Times* in 1974, explained why he felt it was time to sell Capricorn. Feeling that he no longer had the loyalty of New York audiences because of bad critical reviews, he felt it was time to live somewhere else. Regarding his and Barber's relationship, he said:

> And so that is why Sam Barber and I have sold Capricorn, which was a very painful decision to make, since it meant so much to us. Don't forget that Sam and I have known each other ever since we were young students at the Curtis Institute. But once I began traveling all over the world staging my own and other composers' operas, and absenting myself from America for longer and longer periods, both Sam and I felt that the time had come for us to part with Capricorn.
>
> Of course, the moment we sold the house Sam regretted it. He's a bit more sentimental than I am. I think he was unprepared for the emotional shock (quoted in Gruen, *Menotti*, p. 207).

Menotti purchased an eighteenth-century Palladian mansion in Gifford, Scotland, designed by Robert and William Adams. He urged Barber to come live with him there, but this was not to happen until September 1980, a few months before Barber's death.

and his weight. Barber was drawn to the study of yoga, and a notebook kept during this period is filled with quotations from Buddha—apparently chosen selectively to cope with his personal dilemma—on "general unhappiness," "illness and death," "pride and self-importance," and a line of wisdom: "It is pride that inspires ill-feeling at another's success." *

Ballade, Op. 46 (1977)

In August 1974 Barber was asked by the Van Cliburn Foundation to write a short piece for its fifth International Quadrennial Piano Competition, which would take place in 1977 in Fort Worth, Texas, the city in which the Second Symphony had had its genesis many years earlier. The foundation traditionally commissioned works by American composers for the required repertoire of the competition.†

Barber was asked to write a piece six to eight minutes in length, to be submitted to the foundation by March 1977.[51] He was invited also to serve on the panel of judges. The composer was informed: "Mr. Cliburn requests this piece, 'A Ballade,' be written in the beauty and difficulty of the Samuel Barber style."[52] It is not clear whether the title was suggested by Cliburn or Barber.

The $6,000 commission came at a time when Barber's morale was at its lowest. Several years later, in recalling this period of his life, he attributed nearly six years of musical inactivity primarily to depression over the sale of Capricorn.[53] In 1975 Barber purchased a spacious apartment at 907 Fifth Avenue overlooking Central Park. Even the three months he spent each summer at his home in Santa Cristina and the many parties he gave in New York did not seem to offset feelings of restlessness and psychological rootlessness: "In a way, I'm homeless," he told John Gruen.[54] In an attempt to gain control over his life again, he entered into treatment with Dr. Ruth Fox, a psychiatrist who was known for her successful treatment of alcoholism.‡

* Although this notebook is undated, Herranz remembers it was kept by Barber during the mid-seventies. In it are yoga exercises, recipes for carrot soup, and a low-fat diet. On the last few pages of the notebook, Barber listed the milestones in his career—the first time he ever heard an orchestral work of his own (Werner Janssen conducting the New York Philharmonic) and names of conductors who played his works with the Philharmonic over the years (beginning with Rodzinski and ending with Leinsdorf).

† Beginning with its inauguration in 1962, solo works for piano had been composed by Lee Hoiby, Willard Straight, Norman Dello Joio, and Aaron Copland.

‡ Dr. Jack Nelson, interview with the author; Charles Turner, personal memoir of Barber's last ten years; and Valentin Herranz, interview with the author, 16 May 1986, New York. Dr. Fox employed psychodrama in her treatment of alcoholism and introduced the drug Antabuse, an alcohol deterrent, to the United States. Barber's physician, Dr. Jack Nelson, in a telephone conversation with the author, reported that the composer's attendance at these sessions was somewhat sporadic until his deteriorating condition forced him to realize that the only way he would be able to continue to compose was to accept treatment. It is

Beginning a new work had always been difficult for Barber, and now even so short a piece as the Cliburn commission became an inordinate effort that took almost eight or nine months to finish. That the *Ballade* was composed under great stress is suggested by the penmanship of two manuscripts of the piece at the Library of Congress; although the notation is legible, expression markings are uncharacteristically irregular and labored compared to Barber's usually graceful script.

Ballade is strictly symmetrical in design, with outer sections in C minor embracing an agitated middle section.* The "restless" tempo called for at the outset is aided by rhythmic delays that make the right-hand part appear to lag behind the left (see Example 18.11, mm. 1–9). The piece is based on the metamorphosis of a single motive: a chromatically descending four-note pattern (beginning first on E♭, then on C), whose repetitions become increasingly urgent to measure 10, where the rhythm of the motive is augmented and embellished with double trills. The basic theme gains interest through a variety of means: thickening of the harmonic texture, unexpected dissonances, and hammered figurations and embellishments. The middle section, in contrast, presents an agitated outburst in Lisztian rhetoric.

Ballade is deceptive in its apparent simplicity, for it is not lacking virtuosic passages and requires technical skill as well as interpretive nuance. Barber himself is reported to have been pleasantly surprised at Christian Blackshaw's performance in the semifinals of the competition at Fort Worth. "It was the first time I had heard the *Ballade* played well," he said. "Before, I had played it badly myself."† The winner of the competition, which took place 11 to 15 September 1977, was the late Steven De Groote.

Third Essay for Orchestra, Op. 47 (1978)

During their many years of association, Barber and Eugene Ormandy's relationship seemed to swing between problematic and congenial. Barber had on occasion privately expressed his opinion that Ormandy did not treat him very well;[55] yet in later years their correspondence is marked by warmth and appreciation. A series of exchanges between May 1976 and October 1978, though cordial on the surface, demonstrates a situation where

probable that Nelson's compassion for the creative mind was, in large measure, responsible for Barber's renewed and sustained commitment to treatment.

*Phillip Ramey is of the opinion that if Barber had been well, "he would not have offered a literal repetition for the last section, but would have done something more interesting" (interview with the author, 4 April 1986, New York).

†Latryl Ohendalski, "Barber May Not Test Rule after Hearing Playing," *Fort Worth Star Telegram*, 19 September 1977. A policy of the competition was not to allow anyone in or out of Texas Christian University's Landreth Auditorium during a contestant's performance. In an interview prior to the competition, Barber had said that if the playing was terrible, he would leave the hall.

Example 18.11 *Ballade,* Op. 46, title page (G. Schirmer, 1977).

misunderstandings between them resulted in the curtailment of a first performance of the *Third Essay* by the Philadelphia Orchestra and the abandonment of plans for recording of two of Barber's most cherished works, *The Lovers* and *Prayers of Kierkegaard.*

In spring 1976 Barber and Ormandy discussed a possible premiere by the Philadelphia Orchestra of a large-scale work (perhaps sixty minutes in length), for which a wealthy unnamed sponsor was willing to put up a sizable amount of money. At the same time, the composer expressed to the conductor his wish to have recordings made by RCA of the new work, *The Lovers,* and *Prayers of Kierkegaard.* The anonymous wealthy patroness was Audrey Sheldon Poon, who was backed by the Merlin Foundation. An eccentric woman who allegedly fell in love with Barber, Poon was so enthusiastic about his music that she offered $75,000 for the new work and recordings of any works of his preference.* Learning of the commission, Ormandy wrote to Barber:

> It was good to meet you at Carnegie Hall before the Gala concert and to hear from you that the contract between Madame X, your sponsor, and yourself has been signed. . . .
>
> Such large-scale commissions must be carefully prepared, not only by the composer but by all the other forces involved. First, the sponsors, according to you, will give the amount to the Philadelphia Orchestra Association, naturally a round sum of money from which the association would deduct your fee for the commission and turn it over to you. Second, the sponsor, who apparently wants to have a recording made by RCA and our orchestra, would have to pay for two three-hour sessions for the recording, which would be negotiated between the sponsor and RCA. My personal estimate, as I told you over the phone some months ago, would be around $50,000 or $60,000. Third, I, as you know, ask for no fee for myself, but I do make one condition: I must have either a piano copy of the full score, if only a sketch as soon as you finish it, and not until I have seen your score would I be able to tell you when the performance could take place. (Lately every commission we have given was either six months to a year late in delivery, or some were never completed and this I cannot have happen again.) Please understand, I don't want full score, but just sketches so I can see how much time I would need since I have quite a number of other commissioned works that I have to prepare.[56]

Misunderstanding and confusion prevailed when a check to the amount of $40,000 drafted to the Philadelphia Orchestra Association "for the recording of two works by Samuel Barber to be conducted by Eugene Ormandy" was returned to the Merlin Foundation because the orchestra would not accept the specific conditions tied to the contribution. Barber evidently did not fully comprehend that the recording session would have to be negotiated as a separate fee with RCA.† A letter from Ormandy to Boris

* Valentin Herranz, Phillip Ramey, and Charles Turner confirm the strong attachment of Sheldon for Barber. The financial terms of the commission and recordings are discussed in letters from Ormandy to Barber (25 May 1976, 6 December 1976, 21 December 1978, 9 March 1977, 12 April 1977, 18 April 1977, 24 October 1978), Barber to Ormandy (6 April 1977), Ormandy to Wanton Balis, Jr. (29 November 1976, 21 December 1976), Ormandy to Sokoloff (2 December 1976, 21 December 1976), Ormandy to Thomas Shepard (25 May 1976, 19 April 1977), and the Merlin Foundation to the Philadelphia Orchestra Association (13 December 1976). The letters are in the archives of the Philadelphia Orchestra.

† Apparently, the reason the recording sessions would have to be paid for by Barber was that the contract between RCA and the Philadelphia Orchestra was due to expire in May

Sokoloff, manager of the orchestra, discusses the recording arrangements and suggests that the conductor was ambivalent about recording all the works Barber requested:

> I had a long talk with Sam Barber yesterday and asked him to have Mrs. Poon call you and make plans about sending the check for $40,000, made out to the Philadelphia Orchestra Association, to you. . . . She is quite a strange woman. . . . Assuming that we are going to do Barber's new piece, he, naturally, would like to have it recorded by us and would also like to have his "The Lovers" performed at the same time and recorded. He would like to have Tom Krause as soloist, and you will have to find out when he is available and then we will arrange our performances of his works accordingly. He would also like to have both works performed in New York.
>
> I wonder if you agree with me that approximately 60 minutes of Barber might be too much of a good thing. Think about it, please, and let me know.[57]

When Barber learned from Wanton Balis, Jr., president of the Philadelphia Orchestra Association, that they expected $40,000 from the Merlin Foundation over and above his own commission, he was, according to Boris Sokoloff, "quite incensed," saying "it was the first time in his life he had ever heard of the fact that it was necessary to pay an orchestra for performing one of his works."[58] It does seem ironic that the composer who had been recognized earlier that year with the Gold Medal for Music, the highest award of the American Academy and Institute of Arts and Letters, should have to finance recordings of his music himself. Apparently the reason for this was that the composition was not expected to sell enough records to pay anywhere near the recording expenses; "it would have to sell at least 8,000 copies before anyone could make a penny," Ormandy stated.[59] So exasperated was the conductor with the ill-feelings engendered by the commission, he was ready to "forget this composition and suggest that the composer engage another orchestra."[60]

In spite of the reservations expressed to orchestral management, Ormandy continued to act on Barber's behalf and attempted to assuage tensions. First, he wrote Barber of several forthcoming performances by the orchestra of his Violin Concerto and Piano Concerto.* Next, he assured Thomas Z. Shepard, divisional vice-president of RCA, of his willingness to record the newly commissioned work, *The Lovers,* and *Prayers of Kierkegaard,* should the Poon Foundation pay for the project. And finally, he tried to straighten matters out with the sponsor directly.

1978, and it was not known whether there would be a continuation of their professional relationship after then. It was not unusual during this time for recording companies to require advance financing for works that might not guarantee sales.

*Norman Carol played the Violin Concerto with James Levine conducting, 6, 7, and 8 January in Philadelphia, and 11 January in Carnegie Hall, New York. Tedd Joselson played the Piano Concerto on 18, 19, and 22 February with Ormandy conducting at the Academy of Music. Letter from Ormandy to Barber, 21 December 1976.

Early in March 1977, with financial details still unresolved, Ormandy nevertheless went ahead with preparations and wrote to Barber:

> Now we can begin to make plans. Could you let me know, at your convenience, the length of the new commissioned work, the orchestration you will use, extra instruments, if any, and also whether it will require soloists, chorus, or anything else? Until I receive the conductor's score, I will not be able to tell you when the commission can be programmed. Depending on what soloists, etc., you will need, I will try to include New York, Washington, and Baltimore in the first performances.
>
> Please keep in mind I have several other important novelties to prepare and that takes time. Once the matter of your composition has been settled I would like you to tell me what other works should be on the same record. We have a total of sixty minutes on the two sides. Any of the other works you want to record I think should be performed and they will have to be spread out over a period of two or three years. "The Lovers," I believe, is one work you want to record. This, as you know, requires a chorus and a first-class baritone. If possible, I would like to have Krause, but I know he is expensive. This will have to be settled by our management as soon as I hear from you. The lesser parts can be sung by members of the choir. . . . Before I close, I am glad to tell you that Joselson gave a fantastic performance of your Piano Concerto. I feel strongly that it should be one of the works included in the recording.[61]

Barber answered:

> I was glad to hear of the success of the piano concerto. The recording of this, however, could not come under the Poon commission, since this is for works of mine that have not been recorded yet.
>
> I am still very anxious to have Tom Krause and "The Lovers" recorded. I inquired about Krause's fee for the United States, but not from his manager—another one, and he thought his price would be more in the range of $2,000, which does not seem excessive. As you say, the other little solos could be managed by members of the chorus.
>
> This has been a topsy-turvy winter for me and I am apprehensive about my house in Italy. On top of this I have had my wisdom teeth out, which doesn't exactly inspire one to compose. So I cannot answer all your questions about the new work for you; that I will start as soon as I go to Italy in June and spend the summer exclusively on it. All I can say now is that it has no title and will take up one side of a record; no soloists and no extra instruments. I realize that you plan far ahead and I will simply be patient and after it is done you will find a place for it, recording, etc., I hope!
>
> RCA just brought out a new edition of my old "Vanessa" which I am happy about. . . .

> I am still anxious to have "Prayers of Kierkegaard" recorded any time you have a chorus available. There would be funds for that in the Poon Foundation. I will never forget the performance you gave of it.[62]

Ormandy proposed four concerts and one recording session of *The Lovers* for November 1978, but about the possibility of recording *Prayers of Kierkegaard* he said, "It will be difficult to set a date for it now, because in another two years the chorus will be considerably changed and intensive rehearsals would have to take place long before the recording session. What a pity we didn't record it immediately following the New York performance."[63] Ormandy's hesitation was legitimate, but his expression of regret must have seemed a feeble gesture to Barber; for him this work had great personal meaning—musically and spiritually—and he passionately wanted to have it recorded.

By mid-April, however, the Philadelphia Orchestra Association had returned the check from Poon because it was issued with the understanding that the money must be used specifically for recording two works of Barber's—a condition unacceptable to the association. Ormandy wrote to Barber that it would be impossible to continue with plans for the premiere or the recording sessions unless they received another check. He was counting on the composer to explain to his sponsor the necessity of her paying all expenses involved for the engagement of soloists and chorus as well as the recording expenses. Nevertheless, the letter concludes optimistically: "With warm greetings, and awaiting your reply about the approximate date you can mail the score to me so that I can arrange with Boris the dates of the performances."[64] Barber's discouragement and misinterpretation of Ormandy's well-intentioned letter is apparent in the following telephone conversation with Ibel:

> He simply doesn't want my music—and so she [Poon] tore up the check, and she's mad now. It's all gone wrong, I think I have some bad vibrations—like a gypsy once told me—with Philadelphia, not with Mary but with everyone else. You know I've had terrible troubles with the Philadelphia Orchestra; Ormandy was always mean to me.[65]

The situation evidently was irreconcilable; it is not known whether it was Barber or his patroness who wearied of the protracted and ultimately fruitless negotiations with the Philadelphia Orchestra.

In March 1978 Barber celebrated his sixty-eighth birthday with a party in his home. Dr. Jack Nelson remarked on Barber's buoyant demeanor when he announced the forthcoming party.[66] About eighty guests were invited, friends who had been "loyal to him and his music," among them Martha Graham, John Browning, Francis Goelet, Carlos Mosely, Alice Tully, Jack Thatcher, Mary Rockefeller, William Schuman, and Wanda Toscanini Horowitz.* Valentin and his brother prepared a culinary spectacle with gastronomical symbols of Barber's operas: a Roman chariot labeled "Antony and Cleopatra," filled with lobsters and other seafood; and a cake model of the Metropolitan Opera House, in front of which was a fountain labeled "Vanessa." There were numerous toasts, and at the end of the evening, after most of the guests had gone, Barber sat down at the piano and sang some of the songs he had sung for friends on other occasions. He concluded with "Pale Hands I Love," done with an elegant touch of parody. A consistent theme in the accounts given by his friends is that the party was a kind of announcement that he was ready to fight again, to compose again.[67]

Barber wrote his *Third Essay* rather quickly in Italy during the summer of 1978. He received assistance in making the orchestral score from John David Ernst.[68] Audrey Sheldon (by then divorced from Poon and using her maiden name) gave him $60,000 for the commissioned work, which was dedicated to her and performed by the New York Philharmonic on 14 September 1978 for the debut of Zubin Mehta as music director of the orchestra. But the young benefactress was never to hear the work her generosity sponsored, for her life ended tragically in suicide before the premiere of *Third Essay*.

Interviewed before the concert by Phillip Ramey, Barber reluctantly described *Third Essay* as "absolutely abstract music, which is essentially dramatic in character. . . . As far as the overall shape is concerned, it was inspired by a literary form."[69] He acknowledged that, as with his other "Essays," he sought in this piece "above all, to create a unity."[70]

In each of his three musical essays Barber's handling of the form varies, an indication that his concept of the genre he invented was not rigidly fixed. *Essay for Orchestra,* in two parts based on related themes (the second being a diminution of the first), demonstrates less continuity in handling of material than *Second Essay,* which is equivalent to the first movement of a symphony and displays greater integration between themes as well as a more fully realized development section that builds progressively towards a climax. *Third Essay* (deliberately named in order to maintain continuity in titles),[71] written more than thirty years after its earlier counterparts, is longer and was considered by the composer himself to be, in general, less lyric than the other two. It is lavishly scored for a large orchestra: piccolo, two flutes, two oboes, English horn, E♭ clarinet, two clarinets in B♭, bass clarinet, two bassoons, contrabassoon, four horns, three trumpets, euphonium, three trombones, tuba, two harps, piano, an augmented percussion section—two timpani, tam-tams (small and large), bass drum, sheet metal, marimba, xylophone, cymbal, snare drums (high and low), wood block, bells, antique cymbal, bongos—and strings.

*Samuel Barber's Guest Book, 9 March 1978. Included also were members of Barber's therapy group.

Barber authorized the following description of *Third Essay* for program notes for the first performance:[72]

> The concise, tightly made work opens with a rhythmic motive in the percussion that generates certain of the subsequent thematic materials and serves as a kind of rhythmic leitmotif.* A slower section (tranquillo) has a more purely lyric theme in the solo French horn and functions as a contrasting middle part. In the final pages, a climax occurs where different rhythmic ideas are put together.[73]

Third Essay for Orchestra is about rhythm and lyricism and their relationship to each other. It begins with an electrifying twenty-seven bars of percussion only—timpani, tam-tam, bass drum, sheet metal, harps, and piano (Example 18.12). Sequences of fourths characterize the introductory motives upon which, as Barber says, much of the thematic material is based. There is a profusion of cantabile themes, some of great lyric breadth (one, a quotation from *Fadograph of a Yestern Scene*), others merely brief gestures.† The texture is contrapuntal, the tonal language chromatic; development is continuous and often by sequential repetition. A subsidiary theme is a near-quotation from Cleopatra's death aria from *Antony and Cleopatra*, but it is not known whether this was a conscious quotation on Barber's part. After the premiere of the *Third Essay*, his uncertainty about the abrupt conclusion led him to extend slightly the ending in revision.‡

In October 1978 Barber sent the score of *Third Essay* to Ormandy, who promised to review it and asked for a tape of the work.[74] A performance never materialized. A letter written in November 1979 presents a sad postlude to the somewhat troubled working relationship between composer and conductor. John Browning had just played Barber's Piano Con-

* In his interview with Ramey, Barber preferred the word *ostinato*, qualifying his description with "I just hate all these terms. . . . I don't understand how you would use this material at all. If you take a Wagnerian opera, there are one thousand things going on. . . . I don't like 'motto theme' because I think that's old fashioned." To Ramey's suggestion that the material was more a theme than a rhythmic motive, Barber queried, "What would you say about 'da-da-da-dum?' [singing the opening of Beethoven's Fifth Symphony]." Ramey responded "I'd call that more of a motive" (private tape of interview by Phillip Ramey).

† When Ramey pointed out to the composer that *Third Essay* had more themes than either of the earlier two, Barber seemed irritated, remarking: "I haven't analyzed it myself, but if you say so, then it must be true. There are indeed, several lyric themes in this piece. After all, it's not a federal offense" (liner notes, Samuel Barber, *Third Essay for Orchestra*, Op. 47, New York Philharmonic, cond. Zubin Mehta, New World Records, NW 309, 1981).

‡ Phillip Ramey gives the following account of a discussion he had with Barber a few days after the premiere of *Third Essay:*

> He said, "Well, what did you think of the new piece?" And I said, "Shall we have a cup of coffee?" He said something like, "That bad, huh?" And I said, "Oh no, but. . . ." So we sat at the Carnegie Hall Coffee Shop and I told him I thought the music was quite fine as far as it went, but the ending was too abrupt. . . . It should continue. He said, "I've been thinking that too, and somebody else said it to me and that settles it." And he did lengthen it. Not by very much, but he did tinker with it." (Ramey, interviewed by the author, 4 April 1986, New York)

To Audrey Sheldon

THIRD ESSAY

Samuel Barber
Opus 47

♩= 76

Piccolo
Flute 1 2
Oboe 1 2
English Horn
E♭Clarinet
Clarinet 1 2
Bass Clarinet
Bassoon 1 2
Contrabassoon
Horn 1 2 3 4
Trumpet 1 2 3
Euphonium
Trombone 1 2 3
Tuba
Timpani 1 2
ppp cresc. poco a poco
pp
pp cresc. poco a poco
Percussion
Harp 1, 2
Piano

♩= 76

Violin 1 2
Viola
Violoncello
Contrabass

Example 18.12 *Third Essay for Orchestra,* Op. 47, mm. 1–24 (G. Schirmer, 1971).

1
Timp.
Tamtams
ppp (small)
ppp (large) cresc. poco a poco
Tamt.
S
L
Bass Drum
B.D.
pp
ppp
cresc. poco a poco
Metal Sheet
Metal Sheet
cresc. poco a poco
mp
p
pp
a2
Hp. 1,2
p cresc. poco a poco
Pno.
con pedale
2
Marimba
solo
Mar.
f
mf
poco f

certo with the Philadelphia Orchestra; and Ormandy was planning a performance of *Die Natali.* About a year earlier, Barber had been diagnosed as having multiple myeloma, cancer of the lymphatic system.[75] His schedule of chemotherapy treatments prevented him from attending a party in celebration of Ormandy's eightieth birthday. In response to the conductor's invitation, he wrote:

> I still have the sounds of that wonderful performance of my concerto ringing in my ears. I was also very happy to hear from you that you are performing "Die Natale."* . . . My God, how much of my music you have done in all these years. What is Philadelphia going to do without you?[76]

Canzonetta for Oboe and String Orchestra, Op. 48

In the summer of 1978, while still working on the orchestration of the *Third Essay,* Barber began a concerto for oboe and orchestra for the farewell performance of Harold Gomberg, principal oboist with the New York Philharmonic from 1943 to 1977. Gomberg and Barber had been students at the Curtis Institute and maintained a friendship thereafter. The work was one of a series of concertos commissioned by Francis Goelet for members of the New York Philharmonic.†

Barber's failing health made him anxious about composing the piece for Gomberg; Herranz tells of endless starts and stops, where he discarded the music because it was too similar to his other works.[77] Having in mind a three-movement composition, Barber began with what had always seemed easiest for him to write—a lyrical, slow movement.‡ Aware that the andante sostenuto movement could stand as an independent piece if extended, he renamed it Andante for Oboe and Orchestra, ninety-seven measures of which exist in manuscript as a short score.§ Another version in short score, of eight-and-a-half minutes' duration, is marked merely "II," with parts indicated for strings and oboe. In this version the ending is extended another thirty-six measures. Only these short scores were completed before Barber died in January 1981.‖

*This spelling does not appear in any other Barber correspondence that I have seen.

†Charles Turner reports that when Barber learned he had cancer and believed he would not be able to finish the concerto, he offered to return the money to the Philharmonic.

‡John Corigliano remembered Barber telling him at the time that "although he knew he would have no trouble with a slow movement, he as yet had no idea what to do with the fast ones" (program notes, New York Philharmonic, 17–19 December 1981, p. 18).

§Manuscripts are at the Library of Congress and in the private collection of Charles Turner. The manuscript from which Turner worked, indicated as five-and-a-half minutes long, is copied neatly in an unidentified hand, but signed and titled in Barber's hand.

‖Ernst believes that Barber made the short scores to appease Gomberg, who apparently was pressuring him to finish the piece.

In 1980 Barber realized he would not be able to complete the piece and suggested that the extant movement should be titled *Canzonetta for Oboe and String Orchestra.*[78] After Barber's death Paul Wittke, of Schirmer, asked Charles Turner to orchestrate the short score. Turner, Barber's only student and a close friend since the early 1950s, completed the task as dictated by the obvious voices of the short score, leaving only one mark of his own: his choice of instrumentation—three solo violas—for a passage beginning at measure 95 following the cadenza.[79] Turner's fidelity to Barber's intentions led him to protest an alteration that Gomberg attempted to make before the premiere that involved shifting the register of the oboe above the violins to give more prominence to the solo.[80] A minor stir was created when Turner called the *New York Times* to complain about the change prior to the performance, causing conductor Zubin Mehta to restore the original version.[81] At the dress rehearsal, Gomberg produced a cadenza, which Barber had written for him but which had not been written into the score. It was played at the premiere.

In its limited way, the *Canzonetta* offers an appropriate elegy to the conclusion of Barber's career. His affinity and sympathetic writing for the mezzo-soprano voice of the oboe was apparent in his earliest orchestral work, Overture to *The School for Scandal,* and was demonstrated with luminescence in other milestone works—the solo in the second movement of the Violin Concerto, for example, the Intermezzo from *Vanessa,* and passages in *Antony and Cleopatra.* The title *Canzonetta* pays tribute to the vocal inspiration that guided virtually all of his music. Composer John Corigliano, in an analytical program note for the *Canzonetta,* pointed to the interesting dichotomy of harmonic procedures employed by Barber throughout his career—an alternation between "post-Straussian chromaticism and an oft-diatonic, typically American simplicity."[82] Usually, however, when the two elements exist in the same work, they deal with different material. Corigliano described the fusion of the two elements in *Canzonetta,* where one ingenious melody runs throughout:

> At the beginning, it is presented in an absolutely diatonic setting (the first sixteen bars have no accidentals at all, either in solo or accompaniment), but as the piece unfolds the same theme (which, interestingly, bears a rather close resemblance in both melodic and harmonic outline to the opening theme of the Violin Concerto) becomes more angular, changing into a chromatic version of itself. . . . Beginning with a lyric polyphonic introduction (which recurs twice during the course of the work), the *Canzonetta* alternates this intense, chromatic rendition of the theme with the original diatonic treatment, and finally ends as it began, with the simple oboe song.[83]

Called by critics "sweet and modestly luxurious in its lyricism" and "graceful, passionate, and poetic," the work recalls the chief features of the greater musical legacy of Samuel Barber.

* * *

In mid-September 1980, after nearly a year of sporadic hospitalizations, Barber went to Scotland to be with Menotti. After a few weeks, however, he suffered a stroke and was hospitalized in Edinburgh. He was so debilitated by the setback that Herranz came abroad to bring the ailing composer back to New York. The last months of Barber's life were spent in University Hospital and at his home.* Menotti, Herranz, Katharine Fryer, and many friends kept vigil so that he was never alone. Music was brought to his bedside: Ransom Wilson played the flute elegy that became the slow movement of the composer's Piano Concerto; arrangements were made for a New Year's Eve concert to be held in a conference room at the hospital, where a small piano was moved in—Robert de Gaetano played the slow movement of the Piano Sonata, John Browning performed, a string quartet played the *Adagio for Strings*, and a violinist offered some unaccompanied works by Bach. Members of the New York Woodwind Quintet played *Summer Music*. When Barber returned home on 18 January, his bed was moved near a window so that he might see Central Park.

Samuel Osmond Barber II died on 23 January 1981. His family announced his death with few words: "The family and friends record with the greatest sadness the passing of Samuel Barber, who gave them a unique joy and to all the world his music. . . ."[84] He was buried next to his mother in the Barber family plot at the Oaklands Cemetery in West Chester. According to his instructions, his grave is marked by a simple tombstone bearing the inscription: "Samuel Barber / March 9, 1910–January 23, 1981." A plot adjacent to the Barber family's is reserved for Menotti. Barber's will instructs that in the event Menotti chooses to be buried elsewhere, a small tombstone bearing the inscription "To the memory of two friends" will be erected on the empty plot.[85]

Barber left detailed instructions in his will regarding music to be played at his funeral: the service was to begin with the Twelfth Madrigal from Menotti's *The Unicorn, the Gorgon, and the Manticore*, "or such part or parts thereof (preferably including the concluding portion) as my Executors shall determine." He requested there be included also

> the following Bach chorales (the chorale should be played first, followed by the chorale-prelude; page references are to the Barenreiter edition now located in the library of my apartment in New York, New York): "Das alte Jahr vergangen ist" (p. 49); "Christe, Du Lamm Gottes" (pp. 66–67); "O Mensch, bewein dein Suende Gross" (p. 75); "Ich ruf zu dir, Herr Jesu Christ" (p. 119); and such other works or works of music, if any, as my Executors shall choose.[86]

*The records of Dr. Nelson show that Barber was admitted to University Hospital on 9 November 1980 and was discharged on 18 January 1981, five days before his death.

A funeral service was held on 26 January 1981 at the First Presbyterian Church of West Chester and included the music he had requested as well as Barber's own, "Let down the bars, O Death" and *Dover Beach*. The choral works were sung by the Westminster Choir. Memorial services were held in New York on 9 February at St. Bartholomew's Church (see facsimile of program below) and on 3 May 1981 at the Cathedral Church of St. John the Divine.

An obituary by Donal Henahan in the *New York Times* presented Barber as he was then, and still is, conventionally viewed:

> Throughout his career, Samuel Barber was hounded by success. Probably no other American composer enjoyed such early, persistent and such long-lasting acclaim. . . . He was anything but the neglected artist, laboring in obscurity and waiting for the approbation of posterity. Virtually all of his works were recorded. . . .
>
> One reason for the acceptance won by Mr. Barber's music—apart from its undeniable craft and thorough professionalism—was its deep-seated conservatism, which audiences could find congenial even at first hearing. Although he often dealt in pungent dissonances and complex rhythms, like most of his 20th-century contemporaries, there was a lyrical quality even to his strictly instrumental pieces that from the first established him as a neo-Romantic. That earned his music some disdain in avant-garde circles, but Mr. Barber went his own way nonetheless. Most of the century's composing fashions passed him by. He did not adopt twelve-tone music or its serial refinements, he did not dabble in chance or electronics. He wrote nothing that required consulting I Ching. . . .[87]

Henahan's portrait preserves myths about Barber. This study presents evidence that as hounded by success as the composer apparently was, so was he haunted by rigorous self-criticism. Moreover, it was not true that when he died virtually all of Barber's compositions had been recorded—*Prayers of Kierkegaard* was out of print, and *Antony and Cleopatra, The Lovers, To Be Sung on the Water,* and the complete cycle *Despite and Still,* works written at the peak of his career, lay dormant.

* * *

Almost five years earlier, William Schuman, on presenting Barber with the Gold Medal for Music at the American Academy and Institute of Arts and Letters, paid tribute to the composer who was born the same year as he and who had been his friend and colleague since the 1930s:

> The history of the arts is filled with examples of those who expanded the means of expression. There have, however, been other artists who were content to create within established means. In music, for example, such

ORDER OF SERVICE

CHORALE PRELUDES — Johann Sebastian Bach

Ich ruf' zu dir, Herr Jesu Christ
O Mensch bewein dein Sünde Gross

Jack H. Ossewaarde, organ

THE LESSON — Ecclesiasticus 44: 1-7

PRAYERS

The Rev. Thomas D. Bowers

LET DOWN THE BARS, O DEATH (Op. 8, No. 2) — Samuel Barber
TO BE SUNG ON THE WATER (Op. 42, No. 2)

The Choir of St. Bartholomew's Church
Jack H. Ossewaarde, choirmaster

SUMMER MUSIC FOR WOODWIND QUINTET (Op. 31)

Ransom Wilson, flute
Randall Wolfgang, oboe — Gary McGee, clarinet
Richard Vrotney, bassoon — David Jolley, French horn

From the *HERMIT SONGS (Op. 29)*:
THE CRUCIFIXION
THE DESIRE FOR HERMITAGE
DESPITE AND STILL (Op. 41)

Leontyne Price, soprano
David Garvey, piano

VANESSA (Op. 32): Quintet, Act III, Scene 2

Marilyn Zschau, soprano
Rosalind Elias, mezzo-soprano
Alice Garrott, mezzo-soprano
John Aler, tenor
Irwin Densen, bass-baritone

John Browning, piano

PRAYERS OF KIERKEGAARD (Op. 30) — Samuel Barber

Esther Hinds, soprano
The Choir of St. Bartholomew's Church
Marie Bogart, mezzo-soprano — Will Caplinger, tenor
Jack H. Ossewaarde, choirmaster
Dennis Keene, organ

PRAYER CHOSEN BY MR. BARBER
TO BE READ AT HIS FUNERAL

We seem to give him back to Thee, dear Lord, who gavest him to us. Yet as Thou didst not lose him in giving, so we have not lost him by his return. Not as the world givest, givest Thou, O Lover of Souls. For what is Thine is ours, always if we are Thine. What Thou givest Thou takest not away. And life is eternal; and love is immortal; and death is only a horizon, and horizon is nothing save the limit of one's sight. Lift us up, O God, that we may see further; cleanse our eyes that we may see more clearly; draw us closer to Thyself, that we may know ourselves closer to our beloved who are with Thee; and grant that where they are, and Thou art, we too, may one day be. Through Jesus Christ, our Lord. Amen.

The Rev. Thomas D. Bowers

CHORALE PRELUDES — Johann Sebastian Bach

Das alte Jahr vergangen ist
Christe, du Lamm Gottes

Jack H. Ossewaarde, organ

composers would include Bach, Mozart, Mendelssohn, and Brahms. Samuel Barber is in this tradition.

Barber's work is widely recognized and accepted as having enriched the literature of virtually every facet of musical expression. Each piece he has created is characterized by deeply felt emotions couched in the sophisticated terms of a master craftsman. . . .[88]

(facing) Program of memorial service for Barber on 9 February 1981 at St. Bartholomew's Church, New York.

POSTLUDE

Samuel Barber's early indoctrination in the European intellectual and musical tradition was thoroughly compatible with his lifelong creative motivations. He was never compelled to rebel against conventional practices of form, tonality, and lyricism. Those who early or late would label him a conservative, if they mean "reactionary," "unadventurous," and "old-fashioned," do him disservice. The international recognition accorded him during most of his lifetime and the still increasing frequency with which his works are performed today—which gain new significance within the current trend of "New Romanticism"—are testimony to the vitality with which he imbued tonal language and the enduring viability of melody itself. The personal voice that pervades Barber's music is his own, and with it he presents a strong defense against Stravinsky's query "Do we not, in truth, expect the impossible of music when we expect it to express feelings, to translate dramatic situations . . . ?"[1] Throughout his life Barber sought to express emotions in music with conviction and consistency.

Although Barber's music was shaped by a myriad of influences and experiences, this study has shown that one of the heroes of his story is Sidney Homer, who paradoxically reinforced a traditional orientation in his nephew and at the same time was a visionary. The letters of Homer that were selected by Barber for preservation must have held great significance for him. Letter after letter presents explicit messages to the younger composer: the value of sincerity, clarity of expression, reverence for the proven masters, the relinquishment of publicity. Homer preached: "the only thing that counts is finished work . . . work of a quality beyond dispute," choose "serious and vital subjects" with an "international appeal," "you must take into your confidence that vast body of music lovers," "art is common property and a world force." Above all, he told his nephew, listen to the "inner voice that is working with you." It is a rare mentor who can sustain his influence for as long a time as Homer did. The wisdom and optimism that he transmitted to the younger composer for more than twenty-five years fostered Barber's mission, supported his own inclination to adhere unwaveringly to the Romantic style, and inspired the direction of his intellectual environment. While there is no question that Barber's music derives from his own inner conviction, as early as 1926 Homer had written to the sixteen-year old Barber:

> It takes some courage to go into an art which shows you as you are, and no doubt many wonderful souls have shrunk from the ordeal and refused to put their real emotions into art form for others to know.[2]

Barber's words in 1971, almost twenty years after Homer's death, seem to echo that early advice:

> I think that what's been holding composers back a great deal is that they feel they must have a new style every year. This, in my case, would be hopeless. . . . I just go on doing, as they say, my thing. I believe this takes a certain courage.[3]

The steady adherence to one stylistic course over a fifty-year career did not prevent Barber's broadening and deepening as an artist. However, even the elements of modernist language that were incorporated in his work after 1940—increased dissonance, chromaticism, tonal ambiguity, and limited serialism—were only of use to him after they had already found their way into ordinary technique and insofar as they allowed him to pursue without compromise principles of tonality and lyrical expression.

A documentary study of Barber's career becomes a study of patronage in the United States as well. Because he worked almost entirely on commission, we are able to observe the shift in this country during the fifty years of his output from the individual philanthropist and sponsor—Mary Bok, Samuel Fels, John Nicholas Brown, Elizabeth Sprague Coolidge, Serge Koussevitzky—to broader-based financial sources, public institutions, and private foundations—the United States Army Air Force, the League of Composers, the Metropolitan Opera, the Detroit Chamber Music Society, the Alcoa Foundation, the Merlin Foundation, the Girard Bank.

Barber was one of those composers who worked closely with performers and for whom the idiomatic aspect of instrumental and vocal works was an integral part of the conception, and a striking feature of his method of composing was the collaborative relationship between composer and artist. "Performers have always helped me," he acknowledged in 1971. As is demonstrated in his compositions for Horowitz, Browning, and Garbousova, when he began a commission he often conducted a preliminary exploration by inviting soloists to play large portions of their repertoire so that the resulting work would utilize the full resources of the solo instrument and be tailored to the strengths of the particular performer.

Communication to his audience was critical to Barber's work. Again and again it has been shown, contrary to the smooth technical and melodic facility his works suggest, that his instrumental works were produced slowly and with labor. Most often his revisions—on the evidence presented in this study—were motivated by a need to perfect his craft, but some reflect the impact of audience and critical response or the desire to encourage more frequent performance of a work: for example, the reorchestration of *Knoxville: Summer of 1915* for chamber orchestra, revisions of the Second Symphony, the cutting of the skating aria from *Vanessa,* and the reworking of the music for the ballet *Medea* through several versions into its one-movement concert-piece form.

A review of Barber's meteoric rise to fame shows him to be, with Copland, the most frequently performed American composer of his generation from 1941 until the mid-sixties, when the trend toward modernism temporarily made him seem outmoded. It is ironic, however, that while most Americanists at this moment would tend to reject Barber as a banner carrier, he more than once wore the mantle for his country: in Prague in 1946, in England and Germany in the early 1950s, at UNESCO in 1952, and in the Soviet Union in 1962, as the first American composer to attend the biennial Congress of Soviet Composers. In line with John Corigliano's discerning observation about the coexistence in Barber's music of post-Straussian chromaticism and a typically American directness and simplicity, Barber's contribution—indeed his lasting strength—may well prove to be as a conservator of a combined American and European musical tradition.

Works List

The list below provides a chronological overview of Barber's output for the convenience of the reader. Compositions are listed by genre and grouped into published and unpublished works. All editions are published by G. Schirmer, Inc. Most of the unpublished works are at the Library of Congress in Washington, D.C. The title of each work is followed by the date of completion and subsequent arrangements if made or approved by Barber. The names of authors of song texts and libretti, as well as choreographers, are in parentheses following titles of works. The list is substantially the same as my works list in *The New Grove Dictionary of American Music* (Macmillan, 1987) and reprinted in W. W. Norton's Twentieth-Century American Masters series (1988) with several added titles and corrected dates of completion based on new evidence. A more comprehensive descriptive thematic catalogue of Barber's works, including information about manuscripts, commissions, dedications, first performances, and significant recordings, is in progress.

OPERAS
3 published; 1 unpublished

Vanessa, Op. 32 (Menotti), 1957; rev. 1964; arr. for chorus, solo, and duet, "Under the Willow Tree" (1961)

A Hand of Bridge, Op. 35 (Menotti), 1959

Antony and Cleopatra, Op. 40 (Zeffirelli after Shakespeare), 1966; rev. 1974. Concert arias, sop. and orch., "Give me some music," "Death of Cleopatra" (1968); arr. for chorus, "On the Death of Antony," "On the Death of Cleopatra"(1968)

Unpublished

The Rose Tree (Annie Sullivan Brosius Noble), 1920

BALLETS

2 published

Medea ("Serpent Heart," Martha Graham), Op. 23, 1946; revised, *Cave of the Heart,* 1947; rev. orchestral suite, Op. 23, 1947; rev. *Medea's Meditation and Dance of Vengeance,* Op. 23a, 1953

Souvenirs, Op. 28 (Todd Bolender), 1952. See Solo instrumental music.

INCIDENTAL MUSIC

Unpublished

Incidental music for the play *One Day of Spring,* by Mary Kennedy, 1935

ORCHESTRAL MUSIC

17 published; 2 unpublished

Overture to *The School for Scandal,* Op. 5, 1931
Music for a Scene from Shelley, Op. 7, 1933
Symphony in One Movement, Op. 9, 1936
Adagio for Strings, Op. 11 (arr. of String Quartet, mov't 2), 1938; arr. for organ (Strickland, 1949); *Agnus Dei* (arr. for chorus, 1967); arr. for clarinet choir (Lucien Caillet, 1964); arr. for woodwind choir (John O'Reilly, 1967)
Essay for Orchestra, Op. 12, 1937
Concerto for Violin and Orchestra, Op. 14, 1939
Second Essay for Orchestra, Op. 17, 1942
Second Symphony, Op. 19, 1944; mov't 2, *Night Flight,* Op. 19a, 1964
Capricorn Concerto, Op. 21, 1944
Concerto for Violoncello and Orchestra, Op. 22, 1945
Toccata Festiva, Op. 36, 1960
Die Natali, chorale preludes for Christmas, Op. 37, 1960; *Stille Nacht,* arr. for organ, 1960
Concerto for Piano and Orchestra, Op. 38, 1962
Fadograph of a Yestern Scene, Op. 44, 1971
Third Essay for Orchestra, Op. 47, 1978
Canzonetta for Oboe and String Orchestra, Op. 48 (posth.), 1977–78

Unpublished

Concerto for Piano and Orchestra, 1930 (lost)
Horizon, 1945
Adventure, 1954

BAND MUSIC

1 published; 1 unpublished

Commando March, 1943

Unpublished

Funeral March (on the Army Air Corps Song), 1943

CHAMBER MUSIC

7 published; 7 unpublished (1 incomplete)

Serenade for String Quartet, Op. 1, 1928; arr. for string orchestra, 1944
Dover Beach, Op. 3, baritone/contralto and string quartet (Matthew Arnold), 1931
Sonata for Violoncello and Piano, Op. 6, 1932
String Quartet, Op. 11, 1936 (arr. of 2nd mov't, *Adagio for Strings*)
Summer Music for woodwind quintet, Op. 31, 1955
Canzone (Elegy) for flute (or violin) and piano, Op. 38a, 1958
Mutations from Bach for brass choir and timpani, 1967
Variations on Happy Birthday, on the occasion of Eugene Ormandy's seventieth birthday (brass and timpani), RCA limited edition, 1970

Unpublished

Fantasie for Two Pianos, 1924 (also Sonata in Modern Form)
Sonata for Violin and Piano, 1928 (lost)
Commemorative [Wedding] March (violin, cello, and piano), 1941
Song for a New House, for voice, flute, and piano (Shakespeare), 1941
String Quartet (2nd mov't only), 1949

SOLO INSTRUMENTAL MUSIC

10 published; 29 unpublished
For piano unless otherwise indicated.

Three Sketches: Love Song, To My Steinway, Minuet, 1923–24
Suite for Carillon, 1932
Excursions, Op. 20, 1942–44
Souvenirs, Op. 28, four hands, 1951; arr. for piano solo, for two pianos (Gold and Fizdale), and for orch., 1952. See Ballets
Sonata for Piano, Op. 26, 1949
Wondrous Love: Variations on a Shape-note Hymn, Op. 34 (organ), 1958
Nocturne, Op. 33, 1959
Ballade, Op. 46, 1977

Unpublished

Melody in F, 1917
Sadness, 1917
Largo, 1918
War Song, 1918
At Twilight, 1919
Lullaby, 1919
Themes, ca. 1923
Untitled work ("Laughingly and briskly"), ca. 1924
Petite Berceuse, ca. 1924
Prelude to a Tragic Drama, 1925
To Longwood Gardens (organ), 1925
Fresh from West Chester (Some Jazzings): Poison Ivy, a Country Dance (1925), Let's Sit It Out, I'd Rather Watch (1926)
Three Essays, 1926
To Aunt Mamie on her birthday, 1926
Main Street, ca. 1926
Chorale for a New Organ, 1926
Three Chorale Preludes and Partitas for organ, 1927
Two- and three-voice fugues, 1927
Prelude and Fugue in B minor, for organ, 1927
Pieces for Carillon: Round, Allegro, Legend, Dirge, 1930–31
Two Interludes (intermezzi), 1931–32
After the Concert, ca. 1973

CHORAL MUSIC

12 published; 8 unpublished (1 incomplete)

The Virgin Martyrs (Sigebert of Gembloux, trans. Helen Waddell), 1935; Let down the bars, O Death (Emily Dickinson), 1936, Op. 8
Reincarnations, Op. 16 (James Stephens): Mary Hynes, 1937; Anthony O'Daly, The Coolin, 1940
A Stopwatch and an Ordnance Map, Op. 15 (Stephen Spender), 1940
Ad bibinum cum me rogaret ad cenam (V. Fortunatus), for Carl Engel, 1943
Prayers of Kierkegaard, Op. 30 (Søren Kierkegaard), soprano and orchestra, 1954
Easter Chorale (P. Browning), brass choir, timp, org *ad lib,* 1964
Twelfth Night (Laurie Lee); To Be Sung on the Water (Louise Bogan), Op. 42, 1968
The Lovers, Op. 43 (Pablo Neruda), baritone and orchestra, 1971

Unpublished

Christmas Eve: A trio with solos, 1924
Motetto on words from the Book of Job, for four- and eight-part chorus, 1930
Mary Ruane (Stephens), 1936

Peggy Mitchell (Stephens), 1936
God's Grandeur (Gerard Manley Hopkins), 1938
O the mind, the mind has mountains (Hopkins), unfinished, ca. 1939
Ave Maria (after Josquin Desprez), 1940
Long Live Louise and Sidney Homer, 1944

SONGS

38 published; 68 unpublished (2 lost, 1 incomplete)
For solo voice and piano unless otherwise indicated.

Three Songs, Op. 2: The Daisies (James Stephens), 1927; With rue my heart is laden (A. E. Housman), 1928; Bessie Bobtail (James Stephens), 1934

Dover Beach (see chamber works)

Three Songs, Op. 10 (James Joyce): Rain has fallen, Sleep now, 1935; I hear an army, 1936

Four Songs, Op. 13: A Nun Takes the Veil (Hopkins), 1937 (arr. for chorus, Heaven Haven, 1961); The Secrets of the Old (W. B. Yeats), 1938; Sure on this shining night (James Agee), 1938 (arr. for orch. and voice; and for chorus and pf, 1941); Nocturne (Frederic Prokosch), 1940 (arr. for voice and orchestra)

Two Songs, Op. 18: The queen's face on the summery coin (Robert Horan), 1942; Monks and Raisins (J. G. Villa), 1943

Knoxville: Summer of 1915, Op. 24 (Agee), 1948, soprano and orchestra; arr. soprano and chamber orchestra, 1950

Nuvoletta, Op. 25 (Joyce), 1947

Mélodies passagères, Op. 27 (Rainer Maria Rilke): Puisque tout passe, 1950; Un cygne, 1951; Tombeau dans un parc, 1951; Le clocher chante, 1950; Départ, 1950

Hermit Songs, Op. 29 (Irish texts of 8th to 13th centuries): At Saint Patrick's Purgatory (trans. Sean O'Faolain), 1952; Church Bell at Night (trans. Howard Mumford Jones), 1952; Saint Ita's Vision (trans. Chester Kallman), 1953; The Heavenly Banquet (trans. O'Faolain), 1952; The Crucifixion (from "The Speckled Book," trans. Mumford Jones), 1952; Sea-Snatch (trans. W. H. Auden), 1953; Promiscuity (trans. Auden), 1953; The Monk and His Cat (trans. Auden), 1953 (arr. for chorus, 1967); The Praises of God (trans. Auden), 1953; The Desire for Hermitage (trans. O'Faolain), 1953

Andromache's Farewell, Op. 39 (from Euripides: *The Trojan Women,* trans. J. P. Creagh), soprano and orchestra, 1962

Despite and Still, Op. 41, 1968: A Last Song (Robert Graves); My Lizard (Theodore Roethke); In the Wilderness (Graves); Solitary Hotel (Joyce); Despite and Still (Graves)

Three Songs, Op. 45, 1972: Now have I fed and eaten up the rose (Gottfried Keller, trans. Joyce); A Green Lowland of Pianos (Jerzy Harasymowicz, trans. C. Milosz); O boundless, boundless evening (Georg Heym, trans. C. Middleton), 1972

Unpublished

Sometime, 1917
Why Not? (Kitty Parsons), 1917
In the Firelight (Eugene Field), 1918
Isabel (John Greenleaf Whittier), 1919
Prayer (for his mother), 1921
An Old Song (Charles Kingsley), 1921
Hunting Song (John Bennett), with cornet, ca. 1921
Thy Will Be Done, A Sacred Solo (3 verses from "The Wanderer"), voice and organ, ca. 1922
Nursery Songs ("Mother Goose Rhymes set to music"), 1920–23
October-Weather (Barber), ca. 1923
Dere Two Fella Joe, 1924
Minuet, two voices, ca. 1924
My Fairyland (Robert T. Kerlin), ca. 1924
Summer Is Coming (after Alfred Tennyson), 3 voices, ca. 1924
Two Poems of the Wind, 1924 (Fiona Macleod): Little Children of the Wind; Longing
A Slumber Song of the Madonna (Alfred Noyes), voice and organ, 1925
Fantasy in Purple (Langston Hughes), 1925
Lady, When I Behold the Roses (anon.), 1925
La nuit (Alfred Meurath), 1925
Two Songs of Youth, 1925: I Never Thought That Youth Would Go (J. B. Rittenhouse); Invocation to Youth (Laurence Binyon)
An Earnest Suit to His Unkind Mistress Not to Forsake Him (Sir Thomas Wyatt), 1926
Ask Me to Rest (E. H. S. Terry), 1926
Au clair de la lune, 1926
Hey Nonny No (Christ Church MS), 1926
Man (Humbert Wolfe), 1926
Music, When Soft Voices Die (Percy Bysshe Shelley), ca. 1926
Thy Love (Elizabeth Browning), 1926
Watchers (D. Cornwell), 1926
Dance (James Stephens), 1927 (lost)
Mother I Cannot Mind My Wheel (Walter Savage Landor), 1927
Only of Thee and Me (Louis Untermeyer), ca. 1927
Rounds for three voices, 1927: A Lament (Shelley), To Electra (Robert Herrick), Dirge: Weep for the World's Wrong (anon., 1350); Farewell; Not I (Robert Louis Stevenson); Of a Rose Is Al Myn Song (anon., 1350); Sunset (Stevenson), The Moon (Shelley), Sun of the Sleepless (Byron), The Throstle (Tennyson), When Day is Gone (Robert Burns), Late, Late, So Late (Tennyson)
There's nae lark (Algernon C. Swinburne), 1927
The [Passionate] Shepherd to His Love (Christopher Marlowe); The Nymph's Reply [to the Shepherd] (Sir Walter Raleigh), 1928
The Song of Enitharmon Over Los (William Blake), ca. 1934, incomplete
Love at the Door (from Meleager, trans. J. A. Symonds), 1934
Serenader (George Dillon), 1934
Love's Caution (W. H. Davies), 1935

Night Wanderers (Davies), 1935
Peace (from Bhartorihari, trans. P. E. More), 1935
Stopping by Woods on a Snowy Evening (Robert Frost), 1935
Of that so sweet imprisonment (James Joyce), 1935
Strings in the earth and air (Joyce), 1935
Who carries corn and crown (?), ca. 1935
Beggar's Song (W. H. Davies), 1936
In the dark pinewood (Joyce), 1937
Song for a New House (Shakespeare). See chamber works
Between Dark and Dark (Katherine Garrison Chapin), 1942 (lost)

Bibliography

ARCHIVES AND SPECIAL COLLECTIONS

Public Text Collections

The American Academy and Institute of Arts and Letters, New York City. Records of Samuel Barber. Correspondence, press releases, news articles, ceremonial programs and addresses, 1940–81.

The American Academy in Rome, New York Office. Correspondence, newspaper clippings, applications and roster of Samuel Barber, 1935–63. Annual reports, 1935–36, 1936–37.

The Annie Russell Theatre. Rollins College, Winter Park, Florida. Program and clippings about Barber and the music for *One Day of Spring*.

The Curtis Institute of Music, Philadelphia, Pennsylvania.

———. Student Records of Samuel Barber, 1924–33.

———. Faculty Records of Samuel Barber, 1931–42 and 1965–73.

———. Institute catalogues, 1924–33.

———. *Overtones*. Newsletters of the Curtis Institute of Music, October 1929–April 1940; Fiftieth Anniversary Issue, 1 October 1974.

———. Programs of student and faculty recitals at the Curtis Institute, 1924–60. Commencement program, 1934.

———. William Hatton Green clipping file on Samuel Barber. Recital programs, 1919–23; more than 100 articles from *West Chester Daily Local News, Coatesville Record, Philadelphia Evening Bulletin, Philadelphia Inquirer, New York Times, New York Herald Tribune, Newsweek, Musical America, Boston Globe,* etc., 1935–66.

The Library of Congress, Music Division, Washington, D.C. The Samuel Baron Collection. Journal of the New York Woodwind Quintet, 1954–56.

National Personnel Records Center, St. Louis, Missouri. Military Records of Samuel Barber, 1943–45.

The New York Public Library, Astor, Lenox and Tilden Foundations. Dance Collection. Clipping files for *Cave of the Heart* and *Souvenirs.*

———. Music Division. Clipping files for Samuel Barber, Iso Briselli, Leontyne Price, Eleanor Steber, Gama Gilbert, Vladimir Horowitz, John Browning, Jeanne Behrend.

———. Theatre Collection. Annie Russell clipping files.

Philadelphia Orchestra Archives. Clipping files and program notes on Samuel Barber; scrapbooks, correspondence, 1937–85.

Westminster Choir School, Princeton, New Jersey. Bulletins and spring tour schedule, 1938, relating to "God's Grandeur."

Private Text Collections

The Estate of Samuel Barber, Valentin Herranz Collection, New York City. Barber's personal address book, ca. 1960–81.

———. Black copybook, including 3 pp. relating to *Die Natali* and *Andromache's Farewell,* ca. 1958–62.

———. The Curtis Institute of Music Commencement Address by Samuel Barber. Typescript of speech delivered on 12 May 1945.

———. "Dates to be Remembered" (brown leather book), entries include real estate tax schedule; birthdays and anniversaries; royalty payments from G. Schirmer, Inc., and ASCAP, 1958–73.

———. "Fadographs of a Yestern Scene," ca. 1974, 12 pp., typescript memoir of Barber's childhood.

———. Guest book from Barber's last residence, 907 Fifth Avenue, 1975–80.

———. Journal (red clothbound, hardcover book), undated (ca. 1970s), 30 pp., including notes on Buddha, dietary rules, yoga, recipes, and reminiscences of early performances.

———. Loose-leaf notebook, ca. 1960–78, 22 pp., including poetry, list of Barber's works, list of Lieder and folk songs sung by Barber, notes.

———. Travel log, 26 April to 26 June 1955, 10 pp. typescript.

Manfred Ibel, New York City. Miscellaneous reviews from American papers, 1974–77, and European newspapers, 1958; recordings and photographs.

William Strickland, Westport, Connecticut. Personal papers, newspaper clippings on Barber, programs.

Music Collections

Holographs and autograph manuscripts of Samuel Barber

The Estate of Jeanne Behrend, Philadelphia. Holographs of the Two Interludes and *Excursions.*

The Chester County Historical Society, West Chester, Pennsylvania. Holographs of youthful works.

The Library of Congress, Music Division, Washington, D.C. The Serge Koussevitzky Collection, the Elizabeth Sprague Coolidge Collection, and the general collection of the Music Division. Holographs, autograph manuscripts, sketches, copies, libretti; sketchbook (1933–ca. 1943); orchestration notebook; early compositions, 1912–26; school compositions, 1926–27, etc.

The Curtis Institute of Music, Music Library, Philadelphia. Holographs and autograph manuscripts of "With rue my heart is laden," *Reincarnations*, String Quartet (parts), and "Song for a New House."

The Eastman School of Music, Sibley Library, Rochester. Holographs, autograph manuscripts, and copies on loan from G. Schirmer, Inc.

Louise Homer Collection, Katharine Homer Fryer, New York City. Holographs of songs, 1923–27.

The Pierpont Morgan Library, Mary Flagler Cary Music Collection, New York City. "Essay for Strings" [*Adagio for Strings*]; sketches of the third movement of the Piano Sonata; and *Medea*, 4 pp.

LETTERS

Archival Collections

The American Academy and Institute of Arts and Letters, New York City. Correspondence between Samuel Barber and Henry Canby, Douglas Moore, Felicia Geffen, Louise Bogan, and others. 73 letters, November 1940–August 1979.

The American Academy in Rome, New York Office. Correspondence by or relating to Samuel Barber. 10 letters, 1935–63.

The Carnegie Library, Pittsburgh, Pennsylvania. Pittsburgh Symphony Society Files. Correspondence between Seymour Rosen, Arthur M. Doty, and George Sturm, relating to *Fadograph of a Yestern Scene*. 3 letters, July-September, 1971.

The Curtis Institute of Music, Philadelphia, Pennsylvania. Edith Braun to Mr. Gardner, 20 January 1941.

The Georgetown University Library, Special Collections Division, Washington, D.C. Francis and Katherine Biddle Papers. Correspondence from Samuel Barber to Katherine Garrison Chapin [Biddle]. 7 letters, February 1940–November 1942.

The Library of Congress, Music Division, Washington, D.C. Old Correspondence Collection. Correspondence between Oliver Strunk and Samuel Barber, 6 letters, March–April 1937; between Harold D. Spivacke and Samuel Barber, 11 letters, 1943–61; and Mrs. Willem Willecke to Harold Spivacke and Samuel Barber, 2 letters, 14 June 1954.

———. Elizabeth Sprague Coolidge Collection. Correspondence between Samuel Barber and Elizabeth Sprague Coolidge. 10 letters, 1933–34.

———. Serge Koussevitzky Collection. Correspondence between Serge Koussevitzky and Samuel Barber, Colonel Barton K. Yount, Raya Garbousova, Howard C. Bronson, Mary Bok. 65 letters, 1938–55.

———. Alexander Schneider Collection. Samuel Barber to Schneider, 1 January 1943.

Metropolitan Opera Association Archives, New York. Correspondence between Rudolf Bing and Samuel Barber, 4 letters, 1957–63; Barber to Herman Krawitz, 1 letter, ca. 1957; Cecil Beaton to Rudolf Bing, 6 letters, May 1958.

The New York Public Library, Astor, Lenox and Tilden Foundations. Music Division. The Papers and Records of William Schuman. Correspondence between William Schuman and Samuel Barber. 19 letters, 1953–79.
———. Damrosch Collection. Correspondence between Barber and Walter Damrosch. 4 letters, 1939–44.
———. Barber to Grace Martin, 27 April 1957.
———. League of Composers Collection. Barber to Claire Reis, 14 December 1942, 31 December 1965, and 7 April 1970.
The Philadelphia Orchestra Archives, Philadelphia, Pennsylvania. Correspondence between Eugene Ormandy and Samuel Barber, Franklin Roberts, Thomas Shepard, Wanton Balis, Jr., Boris Sokoloff. 23 letters, 1967–79.
Yale University, Music Library. Leonard Burkat Collection. Samuel Barber to Richard Burgin, 8 November 1943; to Leonard Burkat, autumn 1954 and 25 June 1959; and to Charles Münch, 29 June 1955.
———. Quincy Porter Papers. Samuel Barber to Quincy Porter, 19 May 1962.
———. Virgil Thomson Papers. Correspondence between Virgil Thomson and Samuel Barber, 1951–53.
———. Lehmann Engel Collection. Samuel Barber to Mme Carlos Salzedo, 17 September 1934.

Private Collections

Monique de Ruette Arnoldi, Montreal. Samuel Barber to Rosario Scalero, 12 letters, 1928–52; Eusebius Mandyczewski and Barber to Scalero, 1 postcard, 18 August 1928.
The Estate of Samuel Barber, Valentin Herranz Collection, New York City. Samuel Barber to Dr. and Mrs. Roy Barber, 81 letters, 1928–32; to Gustave Schirmer, 11 June 1946.
The Estate of Jeanne Behrend. Samuel Barber to Jeanne Behrend, 19 letters, 1933–51.
John Bitter, Miami. Samuel Barber to John Bitter, 24 July 1980.
Anne S. K. Brown, Providence. Correspondence between Samuel Barber and John Nicholas Brown, Anne Brown, 7 letters, November 1945–March 1946.
Suso Cecchi D'Amico, Rome. Samuel Barber to Suso Cecchi, 2 letters, 1936 and 1939.
Orlando Cole, Philadelphia. Samuel Barber to Orlando Cole, 16 letters, 1935–74.
Katharine Homer Fryer, New York City. Samuel Barber to Fryer, 4 letters, 1963–65; Barber to Sidney Homer, 52 letters, 1943–53; Sidney Homer to Barber, 31 letters, 1922–53.
Manfred Ibel, New York City. Samuel Barber to Ibel, 15 letters, 1971–73.
Henry-Louis de La Grange, Paris. Samuel Barber to La Grange, 24 letters, 1945–73.
William Strickland, Westport, Connecticut. Samuel Barber to Strickland, 40 letters, 1940–61.
Charles Turner, New York City. Samuel Barber to Turner, 8 letters, 1952–73.
Jonathan Williams, Edinburgh. Samuel Barber to Williams, 26 October 1961.

Letters to Author

Ralph Berkowitz, July–October 1983, Albuquerque, New Mexico.
Brunetta Bernard, 11 September 1982, Yarmouth, Maine.
John G. Briggs, Jr., 11 July 1986, Pennsauken, New Jersey.
Anne S. K. Brown, 11 October 1983, Providence, Rhode Island.
Patrick Creagh, 8 December 1988, Florence, Italy.
Suso Cecchi D'Amico, 1 February 1983, Rome, Italy.
Dietrich Fischer-Dieskau, 18 September 1987, Berlin, West Germany.
David Freed, 26 July 1986, Salt Lake City, Utah.
Katherine Harris von Hogendorp, 26 November 1986, Baltimore, Maryland.
Colonel George Howard, 3 August 1985, San Antonio, Texas.
Frank M. Hudson, 17 September 1986, Barrington, New Hampshire.
Werner Janssen, 7 August 1986, Stony Brook, New York.
Milford Myhre, 19 October 1983 and 1 August 1986, Lake Wales, Florida.
Richard Roeckelein, 8 February 1989, Washington, D.C.
Ned Rorem, 16 June 1986, Nantucket, Massachusetts.
Oscar Shumsky, 30 May 1984, New York City.
Stephen Spender, 29 November 1983, London.
Daniel Stehman, 7 April 1988, Hermosa Beach, California.
Virgil Thomson, 8 August 1988, New York City.
Carl Weinrich, 2 May 1984, Princeton, New Jersey.

INTERVIEWS

Interviews with Author

Arroyo, Martina. New York City, 28 November 1987.
Bampton, Rose. New York City, July 1983.
Baron, Samuel. Great Neck, New York, 30 May 1985; Washington, D.C., 18 July 1985.
Baumel, Herbert. Yonkers, New York, 18 May 1984.
Behrend, Jeanne. Philadelphia, 21 September 1982, July 1983.
Bok, Nellie Lee. Philadelphia, 12 May 1982.
Bolender, Todd. Kansas City, Missouri (telephone), 11 July 1987.
Briselli, Iso. Philadelphia, 11 May 1982.
Browning, John. New York City, 22 April 1986.
Callaway, Paul. Washington, D.C. (telephone), 20 June 1987.
Cole, Orlando. Philadelphia, 21 April 1982.
Fryer, Katharine Homer. New York City, 12 January 1983; 9 February 1990.
Garbousova, Raya. New York City, 28 and 30 October 1983.
Harris, Herbert. New York City, 20 May 1986.
Heinsheimer, Hans W. New York City, 21 November 1985.
Herranz, Valentin. New York City, 16 May 1986.
Hoiby, Lee. Long Eddy, New York (telephone), 5 May 1990.
Hollingsworth, Stanley. Pontiac, Michigan (telephone), 12 May 1990.
Ibel, Manfred. New York City, 10 April 1987.

Menotti, Gian Carlo. Philadelphia, 20 April 1982, and numerous telephone conversations between September 1985 and 10 March 1990.
Nelson, M.D., Jack. New York City (telephone), August 1989.
Ramey, Phillip. New York City, 4 April 1986.
Robertson, Muriel. New York City (telephone), 30 October 1986.
Saidenberg, Daniel. New York City, 7 June 1985.
Steber, Eleanor. Belle Terre, New York, 2 September 1983.
Strickland, William. Westport, Connecticut, 31 July 1985.
Turner, Charles. New York City, 8 August 1983, and numerous conversations between 1983 and 1989.
Wolfe, Perry. New York City (telephone), 10 June 1986.

Taped Radio Broadcasts

Samuel Barber by James Fassett. CBS, 19 June 1949, intermission interview, CBS Symphony Orchestra concert, *Knoxville: Summer of 1915*. Motion Picture, Broadcasting, and Recorded Sound Division, Library of Congress, Washington, D.C.
Samuel Barber by Robert Sherman. WQXR Great Artists series, 30 September 1978. Yale University Oral History of American Music.
Samuel Barber and Gian Carlo Menotti by John Gutman. Metropolitan Opera broadcast of *Vanessa,* WQXR, 1 February 1958. New York Public Library, Rodgers and Hammerstein Archives of Recorded Sound.
John Browning, Aaron Copland, Hans Heinsheimer, H. Wiley Hitchcock, Gian Carlo Menotti, Leontyne Price, William Schuman, Virgil Thomson, and Charles Turner by Peter Dickinson; includes excerpts of earlier Barber interviews by Fassett and Sherman. BBC, Barber Retrospective, 23 January 1982. The Institute for Studies in American Music, Brooklyn College, The City University of New York.
John Browning, Eleanor Steber, and Phillip Ramey by Martin Bookspan. WQXR, New York Philharmonic intermission broadcast, 23 January 1983.

SELECTED BOOKS AND ARTICLES

Ardoin, John. "Samuel Barber at Capricorn." *Musical America* (March 1960): 4–5, 46.
———. *The Stages of Menotti.* Chronology, compiled and annotated by Joel Honig. Garden City: Doubleday, 1985.
Barber, Samuel. "Birth Pangs of a First Opera." *New York Times,* 12 January 1958, sec. 2, p. 9.
———. "On Waiting for a Libretto." *Opera News* 22 (27 January 1958): 4–6.
Broder, Nathan. "Current Chronicle." *Musical Quarterly* 36 (April 1950): 276–79.
———. Review of *Prayers of Kierkegaard. Musical Quarterly* 41 (1955): 272.
———. *Samuel Barber.* New York: G. Schirmer, 1956.
Browning, John. "Samuel Barber's Nocturne, Op. 33." *Clavier* (January 1986): 20–21.

Carter, Susan Blinderman. *The Piano Music of Samuel Barber.* Ph.D. diss., Texas Technical University, 1980.

Coleman, Emily. "Samuel Barber and *Vanessa.*" *Theatre Arts* (January 1958): 69–87.

Dailey, William Albert. *Techniques in Composition Used in Contemporary Works for Chorus and Orchestra on Religious Texts as Important Representative Works of the Period from 1952–62.* D.M.A. diss., Catholic University, 1965.

Davis, Alycia Kathleann. "Samuel Barber's 'Hermit Songs,' Op. 29: An Analytical Study." M.A. thesis, Webster University, St. Louis, 1983.

Diamond, David. "Samuel Barber: 'Knoxville: Summer of 1915,' New York: G. Schirmer, Inc., 1949." *Notes* (March 1950): 309.

Dyer, Richard. Liner notes, *Antony and Cleopatra.* New World Records, NW 322–24, 1984.

Fairleigh, James P. "Serialism in Barber's Solo Piano Works." *Piano Quarterly* (Summer 1970): 13–17.

Finkelstein, Sidney. "Samuel Barber." Liner notes for recording of *A Hand of Bridge.* Vanguard 1065.

Freeman, John W. "In the Grand Tradition." *Opera News* (17 September 1966): 40–41.

Friedberg, Ruth. *American Art Song and American Poetry.* 3 vols. Metuchen and London: Scarecrow Press, 1981.

Friedewald, Russell E. *A Formal and Stylistic Analysis of the Published Music of Samuel Barber.* Ph.D. diss., State University of Iowa, 1957.

From the Mail Pouch. *New York Times.* Controversy over Toscanini's broadcast of Barber's music. Letters to the editor from Verna Arvey (25 December 1938), Franco Autori (27 November 1938), Roy Harris (22 November 1938), Alexander Kelberine (20 November 1938), Gian Carlo Menotti (20 November 1938), and Ashley Pettis (13 November 1938).

Gruen, John. "And Where Has Samuel Barber Been. . . ?" *New York Times,* 3 October 1971, sec. 2, p. 15, 21, 30.

———. *Menotti: A Biography.* New York: Macmillan, 1978.

Harrison, Jay. "Entr'acte." Interview with Samuel Barber and John Browning. Program of the Cleveland Orchestra, 24 January 1964, pp. 393–97.

Harrison, Lou. "Forecast and Review." *Modern Music* 22 (November 1944): 31.

Heinsheimer, Hans W. "An Opera Is Born." *Metropolitan Opera 1966–67,* opening program, 16 September 1966, pp. 48–50.

———. "Birth of an Opera." *Saturday Review* (17 September 1966): 49–50, 56–58.

———"The Composing Composer: Samuel Barber." *ASCAP Today* (1968): 4–7.

———. "Vanessa Revisited." *Opera News* (May 1978): 23–25.

———. "Samuel Barber: Maverick Composer." *Keynote* (February 1980): 7–11.

———. "Adagio for Sam." *Opera News* (14 March 1981): 30–31.

Heist, Douglas R. "Harmonic Organization and Sonata Form: The First Movement of Barber's Sonata, Op. 26." *Journal of the American Liszt Society* 27 (Jan.–June 1990): 25–31.

Helm, Everett. " 'Vanessa' in Salzburg." *Saturday Review* (13 September 1958): 65.

Henahan, Donal. "I've Been Composing All My Life, Off and On: A Talk with Samuel Barber." *New York Times,* 28 January 1979, pp. 19 and 24.

Hennessee, Don A. *Samuel Barber: A Bio-Bibliography.* Westport: Greenwood Press, 1985.

Heyman, Barbara. "Samuel Barber, Works List." In *The New Grove Dictionary of American Music.* Edited by H. Wiley Hitchcock and Stanley Sadie. London: Macmillan, 1986. Reprinted updated in *The New Grove Twentieth-Century Masters.* New York: W. W. Norton, 1987.

———. *Samuel Barber: A Documentary Study of His Works.* Ph.D. diss., Graduate School of the City University of New York, 1989.

———. "The Second Time Around, Barber's *Antony and Cleopatra* at the Lyric Opera of Chicago." *Opera News* (7 December 1991): 56–57.

Homer, Anne. *Louise Homer and the Golden Age of Opera.* New York: William Morrow, 1974.

Homer, Sidney. *My Wife and I.* New York: Macmillan, 1939.

———. *Seventeen Songs.* Preface by Samuel Barber. New York: G. Schirmer, [1917] 1943.

Horan, Robert. "American Composers 19: Samuel Barber." *Modern Music* 20 (March-April 1943): 161–69.

———. ". . . And 3 Modern Men Lead a Modern Life in this 'Swiss Chalet.' " *American Home* (July 1946): 36–38.

———. "The Recent Theater of Martha Graham." *Dance Index* 6 (1947): 4–23.

Jackson, Richard. "Samuel Barber." In *The New Grove Dictionary of American Music.* Edited by H. Wiley Hitchcock and Stanley Sadie. London: Macmillan, 1986.

Klein, Howard. "The Birth of an Opera." *New York Times Magazine* (28 August 1966): 32–33, 107–110, 115.

Kolodin, Irving. "Barber, Menotti, and *Vanessa.*" *Saturday Review* (25 January 1958): 41.

———. "Music to My Ears: Barber's Antony, after Zeffirelli." *Saturday Review* (1 October 1966): 35–36.

———. "Music to My Ears." *Saturday Review* (23 October 1971).

———. "Farewell to Capricorn." *Stereo Review* (1 June 1974).

Kozinn, Allan. "Samuel Barber: The Last Interview and the Legacy." *High Fidelity* (June 1981): 43–46, 65–68; (July 1981): 45–47; 80–90.

Kreiling, Jean Louise. *The Songs of Samuel Barber: A Study in Literary Taste and Text-Setting.* Ph.D. diss., University of North Carolina at Chapel Hill, 1986.

Kupferberg, Herbert. "Barber, the Bard, and the Barge." *Atlantic* (September 1966): 126–29.

Lerner, Bennett. "Samuel Barber's Love Song." *Keyboard Classics* (July-August 1986): 4–5.

Mann, Alfred. "Madrigal Awards." *American Choral Review* 29 (Winter 1987): 25.

"Make Mingle with Our Tambourines." Interviews with Samuel Barber, Franco Zeffirelli, Thomas Schippers. *Opera News* 31 (17 September 1966): 31–37.

Menotti, Gian Carlo. "Mail Pouch: 'Vanessa.' " *New York Times,* 15 February 1959, sec. 2, p. 9.

Merkling, Frank. "Two Worlds." *Opera News* (27 January 1958): 9.

Meyerowitz, Jan. "Aus Dem Musikleben." *Musica* 21 (July-August 1967): 176.

Mitropoulos, Dimitri. "Miracle on 39th Street." *Opera News* (27 January 1958): 15.

Porter, Andrew. "Antony's Second Chance." *Music of Three Seasons: 1974–1977*. New York: Farrar, Straus, and Giroux, 1978.

Proceedings of the American Academy and Institute of Arts and Letters, 1977.

Ramey, Phillip. "A Talk with Samuel Barber." Liner notes, *Songs of Samuel Barber and Ned Rorem*. New World Records Recorded Anthology of American Music. NW 229, 1978.

———. "Samuel Barber at Seventy: The Composer Talks About His Vocal Music." *Ovation* (March 1980): 15–20.

———. "Aaron Copland at Eighty." *Ovation* (November 1980): 8–14, 43.

———. "A Talk with Samuel Barber." Liner notes, *Third Essay for Orchestra*, Op. 47. New World Records, NW 309, 1981.

Rhoades, Larry Lynn. *Themes and Variations in Twentieth-Century Organ Literature: Analysis of Variations by Alain, Barber, Distler, Dupré, Duruflé, and Sowerby*. Ph.D. diss., Ohio State University, 1973.

Rorem, Ned. "Looking for Sam." *Stagebill-Carnegie* (February 1983): 14–18, 37.

Sabin, Robert. "Martha Graham Presents New Work 'Serpent Heart,' with score by Samuel Barber, at Columbia Festival." *Dance Observer* (June-July 1946): 73.

Salzman, Eric. "Samuel Barber." *HiFi/Stereo Review* (October 1966): 79–88.

"Samuel Barber: Portrait of a Musical Master." Unpublished monograph. Students in American History Seminar, Henderson High School, West Chester, Pennsylvania, 1982–83.

Schonberg, Harold. "Samuel Barber, 70, Pulitzer Prize-Winning Composer of 'Vanessa,' Dies." *New York Times*, 25 January 1981, pp. 1 and 16.

Sifferman, James Philip. *Samuel Barber's Works for Solo Piano*. D.M.A. diss., University of Texas at Austin, 1982.

Soria, Dorle J. "Artist Life." *Musical America* (September 1974): 5–6.

Tischler, Hans. "Some Remarks on the Use of Twelve-Tone and Fugue Techniques in Samuel Barber's Piano Sonata." *Journal of the American Musicological Society* (Summer 1952): 145–46.

———. "Barber's Piano Sonata, Op. 26." *Music and Letters* 33 (October 1952): 352–53.

"Violets in the Snow: Cecil Beaton." *Opera News* (27 January 1958): 20–21.

Walthen, Lawrence Samuel. *Dissonance Treatment in the Instrumental Music of Samuel Barber*. D.M.A. diss., Northwestern University, 1960.

Zeffirelli, Franco. *Zeffirelli: An Autobiography*. Great Britain and New York: Weidenfeld and Nicolson, 1986.

Notes

Introduction

1. Letter to A. M. Louis de Rouchaud, September 1837, "Lettres d'un bachelier ès musique," in *Pages romantiques,* ed. Jean Chantavoine (Paris: Librarie Félix Alcan, 1912).
2. Barber interviewed by Robert Sherman, WQXR, 30 September 1978.
3. Curtis Institute of Music, 12 May 1945.
4. Barber quoted by John Gruen, "And Where Has Samuel Barber Been. . . ?" *New York Times,* 3 October 1971, sec. 2, p. 15.
5. Interview by Peter Dickinson, BBC, 23 January 1982.

CHAPTER ONE Beginnings

1. Anne Homer, *Louise Homer and the Golden Age of Opera* (New York: William Morrow, 1974), p. 41.
2. Nathan Broder, *Samuel Barber* (New York: G. Schirmer, 1956), p. 11.
3. Anne Homer, *Louise Homer,* p. 370.
4. Ibid., p. 369.
5. Letter to "Ma, Pa, and Sara," 4 July 1930, Andrate.
6. Anne Homer, *Louise Homer,* p. 369; Broder, *Samuel Barber,* p. 10.
7. *West Chester Daily Local News,* 13 July 1921.
8. Anne Homer, *Louise Homer,* p. 411.
9. Samuel Barber, Preface to *Seventeen Songs by Sidney Homer* (New York: G. Schirmer, Inc., 1943).
10. Samuel Barber, "Fadographs of a Yestern Scene" (unpublished memoir, ca. 1974), p. 6.
11. Emily Coleman, "Samuel Barber and *Vanessa,*" *Theatre Arts* (January 1958): 69.

12. *West Chester Daily Local News,* 18 February 1927; Samuel Barber, "On Waiting for a Libretto," *Opera News* (27 January 1958): 4.

13. Phillip Ramey, "Samuel Barber at Seventy," *Ovation* (March 1980): 17.

14. Anne Homer, *Louise Homer,* p. 371.

15. Letter, 19 December 1922.

16. This manuscript and "Nursery Songs" are at the Library of Congress, Music Division, Washington, D.C.

17. John Ardoin, "Samuel Barber at Capricorn," *Musical America* (March 1960): 5.

18. *The Rose Tree,* holograph vocal score, Library of Congress, Music Division.

19. Quoted in Coleman, "Samuel Barber and *Vanessa,*" p. 69.

20. *The Rose Tree,* vocal score, Library of Congress, Music Division.

21. Holograph in the Chester County Historical Society, West Chester.

22. Olive E. Holman (who attended Bible school with Barber), in "Samuel Barber: Portrait of a Musical Master" (unpublished monograph by Henderson High School American History seminar, West Chester, 1983), pp. 24–25.

23. Ibid., p. 5.

24. Broder, *Samuel Barber,* p. 12.

CHAPTER TWO A Serious Student

1. Catalogues of the Curtis Institute of Music, 1924–34, are at the library of the institute.

2. Faculty Record Card, Samuel Barber, Curtis Institute of Music.

3. Menotti, telephone conversation with the author, 11 March 1990.

4. Broder, *Samuel Barber,* p. 12.

5. Letter, Homer to Barber, 9 July 1926.

6. *Overtones,* May 1936, p. 22.

7. Undated letter, Barber to Jeanne Behrend.

8. Menotti, interviewed by Peter Dickinson, BBC broadcast, 23 January 1982.

9. Menotti, BBC broadcast, 23 January 1982, and telephone conversation with the author, 11 March 1990.

10. John Gruen, *Menotti: A Biography* (New York: Macmillan, 1978), p. 21.

11. Samuel Barber, "Fadographs of a Yestern Scene," p. 7.

12. *West Chester Daily Local News,* 18 February 1927.

13. Program of concert, 4 June 1927, George Morris Philips Memorial Chapel, West Chester (shown to the author by Katharine Homer Fryer).

14. Sidney Homer, *My Wife and I* (New York: Macmillan, 1939), p. 254.

15. Diary entry of Katharine Homer Fryer, 28 June 1928.

16. *Songs from the Clay* (London and New York: Macmillan, 1915).

17. "The King of the Fairy Men," in *Seventeen Songs by Sidney Homer* (New York: G. Schirmer, [1917] 1943).

18. The holograph is at the Library of Congress.

19. A photocopy of the program was given to the author by Jeanne Behrend.

CHAPTER THREE Discoveries

1. Letter, Barber to his family, 12 June 1928, SS *de Grasse.*
2. Letter, Barber to his family, 10 June 1928, SS *de Grasse.*
3. Letter, 12 June 1928, SS *de Grasse.*
4. Letter to his family, 14 June 1928, SS *de Grasse.*
5. Undated letter from Montparnasse.
6. Letter to his family, 29 July 1928.
7. Ibid.
8. Letter, Barber to his family, 22 June 1928, Luxembourg Gardens.
9. Ibid.
10. Undated letter from Montparnasse.
11. Letter to his family, 22 June 1928, Luxembourg Gardens.
12. Letter, Barber to his family, 7 July 1928.
13. Letter to his family, 22 July 1928, Gressoney, St. Jean, Italy.
14. Ibid.
15. Ibid.
16. Letter, 8 August 1928, Gressoney.
17. Letter to his family, 29 July 1928, Gressoney.
18. Letter, Barber to his family, 1 August 1928, Gressoney.
19. Letter, Barber to his family, 11 August 1928, Venice. The music is a diplomatic transcription of what appeared in Barber's letter.
20. Letter, Barber to his family, 21 August 1928, Vienna.
21. Ibid.; postcard, Mandyczewski and Barber to Scalero, 18 August 1928, Mönichkirchen. All correspondence from Barber to Scalero cited in this book is from the collection of Monique de Ruette Arnoldi, stepdaughter of Maria Teresa Scalero de Ruette.
22. Letter, Barber to his family, 21 August 1928, Vienna.
23. Ibid.
24. Ibid.
25. Letter to his family, 25 August 1928, Salzburg.
26. Ibid.
27. Letter, Barber to his parents, sister, aunts, and Annie Noble, 4 September 1928, Nürnberg.
28. Ibid.
29. Ibid.
30. Letter, Frank D. Fackenthal to Barber, 11 May 1929, Columbia University Archives.
31. Letter, Homer to Barber, 18 February 1929.
32. Diary entry, 4 May 1929, Katharine Homer.
33. David Freed, letter to the author, 26 July 1986.
34. "School Compositions, 1927–28," Library of Congress, Music Division.
35. Ibid., p. 40.
36. Letter, 18 February 1929.
37. Letter, Barber to Orlando Cole, 15 July 1936. All letters from Barber to Cole are in the personal collection of Orlando Cole, Philadelphia.
38. Letter, Homer to Barber, 7 May 1929.
39. Letter to his parents, 11 August 1929, Gressoney.

40. Letter, 15 July 1936.
41. Letter, 24 October 1936.
42. Charles Mills, "On the Air," *Modern Music* 20 (March–April 1943): 213.
43. *Overtones,* May 1936, p. 25.
44. Letter, Barber to his family, 31 May 1929, "a bordo del 'Conte Grande.' "
45. Ibid.
46. Ibid.
47. Ibid.
48. Letter, Barber to his family, 3 June 1929, Hotel Vesuvius, Naples.
49. Ibid.
50. Ibid.
51. Letter to his family, 7 June 1929, Hotel Excelsior, Florence.
52. Letter, Barber to his family, 9 June 1929, Milan.
53. Letter to "Mamma, Poppa, Sara and Auntie," 16 June 1929, Cadegliano.
54. Ibid.
55. Letter, Barber to his parents, 29 June 1929, Gressoney, St. Jean.
56. Ibid.
57. Letter to "Mamma, Poppa, Sara, and Auntie," 16 June 1929, Cadegliano.
58. Letter to his parents, 9 July 1929, Gressoney, St. Jean.
59. Letter to his parents, 16 July 1929.
60. Letter to his parents, 22 June 1930, Andrate.
61. Letter, Barber to his family, 17 June 1930, Hotel Belvedere, Andrate.
62. Letter, 22 June 1930, Andrate.
63. Letter to his parents, 13 July 1930, Andrate.
64. Ibid.
65. Letter to his family, 17 July 1930, Andrate.
66. Letter, 8 August 1930.
67. Letter, 27 August 1930, Homeland, Bolton-on-Lake-George, New York.
68. Letter to his parents, 9 July 1931, Cadegliano.
69. Letter, 10 November 1931, New York City.
70. "Famed Composer Knows Sam Barber," *West Chester Daily Local News,* 1 October 1931; also quoted by Gama Gilbert in a *New York Times* review of *Music for a Scene from Shelley,* 24 March 1935.
71. Letter to Behrend, 19 September 1938.
72. Barber's black loose-leaf notebook, in collection of Valentin Herranz.
73. Curtis Institute of Music, Barber's Permanent Record Card No. 2.
74. *West Chester Daily Local News,* 16 February 1931.
75. Curtis Institute of Music, Barber's Permanent Record Card No. 2.
76. "Prix de Rome Winner Prepared for Work as Composer with Wide Musical Curriculum," *Musical America* (7 December 1935): 23.
77. Letter, Milford Myhre to the author, 1 August 1986.

CHAPTER FOUR Uncertainties

1. Student records of Samuel Barber, 1924–33, Curtis Institute of Music.
2. Sketchbook, 1930s, Library of Congress, Music Division.

3. Quoted in John N. Burk, program, Boston Symphony Orchestra, 15 February 1941.

4. Slonimsky, liner notes, CBS-Odyssey Y-33230 (unsigned but identical to an earlier release).

5. Letter to his family, 5 June 1931, from on board the SS *Augustus.*

6. Ibid.

7. Letter, 10 June 1931, Hotel Neptune, Pisa.

8. Letters, Barber to his family, 14 June (Hotel Nazionale, Volterra), 15 and 17 June 1931 (Pensione Chiusarelli, Siena).

9. Letter to his family, 20 June 1931, Cadegliano.

10. Letter, Barber to his family, 12 July 1931.

11. Letter, 3 July 1931, Cadegliano.

12. Letter to his family, 6 July 1931, Cadegliano.

13. Letter to his parents, 19 July 1931, Cadegliano.

14. Letter, 23 July 1931, Cadegliano.

15. Letter to his parents, 6 August 1931, Cadegliano.

16. Letter to his parents, 15 August 1931, Cadegliano.

17. Letter to his family, 30 August 1931, Cadegliano.

18. Broder, *Samuel Barber,* p. 21.

19. Barber, "Fadographs," p. 10.

20. Letter, Frank D. Fackenthal to Barber, 6 April 1933 (Columbia University Archives).

21. Letter, 22 April 1933, Palm Beach, Florida.

22. Linton Martin, *Philadelphia Inquirer,* 31 August 1933.

23. *Philadelphia Evening Bulletin,* 31 August 1933.

24. Olin Downes, "Barbirolli Leads Music by Barber," *New York Times,* 31 March 1938.

25. Letter to Sidney Homer, 10 February 1947.

26. Robert Horan, "American Composers 19: Samuel Barber," *Modern Music* 20 (March–April 1943): 165.

27. "Dover Beach," *The Portable Matthew Arnold,* ed. Lionel Trilling (New York: Viking Press, 1949), pp. 165–67.

28. Quoted in Phillip Ramey's liner notes, "Songs of Samuel Barber and Ned Rorem," New World Records NW 229 (1978), a reissue of the 1935 recording of *Dover Beach.* The record also includes *Mélodies passagères,* with Pierre Bernac, baritone, and Francis Poulenc, piano (made in 1962, but never released).

29. Ibid.

30. Ibid.

31. See Friedewald, *A Formal and Stylistic Analysis of the Published Music of Samuel Barber* (Ph.D. diss., Iowa State University, 1957): 16–17.

32. Letter, Barber to Elizabeth Sprague Coolidge, September 1933, written from Cadegliano. Library of Congress, Music Division, Elizabeth Sprague Coolidge Collection.

33. "League of Composers' Concert Heard," *New York Times,* 6 March 1933, p. 16.

34. Ibid.

35. Allan Kozinn, "Samuel Barber: The Last Interview and the Legacy," part 2, *High Fidelity* (July 1981): 45.

36. *Dover Beach,* G. Schirmer, 1936.

37. Barber's letter, quoted in *Overtones*, 1933–34, p. 76.

38. Barber's sketchbook, 1930s, Library of Congress, Music Division.

39. Cole, interview with the author. See also Broder, *Samuel Barber*, p. 27.

40. A photocopy of this program (belonging to Roland Leich) was given to the author by Jeanne Behrend.

41. Letter, early March 1935.

42. Quoted by Ramey in liner notes for "Songs of Samuel Barber."

43. Kozinn, "Samuel Barber: The Last Interview and the Legacy," part 2, p. 45.

44. Letter, Barber to Orlando Cole, December 1935.

45. *American Music Lover*, June 1936; *The Nation*, 17 June 1936.

46. Broder, *Samuel Barber*, p. 23.

47. Letter to Orlando Cole, 15 July 1936.

48. Letter, spring 1938, West Chester (collection of Suso Cecchi d'Amico).

49. Letter, 12 January 1939, St. Augustine, Florida.

CHAPTER FIVE Independence

1. In the collection of Orlando Cole.

2. *Musical America*, 16 October 1936.

3. Cole, interview with the author, 21 April 1982.

4. Ibid.

5. Letter, 16 July 1932, Cadegliano.

6. See Friedewald, *A Formal and Stylistic Analysis*, pp. 176–77.

7. Cole, interview with the author, 21 April 1982.

8. Ibid.

9. *New York Times*, 6 March 1933, p. 16.

10. Letter, Barber to Cole, ca. September or October 1934.

11. Letter, August 1935.

12. "Felix Salmond Appears Here in Cello Recital," *New York Herald Tribune*, 7 February 1937.

13. Letter, 6 May 1936.

14. Undated letter to Mrs. Coolidge, probably September or October 1933, Cadegliano (in the Elizabeth Sprague Coolidge Collection, Library of Congress, Music Division).

15. Letter, 8 September 1934, Bolton, New York.

16. Letter, probably late September or October 1934.

17. Hans Heinsheimer, "The Composing Composer: Samuel Barber," *ASCAP Today* (1968): 7.

18. Broder, *Samuel Barber*, p. 27.

19. Letter, January 1935.

20. Letter, undated, probably January 1935.

21. Cited in Broder, *Samuel Barber*, p. 27–28.

22. News release, 26 January 1935, Barber clipping files, New York Public Library, Music Division.

23. Letter, undated, probably mid-February 1935.

24. Letter, ca. February 1935.

25. Letter, Barber to Cole, late February, 1935.

26. *Overtones,* May 1936, p. 24; "U.S. Musicians Honored: Lady Astor Introduces Them at Reception and Musicale," *New York Times,* 26 June 1935.

27. Cole, interview with the author, 21 April 1982.

28. *Overtones,* May 1936, p. 36.

29. Letter, 23 July 1937, Bolton, New York.

30. Ibid.

31. Letter, 3 October 1933, Cadegliano.

32. Quoted in program notes, New York Philharmonic Society, 24 March 1935.

33. Preface to *Music for a Scene from Shelley* (G. Schirmer, Inc., 1936).

34. Letter of 25 July 1937, quoted in Broder, *Samuel Barber,* p. 89.

35. Letter to Barber, 18 September 1935, Bolton, New York.

36. Olin Downes, *New York Times,* 25 March 1935, p. 13.

37. See sketchbook (1930s), pp. 5–10, Library of Congress, Music Division.

38. Ibid., p. 10.

39. Gama Gilbert, "Philharmonic Plays Youth's Work Today," *Philadelphia Bulletin,* 24 March 1935.

40. Barber's journal (1970s), collection of Valentin Herranz.

41. Barber, interviewed by James Fassett, CBS Symphony Orchestra broadcast, 19 June 1949.

42. "Samuel Barber Music Heard at Carnegie Hall," 25 March 1935.

43. "New York Revels in Superlative Orchestral Concerts, Janssen Gives Barber Novelty," *Musical America* (10 April 1935): 14.

44. Olin Downes, "Janssen Presents New Native Music," *New York Times,* 25 March 1935.

45. NBC Music Research Files, clipping file, New York Public Library, Music Division.

46. *New York Times,* 16 April 1939.

47. *Chicago Daily News,* 3 August 1936.

48. "Mary Kennedy Pays High Tribute to Annie Russell," *Orlando Sentinel-Star,* 12 January 1935.

49. "Author to Play Leading Role in Play," *Orlando Sentinal-Star,* 5 January 1935.

50. Letter to Cole, before Christmas, 1934.

51. Cole, interview with the author, 21 April 1982.

52. *Orlando Sentinel-Star,* 5 January 1935.

53. Archives, Annie Russell Theatre, Professional Artists Series, program, January 24–25, 1935, Rollins College, Winter Park, Florida.

CHAPTER SIX The American Academy

1. Letter, Barber to Cole, December 1934.

2. *Musical Digest,* April 1936; "Samuel Barber Wins Two Musical Awards," *Musical America,* 25 March 1935; "Samuel Barber Wins New Prize," *West Chester Daily Local News,* 7 May 1935; Broder, *Samuel Barber,* p. 29.

3. Broder, *Samuel Barber,* p. 29.

4. Letter, Barber to Jeanne Behrend, 14 August 1935.

5. Letter to Menotti, quoted in Broder, *Samuel Barber,* p. 30.
6. Broder, *Samuel Barber,* p. 30.
7. Letter quoted in Overtones, May 1936, p. 21.
8. *Overtones,* May 1936.
9. Letter, quoted in Broder, *Samuel Barber,* pp. 30–31.
10. *Overtones,* May 1936, p. 22.
11. Broder, *Samuel Barber,* p. 30.
12. *Annual Report of the American Academy in Rome,* 1935–36, p. 34.
13. *Overtones,* May 1936, p. 20.
14. Holograph, Library of Congress, Music Division.
15. See *Collected Songs of Samuel Barber* (New York: G. Schirmer, 1971, 1981).
16. Suso Cecchi d'Amico, letter to the author, 1 February 1983, Rome.
17. Barber, quoted by Ramey, liner notes, "Songs of Samuel Barber," 1978.
18. For an insightful guide to *Finnegans Wake,* see Michael H. Begnal's "The Language of *Finnegans Wake,*" in *A Companion to Joyce Studies,* eds. Zack Bowen and James Carens (Westport: Greenwood Press, 1984).
19. Leslie Carson, *Musical Courier,* 15 February 1953.
20. Barber, interviewed by Philip Ramey, liner notes, "Songs of Samuel Barber," 1978.
21. *High Fidelity* (April 1965): 103. The recording, including Steber, Donald Gramm, Mildred Miller, and John McCollum, was reissued on Desto D-411-12/DST-6411-12.
22. "Barber Songs," Etcetera KTC 1055, released in 1988. The pianist is Tan Crone.
23. New York Philharmonic–Symphony program notes, 4 April 1937.
24. *New York Times,* 14 December 1936.
25. Barber, interviewed by Fassett, CBS, 19 June 1949.
26. *Newsweek,* 3 April 1937.
27. Francis D. Perkins, "Philharmonic Plays Work of Samuel Barber," *New York Herald-Tribune,* 26 March 1937.
28. "Rodzinski Directs Barber Symphony," *New York Times,* 26 March 1937, p. 24.
29. Letter, 6 February 1937, Palm Beach.
30. *New York Times,* 25 July 1937, sec. 2, p. 5.
31. *Newsweek,* 11 April 1938, p. 24.
32. Program, *Salzburger Festspiele* 1937, Erstes Festkonzert, 25 July 1937.
33. *New York Times,* 25 July 1937.
34. "First Time Fever," *Modern Music* (January–February 1939): 84–85.
35. Letter from Koussevitzky, 21 December 1938.
36. *New York Times,* 9 March 1944.
37. These undated and unsigned notes are in the Samuel Barber clipping file at the New York Public Library, Music Division.
38. Letter, 4 January 1943.
39. Letter to Koussevitzky, 24 February 1943.
40. Letter, 11 November 1943.
41. Letter to Koussevitzky, 16 November 1943.
42. Letter, 24 February 1944.

43. Noel Straus, "Barber Symphony Heard in Revision," *New York Times,* 9 March 1944, p. 15.

44. Letter to Homer, 10 February 1947.

45. Letter, Barber to Cole, 6 May 1936.

46. Ibid.

47. Dates are given in Barber's roster at the New York office of the American Academy in Rome.

48. Letter, Menotti to Orlando Cole, September 1936, in the collection of Orlando Cole.

49. Letter, 15 July 1936.

50. Letter to Barber, 17 August 1936.

51. Undated letter, Barber and Menotti to Cole, summer 1936, St. Wolfgang.

52. Letter, probably 19 September 1936.

53. Letter, Menotti to Cole, 19 September 1936.

54. Letter, Barber to Cole, 24 October 1936.

55. Postcard, Barber to Suso Cecchi, October 1936.

56. Letter, Barber to Cole, St. Wolfgang, 24 October 1936.

57. Letter, Barber to Cole, 19 September 1936.

58. Letter, 6 February 1937, Palm Beach.

59. "Composer's Evening: Program of Music by Samuel Barber Given at Casimir Hall," *Philadelphia Evening Bulletin,* 8 March 1937.

60. All correspondence between Strunk and Barber quoted here is in the Library of Congress, Music Division, Old Correspondence Collection.

61. Letter, undated but probably written about 9 April 1937.

62. Howard Taubman, *New York Times,* 16 March 1938.

63. Letter to Cole, written from the Homers' summer home, Bolton, New York, undated but probably August 1938.

64. Ibid.

65. Letter, Barber to Schneider, United States Army, 1 January 1943, Library of Congress, Music Division.

66. Letter, 21 December 1947, Capricorn.

CHAPTER SEVEN Recognition

1. Letter to Barber, 22 April 1933, Palm Beach, Florida.

2. Barber's words, quoted in *Overtones,* February 1934, p. 75.

3. Letter, 11 August 1933, quoted in Broder, *Samuel Barber,* pp. 24–25.

4. Joseph Horowitz, *Understanding Toscanini* (New York: Alfred A. Knopf, 1987), p. 133; and "Toscanini Will Conduct Works by Samuel Barber: First American Compositions He Has Used Since '33," unidentified newspaper, 28 November 1938, New York Public Library, Music Division, Samuel Barber clipping files.

5. Broder, *Samuel Barber,* p. 33.

6. Letter, 19 April 1941, from Winter Park, Florida.

7. Horan, "American Composers 19: Samuel Barber," p. 161.

8. R. L. F. McCombs, Philadelphia Orchestra program, October 1940, in Barber clipping file, New York Public Library, Music Division.

9. Letter to Damrosch, 3 April 1939, Walter Damrosch Collection, New York Public Library, Music Division.
10. Menotti, telephone interview with the author, 11 March 1990.
11. Barber interviewed by Robert Sherman, WQXR, 30 September 1978.
12. Ibid.
13. Broder, *Samuel Barber*, p. 34.
14. *Overtones*, December 1938.
15. "Toscanini Plays Two New Works," *New York Times*, 7 November 1938.
16. Letter to Barber, 12 January 1939, St. Augustine, Florida.
17. Letter, 8 November 1938, printed in "From the Mail Pouch," *New York Times*, 13 November 1938.
18. "Drawn from the Mail Pouch," *New York Times*, 20 November 1938.
19. Ibid.
20. "From the Mail Pouch," *New York Times*, 25 December 1938.
21. Letter, Roy Harris to the music editor, 22 November 1938, *New York Times*, 27 November 1938.
22. Statistics provided by the Philadelphia Orchestra Public Relations Department.
23. Ned Rorem, "Looking for Sam," *Stagebill–Carnegie* (February 1983): 7.
24. Charles Turner, BBC radio broadcast, 23 January 1982.
25. Newspaper item, "Of Two Composers," 12 November 1946, Curtis Institute of Music Library, William Hatton Green clipping file.
26. Letter, Homer to Barber, 15 January 1934, Palm Beach, Florida.
27. Schuman, BBC broadcast, 23 January 1982.
28. Thomson, BBC broadcast, 23 January 1982.
29. See above, chapter 6.
30. Barber, interview with Fassett, CBS, 19 June 1949.
31. Strickland, interview with the author, 31 July 1986.
32. Letter to Strickland, 15 August 1945.
33. See Friedewald, *A Formal and Stylistic Analysis*, pp. 105–8.
34. Quoted in Broder, *Samuel Barber*, p. 51.
35. Letter, 19 January 1938.
36. Barber's sketchbook, 1930s, p. 3. I am indebted to Tim Gura for identifying this text, which is in *The Poems and Prose Of Gerard Manley Hopkins*, ed. W. H. Gardiner (Harmondsworth: Penguin Books, 1953, 1963).
37. The holograph is at the Library of Congress, Music Division.
38. Permanent Record Card of Samuel Barber, Curtis Institute of Music.
39. Patricia McFate, *The Writings of James Stephens: Variations on a Theme of Love* (New York: St. Martin's, 1979), pp. 104–5.
40. Horan, "American Composers 19: Samuel Barber," p. 168.
41. Letter from Stephens to John Quinn, 8 August 1917, in *Letters of James Stephens*, ed. Richard Finneran (New York: Macmillan, 1974), p. 223.
42. Douglas Hyde, *Songs Ascribed to Raftery* (Dublin, 1903), pp. 325–29.
43. Ibid.
44. Horan, "American Composers 19: Samuel Barber," p. 168.
45. Douglas Hyde, *The Love Songs of Connacht*, p. 71.
46. Dated holograph, Library of Congress, Music Division.
47. Letter, 14 November 1942, Georgetown University Library.
48. Letter, 18 February 1943.

49. Alfred Mann, "Madrigal Awards," *American Choral Review* 29 (Winter 1987): 25–26.

50. Barber, *A Stopwatch and an Ordnance Map* (G. Schirmer, 1942), p. 1.

51. Letter, 17 December 1945.

52. Noel Straus, " 'Magnificent' Sung at Carnegie Hall," *New York Herald Tribune,* 18 December 1945.

CHAPTER EIGHT Prelude to War

1. Broder, *Samuel Barber,* p. 35.

2. Ibid.

3. Ibid.

4. Briselli, interview with the author, 20 April 1982.

5. Letter, Oscar Shumsky to the author, 30 May 1984.

6. Letter, Brunetta Bernard (Gama Gilbert's widow) to the author, 11 September 1982.

7. *New York Times,* 29 December 1940, sec. 9, p. 7.

8. Undated handwritten note on Barber's letterhead (166 East 96th Street, New York), Philadelphia Orchestra Archives.

9. Linton Martin, "Albert Spalding Is Soloist with Orchestra at Academy," *Philadelphia Inquirer,* 8 February 1941, p. 12.

10. Henry Pleasants, "Spalding Plays New Barber Concerto," *Philadelphia Evening Bulletin,* 8 February 1941, p. 41.

11. Martin, *Philadelphia Inquirer,* p. 12.

12. Arthur Bronson, *Philadelphia Record,* p. 11.

13. Virgil Thomson, "Academism with Charm," *New York Herald Tribune,* 12 February 1941.

14. Letter, 4 March 1941.

15. Horan, "American Composers 19: Samuel Barber," p. 166.

16. Martin, *Philadelphia Inquirer,* p. 12.

17. Letter, Samuel Barber to Sidney Homer, 7 January 1949.

18. Ibid.

19. Letter, late winter 1949.

20. Letter to Sidney Homer, 7 January 1949.

21. Letter, Barber to Sidney Homer, 8 February 1951, Paris.

22. Information based on records of performances of Barber's works provided by the Philadelphia Orchestra, 18 September 1986.

23. *The Oxford Companion to English Literature,* 4th ed., ed. by Sir Paul Harvey (Oxford: Oxford University Press, 1967, reprinted with corrections in 1981), p. 398.

24. Harold Whitehall, "Sprung Rhythm," *Gerard Manley Hopkins: A Critical Symposium,* by the Kenyon Critics (New York: New Directions, 1944, 1945), p. 54.

25. Arroyo, interview with the author, 28 November 1987.

26. Donal Henahan, "I've Been Composing All My Life Off and On," *New York Times,* 28 January 1979, p. 19. Katharine Fryer also corroborates the incident.

27. Hans W. Heinsheimer, "The Composing Composer: Samuel Barber," *ASCAP Today*, 1968.

28. Letter to Katherine Garrison Chapin, 13 February 1940. Chapin (1890–1977) was married to Francis Biddle, attorney general of the United States 1941–45.

29. *Herald Tribune*, 8 April 1941.

30. Letter to Barber, 15 January 1940, St. Augustine, Florida.

31. Records of the American Academy and Institute of Arts and Letters, New York.

32. Letter, Edith Braun to Mr. Gardiner, 20 January 1941, 1818 Delancey Street, Philadelphia (Curtis Institute of Music Library).

33. The manuscripts are at the Library of Congress, Music Division.

34. Letter, 14 August 1940, from "The Hermit," the Barber family retreat in the Poconos.

35. Letter, 4 March 1941, Winter Park, Florida.

36. Letter, Barber to Chapin, 22 March 1942.

37. Ibid.

38. Letter to Chapin, 30 November 1942.

39. Letter to Chapin, 14 November 1942.

40. "Walter Conducts Trio of 'Seconds,' " *New York Times*, 17 April 1942.

41. "Forecast and Review," *Modern Music* 19 (May-June 1942): 254.

42. Isabel Morse Jones, "Menuhin, Philharmonic Orchestra," *Los Angeles Times*, 7 January 1944.

43. Letter, Olga Naumoff to Barber, 16 December 1941, Serge Koussevitzky Collection, Library of Congress, Music Division.

44. Letter, 20 March 1942, 166 East 96th Street, New York.

45. Letter, 14 September 1942.

46. Letter, 5 October 1942.

47. Letter, dated incorrectly "Jan 4 - 1942." This must have been 1943—a common error so early after the new year is to forget the calendar year has turned. Barber wrote on U.S. Army letterhead.

48. Letters, Barber to Koussevitzky, 27 November 1944, and to Sidney Homer, 3 January 1945.

49. Information provided by the Philadelphia Orchestra, 18 September 1986.

CHAPTER NINE World Cataclysm 1942–45

1. John Selby, "West Chester Composer Is in the Army Now," *Coatesville Record*, 1942.

2. Letter, Barber to William Strickland, spring 1942, 166 East 96th Street, New York.

3. Letter, Barber to Katherine Chapin, 31 March 1942.

4. Letter, 22 March 1942.

5. Letter, Barber to Chapin, 14 November 1942.

6. Robert Ward, "In the Army Now," *Modern Music* 19 (March-April 1942): 168.

7. Ward, "In the Army Now," p. 167.

8. Letters to Strickland, 9 November 1942, and Chapin, 14 November 1942.

9. Letter written after February 1943.

10. Letter, 14 November 1942.

11. Letter to Chapin, 30 November 1942.

12. Letter, 14 November 1942.

13. Letter to Strickland, written after February 1943.

14. The holograph score and corrections are on loan from G. Schirmer to the Sibley Library, Eastman School of Music, Rochester, New York.

15. Frederick Fennell, "Macho Marches," liner notes for Telarc recording DG 10043, 1979.

16. "Band to Play Private Barber's Latest Composition," *West Chester Daily Local News,* 20 May 1943; program, Boston Symphony Orchestra, 29 October 1943, p. 210.

17. Postcard written from Camp Upton, New York, 16 August 1943.

18. Boston Symphony Orchestra program notes, 29–30 October 1943, p. 210.

19. 8 November 1943, Mount Kisco.

20. Moses Smith, "Boston Goes All Out for Premiers," *Modern Music* 21 (January-February 1944): 103–4.

21. Letter to Homer, 11 September 1943.

22. Ibid.

23. Ibid.

24. Ibid.

25. Letter, 27 September 1943.

26. Letter, 16 November 1943.

27. Letter, 29 November 1943.

28. Barber, intermission interview by James Fassett, CBS Symphony Orchestra radio broadcast, 19 June 1949.

29. Barber, interviewed by Eric Salzman, *Hi Fi/Stereo Review* (17 October 1966): 77–89.

30. "Barber's New Symphony," *Boston Globe,* 3 March 1944, p. 22.

31. Letter, 31 January 1944, Capricorn.

32. Letter, 2 February 1944.

33. Letter, Barber to Sidney Homer, 24 February 1944.

34. Letter, 23 February 1944.

35. Laura Haddock, "Boston Hears Symphony Dedicated to the Air Forces," *Christian Science Monitor,* 3 March 1944.

36. Program of the Boston Symphony Orchestra, 3 March 1944.

37. "Barber's New Symphony Definitely 'On the Beam,'" *Boston Globe,* 3 March 1944, p. 22.

38. Ibid.

39. Ibid. Haddock, "Boston Hears Symphony. . . ," *Christian Science Monitor,* 3 March 1944.

40. "Symphony Hall," *Boston Globe,* 4 March 1944.

41. In "Barber's New Symphony. . . ," 3 March 1944, and "Music," 4 March 1944, *Boston Globe;* and L. A. Sloper, "Barber's Second Symphony at First Hearing," *Christian Science Monitor,* 4 March 1944.

42. "New Barber Work Honors Air Forces," *New York Times,* 10 March 1944.

43. Rudolph Elie, Jr., 4 March 1944.

44. *New York Herald Tribune,* 11 March 1944.
45. Ibid.
46. Letter, 23 February 1944.
47. Letter, 21 March 1944.
48. Letter, 18 March 1944, Headquarters, Army Air Forces Training Command, Fort Worth, Texas.
49. Letter, 31 March 1944, Headquarters, Army Air Forces, Washington, D.C.
50. Ibid.
51. Letter, 18 April 1944.
52. Letter, 24 March 1944.
53. *Boston Globe,* 3 March 1944.
54. Letter, 16 December 1946.
55. Letter to Homer, 10 February 1947.
56. Letter, 7 January 1949.
57. Ibid.
58. Letter to Sidney Homer, April 1949.
59. Program, Philadelphia Orchestra, 21 January 1949.
60. "Curtis Institute Begins Two-Day Music Festival at Academy," *Evening Bulletin,* 6 January 1949.
61. *Musical America,* 15 April 1951.
62. Letter, 15 March 1949.
63. Heinsheimer, "The Composing Composer."
64. Ibid.
65. "Notes on the Program," ed. Klaus G. Roy, Cleveland Orchestra, 8–10 October 1964.
66. Ibid.
67. The compact disk recording on Stradivari Classics SCD 8012 includes, also, *Music for a Scene from Shelley,* Overture to *The School for Scandal,* and the *First Essay*. Schenck has been a champion of Barber's music in general.
68. Letter, Barber to Behrend, 19 September 1938, Camden, Maine.
69. Letter, 18 January 1946.
70. Letter, 17 July 1947, clipping files, American Academy of Rome, New York.
71. The list is in a loose-leaf notebook shown to the author by Valentin Herranz.
72. Letter, 22 May 1944, Mount Kisco.
73. Glenn Plaskin, *Horowitz, A Biography* (New York: William Morrow, 1983), p. 229.
74. Victor Berger, "Horowitz Plays in Rare Manner," 29 March 1945, review in unnamed newspaper, Barber clipping file, New York Public Library, Music Division.
75. Postcard, 22 July 1944, Mount Kisco.
76. Notes from concert program, 8 March 1950, University of New Hampshire.
77. Behrend, interview with author, 1 September 1982.
78. Letter from Barber, 20 June 1943, in Spivacke clipping file, Library of Congress, Music Division.
79. Letter, Spivacke to Barber, 23 June 1943, addressed to 52 Broadway, New York City.

80. "Virtuosity Without Offense," *New York Herald Tribune*, 29 March 1945.

81. Rorem, "Looking for Sam," p. 14.

82. Hitchcock, interviewed by Peter Dickinson, BBC radio broadcast, 23 January 1982.

83. Letter to Henry-Louis de La Grange, 5 December 1945, Mount Kisco.

84. Barber's explanatory note to *Excursions,* G. Schirmer, Inc., 1945.

85. Behrend, interview with author, 1 September 1982, Philadelphia.

86. Sifferman, p. 18.

87. Letter, 24 February 1944, Mount Kisco.

88. Ibid.

89. Saidenberg, interview with author, 7 June 1985, New York.

90. Letter, 27 February 1944, Mount Kisco (Damrosch Collection, New York Public Library, Music Division).

91. Telegram to Army Air Forces Headquarters, quoted in letter from Damrosch to Barber, 13 March 1944.

92. Letter, 21 March 1944, Mount Kisco (Damrosch Collection, New York Library, Music Division).

93. Letter, 24 February 1944, Mount Kisco.

94. Saidenberg, interview with the author, 7 June 1985.

95. A holograph sketch and dated finished score, both in pencil, are at the Library of Congress, Music Division.

96. Robert Horan, ". . . And 3 Modern Young Men Lead a Modern Life in this 'Swiss Chalet,' " *American Home* (July 1946): 36–38.

97. Ibid.

98. Ibid.

99. "Samuel Barber: The Last Interview and the Legacy," part 1, *High Fidelity* (June 1981): 44.

100. Letter, 5 December 1945.

101. Quoted in a letter from Barber to Henry-Louis de La Grange, 5 December 1945.

102. Friedewald, *A Formal and Stylistic Analysis*, p. 207.

103. Reviews: Noel Straus, "Saidenberg Leads Little Symphony," *New York Times*, 9 October 1944, p. 17; and *Musical America* (November 1944): 24.

104. Noel Straus, "Saidenberg Leads Little Symphony," *New York Times*, 9 October 1944, p. 17.

105. Lou Harrison, "Forecast and Review," *Modern Music* 22 (November 1944): 31.

106. See, for example, *Gramophone Shop,* record supplement 12 (April 1949): 2; or Edward Downes, program notes of the New York Philharmonic, 30 June 1966.

107. "Big Names in Chicago," *Modern Music* 22 (January-February 1945): 119.

108. Jerome D. Bohm, "Works of Barber Played by Orchestra," unlabeled newsclipping, 8 October 1944, William Hatton Green Collection, Curtis Institute of Music.

109. Letter, 15 April 1947.

110. Letter to Henry-Louis de la Grange, 5 December 1945.

111. Letter to Gustave Schirmer, 11 June 1946, Hotel de la Ville, Rome.

112. Ibid.

CHAPTER TEN Middle Years

1. Letter, 17 March 1945, Mount Kisco.

2. Garbousova, interview with the author, 28 October 1983.

3. Letters, Barber to Koussevitzky, 28 January 1945; Barber to Homer, 17 March 1945.

4. Raya Garbousova, interview with the author, 28 October 1983.

5. "Orchestral Music," *Notes* 11 (December 1953): 146–47, review of the Schirmer miniature score.

6. Letter, Serge Koussevitzky Collection, Library of Congress, Music Division.

7. Letter, 3 August 1945.

8. Letter, 28 September 1945.

9. Letter, 15 November 1945, Mount Kisco.

10. Letter, 26 November 1945.

11. Letter, 5 December 1945, Mount Kisco.

12. Letter, 4 December 1945, Mount Kisco.

13. Letter, Barber to John Nicholas Brown, 1 March 1946 (collection of Anne S. K. Brown); and Garbousova, interview with the author, 28 October 1983.

14. Garbousova, interview with the author, 30 October 1983.

15. Program, Boston Symphony Orchestra, Season 65, 1945–46, 5 April 1946, p. 1355.

16. Liner notes, London ffrr LPS-332.

17. Warren Storey Smith, "Concerto Has Its Debut Here," *Boston Post,* 6 April 1946.

18. *Boston Globe,* 6 April 1946.

19. "Music," *New York Herald Tribune,* 14 April 1946.

20. Olin Downes, *New York Times,* 2 December 1947.

21. Ibid.

22. Stanley Hollingsworth, telephone conversation with the author, 12 May 1990.

23. Letter, Barber to his family, addressed to Sidney Homer, mailed from Rome, 19 December 1950.

24. David W. Moore, "Guide to Records," *American Records Guide* 42 (June 1979): 16.

25. Cole, telephone conversation with the author.

26. Charles Turner, telephone conversation with the author, 13 December 1983.

27. Garbousova, interview with the author, 28 October 1983.

28. Letter to Homer, 17 March 1945.

29. Ibid.

30. Letter, 14 January 1946.

31. Gruen, *Menotti,* 84; *Opera Quarterly* 6, no. 3 (Spring 1989): 44–45.

32. Letter, Coolidge to Graham, 20 January 1944.

33. Letter, 23 January 1944.

34. Records of the Alice M. Ditson Fund, 1945–46, Columbiana Archives, Columbia University.

35. *Great Performances, Dance in America:* "An Evening of Dance and Conversation with Martha Graham," July 1984. Quoted with permission of the Martha Graham Center and Danmarks Radio.

36. Sketch, 1984 bequest of the Estate of Samuel Barber, Library of Congress, Music Division.

37. Letter, 26 November 1945.

38. Letter, 17 December 1945.

39. Letter, 5 December 1945.

40. Letter to Jeanne Behrend, 18 January 1946.

41. Letter, 14 January 1946.

42. Letter, 1 March 1946.

43. Program from Columbia University Music Festival, 10 May 1946.

44. Program from the Second Annual Festival, 10–13 May 1946, Columbiana Archives, Columbia University.

45. McDonagh, *Martha Graham: A Biography* (New York: Praeger, 1973), p. 190.

46. R. Sabin, "Martha Graham Presents New Work 'Serpent Heart,' with Score by Samuel Barber, at Columbia Festival," *Dance Observer* (June-July 1946): 73.

47. Ibid.

48. "Barber Ballet Has Premier," *New York Times,* 11 May 1946.

49. Robert Horan, "The Recent Theater of Martha Graham," *Dance Index* 6 (1947): 15.

50. Donald Fuller, "Columbia's Festival: Hindemith's *Lilacs,*" *Modern Music* 23 (Summer 1946): 200.

51. Letter, 10 February 1947, Mount Kisco.

52. Ibid. A holograph of the score is at the Library of Congress, Music Division.

53. Letter, 21 December 1947.

54. G. Schirmer Study Score No. 53, *Medea,* 1949.

55. Letter, Barber to Sidney Homer, 21 December 1947.

56. Elizabeth Emerson Stine, "Pressler, 19, Pianist Is Acclaimed in Appearance with Orchestra," *Philadelphia Bulletin,* 6 December 1947.

57. Linton Martin, "Palestinian Soloist With Orchestra," *Philadelphia Inquirer,* 6 December 1947.

58. Thomson, "Music," *New York Herald Tribune,* 9 December 1947.

59. Letter to La Grange, 30 January 1948.

60. Thomson, "Music," *New York Herald Tribune,* 9 December 1947.

61. Letter to his family, 23 February 1951, "written while on a train going through the Russian zone—Berlin-Frankfurt," collection of Katharine Homer Fryer.

62. *Medea's Meditation and Dance of Vengeance* (New York: G. Schirmer, 1955).

63. Ibid.

64. "Medea by Barber," *Time* (13 February 1956): 42.

65. Letter, 15 April 1947.

66. Ibid.

67. Barber, interviewed by James Fassett, CBS Symphony Orchestra premiere broadcast of *Knoxville: Summer of 1915,* 19 June 1949.

68. Letter, 15 April 1947.

69. Eleanor Steber, interview with the author, 2 September 1983. Unless otherwise indicated, all quotations and information attributed to Eleanor Steber in this book are taken from this interview.

70. Ibid.

71. Ramey, "Samuel Barber at Seventy," p. 20.
72. Telegram, 9 April 1947.
73. Draft of telegram sent 10 April 1947.
74. Letter, 15 April 1947.
75. Steber, interview with the author.
76. Ibid.
77. Letter, 11 October 1947.
78. Draft of telegram, 22 October 1947.
79. Letter to Koussevitzky, 28 October 1947.
80. Program, New York Philharmonic, 12 November 1959.
81. Letter, 1 April 1948.
82. *Newsweek,* 19 April 1948, p. 85.
83. Ibid.
84. John W. Riley, *Boston Globe,* 10 April 1948.
85. Cable to Barber, 9 April 1948.
86. Letter to Koussevitzky, 26 April 1948.
87. Letter, Barber to Homer, 7 January 1949.
88. Letter, 9 January 1949.
89. Letter, 29 April 1950.
90. Letter, May 1951, Winter Park.
91. Steber, interview with the author.
92. Price, interviewed by Robert Sherman, WQXR, The Listening Room, 30 September 1978.
93. Letter, Charles Turner to Eleanor Steber, 23 January 1983.
94. David Diamond, review of vocal score, *Notes* (March 1950): 309.
95. Glenn Dillard Gunn, "New Barber Sonata Played by Horowitz," *Washington Times-Herald,* 11 January 1950.
96. Letter, Barber to Claire Reis, 31 December 1965, League of Composers Collection, New York Public Library, Music Division; letter from Barber to Homer, 29 April 1950.
97. Alan Rich, "Khrushchev Talks of Modern Music," *New York Times,* 14 April 1962.
98. Glenn Plaskin, *Horowitz* (New York: William Morrow, 1983), p. 229.
99. "The Curse of Being Horowitz," *New York Times,* 23 November 1975.
100. Postcard, 1 December 1947.
101. Letter, 21 December 1947, Capricorn.
102. Letter to Sidney Homer, 14 April 1948, the American Academy, Porta San Pancrazio, Rome.
103. Barber, interviewed by Robert Sherman, WQXR, 30 September 1978.
104. John Browning, "Samuel Barber's Nocturne, Op. 33," *Clavier* (January 1986): 20.
105. Plaskin, *Horowitz,* p. 229.
106. Cited ibid.
107. Letter, 7 January 1949, Mount Kisco.
108. Letter to Homer, written after 22 January 1949, Mount Kisco.
109. Letter, 8 April 1949, Winter Park.
110. Interview with Robert Sherman, WQXR, 30 September 1978.
111. Cited in Plaskin, *Horowitz,* p. 229.
112. Letter, 9 July 1949, Capricorn.

113. Letter, Barber to Homer, 17 January 1950.
114. Gunn, *Washington Times-Herald.*
115. Richard Keith, "New Barber Sonata Done by Horowitz," *Washington Post,* 11 January, 1950.
116. Letter, 21 January 1950.
117. Letter, February 1950.
118. Olin Downes, "Horowitz Offers Barber's Sonata," *New York Times,* 25 January 1950.
119. *Cleveland Plain Dealer,* 7 January 1950.
120. *Atlanta Constitution,* 28 February 1950.
121. Ardoin, "Samuel Barber at Capricorn," p. 5.
122. Review of 1950 edition, N. G. L., *Music Review* 11 (November 1950): 329.
123. This excerpt of Poulenc's diary of his American tour appeared in the Parisian paper *La Table ronde* (June 1950) and was translated by Barber for the *West Chester Daily Local News.*
124. Letter, 26 July 1949.
125. Letter, Barber to Homer, 28 January 1951, Paris.
126. Letter, Homer to Barber, 2 April 1950.

CHAPTER ELEVEN Composer as Conductor

1. Letter to Homer, 29 September 1950.
2. Ibid.
3. Permanent Record Card No. 2, record of private lessons, Curtis Institute of Music.
4. Review in the *Vienna Herald,* 16 February 1934, cited in *Overtones,* 1933–34, pp. 78–79.
5. Letter, 20 October 1944.
6. Letter, 30 October 1944.
7. Letter to Koussevitzky, 27 November 1944, Capricorn.
8. Letter, Barber to Koussevitzky, 21 April 1945.
9. Ibid. For reviews of this concert, see *Capricorn Concerto* in chapter 9 above.
10. Letter, 29 September 1950.
11. Letter, 4 October 1950, Winter Park.
12. Letter, 29 September 1950, Capricorn.
13. Letter to Barber's family, 20 November 1950, Copenhagen.
14. Letter to Barber's family, 24 November 1950, Copenhagen.
15. Letter to Barber's family, 1 December 1950, Copenhagen.
16. Ibid.
17. Ibid.
18. Ibid.
19. Letter, 7 December 1950, London.
20. Letter to Barber's family, 24 November 1950, Copenhagen.
21. Ibid.
22. Letter to Barber's family, 7 December 1950, Bayswater Road, London.

23. Ibid.
24. Letter to Barber's family, 19 December 1950, Hotel Hassler, Rome.
25. Ibid.
26. Ibid.
27. Ibid.
28. Letter, Malko to Strickland, 13 December 1950, London, Kingsway Hall.
29. Letter to Barber's family, 10 January 1951.
30. Ibid.
31. Letter to Barber's family, 13 January 1951.
32. Ibid.
33. Letter, Barber to his family, 28 January 1951, Paris.
34. Ibid.
35. Letter to his family, 8 February 1951, Chez Henry-Louis de La Grange, Paris.
36. Ibid.
37. Turner, telephone discussion with the author, 14 January 1989.
38. Letter to his family, 8 February 1951, Chez Henry-Louis de La Grange, Paris.
39. Ibid.
40. Ibid.
41. Ibid.
42. Letter to Barber's family, 23 February 1951, written while on a train going through the Russian zone—Berlin to Frankfurt.
43. Ibid.
44. Letter, 29 April 1951, Mount Kisco.
45. Letter, 14 September 1951, Mount Kisco.
46. Undated letter, probably written in the autumn of 1952.
47. Quoted in Kozinn, "Samuel Barber: The Last Interview and the Legacy," part 1, p. 46.

CHAPTER TWELVE Song Cycles

1. Letter, 17 January 1950.
2. Letter, Homer to Barber, February 1950.
3. Letter, 2 April 1950.
4. Letter, Barber to Strickland, 25 October 1949.
5. Letter, January 1950.
6. Barber, interviewed by Sherman, WQXR, The Listening Room, 30 September 1978.
7. Barber, interviewed by Phillip Ramey, liner notes, "The Songs of Samuel Barber," 1978.
8. Interview, WQXR, 30 September 1978.
9. *West Chester Daily Local News,* 12 May 1946.
10. Letter, Barber to Strickland, January 1950.
11. Interview with Ramey, liner notes, "The Songs of Samuel Barber."
12. Letter, Barber to Sidney Homer, 29 April 1950, Capricorn.

13. Letter to Sidney Homer, 29 April 1951. The dates of completion are on the holographs.
14. Letter, Barber to his family, 8 March 1951, Hotel Pont Royal, Paris.
15. Ibid.
16. Barber, WQXR, 30 September 1978.
17. Letter, Barber to his family, 8 March 1951.
18. Letter to Homer, 29 April 1951, Mount Kisco.
19. "Current Chronicle," *Musical Quarterly* 38 (July 1952): 436–37.
20. *New York Times,* 11 February 1952.
21. Letter, 13 February 1952.
22. Letter to Strickland, May 1952.
23. Henahan, "I've Been Composing All My Life," p. 24.
24. Charles Turner, interview with the author, 20 February 1987.
25. Letter, 3 February 1952, Capricorn.
26. Letter, 14 May 1952, Capricorn.
27. Letter to his family, 4 July 1952, Cannes.
28. Ibid.
29. Ibid.
30. Letter to Barber's family, 11 July 1952, La Casarella, Calvi, Corsica.
31. Ibid.
32. Letter to Barber's family, 17 July 1952, La Casarella, Calvi, Corsica.
33. Ibid.
34. Letter, 17 August 1952, Villa Waldeck, Gstaad, Switzerland.
35. Ibid.
36. Ibid.
37. Letter, Barber to Homer, 18 November 1952, Capricorn.
38. Todd Bolender, telephone interview with the author, 11 July 1987. Unless otherwise indicated, all quotations and information attributed to Bolender in this book are taken from this interview.
39. Ray Ericson, "Collections and Miscellany," *High Fidelity* (July 1954): 54, review of the Gold and Fizdale recording (Columbia ML 4855).
40. Unsigned review, "Gold and Fizdale Offer Music for 2 Pianos," *New York Times,* 12 March 1953, p. 23.
41. C. J. Luten, "Wonderful Teamwork," *American Record Guide* (May 1954): 284.
42. "Recitals of the Week: Piano Duets," *London Times,* 15 December 1952, p. 9.
43. Bolender, interview with the author.
44. Ibid.
45. Letter, undated, probably November 1952.
46. Letter, 5 May 1953.
47. "Ballet Suite, Op. 28," *Musical Opinion* (August 1954): 651.
48. Bolender, interview with the author.
49. NBC press release, 12 January 1959, for a forthcoming television premiere of the ballet.
50. "The Vamp Puts on Ballet Shoes," *New York Post,* 17 November 1955.
51. Robert Sabin, "New York City Ballet," *Musical America* (1 December 1955): 5.
52. Letter to Homer, 18 November 1952, Capricorn.

53. Letter, 14 May 1952, Capricorn.

54. Letter, 4 July 1952, Cannes.

55. Letter to Homer, 4 July 1952, Cannes.

56. Holographs of all the *Hermit Songs* are in the Elizabeth Sprague Coolidge Collection at the Library of Congress, Music Division.

57. Edited by Philip Schuyler Allen, University of North Carolina Press, 1928, rpt. 1969.

58. London: Kegan Paul, 1951; rev. ed., Penguin Classics, 1986.

59. New York: Viking; London: Jonathan Cape, 1938.

60. Letter, 5 May 1953.

61. Letter to Strickland, 19 July 1953, Capricorn.

62. *The Paris Diary of Ned Rorem* (New York: Braziller, 1966), p. 72.

63. Letters, Mrs. Willem Willecke, music director of South Mountain Association, to Harold Spivacke and to Barber, 14 June 1954; and Barber to Spivacke, 6 July 1954. All this correspondence is in the Old Correspondence Collection at the Library of Congress, Music Division.

64. Jay Harrison, *New York Herald Tribune,* 15 November 1954.

65. Gruen, "Where Has Samuel Barber Been?"

66. Price, BBC broadcast, 23 January 1982.

67. Letter, 27 October 1953, Papers and Records of William Schuman, New York Public Library, Music Division.

68. Perry Wolfe, telephone interview with the author, 10 June 1986. Unless otherwise indicated, all quotations and information attributed to Wolfe in this chapter are taken from this interview.

69. Herbert Harris, interview with the author, 20 May 1986, New York City. Unless otherwise indicated, all quotations and information attributed to Harris in this chapter are taken from this interview.

70. Wolfe, interview with the author.

71. Harris, interview with the author.

72. The holograph at the Library of Congress is dated at the end.

73. Samuel Baron, interview with the author, 18 July 1985.

74. Wolfe, interview with the author.

75. Harris, interview with the author.

CHAPTER THIRTEEN Searches

1. Letter, probably written spring 1953, Rome.

2. Letter from Barber quoted in program notes of the Boston Symphony Orchestra, 3 December 1954, p. 330.

3. Translated by Forrest Williams and Stanley Maron (New York: Philosophical Library, 1949).

4. Excerpts from Barber's letter quoted in program notes of the New Orleans Philharmonic–Symphony Orchestra, 12 April 1966.

5. *The Journals of Søren Kierkegaard,* a selection ed. and trans. by Alexander Dru (London: Oxford University Press, 1938, 1951), pp. 217, 361.

6. Prayer, trans. Walter Lowrie (Oxford University Press, 1940), p. 259.

7. Søren Kierkegaard, *For Self-Examination* and *Judge for Yourselves and Three Discourses* 1851, trans. Walter Lowrie, except for the final discourse, "The Unchangeableness of God," trans. David F. Swenson (Princeton University Press, 1944; London: Humphrey Milford, Oxford University Press), p. 227.

8. Translated by David Swenson, in *For Self-Examination,* p. 227.

9. Review by Nathan Broder, *Musical Quarterly* 41 (April 1955): 228.

10. Letter to Leonard Burkat, autumn 1954, Capricorn, in Leonard Burkat Papers, Yale University Library, New Haven.

11. Undated letter, autumn 1954, from Capricorn, in Leonard Burkat Papers, Yale University Library, New Haven.

12. Letter, January 1955, Capricorn.

13. Olin Downes, "Münch Conducts Work by Barber," *New York Times,* 9 December 1954.

14. Paul Henry Lang, "Music: Boston Symphony," *New York Herald Tribune,* 9 December 1954.

15. Letter to Strickland, January 1955, Capricorn.

16. Letter, 15 February 1955, Capricorn.

17. Ibid.

18. Barber's travel log, April 26 to June 26, 1955, p. 1, in collection of Valentin Herranz.

19. Ibid., pp. 2 and 5.

20. Ibid., p. 7.

21. Ibid., p. 8.

22. Ibid.

23. Ibid., p. 9.

24. Ibid.

25. Letter to Charles Münch, 29 June 1955, Capri, Leonard Burkat Papers, Yale University Library.

26. *New York Times,* 21 September 1953.

27. Karl Haas, president of the society, quoted in "Samuel Barber Commissioned by Detroiters," *Detroit News,* 18 October 1953.

28. Samuel Baron's journal of the New York Woodwind Quintet, 12 January 1955, Samuel Baron Collection, Library of Congress, Music Division.

29. Ibid., 12 January 1955.

30. Ibid., 31 October 1955.

31. Ibid., 14 November 1955.

32. Ibid., 25 November 1955.

33. Josef Mossman, "World Premiere Here to Break Precedents: Unique Concert Full of Firsts," *Detroit News,* 16 March 1956.

34. Program, Chamber Music Society of Detroit, 20 March 1956. Courtesy of the Detroit Public Library.

35. Josef Mossman, "Quintet Given an Encore in Its World Premiere," *Detroit News,* 21 March 1956, p. 24.

36. Baron, journal, 5 April 1956.

37. "Two Premieres Mark Woodwind Concert," *New York Times,* 17 November 1956.

38. Oliver Daniel, "Bloch, Ben-Haim, Barber and Dahl," *Saturday Review,* 12 December 1959.

39. Ibid.

40. Kozinn, "Samuel Barber: The Last Interview and the Legacy," part 2, p. 47.

CHAPTER FOURTEEN *Vanessa*

1. Howard Taubman, " 'Vanessa' at the 'Met,' " *New York Times*, 26 January 1958.
2. Letter, 7 November 1956, Papers and Records of William Schuman, New York Public Library, Music Division.
3. Jay Harrison, "Samuel Barber Discusses 'Vanessa,' " *New York Herald Tribune*, 12 January 1958, p. 6.
4. Coleman, "Samuel Barber and *Vanessa*," p. 86.
5. Letter, 14 September 1942, 166 East 96th St., New York.
6. Barber to Sidney Homer, 24 February 1944, Mount Kisco.
7. Letter, 10 February 1947, Capricorn.
8. Hans Heinsheimer, "*Vanessa* Revisited," *Opera News* (May 1978): 24.
9. Ibid., p. 25.
10. Letter to the author from Stephen Spender, 29 November 1983.
11. Coleman, "Samuel Barber and *Vanessa*," p. 88.
12. Letter, 24 April 1952, Capricorn.
13. Barber, "On Waiting for a Libretto," p. 6.
14. F. M. [Frank Merkling], "Two Worlds," *Opera News* (27 January 1958): 9.
15. Barber, "On Waiting for a Libretto," p. 6.
16. Letter, 18 November 1952, Capricorn.
17. Barber, "On Waiting for a Libretto," p. 6.
18. Coleman, "Samuel Barber and *Vanessa*," p. 86.
19. Barber, "On Waiting for a Libretto," p. 6.
20. Barber's travel log, p. 8.
21. Letter to Olga Koussevitzky, 29 June 1955, "Villa Tuoro," Capri, and Barber's travel log, p. 8.
22. Barber, "On Waiting for a Libretto," p. 6.
23. M[erkling], "Two Worlds," p. 9.
24. Introduction, *Vanessa*, piano-vocal score (G. Schirmer, 1964).
25. M[erkling], "Two Worlds," p. 9.
26. The first draft of the libretto with holograph corrections and changes by Barber and Menotti is at the Library of Congress, Music Division.
27. Barber, "On Waiting for a Libretto," p. 6.
28. Samuel Barber, "Birth Pangs of a First Opera," *New York Times*, 12 January 1958, sec. 2, p. 9.
29. Jay Harrison, "Samuel Barber Discusses 'Vanessa,' " p. 6.
30. Menotti, interviewed on WETA, broadcast 23 July 1989.
31. Louis Calta, "Menotti Writes a 4-Act Libretto," *New York Times*, 7 January 1956.
32. Turner, interview with the author.
33. Barber, "Birth Pangs of a First Opera."
34. Ibid.

35. Ross Parmenter, " 'Met' to Present American Opera," *New York Times*, 6 November 1956, p. 31.

36. John Gruen, "Where Has Samuel Barber Been?" p. 15.

37. "Met Premiere for 'Vanessa,' " *New York Tribune*, 14 March 1957; and "2 Noted Singers Signed by Met," *New York Times*, 23 March 1957.

38. Ibid.

39. Letter to Nikolai Malko, 27 April 1957, Mount Kisco, Pierpont Morgan Library, Mary Flagler Cary Music Collection.

40. Heinsheimer, "The Composing Composer," pp. 4–7.

41. Letters, Barber to Grace Martin, 27 April 1957, and to Manfred Ibel, undated.

42. "Miracle on 39th Street," *Opera News* (27 January 1958): 15.

43. Turner, interview with the author.

44. Barber, "Birth Pangs of a First Opera."

45. Eleanor Steber, interview with the author, 1 September 1983.

46. Ibid.

47. Barber, "Birth Pangs of a First Opera."

48. Steber, interview with the author, 1 September 1983.

49. Ibid.

50. Intermission interview by John Gutman, Metropolitan Opera radio broadcast of *Vanessa*, 1 February 1958, WQXR.

51. "Violets in the Snow: Cecil Beaton," *Opera News* (27 January 1958): 20.

52. Letter, Barber to Homer, 28 November 1950, Hotel Angleterre, Copenhagen.

53. *Vanessa* (New York: G. Schirmer, 1964), p. 1.

54. "Violets in the Snow," pp. 20–21.

55. "Barber, Menotti, and *Vanessa*," *Saturday Review* (25 January 1958): 41.

56. "New York Acclaims 'Vanessa,' " *London Times*, 19 January 1958.

57. " 'Vanessa' Opens at Met," *New York Herald Tribune*, 16 January 1958, p. 10.

58. Miles Kastendieck, "American Opera a Triumph," *New York Journal American*, 16 January 1958; Robert J. Landry, "Met Opera With 'Vanessa' Makes It Big Except in Diction Department," *Variety*, 22 January 1958.

59. Kastendieck, *New York Journal American*, 16 January 1958.

60. Paul Henry Lang, *New York Herald Tribune*, 16 January 1958.

61. Ibid.

62. "Musical Events," 25 January 1958.

63. Barber, "Birth Pangs of a First Opera."

64. Speech delivered on 5 December 1958 by Allan Nevins. The citation was written by Douglas Moore, Papers of Samuel Barber, American Academy and Institute of Arts and Letters.

65. Everett Helm, " 'Vanessa' in Salzburg," *Saturday Review* (13 September 1958): 65.

66. Ibid.

67. Ibid. Howard Taubman, " 'Vanessa' Again," *New York Times*, 18 January 1959, sec. 2, p. 9.

68. Helm, " 'Vanessa' in Salzburg," p. 65.

69. *New York Times*, 24 August 1958.

70. Helm, " 'Vanessa' in Salzburg," p. 65.

71. Ernst Thomas, "Amerika auf den Salzburger Festspielen," *Frankfurter Allgemeine Zeitung,* 19 August 1958, p. 8; Helm, " 'Vanessa' in Salzburg," p. 65; Hubalek, " 'Vanessa', die Plüschoper aus Amerika," *Wien Arbeiter-Zeitung,* 19 August 1958; " 'Vanessa' Criticized," *New York Times,* 19 August 1958.

72. Helm, " 'Vanessa' in Salzburg," p. 66.

73. Thomas, "Amerika auf den Salzburger Festspielen," p. 8.

74. "Mail Pouch: *Vanessa,*" *New York Times,* 15 February 1959, sec. 2, p. 9.

75. K. H. Ruppel, "Salzburger Plüsch, Europäische Erstaufführung von Barbers 'Vanessa' bei den Festspielen," clipping from unnamed paper, shown to the author by Manfred Ibel.

76. Henrik Kralik, "Barbers 'Vanessa'—eine Konzession an das Publikum," *Die Presse,* 19 August 1958.

77. Ibid.

78. " 'Met' Gastspiel in Salzburg: Europa-Premiere der Oper " 'Vanessa,' " *Hamburger Abendblatt,* 18 August 1959, p. 5. Author's translation.

79. Metropolitan Opera press release to Miles Kastendieck, in Metropolitan Opera Association Archives.

80. Ibid.

81. Ibid.

82. "Teatri e concerti," *Musica d'oggi* (July-August 1961): 177–79. Trans. Richard Frank, cited in Hennessee, *Samuel Barber: A Bio-Bibliography,* p. 179.

83. Letter, 3 November 1963, Capricorn, in Metropolitan Opera Association Archives.

84. Michael Kimmelman, "Updating 'Vanessa' in St. Louis," *New York Times,* 14 June 1988.

85. Ibid. Peter Herb, of G. Schirmer, Inc., reports that there are plans for publishing *Vanessa* with the reduced instrumentation.

CHAPTER FIFTEEN Interlude

1. Letter, Richard Roeckelein to the author, 8 February 1989.

2. Ibid.

3. George Pullen Jackson, "The Story of the Sacred Harp, 1844–1944," in *The Sacred Harp,* facsimile edition of the 1860 imprint (Nashville: Broadman Press, 1968), pp. v–xx.

4. Ibid.

5. Letter to the author, 8 February 1989.

6. Browning, "Samuel Barber's Nocturne," p. 21.

7. Gruen, *Menotti,* p. 138. Menotti himself contributed several pseudonymous works to *Album Leaves* between 1959–62 (see John Ardoin, *The Stages of Menotti,* "Chronology," compiled and annotated by Joel Honig [New York: Doubleday, 1985], p. 240).

8. Sidney Finkelstein, "Samuel Barber," liner notes for Vanguard VRS 1065.

9. Ardoin, *Stages of Menotti,* p. 103.

10. Victor Yellin, "Samuel Barber," *Notes* 18 (September 1961): 641.

11. *Philadelphia Bulletin,* 5 October 1960.

12. Ibid.

13. Joseph Whiteford, head of Aeolian Skinner, quoted in *Philadelphia Inquirer,* 10 October 1960.

14. Edwin H. Schloss, program, Philadelphia Orchestra, 30 September 1960.

15. Paul Callaway, telephone interview with the author, September 1987.

16. Samuel Singer, "Philadelphia Dedicates New $150,000 Organ," *Musical Courier* (November 1960): 20.

17. Max de Schauensee, "Orchestra Opens Its 61st Season," *Philadelphia Bulletin,* 1 October 1960.

18. Edwin Schloss, *Philadelphia Inquirer,* 1 October 1960.

19. Max de Schauensee, *Philadelphia Bulletin,* 1 October 1960.

20. Letter, Barber to Spivacke, 10 November 1960 (this and all subsequent correspondence between Barber and Spivacke cited below are at the Library of Congress).

21. Letter, Spivacke to Barber, 21 November 1960.

22. Letter to Harold Spivacke, 29 April 1961, Capricorn.

23. Letter, 3 December 1979, Philadelphia Orchestra Archives.

CHAPTER SIXTEEN Lincoln Center Commissions

1. Program, Cleveland Orchestra, 24 January 1964, p. 395.

2. Heinsheimer, interview with the author, 21 November 1985.

3. Ardoin, "Samuel Barber at Capricorn," p. 5.

4. Browning, "Samuel Barber's Nocturne," p. 20.

5. Barber, interviewed by Jay Harrison, program, Cleveland Orchestra, p. 395.

6. Browning, interview with the author, 22 April 1986, New York.

7. Ibid.

8. Ibid.

9. Ibid.

10. Alan Rich, "Khrushchev Talks of Modern Music," *New York Times,* 14 April 1962; *West Chester Daily Local News,* 16 April 1962.

11. Ibid.

12. *Philharmonic Hall Program,* 1962–63, 24 September 1962, p. 44.

13. Browning, interview with the author, 22 April 1986, New York.

14. Ibid.

15. Browning, interviewed by Martin Bookspan, CBS broadcast of intermission of New York Philharmonic concert, 23 January 1983 (with Eleanor Steber and Phillip Ramey).

16. Browning, interview with the author, 22 April 1986.

17. Ibid.

18. Harold Schonberg, "Music: Barber Concerto," *New York Times,* 25 September 1962.

19. Letter, 3 October 1962, Mount Kisco, Papers and Records of William Schuman, New York Public Library, Music Division.

20. Miles Kastendieck, "Barber Concerto Scores a Hit," *New York Journal-American,* 25 September 1962, p. 20.

21. Louis Biancolli, "Erich Leinsdorf at Lincoln Center," *New York World Telegram and Sun,* 25 September 1962, p. 20.

22. Kastendieck, "Barber Concerto."

23. Ibid.

24. Browning, interviewed by Thomas Cassidy, KFAC, Los Angeles, 20 August 1965.

25. "John Browning," *Current Biography* (May 1969): 10.

26. *New York Times,* 7 May 1963.

27. "Britten, Barber Win Music Awards," *New York Post,* 20 May 1964.

28. Paul Henry Lang, "Boston Symphony," *New York Herald Tribune,* 25 September 1962, p. 16.

29. Sketchbook, Library of Congress, p. 13. Kreiling discusses this work in her dissertation, *The Songs of Samuel Barber: A Study in Literary Taste and Text-Setting* (University of North Carolina at Chapel Hill, 1985), pp. 54–59.

30. Barber, Introduction, *Andromache's Farewell,* G. Schirmer, Inc., 1963.

31. Patrick Creagh, letter to the author, 8 December 1988.

32. Ibid.

33. Martina Arroyo, interview with the author, 28 November 1987, New York City.

34. Ibid.

35. Ibid.

36. Ibid.

37. Ibid.

38. Harriet Johnson, *New York Post,* 5 April 1963; Paul Henry Lang, *New York Herald Tribune,* 5 April 1963; Louis Biancolli, *New York World Telegram and Sun,* 5 April 1963; Miles Kastendieck, *New York Journal American,* 5 April 1963.

39. Harriet Johnson, "Barber's 'Andromache' in Premiere," *New York Post,* 5 April 1963; Miles Kastendieck, "Schippers Unveils Latest by Barber," *New York Journal American,* 5 April 1963; Louis Biancolli, "New Barber Work Hailed at Premiere," *New York World Telegram and Sun,* 5 April 1963.

40. "Music: Schippers Guest Conductor of Philharmonic," *New York Times,* 5 April 1963, p. 30.

41. *New York Times,* 5 April 1963; *Saturday Review,* 20 April 1963.

42. "Musical Events: The Main Stream," *New Yorker,* 13 April 1963.

CHAPTER SEVENTEEN A New Opera House

1. Jan Meyerowitz, "Aus dem Musikleben," *Musica* 21 (July-August 1967): 176.

2. Ibid.

3. Letter, Rudolf Bing to Barber, 15 December 1959, Metropolitan Opera Association Archives.

4. Hans W. Heinsheimer, "Birth of an Opera," *Saturday Review* (17 September 1966): 50.

5. Klein, "Birth of an Opera," p. 32.

6. Letter, Spender to the author, 29 November 1983.
7. Klein, "Birth of an Opera," p. 32.
8. Ibid.
9. Letter to Barber, 1 June 1964, Papers and Records of William Schuman, New York Public Library, Music Division.
10. Menotti, interviewed on "Samuel Barber Retrospective," BBC broadcast, 23 January 1982.
11. Katharine Fryer's diary entry of 19 June 1960.
12. Menotti, BBC broadcast, 23 January 1982.
13. Andrew Porter, "Antony's Second Chance," *Music of Three Seasons: 1974–1977* (New York: Farrar, Straus, and Giroux, 1978), pp. 97–98.
14. Eric Salzman, "Samuel Barber," *HiFi/Stereo Review* (October 1966): 86.
15. Ibid.
16. Klein, "Birth of an Opera," p. 32.
17. Ibid.
18. Heinsheimer, "Birth of an Opera," p. 56.
19. Manfred Ibel, interview with the author, 10 April 1987.
20. Heinsheimer, "Birth of an Opera," p. 56.
21. Katharine Fryer, notes from telephone conversation with Barber ca. July 1964.
22. Heinsheimer, "Birth of an Opera," p. 57.
23. Ibid.
24. Notes dated April 1966, telephone conversation between Barber and Katharine Fryer.
25. Ibid.
26. Lee Hoiby, telephone conversation with the author, 5 May 1990.
27. Klein, "Birth of an Opera," p. 109.
28. Salzman, "Samuel Barber," p. 86.
29. Klein, "Birth of an Opera," p. 109.
30. Richard Dyer, liner notes, *Antony and Cleopatra,* New World Records, NW 322-24, 1984.
31. Hollingsworth, telephone conversation with the author, 12 May 1990.
32. Klein, "Birth of an Opera," p. 110.
33. Emily Coleman, "Leontyne Makes a Date with History," *New York Times,* 11 September 1966, sec. 2, p. 21.
34. Klein, "Birth of an Opera," p. 109.
35. Ibid.
36. Ibid., p. 107; "Make Mingle with Our Tambourines," *Opera News* 31 (17 September 1966): 35.
37. Klein, "Birth of an Opera," p. 107. In contrast, the old opera house had seventy feet of stage from proscenium arch to the rear wall.
38. Schonberg, *New York Times,* 17 September 1966.
39. Charlotte Curtis, "First Lady Adds to Glitter," *New York Times,* 17 September 1966, pp. 1 and 16.
40. Franco Zeffirelli, *Zeffirelli: An Autobiography* (New York: Weidenfeld and Nicolson, 1986), p. 220.
41. Price, interviewed by Peter Dickinson, "Samuel Barber Retrospective," BBC broadcast, 23 January 1982.

42. Klein, "Birth of an Opera," p. 107.

43. Robert Sussman Stewart, "Franco Zeffirelli," *New York Times Magazine* (2 September 1966): 16.

44. Gruen, "Where Has Samuel Barber Been?" p. 15; Hans Heinsheimer, "Adagio for Sam," *Opera News* (14 March 1981): 31.

45. Gruen, "Where Has Samuel Barber Been?" p. 15.

46. Zeffirelli, *Zeffirelli,* p. 219.

47. Herbert Kupferberg, "Barber, the Bard, and the Barge," *Atlantic* (September 1966): 126–29.

48. Gruen, "Where Has Samuel Barber Been?" pp. 15 and 21.

49. Alan Rich, "Barber's Opera: Slick and Chic," *New York/World Journal Tribune,* 2 October 1966, p. 24. See also Sydney Edwards, "Paste amid the Diamonds," *Music and Musicians* 15 (November 1966): 20–21; Roland Gelatt, "New Wine in Old Bottles," *Reporter* 35 (November 1966): 57; Irving Kolodin, "Music to My Ears: Barber's Antony, after Zeffirelli," *Saturday Review* (1 October 1967): 35–36; Lord Harewood, "The New Metropolitan," *Opera* 17 (November 1966): 841–45; James Ringo, "B's A and C," *American Record Guide* (May 1967): 871–72; Winthrop Sargeant, "Musical Events," *New Yorker* (24 September 1966): 114; "Tony and Cleo," *Newsweek* (26 September 1966): 98; Kevin Kelly, "Too Few Arias, Too Late," *Boston Globe* (18 September 1966).

50. Harold C. Schonberg, "Onstage, It Was 'Antony and Cleopatra,' " *New York Times,* 17 September 1966.

51. "Diva Sang for the Old Met Ghosts," *Life* (30 September 1966): 36.

52. Roland Gelatt, "Opening Night at the New Met," *Musical America* 16 (November 1966): 8–10.

53. Sydney Edwards, "Paste amid the Diamonds," pp. 20–21.

54. Ruby Mercer, "The New Metropolitan: A Gala Opening," *Opera Canada* 7 (December 1966): 16–19; Roland Gelatt, "New Wine in Old Bottles," p. 57; Sydney Edwards, "Paste amid the Diamonds"; Shana Alexander, "Culture's Big Super-Event," *Life,* (30 September 1966).

55. The recording is at the Rodgers and Hammerstein Archives of Recorded Sound.

56. Owen Anderson, *Music Journal* 24 (October 1966): 20.

57. Porter, "Antony's Second Chance," p. 98.

58. Ibid.

59. "Music to My Ears."

60. Ibid.

61. Gruen, "Where Has Samuel Barber Been?" p. 21.

62. Dorle J. Soria, "Artist Life," *Musical America* (September 1974): 5.

63. Fryer's diary entry, 11 September 1966.

64. Letter, 19 September 1966, New York.

65. "Recordings in Review: The Best of Barber and of Price," *Saturday Review* 52 (March 1969): 52.

66. "*Antony and Cleopatra* Scenes Please Philharmonic Audience," *New York Times,* 11 December 1971, p. 22.

67. Letter to Turner, 2 June 1972, Festival of Two Worlds, Spoleto.

68. "Revision Underway," *Musical America* (September 1974): 5–6.

69. Hollingsworth, telephone conversation with the author, 12 May 1990.

70. Letter, 31 October 1974, New York.

71. Menotti, interviewed by Peter Dickinson, "Samuel Barber Retrospective," BBC broadcast, 23 January 1982.

72. Donal Henahan, "Juilliard Rehabilitating 'Antony and Cleopatra,'" *New York Times,* 8 February 1975.

73. Soria, "Artist Life," p. 6.

74. Porter, "Antony's Second Chance," p. 101.

75. Henahan, "Juilliard Rehabilitating 'Antony and Cleopatra.'"

76. See Hitchcock, *Music in the United States,* pp. 285–311; and Eric Salzman, *Twentieth-Century Music* (Englewood Cliffs: Prentice Hall, 1988), pp. 166–90.

77. Kate Hevner Mueller, *Twenty-Seven Major American Symphony Orchestras: A History and Analysis of Their Repertoires, Seasons 1842–43 through 1969–70* (Bloomington: Indiana University Studies), p. xxx.

78. New World Records NW 322-24, 1984.

79. Leonardo Pinzuti, "Per amore di quella regina 'Antony and Cleopatra' di Barber a Spoleto," *La nazione,* 27 June 1983. I am grateful to Fred J. Nichols for his translations of all the Italian sources quoted here.

80. Erasmo Valente, "A Spoleto rinasce Cleopatra," *L'unità,* 27 June 1983.

81. Teodoro Celli, "Ecco la prima donna fatale," *Il messagero,* 27 June 1983.

82. Valente, *L'unità.*

83. Celli, *Il messagero.*

84. Celli, *Il messagero;* Enrico Cavallotti, "Ma allora è vivo e vegeto il melodramma oltre oceano," *Il tempo,* 27 June 1983; and Pinzuti, *La nazione.*

85. Cavallotti, *Il tempo.*

86. Ibid.

87. Ibid.

CHAPTER EIGHTEEN The Last Years

1. Menotti, interview with Peter Dickinson, BBC broadcast, 23 January 1982.

2. Heinsheimer, interview with Peter Dickinson, BBC broadcast, 23 January 1982.

3. "Adagio for Sam," p. 31.

4. Postcard to Katharine Homer Fryer, 4 April 1967, Mount Kisco.

5. Letter, 31 October 1974, New York.

6. Letter, Ormandy to Franklin S. Roberts, 22 March 1967.

7. Letter to Barber, 20 December 1967.

8. Robert Graves, "A Last Poem," "In the Wilderness," and "Despite and Still," *Collected Poems* (Garden City: Doubleday, 1965), pp. 3, 158, 127; James Joyce, *Ulysses* (New York: Vintage Books, 1961), p. 684; Theodore Roethke, "My Lizard," *Collected Poems* (Garden City: Doubleday, 1966), p. 217.

9. George Moushon, "Debuts and Reappearances," *High Fidelity/Musical America* (July 1969): 22.

10. Robert Graves, *Collected Poems* (London: Cassell, 1965; Garden City: Doubleday, 1966).

11. Theodore Roethke, *Collected Poems* (Garden City: Doubleday, 1966), p. 217. For a detailed discussion of this song, see Kreiling, pp. 205–9.

12. Ramey, "Samuel Barber at Seventy," p. 19.
13. James Joyce, *Ulysses* (New York: Vintage, 1961), p. 684.
14. "Leontyne Price Excels in Recital sans Opera," *New York Times,* 28 April 1969.
15. Hans Heinsheimer, interview with the author, 21 November 1985.
16. Heinsheimer, interview with Peter Dickinson, BBC broadcast, 23 January 1982.
17. *20 Poemas de amor y una Canción desesperada,* first published in Chile, 1924; trans. W. S. Merwin (Great Britain: Jonathan Cape, 1969; England and New York: Penguin Books, 1976; 1985 reprint).
18. Preface to the commemorative edition of *Cien Sonetos de Amor* (Private Edition, Santiago and Losada, Buenos Aires, 1959), after the sale of the millionth copy in Spanish; cited in George K. Diehl's program notes for the Philadelphia Orchestra, 22 September 1971.
19. Pablo Neruda, *Twenty Love Poems Based on the Spanish of Pablo Neruda,* in *Songs,* trans. Logue (London: Hutchinson, 1959); *Twenty Love Poems and A Song of Despair,* trans. Merwin (Great Britain: Jonathan Cape, 1969).
20. The holographs of the text are at the Library of Congress, Music Division.
21. Barber, quoted by Daniel Webster for the *Philadelphia Inquirer,* 19 September 1971.
22. Daniel Webster, "Samuel Barber: Reading Love Poems in the Board Room," *Philadelphia Inquirer,* 19 September 1971.
23. Dean Dougherty, *Philadelphia Daily Planet,* 28 September 1971.
24. Daniel Webster, *Philadelphia Inquirer,* 23 September 1971, p. 8.
25. Herranz, interview with the author, 16 May 1986.
26. "Ormandy Gets Ovation," *Philadelphia Bulletin,* 23 September 1971; Henahan, "Emphasis Is on the Voice in Philadelphian's Concert," *New York Times,* 7 October 1971.
27. Schonberg, *New York Times,* 7 October 1971.
28. "Music to My Ears," *Saturday Review* (23 October 1971).
29. Henahan, "I've Been Composing All My Life."
30. Letter to Ibel, 11 June 1971, Santa Cristina.
31. Letter, 28 June 1971, Santa Cristina.
32. Letter to Manfred Ibel, 15 July 1971.
33. Letter from George Sturm, of G. Schirmer, Inc., to Seymour Rosen, 29 July 1971.
34. Ibid. Frederick Dorian of Carnegie Mellon University wrote the notes on the program, which presented Beethoven's Overture, *Weihe des Hauses,* followed by Barber's work and Mahler's Symphony No. 2.
35. Letter, Barber to Manfred Ibel, 24 July 1971, Santa Cristina.
36. James Joyce, *Finnegans Wake* (Harmondsworth, England: Penguin Books, 1984), pp. 6–7.
37. Information provided by G. Schirmer, Inc., 1 February 1988.
38. This is confirmed by numerous letters written by Barber to Ibel between 1971 and 1972.
39. Letter, 13 March 1972, Spoleto.
40. Letter, 2 June 1972, from Festival of Two Worlds, Spoleto.
41. Ibid.
42. Letter, 27 July 1972.

43. Kreiling (p. 299, table 1) gives Keller's original German text with a literal English translation, Schoeck's abbreviated version, and Joyce's translation of Schoeck's song text. She believes Barber's source to be Herbert Gorman's biography of Joyce (New York: Farrar and Rinehart, Inc., 1939) as it was, until 1983, the only known source for the translation.

44. Letter, 12 February 1973.

45. Letter to the author from Fischer-Dieskau, 18 September 1987, Berlin.

46. Donal Henahan, "Music: Season's Finale," *New York Times,* 2 May 1974.

47. Letter, Barber to Ibel, 4 April 1973, Spoleto.

48. Letter, Barber to Ibel, 10 July 1973, Santa Cristina.

49. Henahan, "I've Been Composing All My Life."

50. Soria, "Artist Life," p. 5.

51. Letter, to Barber from Catherine L. Russell, executive secretary of the Van Cliburn Foundation, 12 September 1974.

52. Ibid.

53. Henahan, "I've Been Composing All My Life."

54. Gruen, *Menotti,* p. 207.

55. Telephone conversation between Barber and Manfred Ibel, 1976.

56. Letter, Eugene Ormandy to Barber, 25 May 1976. All correspondence between Barber and Ormandy cited in this chapter is in the Philadelphia Orchestra Archives.

57. Letter, 2 December 1976.

58. Letter, Ormandy to Sokoloff, 20 December 1976.

59. Memo, Ormandy to Balis and Sokoloff, 21 December 1976.

60. Ibid.

61. Letter, 9 March 1977.

62. Letter, Barber to Ormandy, 6 April 1977, 907 Fifth Avenue, New York.

63. Letter, Ormandy to Barber, 12 April 1977.

64. Letter, Ormandy to Barber, 18 April 1977.

65. Telephone conversation, April 1977 (provided by Manfred Ibel).

66. Nelson, telephone interview with the author.

67. Charles Turner, personal memoir of Barber's last ten years.

68. John David Ernst, telephone conversation with the author, October 1989.

69. Ramey, program, New York Philharmonic, 14 September 1978.

70. Barber, quoted by Phillip Ramey, "A Talk with Samuel Barber," liner notes, *Third Essay for Orchestra,* Opus 47, New York Philharmonic, cond. Zubin Mehta, New World Records, NW 309, 1981.

71. Ramey, telephone interview with the author, 15 January 1988.

72. Ramey, program, New York Philharmonic, 14 September 1978.

73. Ibid.

74. Letter, Ormandy to Barber, 24 October 1978.

75. Dr. Jack Nelson, telephone interview with the author.

76. Letter, Barber to Ormandy, 16 November 1979.

77. Herranz, interview with the author, 16 May 1986.

78. John Corigliano, program, New York Philharmonic, 17–19 December 1981.

79. Turner, interview with the author, 8 August 1983.

80. Ibid.

81. John Rockwell, "Philharmonic: 4 Pieces by Modern Composers," *New York Times,* 20 December 1981.

82. Corigliano, program, New York Philharmonic, 17–19 December 1981.

83. Ibid.

84. Obituary, *New York Times,* 25 January 1981.

85. Records of the New York State Surrogate's Court.

86. Will of Samuel Barber, p. 2, Records of the New York State Surrogate's Court. Gian Carlo Menotti is the executor of Barber's estate.

87. Donal Henahan, "Samuel Barber, 70, Pulitzer Prize-Winning Composer of 'Vanessa,' Dies," *New York Times,* 24 January 1981, pp. 1 and 16.

88. William Schuman, Speech at the Joint Ceremonial, 19 May 1976, *Proceedings of the American Academy and Institute of Arts and Letters,* 1977, p. 26.

Postlude

1. *Poetics of Music* (Cambridge, MA: Harvard University Press, 1942), p. 77.
2. Letter, 9 July 1926, Bolton, New York.
3. Gruen, "Where Has Samuel Barber Been?"

Index